Personalized Information Retrieval and Access: Concepts, Methods, and Practices

Rafael Andrés González
Delft University of Technology, The Netherlands

Nong Chen
Delft University of Technology, The Netherlands

Ajantha Dahanayake
Georgia College & State University, USA

 **INFORMATION SCIENCE REFERENCE**

Hershey · New York

Acquisitions Editor:	Kristin Klinger
Development Editor:	Kristin Roth
Senior Managing Editor:	Jennifer Neidig
Managing Editor:	Jamie Snavely
Assistant Managing Editor:	Carole Coulson
Copy Editor:	Larissa Vinci
Typesetter:	Larissa Vinci
Cover Design:	Lisa Tosheff
Printed at:	Yurchak Printing Inc.

Published in the United States of America by
Information Science Reference (an imprint of IGI Global)
701 E. Chocolate Avenue, Suite 200
Hershey PA 17033
Tel: 717-533-8845
Fax: 717-533-8661
E-mail: cust@igi-global.com
Web site: http://www.igi-global.com

and in the United Kingdom by
Information Science Reference (an imprint of IGI Global)
3 Henrietta Street
Covent Garden
London WC2E 8LU
Tel: 44 20 7240 0856
Fax: 44 20 7379 0609
Web site: http://www.eurospanbookstore.com

Library of Congress Cataloging-in-Publication Data

Personalized information retrieval and access : concepts, methods and practices / Rafael Andres Gonzalez Rivera, Nong Chen, and Ajantha Dahanayake, editors.

p. cm.

Summary: "This book surveys the main concepts, methods, and practices of personalized information retrieval and access in today's data intensive, dynamic, and distributed environment, and provides students, researchers, and practitioners with authoritative coverage of recent technological advances that are shaping the future of globally distributed information retrieval and anywhere, anytime information access"-- Provided by publisher.

Includes bibliographical references and index.

ISBN-13: 978-1-59904-510-8 (hbk.)

ISBN-13: 978-1-59904-512-2 (ebook)

1. Database searching. 2. Information retrieval. 3. Web services. I. Gonzales Rivera, Rafael Andres. II. Chen, Nong, 1976- III. Dahanayake, Ajantha, 1954-

QA76.9.D3P495123 2008

025.5'24--dc22

2007036852

British Cataloguing in Publication Data
A Cataloguing in Publication record for this book is available from the British Library.

Table of Contents

Preface xii

Acknowledgment xx

Section I
Concepts

Chapter I
Learning Personalized Ontologies from Text: A Review on an Inherently Transdisciplinary Area 1
    Shan Chen, University of Technology, Sydney, Australia
    Mary-Anne Williams, University of Technology, Sydney, Australia

Chapter II
Overview of Design Options for Neighborhood-Based Collaborative Filtering Systems 30
    Nikos Manouselis, Informatics Laboratory, Agricultural University of Athens, Greece
    Constantina Costopoulou, Informatics Laboratory, Agricultural University of Athens, Greece

Chapter III
Exploring Information Management Problems in the Domain of Critical Incidents 55
    Rafael Andrés Gonzalez, Delft University of Technology, The Netherlands

Chapter IV
Mining for Web Personalization 77
    Penelope Markellou, University of Patras, Greece
    Maria Rigou, University of Patras, Greece
    Spiros Sirmakessis, University of Patras, Greece

Chapter V
Clustering Web Information Sources.. 98
    Athena Vakali, Aristotle University of Thessaloniki, Greece
    George Pallis, Aristotle University of Thessaloniki, Greece
    Lefteris Angelis, Aristotle University of Thessaloniki, Greece

Section II
Methods and Practices

Chapter VI

A Conceptual Structure for Designing Personalized Information Seeking and Retrieval Systems
in Data Intensive Domains... 119

Nong Chen, Delft University of Technology, The Netherlands
Ajantha Dahanayake, Georgia College & State University, USA

Chapter VII

Privacy Control Requirements for Context-Aware Mobile Services 151

Amr Ali Eldin, Accenture BV, The Netherlands
Zoran Stojanovic, IBM Nederland BV, The Netherlands

Chapter VIII

User and Context-Aware Quality Filters Based on Web Metadata Retrieval..................... 167

Ricardo Barros, Federal University of Rio de Janeiro, Brazil
Geraldo Xexéo, Federal University of Rio de Janeiro, Brazil
Wallace A. Pinheiro, Federal University of Rio de Janeiro, Brazil
Jano de Souza, Federal University of Rio de Janeiro, Brazil

Chapter IX

Personalized Content-Based Image Retrieval 194

Iker Gondra, St. Francis Xavier University, Canada

Chapter X

Service-Oriented Architectures for Context-Aware Information Retrieval and Access 220

Lu Yan, University College London, UK

Chapter XI

On Personalizing Web Services Using Context.. 232

Zakaria Maamar, Zayed University, UAE
Soraya Kouadri Mostéefaoui, Fribourg University, Switzerland
Qusay H. Mahmoud, Guelph University, Canada

Chapter XII

Role-Based Multi-Agent Systems.. 254

Haibin Zhu, Nipissing University, Canada
MengChu Zhou, New Jersey Institute of Technology, USA

Chapter XIII
Towards a Context Definition for Multi-Agent Systems 286
    Tarek Ben Mena, RIADI-ENSI, Tunisia & GRIC-IRIT, France
    Narjès Bellamine-Ben Saoud, RIADI-ENSI, Tunisia
    Mohamed Ben Ahmed, RIADI-ENSI, Tunisia
    Bernard Pavard, GRIC-IRIT, France

Compilation of References 308

About the Contributors 342

Index 347

Detailed Table of Contents

Preface xii

Acknowledgment xx

Section I
Concepts

Chapter I
Learning Personalized Ontologies from Text: A Review on an Inherently Transdisciplinary Area 1
Shan Chen, University of Technology, Sydney, Australia
Mary-Anne Williams, University of Technology, Sydney, Australia

Ontology learning has been identified as an inherently transdisciplinary area. Personalized ontology learning for Web personalization involves Web technologies and therefore presents more challenges. This chapter presents a review of the main concepts of ontologies and the state of the art in the area of ontology learning from text. It provides an overview of Web personalization, and identifies issues and describes approaches for learning personalized ontologies. The goal of this survey is—through the study of the main concepts, existing methods, and practices of the area—to identify new connections with other areas for the future success of establishing principles for this new transdisciplinary area. As a result, the chapter is concluded by presenting a number of possible future research directions.

Chapter II
Overview of Design Options for Neighborhood-Based Collaborative Filtering Systems 30
Nikos Manouselis, Informatics Laboratory, Agricultural University of Athens, Greece
Constantina Costopoulou, Informatics Laboratory, Agricultural University of Athens, Greece

The problem of collaborative filtering is to predict how well a user will like an item that he or she has not rated, given a set of historical ratings for this and other items from a community of users. A plethora of collaborative filtering algorithms have been proposed in related literature. One of the most prevalent families of collaborative filtering algorithms are neighborhood-based ones, which calculate a prediction of how much a user will like a particular item, based on how other users with similar preferences have rated this item. This chapter aims to provide an overview of various proposed design options for neighborhood-based collaborative filtering systems, in order to facilitate their better understanding, as well as their study and implementation by recommender systems' researchers and developers. For this purpose, the chapter extends a series of design stages of neighborhood-based algorithms, as they have been initially identified by related literature on collaborative filtering systems. Then, it reviews proposed alternatives for each design stage and provides an overview of potential design options.

Chapter III
Exploring Information Management Problems in the Domain of Critical Incidents 55
    Rafael Andrés Gonzalez, Delft University of Technology, The Netherlands

In this chapter, information management problems and some of the computer-based solutions offered to deal with them are presented. The claim is that exploring the information problem as a three-fold issue, composed of heterogeneity, overload, and dynamics, will contribute to an improved understanding of information management problems. On the other hand, it presents a set of computer-based solutions that are available to tackle these problems: information discovery and retrieval, information filtering, information fusion, and information personalization. In addition, this chapter argues that a rich and interesting domain for exploring information management problems is critical incident management, due to its complexity, requirements, and the nature of the information it deals with.

Chapter IV
Mining for Web Personalization 77
    Penelope Markellou, University of Patras, Greece
    Maria Rigou, University of Patras, Greece
    Spiros Sirmakessis, University of Patras, Greece

The Web has become a huge repository of information and keeps growing exponentially under no editorial control, while the human capability to find, read, and understand content remains constant. Providing people with access to information is not the problem; the problem is that people with varying needs and preferences navigate through large Web structures, missing the goal of their inquiry. Web personalization is one of the most promising approaches for alleviating this information overload, providing tailored Web experiences. This chapter explores the different faces of personalization, traces back its roots, and follows its progress. It describes the modules typically comprising a personalization process, demonstrates its close relation to Web mining, depicts the technical issues that arise, recommends solutions when possible, and discusses the effectiveness of personalization and related concerns. Moreover, the chapter illustrates current trends in the field, suggesting directions that may lead to new scientific results.

Chapter V
Clustering Web Information Sources.. 98
    Athena Vakali, Aristotle University of Thessaloniki, Greece
    George Pallis, Aristotle University of Thessaloniki, Greece
    Lefteris Angelis, Aristotle University of Thessaloniki, Greece

The explosive growth of the Web scale has drastically increased information circulation and dissemination rates. As the number of both Web users and Web sources grows significantly everyday, crucial data management issues, such as clustering on the Web, should be addressed and analyzed. Clustering has been proposed towards improving both the information availability and the Web users' personalization.

Clusters on the Web are either users' sessions or Web information sources, which are managed in a variation of applications and implementations testbeds. This chapter focuses on the topic of clustering information over the Web, in an effort to overview and survey the theoretical background and the adopted practices of most popular emerging and challenging clustering research efforts. An up-to-date survey of the existing clustering schemes is given, to be of use for both researchers and practitioners interested in the area of Web data mining.

Section II
Methods and Practices

Chapter VI
A Conceptual Structure for Designing Personalized Information Seeking and Retrieval Systems
in Data Intensive Domains.. 119
Nong Chen, Delft University of Technology, The Netherlands
Ajantha Dahanayake, Georgia College & State University, USA

Personalized information seeking and retrieval is regarded as the solution to the problem of information overload in domains such as crisis response and medical networks. Personalization algorithms and techniques are maturing, but their centralized implementation solutions are becoming less efficient for dealing with ever-changing user information needs in data-intensive, dynamic, and distributed environments. In this chapter, we present a conceptual structure for designing personalized, multidisciplinary information seeking and retrieval systems. This conceptual structure is capable of serving as a bridge between information needs coming from an organizational process, and existing implementations of information access services, software, applications, and technical infrastructure; it is also capable of sufficiently describing and inferring users' personalized information needs. We believe that it offers a new way of thinking about the retrieval of personalized information.

Chapter VII
Privacy Control Requirements for Context-Aware Mobile Services 151
Amr Ali Eldin, Accenture BV, The Netherlands
Zoran Stojanovic, IBM Nederland BV, The Netherlands

With the rapid developments of mobile telecommunications technology over the last two decades, a new computing paradigm known as 'anywhere and anytime' or 'ubiquitous' computing has evolved. Consequently, attention has been given not only to extending current Web services and mobile service models and architectures, but increasingly also to make these services context-aware. Privacy represents one of the hot topics that has questioned the success of these services. In this chapter, we discuss the different requirements of privacy control in context-aware service architectures. Further, we present the different functionalities needed to facilitate this control. The main objective of this control is to help end users make consent decisions regarding their private information collection under conditions of uncertainty. The proposed functionalities have been prototyped and integrated in a UMTS location-based mobile services testbed platform on a university campus. Users have experienced the services in real time. A survey of users' responses on the privacy functionality has been carried out and analyzed as well. Users' collected response on the privacy functionality was positive in most cases. Additionally, results obtained reflected the feasibility and usability of this approach.

Chapter VIII

User and Context-Aware Quality Filters Based on Web Metadata Retrieval 167

Ricardo Barros, Federal University of Rio de Janeiro, Brazil
Geraldo Xexéo, Federal University of Rio de Janeiro, Brazil
Wallace A. Pinheiro, Federal University of Rio de Janeiro, Brazil
Jano de Souza, Federal University of Rio de Janeiro, Brazil

This chapter addresses the issues regarding the large amount and low quality of Web information by proposing a methodology that adopts user and context-aware quality filters based on Web metadata retrieval. This starts with an initial evaluation and adjusts it to consider context characteristics and user perspectives to obtain aggregated evaluation values.

Chapter IX

Personalized Content-Based Image Retrieval 194

Iker Gondra, St. Francis Xavier University, Canada

In content-based image retrieval (CBIR), a set of low-level features are extracted from an image to represent its visual content. Retrieval is performed by image example, where a query image is given as input by the user and an appropriate similarity measure is used to find the best matches in the corresponding feature space. This approach suffers from the fact that there is a large discrepancy between the low-level visual features that one can extract from an image and the semantic interpretation of the image's content that a particular user may have in a given situation. That is, users seek semantic similarity, but we can only provide similarity based on low-level visual features extracted from the raw pixel data, a situation known as the semantic gap. The selection of an appropriate similarity measure is thus an important problem. Since visual content can be represented by different attributes, the combination and importance of each set of features varies according to the user's semantic intent. Thus, the retrieval strategy should be adaptive so that it can accommodate the preferences of different users.

Chapter X

Service-Oriented Architectures for Context-Aware Information Retrieval and Access 220

Lu Yan, University College London, UK

Humans are quite successful at conveying ideas to each other and retrieving information from interactions appropriately. This is due to many factors: the richness of the language they share, the common understanding of how the world works, and an implicit understanding of everyday situations. When humans talk with humans, they are able to use implicit situational information (i.e., context) to enhance the information exchange process. Context plays a vital part in adaptive and personalized information retrieval and access. Unfortunately, computer communications lacks this ability to provide auxiliary context in addition to the substantial content of information. As computers are becoming more and more ubiquitous and mobile, there is a need and possibility to provide information "personalized, any time, and anywhere." In these scenarios, large amounts of information circulate in order to create smart and proactive environments that will significantly enhance both the work and leisure experiences of people. Context-awareness plays an important role in enabling personalized information retrieval and access according to the current situation with minimal human intervention. Although context-aware information retrieval systems have been researched for a decade, the rise of mobile and ubiquitous computing put new challenges to issue, and therefore we are motivated to come up with new solutions to achieve non-intrusive, personalized information access on the mobile service platforms and heterogeneous wireless environments.

Chapter XI

On Personalizing Web Services Using Context.. 232

Zakaria Maamar, Zayed University, UAE
Soraya Kouadri Mostéefaoui, Fribourg University, Switzerland
Qusay H. Mahmoud, Guelph University, Canada

This chapter presents a context-based approach for Web services personalization so that user preferences are accommodated. Preferences are of different types varying from when the execution of a Web service should start to where the outcome of this execution should be delivered according to user location. Besides user preferences, this chapter will discuss that the computing resources on which the Web services operate have an impact on their personalization. Indeed resources schedule the execution requests that originate from multiple Web services. To track the personalization of a Web service from a temporal perspective (i.e., what did happen, what is happening, and what will happen), three types of contexts are devised and referred to as user context, Web service context, and resource context.

Chapter XII

Role-Based Multi-Agent Systems... 254

Haibin Zhu, Nipissing University, Canada
MengChu Zhou, New Jersey Institute of Technology, USA

In this chapter, the authors introduce roles as a means to support interaction and collaboration among agents in multi-agent systems. They review the application of roles in current agent systems at first, then describe the fundamental principles of role-based collaboration and propose the basic methodologies of how to apply roles into agent systems (i.e., the revised E-CARGO model). After that, they demonstrate a case study: a soccer robot team designed with role specifications. Finally, the authors present the potentiality to apply roles into information personalization.

Chapter XIII

Towards a Context Definition for Multi-Agent Systems 286

Tarek Ben Mena, RIADI-ENSI, Tunisia & GRIC-IRIT, France
Narjès Bellamine-Ben Saoud, RIADI-ENSI, Tunisia
Mohamed Ben Ahmed, RIADI-ENSI, Tunisia
Bernard Pavard, GRIC-IRIT, France

This chapter aims to define context notion for multi-agent systems (MAS). Starting from the state of the art on context in different disciplines, the authors present context as a generic and abstract notion.

They argue that context depends on three characteristics: domain, entity, and problem. By specifying this definition with MAS, they initially consider context from an extensional point of view as three components—actant, role, and situation—and then from an intensional one, which represents the context model for agents in MAS which consist of information on environment, other objects, agents, and relations between them. Therefore, they underline a new way of representing agent knowledge, building context on this knowledge, and using it. Furthermore, the authors prove the applicability of contextual agent solution for other research fields, particularly in personalized information retrieval by taking into account as agents: crawlers and as objects: documents.

Compilation of References 308

About the Contributors 342

Index 347

Preface

The existence of large volumes of globally distributed information and the availability of various computing devices, many of which are mobile, present the possibility of anywhere-anytime access to information. This enables individuals and organizations to coordinate and improve their knowledge over various autonomous locations. However, the amount and nature of information can result in overload problems, in heterogeneity of formats and sources, in rapidly changing content, and in uncertain user information needs. Individuals and organizations may thus be faced with increasing difficulty in finding the "right information" in the "right format" at the "right time."

In an already classic paper, Imielinski and Badrinath (1994) presented the trends and challenges surrounding mobile computing, which they said held the promise of access to information "anywhere and at any time." The idea was that mobile or nomadic computing was possible thanks to mobile computers having access to wireless connections to information networks, resulting in more collaborative forms of computing. What Imielinski and Badrinath presented as challenges continue to be critical issues in the development of mobile applications and information services today. They pointed at heterogeneity as a result of the massive scale of mobile environments, they mentioned the need for dynamic reconfiguration of services in response to client mobility, and they reminded us of the privacy and security implications of mobility. Consequently, they argued that mobility would have far-reaching consequences for systems design, and indeed they were right. This book finds motivation on those issues, focusing on the subject of information retrieval and access—personalization in particular.

Chapters IV, VII, and X of this book explicitly address mobility challenges and propose ways to deal with them. Mobility is currently tied, from a telecommunications perspective, with next-generation wireless technologies that promise ubiquitous networking and mobile computing on a large scale, providing high-bandwidth data services and wireless Internet (Pierre, 2001). This can be grouped under the term "mobile next-generation networks (NGNs)" (Huber, 2004), which refers to the convergence of the Internet and intranets with mobile networks and with media and broadcasting technologies (Universal Mobile Telecommunication System, or UMTS, among them). Mobility can be defined as the ability to access services, normally accessible in a wired manner, from anywhere (Pierre, 2001). Mobile computing uses such mobility to allow users of portable devices to access information services through a shared infrastructure, regardless of location or movement (Pierre, 2001). Mobility can be further specified into the following types:

- **Terminal mobility:** The ability to locate and identify mobile terminals as they move, to allow them access to telecommunication services (Pierre, 2001).

- **Personal mobility:** Centers around users carrying a personal unique subscription identity and the system's capability to provide services according to the user profile (El-Khatib, Zhang, Hadibi, & Bochman, 2004; Pierre, 2001).
- **Service mobility:** The capacity of a network to provide subscribed services at the terminal or location determined by users (Pierre, 2001); this allows the possibility of suspending a service and resuming it on another device (El-Khatib et al., 2004).

Ubiquitous computing, for some the next wave after the "Internet wave," uses the advances in mobile computing and integrates them with pervasive computing, which refers to the acquiring of context from the environment to dynamically and accordingly build computing models (Singh, Pradkar, & Lee, 2006). The result is a global computing environment that is defined as ubiquitous computing. This novel computing paradigm has the goal of embedding small and highly specialized devices within day-to-day environments so that they operate seamlessly and become transparent (invisible) to offline or online users (Singh et al., 2006; Huber, 2004). Ubiquitous computing integrates several technologies, which include embedded systems, service discovery, wireless networking, and personal computing (El-Khatib et al., 2004).

Research in ubiquitous computing has shown three main focuses: (1) how to provide users with personalized information or services based on users' profiles, (2) how to provide services or devices with context-awareness ability to adapt the service behaviors or device behaviors according to various situations, or (3) a combination of the above. Therefore, personalization and context-awareness are of special importance for the development of ubiquitous computing.

Personalization reflects a design philosophy that focuses on the delivery of a contextual user experience (Hyldegaard & Seiden, 2004). Personalization, in the context of ubiquitous computing, is generally meant to denote the ability to customize the user interface, the information content, the information channels, and the services provided according to the individual user's needs, personal interests, and preferences (Hyldegaard & Seiden, 2004). Adding personalized functions into Internet-enabled information retrieval and access applications—for example, search engines or e-services—is becoming one of the competitive advantages used to attract users to survive in the current competitive business world. There are several personalization strategies, such as interface personalization, link personalization, content personalization, and context personalization. Personalization models, methods, and techniques built based on solid mathematic foundations and advanced programming languages are studied in the field, with the aim of providing feasible solutions to solve the problem of inappropriate information overload at the technological level, ranging from simple user-controlled information personalization to autonomous system-controlled adaptation.

Context-awareness is the second important issue of mobile and ubiquitous computing, because this type of computing requires sharing knowledge between individual environments and providing services that take the environmental characteristics and constraints into account. A human user is typically associated with many environments and consequently adopts different roles in each one; the system should then transparently recognize this role (Singh et al., 2006). The context itself can be defined as a piece of information that can be used to characterize the situation of a participant, so by sensing this context, applications can present contextual information to users or modify their behavior according to the environmental changes (Singh et al., 2006). A true ubiquitous system should provide the best possible service(s) based on the user role and its associated privileges, restrictions, location, and time. This requires a complete description of profiles and personalization of the resulting service. Profiles can be of the following types (El-Khatib et al., 2004):

- **User profile:** Personal properties and preferences.
- **Content profile:** Metadata about the content, including storage features, available variants, author and production, and usage (metadata is a topic addressed by Chapter VIII).
- **Context profile:** Dynamic information that is part of the context or status of the user, including physical, social, and organizational information.
- **Device profile:** Hardware and software characteristics of a computing device.
- **Network profile:** Resources and capabilities of the communication network.
- **Intermediaries profile:** Description of all adaptation services that intermediaries can provide.

Context-awareness and personalization are topics treated in Chapters I, III, IV, V, VI, VII, X, XI, and XIII of this book. Among the specific applications of context-awareness and personalization is collaborative filtering and recommendation, treated in Chapters II and III. Collaborative recommendation is a personalization technique that keeps track of user preferences and uses them to offer new suggestions in e-commerce or information access scenarios (O'Mahoney, Hurley, Kushmerick, & Silvestre, 2004). The idea is to recommend items to a target customer, by looking at customers who have expressed similar preferences. This helps individuals more effectively identify content of interest from a potentially overwhelming set of choices (Herlocker, Konstan, Terveen, & Riedl, 2004).

Some of the recent technologies on which personalized information services, context-awareness, and ubiquitous computing in general are grounded are: software components, service orientation, and multi-agent systems. A software component is any coherent design unit which may be packaged, sold, stored, assigned to a person or team (for development), maintained, and perhaps most importantly, reused (Meling, Montgomery, Ponnusamy, Wong, & Mehandjiska, 2000). Component-based development (or CBD for short) includes improvements in: quality, throughput, performance, reliability and interoperability, reducing development, documentation, maintenance, and staff training time and cost (Herzum & Sims, 2000; Szyperski, 2002). Most recent trends in software engineering show that future developments will follow in the CBD path. This argument is partially confirmed by the large amount of component development technologies that have existed for some years now (CORBA, EJB, DCOM, and .NET, among others), and also by the increasing amount of components available in the market (Andrews, Ghosh, & Choi, 2002). Services, and especially Web services, can be thought of as an evolution of the component notion (Apperly et al., 2003). By using interfaces and Web-enabled standards for discovery and representation, services (e.g., information services) are offered for consumption to different applications, making service consumption truly aligned with the possibilities of ubiquitous computing. In addition to components and services, software agents are another technology that can underlie mobile and ubiquitous computing. Agent technology is possible due to the convergence of artificial intelligence (which deals with autonomy and intelligence in agent behavior) and distributed object systems (which extend with mobility the object-oriented approach) (Marinescu, 2002). As such, an agent can be seen as a reactive program defined by autonomy (or agency), mobility, and intelligence (inference, planning, and learning capabilities). An agent can also be described in human-like terms of knowledge—knowledge of itself; knowledge of other agents, goals, or possible solutions; and knowledge of its own desires, commitments, and intentions—and capabilities (communication and reasoning) (Shakshuki, Ghenniwa, & Kamel, 2003). In this book, components and services related to context-awareness and personalization are treated in Chapters VI, VII, and XI. Agents are treated in several chapters, due to their prominence in modern software technology. In particular, Chapters III, XII, and XIII mention agent-based solutions to some of the challenges that will be presented in the next section of this preface.

INFORMATION MANAGEMENT CHALLENGES

Mobility, ubiquitous computing, personalization, and context-awareness present a wide array of challenges related to telecommunication networks, device software, data management, and human and social issues related to this new form of exchanging information, collaborating, and consuming services. This book gives special attention to the challenges of information volume and overload, and to information heterogeneity. It also considers challenges with regards to information quality and dynamics, and to privacy in context-awareness. This is also linked to changing and uncertain information needs that add additional requirements to information service design.

As mentioned earlier, the volume of information carries with it issues of storage, distribution, and retrieval from the data management perspective, but also carries with it the possibility of information overload at the individual or group user level. This challenge is discussed in Chapters I, III, IV, VI, and VIII of this book, and in Chapter IX with special emphasis on image collections.

Another challenge already mentioned is that of information heterogeneity. Whether due to volume or not, heterogeneity implies a variety of data formats, sources, authors, languages, and other characteristics that determine the potential usage and interpretation of information. The use of standards, filters, translation templates, and other means may help in dealing with this issue. Chapters III, VI, and VIII consider it as part of their concerns.

Because of the volume and heterogeneity of information, in addition to a changing business environment and the changing nature of globally distributed information, information needs may also be unclear. If we add the existence of an ill-structured problem as motivation, then uncertainty (and changes) in information needs, and their associated queries, is another challenge to be considered. This is treated in Chapters VI and VIII of this book.

Besides volume, heterogeneity, and changing needs, there is another issue related to the quality of information. The trustworthiness, length, media format, digital resolution, or tractability of a piece of information are also important. Defining what quality of information is, what its attributes are, and how it should be included in the information-seeking and retrieval process is a challenge. Part of this challenge is addressed in Chapter VIII.

The last two challenges of interest for this book are information dynamics, treated in Chapter III, and privacy in context-aware solutions, the subject of Chapter VII. Information dynamics relates to the fact that information flows in a global and distributed environment, so it is far from being a static repository, and information seeking and retrieval should take this into account. It also means that information itself is subject to modifications, adaptations, additions, and revisions that make each information unit also independently dynamic. With regards to context-awareness, personalization and mobile or ubiquitous computing should take into account privacy as a very relevant requirement, which might conflict with the goals of context-aware services, but which can also be embedded into the service without compromising the identity, profile, or history of the users.

This book compiles several approaches to deal with the challenges just mentioned. This is the subject of the next section in this preface.

TACKLING THE CHALLENGES

This book presents concepts, approaches, architectures, and models that contribute to dealing with the challenges of mobility and ubiquity. Personalized information retrieval and access is regarded as a remedy when it comes to relieving the problem of information overload. Many personalization algorithms and techniques have emerged in different research directions, including user modeling, data mining, user profiling, context-aware computing, information visualization, and their combinations. Equipped with advanced personalization techniques and algorithms, many academic and commercial off-the-shelf information search services and tools are available to effectively filter out irrelevant information, and to rank and present information in a user-preferred way.

However, as shown earlier, dynamic and distributed environments challenge those personalized information search applications. Although the personalization techniques and algorithms are becoming mature, their centralized implementation is becoming less efficient to support the rapidly changing information needs taking place in dynamic and distributed environments. Changes in an organizational or a personal information need may lead to a need to redesign a complete application. Therefore, there is a requirement of designing personalized information retrieval and access in an agile and flexible way, which can be adapted easily to satisfy personalized organizational information needs with minimum effort.

This book presents approaches centered around service orientation, multi-agent systems, information retrieval and information filtering, in addition to intelligent techniques and ontologies to overcome some of these challenges.

Service orientation is taken as a design principle or underlying approach in Chapters VI, VII, X, and XI. Multi-agent systems are treated in Chapter XII from a role-based perspective to personalization; in Chapter III they are included in several of the examples provided; in Chapter XIII, a context model for multi-agent systems is provided. Information retrieval, from a content-based view, is treated in Chapter IX; from a personalization view, information retrieval is part of Chapters III and VI. Information filtering is also a part of the solutions. In Chapters II and III, filtering is discussed, giving special attention to collaborative filtering; context-aware filtering is the subject of Chapter VIII, and the issue of privacy is dealt with in Chapter VII. Three chapters address personalization in the specific context of the Web: Chapters IV and V treat personalization for Web data mining, and Chapter XI presents an approach for creating context-aware personalized Web services. A final approach treated in this book regards the role of ontologies; this is a subject treated in Chapters I and III.

This book agrees with Pierre (2001) in his statement that the delivery of information is the most powerful tool in building a knowledge-based economy. The convergence of solutions, like the ones presented in this book, can help improve the understanding of the new challenges of ubiquitous computing on top of those already existing in the already global, distributed information infrastructure of the Internet. By scaffolding this new paradigm of information access, exchange, and service provision and access, individuals and organizations will be able to harness the full potential of existing and emergent information technology, thus being a part of the construction and operation of the knowledge-based economy.

ORGANIZATION OF THE BOOK

The book is organized into two sections. The first section includes five chapters with a primarily conceptual contribution which present some of the issues, definitions, and accounts of literature which provide a theoretical background for the rest of the book, and show issues and trends for research and practice. The chapters of this first part are briefly presented as follows.

Chapter I, "Learning Personalized Ontologies from Text: A Review on an Inherently Transdisciplinary Area," presents the issue of information overload and personalized information retrieval and access (specifically for the Web) as a countermeasure. It views personalization as appropriately coupled to the Semantic Web, and thus ontology is at its foundation. The result proposed is to create personalized ontologies, which can be built through learning techniques. The authors review the methods, concepts, and practices of learning personalized ontologies, and highlight contextual information extraction and personalized Web services as future trends in this area.

Chapter II, "Overview of Design Options for Neighborhood-Based Collaborative Filtering Systems," focuses on collaborative filtering as a subtype of filtering systems (the other being cognitive filtering) and explores neighborhood-based techniques for this kind of filtering. The chapter provides an overview of different design options of neighborhood-based collaborative filtering systems, presented in line with the stages of collaborative filtering to highlight the design options relevant to the appropriate stage.

Chapter III, "Exploring Information Management Problems in the Domain of Critical Incidents," presents an understanding of information management problems as divided into heterogeneity, overload, and dynamics. On the other hand, it presents computer-based solutions to deal with those information management problems: information discovery and retrieval, information filtering, information fusion, and information personalization. In addition to this review of problems and solutions, the chapter finally argues that exploring these issues in the domain of critical incident management helps cover the complexities of information management.

Chapter IV, "Mining for Web Personalization," offers an introduction to information personalization, underlining the question of whether personalization is just hype or a real opportunity to deal with an increasing volume of information on the Web and the resulting information overload that comes with such a growing repository. By presenting Web mining as a method for Web information personalization, this chapter argues that personalization can be a real opportunity for the present and the future.

Chapter V, "Clustering Web Information Sources," contributes an overview of clustering for improving personalization to support the area of Web data mining. It discusses personalization in the context of the growing Web and presents Web clustering as an approach to support personalization. It separates Web document clustering from user clustering, and then presents a literature survey of several approaches and algorithms to deal with these types of clustering, covering the processes and methods that are available and how they can be integrated.

The second section of the book consists of eight more chapters which present particular solutions (approaches, architectures, conceptual models, and prototypes) in the context of information personalization and its surrounding topics as presented in the beginning of this preface. A short description of these eight chapters follows.

Chapter VI, "A Conceptual Structure for Designing Personalized Information Seeking and Retrieval Systems in Data-Intensive Domains," starts by highlighting information overload and heterogeneity issues, in addition to changing information needs. The problem is providing anywhere/anytime information access in data-intensive domains (e.g., crisis response). The proposed solution is situated in the context of mobility and software component and services. The chapter presents a conceptual structure which should act as a bridge between personalized information needs and implementation of information services.

Chapter VII, "Privacy Control Requirements for Context-Aware Mobile Services," focuses on the privacy implications of context-awareness as a part of ubiquitous computing. The challenge is how to implement privacy requirements in context-aware services. The chapter presents a UMTS location-based mobile services testbed on a university campus in which a prototype is used to test the basic functionality of helping automate the process of getting user consent in acquiring context data.

Chapter VIII, "User and Context-Aware Quality Filters Based on Web Metadata Retrieval," starts by presenting the volume of information on the Web as a challenge, resulting in information quality variability and uncertain information needs. By integrating the use of Web metadata and fuzzy theory into an ontology and architecture, the chapter proposes a user and context-aware quality filter. This filter is illustrated in an example of a query (in the economics domain).

Chapter IX, "Personalized Content-Based Image Retrieval," reminds us of the growth of digital media (image collections in particular) in information networks and how this type of media cannot easily be described with text. Content-based retrieval uses image information, such as color, texture, and shape, but this results in a "semantic-similarity" challenge. This challenge is tackled in the chapter through the use of relevance feedback learning, and tested with the classic measures of precision and recall using a content-based image retrieval system that uses an image segment as query input.

Chapter X, "Service-Oriented Architectures for Context-Aware Information Retrieval and Access," presents context as a natural part of human interaction, which, as described in the beginning of this Preface, is a fundamental aspect of mobility and ubiquitous computing. The chapter proposes the use of a service-oriented architecture to make use of different services along with context-aware action systems, exemplified with the implementation of a conference assistant system.

Chapter XI, "On Personalizing Web Services Using Context," also combines services and context awareness. Focusing on Web services, this chapter contains an approach that divides context into three types: user context, Web service context, and resource context. Each of these contexts addresses user preferences, Web service composition, and computing resources, respectively.

Chapter XII, "Role-Based Multi-Agent Systems," discusses the understanding of the notion of 'roles' from organization theory and its use as a modeling mechanism for multi-agent systems. As a result of the specification of roles, the E-CARGO (Environment, Classes, Agents, Roles, Groups, and Objects) environment is extended and presented as an architecture for role-based multi-agent systems that can provide a contribution to roles as preferences in a multi-agent-based personalization system.

Chapter XIII, "Towards a Context Definition for Multi-Agent Systems," aims at redefining context for multi-agent systems. By presenting an object model for the notion of 'context', the authors contribute to an improvement in the understanding and use of this concept in the field of artificial intelligence. The model is applied to an example of an agent-based virtual environment of accident emergency rescue. Regarding the implications of integrating the concept of 'context' into the multi-agent systems, the latter can be better exploited in the context of personalization and context-aware information services.

REFERENCES

Andrews, A., Ghosh, S., & Choi, E. (2002). A model for understanding software components. *Proceedings of the International Conference on Software Maintenance* (pp. 359-368).

Apperly, H., Hofman, R., Latchem, S., Maybank, B., McGibbon, B., Piper, D., Simons, C., & Hoffman, R. (2003). *Service- and component-based development: Using the select perspective and UML.* Boston: Addison-Wesley.

El-Khatib, K., Zhang, Z., Hadibi, N., & Bochman, G. (2004). Personal and service mobility in ubiquitous computing environments. *Wireless Communications and Mobile Computing, 4*(6), 595-607.

Herlocker, J., Konstan, J., Terveen, L., & Riedl, J. (2004). Evaluating collaborative filtering recommender systems. *ACM Transactions on Information Systems, 22*(1), 5-53.

Herzum, P., & Sims, O. (2000). *Business component factory.* New York: John Wiley & Sons.

Huber, J. (2004). Mobile next-generation networks. *IEEE Multimedia, 11*(1), 72-83.

Hyldegaard, J., & Seiden, P. (2004). My e-journal—exploring the usefulness of personalized access to scholarly articles and services. *Information Research, 9*(3), paper 181.

Imielinski, T., & Badrinath, B. (1994). Mobile wireless computing. *Communications of the ACM, 37*(10), 18-28.

Marinescu, D. (2002). *Internet-based workflow management: Toward a Semantic Web.* New York: John Wiley & Sons.

Meling, R., Montgomery, E., Ponnusamy, P., Wong, E., & Mehandjiska, D. (2000). Storing and retrieving software components: A component description manager. *Proceedings of the Australian Conference on Software Engineering* (pp. 107-117).

O'Mahoney, M., Hurley, N., Kushmerick, N., & Silvestre, G. (2004). Collaborative recommendation: A robustness analysis. *ACM Transactions on Internet Technology, 4*(4), 344-377.

Pierre, S. (2001). Mobile computing and ubiquitous networking: Concepts, technologies and challenges. *Telematics and Informatics, 18*(2-3), 109-131.

Shakshuki, E., Ghenniwa, H., & Kamel, M. (2003). An architecture for cooperative information systems. *Knowledge-Based Systems, 16,* 17-27.

Singh, S., Pradkar, S., & Lee, Y. (2006). Ubiquitous computing: Connecting pervasive computing through Semantic Web. *Information Systems and E-Business Management, 4*(4), 421-439.

Szyperski, C. (2002). *Component software: Beyond object-oriented programming* (2nd ed.). New York: ACM Press/Addison-Wesley.

Acknowledgment

The editors would like to acknowledge the help of all involved in the collation and review process of the book, without whose support the project could not have been satisfactorily completed.

First, we would like to thank all of the authors for their insights and excellent contributions to this book, and also for their cooperation throughout the process. They deserve the greatest appreciation because their contributions were essential in this book. It was a wonderful experience to work with them. Most of the authors of chapters included in this book also served as referees for articles written by other authors. Thanks to all those who assisted us in the reviewing process by providing constructive and comprehensive reviews.

Special thanks also go to all the staff at IGI Global, whose contributions throughout the whole process from inception of the initial idea to final publication have been invaluable. In particular, to Lynley Lapp, Ross A. Miller, and Jessica Thompson, who continuously prodded via e-mail to keep the project on schedule, and to Jan Travers, Mehdi Khosrow-Pour, and Kristin Roth, who accepted our proposal and invited us to take on this project.

We would like to show our appreciation to the staff members of Systems Engineering Group at the Faculty of Technology, Policy and Management at Delft University of Technology. Their support was vital in achieving the completeness of this book.

In closing, we wish to express our gratitude to our families for their unfailing patience, support, and love.

Rafael González, Delft University of Technology, The Netherlands
Nong Chen, Delft University of Technology, The Netherlands
Prof. Dr. Ajantha Dahanayake, Georgia College & State University, USA

November 2007

Section I
Concepts

Chapter I
Learning Personalized Ontologies from Text:
A Review on an Inherently Transdisciplinary Area

Shan Chen
University of Technology, Sydney, Australia

Mary-Anne Williams
University of Technology, Sydney, Australia

ABSTRACT

Ontology learning has been identified as an inherently transdisciplinary area. Personalized ontology learning for Web personalization involves Web technologies and therefore presents more challenges. This chapter presents a review of the main concepts of ontologies and the state of the art in the area of ontology learning from text. It provides an overview of Web personalization, and identifies issues and describes approaches for learning personalized ontologies. The goal of this survey is—through the study of the main concepts, existing methods, and practices of the area—to identify new connections with other areas for the future success of establishing principles for this new transdisciplinary area. As a result, the chapter is concluded by presenting a number of possible future research directions.

INTRODUCTION

The success of the Web today has changed the way we receive and access information. While the Web has become the de facto information resource, it leads to an information overload problem in our everyday life and business. The enormous volume of information available on the Web, the broad coverage of the Web content, the phenomenal number of Web users and businesses, and their continued rapid growth have presented a major challenge to the Web community: how to find relevant information appropriate to individual needs. This is regarded as a problem of Web personalization, which deals with personalized information retrieval and access.

The Semantic Web is being developed as an extension to the current Web. It introduces a semantic layer over existing Web content, to support information processing and accessing more effectively. The semantic layer transforms Web content into a semantic information space that can provide a shared common understanding across humans and machines. The foundation of such a layer is provided by ontologies. Personalized ontologies, as the name suggests, are personalized to each user, and can be used to improve the efficiency of data retrieving and accessing to better meet individual needs. When applied to the Web, personalized ontologies can facilitate Web data discovery for individuals, for example, finding out about users' interests and preferences for e-business.

Building ontologies is a difficult task. Although many efforts have been attempted, many research issues remain open. Ontology learning is a new research area that aims to develop methodologies and tools for constructing ontologies in an engineering manner with a higher degree of automation. It is transdisciplinary and integrates techniques from knowledge representation, machine learning, statistics, logic, natural language processing, information extraction, and information retrieval. In the context of the Web, the problem of learning personalized ontologies has raised many new issues. In particular we consider the following issues:

- **Richness of semantic representation:** Can the user's interests and preferences be represented in a richer, more precise, and less ambiguous way than a keyword/item-based model?
- **Dependency of context:** Can the user's interests and preferences be captured with the background knowledge of the Web page?
- **Dynamic capture of user's interests:** Can the user's interests and preferences be captured dynamically to reflect the new content of the Web page?

- **Validity of the Built Ontologies:** What level of validity are the built ontologies, in terms of quality or accuracy in representing user's interests and preferences?

The goal of this chapter is to survey the main concepts, existing methods, and practices of learning personalized ontologies, with a focus on dealing with the issues described above. The survey will involve techniques from areas of ontology engineering, information extraction, information retrieval, unsupervised machine learning (e.g., neural networks and hierarchical clustering), and personalization. The rest of this chapter is organized as follows. The next section presents a review of the main concepts of ontologies, followed by a section that studies the state of the art in the area of *ontology learning*. Then, an overview of Web personalization, and issues and approaches for learning personalized ontologies are presented. Finally, a number of future research directions are described.

ONTOLOGIES: DEFINITIONS AND OVERVIEW

The importance of ontologies has been recognized in the computer science community. A good example is the key role they play in building Semantic Web applications. However, there are still different arguments as to the meaning of the term ontology. To begin the review, a study of the related concepts and clarification of the terminologies is necessary. This section is to provide an introduction and overview for such purpose.

The Origin

Attention should first be given to the distinction between the notions of *Ontology* (with capital "O") and *ontology* (with lower case "o") (Guarino,

1998). The former is the philosophy that studies the nature of beings, while the latter refers to an object that accounts for a view of the world within a certain context (Gruber, 1993). According to the Oxford English Dictionary (*www.oed.com*), *ontology* (with small "o") is a countable noun. It is "a theory or conception relating to the nature of being."

The Notion of Ontologies in Computer Science

In computer science, ontologies were first developed in *artificial intelligence* (AI), which is a field for reasoning about models of the world. AI researchers use the term "ontology" to describe the world that is being represented within a context. Since its first usage in computer science, the definition of ontology has changed and evolved over time. The most common citation in the literature is attributed to Gruber's (1993) definition that specifies an ontology as "an explicit specification of a conceptualization." Borst (1997) refined this definition to "a formal specification of a shared conceptualization." Studer, Benjamins, and Fensel (1998) further developed the above two definitions to be more specific:

An ontology is a formal, explicit specification of a shared conceptualisation. Conceptualisation refers to an abstract model of some phenomenon in the world by having identified the relevant concepts of that phenomenon. Explicit means that the type of concepts used, and the constraints on their use are explicitly defined. Formal refers to the fact that the ontology should be machine readable, which excludes natural language. Shared reflects the notion that an ontology captures consensual knowledge, that is, it is not private of some individual, but accepted by a group.

It can be seen that the term "conceptualization" is central to these definitions. The concept of conceptualization comes from the field of AI, which consists of a set of objects assumed to exist in a given domain and the inter-relationships of these objects. The set of objects and their interrelationships are expressed in a declarative formal vocabulary that represents the knowledge of the given domain (Genesereth & Nilsson, 1987). With the account for the *meaning* of relevant objects and relations, a conceptualization is seen as a set of rules describing the structure of a piece of reality (Guarino & Giaretta, 1995). In other words, a conceptualization is an abstract model that represents a piece of reality (Pinto & Martins, 2004) and can be used to communicate meanings among agents (Maedche, 2003).

A "shared conceptualization" promises a common understanding among agents in the communication. To fulfill this requirement, agreements about objects and relations being communicated must exist (Gruber, 1993). Given that the underlying concept of an ontology is to provide a *shared conceptualization* of the world that is being represented, an ontology promises a shared and common understanding among agents by capturing *consensual* knowledge in a general and formal manner (Corcho, Fernández-López, & Gómez-Pérez, 2003).

Therefore, fundamental to the notion of a *computer science ontology* (denoted as the term "ontology" in the rest of this chapter, unless otherwise specified) is *conceptualization* and *communication*. To reach a common conclusion in the communication, accurate, consistent, and meaningful distinctions among concepts and relations in the ontology must be made. To meet this requirement, logic-based languages are usually employed to express ontologies. However, logical theories are mainly used by skilled or trained people and inference engines. This conflicts with the fact that ontologies are used by human and machine agents. To minimize possible misunderstandings, ontologies should allow direct mappings to natural languages. In an attempt to address this issue, Maedche (2003) has proposed an ontology structure for formalizing domain theory and a lexicon to discover semantics for communication:

Ontology Structure

An ontology structure is a 5-tuple $O := \{C, R, H^C, rel, A^O\}$*, consisting of:*

- *Two disjoint sets* C *and* R *whose elements are called concepts and relations, respectively.*
- *A concept hierarchy* $H^C : H^C$ *is a directed relation* $H^C \subseteq C \times C$ *which is called concept hierarchy or taxonomy.* $H^C(C_1, C_2)$ *means that* C_1 *is a subconcept of* C_2.
- *A function* $rel : R \to C \times C$ *that relates concepts non-taxonomically. The function* $dom : R \to C$ *with* $dom(R) := \Pi_1(rel(R))$ *gives the domain of R, and* $range : R \to C$ *with* $range(R) := \Pi_2(rel(R))$ *give its range. For* $rel(R) = (C_1, C_2)$ *one may also write* $R(C_1, C_2)$.
- *A set of ontology axioms* A^O*, expressed in an appropriate logical language, e.g., first order logic.* (p. 18)

Lexicon for Ontology Structure

A lexicon for the ontology structure $O := \{C, R, H^C, rel, A^O\}$ *is a 4-tuple* $L := \{L^C, L^R, F, G\}$ *consisting of:*

- *Two sets* L^C *and* L^R*, whose elements are called lexical entries for concepts and relations, respectively.*
- *Two relations* $F \subseteq L^C \times C$ *and* $G \subseteq L^R \times R$ *called references for concepts and relations, respectively. Based on* F*, let for* $L \in L^C$*,* $F(L) = \{C \in C \mid (L, C) \in F\}$ *and for* $F^{-1}(C) = \{L \in L^C \mid L, C) \in F\}$*,* G *and* G^{-1} *are defined analogously."* (p. 18)

Note that the definition allows concept references separated from concept denotations. This separation enables avoiding an instantaneous conflict when merging very domain-specific ontologies—a fundamental requirement of the Semantic Web (Maedche & Staab, 2001). The inclusion of a lexicon makes an ontology representation explicitly at a lexical level, enabling a direct mapping to a natural language. An example can be found in Maedche (2003).

Classification of Ontologies

The notion of ontology is sometimes "diluted" to the simplest case, in which *taxonomies* are considered full ontologies (Guarino, 1998; Studer et al., 1998). For example, Lassila and McGuinness (2001) consider the Yahoo! Directory (www. yahoo.com) as ontologies based on the consensual conceptualization it provides for a given domain. To clarify the concept, the ontology community develops two criteria to categorize the ontologies: the depth of the domain model and the amount of restrictions on domain semantics (Corcho et al., 2003). Based on these criteria, ontologies can be lightweight or heavyweight (Corcho et al., 2003; Gómez-Pérez, Fernández-López, & Corcho, 2004). *Lightweight ontologies* describe concepts and relationships that hold among them. *Heavyweight ontologies* add axioms with constraints to lightweight ontologies. Generally, lightweight ontologies hold simple relations such as "is-a" relation. Heavyweight ontologies offer the ability to include other complex types of relations (Guarino, 1998; Corcho et al., 2003; Gómez-Pérez et al., 2004). The Cyc (Lenat, 1995) ontology is a good example of a heavyweight ontology. With the intention of covering common-sense knowledge, Cyc organizes the knowledge under *microtheories,* each of which is an ontology for a specific domain.

Another popular classification system proposes to use the "subject of conceptualization" as the main criterion (Guarino, 1998; Sure & Studer, 2002b; Gómez-Pérez et al., 2004). By considering the level of generality (Guarino, 1998), ontologies are distinguished as follows:

- *Top-level ontology,* which is the vocabulary of highly generic concepts and is independent of a particular problem or domain. This kind of ontology is also known as *foundational ontology* (Sure & Studer, 2002b) or *upper-level* ontology (Gómez-Pérez et al., 2004).
- *Domain ontology,* which is the vocabulary of a given domain. The vocabulary is a specialization of concepts introduced in the related top-level ontology.
- *Task ontology,* which is the vocabulary of a given task or activity. The vocabulary is a specialization of concepts introduced in the related top-level ontology.
- *Application ontology,* which is the vocabulary of very specific concepts related to a particular domain and task. Such concepts often correspond to roles played by domain entities for a certain activity.

Methodologies

Ontology building is a challenging task. A number of methodologies have been proposed to guide the building. However, different approaches focus on different aspects of the building process. For example, KACTUS (Schreiber, Wielinga, & Jansweijer,1995) is built by an abstraction process from an initial knowledge base, while SENSUS (Swartout, Patil, Knight, & Russ, 1997) builds the skeleton of the ontology automatically from a large ontology. To compare the different approaches, Corcho et al. (2003) take account of the degree of dependency of the built ontology and its application. This is measured by the dependency of the development process and the uses of the ontology. In this aspect, KACTUS and

On-To-Knowledge (OTK) (Fernández-López & Gómez-Pérez, 2002; Sure & Studer, 2002a) are application driven (Schreiber et al.,1995), hence they are application dependent. TOVE (Grűninger & Fox, 1995) and SENSUS are semi-application dependent, while Cyc (Lenat & Guha, 1989; Lenat, 1995), Skeletal (Uschold & Grűninger, 1996), and METHONTOLOGY (Fernández-López, Gómez-Pérez, & Juristo, 1997; Fernández-López, Gómez-Pérez, Sierra, & Sierra, 1999) are application independent.

Of these approaches, TOVE has a higher degree of formality. It has been applied and tested in business domains. However, as in Seletal and KACTUS, TOVE does not provide much guidance for naive ontology builders. OTK identifies most processes of ontology development, focusing on knowledge management applications. Compared to these approaches, METHONTOLOGY provides better guidance for each process. It focuses on acquisition and conceptualization, and enables ontology construction at the knowledge level. It was used by the Foundation for Intelligent Physical Agents (FIPA) (*www.fipa.org*) for constructing ontologies. Moreover, METHONTOLOGY is the methodology that has most compliance with the IEEE standard of software development (IEEE, 1996).

None of these approaches can be considered as mature, when compared to software engineering and knowledge engineering methodologies. The major issue is that these proposals are not unified; each methodology or method follows a different approach. The need for creating a consensual methodology for ontology construction has been noted. Collaboration between different groups to unify different approaches is thus proposed (Corcho et al., 2003). A good attempt is an engineering approach, which develops an ontology construction process as an engineering task, namely *ontology engineering.* In the next sub-section we present this approach.

Ontology Engineering

An ontology engineering (OE) approach provides "a basis of building models of all things, in which information science is interested, in the world" (Mizoguchi, Ikeda, & Sinitsa, 1997). This approach consists of a set of processes related to the development of ontologies for a particular domain and methodologies to guide the construction process. The set of processes is referred to as an *ontology lifecycle.* According to Pinto and Martins (2004), these processes are specification, conceptualization, formalization, implementation, maintenance, knowledge acquisition, evaluation, and documentation. Each of these processes fulfills a task as follows:

- *Specification* identifies the purpose and scope of the ontology;
- *Conceptualization* describes the ontology in a conceptual model;
- *Formalization* transforms the conceptual model from a descriptive model into a formalized model;
- *Implementation* implements the formalized ontology in a knowledge representation language;
- *Maintenance* updates the implemented ontology;
- *Knowledge acquisition* acquires knowledge about the subject;
- *Evaluation* evaluates the quality of the built ontology from a technical perspective; and
- *Documentation* documents terms represented in the ontology, and the relationships among these terms and reports of what was done and how it was done.

Superficially, these activities are similar to software engineering activities (IEEE, 1996), however they differ in two main aspects: knowledge acquisition and design activities. Knowledge acquisition is an essential part of OE processes; it came to software engineering only recently and is seldom presented. Design activities in software engineering are divided into conceptualization and formalization activities in OE. Conceptualization activities capture the domain image in an abstract model, while formalization activities enable the ease of implementation, and in some cases allow automation. On the other hand, evaluation is performed throughout the lifetime. During the development of an ontology, one can go back from any activity to any previous activity of the development process, when an unsatisfied evaluation is found. This is different from software development that has an iterative lifecycle.

Towards an engineering discipline, in addition to identifying the set of processes, methodologies to guide the construction of ontologies are required. Recently, the emergence of the Semantic Web has introduced new requirements for the way ontologies are built. In other words, when ontologies are built for the Semantic Web, new issues need to be considered (Pinto & Martins, 2004; Maedche, 2003). Given the fact that the Semantic Web is a "meta-Web" of the current Web, to realize it a large number of domain-specific ontologies need to be built. Building domain-specific ontologies requires domain experts to contribute domain knowledge. Therefore, domain experts, together with ontology engineers, will be the developers of ontologies. The role of domain experts is to model and maintain ontologies. On the other hand, since the purpose of the Semantic Web is to support better information process and access to the existing Web content, it is to be used by humans and machines in different applications (Maedche, 2003).

With these two issues in mind, Maedche (2003) has proposed a layered framework. The framework is based on the distinction between the notions of "general" and "specific" in a domain of interest: while *ontologies* are to capture the conceptual structures of the domain, *knowledge bases* aim to specify given concrete states. Since knowledge bases describing particular circumstances can be defined on top of ontologies, a knowledge base can be instantiated using an ontology structure. Therefore, a knowledge base structure can be formally defined as follows (Maedche, 2003):

Knowledge Base Structure

A knowledge base structure is a 4-tuple $KB:=\{O,I, inst, instr\}$, *that consists of:*

- *An ontology* $O:=\{C,R,H^C,rel,A^O\}$.
- *A set* I *whose elements are called instances.*
- *A function* $inst:C \to 2^I$ *called concept instantiation. For* $inst(C)=I$ *one may also write* $C(I)$.
- *A function* $instr:R \to 2^{I \times I}$ *called relation instantiation. For* $instr(R)=\{I_1,I_2\}$ *one may also write* $R(I_1,I_2)$. *(p. 20)*

Similar to the ontology structure O, a lexicon is defined for a given knowledge base structure KB:

Lexicon for Knowledge Base Structure

A lexicon for knowledge base structure $KB:=\{O,I,inst,instr\}$ *is a tuple* $L^{KB}:=(L^I,J)$ *consisting of:*

- *A set* L^I *whose elements are called lexical entries for instances, respectively.*
- *A relation* $J \subseteq L^I \times I$ *reference for instances, respectively. Based on* J, *let for* $L \in L^I$, $J(L)=\{I \in I \mid (L,I) \in J\}$ *and for* $J^{-1}(I)=\{L \in L^I \mid (L,I) \in J\}$. *(p. 20)*

A *layered* approach is thus proposed based on the ontology structure O, the knowledge base structure KB, and their corresponding lexicons L and L^{KB}, respectively. The layered framework consists of three layers. From bottom to the top, they are:

The first layer comprises lexical entries for concepts L^C, relations L^R, and instances L^{KB}.

The second layer includes elements from:

- **Ontology structure** O: The set of concepts C referenced by L^C, the set of relations R referenced by L^R, the concept taxonomy defined by statements such as $H^C(C_1, C_2)$, and non-taxonomic relations defined by statements such as $R(C_1, C_2)$.
- **Knowledge base structure** KB: The set of instances I referenced by L^{KB}, the set of concept $C(I)$, and relation instantiations $R(I_1, I_2)$.

The third layer is the set of ontological axioms A^O.

The layered framework supports incremental and cyclic development of ontologies. The incremental model is based on the interaction between layers, and the dependency or overlap between ontology and knowledge base. Advantages of this layered approach can be seen from the following aspects (Maedche, 2003):

- The ontology structure supports ontology representation for the Semantic Web; together with the knowledge base structure, it can be transformed into different concrete ontology representation languages such as the W3C standard resource description framework RDF(S). Using a language that supports inference mechanisms enables using ontology to reasoning about the Semantic Web and thus improves the effectiveness of Web information process and access.
- The lexicon layer provides an explicit lexical representation. This fulfills the requirement of communication about ontologies between humans and machines. While formal semantics is an important building block of ontologies, the lexical entries take the role of references to them.

We can see that these two advantages benefit the development of Semantic Web applications. However, their corresponding drawbacks also need to be noted: the separation of ontology and knowledge base structures might have no strict boundary in reality. This can result in some overlap between the two and lead to overhead in the development or redundancy in the application. In addition, the explicit representation at the lexical level restricts ontologies to natural language applications.

An important issue has been raised: what types of data can be used to build ontologies? Generally, ontologies can be built from different types of source data. The current trend is to learn ontologies from natural language textual data. The motivation comes from the following understandings:

- With the rapid increase of digital resources, valuable information tends to be stored in free text format. Therefore, the ability to capture a domain image from raw textual data has a higher value of using and sharing domain knowledge. Such a domain image can be presented in the form of ontologies (Chen, 2006). On the other hand, much of the Web content data is unstructured textual data (Kosala & Blockeel, 2000). Capturing the content of Web data in ontologies is the first step towards the building of Semantic Web applications. Thus, natural language text is considered as the most important source data of ontologies for the Semantic Web (Maedche, 2003).

- Although techniques and tools for ontology construction have been developed over the last decade, they provide little support to building ontologies in an efficient engineering manner. Many relevant ontologies were constructed in a more manual manner than an engineering task (Pinto & Martins, 2004; Celjuska, 2004). The labor-intensive and time-consuming manual construction has introduced a serious knowledge acquisition bottleneck in building ontologies. How to develop large and adequate ontologies within short timeframes to keep the cost down is an open question in the research community. One way to address this issue is to develop automatic techniques and tools for the construction of ontologies. However, current technologies do not support fully automatic processes. While automatic construction of ontologies remains in the distant future, achieving semi-automation has become a compelling goal. When building ontologies from textual data, existing unsupervised machine learning techniques can be integrated into the process to achieve a higher degree of automation. This integration process is often referred to as *ontology learning*.

The role of ontology learning has been recognized as an important process in ontology engineering; in particular, a semi-automatic learning process is considered to simplify the process of ontology engineering. In the next section we present the state of the art in ontology learning.

ONTOLOGY LEARNING FROM TEXT

Ontology learning has emerged as a new area aiming at the integration of multiple disciplines, to develop methodologies and techniques that can be used to facilitate the ontology construction process (Maedche, 2003). Generally, ontology learning is concerned with knowledge acquisition (Buitelaar, Cimiano, & Magnini, 2005). However, there is no consensus about the precise tasks an ontology learning framework needs included (Buitelaar et al., 2005). In the context of learning ontologies from text, Buitelaar et al. (2005) have made the first attempt that contributes to the understanding of ontology learning tasks. By analyzing the fundamental requirement of an ontology structure, they have proposed a set of subtasks. These subtasks are organized in a *layer cake* with an increasing order of complexity of the learning target. From the simplest task sitting at the bottom layer to the complex task at the top layer, these subtasks learn *terms, synonyms, concepts, concept hierarchies, relations,* and *rules.* The state of the art of these subtasks is presented below.

Layer 1: Terms

This layer is concerned with term extraction from text. When free text is used as the source of data for creating ontologies, the task of ontology learning is concerned with knowledge acquisition from text. Term extraction is designed to identify relevant terms from text. The most commonly used technique is of *feature selection,* which is a process that selects a subset of the original feature set according to a given criteria (Liu, Liu, Chen, & Ma, 2003). The aim of the process is to derive a reliable feature set that retains the original meaning of terms, help remove noise from source data, and provide a better understanding of the source data (Ankolekar, Seo, & Sycara, 2003; Liu et al., 2003; Osiski, 2004).

The extraction process is based on the weights of terms. Such weights reflect the importance of the associated terms in the text. The technique used to derive such a weight is called *term weighting.* Many term weighting schemes have been proposed. Among these, the most popular ones are *Term Frequency* (TF) and *Term Frequency-Inverse Document Frequency* (TF-IDF). According to Salton and McGill (1983), TF is a measure of proportion to the standard occurrence frequency of each term in the document. The *Inverse Document Frequency* (IDF) is the proportion to the total number of documents to which the term is assigned. IDF is often used with the TF to measure the similarity between documents, a scheme that is referred to as TF-IDF. *Document Frequency* (DF) (Salton & McGill, 1983) was originally used in the field of information retrieval. For a given document collection, it is defined as the number of documents that contain a term. The idea behind *Document Frequency Thresholding* (DFT) is the assumption that rare terms make no contribution either to the category prediction or in the global performance. When used as a threshold, each unique term in the training set is compared to its DF. Terms are selected if their DFs are greater than some pre-determined threshold. For text categorization, it is simple and effective. It can be easily scaled to a large dataset with linear time complexity (Yang & Pedersen, 1997). Since it does not require class information, it can be applied to text clustering. The drawback is that each term is given the same importance in different documents to which they belong. For example, there might be common terms that are of high DF but uniformly distributed over different classes (Liu et al., 2003).

Term Strength (TS) (Yang, 1995; Yang & Pedersen, 1997; Liu et al., 2003) measures term importance based on the term's co-occurrences in pairs of related documents in the collection. It is computed as the probability of a term in a document related to any documents that contain the term. Let d_i, d_j be an arbitrary pair of related documents, and t a term, then the TS of term t is defined as $TS(t)=P_r(t\in d_i \mid t\in d_j)$, where P_r is the probability of $t\in d_i$ to $t\in d_j$.

The selection of a pair of related documents d_i and d_j is based on the similarity between these documents. If the similarity value is above a threshold, then d_i and d_j are related documents. Thus, a similarity measure and a threshold parameter are required for the TS calculation. Since the computation of similarity is performed on every possible pair of documents, the time complexity is quadratic in the number of training documents.

Term Contribution (TC) (Liu et al., 2003) computes the contribution of a term by document similarity using the dot product:

$$sim(d_i, d_j) = \sum_t f(t, d_i) \times f(t, d_j),$$

where $f(t,d)$ denotes the tf*idf (Salton & McGill, 1983) weight of term t in document d. The TC of a term in a dataset is then defined as its overall contribution to the documents' similarities:

$$TC(t) = \sum_{i,j} f(t,d_i) \times f(t,d_j).$$

If the weights of all terms are equal, set $f(t,d)=1$, then the value $TC(t)$ can be written as $TC(t)=DF(t)(DF(t)-1)$. When $DF(t)$ is a positive integer, the transformation increases monotonously. Thus, DF is a special case of TC. TC has a time complexity of $O(MN^2)$, where M is the dimension of the features and N the average number of documents in which per term occurs.

Liu et al. (2003) have found that TS and TC are better than DF. Compared to TS, TC has a lower time complexity. It is recommended as a better choice than TS as an unsupervised feature selection method for text clustering. These authors have also proposed an iterative feature selection method by utilizing some supervised methods. Details about this method can be found in Liu et al. (2003).

Works on this layer applied to ontology learning have been limited. The main issue is that the learning process is only concerned with the extraction of relevant terms. This can easily result in a lack of identifying terms' internal semantic relations. For example, natural language text often contains a certain amount of synonyms. Thus, learning synonyms is important for knowledge acquisition from text.

Layer 2: Synonyms

A synonym is "a word having the same sense as another" (www.oed.com). Therefore, synonyms can reveal semantic similarity of terms. The main problem of this learning task is the identification of the correct sense of a term in the given context. This issue is referred to as *word sense disambiguation* (WSD), which was originally considered as one of the linguistic problems in traditional text

analysis. In the context of ontology learning, efforts have been channeled into utilizing WordNet (Fellbaum, 1998; WordNet, n.d.) and clustering algorithms.

WordNet is a lexical reference system. Inspired by current psycholinguistic theories of human lexical memory, WordNet organizes English nouns, verbs, adjectives, and adverbs into synonym sets, each representing one underlying lexical concept, referred to as *synset*. A word with multiple senses belongs to multiple synsets. WordNet consists of 115,424 concepts and 152,059 lexical words. Different relations (e.g., hypernym, hyponym, meronym, and holonym relations) are used to link the synonym sets in the form of ontologies. Since synsets are the basic building blocks of WordNet, the basic semantic relation in WordNet is synonymy (Fellbaum, 1998; WordNet, n.d.). Since WordNet is a linguistic resource for general-purpose reference and it is free to be downloaded and accessed online, it has attracted much attention by the research community. However, its "static" content and "general-purpose only" restrict its use in a particular domain where domain-specific terms are references to the domain knowledge. Clustering techniques are therefore utilized to enable the *dynamic* acquisition of synonyms. On the other hand, recent research has found that ambiguous terms might have very specific meanings in some domain areas (Buitelaar et al., 2005). A learning approach at this layer needs to take these issues into account during the learning process.

Layer 3: Concepts

Recall that *concepts* and their inter-relationships are the fundamental elements of an ontology. In WordNet, a set of synonyms called *synset* is defined as a concept. Much research such as Hotho, Staab, and Stumme (2003) and Chen, Alahakoon, and Indrawan (2005) has followed this practice. From a linguistic point of view, some of these works overlap with the learning of terms and synonyms (Layers 2 and 3). Buitelaar et al. (2005) see a concept as a compound of:

- An intentional definition of the concept,
- A set of concept instances, and
- A set of linguistic realization.

In the case of natural language textual data, terms are linguistic realizations of concepts. In this light, ontology population (Etzioni et al., 2004) addresses the problem of learning concepts in an extensional context. With regard to the intentional definition, concept properties such as its relationship to other concepts must be included. In addition, a description of the concept is also required. While OntoLearn (Navigli, Velardi, & Gangemi, 2003; Missikof, Navigli, & Velardi, 2002) is one of the few works that can be found on learning glosses for domain-specific concepts, learning relationships between concepts is considered a set of distinct tasks. Since relations in an ontology can vary, what kind of relations an ontology can hold depends on the application domain and the purpose of building the ontology. Often, concepts hold some taxonomic relationships among themselves. Each concept in the taxonomy is usually corresponding to different modules or sub-ontologies. Such a hierarchical architecture enables decomposition of the domain knowledge. Therefore, taxonomies are considered key components of ontologies. Learning taxonomic relations is seen as a key task in learning ontologies. In the *layer cake* framework, it is referred to as *concept hierarchies* at Layer 4.

Layer 4: Concept Hierarchies

Concept hierarchies are presented in taxonomies. A taxonomy is a classification of similarities. A taxonomic relation is subsumption, of which concept *A* subsumes concept *B*, if and only if any instances of *B* are necessarily instances of *A* (Gandon, 2002). In other words, a taxonomy holds *is-a* relations. According to Uschold and Grüninger

(1996), three approaches can be used to build a taxonomy of concepts. These approaches are:

- *Top-down* identifies concepts from the most general to the most specific;
- *Bottom-up* identifies concepts from the most specific to the most general; and
- *Combination* (also known as *middle-out*) identifies the more salient concepts first, then generalizes and specializes them appropriately.

These approaches have been employed by many methodologies for identifying concepts. For example, KACTUS uses a top-down approach. Skeletal, TOVE, and METHONTOLOGY use a combination approach. The OTK does not fix a strategy, but rather, it chooses a strategy according to the application.

The choice of an approach is based on the domain, source data, and the purpose of building ontologies. Each approach results in a different level of detail. Top-down provides high-level philosophical considerations, making coherence maintenance facilitate. It enables better control of the level of detail and the reuse of ontologies. However, a risk of less stability and a miss of the commonality inherent in the complex web of interconnected concepts exist. Bottom-up tailors ontologies with fine-grained concepts. The trade-off is the higher overall effort and the difficulty of spotting commonality from the related concepts. Combination encourages the emergence of thematic fields, enhancing the modularity and stability of the result. It offers a balance of the level of detail. While this approach is being acknowledged as a better approach, it suffers from the workload of identifying the most relevant concepts (Uschold & Grüninger, 1996; Gandon, 2002).

Researchers have addressed the problem by integrating clustering and related techniques to form hierarchical clusters and label them. Labels are then extracted and presented in taxonomies.

The motivation of this line is to utilize unsupervised hierarchical clustering techniques to achieve a higher degree of automation in the learning process. As Maedche and Staab (2000) have noted, common approaches currently being researched are to collect relevant concepts and cluster them into a hierarchy using combinations of statistic and linguistic data. For example, ASIUM (Faure & Nédellec, 1998) is a semi-automatic system that learns semantic knowledge from text. It forms basic clusters by head words that occur with the same verb after the same preposition or with the same syntactical role. Using these classes as input, ASIUM builds an ontology level by level. It aggregates the clusters and extracts concepts from newly formed clusters to represent the ontology of the domain. At each level the number of clusters to be aggregated is restricted to two. This restriction may lead to an enormous number of useless classes. Hence, a process of removing all useless classes is performed in a post-processing phase. Experiments have shown that ASIUM performs well on a corpus of cooking recipes; however, the nature of the algorithm might not give a promising result in a general domain (Celjuska, 2004). Based on a top-down fashion, Khan and Luo (2002) modify the self-organizing tree (SOTA) (Dopazo & Carazo, 1997) with the extension of topic tracking to construct a hierarchy. An automatic concept selection algorithm from WordNet (Fellbaum, 1998; WordNet, n.d.) is integrated into their model for labeling.

While these approaches attempt to address the problem of *knowledge acquisition bottleneck* by targeting a higher degree of automatic process, there is a lack of consideration given to the resultant ontologies in the *level of meeting the requirements or expectations*. For example, what is the impact of the resultant hierarchy on the target ontology, e.g., ASIUM uses a bottom-up process that will result in very fine clusters that may not meet the requirements of a practical application. When labeling clusters, how do you identify the abstraction level of clusters and the relationship between layers so that they can reflect the taxonomic structure that will be used to construct the ontology? These two issues are referred to as *taxonomic problem* and *semantic problem,* respectively (Chen, 2006).

It is apparent that the *taxonomic problem* is closely related to the clustering techniques employed. To address the issue carefully, selection of a clustering algorithm is required. Dimensions to be considered are the *degree of automation* and the ability to provide an *adaptable hierarchy architecture*. Since labels are based on the resultant clusters, the *abstraction level of clusters* and the *number of layers in the hierarchy* will have an impact on the semantic issues. Therefore, the clustering algorithm also needs to take these two dimensions into account. The Hierarchical GSOM Clustering (BHGSOM) (Chen et al., 2006) is a good example attempting to address these issues. It makes use of the spread factor of an unsupervised neural network model called Growing Self-Organizing Map (GSOM) (Alahakoon, Halgamuge, & Srinivasan, 2000). The model minimizes the workload needed for discovering necessary layers in the hierarchy, implicitly supporting the ability to identify and limit the depth of the target taxonomies.

The *semantic problem* requires semantic commitments that are methods to guide the construction of taxonomies. In the context of using a clustering approach, it is more specifically in the guiding of labeling process. Works at this level can be found in the *semantic commitment* (Bachimont, Isaac, & Troncy, 2002) and the *OntoDiscFM* (Chen, 2006).

Semantic Commitment

Bachimont et al. (2002) first proposed a natural language methodology called *semantic commitment* to guide the construction of taxonomies. The method takes a semantic approach to normalize the meaning of the concepts, which are the knowledge primitives of the ontology in a natural way by using natural language. It consists of three steps:

- *Semantic normalization* of terms that will be used later in the constructed ontology, by choosing linguistic labels and specifying the meaning of these labels used for naming the concepts. A taxonomy of notions is produced by using four principles of differential semantics:

    - *Similarity with parent (swp)*, the reason the notion inherits properties of the one that subsumes it;
    - *Similarity with siblings (sws)*, a property to compare the notion with its siblings;
    - *Difference with siblings (dws)*, a property to distinguish the notion from its siblings; and
    - *Difference with parent (dwp)*, a property to distinguish the notion from its parent.

Interestingly, the authors have found that the *swp* and *sws* are shared among the notions of the same siblings. The *dwp* is the sum of *sws* and *dws*. The meaning of each node in the taxonomy is all the similarities and differences attached to all the notions from the most generic root to this node.

- *Knowledge formalization* of primitives obtained, where notions become concepts, performing as formal primitives, and become part of a referential ontology. Each concept has a set of domain objects. Hence, set operations can be used to obtain new concepts.
- *Ontology computation*, where possible computational operations are performed on the referential concepts.

The semantic commitment approach has been implemented in a prototype and applied to build several ontologies. However, since semantic matching is based on a specific context, the contracted ontology is valid only for a domain or task. In addition to a limit on the scope, the approach takes domain terms as input source, requiring other tools to discover domain terms.

OntoDiscFM (Chen, 2006) is a hybrid framework for ontology discovery, which is a process of learning important lexical entries from a given set of text documents. Each of the learned lexical entries and relationships represent the underlying concepts and their taxonomic relationships that are contained in the documents. The learning process takes a clustering approach on a semantics base by integrating the lexical database WordNet and the neural network model BHGSOM. To improve the clustering performance and integrate the clusters into ontologies at the semantic level, three components called Semantic Feature Extraction, Cluster Labeling, and Taxonomy Refining are developed, with the semantic aspect highlighted below:

- *Semantic feature extraction* extracts relevant features at the semantic level taking into account background knowledge of the source data. The extraction is supported by:

    - A *concept tree* that identifies the scope of background knowledge for a given concept,
    - A *concept hierarchy* that narrows the scope of background knowledge for identifying an appropriate concept in the concept tree,
    - A *stopping criterion* that determines the appropriate generalization of a concept in the concept tree,
    - A *context factor* that identifies the degree of generalization of a layer in the concept tree, and
    - A *lookup table* that contains semantics of the source data and their background knowledge. It is used to support the semantic labeling and refining.

- *Cluster labeling* uses a semantically driven approach to label clusters. Labels contain background knowledge derived from the source data for clustering. Such labels cannot only uncover the meaning of clusters, but also reveal the relationship between layers of the hierarchy, providing a "foundation" for extracting taxonomy of concepts.
- *Taxonomy refining* uses a set of heuristic criteria for refining taxonomies based on the semantics and background knowledge. With human intervention and domain knowledge input, it ensures the fineness of labels from an ontology perspective.

The semantic approach taken in labeling and refining components has initiated a research attempt in presenting taxonomic skeletons with a "self-presenting" manner, which is the use of the semantic references learned from the source data. This semantics-based approach retains the information contained in the source data at a higher level.

In summary, taxonomies are key components of ontologies. Learning taxonomies is a key task in ontology learning. Works on this layer have been carried out; however, there remain issues. More research is required, in particular addressing the taxonomic problem and the semantic problem.

Layer 5: Relations

The task of this layer is to learn non-taxonomic relations. Although taxonomic relations is the key relation in ontologies, non-taxonomic relations may also play important roles in some application domains, for example, *part-of* relations in medical domains (e.g., an ontology for describing human body structure). Learning non-taxonomic relations is difficult, since what type of relations can be extracted is unknown. In other words, the extraction is often used to discover new relationships between concepts. In case of natural language text as the source of data, statistical and linguistic analysis techniques are often used.

While non-taxonomic relation extraction is mostly in the acquisition of selection restrictions for verb arguments (Buitelaar et al., 2005), taxonomic relations usually hold between nouns. A novel approach making use of the taxonomies for discovering non-taxonomic relations has been proposed by Maedche and Staab (2000). The authors use a generalized association rule algorithm by analyzing statistical information about the linguistic output. They use background knowledge from the domain taxonomy to determine the appropriate level of abstraction at which to define the relations.

Non-taxonomic relations appear as an important building block of ontologies. In some particular domain, it can be a major building block. However, work at this layer is still not well researched. More efforts are required.

Layer 6: Rules

The task at this layer is to learn rules from source data. Work in this area is rather rare. Recently, noticeable attention was raised by the PASCAL Recognizing Textual Entailment (RTE) Challenge (Dagan, Glickman, & Magnini, 2005). The motivation behind the RTE is that natural language can have variability of semantic expressions. Different texts can represent or infer the same meaning, often resulting in many-to-many relations between language expressions and meanings. A model that can recognize mappings between different text variants and a particular target meaning is needed. In other words, it is used to recognize whether the meaning of one text fragment can be inferred from the other. The RTE has been proposed as a generic task that captures major semantic inference needs across applications processing natural languages.

Although works in this area remain under-researched, the RTE has made an initial attempt to address the problem of learning semantic entailments for natural language applications such as question answering, information retrieval, information extraction, and (multi) document summarization. This research effort has greatly increased the awareness of the problem and could open up many new possibilities for the research community.

From the above study we can see that learning of terms, synonyms, concepts, and concept hierarchies are closely related to natural language processing and text clustering. Depending on definitions, these processes may overlap to some extent. There are taxonomic relations and non-taxonomic relations. While the former is necessary, the latter can vary, depending on the target and the application domain. The extraction of rules is a new area in ontology learning. The RTE has initiated an attempt in learning semantic entailments. All these learning tasks constitute the complex task of ontology learning. Central to the problem of these learning sub-tasks is the *semantic problem.* Ontology learning should aim at a higher degree of richness of semantic representation.

LEARNING ONTOLOGIES FOR PERSONALIZATION

To understand how ontologies can be applied to personalization, we start this section by introducing what personalization is in general, and Web personalization more specifically. Then, we discuss how techniques presented above can be utilized to learn personalized ontologies as a means to personalization processes and services.

Personalization

Personalization is a process of customizing information access to end users. It has been regarded as one of the approaches to the problem of information overload. With the rapid increase

of information available online, personalization has become a key component of Web applications to tailor information content, structure, and presentation to the needs of a particular user or a group of users (Mobasher, Cooley, & Srivastava, 2000; Eirinaki & Vazirgiannis, 2003). A simple example is to create a personal gateway to a Web mail client such as Google or Yahoo! mail. This kind of personalization requires the user to specify the settings. More complex examples targeting automatic adjustment of information to meet the user's requirements can be found in e-business applications. For example, Amazon's (www.amazon.com) recommendation provides suggestions of books according to the similarities in the user's purchase history.

The type of personalization applied to the Web can be any action—for example, browsing the Web, trading stocks, or purchasing a book—that makes a user's Web experience personalized to his or her taste (Mobasher et al., 2000). Eirinaki and Vazirgiannis (2003) define a Web personalization process in four steps: collecting Web data, modeling and categorizing the collected data, analyzing the collected data, and determining actions to be performed. In the following we give an overview of the first three processes, which are essential steps before a personalized action can be performed.

Web Data

Web data can vary. Generally, there are content data, structure data, usage data, and user profile data. *Content data* can be text, images, or structured data presented to the end user. *Structure data* represents the structure of the content, for example, HTML or XML tags used within a page and hyperlinks that connect pages. *Usage data* is data about a user's Web experience such as IP address, access time, and path accessed. *User profile data* provides user data such as demographic information, and the interests and preferences of the user. Such information can be obtained from the user's input (e.g., registration form or questionnaires) or inferred by analyzing Web logs (Eirinaki & Vazirgiannis, 2003).

Modeling and Categorizing Web Data

Depending on the application domain, the collected data is pre-processed, for example, data cleaning and important features extraction. The processed data is then classified in conceptual categories for analyzing in the next step. Data mining techniques such as clustering, classification, and the related data pre-processing techniques can be utilized to fulfill the tasks at this step.

Analyzing Web Data

Existing analysis techniques have been largely focused on filtering and Web mining aspects. *Filtering* approaches include content-based filtering, collaborative filtering, and rule-base filtering. A *content-based filtering system* tracks a user's browsing behavior to discover his or her personal preferences (Eirinaki & Vazirgiannis, 2003; Pierrakos, Paliouras, Papatheodorou, & Spyropoulos, 2003). Often machine learning techniques are applied to Web content data. This can benefit the learning of the user's interest from the content of Web pages. A *collaborative filtering system* relies on the user's input. For example, input includes the rating of objects and explicitly expressing their preferences and interests. By making an assumption that users with similar behaviors have similar interests, collaborative filtering searches for common preferences of different users then returns information predicted to be of interest for the users. A *rule-based filtering system* requires users to answer a set of questions derived from a decision tree. The users' answers are then used as rules to filter out information that is not of interest.

Web mining is a research area that develops techniques and methods to discover knowledge from the Web. Works in this area can be divided into three sub-areas (Kosala & Blockeel, 2000): Web content mining, Web usage mining, and Web structure mining. *Web content mining* is to discover knowledge from the content of Web pages, *Web usage mining* analyzes Web usage data to discover usage patterns, and *Web structure mining* aims at mining the structure of the Web graph. Of these three mining spaces, Web usage mining concerned with user behaviors has a close relationship to the Web personalization. Since usage data are often collected when a user browses a Web site, they can capture the user's navigation behaviors. Web usage mining based on such data is an approach to discover users' interests, and thus it can be used for Web personalization.

The Role of Ontologies in Personalization

An important issue to a personalization process is the degree of automation. In other words, does the process require human involvement, and if so, to what degree. Like any artificial complex systems, a manual process is very labor intensive and time consuming. In the Web environment, a lower degree of automation will introduce a bottleneck in discovering interesting patterns for personalization.

Rule-based filtering and collaborative filtering approaches rely heavily on the users' participation to collect their profiles. This is very subjective since users may be reluctant to give true and/or complete data. In addition, users' interests and preferences may change over time, so the collected data can be easily out of date (Mobasher et al., 2000). Content-based filtering and Web usage mining approaches attempt to apply machine learning methods to alleviate this problem. The main problem with content-based filtering is the difficulty to analyze page content and reach a level of quality or accuracy that can be achieved by human experts. Since much of the Web content data is unstructured textual data, content-based filtering involves analysis of textual data. Taking a machine learning approach for text analysis has the difficulty of capturing semantic similarities. On the other hand, when there are limited textual contents, the semantic problem can be critical. Web mining usage approaches rely on the Web log data that captures users' navigation behaviors. Such data can facilitate the exploitation of usage patterns *dynamically.* Integrating unsupervised learning techniques into the approach enable automatic construction of user models. However, the fact that this group of techniques relies solely on usage data can result in failure to understanding the *meaning* of the user's interests. Consider that Sonja is reading a news article on *The Australian* newspaper Web site. The usage data captures her Web experience of browsing the Web site of the newspaper; however, it fails to capture the context of the story that has interested her. To better understand Sonja's interests, we need to look inside the story. This feature is not supported by usage mining techniques, but the content-based model. Thus, exploiting multiple sources of information, for example, the combination of usage data and Web page contents, is the key to building an efficient personalization system.

When applying a content-based filtering approach to the above example, we found that the article Sonja is reading describes kangaroo, koala, possum, and echidnas. Therefore we say that Sonja is interested in these animals. Given our knowledge that these animals are Australian animals, we can infer that Sonja is interested in Australian animals. However, without we humans involved, it would be difficult to predict "Australian animal" as a "general" interest of Sonja. This is a problem of *context* in natural language processing. In addition, if Sonja is interested in Australian animals, is she also interested in other animals? An issue raised here is: how can her interests be represented at an appropriate level of *granularity*, for example, "Australian animal" or "animal"? Building personalized ontologies

from Web textual data is one way to address these problems.

Taxonomies are key components of ontologies. An ontology with taxonomic relations provides the ability to represent users' interests and preferences in a richer, more precise, and less ambiguous manner than a keyword-based model. With taxonomic relations, an ontology organizes users' interests and preferences at different levels of granularity in a hierarchical structure. In other words, users' interests and preferences can be represented from coarse to fine-grained—for example, interests for broad topics such as traveling and working in China or Australia vs. preference for traveling and working in particular cities such as Beijing, Shanghai, Sydney, and Melbourne. However, it can be assumed that a user interested in *knowledge representation and reasoning* techniques is interested in the area of *artificial intelligence.* Integrating ontology learning techniques into content-based filtering and Web content mining process (to a certain extent, the former overlaps with the latter), together with Web usage mining techniques to learn ontologies, can better discover an individual user's interests and preferences, explicitly or implicitly, at a conceptual level. Since ontologies are learned from Web data that reflects an individual user's Web experience, they are personalized and can be referred to as personalized ontologies. Such personalized ontologies can enhance the information retrieval process by complementing implicit preferences to explicit requests.

On the other hand, ontologies promise a shared and common understanding across humans and machines. The ability to provide formal, machine-readable concepts can benefit personalization systems. Ontology-related languages such as RDF, OWL, and SRWL, which support inference mechanisms, can be used to improve the effectiveness of the personalization process.

How Personalized Ontologies Can Be Learned

As studied in the previous section, there are different levels of complexity on ontology learning tasks. According to the definition earlier, learning of concepts and relations is the fundamental task of learning an ontology. In the above example, learning the concept of "Australian animal" and its relationships to "kangaroo", "koala", "possum", and "echidnas", as well as the relationships among these animals, is the key towards building an ontology to represent Sonja's interests. One of the main problems of this process is how to learn the concept "Australian animal" when the wording does not appear in the source data. In other words, the concept "Australian animal" is hidden behind the concepts of "kangaroo", "koala", "possum", and "echidnas". In this scenario, the concept of "Australian animal" is referred to as the *background knowledge* (Chen, 2006; Chen et al., 2005; Hotho et al., 2003) or *contextual information* (Lau, Hao, Tang, & Zhou, 2007; Zadrozny, 1995) of "kangaroo," "koala," "possum," and "echidnas." When we humans read the article, we can easily find out this contextual information based on our knowledge. However, can it be achieved without humans involved? This is a problem related to the *semantic problem.* The other challenge is: is Sonja interested in all of the animals? This is a difficult question since even we humans cannot give a perfect answer. Apparently this is related to the *taxonomic problem.* An efficient solution addressing these issues, combined with filtering and Web mining techniques, can lead to better quality or accuracy of personalized ontologies that are learned.

A number of attempts to address these issues from different aspects have been reported. Techniques from natural language processing, formal concept analysis (Ganter, 1999), and text clustering have been integrated or extended into these works to improve the quality of automatically learning taxonomies (Bloehdorn, Cimiano,

& Hotho, 2006). In the following sub-sections we study these research initiatives to understand how personalized ontologies can be learned in practice.

Formal Concept Analysis Approach

Formal Concept Analysis (FCA) (Ganter, 1999) is a systematic method mainly used for data analysis. It offers the ability to derive implicit inter-relationships between objects characterized by a set of attributes. Data is organized into several units, each of which is a formal abstraction of concepts. Central to the FCA is the notion of a formal context that includes the common attributes of a set of objects in the same class. As FCA provides an intentional description for the abstract concepts (data units), it can be used as a conceptual clustering technique.

Based on the FCA, Cimiano, Hotho, and Staab (2005) have proposed automatic taxonomy learning from domain-specific text. With this approach, part-of-speech is tagged. Each sentence in the corpus is then parsed to a tree, from which verb/subject, verb/object, and verb/prepositional phrase dependencies are extracted. The verb and the head of the subject, object, or prepositional phrase are extracted as pairs such that the verb and the heads are lemmatized. The corresponding verbs for each head are then used as the attributes for building the formal context. The approach not only does output clusters, but also an intentional description for each cluster. However, a main shortcoming of using FCA is that it produces a large lattice which can become an exponential size of the context and lead to an exponential time complexity. In other words, the resultant taxonomy may be too large to reflect the knowledge of the source data. Hence, the *taxonomic problem* remains an issue with FCA-based approaches.

Hierarchical Clustering Approach

Clustering is a division of data into clusters based on the similarity of features (Berkhin, 2002). Hierarchical clustering builds a tree of clusters, which are changed on the similarity level. In other words, clusters at one level are different from those at another level. Representing data on such structure enables exploring data on different levels of granularity, providing a more intuitive view that is close to the way humans view the world (Chen et al., 2006). Thus, hierarchical clustering is one of the efficient ways to learn taxonomic concepts from textual data (Chen, 2006; Chen et al., 2004, 2005).

Hierarchical clusters can be built using a bottom-up or top-down mechanism. Traditionally, hierarchical clustering techniques are categorized into *agglomerative* and *divisive* approaches (Kaufman & Rousseeuw, 1990; Jain, Murty, & Flynn, 1999), where:

- *Agglomerative clustering* starts with one-point clusters and recursively merges the two most similar clusters until all the clusters are encapsulated into one final cluster (Kaufman & Rousseeuw, 1990), or an appropriate stopping criterion is achieved (Jain et al., 1999).
- *Divisive clustering* considers the entire dataset as one cluster and then recursively splits it into smaller clusters until an appropriate stopping criterion is achieved.

Details of clustering techniques and hierarchical text clustering techniques relevant to ontology learning can be found in Berkhin (2002) and Chen (2006), respectively.

The Taxonomy Generation method (Chuang & Chien, 2005) is a clustering-based approach. The approach takes text segments as queries input into a real-world search engine, then uses the highly ranked search-result snippets as the contexts of input text segments. The motivation behind this idea is to exploit the Web. Short text segments usually do not contain sufficient information to extract reliable features, especially the contextual information. The authors believe that adequate information can be retrieved from large amounts of Web pages, as there are huge amounts of the available online indexed information. A agglomerative hierarchical clustering is developed to cluster text segments into a binary-tree hierarchy, which is then converted into a multi-way-tree hierarchy by using a top-down fashion based on the Min-Max partitioning principle. The approach offers a higher chance to obtain adequate information for a text segment. However, the shortcomings are also apparent: it solely relies on a search engine and requires a lot of Web access in order to use the search results.

OntoLearn (Navigli et al., 2003; Missikof et al., 2002) was developed to automatically learn ontologies from domain texts. It consists of three phases:

1. Extracting terminologies from a corpus of domain text, then using natural language processing and statistical techniques to filter out the extracted terminologies that are not domain-specific for the target domain.
2. Semantically interpreting terms to determine the appropriate sense (concept) for each component of a complex term, then identifying semantic relations among these concepts by using WordNet and SemCor (in Missikof et al., 2002). A domain concept forest (DCF) is created to represent taxonomic and other semantic relations among the complex domain concepts.
3. Creating a specialized view of WordNet. The DCF is used as a complementary component to expand a core domain ontology. If domain ontologies are not available, the DCF is integrated into WordNet to create a domain ontology. The integration is achieved by attaching the domain concept trees of the DCF to the appropriate nodes in WordNet,

then it removes all branches that do not contain a domain node from the WordNet.

OntoLearn has been applied to automatically translate multiword terms from English to Italian. However, limitations exist. At the first phase, extracted terminologies are filtered by a comparative analysis across different domains and filter out those used in the target domain but not seen in other domains. To a certain extent, this relies on the contents of other domain corpus. More importantly, the involvements of analysis of other domain corpus increase the complexity. Another shortcoming with this approach is the static semantic relation extraction, since the relations are derived solely based on WordNet and SemCor. Thus, the *semantic problem* requires an improvement to the approach.

OntoEdit (Maedche, 2003; Maedche & Staab, 2001) is a semi-automatic approach for ontology learning. The learning process is based on the ontology structure O and its lexicon L (see the definition earlier). It begins with a extraction of lexical entries in L and concepts in C. Traditional text processing TF-IDF and shallow processing techniques are used to extract the L. Each entry in L is considered as a potential candidate for a concept in C. Based on a hierarchical clustering model, a taxonomy (conceptual hierarchy H^C) is extracted. The non-taxonomic relations R are then learned by using H^C as a background knowledge resource and association rule mining technique. The approach allows import and reuse of existing ontologies. This process requires merging existing semantic structures of defined mapping rules between structures. It is performed at the first step of the whole ontology learning process. Note that the "internal" background knowledge (learned from the source data) is employed for labeling in the hierarchical clustering model and the relations R learning process.

Self-Organizing Map-Based Approach

Self-Organizing Map (SOM) (Kohonen, 1989) is an unsupervised neural network model that maps high-dimensional input space to low-dimensional output space. When the resulting map is a two-dimensional topology, the intuitive visualization provides good exploration possibilities. It has been found that it has certain advantages for clustering high-dimensional data such as texts (Alahakoon et al., 2000; Nurnberger, 2001; Dittenbach, Merkl, & Rauber, 2002; Rauber & Merkl, 1999). In the context of learning ontologies from text, SOM and its variants have been utilized to learning clusters and mining semantics from textual data.

Dittenbach, Berger, and Merll (2004) have proposed to improve domain ontologies by using SOM to exploit hidden semantics from domain text documents. By encoding word contexts of terms in an artificial data set of three-word sentences consisting of nouns, verbs, and adverbs (e.g., "John walks fast"), terms are clustered based on their syntactic categories, namely nouns, verbs, and others (all other words). Each of these syntactic categories consists of a set of semantic classes. A semantic class is a group of relevant terms according to their semantic similarities that are measured by using statistical context analysis. These semantic and syntactic classes are presented on the resultant map. Such a map provides an intuitive view of the semantic relations among terms. It can also facilitate discovering synonyms, adding new relations among concepts, and detecting new concepts that can be added to the target ontology. However, the pre-fixed size of the output space (a requirement of learning SOM clusters) can result in distort clusters, leading to inappropriate concepts and relations discovered. Since the visual map cannot tell the user what the resultant clusters are and where their boundaries are (Rauber & Merkl, 1999), the discovery of semantic relations from the map relies on human input. In addition, it is well known that SOM lacks in providing hierarchical architecture. Using the standard SOM model limits this approach applied to learning taxonomic relations.

The advantages and disadvantages of using SOM have been noted. Many research attempts have been reported. However, in the aspect of building hierarchical architecture, many of the existing techniques make no contribution to the fundamental structure of the standard SOM. As a result they inherit the static architecture from the standard SOM (Chen, 2006). BHGSOM (Chen, 2006; Chen et al., 2006) attempts to address these issues to support learning ontologies from text. It is built on the GSOM algorithm, which is a SOM variant that can produce an adaptive architecture and has potential to build hierarchical clusters.

Using BHGSOM as the hierarchical clustering base, Chen (2006) proposed a hybrid framework called OntoDiscFM to discover taxonomic skeletons for target ontologies. In an attempt to address the semantic problem and the taxonomic problem in a single mode, the framework introduces several novel concepts, combined with background knowledge, to detect the appropriate abstraction level of a concept with the goal of maximally retaining the original meaning of words and their inter-relationships. The initial background knowledge is derived from Word-Net. Newly created ontologies are then used as a new background knowledge resource. Another novel aspect with this framework is that it learns semantic references from the source data to present taxonomies in a "self-presenting" manner; thus, it retains the information contained in the source data at a higher level. In addition, the set of semantic references is also utilized to support the discovery of a multiple inheritance relations, which is one of the critical issues in ontology-based systems but is still under-researched. Moreover, these references are used to guide the validation at the semantic level. On the other hand, the approach has the potential to address the incremental update issue by dynamically updating the semantic references. A limitation but interesting point is the relationship between the layer and the context factor. A context factor is used to identify the level of abstraction that a candidate concept should be. A linear scale of 10 between different layers of abstraction is given in the framework. Whether there are better scales for this parameter is a research question with this framework. The multiple inheritance gives another possibility to further research in combination with logical theories. Other challenges include exploiting more parts-of-speech in addition to the noun (the only part-of-speech exploited), integrating appropriate *word sense disambiguation* algorithms postponed in the framework, and considering semantic relations other than the *is-a* relation.

Discussion

Combined with filtering and Web mining techniques, personalized ontologies can be learned from Web content data. Since much of the Web content data is unstructured textual data, the fundamental problem of learning personalized ontologies can be seen as the problem of learning ontologies from text. In this chapter, we focus on learning taxonomies, the core component for ontologies. A taxonomy of a personalized ontology can represent the user's interests and preferences on different levels of granularity. Such a representation is richer, more precise, and less ambiguous than a keyword/item-based model.

The above study highlights the important role of unsupervised hierarchical clustering in learning taxonomic concepts for ontologies. Therefore, selection of a hierarchical clustering model is critical. Not only do we need to consider algorithm issues such as agglomerative clustering vs. divisive clustering, but also knowing how it can address the *taxonomic problem* from an ontology's perspective. On the other hand, the *semantic problem* is a fundamental issue. It involves the problem of context, meaning the ability to discover the user's interests and preferences hidden in the source data. The context problem is extended to a validation problem when the ontologies are built.

This is a question about whether the validation can be processed at the semantic level to ensure the built ontologies capture the user's interests and preferences semantically.

Research initiatives have shown that these problems can be addressed from different aspects by using different techniques such as FCA, traditional hierarchical clustering approaches, or SOM-based techniques with labeling algorithms, and different resources such as WordNet or domain-specific ontologies. However, one's advantage might become the disadvantage of another. For example, FCA-based approaches can achieve automatic learning processes and derive an appropriate abstraction level of concepts; however, it may fail to address the taxonomic problem. The OntoLearn automatically performs the process with larger complexity and the dependence of WordNet and SemCor. OntoEdit allows reuse of existing ontologies, but requires human intervention. It uses background knowledge learned from the source data, but does not consider background knowledge during feature extraction. We can see that none of these approaches addresses the taxonomic problem and the semantic problem in a single model. The OntoDiscFM is developed to tackle this issue. It utilizes background knowledge during the whole process, addressing the semantic and taxonomic issues within a single model. Moreover, it supports multiple inheritance and validation at the semantic level. However, the design of a more appropriate context factor scale requires more efforts.

An important issue with taking a hierarchical clustering approach is the need of pre-processing source data. Since existing clustering algorithms require input in numeric form, coding text and scaling them to numbers can result in the loss of semantics ("meaning") in text. Therefore, careful pre-processing is essential. A common approach is to perform term extraction. Advanced techniques consider synonym/concept extraction with background knowledge (Chen, 2006; Chen et al., 2005). Another important issue is the post-processing of

resultant clusters, referred to as cluster labeling, a semantic problem. Background knowledge has been found that shows certain advantages to the semantic problem (Chen, 2006; Maedche, 2003; Maedche & Staab, 2001).

The issue of dynamically capturing the user's interests and preferences to reflect the new content of Web pages is regarded as the problem of ontology evolution. Although the OntoDiscFM has the potential to address the incremental update issue by dynamically updating the semantic references, it does not address many sub-problems of ontology evolution such as ontology versioning, merging, and alignment. As the Web becomes increasingly complex, it can lead to unreliable, inconsistent, invalid, and outdated information. To keep the constructed personalized ontologies up to date, issues like "how can the user's new interests and preferences be accommodated and still retain the logical integrity of the ontology" and "how can a collection of ontologies of the user be maintained consistently during the revision process" must be taken into account. *Belief revision* (Alchourrón, Gärdenfors, & Makinson, 1985; Benferhat, Kaci, Berre, & Williams, 2004; Williams, 1997, 1998) is a possible solution to such issues. It describes the change process in non-monotonic knowledge bases, providing mechanisms to incorporate new information into the knowledge base without compromising its integrity. It also deals with inconsistency when the new knowledge needs to be revised (Kang & Lau, 2004; Williams, 1998). One well-known model in belief revision is called AGM (Alchourrón et al., 1985), a formal framework based on the principle of *minimal change* to model ideal and rational changes to repositories of information. It provides potential direction on how ontologies should evolve (Foo, 1995). However, changes are modeled in fixed logical theories that involve addition and removal of facts (Williams, 1998). All potential facts and theories are assumed to reside within a given ontology (Foo, 1995). Following the principle of minimal change, Heflin and Hendler (2000) have proposed an approach called DMA to minimize the loss of information. Kang and Lau (2004) have discussed the feasibility of using the concept of belief revision based on the AGM model for ontology revision. As the authors have pointed out, investigation of maintaining ontology versions and a library to handle issues in ontology revision is needed. More research efforts are required before principles can be established and exploited.

In summary, techniques of ontology learning from text can be utilized, together with filtering and Web mining techniques to learning personalized ontologies for Web personalization. Research efforts have been reported; however, more work is still required. In the next section we describe possible future research works in this area.

FUTURE RESEARCH DIRECTIONS

Ontology learning has been identified as an inherently transdisciplinary area. Personalized ontology learning for personalization involves Web technologies and therefore presents more challenges. Establishing new connections with other areas is an important step towards the success of establishing principles. The future directions presented below may open up many opportunities to the research community.

Contextual Information Extraction

Contextual information plays an important role in the quality and accuracy of personalization systems. Contextual information learning involves issues such as degree of automation vs. level of quality and accuracy. How to automatically extract contexts at a higher level of quality and accuracy is still an open question. Exploiting this problem would lead to a valuable contribution to future work.

Ontology Evolution

Since a user's needs, interests, and preferences change over time, personalized ontologies must also evolve. More work needs to be conducted to understand ontology dynamics and to build personalized applications which are elaboration tolerant (McCarthy, 2003). An exciting application domain in which ontology evolution is crucial is robotics. Robots with an explicit representation about their knowledge are enabled because it allows them to ground their representations more effectively and to reason about their representations (Gärdenfors & Williams, 2003; Williams, Gärdenfors, McCarthy, Karol, & Stanton, 2005).

Parts-of-Speech

Most existing works have focused on extracting noun information. Although nouns play a key role in the information obtaining, other parts-of-speech such as verbs, adjectives, and adverbs are also important, especially for learning semantic relations other than the "is-a" relation. Therefore, work on parts-of-speech is expected to generate potential future research fruits.

Word Sense Disambiguation

Word sense disambiguation (WSD) is necessary for natural language analysis. There is a research community dedicated to the WSD, which is a richer and expensive research topic. WSD in the ontology learning processes would open up many possibilities.

Semantic Relations and Rules

As studied above, there are few works on learning non-taxonomic relations and rules for ontologies. These two elements are important building blocks of ontologies to handle complex cases. Significant research work is expected to yield important results in the near future.

Multiple Inheritance

Multiple inheritance is an important issue in building ontologies. It is a problem that is strongly connected to the semantic problem and the taxonomic problem. There is also the potential to integrate fuzzy logic. To the best of our knowledge, very few efforts have been reported. In reality, multiple inheritance is prevalent and therefore research needs to be directed into this area particularly for ontology learning and personalization applications.

Personalized Web Services

Web services can enhance e-business management. While this is not a new concept, there remain potential developments such as how to use personalized ontologies to enable agents to automatically and efficiently compose Web services for personalization systems. On the other hand, to enable a service sharing context with other services, for example when it is requested to connect to a third-party Web service, it is essential to establish standard representations for the shared context. Can personalized ontologies dynamically capture the shared context and be the standard representations? Exploiting such issues to develop personalized Web services to enhance e-business management would be valuable.

Multi-Linguistics Web Personalization

The Web is worldwide. There are many types of natural languages used on the Web. Works presented in this chapter are applicable to English language only. Exploiting techniques that can be applied to languages other than English-like such as Chinese is still under-researched. Different languages may require different techniques to

support. Multiple linguistics personalization is a challenging future direction in the area of Web personalization.

REFERENCES

Alahakoon, D., Halgamuge, S.K., & Srinivasan, B. (2000). Dynamic self-organizing-maps with controlled growth for knowledge discovery. *IEEE Transactions on Neural Networks, 11*(3), 601–614.

Alchourrón, C.E., Gärdenfors, P., & Makinson, D. (1985). On the logic of theory change: Partial meet contraction and revision functions. *Journal of Symbolic Logic, 50*(2), 510–530.

Ankolekar, A., Seo, Y.-W., & Sycara, K. (2003). Investigating semantic knowledge for text learning. *Proceedings of the ACM SIGIR Workshop on the Semantic Web*. Retrieved from http://www-cgi.cs.cmu.edu/~softagents/papers/ywseo_sigir_03.pdf

Bachimont, B., Isaac, A., & Troncy, R. (2002). Semantic commitment for designing ontologies: A proposal. *Proceedings of the 13th International Conference on Knowledge Engineering and Knowledge Management. Ontologies and the Semantic Web* (EKAW'02) (pp. 114–121). London: Springer-Verlag.

Benferhat, S., Kaci, S., Berre, D.L., & Williams, M.-A. (2004). Weakening conflicting information for iterated revision and knowledge integration. *Artificial Intelligence, 153*(1–2), 339-371.

Berkhin, P. (2002). *Survey of clustering data mining techniques*. Technical Report, Accrue Software, USA. Retrieved from http://www.accrue.com/products/rp_cluster_review.pdf

Bloehdorn, S., Cimiano, P., & Hotho, A. (2006, March 9–11). Learning ontologies to improve text clustering and classification. In M. Spiliopoulou,

R. Kruse, A. Nurnberger, C. Borgelt, & W. Gaul (Eds.), *From Data and Information Analysis to Knowledge Engineering: Proceedings of the 29ᵗʰ Annual Conference of the German Classification Society* (GFKL 2005) (vol. 30, pp. 334–341), Magdeburg, Germany. Berlin: Springer-Verlag.

Borst, P. (1997). *Construction of engineering ontologies for knowledge sharing and reuse.* Unpublished Doctoral Dissertation, Universiteit Twente, the Netherlands.

Buitelaar, P., Cimiano, P., & Magnini, B. (Eds.). (2005). *Ontology learning from text: Methods, evaluation and applications.* Amsterdam: IOS Press.

Celjuska, D. (2004). *Semi-automatic construction of ontologies from text.* Unpublished Master's Thesis, Technical University Koice, Slovak Republic.

Chen, S. (2006). *Ontology discovery from text: A hybrid framework.* Unpublished Master's Thesis, Monash University, Australia.

Chen, S., Alahakoon, D., & Indrawan, M. (2004). An unsupervised neural network approach for ontology discovery from text. *Proceedings of the Workshop on Semantic Web Mining and Reasoning* (SWMR 2004) (pp. 1–8), Beijing.

Chen, S., Alahakoon, D., & Indrawan, M. (2005). Background knowledge driven ontology discovery. *Proceedings of the 2005 IEEE International Conference on E-Technology, E-Commerce and E-Service* (EEE'05) (pp. 202–207).

Chen, S., Alahakoon, D., & Indrawan, M. (2006). Building an adaptive hierarchy of clusters for text data. *Proceedings of the International Conference on Intelligent Agents, Web Technology and Internet Commerce* (IAWTIC'2005) (pp. 7–12).

Chuang, S.-L., & Chien, L.-F. (2005). Taxonomy generation for text segments: A practical Web-based approach. *ACM Transactions on Information Systems, 23*(4), 363–396.

Cimiano, P., Hotho, A., & Staab, S. (2005). Learning concept hierarchies from text corpora using formal concept analysis. *Journal of Artificial Intelligence Research, 24,* 305–339.

Corcho, O., Fernández-López, M., & Gómez-Pérez, A. (2003). Methodologies, tools and languages for building ontologies: Where is their meeting point? *Data Knowledge Engineering, 46*(1), 41–64.

Dagan, I., Glickman, O., & Magnini, B. (2005, April 11–13). The PASCAL recognising textual entailment challenge. *Revised Selected Papers of the Machine Learning Challenges, Evaluating Predictive Uncertainty, Visual Object Classification and Recognizing Textual Entailment, 1st PASCAL Machine Learning Challenges Workshop* (MLCW 2005) (vol. 3944, pp. 177–190), Southampton, UK. Berlin: Springer-Verlag.

Dittenbach, M., Berger, H., & Merll, D. (2004). Improving domain ontologies by mining semantics from text. *Proceedings of the 1st Asian-Pacific Conference on Conceptual Modeling* (APCCM'04) (pp. 91–100). Darlinghurst, Australia: Australian Computer Society.

Dittenbach, M., Merkl, D., & Rauber, A. (2002). Organizing and exploring high-dimensional data with the growing hierarchical self-organizing map. In L. Wang, S. Halgamuge, & X. Yao (Eds.), *Proceedings of the 1ˢᵗ International Conference on Fuzzy Systems and Knowledge Discovery* (FSKD 2002) (vol. 2, pp. 626–630), Singapore.

Dopazo, J., & Carazo, J.M. (1997). Phylogenetic reconstruction using an unsupervised growing neural network that adopts the topology of a phylogenetic tree. *Journal of Molecular Evolution, 44,* 226–233.

Eirinaki, M., & Vazirgiannis, M. (2003). Web mining for Web personalization. *ACM Transactions on Internet Technology, 3*(1), 1–27.

Etzioni, O., Cafarella, M., Downey, D., Kok, S., Popescu, A.-M., Shaked, T. et al. (2004). Web-scale information extraction in Knowitall: (preliminary results). *Proceedings of the 13th International Conference on the World Wide Web* (WWW'04) (pp. 100–110). New York: ACM Press.

Faure, D., & Nédellec, C. (1998). ASIUM: Learning subcategorization frames and restrictions of selection. In Y. Kodratoff (Ed.), *Proceedings of the 10th Conference on Machine Learning, Workshop on Text Mining* (ECML'98), Chemnitz, Germany.

Fellbaum, C. (Ed.). (1998). *WordNet: An electronic lexical database*. Cambridge, MA: MIT Press.

Fernández-López, M., & Gómez-Pérez, A. (2002). *OntoWeb—a survey on methodologies for developing, maintaining, evaluating and reengineering ontologies*. OntoWeb Deliverable 1.4, IST Programme of the Commission of the European Communities, IST-2000-29243.

Fernández-López, M., Gómez-Pérez, A., & Juristo, N. (1997). METHONTOLOGY: From ontological art towards ontological engineering. *Proceedings of the Symposium on Ontological Engineering of AAAI* (pp. 33–40), Stanford, CA.

Fernández-López, M., Gómez-Pérez, A., Sierra, J.P., & Sierra, A.P. (1999). Building a chemical ontology using methontology and the ontology design environment. *IEEE Intelligent Systems, 14*(1), 37–46.

Foo, N.Y. (1995, August 14–18). Ontology revision. In G. Ellis, R. Levinson, W. Rich, & J.F. Sowa (Eds.), *Proceedings of Conceptual Structures: Applications, Implementation and Theory, the 3rd International Conference on Conceptual Structures* (ICCS'95) (pp. 16–31), Santa Cruz, CA.

Gandon, F. (2002). *Ontology engineering: A survey and a return on experience*. Rapport de Recherche No. 4396, INRIA.

Ganter, B. (1999). *The Dresden formal concept analysis page*. Retrieved February 21, 2005, from http://www.math.tu-dresden.de/~ganter/fba.html

Gärdenfors, P., & Williams, M.-A. (2003). Building rich and grounded robot world models from sensors and knowledge resources: A conceptual spaces approach. *Proceedings of the 2nd International Symposium on Autonomous Mini-Robots for Research and Edutainment* (pp. 34–45).

Genesereth, M.R., & Nilsson, N.J. (1987). *Logical foundations of artificial intelligence*. San Francisco: Morgan Kaufmann.

Gómez-Pérez, A., Fernández-López, M., & Corcho, O. (2004). *Ontological engineering: With examples from the areas of knowledge management, e-commerce and the Semantic Web (advanced information and knowledge processing)*. London/New York: Springer-Verlag.

Gruber, T.R. (1993). A translation approach to portable ontology specifications. *Knowledge Acquisition, 5*(2), 199–220.

Grüninger, M., & Fox, M. (1995). Methodology for the design and evaluation of ontologies. *Proceedings of IJCAI'95, Workshop on Basic Ontological Issues in Knowledge Sharing*.

Guarino, N. (1998). Formal ontology and information systems. *Proceedings of the 1st International Conference on Formal Ontologies in Information Systems* (FOIS'98) (pp. 3–5), Trento, Italy. Amsterdam: IOS Press.

Guarino, N., & Giaretta, P. (1995). Ontologies and knowledge bases: Towards a terminological clarification. In N.J.I. Mars (Ed.), *Towards very large knowledge bases* (pp. 25–32). Amsterdam: IOS Press.

Heflin, J., & Hendler, J.A. (2000). Dynamic ontologies on the Web. *Proceedings of the 17th National Conference on Artificial Intelligence and 12th Conference on Innovative Applications of Artificial Intelligence* (pp. 443–449). Cambridge, MA: AAAI Press/MIT Press.

Hotho, A., Staab, S., & Stumme, G. (2003). WordNet improves text document clustering. *Proceedings of the SIGIR 2003 Semantic Web Workshop, 26th Annual International ACM SIGIR Conference.*

IEEE. (1996). *IEEE standard for developing software life cycle processes.* Standard 1074-1995, IEEE Computer Society, USA.

Jain, A.K., Murty, M.N., & Flynn, P.J. (1999). Data clustering: A review. *ACM Computing Surveys, 31*(3), 264–323.

Kang, S.H., & Lau, S.K. (2004, September 20–25). Ontology revision using the concept of belief revision. *Proceedings of the 8th International Conference on Knowledge-Based Intelligent Information and Engineering Systems* (KES 2004) (pt. 3, pp. 8–15), Wellington, New Zealand.

Kaufman, L., & Rousseeuw, P.J. (1990). *Finding groups in data: An introduction to cluster analysis.* New York: John Wiley & Sons.

Khan, L., & Luo, F. (2002). Ontology construction for information selection. *Proceedings of the 14th IEEE International Conference on Tools with Artificial Intelligence* (ICTAI'02) (pp. 122–127), Washington, DC.

Kohonen, T. (1989). *Self-organization and associative memory* (3rd ed.). New York: Springer-Verlag.

Kosala, R., & Blockeel, H. (2000). Web mining research: A survey. *SIGKDD Explor. Newsletter, 2*(1), 1–15.

Lassila, O., & McGuinness, D. (2001). *The role of frame-based representation on the Semantic Web.* Technical Report No. KSL-01-02, Stanford University, USA.

Lau, R.Y.K., Hao, J.X., Tang, M., & Zhou, X. (2007, January 3–6). Towards context-sensitive domain ontology extraction. *Abstract Proceedings of the 40th Hawaii International Conference on Systems Science* (HICSS-40 2007) (p. 60), Waikoloa, Big Island, HI.

Lenat, D.B. (1995). CYC: A large-scale investment in knowledge infrastructure. *Communications of the ACM, 38* (11), 33–38.

Lenat, D.B., & Guha, R.V. (1989). *Building large knowledge-based systems: Representation and inference in the Cyc Project.* Boston: Addison-Wesley Longman.

Liu, T., Liu, S., Chen, Z., & Ma, W.-Y. (2003). An evaluation on feature selection for text clustering. *Proceedings of the 20th International Conference on Machine Learning* (ICML 2003) (pp. 488–495).

Maedche, A. (2003). *Ontology learning for the Semantic Web.* Boston: Kluwer Academic.

Maedche, A., & Staab, S. (2000). Discovering conceptual relations from text. *Proceedings of ECAI* (pp. 321–325).

Maedche, A., & Staab, S. (2001). Ontology learning for the Semantic Web. *IEEE Intelligent Systems, 16*(2), 72–79.

McCarthy, J. (2003). *Elaboration tolerance.* Retrieved May 17, 2007, from *http://www-formal.stanford.edu/jmc/elaboration/elaboration.html*

Missikof, M., Navigli, R., & Velardi, P. (2002). Integrated approach to Web ontology learning and engineering. *Computer, 35*(11), 60–63.

Mizoguchi, R., Ikeda, M., & Sinitsa, K. (1997). Roles of shared ontology in AI-ED research. *Proceedings of the Conference on Intelligence, Conceptualization, Standardization, and Reusability* (AI-ED97) (pp. 537–544).

Mobasher, B., Cooley, R., & Srivastava, J. (2000). Automatic personalization based on Web usage mining. *Communications of the ACM, 43*(8), 142–151.

Navigli, R., Velardi, P., & Gangemi, A. (2003). Ontology learning and its application to automated terminology translation. *IEEE Intelligent Systems, 18*(1), 22–31.

Nurnberger, A. (2001). Clustering of document collections using a growing self-organizing map. *Proceedings of the BISC International Workshop on Fuzzy Logic and the Internet* (FLINT 2001) (pp. 136–141).

Osiski, S. (2004). *Dimensionality reduction techniques for search results clustering.* Unpublished Master's Thesis, Department of Computer Science, University of Sheffield, UK.

Pierrakos, D., Paliouras, G., Papatheodorou, C., & Spyropoulos, C.D. (2003). Web usage mining as a tool for personalization: A survey. *User Modeling and User-Adapted Interaction, 13*(4), 311–372.

Pinto, H.S., & Martins, J.P. (2004). Ontologies: How can they be built? *Knowledge and Information Systems, 6*(4), 441–464.

Rauber, A., & Merkl, D. (1999). Using self-organizing maps to organize document archives and to characterize subject matter: How to make a map tell the news of the world. *Proceedings of the 10th International Conference on Database and Expert Systems Applications* (DEXA'99) (pp. 302–311). London: Springer-Verlag.

Salton, G., & McGill, M. (1983). *Introduction to modern information retrieval.* New York: McGraw-Hill.

Schreiber, A.T., Wielinga, B.J., & Jansweijer, W.H.J. (1995). The KACTUS view on the 'O' word. *Proceedings of the IJCAI Workshop on Basic Ontological Issues in Knowledge Sharing.*

Studer, R., Benjamins, V.R., & Fensel, D. (1998). Knowledge engineering: Principles and methods. *Data Knowledge Engineering, 25*(1–2), 161–197.

Sure, Y., & Studer, R. (2002a). *On-To-Knowledge methodology—expanded version.* Technical

Report No. OTK/2001/D17/v1.0, Institute AIFB, University of Karlsruhe, Germany.

Sure, Y., & Studer, R. (2002b). *On-To-Knowledge methodology—final version.* Technical Report No. OTK/2002/D18/v1.0, Institute AIFB, University of Karlsruhe, Germany.

Swartout, B., Patil, R., Knight, K., & Russ, T. (1997). Toward distributed use of large-scale ontologies. *Proceedings of the Symposium on Ontological Engineering of AAAI* (pp. 138–148), Stanford University, USA.

Uschold, M., & Grüninger, M. (1996). Ontologies: Principles, methods, and applications. *Knowledge Engineering Review, 11*(2), 93–155.

Williams, M.-A. (1997). Anytime belief revision. *Proceedings of the International Joint Conference on Artificial Intelligence* (pp. 74–80).

Williams, M.-A. (1998). Applications of belief revision. *Proceedings of the International Seminar on Logic Databases and the Meaning of Change, Transactions and Change in Logic Databases* (ILPS'97) (pp. 287–316). London: Springer-Verlag.

Williams, M.-A., Gärdenfors, P., McCarthy, J., Karol, A., & Stanton, C. (2005). A framework for grounding representations. *Proceedings of the IJCAI Workshop on Agents in Real-Time and Dynamic Environments.*

WordNet. (n.d.). Retrieved July 5, 2004, from http://www.cogsci.princeton.edu /wn/

Yang, Y. (1995). Noise reduction in a statistical approach to text categorization. In E.A. Fox, P. Ingwersen, & R. Fidel (Eds.), *Proceedings of the 18th ACM International Conference on Research and Development in Information Retrieval* (SIGIR-95) (pp. 256–263), Seattle, WA. New York: ACM Press.

Yang, Y., & Pedersen, J.O. (1997). A comparative study on feature selection in text categorization.

Proceedings of the 14th International Conference on Machine Learning (ICML'97) (pp. 412–420). San Francisco: Morgan Kaufmann.

Zadrozny, W. (1995). *Context and ontology in understanding of dialogs.* CoRR, cmp-lg/9505032.

ADDITIONAL READING

Anderberg, M.R. (1973). *Cluster analysis for applications.* New York/London: Academic Press.

Antoniou, G., & Harmelen, F. (2004). *A Semantic Web primer (cooperative information systems).* Cambridge, MA: MIT Press.

Berners-Lee, T., Hendler, J., & Lassila, O. (2001). The Semantic Web. *Scientific American, 284*(5).

Bigus, J.P. (1996). *Data mining with neural networks: Solving business problems from application development to decision support.* Hightstown, NJ: McGraw-Hill.

Cimiano, P. (2006). *Ontology learning and population from text: Algorithms, evaluation and applications.* New York: Springer-Verlag.

Ehrig, M. (2006). *Ontology alignment: Bridging the semantic gap (Semantic Web and beyond).* New York: Springer-Verlag.

Fensel, D., Lausen, H., Polleres, A., Bruijn, J., Stollberg, M., Roman, D. et al. (2006). *Enabling Semantic Web services: The Web service modeling ontology.* New York: Springer-Verlag.

Fernández-López, M. (1999). Overview of methodologies for building ontologies. *Proceedings of the IJCAI99 Workshop on Ontologies and Problem-Solving Methods: Lessons Learned and Future Trends.*

Gruber, T.R. (1995). Toward principles for the design of ontologies used for knowledge shar-ing. *International Journal of Human-Computer Studies, 43*(5–6), 907–928.

Han, J., & Kamber, M. (2001). *Data mining: Concepts and techniques.* San Francisco: Morgan Kaufmann.

Hartigan, J.A. (1975). *Clustering algorithms.* New York: John Wiley & Sons.

Jain, A.K., Duin, R.P.W., & Mao, J. (2000). Statistical pattern recognition: A review. *IEEE Transactions on Pattern Analysis and Machine Intelligence, 22*(1), 437.

Noy, N.F., & Hafner, C.D. (1997). The state of the art in ontology design: A survey and comparative review. *AI Magazine, 18*(3), 53–74.

Pal, N., & Rangaswamy, A. (Eds.). (2003). *The power of one: Gaining business value from personalization technologies.* eBRC Press.

Pashtan, A. (2005). *Mobile Web services.* New York: Cambridge University Press.

Peppers, D., Rogers, M., & Kasanoff, B. (2002). *Making it personal: How to profit from personalization without invading privacy.* New York: Perseus Books.

Poli, R., & Simons, P. (2006). *Formal ontology.* Berlin: Springer-Verlag (Nijhoff International Philosophy Series).

Russell, S., & Norvig, P. (2003). *Artificial intelligence: A modern approach* (2nd ed.). Englewood Cliffs, NJ: Prentice Hall.

Sanchez, E. (2006). *Fuzzy logic and the Semantic Web (capturing intelligence).* New York: Elsevier Science.

Sharman, R., Kishore, R., & Ramesh, R. (Eds.). (2006). *Ontologies: A handbook of principles, concepts and applications in information systems.* New York: Springer-Verlag (Integrated Series in Information Systems).

Chapter II
Overview of Design Options for Neighborhood–Based Collaborative Filtering Systems

Nikos Manouselis
Informatics Laboratory, Agricultural University of Athens, Greece

Constantina Costopoulou
Informatics Laboratory, Agricultural University of Athens, Greece

ABSTRACT

The problem of collaborative filtering is to predict how well a user will like an item that he or she has not rated, given a set of historical ratings for this and other items from a community of users. A plethora of collaborative filtering algorithms have been proposed in related literature. One of the most prevalent families of collaborative filtering algorithms are neighborhood-based ones, which calculate a prediction of how much a user will like a particular item, based on how other users with similar preferences have rated this item. This chapter aims to provide an overview of various proposed design options for neighborhood-based collaborative filtering systems, in order to facilitate their better understanding, as well as their study and implementation by recommender systems' researchers and developers. For this purpose, the chapter extends a series of design stages of neighborhood-based algorithms, as they have been initially identified by related literature on collaborative filtering systems. Then, it reviews proposed alternatives for each design stage and provides an overview of potential design options.

INTRODUCTION

About two decades ago, Malone, Grant, Turbak, Brobst, and Cohen (1987) provided an overview of intelligent information sharing systems, iden-tifying a fundamental categorization of systems that support access to highly dynamic informa-tion resources (Belkin & Croft, 1992; Baudisch, 2001; Hanani, Shapira, & Shoval, 2001). More specifically, they distinguished:

1. *Cognitive filtering* systems such as the ones that characterize the contents of an information resource (shortly referred to as an *item*) and the information needs of potential item users, and then use these representations to intelligently match items to users; and

2. *Sociological filtering* systems such as the ones that are working based on the personal and organizational interrelationships of individuals in a community.

Early information sharing systems belonged to the first category and were based on text-based filtering, which works by selecting relevant items according to a set of textual keywords. *Collaborative filtering* systems were first introduced as representatives of the second category. They addressed two shortcomings of text-based systems (Konstan, 2004):

1. The often overwhelming number of on-topic items (ones that would be all selected by a keyword filter) which has been addressed by the introduction of further evaluating the items based on human judgment about their quality, and

2. The issue of filtering non-text items which has been addressed by judging them on subjective criteria such as human taste.

In general, the problem of collaborative filtering is to predict how well a user will like an item that he has not rated (also called "evaluated" in the rest of this chapter), given a set of historical ratings for this and other items from a community of users (Herlocker, Konstan, & Riedl, 2002; Adomavicius & Tuzhilin, 2005). The problem space can be formulated as a matrix of users vs. items (or *user-rating* matrix), with each cell storing a user's rating on a specific item. Under this formulation, the problem refers to predicting the values for specific empty cells (i.e., predict a user's rating for an item).

A plethora of collaborative filtering algorithms have been proposed in related literature. The most popular approach is the adoption of traditional neighborhood-based techniques (Cover & Hart, 1967), which are appropriately adapted to suit collaborative filtering needs and to produce a rating prediction based on the ratings of a relatively small number of neighbors with preferences similar to the ones of the targeted user. Different aspects of neighborhood-based algorithms are explored by various researchers, leading to a wide variety of proposed design options for a collaborative filtering system. On the other hand, since the study of Herlocker et al. (2002), there has not appeared in the literature an overview of the various proposed design options and how they can be considered for implementation in an integrated manner.

In this direction, this chapter aims to provide an overview of various proposed design options for neighborhood-based collaborative filtering systems, in order to facilitate their better understanding, as well as their study and implementation by recommender systems' researchers and developers. For this purpose, the chapter builds upon a series of design stages for neighborhood-based collaborative filtering algorithms, as they have been initially identified by related literature (Herlocker et al., 2002; Vozalis & Margaritis, 2003; Sarwar, Karypis, Konstan, & Riedl, 2000) and enhanced by our study (Manouselis & Costopoulou, 2006a). Then it reviews proposed alternatives for each design stage and provides an overview of potential design options.

More specifically, the chapter is structured as it follows: In the next section, the background of this study is presented, by introducing neighborhood-based algorithms for single-attribute collaborative filtering and outlining seven generic stages of a neighborhood-based algorithm. Each stage is further discussed, and methods for its implementation are reviewed. We next provide a synopsis of the reviewed design options, identify possible further extensions, and present the conclusions of this study. The final section outlines directions for future research.

BACKGROUND

Collaborative filtering systems make up one of the major classes of *recommender systems*. These can be defined as any system that produces individualized recommendations as output or has the effect of guiding the user in a personalized way to interesting or useful items in a large space of possible options (Burke, 2002). As related studies indicate, the methods that may be engaged in recommender systems generally include (Schafer et al., 2001; Adomavicius & Tuzhilin, 2005; Manouselis & Costopoulou, 2007a):

- Raw retrieval of items where no particular personalization method is engaged and recommended items are presented as results of typical search queries. For example, the results returned in some query in Google (*www.google.com*) will be the same for all users, if they use the same keywords and are from the same geographical area.
- Manual selection of recommendations, for example when some experts, opinion leaders, or plain users recommend a list of items to all users. A characteristic example is Amazon's Listmania feature (*www.amazon.com/listmania*), where some user selects and proposes to other users a list of recommended items of a specific category (e.g., "Recommended Family Books" by Megan Destra).
- Content-based recommendation methods which characterize the contents of the item and the information needs of potential item users, and then use these representations to match items to users—for example, the news personalization service of Findory.com, which monitors articles that users read in order to propose them with related articles, books, or blogs.
- Collaborative filtering recommendation methods that recommend items to a user according to what people with similar tastes and preferences liked in the past. One of the most well-known systems is MovieLens (movielens.umn.edu), which was developed at the University of Minnesota and proposes movies to users according to the ratings they provide for movies they have seen and the ratings that other users with similar tastes have provided.
- Hybrid approaches that combine some of the above methods. For instance, Amazon's recommendation services are now using a combination of the above methods, including both a collaborative filtering and a content-based recommendation service.

Collaborative filtering systems constitute a large majority of recommender systems and have found their way into many implemented systems (Adomavicius & Tuzhilin, 2005). Instead of performing content indexing or content analysis, collaborative filtering systems rely entirely on interest ratings from the members of a participating community (Herlocker et al., 2002). They can be considered complementary to content-based systems, since they aim at learning predictive models of user preferences, interests, or behaviors from community data—that is, a database of available user preferences.

Conceptual Definition

As mentioned earlier, in the problem of collaborative filtering, the problem space can be formulated as a user-rating matrix, with each cell storing a user's rating on a specific item (Herlocker et al., 2002). Under this formulation, the problem of predicting how well a user will like an item that he or she has not rated actually refers to predicting the values for specific empty cells of the user-rating matrix. As Herlocker et al. (2002) state, in collaborative filtering the user-rating matrix is generally very sparse, since each user will only have rated a small percentage of the total number of items. Table 1 illustrates a classic example of a user-

Table 1. An example of a user-item matrix, where each filled cell represents a user's rating for an item (inspired by the example given by Herlocker et al., 2002)

	Spiderman 3	**Hoop dreams**	**Contact**	**Half Nelson**
Nikos	5		5	4
Tina	2	5		3
Mary		2	4	2
Poly	5	1	5	?

rating matrix that demonstrates how predictions are being computed for movies in a collaborative filtering system. In this example, a collaborative filtering system would try to predict the rating Poly would give to the movie Half Nelson.

Formal Definition

The collaborative filtering problem may be more formally formulated as follows (Adomavicius & Tuzhilin, 2005; Manouselis & Costopoulou, 2006a): let C be the set of all users and S the set of all possible items that can be recommended. We define as $U^c(s)$ a utility function $U^c(s): C \times S \to \Re^+$ that measures the appropriateness of recommending an item s to user c. It is assumed that this function is not known for the whole C x S space, but only on some subset of it. Therefore, in the context of recommendation, we want each user $c \in C$ to be able (Manouselis & Costopoulou, 2006a) to estimate (or approach) the utility function $U^c(x)$ for an item x of the space S for which $U^c(x)$ is not yet known, or to choose a set of items $x \in S' \subseteq S$ that will maximize $U^c(x)$.

The aim of collaborative filtering is then to predict the utility of items for a particular user (called *active user*), based on the items previously evaluated by other users (Adomavicius & Tuzhilin, 2005). That is, the utility $U^a(x)$ of item x for the active user a is estimated based on the utilities $U^c(x)$ assigned to item x by those users $c \in C$ who

are 'similar' to user a. For single-attribute collaborative filtering (which is examined in this section), it corresponds to the prediction of the rating $U^a(x) = r^a(x) = r_{a,x}$, according to the ratings $U^c(x) = r^c(x) = r_{c,x}$ provided by the users $c \in C$ who are 'similar' to user a (where a rating is allowed to take values in a defined $[r_{min}, ..., r_{max}]$).

Collaborative Filtering Algorithms

Several algorithmic approaches have been applied to support prediction of unknown ratings in collaborative filtering. In general, they can be distinguished to memory-based (or heuristic-based) approaches and to model-based approaches (Breese, Heckerman, & Kadie, 1998; Adomavicius & Tuzhilin, 2005). Memory-based algorithms operate as heuristics that make rating predictions based on the entire collection of previously rated items by the users. In contrast, model-based algorithms use the collection of ratings in order to build a model, which is then used to make rating predictions. Model-based systems mostly include clustering models (Roh, Oh, & Han, 2003; Cho, Cho, & Kim, 2005; Martin-Guerrero et al., 2006), support vector machines (Maritza, Gonzalez-Caro, Perez-Alcazar, Garcia-Diaz, & Delgado, 2004), Bayesian networks (Breese et al., 1998), probabilistic latent semantic analysis (Hoffman, 2003), binary logistic regression (Lee, Jun, Lee, & Kim, 2005; Kim, Yum, & Kim, 2005), and data mining techniques such as decision tree induction and association rule mining (Cho, Kim, & Kim, 2002; Kim et al., 2005). Memory-based systems are usually built upon user-to-user algorithms (Resnick, Iacovou, Suchak, Bergstrom, & Riedl, 1994; Shardanand & Maes, 1995; Konstan et al., 1997; Min & Han, 2005), item-to-item algorithms (Deshpande & Karypis, 2004; Miller, Konstan, & Riedl, 2004), and probabilistic algorithms (Yu, Schwaighofer, Tresp, Xu, & Kriegel, 2004). There are also some hybrid approaches, combining these two types of collaborative-filtering algorithms (Xue et al., 2005).

In this chapter, the focus is on memory-based algorithms, which are still the most popular ones. The main reason for their popularity is that they are simple and intuitive on a conceptual level, while avoiding the complications of a computationally expensive model-building stage (Adomavicius & Tuzhilin, 2005). The most prevalent memory-based algorithms used in collaborative filtering are the so-called *neighborhood-based* ones (Herlocker et al., 2002; Zeng, Xing, Zhou, & Zheng, 2004). These have their roots in instance-based learning (IBL) techniques that are very popular in machine learning applications (Aha, Kibler, & Albert, 1991). The nearest neighbor algorithm is one of the most straightforward IBL algorithms (Cover & Hart, 1967). During generalization, IBL algorithms use a function that represents the distance between one distance and another (also called a similarity function) to determine how close a new instance is to stored instances, and use the nearest instance or instances to predict the target (Yu, Xu, Ester, & Kriegel, 2003).

Collaborative Filtering Stages

The plethora of proposed approaches in neighborhood-based algorithms for collaborative filtering engages various methods and techniques at each stage of an algorithm. Building upon the stages of neighborhood-based algorithms that have been initially identified by related literature (Herlocker

et al., 2002; Vozalis & Margaritis, 2003; Sarwar et al., 2000), we have identified the following stages (Manouselis & Costopoulou, 2006a):

- **Stage A—Data preparation:** Some algorithms apply some data processing/preparation technique in order to face the problem of sparsity in the user-item matrix. This stage is not considered a part of the algorithm, but an initial preparation phase.
- **Stage B—Similarity calculation:** This is the core stage of the algorithm, where the method for calculating the similarity between the examined user and the rest of the users is calculated.
- **Stage C—Feature weighting:** This concerns the engagement of a feature weighting method, which further weights similarity according to the characteristics of each user.
- **Stage D—Similarity processing:** An additional stage where similarity is furthermore weighted, according to some heuristic criteria.
- **Stage E—Neighborhood formation/selection:** This refers to the method engaged for the selection of the set of users to be considered for producing the prediction (neighborhood formation).
- **Stage F—Contributing ratings normalization:** A stage normalizing the ratings that the users in the neighborhood have provided for the unknown item, before these are used to formulate a prediction for the examined user.
- **Stage G—Combining ratings for prediction:** The final stage, using some method to combine the ratings that the users in the neighborhood have provided for the unknown item, in order to predict its utility for the examined user.

For each one of these design stages, methods and techniques that have been proposed so far in the literature will be reviewed in the following sections of this chapter.

DATA PREPARATION

This preliminary stage refers to the preparation of the user-item matrix, in order to address problems of sparsity and thus to improve the performance of the algorithms. The following approaches may be followed.

None

In classic collaborative filtering algorithms, the input data is the original user-rating matrix, where no processing is being applied. Characteristic examples are the algorithms of Herlocker et al. (2002) and Shardanand and Maes (1995).

Default Voting

Default voting refers to the usage of a technique introduced by Breese et al. (1998), in order to address the sparsity problem. It arose from the observation that when there are relatively few ratings (votes) for either the active user or each of the other examined users, the algorithm is not able to perform well (and sometimes not able to produce a prediction at all), since it operates on the intersection of the items both individuals have rated. The technique assumes some default rating r_{fill-n} for items that have been rated by one user but for which there are no explicit ratings from the other one. In addition, it assumes the same default rating value r_{fill-n} for some number of additional items that neither user has rated. According to Breese et al. (1998), this has the effect of assuming that there is some additional number of unspecified items that neither user has voted on, but both would nonetheless agree on. In most cases, the default rating value will reflect a neutral or somewhat negative preference for these unobserved items. According to Sarwar (2001),

the following schemes can be used in order to implement default voting in a neighborhood-based algorithm (Vozalis & Margaritis, 2003):

- **User-average scheme:** In this scheme, we calculate the average user rating:

$$\overline{r_{c,mean}} = \frac{\sum_{v=1}^{\hat{s}_c} r_{c,v}}{s_c} \qquad (1)$$

for each user c, where $\hat{s}_c \in \Re^+$ is the number of items that this user has rated in the past (if $\hat{s}_c = 0$, then a default rating such as $r_{fill-n} = \frac{r_{max} - r_{min}}{2}$ can be assigned). Then, this average user rating is used to replace the missing values for the particular user c. This approach is based on the idea that a user's rating for a new item can be simply predicted if we take into account the $\hat{s}_c$ past ratings of this user. Therefore, for each item $s \in S$, the assumed rating for user c is calculated from:

$$r_{fill-in} = \begin{cases} \overline{r_{c,mean}}, & \text{if user } c \text{ has not rated item } s \\ r_{c,s}, & \text{if user } c \text{ has rated item } s \text{ with } r_{c,s} \end{cases}$$

$$(2)$$

- **Item-average scheme:** In this scheme, an item average:

$$\overline{r_{mean,s}} = \frac{\sum_{v=1}^{\hat{c}_s} r_{v,s}}{\hat{c}_s} \qquad (3)$$

is calculated as a fill-in value for an item s, using the ratings that $\hat{c}_s \in \Re^+$ users (who have previously rated item s) have provided. Similarly, if $\hat{c}_s = 0$, then a default rating such as:

$$r_{fill-in} = \frac{r_{max} - r_{min}}{2} \qquad (4)$$

can be assigned. If not, for each item $s \in S$, the assumed rating for user c is calculated from:

$$r_{fill-in} = \begin{cases} \overline{r_{mean,s}} & \text{, if user } c \text{ has not rated item } s \\ r_{c,s} & \text{, if user } c \text{ has rated item } s \text{ with } r_{c,s} \end{cases} \qquad (5)$$

- **Composite scheme:** In this scheme, collected information about both the users and the items contributes to the default voting value. The main idea behind this approach is that it uses the average of user c on item s and then adds a correction factor according to how the specific item has been rated by other users. More formally, assuming that there exists a set C' with $\hat{c}_s$ users ($C' = \{c_1, c_2, ..., c_{\hat{c}_s}\}$) who have all rated item s in the past, then the correction term that is introduced for some user $c_v \in C'\,(1 \le v \le \hat{c}_s)$ can be calculated as $\delta_v = r_{c_v,s} - \overline{r_{mean,s}}$. The fill-in value (called composite rating) can be then calculated from the following formula:

$$r_{fill-in} = \begin{cases} \overline{r_{c,mean}} + \dfrac{\sum_{v=1}^{\hat{c}_s} \delta_v}{\hat{c}_s} & \text{, if user } c \text{ has not rated item } s \\ r_{c,s} & \text{, if user } c \text{ has rated item } s \text{ with } r_{c,s} \end{cases} \qquad (6)$$

If the two mean rating factors (i.e., $\overline{r_{c,mean}}$ and $\overline{r_{mean,s}}$) are interchanged and an appropriate modification is introduced in δ_v (with $1 \le v \le \hat{s}_c$), a similar composite rating formula can be produced (Vozalis & Margaritis, 2003). Experiments from Sarwar (2001) have indicated that the composite scheme has the best predicting accuracy from

all three. Nevertheless, its main drawback is that it requires intensive calculations in order to be computed for all missing values in the original user-item matrix.

Data Blurring

The method of data blurring (Kim, Kim, & Herlocker, 2004) was proposed as appropriate for completing missing values of the user-item matrix in cases when items can be distinguished among classes (e.g., genres). The underlying assumption is that a user will prefer a particular item if the other items of the same genre are preferred. Kim et al. (2004) apply data blurring for items that are described by multiple features (attributes). The basic concept is that if a user prefers an item with feature value $j^{desired}$, then it can be inferred that the user will also have some preference for other items that have value $j^{desired}$ on this feature. Kim et al. (2004) presented a formal way for computing blurring values based on binary preferences (items are either 'preferred' or 'unknown'). They define that the probability that an item s will be preferred by a user c (i.e., that it would receive a rating $r_{c,s} \ge j^{desired}$, where $r_{min} \le j^{desired} \le r_{max}$) can be defined as $P_{c,s} = 1$, whereas the probability that it will not be preferred (i.e., $r_{c,s} < j^{desired}$) can be defined as $P_{c,s} = 0$. Then, they engage two techniques: row-wise blurring that fills unknown ratings by using previous ratings on items of this class, and column-wise blurring that fills unknown ratings by using previous ratings by users on the items of this class. For the case that we examine—that is, multi-valued ratings upon a single attribute—the calculation of the data blurring values can be calculated as it follows:

- **Row-wise:** The probability that for the particular item s the user c has some preferred value $j^{desired}$ can be related to the probability that the items in the class of s have been rated with value $j^{desired}$ by the rest of the users. It can be calculated using the distribution of ratings from all users that have rated the items of its class.

- **Column-wise:** The probability that for the particular item s the user c has some preferred value $j^{desired}$ can be related to the probability that the user has provided value $j^{desired}$ to the set of items that belong to the same class with item s. Again, it can be calculated using the distribution of ratings that this user has provided to the items of its class.

Dimensionality Reduction

The dimensionality reduction approaches remove unrepresentative or insignificant users or items in order to condense the user-item matrix. A characteristic approach is aggregating items into classes of related items, and considering the ratings that users give upon those classes, in order to produce more dense matrixes which are transformed from user-item to user-class ones (Zeng et al., 2004). Techniques such as singular value decomposition (SVD) (Sarwar et al., 2000), principal component analysis (PCA) (Goldberg, Roeder, Gupta, & Perkins, 2001), or latent semantic indexing (LSI) (Hoffman, 2003) may be used for this purpose. However, potentially useful information may be lost during the reduction process (Papagelis, Rousidis, Plexousakis, & Theoharopoulos, 2005).

SIMILARITY CALCULATION

At this stage, a particular method is engaged to calculate the similarity between two users (the active user and each other user that has provided a rating on the unknown item) based on the $y \in \Re^{+}$ items they have both rated in the past (if $y = 0$, then the similarity of a with this user cannot be calculated, and this user is ignored from the calculation of the prediction). The method to be selected calculates the similarity using the ratings on these co-rated items. Several approaches have been identified in the literature.

Closeness

A rather simple approach that can be found in related literature is the one used in the LikeMinds system (Greening, 1997; Aggarwal, Wolf, Wu, & Yu, 1999). It calculates similarity based on the absolute value of the difference between ratings. More specifically, considering the active user a and another user c, LikeMinds defines a *closeness* function $C(|r_{a,s} - r_{c,s}|)$ that is based on the absolute value of the difference between two ratings for an item s. The *closeness value total* $CVT_{a,c}$ is defined as the sum of all closeness function values, over all items rated in common between two users a and c: $CVT_{a,c} = \sum_{i=1}^{y} C(|r_{a,i} - r_{c,i}|)$. Then, the similarity between the two users can be computed as a scaled average value of $CVT_{a,c}$, such as:

$$sim(a,c) = \frac{CVT_{a,c}}{y} \qquad (7)$$

$$sim(a,c) = \frac{CVT_{a,c}}{y} \cdot \log_2 y \qquad (8)$$

The first is a simple arithmetic mean, whereas the second calculation is the logarithmically scaled average value of the closeness function values.

L1-Norm

Another simple measure of similarity between the vectors of the y co-rated items of two users (i.e., $\vec{r}^a = [r_{a,1},...,r_{a,y}]$ and $\vec{r}^c = [r_{c,1},...,r_{c,y}]$, where for simplicity reasons we use the notation $r_{c,i}$ to refer to the ratings of the item c_i with $i \in [1,...,y]$), is the L1-Norm (Spertus, Sahami, & Buyukkokten, 2005). This is computed using the following formula:

$$sim(a,c) = L1(\vec{r}^a, \vec{r}^c) = \frac{\vec{r}^a \cdot \vec{r}^c}{\|\vec{r}^a\|_1 \cdot \|\vec{r}^c\|_1} = \frac{\sum_{i=1}^{y} f_i^2 (r_{a,i} \cdot r_{c,i})}{\sum_{i=1}^{y} f_i^2 r_{a,i}^2 \cdot \sum_{i=1}^{y} f_i^2 r_{c,i}^2}$$

$$(9)$$

The weighting factor f_i depends on whether a feature weighting method is engaged in the following stage. At this point, we are not concerned about how this factor is calculated (e.g., it may be assumed that f_i is equal to '1' and that it does not affect the calculation of similarity).

Mean Square Differences

One of the first approaches was the one used by Shardanand and Maes (1995), which calculates the similarity of two users, according to the mean squared distance of the ratings upon each co-rated item. The formula used is:

$$sim(a,c) = \frac{\sum_{i=1}^{y} f_i^2 \left(r_{a,i} - r_{c,i}\right)^2}{y \sum_{i=1}^{y} f_i^2} \tag{10}$$

Euclidian Distance

Another elementary approach is the one engaging the Euclidian distance formula in order to measure the distance between the ratings of the active user to the ratings of some other user (Kim & Yang, 2004). According to the following formula, the larger the distance, the smaller the similarity between the two users is:

$$sim(a,c) = 1 - \sqrt{\frac{\sum_{i=1}^{y} f_i^2 \left(r_{a,i} - r_{c,i}\right)^2}{\sum_{i=1}^{y} f_i^2}} \tag{11}$$

Vector/Cosine Similarity

One of the most popular similarity metrics in information retrieval literature is the cosine similarity measure between two vectors, also referred to as the L2-Norm (Spertus et al., 2005). In collaborative filtering (Breese et al., 1998; Sarwar et al., 2000; Adomavicius & Tuzhilin, 2005; Delgado & Ishii, 1999), it is used to measure the similarity between the vector of active user's ratings $\vec{r}^a$ and

the vector of some other user's ratings $\vec{r}^c$ of the y co-rated items:

$$sim(a,c) = \cos\left(\vec{r}^a, \vec{r}^c\right) = \frac{\vec{r}^a \cdot \vec{r}^c}{\left\|\vec{r}^a\right\|_2 \cdot \left\|\vec{r}^c\right\|_2} = \frac{\sum_{i=1}^{y} f_i^2 \left(r_{a,i} \cdot r_{c,i}\right)}{\sqrt{\sum_{i=1}^{y} f_i^2 r_{a,i}^2} \cdot \sqrt{\sum_{i=1}^{y} f_i^2 r_{c,i}^2}} \tag{12}$$

Pearson Correlation

The most popular similarity metric used in collaborative filtering algorithms (Resnick et al., 1994; Sarwar et al., 2000; Herlocker et al., 2002; Papagelis & Plexousakis, 2005) is the Pearson correlation factor between the set of ratings that the active user has provided in the past, and the set of ratings that the other user has provided. It is calculated using the following formula:

$$sim(a,c) = \frac{\sum_{i=1}^{y} f_i^2 \left(r_{a,i} - \overline{r_{a,mean}}\right)\left(r_{c,i} - \overline{r_{c,mean}}\right)}{\sqrt{\sum_{i=1}^{y} f_i^2 \left(r_{a,i} - \overline{r_{a,mean}}\right)^2 \cdot \sum_{i=1}^{y} f_i^2 \left(r_{c,i} - \overline{r_{c,mean}}\right)^2}} \tag{13}$$

where (as mentioned earlier) $\overline{r_{a,mean}}$ is the mean value of the ratings of the active user, and $\overline{r_{c,mean}}$ the mean value of the ratings of the other user.

Constrained Pearson Correlation

A variation of the previous formula, where a constant is used instead of the mean ratings of the users, is the constrained Pearson correlation factor. It was introduced by Shardanand and Maes (1995), and it calculates similarity using one of the following formulas:

$$sim(a,c) = \frac{\sum_{i=1}^{y} f_i^2 \left(r_{a,i} - mid\right)\left(r_{c,i} - mid\right)}{\sqrt{\sum_{i=1}^{y} f_i^2 \left(r_{a,i} - mid\right)^2 \cdot \sum_{i=1}^{y} f_i^2 \left(r_{c,i} - mid\right)^2}} \tag{14}$$

where *mid* is the middle of the evaluation scale used for the rating, or

$$sim(a,c) = \frac{\sum_{i=1}^{y} f_i^2 (r_{a,i} - median_a)(r_{c,i} - median_c)}{\sqrt{\sum_{i=1}^{y} f_i^2 (r_{a,i} - median_a)^2 \cdot \sum_{i=1}^{y} f_i^2 (r_{c,i} - median_c)^2}}$$

$$(15)$$

where the median of each user's ratings is used.

Spearman Correlation

A similar approach is using the Spearman rank correlation coefficient in order to compute a measure of correlations between the ranks that ratings have for each user, instead of rating values (Herlocker et al., 2002). To compute Spearman's correlation, each user's list of ratings is converted to a list of ranks, where the user's highest rating gets rank '1'. Tied ratings get the average of the ranks for their spot. Then similarity is calculated using the following formula:

$$sim(a,c) = \frac{\sum_{i=1}^{y} f_i^2 (k_{a,i} - \overline{k_{a,mean}})(k_{c,i} - \overline{k_{c,mean}})}{\sqrt{\sum_{i=1}^{y} f_i^2 (k_{a,i} - \overline{k_{a,mean}})^2 \cdot \sum_{i=1}^{y} f_i^2 (k_{c,i} - \overline{k_{c,mean}})^2}}$$

$$(16)$$

where $k_{a,i}$ represents the rank of the active user's rating of item i, and $k_{c,i}$ the rank of the other user's rating of item i. With $\overline{k_{a,mean}}$ and $\overline{k_{c,mean}}$ the formula refers to the average rank positions that the items have for users a and c, respectively.

Variance Weighting

Variance weighting is a modification of the mean squared difference method which incorporates an item variance weight factor. It was proposed by Herlocker et al. (2002), who calculated a variance weight for each item and then added a normalizing factor var_i in the denominator. The following formula occurred for the calculation of the similarity:

$$sim(a,c) = \frac{\sum_{i=1}^{y} f_i^2 \upsilon_i (r_{a,i} - r_{c,i})^2}{\sum_{i=1}^{y} f_i^2 \upsilon_i}$$

$$(17)$$

where the item variance weight factor is calculated using the following formulas:

$$\upsilon_i = \frac{var_i - var_{min}}{var_{max}} \ (1 \le i \le y)$$

$$(18)$$

$$var_i = \frac{\sum_{v=1}^{\hat{c}_{max}} (r_{v,i} - \overline{r_{mean,i}})^2}{\hat{c}_{max} - 1}$$

$$(19)$$

In the above formulas, $\hat{c}_{max}$ is the total number of users considered in the system, $\overline{r_{mean,i}}$ is (as noted earlier) the mean value of ratings that has been given to item i, and var_{min} and var_{max} are selected as the minimum and maximum values of the variance of all examined items that users a and c have rated. By incorporating a variance weighting factor, Herlocker et al. (2002) aimed to increase the influence of items with high variance in ratings, decrease the influence of items with low variance, and thus improve the performance of the algorithm.

Clark's Distance

A distance metric that was recently proposed for recommender systems is Clark's distance (de la Rosa, Montaner, & Lopez, 2006). It is calculated using the following formula:

$$sim(a,c) = \sqrt{\frac{\sum_{i=1}^{y} f_i^2 \left(\frac{|r_{a,i} - r_{c,i}|}{|r_{a,i} + r_{c,i}|} \right)^2}{\sum_{i=1}^{y} f_i^2}}$$

$$(20)$$

Probabilistic Rating Pattern

The motivation of this approach comes from the fact that two users with very similar preferences on items may have very different rating schemes (Jin, Zhai, & Callan, 2003). For a rating $r_{c,s} = r^c(s)$ that a user c provides for an item s, Jin et al. (2003) define the probability $P^c(s)$ that the user actually prefers the particular item. This means that even if two different users provide the same rating value, the probability that they would actually select this item from the set of available ones could be different. In this case, the aim is to find the distribution of probability $P^c(s)$, considering rating $r^c(s)$. For simplicity reasons, Jin et al. (2003) consider this as a Gaussian distribution $N(\mu(r^c(s),c),\sigma(r^c(s),c))$, which centers at $\mu(r^c(s),c)$ with a width of $\sigma(r^c(s),c)$. Jin et al. (2003) have therefore proposed the separation (decoupling) of the preference model from the rating scheme, and for measuring similarity they have defined two different similarity notions: the similarity between the preference patterns ($sim^P(a,c)$) and the similarity of the rating patterns ($sim^R(a,c)$).

- **Rating pattern similarity:** Jin et al. (2003) define the similarity of users a and c as the likelihood of mistaking user a as user c, giving the rating pattern of a. Assuming that the user selects a rating $j \in [r_{min},...,r_{max}]$, we define the rating pattern as $\tilde{R}(c) = \{C(j,c) 1 \le j \le r_{max}\}$, where $C(R,c)$ is the count of items rated with value j. With these definitions, $sim^R(a,c)$ can be defined as (Jin et al., 2003):

$$sim^R(a,c) = p(c \mid \tilde{R}(a)) = \frac{p(\tilde{R}(a)|c)p(c)}{p(\tilde{R}(a))} \approx \frac{p(\tilde{R}(a)|c)}{\sum_{c'} p(\tilde{R}(a)|c')}$$
(21)

where $\sum_{c'} p(\tilde{R}(a)|c')$ is the sum of probabilities that any other user $c' \in C$ has rated items with a pattern $\tilde{R}(a)$ (i.e., identical to the one of user a). This last step also requires the assumption that every user has the same prior $p(a)$. By assuming that every rating is generated independently of others, $p(\tilde{R}(a)|c)$ can be expressed as:

$$p(\tilde{R}(a)|c) = \prod_{j=r_{min}}^{r_{max}} p(j|c)^{C(j,a)}$$
(22)

where $p(j|c)$ stands for the likelihood for user a to come up with rating j for an arbi-

trary item, and $C(j,a)$ is the count of items that a has rated with j.

- **Preference pattern similarity:** The preference similarity of user a and user c, $sim^P(a,c)$, can be computed as the likelihood of mistaking user c as user a, given the preference pattern of a. Let S^a be the set of items that are rated by user a. The preference pattern of user a $\tilde{P}(a)$ is defined as (Jin et al., 2003):

$$\tilde{P}(a) = \{P_a(s) | \forall s \in S^a\} = \{\mu(r^a(s),a) | \forall s \in S^a\}$$
(23)

The preference similarity of users a and c can be similarly written as:

$$sim^P(a,c) = p(c \mid \tilde{P}(a)) = \frac{p(\tilde{P}(a)|c)p(c)}{p(\tilde{P}(a))} \approx \frac{p(\tilde{P}(a)|c)}{\sum_{c'} p(\tilde{P}(a)|c')}$$
(24)

Similarly, $\sum_{c'} p(\tilde{P}(a)|c')$ is the sum of probabilities that any other user $c' \in C$ has a preference pattern $\tilde{P}(a)$ (i.e., identical to the one of user a). Assuming that each item is generated independently from others, $p(\tilde{P}(a)|c)$ can be expressed as:

$$p(\tilde{P}(a)|c) = \prod_{s \in S^a} \mu(r^c(s),c)^{\mu(r^a(s),a)}$$
(25)

Jin et al. (2003) have calculated $\mu(r^c(s),c) = P^c(j \le r^c(s)|c) - P^c(j = r^c(s)|c)/2$, where $P^c(j \le r^c(s)|c)$ is the likelihood for user c to rate any item no higher than the rating $r^c(s)$, and $P^c(j = r^c(s)|c)$ is the likelihood for user c to rate any item as $r^c(s)$.

A problem occurs in the calculation of $sim^P(a,c)$ when there are items that are rated by user a but not rated by user c. In that case, there will not be enough rating information for user c on the item. This corresponds to the missing data issue discussed in the Data Preparation stage, and is appropriately addressed at that stage. If not, the similarity cannot be calculated.

Other Metrics

Information theory has motivated other measures of correlation, such as "mutual information" (Cover & Thomas, 1991; Spertus et al., 2005), Salton's (1989), and logg-odds (Spertus et al., 2005). These measures have been experimentally investigated in the study of Spertus et al. (2005), and have been found to have strong correlations with other simpler metrics (and mainly with L1-Norm), thus they are not further examined here.

FEATURE WEIGHTING

As indicated before, collaborative filtering is built on the assumption that a good way to predict the preferences of the active user for a target item is to find other users who have similar preferences, and then use those similar users' preferences for the target item in order to make a prediction. The similarity measure is therefore based on preference patterns of users. Thus, a set of user's ratings can be considered as features related to this user. Hence, feature weighting methods have been introduced, aiming to improve the accuracy of the prediction (Yu, Wen, Xu, & Ester, 2001; Zeng et al., 2004). These methods focus on the 'good' items, while removing the 'bad' ones or reducing their impact. Ratings on a 'good' item are those considered highly relevant to the preference of the target item, while 'bad' ratings are irrelevant or noisy in prediction for the target item. Feature weighting is introduced if the weighting factor f_i in the formulas used for the calculation of similarity is assigned a value according to some particular technique. In all the formulas that follow, i refers to the specific item being examined and therefore is allowed to take values between $1 \leq i \leq y$.

None

As mentioned earlier, in most algorithms (e.g., Herlocker et al., 2002), no feature weighting is engaged. Therefore the weighting factor f_i is assigned the value '1'.

Inverse User Frequency

The idea behind this technique is borrowed from information retrieval and aims to reduce the weight for commonly occurring items, capturing the intuition that they are not useful in distinguishing preferences among users, whereas less frequently appearing items may be more indicative. Breese et al. (1998) first applied such a transformation, assuming that universally liked items will not be as useful in capturing similarity as less common items. They have defined inverse frequency weight as:

$$f_i = \log \frac{\hat{c}_{max}}{\hat{c}_i} \qquad (26)$$

where $\hat{c}_i$ is the number of users that have rated item i, and $\hat{c}_{max}$ is the total number of users in the system.

Entropy

Another approach for feature weighting is the one proposed by Yu et al. (2001, 2003). It is based on the concept of entropy as a measure of uncertainty of a random variable. It claims that the diversity (or distribution) of users' ratings to a specific item is apparently meaningful for collaborative filtering. Yu et al. (2001, 2003) propose the following entropy-based weighting method for collaborative filtering:

$$f_i = \frac{H_i}{H_{i,max}} = \frac{-\sum_{j=r_{min}}^{r_{max}} p_{j,i} \cdot \log_2 p_{j,i}}{H_{i,max}} \qquad (27)$$

where H_i is the entropy of item i, $p_{j,i}$ is the probability of ratings on item i to take the value j (distribution of ratings upon scales $[r_{min},\ldots,r_{max}]$), and $H_{i,max}$ represents the maximum entropy which assumes that the distributions over all scales of ratings are identical. Thus, a large value of f_i means diverse preference for item i, and hence more emphasis should be put on the ratings of this i during the prediction. However, the proposed entropy-based weighting scheme may encounter the risk that there is no significant difference of entropy from item to item.

SIMILARITY PROCESSING

This stage deals with a further processing of the calculated similarities in order to put more emphasis to some particular similarities and to devalue some other ones.

None

Not all algorithms engage the stage of similarity processing. Many of the proposed algorithms (e.g., Shardanand & Maes, 1995) do not further process the calculated similarities, and use them as they are:

$$sim'(a, c) = sim(a, c) \qquad (28)$$

Case Amplification

Breese et al. (1998) have proposed this similarity processing technique. Case amplification emphasizes higher similarity weights and punishes low ones. It transforms the calculated weights as follows:

$$sim'(a,c) = \begin{cases} (sim(a,c))^q & , \text{if } sim(a,c) \geq 0 \\ -(|sim(a,c)|^q) & , \text{if } sim(a,c) \prec 0 \end{cases}$$

$$(29)$$

where $q \in \Re^+$. A typical value for q that Breese et al. (1998) used for their experiments was $q=2.5$.

Significance Weighting

Another technique that processes the similarity weights in order to appropriately devalue those that are based on a small number of co-rated items between the active user and the other user is significance weighting. This technique was applied by Herlocker et al. (2002) and is calculated using the following formula:

$$sim'(a,c) = \begin{cases} \dfrac{sim(a,c) \cdot y}{b_y} & , \text{if } y \prec b_y \\ sim(a,c) & , \text{if } y \geq b_y \end{cases}$$

$$(30)$$

where b_y is a threshold, also referred to as a *penalty constant* (Zeng et al., 2004), which denotes the number of co-rated items that are considered satisfactory in order for the similarity not to be changed.

Aspect Model

In a similar manner and using some instance selection method, the most relevant users for a particular targeted item can be identified, in order to help narrow down the possible set of potential neighbors. Zeng et al. (2004) study how an aspect model (a latent class statistical-mixture model) can be used to facilitate the instance selection. In the aspect model, user $c \in C = \{c_1,...,c_{\hat{c}_{max}}\}$, together with the items they rate $s \in S = \{s_1,...,s_{\hat{s}_{max}}\}$, forms an observation (c,s) which is associated with one latent class variable $l \in L = \{l_1,...,l_K\}$. The working assumption is that c and s are independent and conditioned on l. The similarities are recalculated according to the following formula:

$$sim'(a,c) = sim(a,c) \cdot p(c,s) \qquad (31)$$

where the relevance $p(c,s)$ of user c to item s based on the aspect model of Zeng et al. (2004) is calculated from:

$$p(c,s) = p(s)\sum_{l\in L}\frac{p(l\mid c)p(l\mid s)}{p(l)} \qquad (32)$$

where $p(l\mid c)$ and $p(l\mid s)$ are class-conditioned multinomial distributions, and $p(l)$ the class's prior probabilities. In this equation:

- $p(s)$ can be ignored because it has no impact on the ranking of the relevancy between users and the target item.
- $p(l\mid s)$ can be calculated in various ways—for example, for text items using a naive Bayesian classification method or for other types of items using a manual classification in classes (e.g., using an ontology taxonomy).
- The rating of user c on class l divided by the total rating of the user on all classes is utilized to represent $p(l\mid c)$, which can be written (Zeng et al., 2004) as:

$$p(l\mid c) \approx \frac{u_{c,l}}{\sum_{k=1}^{K}u_{c,k}} \qquad (33)$$

where K is the number of classes, $u_{c,l}$ is the rating of user c on class l, and $u_{c,k}$ is the rating of user c on class l_k.

- $p(l)$ is represented as the number of items belonging to class l divided by the total number of items belonging to all classes. That is:

$$p(l) \approx \frac{N_l}{\sum_{k=1}^{K}N_k} = \frac{N_l}{N} \qquad (34)$$

NEIGHBORHOOD FORMATION/SELECTION

This is one of the core stages in a neighborhood-based algorithm, since it deals with how the neighborhood of the active user (that is, the set of users that are considered more "similar" to the active user) is selected. Two basic methods are usually engaged for selecting the neighbors and formulating the neighborhood.

Similarity Threshold (or Correlation Weight Threshold)

The first approach defines a threshold value $threshold_{cw}$ for the similarity, which is also called 'correlation weight threshold' (Herlocker et al., 2002) or 'user frequency threshold' (Zeng et al., 2004). Each user c having a similarity to the active user a with value $sim'(a, c)$ equal or higher with this threshold is included in the neighborhood ($sim'(a,c) \geq threshold_{cw}$). This method aims to include in the neighborhood only the m neighbors with a high similarity to the active user.

Maximum Number of Neighbors

The second approach defines a pre-determined maximum number of neighbors M, called maximum number of neighbors (Herlocker et al., 2002), which will be considered for the prediction. That is, the users are ranked into a list according to their similarity value. Here m takes the constant value M. The method aims to restrict the number of neighbors that will be considered for the prediction, in the case of large numbers of users. Two particular techniques are used (Sarwar et al., 2000; Vozalis & Margaritis, 2003):

1. **Center-based scheme (Classic):** This is the typical maximum number of neighbors' selection scheme introduced by Herlocker et al. (2002). The center-based scheme creates a neighborhood of size M for the active user a, by simply selecting those users that have the M highest similarity values with the active user a.
2. **Aggregate-neighborhood scheme:** This scheme creates a neighborhood of users not by finding the users who are closest to the active user, but by identifying users who are closest to the center point $\bar{C}$ (centroid) of the current neighborhood. It is a scheme that is proven to be beneficial in very sparse user-item matrices. This scheme forms a

neighborhood of size M by first picking the user that is closest to the active user a. The procedure for selecting the next M-1 neighbors resumes in the following manner (Vozalis & Margaritis, 2003):

a.   Assume that at a certain point, the current neighborhood consists of h users, where clearly $h < M$.
b.   The centroid of the current neighborhood is computed as:

$$\vec{C} = \frac{1}{h}\sum_{j=1}^{h} c_j \qquad (35)$$

c.   A new user will be selected for the neighborhood only if he or she is closest to the user that serves as the current centroid.
d.   The neighborhood grows to h+1 users and the centroid is recalculated. The process continues until the size of the neighborhood becomes M.

In addition, two ways for defining the maximum number of neighbors M have been followed (Zeng et al., 2004): first, by defining M as an absolute number, independent from the total number of users in the system; and second, by defining M as a percentage the users currently using the system (e.g., the most relevant 5%).

Clustering-Based Selection

The k-nearest neighbor technique (also referred to as the k-means algorithm) creates k clusters, each of which consists of users who have similar preferences among them. The aim of this technique is to create clusters of users with similar preferences, and then identify the cluster with which the active user is more similar (and therefore use this as a neighborhood). In the first pass, the algorithm arbitrarily takes the first k users as the initial centroids of the k clusters. Then, each user is assigned to a cluster in such a way that the distance between the user and the cluster centroid is minimized. The distance is usually calculated based on the Euclidian (Kim & Yang, 2004) or the Pearson (Xue et al., 2005) similarity measures. Then, a new centroid is calculated for each cluster, based on the users currently in it. After finding the center of each cluster, the distance between the center and each user is computed as before, in order to find the customer in which the user should belong. Recalculating the means and computing the distances are repeated until a terminating condition is met. The condition is generally how far each new center has moved from the previous center—that is, if all the new centers moved within a certain distance, the loop can be terminated. When this occurs, the cluster with the shortest distance from its centroid to the active user is selected. The neighborhood used for prediction is the one formed by the users in the selected cluster.

CONTRIBUTING RATINGS NORMALIZATION

The next stage concerns the transformation or normalization of the ratings that the users in the neighborhood have provided for the target item x. It may take place for various reasons, such as for normalizing the effect of having great variances in the way users have used the evaluation scale to rate the target item.

None

The first option is to use no normalization (Herlocker et al., 2002). The ratings are considered for producing a prediction, as they have been provided by the neighbors ($\tilde{r}_{d,x} = r_{d,x}$).

Gaussian Normalization

The second option is to engage a method that considers two factors that may lead to variance in the ratings of users with similar interests (Jin & Si, 2004). The first factor is the shift of average ratings, the fact that some users are more 'tolerant' and tend to give higher ratings than others. As a result, the average ratings of those 'tolerant' users are usually higher than other rigorous users. This factor can be accounted by subtracting ratings of each user from the average rating of the user. The second factor is the use of different rating scales, related to the fact that 'conservative' users tend to assign items to a narrow range of rating values, whereas 'liberal' users tend to assign items with a wider range of rating values. This factor can be accounted by dividing the ratings of each user by the variance in his or her ratings. Combining the above, the calculation of the normalized rating $\tilde{r}_{d,x}$ of a neighbor d for item x may be given by:

$$\tilde{r}_{d,x} = \frac{r_{d,x} - \overline{r_{d,mean}}}{\sqrt{\sum_{i=1}^{\hat{s}_d}\left(r_{d,i} - \overline{r_{d,mean}}\right)^2}} \qquad (36)$$

where (as previously) $\hat{s}_d$ refers to the number of items that user d has rated. Since this normalization method essentially normalizes the rating distribution of a user to a Gaussian distribution, Jin and Si (2004) proposed to refer to it as the Gaussian normalization method.

Decoupling Normalization

The third option normalizes the contributed rating of an item according to the probability that this item was favored by the particular neighbor. This probabilistic measurement can be determined based on the following two assumptions:

1. When a large portion of items are rated by a user with a rating value less than j, then the

items that will be rated with j are probably favored by the user; and

2. When more items are rated with the rating value j, then it becomes less likely that these items are favored by the user.

Based on these two assumptions, Jin and Si (2004) and Jin et al. (2003) have proposed a formula called 'halfway accumulative distribution', in order to calculate the probability that measures how likely the item x will be favored by a specific neighbor. The formal expression of the formula is:

$$p^{favors}(x) = p_d\left(r_{d,x} \le j^d\right) - \frac{p_d\left(r_{d,x} = j^d\right)}{2} \qquad (37)$$

where $p_d\left(r_{d,x} \le j^d\right)$ can be practically calculated as the percentage of items that d has rated with no more than j^d, and $p_d\left(r_{d,x} = j^d\right)$ can be practically calculated as the percentage of items that have been rated with j^d. The value of j^d may be either manually determined, or it can be defined as the rating value the majority of items received by this user. Then, the contributed rating is normalized as:

$$\tilde{r}_{d,x} = r_{d,x} \cdot p^{favors}(x) \qquad (38)$$

This method has been called the 'decoupling normalization method' by Jin and Si (2004) and Jin et al. (2003).

Belief-Distribution Normalization

This improvement of neighborhood-based algorithms was introduced by McLaughlin and Herlocker (2004). It aims to identify possible inconsistencies in the ratings that users have provided, for example, due to mistakes, change in taste, or change of mood. For this purpose, they have mapped each rating to a discrete belief distribution, representing a belief of user c's rating on item x.

In this manner, instead of using each neighbor's rating on x, the rating on which the user has the maximum belief value can be used. That is, $\tilde{r}_{d,x} = j^{belief}$, where j^{belief} is selected as the value of the rating scale j ($r_{min} \leq j \leq r_{max}$) for which the belief distribution is maximum—that is, $j^{belief} = \max(belief_{d,x}(j))$. Therefore, for a neighbor d we construct a vector $\vec{B}_{d,x}$ of belief distributions upon the rating scale as far as item x is concerned:

$$\vec{B}_{d,x} = [belief_{d,x}(r_{min}),...,belief_{d,x}(r_{max})] \quad (39)$$

The belief distribution can be constructed in several ways, for example, manually or by calculating the distance of a rating scale to the mean rating of the user (McLaughlin & Herlocker, 2004).

COMBINING RATINGS FOR PREDICTION

The final stage of neighborhood-based algorithms is the combination of the ratings that the neighbors have provided in order to produce a prediction $U^a(x)$ of the rating the active user would give to the target item x. Several methods have been proposed for this stage.

Simple Arithmetic Mean

The simplest method is the calculation of the simple arithmetic mean of the ratings of the neighbors, according to the formula (Herlocker et al., 2002):

$$U^a(x) = \frac{\sum_{d=1}^{m} \tilde{r}_{d,x}}{m} \quad (40)$$

where m is the number of users in the neighborhood.

Weighted Mean

One of the most popular methods (Greening, 1997) is extending the arithmetic mean method by weighting the rating of each neighbor by the similarity this user has with the active user. The formula used for the calculation is:

$$U^a(x) = \frac{\sum_{d=1}^{m} r_{d,x} \cdot sim'(a,d)}{\sum_{d=1}^{m} sim'(a,d)} \quad (41)$$

Deviation-from-Mean

Another very popular method, first introduced in the GroupLens system and then used in numerous systems (Konstan et al., 1997; Resnick et al., 1994; Delgado & Ishii, 1999; Zeng et al., 2004; Papagelis & Plexousakis, 2005; Tsai, Chiu, Lee, & Wang, 2006), is the one that performs a weighted average of deviations from the neighbor's mean, according to the formula (Herlocker et al., 2002):

$$U^a(x) = \overline{r_{a,mean}} + \frac{\sum_{d=1}^{m} \left[(r_{d,x} - \overline{r_{d,mean}}) sim'(a,d) \right]}{\sum_{d=1}^{m} sim'(a,d)} \quad (42)$$

where $\overline{r_{d,mean}}$ is the mean value of the ratings that each neighbor has provided in the past.

Z-Score

An extension of the above method is to account for the differences in spread between users' rating distributions, by converting ratings to z-scores (ratings with mean '0' and standard deviation '1'). Herlocker et al. (2002) have provided the following formula for this purpose:

$$U^a(x) = \overline{r_{a,mean}} + \sigma^a \cdot \frac{\sum_{d=1}^{m} \left[\frac{(\tilde{r}_{d,x} - \overline{r_{d,mean}})}{\sigma^d} \cdot sim'(a,d) \right]}{\sum_{d=1}^{m} sim'(a,d)} \quad (43)$$

Table 2. Overview of design options for neighborhood-based collaborative filtering

Design Options	Representative References
Data Preparation Stage	
None	Herlocker et al. (2002), Shardanand & Maes (1995)
Default voting	Breese et al. (1998), Sarwar (2001), Vozalis & Margaritis (2003)
Data blurring	Kim et al. (2004)
Dimensionality reduction	Sarwar et al. (2000), Goldberg et al. (2001), Hoffman (2003), Zeng et al. (2004), Papagelis et al. (2005)
Similarity Calculation Stage	
Closeness	Greening (1997), Aggarwal et al. (1999)
L1-Norm	Spertus et al. (2005)
Mean square differences	Shardanand & Maes (1995)
Euclidian distance	Kim & Yang (2004)
Vector/Cosine similarity	Breese et al. (1998), Sarwar et al. (2000), Adomavicius & Tuzhilin (2005), Spertus et al. (2005)
Pearson correlation	Resnick et al. (1994), Herlocker et al. (2002), Sarwar et al. (2000), Papagelis & Plexousakis (2005)
Constrained Pearson correlation	Shardanand & Maes (1995)
Spearman correlation	Herlocker et al. (2002)
Variance weighting	Herlocker et al. (2002)
Clarck's distance	de la Rosa et al. (2006)
Probabilistic rating pattern	Jin et al. (2003)
Information theory metrics	Spertus et al. (2005)
Feature Weighting Stage	
None	Herlocker et al. (2002)
Inverse user frequency	Breese et al. (1998)
Entropy	Yu et al. (2001; 2003)
Similarity Processing Stage	
None	Shardanand & Maes (1995)
Case amplification	Breese et al. (1998)
Significance weighting	Herlocker et al. (2002), Zeng et al. (2004)
Aspect model	Zeng et al. (2004)
Neighborhood Formation/Selection Stage	
Similarity (or correlation weight) threshold	Herlocker et al. (2002)
Maximum number of neighbors	Herlocker et al. (2002), Sarwar et al. (2000), Vozalis & Margaritis (2003)
Clustering-based selection	Kim & Yang (2004), Xue et al. (2005)

continued on following page

Table 2. continued

Contributing Ratings Normalization Stage	
None	Herlocker et al. (2002)
Gaussian normalization	Jin & Si (2004)
Decoupling normalization	Jin & Si (2004), Jin et al. (2003)
Belief-distribution normalization	McLaughlin & Herlocker (2004)
Combining Ratings for Prediction Stage	
Simple arithmetic mean	Herlocker et al. (2002)
Weighted mean	Greening (1997)
Deviation-from-mean	Konstan et al. (1997), Resnick et al. (1994), Delgado & Ishii (1999), Herlocker et al. (2002), Zeng et al. (2004), Papagelis & Plexousakis (2005), Tsai et al. (2006)
Z-score	Herlocker et al. (2002)
Belief distribution for prediction	McLaughlin & Herlocker (2004)

where $s^a = \sqrt{\sum_{i=1}^{\bar{s}_a} \left(r_{a,i} - \overline{r_{a,mean}} \right)^2}$ is the standard deviation of the ratings of the active user and the standard deviation of the ratings of the neighbor.

Belief-Distribution Prediction

Apart from using the belief distribution vector that McLaughlin and Herlocker (2004) have proposed for normalization purposes, it can also be used for the calculation of the prediction. More specifically, instead of predicting $U^a(x)$ by using the normalized ratings $\tilde{r}_{d,x}$ that each neighbor d has provided on x, they propose to select the rating value on which there is maximum belief. That is:

$$U^a(x) = j^{belief} = \max\left(belief_{a,x}(j)\right) \qquad (44)$$

where j^{belief} is selected as the rating scale $j(r_{min} \le j \le r_{max})$ for which the belief distribution is maximum.

To calculate the belief distribution vector $\bar{B}_{a,x}$ of the active user a, McLaughlin and Herlocker

(2004) have used a sum of the belief difference distributions of all neighbors, weighted with the similarity values for each neighbor. The weighting is complemented by combining each neighbor's belief distribution with the uniform belief distribution. The intuition behind this weighting is that the less similar a neighbor is to the active user, the less belief there will be that the neighbor's observed rating is the correct rating for the user. The formula used to calculate the belief distribution vector $\bar{B}_{a,x}$ is:

$$\bar{B}_{a,x} = \frac{\gamma + \sum_{d=1}^{m} \left[sim'(a,d) \cdot \bar{B}_{d,x} + \left((1 - sim'(a,d)) \cdot \gamma \right) \right]}{m+1}$$

$$(45)$$

In this formula, the uniform belief distribution (represented here as γ) can be thought of as a null vote with a similarity weight of '1'. According to McLaughlin and Herlocker (2004), it provides a threshold that the subsequent weights must overcome in order to predict a high confidence rating.

CONCLUSION

Considering all of the above options during the design of a neighborhood-based algorithm for collaborative filtering can lead to a variety of available design options for the developer to choose from. Table 2 provides an overview of the design options that we have examined in the previous sections. Other options to explore in the future might also include adding the time factor in order to differentiate user preferences in various time slots (e.g., Cho et al., 2005). Another option is the introduction of an adaptive component to the algorithm, which can be revising/recalculating the similarities in each step (e.g., after a prediction or the submission of a new rating), according to the previous step results (Delgado & Ishii, 1999; Nakamura & Abe, 1998). Furthermore, multiple similarity measures may be calculated and combined in order to formulate the neighborhood. For example, Jin et al. (2003) first measure the rating similarity and the preference similarity between two users, but then they combine them in order to produce a prediction.

This chapter focused on a category of information retrieval systems with a long tradition—collaborative filtering ones. It particular, studied issues related to one of the most prevalent families of algorithms for collaborative filtering—that is, neighborhood-based ones. Since 1995, when the first neighborhood-based approaches for collaborative filtering systems appeared (Shardanand & Maes, 1995), a plethora of methods for implementing such algorithms have been proposed. The chapter identified and extended seven generic algorithmic stages that have been found in related literature (Herlocker et al., 2002; Vozalis & Margaritis, 2003; Sarwar et al., 2000). Then it performed a review and discussion of design options for each stage of the algorithms based on approaches found in relevant literature. This study could serve as a basis for further extending the stages of neighborhood-based collaborative filtering systems. By providing an organized overview of available options, it may also help developers of such systems to study and select the ones they find appropriate for implementation in their systems.

FUTURE RESEARCH DIRECTIONS

The work presented in this chapter could be further extended as far as the implementation of proposed design options is concerned. More specifically, we previously introduced a simulation environment that allows for the experimental investigation of some of the examined design options for collaborative filtering algorithms (Manouselis & Costopoulou, 2006b). The rationale for such a tool is that collaborative filtering researchers and implementers could benefit from having a simulation environment that they could use to parameterize and test various design options for the algorithms they wish to implement. In this way, a variety of design options can be experimentally tested under conditions simulating the expected actual ones, before the final system is deployed. In this context, we plan to further develop the prototype of the simulation environment, so that it provides all examined designed options as variations of tested algorithms. In addition, we are interested in exploring how the examined design options are applied in the case of multi-attribute collaborative filtering algorithms. In previous work, we have developed and tested some of the examined options inside proposed multi-attribute utility algorithms for collaborative filtering (Manouselis & Costopoulou, 2007b). It is our intention to explore how the rest of the design options fit in the context of multi-attribute algorithms as well (Manouselis & Costopoulou, 2007a).

REFERENCES

Adomavicius, G., & Tuzhilin, A. (2005). Towards the next generation of recommender systems: A survey of the state-of-the-art and possible extensions. *IEEE Transactions on Knowledge and Data Engineering, 17*(6), 734–749.

Aggarwal, C.C., Wolf, J.L., Wu, K.-L., & Yu, P.S. (1999). Horting hatches an egg: A new graph-theoretic approach to collaborative filtering. *Proceedings of the ACM SIGKDD International Conference on Knowledge Discovery and Data Mining.*

Aha, D.W., Kibler, D., & Albert, M.K. (1991). Instance-based learning algorithms. *Machine Learning, 6,* 37–66.

Baudisch, P. (2001). *Dynamic information filtering.* PhD Thesis, Darmstad Technical University (GMD Research Series, 16), Germany.

Belkin, N.J., & Croft, W.B. (1992). Information filtering and information retrieval: Two sides of the same coin? *Communications of the ACM, 35*(12), 29–38.

Breese, J.S., Heckerman, D., & Kadie, C. (1998). Empirical analysis of predictive algorithms for collaborative filtering. *Proceedings of the 14th Conference on Uncertainty in Artificial Intelligence.*

Burke, R. (2002). Hybrid recommender systems: Survey and experiments. *User Modeling and User-Adapted Interaction, 12,* 331–370.

Cho, Y.B., Cho, Y.H., & Kim, S.H. (2005). Mining changes in customer buying behavior for collaborative recommendations. *Expert Systems with Applications, 28,* 359–369.

Cho, Y.H., Kim, J.K., & Kim, S.H. (2002). A personalized recommender system based on Web usage mining and decision tree induction. *Expert System with Applications, 23,* 329–342.

Cover, T.M., & Hart, P.E. (1967). Nearest neighbor pattern classification. *IEEE Transactions on Information Theory, 13*(1), 21–27.

Cover, T.M., & Thomas, J.A. (1991). *Elements of information theory.* New York: John Wiley & Sons.

de la Rosa, J.L., Montaner, M., & Lopez, J.M. (2006). Opinion based filtering. *Proceedings of the International Workshop on Recommender Systems, 17th European Conference on Artificial Intelligence* (ECAI 2006), Riva del Garda, Italy.

Delgado, J., & Ishii, N. (1999). Memory-based weighted-majority prediction for recommender systems. *Proceedings of the ACM-SIGIR'99 Recommender Systems Workshop,* Berkeley, CA.

Deshpande, M., & Karypis, G. (2004). Item-based Top-N recommendation algorithms. *ACM Transactions on Information Systems, 22*(1), 143–177.

Goldberg, K., Roeder, T., Gupta, D., & Perkins, C. (2001). Eigentaste: A constant time collaborative filtering algorithm. *Information Retrieval Journal, 4*(2), 133–151.

Greening, D. (1997). *Building consumer trust with accurate product recommendations.* LikeMinds White Paper, LMWSWP-210-6966.

Hanani, U., Shapira, B., & Shoval, P. (2001). Information filtering: Overview of issues, research and systems. *User Modeling and User-Adapted Interaction, 11,* 203–259.

Herlocker, J., Konstan, J.A., & Riedl, J. (2002). An empirical analysis of design choices in neighborhood-based collaborative filtering algorithms. *Information Retrieval, 5,* 287–310.

Hoffman, T. (2003). Collaborative filtering via Gaussian probabilistic latent semantic analysis. *Proceedings of the International ACM SIGIR Conference on Research and Development in Information Retrieval* (SIGIR'03), Toronto, Canada.

Jin, R., & Si, L. (2004). A study of methods for normalizing user ratings in collaborative filtering. *Proceedings of the International ACM SIGIR Conference on Research and Development in Information Retrieval* (SIGIR'04), Sheffield, UK.

Jin, R., Zhai, C., & Callan, J. (2003). Collaborative filtering with decoupled models for preferences and ratings. *Proceedings of CIKM'03*, New Orleans, LA.

Kim, H., Kim, J., & Herlocker, J. (2004). Feature-based prediction of unknown preferences for nearest-neighbor collaborative filtering. *Proceedings of the IEEE International Conference on Data Mining* (ICDM'04).

Kim, T.-H., & Yang, S.-B. (2004). Using attributes to improve prediction quality in collaborative filtering. *Proceedings of the 5th International Conference on E-Commerce and Web Technologies* (EC-Web 2004), Zaragoza, Spain.

Kim, Y.S., Yum, B.-J., & Kim, S.M. (2005). Development of a recommender system based on navigational and behavioral patterns of customers in e-commerce sites. *Expert Systems with Applications, 28,* 381–393.

Konstan, J.A. (2004). Introduction to recommender systems: Algorithms and evaluation. *ACM Transactions on Information Systems, 22*(1), 1–4.

Konstan, J.A., Miller, B.N., Maltz, D., Herlocker, J.L., Gordon, L.R., & Riedl, J. (1997). Grouplens: Applying collaborative filtering to Usenet news. *Communications of the ACM, 40*(3), 77–87.

Lee, J.-S., Jun, C.-H., Lee, J., & Kim, S. (2005). Classification-based collaborative filtering using market basket data. *Expert Systems with Applications, 29,* 700–704.

Malone, T., Grant, K., Turbak, F., Brobst, S., & Cohen, M. (1987). Intelligent information sharing systems. *Communications of the ACM, 30*(5), 390–402.

Manouselis, N., & Costopoulou, C. (2007a). Analysis and classification of multi-criteria recommender systems. *World Wide Web: Internet and Web Information Systems, Special Issue on Multi-Channel Adaptive Information Systems on the World Wide Web.*

Manouselis, N., & Costopoulou, C. (2006a). *Designing multi-attribute utility algorithms for collaborative filtering.* Technical Report No. 181, Informatics Laboratory, Agricultural University of Athens, Greece.

Manouselis, N., & Costopoulou, C. (2006b). A Web-based testing tool for multi-criteria recommender systems. *Engineering Letters, Special Issue on Web Engineering, 13*(3).

Manouselis, N., & Costopoulou, C. (2007b). Experimental analysis of design choices in multi-attribute utility collaborative filtering. *International Journal of Pattern Recognition and Artificial Intelligence, Special Issue on Personalization Techniques for Recommender Systems and Intelligent User Interfaces, 21*(2), 311–331.

Maritza, L., Gonzalez-Caro, C.N., Perez-Alcazar, J.J., Garcia-Diaz, J.C., & Delgado, J. (2004). A comparison of several predictive algorithms for collaborative filtering on multi-valued ratings. *Proceedings of the 2004 ACM Symposium on Applied Computing* (SAC'04), Nicosia, Cyprus.

Martin-Guerrero, J.D., Palomares, A., Balaguer-Ballester, E., Soria-Olivas, E., Gomez-Sanchis, J., & Soriano-Asensi, A. (2006). Studying the feasibility of a recommender in a citizen Web portal based on user modeling and clustering algorithms. *Expert Systems with Applications, 30*(2), 299–312.

McLaughlin, M.R., & Herlocker, J.L. (2004). A collaborative filtering algorithm and evaluation metric that accurately model the user experience. *Proceedings of the International ACM SIGIR Conference on Research and Development in Information Retrieval* (SIGIR'04), Sheffield, UK.

Miller, B.N., Konstan, J.A., & Riedl, J. (2004). PocketLens: Toward a personal recommender system. *ACM Transactions on Information Systems, 22*(3), 437–476.

Min, S.-H., & Han, I. (2005). Detection of the customer time-invariant pattern for improving recommender systems. *Expert Systems with Applications, 28,* 189–199.

Nakamura, A., & Abe, N. (1998). Collaborative filtering using weighted majority prediction algorithms. *Proceedings of the 15th International Conference on Machine Learning* (ICML'98). San Francisco: Morgan Kaufman.

Papagelis, M., & Plexousakis, D. (2005). Qualitative analysis of user-based and item-based prediction algorithms for recommendation agents. *Engineering Applications of Artificial Intelligence, 18,* 781–789.

Papagelis, M., Rousidis, I., Plexousakis, D., & Theoharopoulos, E. (2005). Incremental collaborative filtering for highly-scalable recommendation algorithms. *Proceedings of ISMIS 2005* (pp. 553–561). Berlin: Springer-Verlag (LNAI 3488).

Resnick, P., Iacovou, N., Suchak, M., Bergstrom, P., & Riedl, J. (1994). GroupLens: An open architecture for collaborative filtering. *Proceedings of ACM CSCW'94* (pp. 175–186).

Roh, T.H., Oh, K.J., & Han, I. (2003). The collaborative filtering recommendation based on SOM cluster-indexing CBR. *Expert Systems with Applications, 25,* 413–423.

Salton, G. (1989). *Automatic text processing: The transformation, analysis and retrieval of information by computer.* Reading, MA: Addison-Wesley.

Sarwar, B.M. (2001). *Sparsity, scalability, and distribution in recommender systems.* PhD Thesis, University of Minnesota, USA.

Sarwar, B., Karypis, G., Konstan, J., & Riedl, J. (2000). Analysis of recommendation algorithms for e-commerce. *Proceedings of ACM EC'00,* Minneapolis, MN.

Shardanand, U., & Maes, P. (1995). Social information filtering: Algorithms for automatic 'word of mouth'. *Proceedings of the Conference on Human Factors in Computing Systems* (CHI'95), Denver CO.

Spertus, E., Sahami, M., & Buyukkokten, O. (2005, August 21–24). Evaluating similarity measures: A large-scale study in the Orkut Social Network. *Proceedings of KDD'05.*

Tsai, K.H., Chiu, T.K., Lee, M.C., & Wang, T.I. (2006). A learning objects recommendation model based on the preference and ontological approaches. *Proceedings of the 6th IEEE International Conference on Advanced Learning Technologies* (ICALT'06).

Vozalis, E., & Margaritis, K.G. (2003). Analysis of recommender systems' algorithms. *Proceedings of the 6th Hellenic-European Conference on Computer Mathematics and its Applications* (HERCMA), Athens, Greece.

Xue, G.-R., Lin, C., Yang, Q., Xi, W., Zeng, H.-J., Yu, Y., & Chen, Z. (2005). Scalable collaborative filtering using cluster-based smoothing. *Proceedings of the 2005 Conference on Research and Development in Information Retrieval* (SIGIR 2005), Salvador, Brazil.

Yu, K., Schwaighofer, A., Tresp, V., Xu, X., & Kriegel, H.-P. (2004). Probabilistic memory-based collaborative filtering. *IEEE Transactions on Knowledge and Data Engineering, 16*(1), 56–68.

Yu, K., Wen, Z., Xu, X., & Ester, M. (2001). Feature weighting and instance selection for collaborative filtering. *Proceedings of the 2nd International Workshop on Management of Information on the Web—Web Data and Text Mining* (MIW'01).

Yu, K., Xu, X., Ester, M., & Kriegel, H.-P. (2003). Feature weighting and instance selection for collaborative filtering: An information-theoretic approach. *Knowledge and Information Systems, 5*(2), 201–224.

Zeng, C., Xing, C.-X., Zhou, L.-Z., & Zheng, X.-H. (2004). Similarity measure and instance selection for collaborative filtering. *International Journal of Electronic Commerce, 8*(4), 115–129.

ADDITIONAL READING

Adomavicius, G., & Kwon, Y. (2007). New recommendation techniques for multi-criteria rating systems. *IEEE Intelligent Systems, Special Issue on Recommender Systems, 20*(3).

Adomavicius, G., Sankaranarayanan, R., Sen, S., & Tuzhilin, A. (2005). Incorporating contextual information in recommender systems using a multidimensional approach. *ACM Transactions on Information Systems, 23*(1), 103–145.

Balabanovic, M., & Shoham, Y. (1997). Content-based collaborative recommendation. *Communications of the ACM, 40*(3), 66–72.

Burke, R., Mobasher, B., Zabicki, R., & Bhaumik, R. (2005). Identifying attack models for secure recommendation. *Proceedings of Beyond Personalization: A Workshop on the Next Generation of Recommender Systems,* San Diego, CA.

Cantador, I., Fernandez, M., & Castells, P. (2006). A collaborative recommendation framework for ontology evaluation and reuse. *Proceedings of the International Workshop on Recommender Systems, 17th European Conference on Artificial Intelligence* (ECAI 2006), Riva del Garda, Italy.

Felfernig, A., Friedrich, G., Jannach, D., & Zanker, M. (2007). An integrated environment for the development of knowledge-based recommender applications. *International Journal of Electronic Commerce, Special Issue on Recommender Systems, 11*(2), 11–34.

Herlocker, J.L., Konstan, J.A., Terveen, L.G., & Riedl, J.T. (2004). Evaluating collaborative filtering recommender systems. *ACM Transactions on Information Systems, 22*(1), 5–53.

Huang, Z., Chen, H., & Zeng, D. (2004). Applying associative retrieval techniques to alleviate the sparsity problem in collaborative filtering. *ACM Transactions on Information Systems, 22*(1), 116–142.

Iijima, J., & Ho, S. (in press). Common structure and properties of filtering systems. *Electronic Commerce and Applications.*

Kramer, R., Modsching, M., ten Hagen, K., & Gretzel, U. (2006). Evaluating different preference elicitation methods for a mobile recommender system in a field trial. *Proceedings of the International Workshop on Recommender Systems, 17th European Conference on Artificial Intelligence* (ECAI 2006), Riva del Garda, Italy.

Kwon, O.B. (2003). 'I know what you need to buy': Context-aware multimedia-based recommendation system. *Expert Systems with Applications, 25,* 387–400.

Li, Y., Lu, L., & Xuefeng, L. (2005). A hybrid collaborative filtering method for multiple-interests and multiple-content recommendation in e-commerce. *Expert Systems with Applications, 28,* 67–77.

Lihua, W., Lu, L., Jing, L., & Zongyong, L. (2005). Modeling multiple interests by an improved GCS approach. *Expert Systems with Applications, 29*(4), 757–767.

Middleton, S.E., Shadbolt, N.R., & Roure, D.C. (2004). Ontological user profiling in recommender systems. *ACM Transactions on Information Systems, 22*(1), 54–88.

Mirza, B.J., Keller, B.J., & Ramakrishnan, N. (2003). Studying recommendation algorithms by graph analysis. *Journal of Intelligent Information Systems, 20*(2), 131–160.

Montaner, M., Lopez, B., & de la Rosa, J.L. (2003). A taxonomy of recommender agents on the Internet. *Artificial Intelligence Review, 19,* 285–330.

O'Mahony, M., Hurley, N., Kushmerick, N., & Silvestre, G. (2004). Collaborative recommendation: a robustness analysis. *ACM Transactions on Internet Technology, 4*(4), 344–377.

Pennock, D.M., & Horvitz, E. (1999). Analysis of the axiomatic foundations of collaborative filtering. *Proceedings of the AAAI Workshop on Artificial Intelligence for Electronic Commerce,* Orlando, FL.

Perugini, S., Goncalves, M.A., & Fox, E.A. (2004). Recommender systems research: A connection-centric survey. *Journal of Intelligent Information Systems, 23*(2), 107–143.

Resnick, P., & Varian, H.R. (1997). Recommender systems. *Communications of the ACM, 40*(3), 56–58.

Schafer, J.B., Konstan, J.A., & Riedl, J. (2001). E-commerce recommendation applications. *Data Mining and Knowledge Discovery, 5,* 115–153.

Vuorikari, R., Manouselis, N., & Duval, E. (in press). Using metadata for storing, sharing, and reusing evaluations in social recommendation: The case of learning resources. In D.H. Go & S. Foo (Eds.), *Social information retrieval systems: Emerging technologies and applications for searching the Web effectively.* Hershey, PA: Idea Group.

Wei, C.-P., Shaw, M.J., & Easley, R.F. (2002). A survey of recommendation systems in electronic commerce. In R.T. Rust & P.K. Kannan (Eds.), *E-service: New directions in theory and practice.* Armonk, NY: M.E. Sharpe.

Yuan, S.-T., & Cheng, C. (2004). Ontology-based personalized couple clustering for heterogeneous product recommendation in mobile marketing. *Expert Systems with Applications, 26,* 461–476.

Yuan, S.-T., & Tsao, Y.W. (2003). A recommendation mechanism for contextualized mobile advertising. *Expert Systems with Applications, 24,* 399–414.

Chapter III
Exploring Information Management Problems in the Domain of Critical Incidents

Rafael A. Gonzalez
Delft University of Technology, The Netherlands

ABSTRACT

In this chapter, information management problems and some of the computer-based solutions offered to deal with them are presented. The claim is that exploring the information problem as a three-fold issue, composed of heterogeneity, overload, and dynamics, will contribute to an improved understanding of information management problems. On the other hand, it presents a set of computer-based solutions that are available to tackle these problems: information discovery and retrieval, information filtering, information fusion, and information personalization. In addition, this chapter argues that a rich and interesting domain for exploring information management problems is critical incident management, due to its complexity, requirements, and the nature of the information it deals with.

INTRODUCTION

There is more than one information problem. Information is one of those concepts that encompasses many possible views and approaches. Consequently, probably the first information problem is to know what exactly information is (van Rijsbergen & Lalmas, 1996; Burgin, 2003). This issue has been treated with an information theory perspective, with information measurements in mind, or with philosophical, communica-tion, sociological, or mathematical lenses. There are general definitions of information (studied recently from the unified theory of information perspective) or domain-specific definitions of information. In classic information (communication) theory, information measurement was defined originally by Shannon as the entropy measure of information and is now typically defined as that property of data which represents effects of processing of them (data) (Hayes, 1993). It has also been defined as the value attached or instantiated to a characteristic or variable returned by a function or produced by a process (Losee, 1997). Within the information retrieval domain, information as a concept has been addressed by studying the information that one object contains about another object. This shifts the focus from measurement or procedural views, to concentrate on the information flow between objects, which is seen as the key component of an information retrieval system (van Rijsbergen & Lalmas, 1996).

Information may also be seen as a vessel, channel, or flow related to knowledge in all fields. Indeed, data, information and knowledge are often differentiated, but also presented as complementary as if each is a further abstraction of the previous one (e.g., information as meaningful data, or knowledge as applied or understood information). This is why many of the problems in all fields of knowledge can be seen as an information problem (or a language problem) in which semantics, interpretations, worldviews, and distortions all contribute to confusion, ambiguity, or onto-epistemological sources of conflicts of consistency, definition, and truth. The work of Foucault, Wittgenstein, Gadamer, Chomsky, and many other philosophers or epistemologists are testament to the importance of these issues, but this approach is outside the scope of this chapter (see "Additional Reading") as it is of philosophical nature. Rather, the interest of this chapter is to explore information problems within the computer-supported information management domain.

When information management (storing, finding, exchanging, and using information) is mediated with computers, the generic information problems are inherited, but are also complemented with problems of representation (e.g., how to use types or how to balance machine vs. man readability), description (e.g., how formal should it be or how metadata should be used), and exchange (e.g., how to handle synchronization or how to deal with centralization vs. distribution), among others. Technology also poses new challenges for

handling information because, while it supports traditional information management tasks, it has also made available a wide and increasingly cheaper array of mechanisms to support that management. Today, the sheer multitude, diversity, and dynamic nature of information sources, especially on the Internet, makes finding and accessing any specific piece of information extremely difficult (Huokka & Harada, 1998, p. 91). In this chapter, the information problem is presented as composed of three dimensions: heterogeneity, overload, and dynamics. All three dimensions are related to the nature of information, to its context, to its flow, and to the technology used to support its storage and exchange. Of course, as the beginning of this introduction suggests, there are many other possible information problems, or dimensions or categories. The claim of this chapter is that to explore these problems in computer-supported information management, it is useful to begin by looking at these three dimensions: heterogeneity, overload, and dynamics. Another claim is that to do so with a particular domain in mind can also contribute to make this exploration richer and more interesting.

One domain which can aid in the understanding of information problems and their associated solutions is that of critical incidents (crises, emergencies)—because of their complexity and the particular and urgent needs for information they pose—and the nature of the information itself. This chapter will use this domain to explore some of the practical implications of the information problem and its solutions.

The structure of this chapter will be as follows. The next section explains the proposed understanding of the "information problem" by discussing the notions of information heterogeneity, information overload, and information dynamics as subsections. We then take the opposite approach by presenting some of the solutions that are available to deal with the information problem (as described in the second section). In particular, four subsections will treat the following types of solutions: information discovery and retrieval, information filtering, information fusion, and information personalization. For each type of solution, there is at least one example of a working system or approach from the research literature (for commercial applications, the reader can refer to the "Additional Reading" section).

Following this brief account of solutions to the information problem, we relate the information problems of the second section to the domain of critical incidents, followed by some examples of how they can be dealt with (solutions specific to critical incident management). The conclusion summarizes and highlights the main contributions of this chapter. In the end, an extra section briefly discusses research trends related to the information problems, their solutions, and the domain of critical incidents. In addition to the references, a suggested list of further reading is also offered.

THE "INFORMATION PROBLEM"

There exists the notion that evolution has given rise to more "intelligent" creatures due to the increase in their information processing capacity (Roth & Dicke, 2005). Although there is no accepted measure of biological complexity (Szathmáry & Maynard Smith, 1995), it seems to be linked with changes in language, information storage, and transmission, giving rise to more behavioral variety (Szathmáry & Maynard Smith, 1995). Although there could hardly be any proof of biological evolution in humans during the history of mankind, there is an accepted view that culture and society have evolved, becoming more complex (in the sense just presented). Stepping aside from the debate on linking evolution with "progress," there is a clear increase in our capacity to store and communicate information. Just as the book is an extension of memory and imagination for Borges (1979), and electric circuitry, an extension of the central nervous system, for McLuhan and Fiore

(1967), there are now claims that the Internet—or more specifically, popular search engines are an extension of the brain. It follows that as a group we potentially have the means to behave more "intelligently," but this does not come for free; it poses several challenges that may be regarded as part of the information problem.

Although "the information problem" is not a standard term, it may be regarded as the set of problems or issues related to information management. In the so-called Dark Ages, for instance, the information problem could have been mainly equated to a lack of information. From one point of view, the main issue was access to information, which is why the printing press changed history, by enabling mass distribution of books. It should be noted, by the way, that this is a Western vision: the impact of the printing press is one of the milestones of the end of medieval Europe, despite the fact that similar technology already existed in China centuries earlier.

From a different viewpoint, the problem was information (knowledge) production, or the lack thereof; but the more we learn about this time period, the more we realize that the problem was access (distribution) rather than production (creation), although it does follow that without access, production is slower and more difficult. In our days, new technologies have shifted the focus of the information problem. Since access to information is no longer an impediment—however, it is still an issue from a socio-political point of view, for example, the *digital divide*—then the question is how to deal with such an enormous amount of stored, lightweight, and in many cases free information.

In what follows, the understanding of the information problem follows from this modern perspective, and the dimensions or components suggested to explore it are: heterogeneity, overload, and dynamics. Information comes from many different places, in different languages, formats, and media types, and is accessible by different means: this is the heterogeneity component.

Information storage has increased impressively and digital technology has made this possible without occupying relevant physical space and making site-dependence increasingly a thing of the past. As new information becomes available, it finds its way into the Internet; news and scientific publications are increasingly becoming distributed primarily through the Web, and the trend in other categories and media types can only grow. As we no longer require special effort to access resources in one of a few libraries or repositories, but are confronted with countless resources at a click of the mouse, our problem is quite different from the one faced by the people in the Dark Ages, and our capacity to browse and assimilate this information is in many instances overwhelmed: this is the overload component. Furthermore, even if we are able to understand (overcoming language and format barriers, i.e., heterogeneity) and assimilate information (overcoming overload), we must deal with another issue: information does not remain static for us to process in our time. Information changes continuously, it is updated, it becomes obsolete, it gets refuted, it is complemented, it is integrated, it is commented, and it is exchanged continuously: this is the dynamics component. The following subsections will look into the three dimensions of the information problem with more detail.

Information Heterogeneity

In a small closed system with a limited boundary, information handling is a fairly manageable task, since we know the extent, nature, and scope of the information we are dealing with. However, with large volumes of information sources encompassing a large geographic area and covering different organizational entities, information gathering and fusing can be daunting (Bui, Cho, Sankaran, & Sovereign, 2000). The heterogeneity that results from this can manifest itself in terms of different languages, electronic formats, source disciplines, nature of providers (and their associated trustwor-

thiness), media types, or onto-epistemological assumptions.

Heterogeneity, from a technical perspective, is due to differences in hardware, software, and communication systems. For example, heterogeneities due to differences in database management systems result from differences in data model, database schema, constraints, and query language (Lenz, 1998). From a semantic perspective, heterogeneity occurs if there is a lack or disagreement about the definition, meaning, interpretation, transformation, restriction, or intended use of data (Lenz, 1998). Although both types of heterogeneity can be tackled with technical integration schemas—which have developed abundantly ever since XML (eXtensible Markup Language) technology is widespread—the process of providing integration or fusion of heterogeneous data sources is different when disagreement resides on data formats or models than when it resides on definitions, interpretations, or uses.

If we want to find out about a topic or satisfy an information need in general, we may find numerous different resources: books, images, movies, and newspaper articles—from different countries, in different languages, and with different intentionality. At first this may seem a scary prospect; however, if we are studying the topic in detail or need in-depth information to draw conclusions or make decisions, we will probably hope to find all these different resources. Most of us are grateful that recent technological advances have resulted in large amounts of heterogeneous information, because it allows us to find hidden events of interest by inferring them from large quantities of heterogeneous and noisy evidence (Pavlin, de Oude, & Nunnink, 2005). This means that heterogeneity is not automatically a negative issue, but simply an issue that can be desirable or undesirable. The right level of heterogeneity or manageable diversity depends on the type of information, the quantity, the person or persons receiving it, the supporting systems, and the task or need at hand.

In a similar manner, redundancy has been treated in information theory or computer science as a delicate topic. It can readily be treated as undesirable, when seen as unnecessary repetition. But in education and research, for instance, accessing the same information at different times, through different media, or with different perspectives is most commonly seen as positive. Heterogeneity and diversity are thus multifaceted issues, but the main point is that they are unavoidable.

Information Overload

Information overload conveys the notion of receiving too much information and is related to cognitive, sensory, communication, or knowledge overload (Eppler & Mengis, 2004). At an individual or group level, the cognitive load can be too high to allow for effective or efficient information processing. Our senses, even when aided by technology, also have a threshold over which we automatically begin to filter or block out external input in order to be able to make sense of reality. Interpersonal or technology-aided channels and media of communication also have a limit to the capacity of information exchange they can handle. Our existing knowledge, intellectual abilities, and personality also constitute a boundary over which knowledge will be difficult

to construct or integrate. These issues have been studied from the psychological perspective, as is to be expected, but also have social, technological, managerial, and group decision-making views or dimensions.

As with heterogeneity, information overload is also subject to a delicate balance, meaning that the actual variable here is load (not overload) and that there is a point in which such load becomes too much to handle. To clarify, when compared to the accuracy of decision making, based on available information, this can be seen graphically as the so-called "inverted U-curve" presented in Figure 1a. As can be seen, decisions become more accurate as we have access to more data to inform that decision. There is a point at which our decision will be as accurate as possible, because we have reached an optimal balance of necessary and sufficient information, but over that point, decision accuracy will quickly drop. If we are exposed to unnecessary or more than sufficient information, we will still have to maneuver through it, so the possibility of inconsistencies, time delays, communication bottlenecks, or cognitive pressures will increase, resulting in poorer decision accuracy as a result of this overload.

A similar way of conceiving the information overload phenomenon compares the individual's information processing capacity with the informa-

Figure 1. (a) Inverted U-curve of information overload (Eppler & Mengis, 2004, p. 326); (b) Inverted U-curve of information overload shifted under pressure

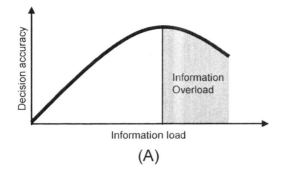
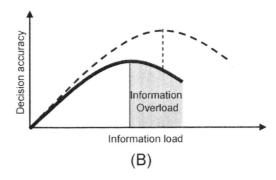

(A)   (B)

tion processing requirements (Eppler & Mengis, 2004). With these variables considered, information overload can be seen as a result of more information processing requirements and/or less information processing capacity. These can both be defined in individual or group terms and can both be altered with technological support.

Others conceive overload as a subjective experience in which feelings (stress, confusion, pressure, anxiety, motivation) signal the occurrence of overload. This means that one person may be exposed to overload while another may be able to deal with the situation even if they both share the same context. It also means that under normal conditions, an individual or a group may be able to handle a certain amount and type of information, but given additional pressures, such as those related to critical incidents, their information processing capacity will decrease from its normal level and overload will come faster. This would mean that the point at which overload is reached will shift to the left, as shown in Figure 1b, immediately implying that our tolerance for less-than-optimal decision making will have to increase, among other things.

As with other issues discussed so far, information technology (IT) is a double-edged sword. Although IT support can increase the information processing capacity, quite often it increases the information processing requirements. For example, the enormous amount of information in the World Wide Web induces the problem of information overload since there is too much for people to digest (Tu & Hsiang, 2000). And we have all experienced more or less overload due to e-mail use. Later on, the other point of the sword will be considered by mentioning some technology-based solutions to the overload problem, but the irony lies in that most information processing technology is meant to deal with technology-induced overload, leaving us no option but to fight fire with fire.

If such a dilemma is not enough, there is another: traditionally lateral relationships (those between people that are not formally related) have been seen as useful tools for dealing with information overload. The assumption is that by collaborating with others, we share the load, and the result is the emergence of higher information processing capacity (Galbraith, 1974). However, recently it has been found that this focus on collaborative and interdisciplinary work is a cause rather than a countermeasure of information overload, manifested in increased meeting times, increased conflict, and increased need for information (Eppler & Mengis, 2004; Galbraith, Downey, & Kates, 2002). For example, participating in a community of practice may offer an interesting knowledge sharing opportunity, but it also requires time and may delay decision making.

Information Dynamics

Some people may believe that historians or archeologists have privileged jobs, in the sense that they are dealing with past events that will not change and they can only learn more about them in a cumulative manner. A historian will tell us, however, that this is far from the truth, that theory, research methods, consistency, and quality all change in the field constantly, and they have to keep themselves updated to remain in the game like the rest of us. If this is the outlook for historians, we can only assume that no one is exempt from dealing with dynamic information.

Although there are many information units which remain static, such as published material or films, these can seldom be understood in isolation, and even then, new critical editions, remakes, comments, or references pop-up without end to alter the original material through its context. With regards to electronic material, it gets even worse (but more interesting and challenging as well), because it is not only the context, but the actual document that can change with time. This prompts a reevaluation of the so-called borderline issues and brings into question Latour's notion of documents as immutable mobiles, because it is precisely mutability, which makes electronic documents innovative (Brown & Duguid, 1994).

In addition to the documents themselves being dynamic, information flow is also quite dynamic. Information flows take place within social networks whose nature (components and relationships) is sometimes difficult to establish (Huberman & Adamic, 2004). Since the way information spreads determines the speed by which individuals can act and plan their future activities (Huberman & Adamic, 2004), the flow is an interesting study object in itself. For example, the way information spreads is not unlike how a disease spreads, which is why epidemic models on social network graphs are relevant to study information flows (Huberman & Adamic, 2004). Again the bipolar nature of information problems makes its appearance: this dynamic behavior may be desirable, since it allows us access to remote information, without complete knowledge of the path towards it. However, it can also be challenging, because it may be difficult to trace or find information within a complex network, and there is no guarantee that we will find it even though it is out there.

Agrawala, Larsen, and Szajda (2000) propose information dynamics as an information-centric (as opposed to process-centric) approach to systems design in which the time-dependence of information is stressed. The principles of this framework are: the distinction between information and its representation, the value of information in context, and the changing value of information through time. The first principle highlights the significance of information in a computer-based setting, since computers are only able to process limited representations of information, prompting the need to consider implicit information. The principle of value in context reminds us that the value of information is dependent on its usage and is affected by its movement, representation, and storage, among others. The principle of changing of value in time is perhaps the most relevant in terms of dynamics, because it states that the value

of information changes as times goes by (typically, but not always decreasing); this is self-evident during critical incidents where opportune information is of very high value, but it quickly drops as time passes. Time here can have two connotations: it is either relative to a universal time or clock, or its is understood causally as events unfold, tying each other sequentially.

After describing the proposed conception of "the information problem" as composed of information heterogeneity, information overload, and information dynamics, the next section turns to some of the solutions to these problems from an information management perspective.

SOLUTIONS TO THE INFORMATION PROBLEM

An attempt at making a one-to-one relationship between information problems and solutions is possible. It could be argued that information fusion counters heterogeneity, that information personalization and filtering counter overload, and that information discovery and retrieval deal with dynamics. However, in the same way as most information management (to group these solutions somewhat vaguely) is a composite of many approaches and technologies, the components of the information problem are also related to each other. On the other hand, problems as well as solutions are also related to each other. For example, Malone, Grant, Turbak, Brobost, and Cohen (1987) present information filtering in the context of the "information sharing" problem, which has to do with the distribution of information that reaches people to whom it is valuable without interfering with those to whom it is not. This adds another dimension to the information problem, which is related to overload (the challenge here being to reduce overload by routing messages appropriately) and to heterogeneity (messages come from different sources and this requires filtering). For this reason, and for the sake of presentation clarity, this section presents the solutions (or rather, approaches to solve the information problems) separately, and although sometimes it will be clear which specific problem they deal with, in general there is a network of relationships among and in between information problems and solutions.

Information Discovery and Retrieval

The boundary dividing information discovery, filtering, and retrieval is not clear-cut. In a simplified form, one could see discovery as the first objective (to find the information needed), retrieval as the second objective (to get the information found, or its description for further consideration), and filtering as a third and perhaps optional objective (to limit the search results to a more manageable set). However, most information filtering systems are part of a wider information retrieval system, and both typically use an information discovery service at some point; also, filtering may be applied to the query, the reply, or the end user presentation set. To further understand the relationship, information retrieval in the Web context can be seen in itself as a filter, providing more interesting results and less uninteresting results, as well as suggesting interesting URLs (Tu & Hsiang, 2000). This component for suggestions also links retrieval to recommendation, which can be a form of personalization.

Despite this overlap between information management strategies or components, there are some differences between information retrieval and discovery. The information retrieval field has traditionally focused on searching relevant documents in fixed (usually textual) document collections, and users are presumed to have a very clear understanding of their information need, evidenced in the well-known measures of retrieval effectiveness: precision and recall (Proper & Bruza, 1999). This is different from discovery, which is typically associated to open

networked environments where there is no fixed set of documents and no guarantee that they will be textual (Proper & Bruza, 1999). Perhaps the distinction between information retrieval and information discovery (or resource discovery) is a result of the Internet, which prompted new approaches, technologies, and research paths different from those in "pre-Internet" information science. However, this growth of open distributed systems has also altered information retrieval itself, and current retrieval systems are very different from those used in the 1950s and 1960s for static batch processing systems (Spink & Saracevic, 1997).

Information retrieval has been regarded as simply document retrieval because, in reality, it was thought that retrieving a document merely pointed to a potential source of information, without providing explicit information (changing the knowledge of the user) (van Rijsbergen & Lalmas, 1996). More recently, though, the retrieval result is thought of as information about information. This process is carried out through indexing, which is a common technique for both retrieval and discovery.

Indexing is the process of developing a document representation by assigning content descriptors or terms to the documents (Gudivada et al., 1997, p. 59). Since information retrieval is about matching a query to a document (or resource), this matching is done through the index. The matching principles (or information retrieval models) can be classified as follows (Belkin & Croft, 1992):

- **Exact match:** A one-to-one, direct, and exact match between the query and the index terms results in retrieving the documents associated with those terms and those terms alone.
- **Best-match:** Since exact matches exclude documents that do not precisely match the query, thus hampering effectiveness (since queries are seldom perfect to begin with),

best-matches provide close matches and rank them in order not to give exact and close matches the same relevance. A vector is used to represent both the query and the document, and then the two are compared to establish similarity which is then quantified to provide the ranked results.

- **Probabilistic:** These models stem from the principle that the function of an information retrieval system is to rank the documents in the order of their probability of relevance to the query, according to evidence such as the statistical distribution of terms in relevant and non-relevant documents.

An extension of these basic principles is justified by the argument that if an index term is good enough to discriminate relevant from non-relevant documents, then a closely associated index term is likely also to provide this utility (van Rijsbergen & Lalmas, 1996). The information retrieval system can then be improved by adding more algorithms that integrate closely related index terms to the matching process. It follows that index building has become more sophisticated through XML, Web crawlers, clustering, or co-word analysis, among others; but the basic principle remains the same: it is more efficient to search an index of the content than the content itself.

Example 1

Tu and Hsiang (2000) have proposed an architecture for intelligent/interactive information retrieval (IIR) agents that integrate several Web IR issues. The agents would have features such as: intelligent/interactive search, navigational guide, information auto-notification, personal information management, dynamic personalized Web pages, and reading-aid tools (dictionary, encyclopedia, translation). In the proposed architecture, agents collaborate to perform intelligent search, auto-notification, navigation guide, and personal information management.

Example 2

Another architecture presented by Shakshuki, Ghenniwa, and Kamel (2003) supports a multi-agent system that is based on autonomous and heterogeneous architecture. This system assists users in the process of locating and retrieving information from distributed information systems. It acts as a mediator between the user and the information environment, and is layered into a multi-tier architecture. At the middle tier, the agents in this system—broker agents—act as 'middlemen' between the agents of the other tiers and communicate using Knowledge Query Manipulation Language (KQML). User agents allow users to interact with the system environment (receiving queries and delivering results) and have a dynamic concept-quality vector to build models of information resources adapted to users' preferences. Resource agents represent information sources or providers (receiving queries and identifying matching resources).

Information Filtering

The idea of information filtering is quite straightforward. A filter, which can be anywhere from automatic and intelligent to personal and intuitive, is applied to a set in order to obtain a smaller set that is supposed to be more relevant or pertinent according to an information need. Apart from the already mentioned difference between information retrieval and discovery, there is also a larger difference between information retrieval (IR) and information filtering (IF):

- IF systems deal with (multimedia) textual information (Belkin & Croft, 1992).
- Traditional IR systems are meant for relatively static databases, while IF is meant for very large dynamic databases, such as the WWW, where timeliness and privacy are more of a concern (Belkin & Croft, 1992).

- IF systems typically consider streams of data from remote sources (Belkin & Croft, 1992).
- IF systems are based on profiles (individual or group information preferences) for long-term users, as opposed to IR, which assumes ad hoc, one-time users (Belkin & Croft, 1992; Hanani, Shapira, & Shoval, 2001).
- IF systems are often meant to filter out data (remove it), rather than find it, as in IR systems (Belkin & Croft, 1992; Hanani et al., 2001), although some define IF in terms of selection too (Malone et al., 1987; Atoji, Koiso, & Nishida, 2000).
- Information needs are represented as queries in IR and as profiles in IF (Belkin & Croft, 1992; Hanani et al., 2001).

The basic strategies of information filtering are (Malone et al., 1987; Hanani et al., 2001):

- Cognitive filtering selects information according to the interests of the user, matching messages and recipients through areas of interest (content-based) or through more than just areas of interest (properties-based).
- Social (or sociological) filtering is based on selection according to the organization or community to which the user belongs. When the filtering criteria includes the sender as well as the topics of the message for matching it with the recipient, then it comes very close to properties-based cognitive filtering. More recently, it can also be regarded as collaborative filtering, which will be discussed shortly.
- Economic filtering takes a monetary approach by selecting, after assessing the profit vs. the cost of getting the information or after assessing the value that the information might have for the user, for example by estimating its cost in relation to its length.

Since content-based filtering is difficult for computers (especially when no formal ontology is available), collaborative filtering is one way to allow people to collaborate in filtering by sharing their reactions to documents (Atoji et al., 2000). The system simply allows the users to share this information, but filtering is done by the user community (through word of mouth, ratings, and recommendations), not by the system. In this sense, the filtering system becomes a recommendation system which filters not based on the content of the documents or resources, but under the assumption that if a user's interests are similar to those of another user (typically because they rate or buy items similarly), then the items preferred by one can be recommended to the other (Shahabi & Chen, 2003). Some of the user tasks (or behaviors) that may be performed within a collaborative filtering recommender system, and that should be considered for design and evaluation, are (Herlocker, Konstan, Terveen, & Riedl, 2004):

- **Annotation in context:** Posting comments linked to an item to determine its worthiness.
- **Find good items:** The system provides a ranked list of recommended items, highlighting those with the highest likelihood of being found worthy by users.
- **Find all good items:** In some cases, users are willing to deal with overload in order not to miss any potentially interesting items.
- **Recommend sequence:** Instead of rating items individually, items (e.g., songs, documents) are evaluated according to a sequence which is then recommended to be followed by others.
- **Just browsing:** In some cases, the user intention is not specific.
- **Find credible recommender:** Users do not automatically trust every recommender, so they use different strategies to find a recommender with similar interests or taste.

- **Improve profile:** By providing ratings, the users themselves improve their own profile and, as a consequence, the quality of the recommendations they receive.
- **Express self:** Some users provide rating and comments not to improve their profiles, but to be able to express themselves (this may of course have different issues regarding anonymity and privacy).
- **Help others:** Some users contribute simply to contribute to the user community.
- **Influence others:** Another motivation for participating is encouraging other users to view (or not) a particular item.

With regards to the algorithmic and representational approaches underlying the information filtering systems, these can follow a statistical or knowledge-based concept (Hanani et al., 2001). Statistical concept IF systems use a weighed vector of index terms to represent user profiles, then use a statistical algorithm to compute similarity between a vector representing a data item and the user profile vector, and finally use a learning component for incorporating user feedback. Knowledge-based IF systems use artificial intelligence techniques by representing user needs as production rules (filtering patterns), by using artificial neural networks trained by the user, and by using evolutionary genetic-based algorithms in which a gene represents a term, an individual is a document, and the community represents the profile.

Example

The Amalthea system (Moukas, 1997) uses information filtering and information discovery agents. The first is responsible for personalization of the system and keeping track of the users' interests. The latter is responsible for finding and fetching the information that the user needs. The system uses an economic filtering approach by giving the filtering agents a reward (credit) when they

suggest a valuable item (positive feedback). This is further used to enable the multi-agent system to evolve (improve) by giving the agents with more credit a higher chance of reproducing (creating more agents). The newly created agents will share a "genotype" with their parents, which is essentially an augmented keyword vector where relevance weights (for each keyword) become increasingly accurate through the evolution process. Of course, the reverse is also part of the system: agents that are not given credit end up being removed.

Information Fusion

Both overload and heterogeneity may prompt the need for fusing information sources. By fusing similar documents into a single summary, we are saving time in searching and processing this information (in the way many literature reviews are conducted by humans). This can be done automatically from Internet sources, for example for a particular news event (Barzilay, McKeown, & Elhadad, 1999; Hunter & Liu, 2006). The main advantage or utility of using information fusion is decision-support, because the outcome is often a decision based on different sources of information. Information fusion can then be understood as a process that accepts some data (form multiple sources) and produces some outputs (decisions) (Kokar, Tomasik, & Weyman, 2004).

Information fusion can be defined as merging several sources of information to answer questions of interest and make proper decisions with one of several aims: to improve current knowledge of the state of the world, to update information on a case of interest, to establish the global point of view of a group, or to derive generic knowledge from data (Dubois & Prade, 2004, p. 144). Another way to classify the aims of fusion is as: reduction of dimensionality, improvement of precision and certainty, and increased reliability (Valet, Mauris, & Bolon, 2001). And in an even more general sense, the aim of fusion is to obtain information of greater quality, but the exact meaning of quality remains an ambiguous notion (Valet et al., 2001), as in the case of critical incident management, where information needs and uses differ in between response agencies.

One way in which information fusion systems can be viewed is on three levels (Valet et al., 2001). The *signal level* aggregates raw data directly from the sources, without transforming it. The *feature level* extracts features (descriptors) from the data before fusing it. The *decision level* fuses the decisions proposed by each input datum. Another way to interpret these levels is by considering decision-level fusion as a subclass of data-level fusion (Kokar et al., 2004)

Some of the challenges that information fusion systems have are: discovering the sources at runtime, having a complex world model to deal with heterogeneous sources, creating such models at runtime, and avoiding central models to prevent bottlenecks in communication (Pavlin et al., 2005). The convergence of distributed systems, agent technology, and intelligent sensors may come together for dealing with such challenges.

A couple of terms that are closely related to information fusion are information merging and integration, although one should be careful of the knowledge domain in which they are used. Information integration, for instance, refers to the physical (through warehousing) or logical bringing together of complementary data that come from heterogeneous sources: from very structured (e.g., databases) to semi-structured (e.g., XML) to unstructured (e.g., Web resources) (Jhingran, Mattos, & Pirahesh, 2002).

Example 1

One increasingly popular approach to integrating Web data is using the RDF Site Summary (RSS). RDF (Resource Description Framework) is an XML-based suite of specifications which, along with OWL (Web Ontology Language), constitute the basic Semantic Web Standards developed by the W3C (World Wide Web Consortium) (*www.*

w3.org/RDF). The RSS conforms with RDF and is a syndication format that describes a "channel" consisting of URL-retrievable items, consisting of title, link, and description (*web.resource. org/rss/1.0/spec*). RSS has been used for news headlines, but now is being adopted to syndicate Weblogs or podcasts, among others. An RSS feed can read another XML-based metadata set, such as DublinCore (*dublincore.org*), to maintain a user or external system updated with distributed Web data. It is thus a solution to both heterogeneity and dynamics (by constantly updating), but it can actually be a source of overload.

Example 2

Since fusion typically integrates information or data from multiple sources or sensors, agents are potentially well suited for supporting fusion systems by representing sensors or information sources as proxies; by adding a fusion layer to existing systems; or by exchanging information, exploiting the increasingly efficient and scalable means of message exchange in multi-agent systems. One such system is proposed by Pavlin et al. (2005): Distributed Perception Networks (DPNs) for distributed situation assessment. DPNs are multi-agent systems that implement a logical layer on top of an existing sensory, communication, and processing/storage infrastructure, in which agents wrap heterogeneous, spatially dispersed information sources and integrate them into complex inference systems. Sensor agents interpret raw data; fusion agents use local world models (encoded through Bayesian networks) for high-level information fusion; DPN agents organize and integrate the Bayesian networks (BN) at runtime into complex causal models to provide mapping between symptoms and hypotheses. Local inference is combined with inter-agent message passing for distributed belief propagation. An example application is to quickly provide a decision maker with relevant information about the presence of a toxic gas, from multiple sources (sensors, databases, Web pages).

Information Personalization

Information personalization can be an extension or a result of using information retrieval, filtering, and/or fusion systems. In truth then it is not a separate category of what here are regarded as solutions to the "information problem." Nonetheless, it has been regarded as a separate avenue for research and commercial applications, which is why it is presented explicitly. In simple terms, information personalization is the dynamic adaptation of generic information content to a personalized information content, to suit an individual's characteristics, such as demographics, knowledge, skills, capabilities, interests, preferences, needs, goals, plans, and behavior (Abidi & Chong, 2004, pp. 261–262). Personalization can occur at the content, structure, or presentation levels (Abidi & Chong, 2004), typically based on constraints linked to a profile. Information personalization is a popular remedy to customize the Web environment and alleviate the overload produced by this large collection of semi- or unstructured information sources (Shahabi & Chen, 2003). Personalized information systems provide customized responses to individual requests, adapting results to preferences, goals, and capacities (Petit-Rozé & Grislin-Le Strugeon, 2006). This means these systems are able to access and select data, know about the users (and learn about them), and establish pertinence of data according to user needs.

Personalization systems for the Web can customize responses based on page importance, query refinement, or meta-searching (Shahabi & Chen, 2003). Page importance is based on ranking algorithms and gives access primarily to the highly rated sources. Query refinement uses existing search engine algorithms, but modifies the queries of the user according to their profile, forwards them to the engine, and refines the reply before presenting it back to the user. Meta-searching is another approach, which gathers replies to a query from various search systems; as overload can potentially be intensified by doing this, personalization comes in to refine or merge the result. As can be seen, personalization is strongly related to discovery, retrieval, filtering, and fusion.

One of the most common applications of personalization is recommendation tools. The idea is that the system not only reacts to a user request, but can also proactively suggest relevant information according to the user profile. At the moment such applications are used mainly for e-commerce, but have received limited attention for Web search systems (Shahabi & Chen, 2003). The reason for this is that in using e-commerce, users typically enter (or at least finally place an order) by using a profile, which includes registering their e-mail that can be used later to send suggestions. Of course, for public use (such as free Web search engines), privacy issues are also a source of concern.

Example 1

In an agent-based personalization system presented by Petit-Rozé and Grislin-Le Strugeon (2006), the main functions of an information agent are: information acquisition and management (retrieval); information synthesis and presentation (filtering); and intelligent user assistance (interface or assistant agents), which shows what was already pointed out in the beginning of this section, that the problems and solutions related to information are typically related to each other or part of a larger whole. The focus is however on personalization. In this approach, agent characteristics include: proactivity (triggering actions not explicitly requested), uncertainty management (inferring from incomplete knowledge and past experience), autonomy (dealing with distributed data, knowledge, and resources), and social abilities (performing tasks interacting with distributed entities in multi-agent systems). Their MAPIS

(Multi-Agent Personalized Information System) provides personalized access to an information set, by interacting with both users and information sources. The MAPIS system bases its personalization process on the management and processing of data about the information domain, the history of requests and responses, and the users. The users are modeled according to the characteristics required to complete the personalization. Assistant agents carry out distinct activities according to the type of request received (subscription or request). They transfer activities towards both the Profile and the Solver agents. The Solver agents work on the simultaneous tasks of data profiling and data retrieval. The approach assigns stereotypes to instantiate user profiles the first time, and later on adjusts importance and confidence weights. Personalization occurs in several steps: data and profiles are selected separately. Selected data is further filtered according to the profile and then adapted to interface format.

Example 2

An earlier proposal which sits in between retrieval and personalization is that of just-in-time information retrieval agents (JITIR agents) that proactively present information based on a person's context, continuously watching a person's environment and presenting information that may be useful without requiring any action on the part of the user (Rhodes & Maes, 2000). It is important to point out that according to this proposal, the agent not only helps in substituting traditional search tools, but actually changes the way in which people use information.

The issues related to information management (or information problems), namely heterogeneity, overload, and dynamics, were presented in the second section of this chapter. The main approaches for dealing with these issues, namely retrieval, filtering, fusion, and personalization, have just been presented. The next step in this chapter is to briefly explore these issues and approaches in a real-world domain, which is very appropriate for illustrating the nuances and possibilities of the previous two sections: critical incident management.

INFORMATION ISSUES IN CRITICAL INCIDENT MANAGEMENT

This section will use the term "critical incidents," rather than crises, emergencies, disasters, or extreme events, but in this context they can be regarded as interchangeable concepts. A critical incident can be defined as: "any manmade or natural event or situation that threatens people, property, business, or the community and occurs outside the normal scope of routine business operations" (Michigan State University School of Criminal Justice, 2000, p. 37). A key characteristic of critical incidents is their complexity. Failure or instability in factors such as climate change, health crises, and the increasing hyper-complexity of ICTs (information and communication technologies) might trigger cascading impacts through unexpected pathways in supply networks and trading systems (Barnes & Oloruntoba, 2005). One failure in an operational system may trigger failure in interdependent systems of electrical power, communications, transportation, water, gas, and sewage; this may stagger the operational capacity of a whole region and create new dangers for the population (Comfort, Ko, & Zagorecki, 2004). If it is a major disaster, potentially the whole socio-technical system of a region or community may collapse (Comfort et al., 2004). On top of this, when the situation becomes a multi-incident event, then its response also becomes far more complicated (Chen, Sharman, Rao, & Upadhyaya, 2005). Accurate, complete, and timely information is of evident value for the assessment, planning, response, and learning efforts, but sources are unknown, quantities grow quickly and unexpectedly, sharing is not pre-established, and relationships not clear, making management of crisis information a very difficult task, but also a very rich domain for studying information problems and solutions.

Information Problems in Critical Incidents

All phases of emergency management are information and communication intensive, imposing heavy demands on the information technologies that support them (Jenvald, Morin, & Kincaid, 2001). In this section, some of the information-related challenges associated with critical incidents are presented, using the same three components suggested in the first part of this chapter: heterogeneity, overload, and dynamics.

Information Heterogeneity

Information production, sharing, and interpretation is difficult during a critical incident because of the many different agencies that usually take part in the response. In "normal" incidents, the response can be handled by regular public emergency services; a large-scale event, however, is usually beyond their capacity (Liu, 2004). As an example, consider some of the agencies that are typically involved in a disaster relief operation: UNICEF (the United Nations Children's Fund to take care of child victims), UNDP (the United Nations Development Program for infrastructure and economic development after initial response), NGOs (non-government organizations of different natures, such as Medecins Sans Frontiers), the military forces of different contributing countries (and United Nations Peacekeeping forces along the local armed forces), regional organizations, national government, government agencies, Red Cross (Red Crescent), WHO (World Health Organization), relief agencies, and many others. The presence of many different agencies results in goal conflicts, cultural differences, and competition over resources (Bui et al., 2000). For example, one agency may be interested in immediate relief efforts, while another may be interested in long-term reconstruction, making them not only conflict in the site, but also making their information needs quite distinct. Cultural differences may result in mistrust, misrepresentation of facts, and differences in perception and values, which are all issues related to information management. From a purely technological perspective, this also means their communication devices will be different, their language will sometimes differ, their access and training in information systems use will not be leveled, and standards will not be easy (if at all possible) to create in advance.

Information Overload

Even if systems have been implemented for dealing with the incident, a constraint we cannot do away with is the cognitive limitation of humans interacting with the system and with each other. To deal with complexity the system needs to be complex enough, but also simple enough for it to be fault-tolerant and not slow or too costly or too interfering for systems in regular operation. Critical incidents are unpredictable, which is not to say always unanticipated. This means that information regarding a critical incident is always non-existing before the actual incident occurs. There may be historical data of similar incidents, simulation data, lessons learned, contingency plans to follow, predictions, and updated sensor information for early warning, but none of these will be enough for making complete sense of the incident once it occurs. This initial lack of information quickly turns into overload, because, for example, when a large-scale disaster happens, a great deal of information occurs in a short time (Atoji et al., 2000). The fact that the response is a task full of uncertainty means that more information will have to be processed for decision making. At the same time, the pressure of acting quickly and preventing further loss places additional cognitive constraints on decision makers.

Information Dynamics

One of the difficulties with the complexity of crises (before an incident actually occurs) is that warning signs may be invisible (Barnes & Oloruntoba, 2005) or visible only when too late for a proper response. This forces response networks to improvise in the face of a non-existing or non-permanent structure for dealing with the critical incident (Steinberg & Cruz, 2004). In the actual response it is often the case that response services are reconfigured, updated, or revoked (Chen et al., 2005). Besides complexity of the incident itself, emergency related information has a different nature to other types of information; besides increasing rapidly after the incident, it is unique for each incident (establishing categories in advance is a difficult task), and the situation changes so quickly that respondents (and managers) need to know how the information is linked in terms of time and causal relationships (Atoji et al., 2000). Other special characteristics are: national security and safety imply assessing releasability and transparency of the information, cultural and technological incompatibilities may hinder the response, and standards are difficult to achieve (Bui et al., 2000).

Examples of Solutions to Information Problems in Critical Incident Management

Disasters are one of those human and organizational circumstances when free dissemination of timely and pertinent information is essential to prevent avoidable loss of life and property (Bui et al., 2000; Goh & Fung, 2005). Thus, many proposals and systems have been developed through the years to improve information management in critical incidents. It is possible to classify these solutions in terms of the approaches presented earlier (discovery and retrieval, filtering, fusion, and personalization). However, since these are often related to each other or built on top of each other, such classification is not as easy (or helpful) when it comes to actual systems or frameworks. The examples that follow can be placed in more than one of those approaches, but they all share the same application domain, which is the focus of this section.

Example 1

The first is CCNet, based on an Automated Knowledge Extraction Agent (AKEA), which was started during the 2003 SARS crisis, and uses a conversational software robot—AINI (Artificial Intelligence Neural-network Identity)—to inform users of crisis-related information, providing a sense of familiarity and comfort (Goh & Fung, 2005). AINI's knowledge base consists of a common base, an expression emotion database, a customer knowledge base, and an Alert-News knowledge base. AIML (an XML language, based on ALICE) is used to represent AINI's common knowledge base. The Expression Emotion Database is used to identify and classify emotions within the context of the conversation between the user and the software robot. The AlertNews knowledge base provides news and information to users via mobile devices. A syntactic preprocessor uses online news documents (in HTML) as input, cleans them, identifies dependencies in the words, and feeds it into the CCNet news repository, which is then intended for use by the robot to read search results to the users. This system then combines some of the topics treated earlier: it is an agent-based information retrieval, fusion, and filtering system for crisis communication.

Example 2

The second system, COSMOA, is a multi-agent system based on ontology that supports the decision-making process during the medical response to a large-scale incident (Bloodsworth & Greenwood, 2005). It simulates the monitoring of a range of news feeds in addition to emergency service reports of incidents in order to determine that it has taken place and the nature of this incident. Using the available information, as it comes into the system, it then predicts the potential number of casualties and likely injuries using heuristics and other methods. The system also regularly collects data from each local hospital within the area of the emergency plan to determine its capacity and the current facilities that they can offer within the context of the incident. Then, a Web-based schedule is produced setting out which hospital will handle each type of casualty. This system is feasible because it focuses only on medical response, but simplifies information sources to news feeds and may conflict with the systems of other agencies, especially when there is a combined response in which lines of authority are unclear.

Example 3

A framework for effective dissemination of incident reports and lessons learned from real emergency-related operations and exercises was proposed by Jenvald et al. (2001). This framework defines mechanisms for Web-based information exchange, providing a foundation for analyzing information needs and flows based on user data. It includes a generic information processor (GIP) used as a basic entity for modeling both sources and users through document types, a unique name (to identify and locate the information it publishes), and associated virtual archives. The virtual archives describe the input information the GIP requires to generate its output documents (thus enabling the representation of information needs and flows). As an example, an implementation of the framework was built to represent the information flow at a task force training exercise, in which an instrumentation system collects and visualizes exercise data. Units and observers

represent data sources, and the *exercise control* collects and compiles this data using the system to produce a mission history that can be fed back to the units and observers by means of GIPs to help them learn from the exercise.

Example 4

Finally, a more ambitious project is a plan for a global information network (GIN), which considers that any system devised to manage humanitarian assistance/disaster relief should ensure that information flows freely and that decision makers act on such information without fail (Bui et al., 2000). GIN can assist disaster planners and managers by offering information, cognition, collaboration/coordination, and decision focus, and by providing these not only during the crisis response phase, but during pre- and post-crisis phases as well. The GIN implementation would include a physical command center with telecommunication lines connecting to expert advice groups from around the world. The GIN would link to knowledge and data warehouses covering the range of information required in disaster situations. Field sensors would be connected to the network bringing the latest information. The knowledge bases would have information on the social/cultural/organizational characteristics of the agencies involved, and the system would provide linkage fostering productive communication, negotiation, and faster conflict resolution. Software agents would be used to detect patterns in data and knowledge warehouses for mining. Application software, groupware, decision support, modeling, and statistical systems would be made available. Multimedia capabilities would also be incorporated. If realized, a complete and tested system of this type would offer a holistic solution to the information problem in critical incident management. Of course, even if all the technology is available to realize this system, it would still have to deal with the cultural, technological, and social incompatibilities of potential user agencies, making the challenge more than just a technology problem.

CONCLUSION

This chapter has presented an understanding of the information problem as composed of three dimensions. Information heterogeneity relates to the different and potentially conflicting sources and types of information. Information overload is associated to the limit at which a person or group can no longer adequately process incoming information. Information dynamics denotes the changing nature of information and the highly dynamic flow of it within a complex network. These are issues that become more evident and widespread in the context of the Internet and more critical in the face of crises or emergencies. However, for some time there have been different approaches to deal with these issues, including information discovery/retrieval, information fusion, information filtering, and information personalization.

Information problems and their associated solutions are not easy to decompose because they are strongly related to each other. Furthermore, the types of solutions presented also feedback on the information management scenario, increasing or creating new problems themselves. This calls for a holistic and multidisciplinary study of the field in which the role of standards, ontologies, and social network analysis (presented in the Future Research Directions) may contribute to better design solutions and more effectively deal with information problems.

This chapter argues that a good arena to grasp these problems from both a challenging and rich perspective is critical incident management, because of its complexity and the fact that it is a data-intensive, open, distributed domain. Good information management in this field will not only contribute to better response and improved decision making, but will allow for more structured learning to prevent or mitigate future emergencies. It would be interesting to see how a larger set of existing emergency or crisis-related solutions fit into the information problem dimensions and types of solutions offered in this chapter. This could contribute to a more coherent body of knowledge of information management in the critical incident management domain.

FUTURE RESEARCH DIRECTIONS

The Internet still holds the power of serving two of the most important functions in the modern world: as a giant virtual storehouse of data, information, and knowledge; and as the true information superhighway (Goh & Fung, 2005). However, some promises have fallen short. According to the initial idea of the Semantic Web, for instance, information could be derived from data through a semantic theory for interpreting symbols, in which the logical connection of terms establishes interoperability between systems (Shadbolt, Berners-Lee, & Hall, 2006). This was supposed to become a reality, among other things, by using agents. A classic application of agents to deal with information overload (Maes, 1994) was aimed at replacing the metaphor of direct manipulation, which requires information systems users to initiate all tasks explicitly and to monitor all events. Autonomous agents would help introduce the alternative: indirect management, in which an agent would act in behalf of the user. Although the promise has not exactly been fulfilled, the idea is still valid and underlies most agent-based approaches in human-agent systems.

Despite the setbacks, some believe (Shadbolt et al., 2006) that through ontology and standards, the Semantic Web is still possible in its full potential, and the path is already delineated by efforts (mostly from the World Wide Web Consortium) such as: RDF (Resource Description Framework), URI (Uniform Resource Identifiers), and OWL (Web Ontology Language). However, these growing standards still need uptake from committed practice communities. This poses the question of the cost of developing and maintaining ontologies, which should not be a problem considering that the productivity gain is higher and that as the user base increases, cost decreases (spreads out). The convergence of agent technology and Semantic Web principles is still a fertile research area for the information management field. It remains to be seen whether this holds true for critical incidents.

There is a second trend worth highlighting. Since relationships are important for the acquisition of information, and knowledge creation is a social process, it is important to understand the social component of information seeking and sharing. Borgatti and Cross (2003), through social network analysis, have found that three enduring relational characteristics are predictive of the behavior of information seeking: knowing what another person knows, valuing what another person knows in relation to one's work, and being able to gain timely access to that knowledge. Relational conditions of knowing and access can be developed both virtually (through computer mediation) and physically (e.g., with open office environments) (Borgatti & Cross, 2003; Galbraith, 2002). Information flows and dynamics will continue to be studied under the social network analysis approach—for example, through e-mail (Huberman & Adamic, 2004), and by using simulation to explore the behavior of the networks, to find paths, and to explore relationships. The principles behind social networks, such as scale-free graphs and "small-world" behavior, will also continue to have an impact on the way real networks are designed, retrieval algorithms are developed, and efficiency improved. By combining these ideas with agent-based technology and the developments in distributed systems (P2P architectures), information management systems will increasingly become decentralized and support information sharing on open, heterogeneous environments. Whether these trends will conflict or converge with the previously mentioned effort to continue work on standards and ontologies is yet to be seen.

REFERENCES

Abidi, S., & Chong, Y. (2004). Constraint satisfaction methods for information personalization. *Lecture Notes in Artificial Intelligence, 3060,* 261–276.

Agrawala, A.K., Larsen, R.L., & Szajda, D. (2000). Information dynamics: An information-centric approach to system design. *Proceedings of the International Conference on Virtual Worlds and Simulation,* San Diego, CA.

Atoji, Y., Koiso, T., & Nishida, S. (2000). Information filtering for emergency management. *Proceedings of the 2000 IEEE International Workshop on Robot and Human Interactive Communication.*

Barnes, P., & Oloruntoba, R. (2005). Assurance of security in maritime supply chains: Conceptual issues of vulnerability and crisis management. *Journal of Information Management, 11,* 519–540.

Barzilay, R., McKeown, K., & Elhadad, M. (1999). Information fusion in the context of multi-document summarization. *Proceedings of the 37th Annual Meeting of the Association for Computational Linguistics on Computational Linguistics* (pp. 550–557).

Belkin, N.J., & Croft, W.B. (1992). Information filtering and information retrieval: Two sides of the same coin? *Communications of the ACM, 35*(12), 29–38.

Bloodsworth, P., & Greenwood, S. (2005). COSMOA: An ontology-centric multi-agent system for coordinating medical responses to large-scale disasters. *AI Communications, 18,* 229–240.

Borgatti, S.P., & Cross, R. (2003). A relational view of information seeking and learning in social networks. *Management Science, 49*(4), 432–445.

Borges, J.L. (1979). *Borges oral, emcee.* Buenos Aires: Alianza.

Brown, J., & Duguid, O. (1994). Borderline issues: Social and material aspects of design. *Human-Computer Interaction, 9,* 3–36.

Bui, T., Cho, S., Sankaran, S., & Sovereign, M. (2000). A framework for designing a global information network for multinational humanitarian assistance/disaster relief. *Information Systems Frontiers,* 1(4), 427–442.

Burgin, M. (2003). Information theory: A mutlifaceted model of information. *Entropy, 5*(2), 146–160.

Chen, R., Sharman, R., Rao, H.R., & Upadhyaya, S. (2005). Design principles of coordinated multi-incident emergency response systems. In P. Kantor et al. (Eds.), *Proceedings of the IEEE International Conference on Intelligence and Security Informatics* (ISI 2005) (pp. 19–20). Berlin: Springer-Verlag.

Comfort, L., Ko, K., & Zagorecki, A. (2004). Coordination in rapidly evolving disaster response systems: The role of information. *American Behavioral Scientist, 48*(3), 295–313.

Dubois, D., & Prade, H. (2004). On the use of aggregation operations in information fusion processes. *Fuzzy Sets and Systems, 142*(1), 143–161.

Eppler, M., & Mengis, J. (2004). The concept of information overload: A review of literature from organization science, accounting, marketing, MIS, and related disciplines. *The Information Society, 20*(5), 325–344.

Galbraith, J. (1974). Organization design: An information processing view. *Interfaces, 4*(3), 28–36.

Galbraith, J., Downey, D., & Kates, A. (2002). How networks undergird the lateral capability of an organization—where the work gets done. *Journal of Organizational Excellence, 21*(2), 67–78.

Goh, O., & Fung, C. (2005). Automated knowledge extraction from Internet for a crisis communication portal. *Lecture Notes in Artificial Intelligence, 3614,* 1226–1235.

Hanani, U., Shapira, B., & Shoval, P. (2001). Information filtering: Overview of issues, research and systems. *User Modeling and User-Adapted Interaction, 11*(3), 203–259.

Hayes, R.M. (1993). Measurement of information. *Information Processing & Management, 29*(1), 1–11.

Herlocker, J.L., Konstan, J.A., Terveen, L.G., & Riedl, J.T. (2004). Evaluating collaborative filtering recommender systems. *ACM Transactions in Information Systems, 22*(1), 5–53.

Huberman, B., & Adamic, L. (2004). Information dynamics in the networked world. *Lecture Notes in Physics, 650,* 371–398.

Hunter, A., & Liu, W. (2006). Fusion rules for merging uncertain information. *Information Fusion, 7*(1), 97–134.

Huokka, D., & Harada, L. (1998). Matchmaking for information agents. In M. Huhns & M. Singh (Eds.), *Readings in agents.* San Francisco: Morgan Kaufmann.

Jenvald, J., Morin, M., & Kincaid, J.P. (2001). A framework for Web-based dissemination of models and lessons learned from emergency-response exercises and operations. *International Journal of Emergency Management, 1*(1), 82–94.

Jhingran, A.D., Mattos, N., & Pirahesh, H. (2002). Information integration: A research agenda. *IBM Systems Journal, 41*(4), 555–562.

Kokar, M., Tomasik, J., & Weyman, J. (2004). Formalizing classes of information fusion systems. *Information Fusion, 5*(3), 189–202.

Lenz, H. (1998). Multi-data sources and data fusion. *Proceedings of the International Seminar on New Techniques & Technologies for Statistics (NTTS '98)* (pp. 139–146), Sorrento.

Liu, K. (2004). Agent-based resource discovery architecture for environmental emergency management. *Expert Systems with Applications, 27,* 77–95.

Losee, R.M. (1997). A discipline independent definition of information. *Journal of the American Society for Information Science, 48*(3), 254–269.

Malone, T.W., Grant, K.R., Turbak, F.A., Brobost, S.A., & Cohen, M.D. (1987). Intelligent information-sharing systems. *Communications of the ACM, 30*(5), 390–402.

Maes, P. (1994). Agents that reduce work and information overload. *Communications of the ACM, 37*(7), 30–40.

Marinescu, D. (2002). *Internet-based workflow management: Toward a semantic we.* New York: John Wiley & Sons.

McLuhan, M., & Fiore, Q. (1967). *The medium is the massage.* London: Penguin.

Michigan State University School of Criminal Justice. (2000). *Critical incident protocol—a public and private partnership.* Retrieved December 18, 2006, from *http://www.cj.msu.edu/%7Eoutreach/CIP/CIP.pdf*

Moukas, A. (1997). Amalthea: Information discovery and filtering using a multiagent evolving ecosystem. *Applied Artificial Intelligence, 11,* 437–457.

Pavlin, G., de Oude, P., & Nunnink, J. (2005). A MAS approach to fusion of heterogeneous information. *Proceedings of the 2005 IEEE/WIC/ACM International Conference on Web Intelligence (WI'05)* (pp. 802–804).

Petit-Rozé, C., & Grislin-Le Strugeon, E. (2006). MAPIS, a multi-agent system for information personalization. *Information and Software Technology, 48,* 107–120.

Proper, H.A., & Bruza, P.D. (1999). What is information discovery about? *Journal of the American Society for Information Science, 50*(9), 737–750.

Rhodes, B.J., & Maes, P. (2000). Just-in-time information retrieval agents. *IBM Systems Journal, 39*(3–4), 685–704.

Roth, G., & Dicke, U. (2005). Evolution of the brain and intelligence. *Trends in Cognitive Sciences, 9*(5), 250–257.

Shadbolt, N., Berners-Lee, T., & Hall, W. (2006). The Semantic Web revisited. *IEEE Intelligent Systems, 21*(3), 96–101.

Shahabi, C., & Chen, Y. (2003). Web information personalization: Challenges and approaches. *Lecture Notes in Computer Science, 2822,* 5–15.

Shakshuki, E., Ghenniwa, H., & Kamel, M. (2003). An architecture for cooperative information systems. *Knowledge-Based Systems, 16,* 17–27.

Spink, A., & Saracevic, T. (1997). Interaction in information retrieval: Selection and effectiveness of search terms. *Journal of the American Society for Information Science, 48*(8), 741–761.

Steinberg, L., & Cruz, A. (2004). When natural and technological disasters collide: Lessons from the Turkey earthquake of August 17, 1999. *Natural Hazards Review, 5*(3).

Szathmáry, E., & Maynard Smith, J. (1995). The major evolutionary transitions. *Nature, 374*(16), 227–232.

Tu, H., & Hsiang, J. (2000). An architecture and category knowledge for intelligent information retrieval agents. *Decision Support Systems, 28*(3), 255–268.

Valet, L., Mauris, G., & Bolon, P. (2001). A statistical overview of recent literature in information fusion. *IEEE AESS Systems Magazine, 16*(3), 7–14.

van Rijsbergen, C.J., & Lalmas, M. (1996). Information calculus for information retrieval. *Journal of the American Society for Information Science, 47*(5), 385–398.

ADDITIONAL READING

For an early account on the concept of information and the philosophical foundations of information science:

Belkin, N.J. (1978). Information concepts for information science. *Journal of Documentation, 34*(1), 55–85.

Capurro, R. (1992). What is information science for? A philosophical reflection. In P. Vakkari & B. Cronin (Eds.), *Conceptions of library and information science. Historical, empirical and theoretical perspectives.* London: Taylor Graham.

Capurro, R., & Hjørland, B. (2003). The concept of information. *Annual Review of Information Science and Technology, 37,* 343–411.

For an early account of information retrieval on the World Wide Web:

Gudivada, V., Raghavan, V., Grosky, W., & Kasanagottu, R. (1997). Information retrieval on the World Wide Web. *IEEE Internet Computing, 1*(5), 58–68.

For information retrieval and filtering from an agent-based perspective:

Decker, K.S., & Sycara, K. (1997). Intelligent adaptive information agents. *Journal of Intelligent Information Systems, 9,* 239–260.

For an extended account of information filtering systems, including a review of commercial applications (up until the year of publication):

Hanani, U., Shapira, B., & Shoval, P. (2001). Information filtering: Overview of issues, research and systems. *User Modeling and User-Adapted Interaction, 11*(3), 203–259.

For a brief introduction of the basic problem of information seeking:

Belkin N.J. (2000). Helping people find what they don't know. *Communications of the ACM, 43*(8), 58–61.

Chapter IV
Mining for Web Personalization

Penelope Markellou
University of Patras, Greece

Maria Rigou
University of Patras, Greece

Spiros Sirmakessis
University of Patras, Greece

ABSTRACT

The Web has become a huge repository of information and keeps growing exponentially under no editorial control, while the human capability to find, read and understand content remains constant. Providing people with access to information is not the problem; the problem is that people with varying needs and preferences navigate through large Web structures, missing the goal of their inquiry. Web personalization is one of the most promising approaches for alleviating this information overload, providing tailored Web experiences. This chapter explores the different faces of personalization, traces back its roots and follows its progress. It describes the modules typically comprising a personalization process, demonstrates its close relation to Web mining, depicts the technical issues that arise, recommends solutions when possible, and discusses the effectiveness of personalization and the related concerns. Moreover, the chapter illustrates current trends in the field suggesting directions that may lead to new scientific results.

INTRODUCTION

Technological innovation has led to an explosive growth of recorded information, with the Web being a huge repository under no editorial control. More and more people everyday browse

through it in an effort to satisfy their "primitive" need for information, as humans might properly be characterized as a species of *Informavores* who "have gained an adaptive advantage because they are hungry for further information about the world they inhabit (and about themselves)"

(Dennett, 1991, p. 181). Based on the observation that humans actively seek, gather, share and consume information to a degree unapproached by other organisms, Pirolli and Card (1999, p. 3) took the informavores approach one step further and introduced the *Information Foraging Theory[1]* according to which, "when feasible, natural information systems evolve towards stable states that maximize gains of valuable information per unit cost" (see also Resnikoff, 1989). Under the information foraging assumption, people need information and the Web today provides open access to a large volume. Thus providing people with access to more information is not the problem; the problem is that more and more people with varying needs and preferences navigate through large and complicated Web structures, missing -in many cases- the goal of their inquiry. The challenge today is how to concentrate human attention on information that is useful (maximizing gains of valuable information per unit cost), a point eloquently made by H.A. Simon (as quoted by Hal Varian in 1995, p. 200), "...what information consumes is rather obvious: it consumes the attention of its recipients. Hence a wealth of information creates a poverty of attention and a need to allocate that attention efficiently among the overabundance of information sources that might consume it."

Personalization can be the solution to this information overload problem, as its objective is to provide users with what they want or need, without having to ask (or search) for it explicitly (Mulvenna et al., 2000). It is a multidiscipline area deploying techniques from various scientific fields for putting together data and producing personalized output for individual users or groups of users. These fields comprise information retrieval, user modeling, artificial intelligence, databases, and more. Personalization on the Web covers a broad area, ranging from check-box customization to recommender systems and adaptive Websites. The spectrum from customizable Websites (in which users are allowed, usually manually, to configure the site in order to better suit their preferences) to adaptive ones (the site undertakes to automatically produce all adaptations according to the user profile, recorded history, etc.) is wide and personalization nowadays has moved towards the latter end. We meet cases of personalization in use in e-commerce applications (product recommendations for cross-selling and up-selling, one-to-one marketing, personalized pricing, store-front page customization, etc.), in information portals (home page customization such as *my.yahoo.com*, etc.), in search engines (in which returned results are filtered and/or sorted according to the profile of the specific user or group of users), and e-learning applications (topic recommendations, student/teacher/administrator views, content adaptations based on student level and skills, etc.). And while recently there has been a lot of talking about personalization, one has to wonder whether it is hype or an actual opportunity. Doug Riecken, in his editorial article in the *Communications of the ACM Special Issue on Personalization* (2000), claims that it should be considered as an opportunity, but it must be defined clearly and it must be designed to be useful and usable, conditions that in the traditional HCI field (Nielsen, 1994) are interpreted as allowing users to achieve their goals (or perform their tasks) in little time, with a low error rate, and while experiencing high subjective satisfaction.

The personalization technology is fast evolving and its use spreads quickly. In the years to come all Web applications will embed personalization components, and this philosophy will be part and parcel of many everyday life tasks (e.g., ambient computing, house of tomorrow). We are now at the phase of exploring the possibilities and potential pitfalls of personalization as implemented and designed so far. In our opinion this is a good point to review the progress, learn from our mistakes, and think about the "gray" areas and the controversies before planning for the future. This chapter aims to define personalization, describe its modules, demonstrate the close relation between personalization and Web mining, depict the technical issues that arise, recommend solutions when possible, and discuss its effectiveness, as well as the related concerns. Moreover, our goal is to illustrate the future trends in the field and suggest in this way directions that may lead us to new scientific results.

MOTIVATION FOR PERSONALIZATION

Taking things from the beginning, the roots of personalization—as we interpret it today—are traced back to the introduction of *adaptive hypermedia applications* in Brusilovsky's work of 1996 and its updated version of 2001. Adaptive hypermedia were introduced as an alternative to the traditional "one-size-fits-all" approach, building a model of the goals, preferences and knowledge of each individual user, and using this model throughout the interaction, in order to adapt to the user's specific needs.

Adaptations are differentiated depending on the amount of control a user has over them. Four distinct roles are defined in the process: adaptation *initiator*, *proposer*, *selector* and *producer* (Dieterich et al., 1993). Systems in which the user is in control of initiation, proposal, selection and production of the adaptation are called *adaptable* (Oppermann, 1994) ("in control" thereby meaning that the user can perform these functions, but can also opt to let the system perform some of them). In contrast, systems that perform all steps autonomously are called *adaptive*. Adaptability and adaptivity can coexist in the same application and the final tuning between the two should be decided taking into account convenience for the user, demands on the user, irritation of the user and the consequences of false adaptation. User control may be provided on a general level (users can allow or disallow adaptation at large), on a type level (users can approve or disapprove that

certain types of adaptation take place) or on a case-by-case basis (Kobsa & Pohl, 2001).

As already mentioned, initial attempts of implementing personalization were limited to *check-box personalization,* in which portals allowed the users to select the links they would like on their "personal" pages, but this has proved of limited use since it depends on the users knowing in advance the content of their interest. Moving towards more intelligent (or AI) approaches, *collaborative filtering* was deployed for implementing personalization based on knowledge about likes and dislikes of past users that are considered similar to the current one (using a certain similarity measure). These techniques required users to input personal information about their interests, needs and/or preferences, but this posed in many cases a big obstacle, since Web users are not usually cooperative in revealing these types of data. Due to such problems, researchers resorted to *observational personalization,* which is based on the assumption that we can find clues about how to personalize information, services or products in records of users' previous navigational behavior (Mulvenna et al., 2000). This is the point at which *Web mining* comes into play; Web mining is defined as the use of data mining techniques for discovering and extracting information from Web documents and services and is distinguished as *Web content, structure* or *usage mining* depending on which part of the Web is mined (Kosala & Blockeel, 2000). In the majority of cases, Web applications base personalization on Web usage mining, which undertakes the task of gathering and extracting all data required for constructing and maintaining user profiles based on the behavior of each user as recorded in server logs.

Now that all necessary introductions are in place, we may proceed with formally introducing the central concept of this chapter. Defining a scientific discipline is always a controversial task, and personalization is no exception to this rule as, in the related bibliography, one may come across many definitions; we already referred to the definition found in Mulvenna et al. (2000) and we indicatively also quote the following one, which follows a more user-centric approach: "Personalization is a process that changes the functionality, interface, information content, or distinctiveness of a system to increase its personal relevance to an individual" (Blom, 2000). Eirinaki and Vazirgiannis (2003, p. 1) define it in a way that addresses adequately all primary aspects of personalization as perceived in the specific context of this book: "Personalization is defined as any action that adapts the information or services provided by a web site to the knowledge gained from the users' navigational behavior and individual interests, in combination with the content and *the* structure of the web site". For the remainder of the chapter, we will use this as our working personalization definition.

PERSONALIZATION PROCESS DECOMPOSED

In this section we discuss the overall personalization process in terms of the discrete modules comprising it: *data acquisition*, *data analysis* and *personalized output*. We describe in detail the objectives of each module and review the approaches taken so far by scientists working in the field, the obstacles met, and when possible, the solutions recommended.

Data Acquisition

In the large majority of cases, Web personalization is a data-intensive task that is based on three general types of data: data about the user, data about the Website usage and data about the software and hardware available on the user's side.

User data. This category denotes information about personal characteristics of the user. Several such types of data have been used in personalization applications, such as:

- *Demographics* (name, phone number, geographic information, age, sex, education, income, etc.);
- *User's knowledge* of concepts and relationships between concepts in an application domain (input that has been of extensive use in natural language processing systems) or domain specific expertise;
- *Skills and capabilities* (in the sense that apart from "what" the user knows, in many cases it is of equal importance to know what the user knows "how" to do, or even further, to distinguish between what the user is familiar with and what she can actually accomplish);
- *Interests and preferences*;
- *Goals and plans* (plan recognition techniques and identified goals allow the Website to predict the user's interests and needs and adjust its contents for easier and faster goal achievement).

There are two general approaches for acquiring user data of the types described above: either the user is asked *explicitly* to provide the data (using questionnaires, fill-in preference dialogs, or even via machine readable data-carriers, such as smart cards), or the system *implicitly* derives such information without initiating any interaction with the user (using acquisition rules, plan recognition, and stereotype reasoning).

Usage data. Usage data may be directly observed and recorded, or acquired by analyzing observable data (whose amount and detail vary depending on the technologies used during Website implementation, i.e., java applets, etc.), a process already referenced in this chapter as Web usage mining. Usage data may either be:

Observable data comprising selective actions like clicking on an link, data regarding the temporal viewing behavior, ratings (using a binary or a limited, discrete scale) and other confirmatory or disconfirmatory actions (making purchases, e-mailing/saving/printing a document, book-marking a Web page and more), or

Data that derive from further processing the observed and regarded usage regularities (measurements of frequency of selecting an option/link/service, production of suggestions/recommendations based on situation-action correlations, or variations of this approach, for instance recording action sequences).

Environment data. On the client side, the range of different hardware and software used is large and keeps growing with the widespread use of mobile phones and personal digital assistants (PDAs) for accessing the Web. Thus in many cases the adaptations to be produced should also take into account such information. Environment data address information about the available *software* and *hardware* at the client computer (browser version and platform, availability of plug-ins, firewalls preventing applets from executing, available bandwidth, processing speed, display and input devices, etc.), as well as *locale* (geographical information in order to adjust the language, or other locale specific content).

After data have been acquired (a process that is in continuous execution for most of the cases), they need to be transformed into some form of internal representation (modeling) that will allow for further processing and easy update. Such internal representation models are used for constructing individual or aggregate (when working with groups of users) profiles, a process termed *user profiling* in the relative literature. Profiles may be *static* or *dynamic* based on whether -- and how often -- they are updated. Static profiles are usually acquired explicitly while dynamic ones are acquired implicitly by recording and analyzing user navigational behavior. In both approaches, we have to deal with different but equally serious problems. In the case of explicit profiling, users are often negative about filling in questionnaires and revealing personal information online; they comply only when required and even then the

data submitted may be false. On the other hand, in implicit profiling, even though our source of information is not biased by the users' negative attitude, the problems encountered derive once again from the invaded privacy concern and the loss of anonymity, as personalization is striving to identify the user, record the user's online behavior in as much detail as possible and extract needs and preferences in a way the user cannot notice, understand or control. The problem of loss of control is observed in situations in which the user is not in control of when and what change occurs and it is referenced in numerous HCI resources, such as Kramer et al. (2000), Mesquita et al. (2002), and Nielsen (1998) as a usability degrading factor. A more detailed discussion on the issues of privacy and locus of control can be found later in this chapter, under "Trends and Challenges in Personalization Research."

Data Analysis

User profiling dramatically affects the kinds of analysis that can be applied after the phase of data acquisition in order to reach secondary inferences and accomplish more sophisticated personalization. The techniques that may be applied for further analyzing and expanding user profiles so as to derive inferences vary and come from numerous scientific areas that comprise artificial intelligence, machine learning, statistics, and information retrieval. In this chapter, we follow the approach of information retrieval and set our focus on deploying Web mining for analyzing user behavior and inferring "interesting" patterns, similarities, clusters and correlations among users and/or page requests. In the past years, several researchers have applied *Web usage mining* for constructing user profiles and making personalization decisions. Web usage mining uses server logs as its source of information and the process of deriving valuable information from them progresses according to the following phases (Srivastava et al., 2000): data preparation and preprocessing, pattern discovery and pattern analysis.

Data Preparation and Preprocessing

The objective of this phase is to derive a set of server sessions from raw usage data, as recorded in the form of Web server logs. Before proceeding with a more detailed description of data preparation, it is necessary to give a set of data abstractions as introduced by the W3C[a] (World Wide Web Consortium) for describing Web usage. A *server session* is defined as a set of page views served due to a series of HTTP requests from a single user to a single Web server. A *page view* is a set of page files that contribute to a single display in a Web browser window (the definition of the page view is necessary because for analyzing user behavior what is of value is the aggregate page view and not each one of the consecutive separate requests that are generated automatically for acquiring parts of the page view such as scripts, graphics, etc.). Determining which log entries refer to a single page view (a problem known as *page view identification*) requires information about the site structuring and contents. A sequential series of page view requests is termed *click-stream* and it is its full contents that we ideally need to know for reliable conclusions. A *user session* is the click-stream of page views for a single user across the entire Web, while a *server session* is the set of page views in a user session for a particular Website.

During data preparation the task is to identify the log data entries that refer to graphics or traffic automatically generated by spiders and agents. These entries in most of the cases are removed from the log data, as they do not reveal actual usage information. Nevertheless, the final decision on the best way to handle them depends on the specific application. After cleaning, log entries are usually parsed into data fields for easier manipulation.

Apart from removing entries from the log data, in many cases data preparation also includes enhancing the usage information by adding the missing clicks to the user click-stream. The reason dictating this task is client and proxy caching, which cause many requests not to be recorded in the server logs and to be served by the cached page views. The process of restoring the complete click-stream is called *path completion* and it is the last step for preprocessing usage data. Missing page view requests can be detected when the referrer page file for a page view is not part of the previous page view. The only sound way to have the complete user path is by using either a software agent or a modified browser on the client-side. In all other cases the available solutions (using for instance, apart from the referrer field, data about the link structure of the site) are heuristic in nature and cannot guarantee accuracy.

Except for the path completion issue, there remains a set of other technical obstacles that must be overcome during data preparation and preprocessing. More specifically, a major such issue is *user identification*. A number of methods are deployed for user identification and the overall assessment is that the more accurate a method is, the higher the privacy invasion problem it faces. Assuming that each IP address/agent pair identifies a unique user is not always the case, as many users may use the same computer to access the Web and the same user may access the Web from various computers. An embedded session ID requires dynamic sites and while it distinguishes the various users from the same IP/Agent, it fails to identify the same user from different IPs. Cookies and software agents accomplish both objectives, but are usually not well accepted (or even rejected and disabled) by most users. Registration also provides reliable identification but not all users are willing to go through such a procedure or recall logins and passwords. Alternatively, modified browsers may provide accurate records of user behavior even across Websites, but they are not a realistic solution in the majority of cases as they require installation and only a limited number of users will install and use them.

Last but not least, there arises the issue of *session identification*. Trivial solutions tackle this by setting a minimum time threshold and assuming that subsequent requests from the same user exceeding it belong to different sessions (or use a maximum threshold for concluding respectively).

Pattern Discovery

Pattern discovery aims to detect interesting patterns in the preprocessed Web usage data by deploying statistical and data mining methods. These methods usually comprise (Eirinaki & Vazirgiannis, 2003):

- **Association rule mining:** A technique used for finding frequent patterns, associations and correlations among sets of items. In the Web personalization domain, this method may indicate correlations between pages not directly connected and reveal previously unknown associations between groups of users with specific interests. Such information may prove valuable for e-commerce stores in order to improve customer relationship management (CRM).

- **Clustering:** A method used for grouping together items that have similar characteristics. In our case items may either be users (that demonstrate similar online behavior) or pages (that are similarity utilized by users).

- **Classification:** A process that learns to assign data items to one of several predefined

Figure 1. Personalization based on Web mining

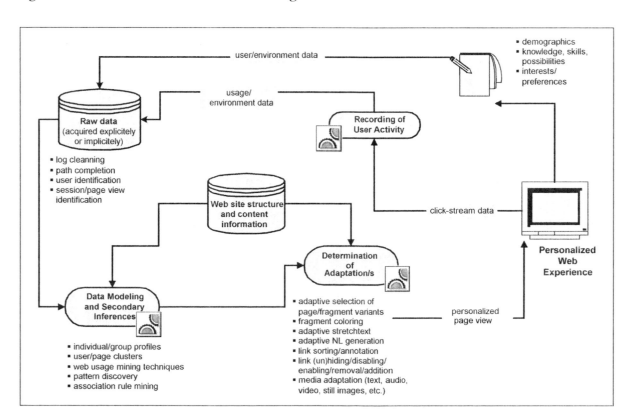

classes. Classes usually represent different user profiles, and classification is performed using selected features with high discriminative ability as refers to the set of classes describing each profile.

- **Sequential pattern discovery:** An extension to the association rule mining technique, used for revealing patterns of co-occurrence, thus incorporating the notion of time sequence. A pattern in this case may be a Web page or a set of pages accessed immediately after another set of pages.

Pattern Analysis

In this final phase the objective is to convert discovered rules, patterns and statistics into *knowledge* or insight involving the Website being analyzed. Knowledge here is an abstract notion that in essence describes the transformation from information to understanding; it is thus highly dependent on the human performing the analysis and reaching conclusions. In most of the cases, visualization techniques are used for "communicating" better the knowledge to the analyst.

Figure 1 provides a summarized representation of all described subtasks comprising the process of Web personalization based on usage mining.

The techniques mentioned so far for performing the various phases of data analysis apply Web usage mining in order to deliver Web personalization. This approach is indeed superior to other more traditional methods (such as collaborative or content based filtering) in terms of both scalability and reliance on objective input data (and not, for instance, on subjective user ratings). Nevertheless, usage-based personalization can also be problematic when little usage data are available pertaining to some objects, or when the site content changes regularly. Mobasher et al. (2000a) claims that for more effective personalization, both usage and content attributes of a site must be integrated into the data analysis phase and be used uniformly as

the basis of all personalization decisions. This way semantic knowledge is incorporated into the process by representing domain ontologies in the preprocessing and pattern discovery phases, and using effective techniques to obtain uniform profiles representation and show how to use such profiles for performing real-time personalization (Mobasher & Dai, 2001).

Personalized Output

After gathering the appropriate input data (about the user, the usage and/or the usage environment), storing them using an adequate representation and analyzing them for reaching secondary inferences, what remains is to explore and decide upon the kind of adaptations the Website will deploy in order to personalize itself. These adaptations can take place at different levels:

- **Content:** Typical applications of such adaptations are optional explanations and additional information, personalized recommendations, theory driven presentation, and more. Techniques used for producing such adaptations include adaptive selection of Web page (or page fragment) variants, fragment coloring, adaptive stretch-text, and adaptive natural language generation.
- **Structure:** It refers to changes in the link structure of hypermedia documents or their presentation. Techniques deployed for producing this kind of adaptation comprise adaptive link sorting, annotation, hiding and unhiding, disabling and enabling, and removal/addition. Adaptations of structure are widely used for producing adaptive recommendations (for products, information or navigation), as well as constructing personal views and spaces.
- **Presentation and media format:** In this type of personalized output the informational content ideally stays the same, but its

format and layout changes (for example from images to text, from text to audio, from video to still images). This type of adaptations is widely used for Web access through PDAs or mobile phones, or in Websites that cater to handicapped persons.

In the majority of cases, personalized Websites deploy hybrid adaptation techniques.

Personalization requires the manipulation of large amounts of data and processing them at a speed that allows for low response times, so that adaptations take effect as soon as possible and the process remains transparent to the user. At the same time, in most personalization scenarios, and with the purpose of keeping the processing time very low, parts of the process are executed offline. An effect of this case is that the system delays in updating changing user profiles, since it is only natural that user preferences and even more often user needs change over time, requiring corresponding updates to the profiles. The trade-off between low response times and keeping profiles updated is usually determined on an application basis, according to the specific precision and speed requirements, or in other words, the fault and delay tolerance.

THEORY IN ACTION: TOOLS AND STANDARDS

From the previous, it is obvious that personalizing the Web experience for users by addressing individual needs and preferences is a challenging task for the Web industry. Web-based applications (e.g., portals, e-commerce sites, e-learning environments, etc.) can improve their performance by using attractive new tools such as dynamic recommendations based on individual characteristics and recorded navigational history. However, the question that arises is how this can be actually accomplished. Both the Web industry and researchers from diverse scientific areas

have focused on various aspects of the topic. The research approaches, and the commercial tools that deliver personalized Web experiences based on business rules, Website content and structure, as well as the user behavior recorded in Web log files are numerous. This section provides a tour around the most well known applications of Web personalization both at a research and a commercial level.

Letizia (Lieberman, 1995), one of the first intelligent agents, assists Web search and offers personalized lists of URLs close to the page being read using personal state, history and preferences (contents of current and visited pages). More specifically, the agent automates a browsing strategy consisting of a best-first search augmented by heuristics inferring user interest from her behavior.

WebWatcher (Armstrong et al., 1995; Joachims et al., 1997) comprises a "tour guide" Web agent that highlights hyperlinks in pages based on the declared interests and path traversal pattern of the current user, as well as previous similar users. WebWatcher incorporates three learning approaches: (a) learning from previous tours, (b) learning from the hypertext structure and (c) combination of the first two approaches.

A recommendation system that assists Web search and personalizes the results of a query based on personal history and preferences (contents and ratings of visited pages) is *Fab* (Balabanovic & Shoham, 1997). By combining both collaborative and content-based techniques, it succeeds to eliminate many of the weaknesses found in each approach.

Humos/Wifs (Ambrosini et al., 1997) has two components, the Hybrid User Modeling Subsystem and the Web-oriented Information Filtering Subsystem, assisting Web search and personalizing the results of a query based on an internal representation of user interests (inferred by the system through a dialogue). It uses a hybrid approach to user modeling (integration of case-based components and artificial neural network) and takes advantage of semantic networks, as well as a well-structured database, in order to perform accurate filtering.

Another agent that learns users' preferences by looking at their visit records and then provides them with updated information about the Website is *SiteHelper* (Ngu & Wu, 1997). The agent carries out two types of incremental learning: interactive learning, by asking user for feedback, and silent learning, by using the log files.

Personal WebWatcher (Mladenic, 1999) is a "personal" agent, inspired basically by Web-Watcher, that assists Web browsing and highlights useful links from the current page using personal history (content of visited pages), while *Let's Browse* (Lieberman et al., 1999) implemented as an extension to Letizia, supports automatic detection of the presence of users, automated "channel surfing" browsing, dynamic display of the user profiles and explanation of recommendations.

The use of *association rules* was first proposed in Agrawal et al. (1993) and Agrawal and Srikant (1994). Chen et al. (1998) use association rules algorithms to discover "interesting" correlations among user sessions, while the definition of a session as a set of *maximal forward references* (meaning a sequence of Web pages accessed by a user) was introduced in Chen et al. (1996). This work is also the basis of *SpeedTracer* (Wu et al., 1998), which uses referrer and agent information in the pre-processing routines to identify users and server sessions in the absence of additional client side information, and then identifies the most frequently visited groups of Web pages. Krishnan et al. (1998) describe *path-profiling* techniques in order to predict future request behaviors. Thus content can be dynamically generated before the user requests it.

Manber et al. (2000) presents *Yahoo! personalization experience*. Yahoo! was one of the first Websites to use personalization on a large scale. This work studies three examples of per-sonalization: Yahoo! Companion, Inside Yahoo! Search and My Yahoo! application, which were introduced in July 1996.

Cingil et al. (2000) describe the need for *interoperability* when mining the Web and how the various *standards* can be used for achieving personalization. Furthermore, he establishes an architecture for providing Web servers with automatically generated, machine processable, dynamic user profiles, while conforming to users' privacy preferences.

Mobasher et al. (2000b) describe a general architecture for automatic Web personalization using Web usage mining techniques. *WebPersonalizer* (Figure 2) is an advanced system aiming at mining Web log files to discover knowledge for the production of personalized recommendations for the current user based on her similarities with previous users. These user preferences are automatically learned from Web usage data, eliminating in this way the subjectivity from profile data, as well as keeping them updated. The pre-processing steps outlined in Cooley et al. (1999a) are used to convert the server logs into server sessions. The system recommends pages from clusters that closely match the current session.

For personalizing a site according to the requirements of each user, Spiliopoulou (2000) describes a process based on discovering and analyzing *user navigational patterns*. Mining these patterns, we can gain insight into a Web site's usage and optimality with respect to its current user population.

Usage patterns extracted from Web data have been applied to a wide range of applications. *WebSIFT* (Cooley et al., 1997, 1999b, 2000) is a Website information filter system that combines usage, content, and structure information about a Website. The information filter automatically identifies the discovered patterns that have a high degree of subjective interestingness.

Figure 2. A general architecture for usage-based Web personalization (Mobasher et al., 2000b)

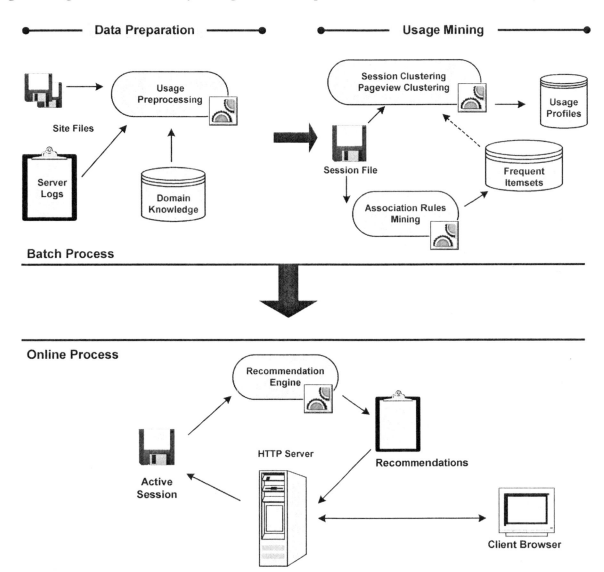

Web Utilization Miner - WUM) (Spiliopoulou et al., 1999a, 1999b; Spiliopoulou & Faulstich, 1998; Spiliopoulou & Pohle, 2000) () specifies, discovers, and visualizes interesting navigation patterns. In WUM the concept of navigation patterns includes both the sequence of events that satisfies the expert's constraints and the routes connecting those events.

Another Web usage miner designed for e-commerce applications is *MIDAS* (Buchner et al., 1999), in which a navigation pattern is a sequence of events satisfying the constraints posed by an expert who can specify, in a powerful mining language, which patterns have potential interest.

IndexFinder (Perkowitz & Etzioni, 2000b) is a Web management assistant, a system that can process massive amounts of data about site usage and suggest useful adaptations to the Web master. This assistant develops adaptive Websites that semi-automatically improve their organization and presentation by learning from visitor access patterns. Adaptive Websites are

Table 1. Commercial applications

Commercial applications		
Vendor	**Application**	**Description**
Accrue Software Inc. *http://www.accrue.com*	Accrue G2, Accrue Insight, Pilot Suite, Pilot Hit List	Analytic tools that allow companies to transform volumes of complex Web data into actionable information for building long-term, multi-channel customer relationships (by capturing users' decision-making process and behavior patterns).
Blue Martini Software Inc. *http://www.bluemartini.com*	Blue Martini Marketing	A comprehensive solution for customer analysis and marketing automation. Companies use the software to create a unified picture of customers, analyze their behavior for patterns and insights, and implement those insights through personalization and outbound marketing.
Coremetrics Inc. *http://www.coremetrics.com*	Coremetrics Marketforce	An online marketing analytics platform that captures and stores all visitor and customer activity to build LIVE (Lifetime Individual Visitor Experience) Profiles that serve as the foundation for all successful marketing initiatives (featuring essential tools to increase online sales, maximize marketing return on investment (ROI), and optimize site design).
E.piphany *http://www.epiphany.com*	E.piphany E.6	Integrated tool that merges analytical/operational CRM capabilities to drive intelligent, effective, and personalized interactions with customers on any touch point (including applications for marketing, sales, service, etc.).
Elytics Inc. *http://www.elytics.com*	Elytics Analysis Suite	Powerful customer-centric analytics tools and innovative visualization applications that allow companies to measure and optimize e-channel performance by improving customer segment response to online initiatives, marketing campaign and tactic effectiveness, content effectiveness, registration browse-to-buy conversions, and so forth.
IBM Corporation *http://www.ibm.com*	WebSphere Personalization, SurfAid (Express. Analysis, Business Integration)	Tools that allow Website content personalization matching the unique needs and interests of each visitor. By analyzing Web traffic and visitor behavior companies may gain rapid feedback in regard to site traffic, marketing campaigns, visitor geographies, site navigation and design effectiveness, visitor loyalty, site stickiness, and so forth.
Lumio Software *http://www.lumio.com*	Re:cognition Product Suite, Re:action, Re:search, Re:collect	Suite for optimizing customer experience by personalization/customization. It enhances the effectiveness of e-businesses by supporting behavioral data collection-analysis-storage, real-time knowledge deployment and key performance indicators measurement to continuously monitor the quality of the interactions with customers.
NCR Corporation *http://www.ncr.com*	Teradata Warehouse	Analytical CRM solution suite that enables personalized customer dialogues by event-driven optimization and achieving higher revenue and profitability while improving customer satisfaction.

continued on following page

Table 1. continued

Net Perceptions http://www.netperceptions.com	NetP 7	NetP 7 powers one-to-one interactions driving product penetration and increased revenue via call center, Website, outbound e-mail campaigns, and direct mail by delivering personalized offers to customers. It contains advanced analytics to build statistical models based on historical transaction data that form the basis for effective cross-sell, up-sell, targeted customer lists and alternative product recommendations for out-of-stock items.
NetIQ Corporation http://www.netiq.com	WebTrends Intelligence Suite, WebTrends Log Analyzer Series	Web analytics solutions that deliver key insight into every element of Web visitor activity, allowing organizations to make smarter decisions in order to acquire, convert and retain more customers, resulting in higher returns on infrastructure and marketing investments and improved visitor-to-customer conversion rates.
Quest Software http://www.quest.com	Funnel Web Analyzer, Funnel Web Profiler	User profiling and Website traffic analysis tools that optimize Websites by analyzing how users interact with them and make informed decisions about what changes will improve users' experience (Client Click Stream analysis feature).
Sane Solutions http://www.sane.com	NetTracker 6.0 (Business Objects, Cognos, MicroStrategy)	NetTracker empowers business companies with easy-to-use, instant ad hoc analysis capabilities for answering very specific questions about individual visitors.
SAS http://www.sas.com	SAS Value Chain Analytics, SAS IntelliVisor, Enterprise Miner	Services for providing customized information, improving effectiveness of marketing campaigns by data mining and analytical techniques. They also help companies to reveal trends, explain known outcomes, predict future outcomes and identify factors that can secure a desired effect, all from collected demographic data and customer buying patterns.
SPSS Inc. http://www.spss.com	NetGenesis	A Web analytic software that interprets and explains customer behavior. It gathers and manages vast amounts of data, identifies which content brings the most value, builds loyal customers and determines the effectiveness of commerce and marketing campaigns. It addresses the distinct and complex needs of large businesses with dynamic, transaction driven and highly personalized Websites.
WebSideStory Inc. http://www.websidestory.com	HitBox Services Suite (Enterprise, Commerce, Wireless Website Analysis)	A broad range of market-proven services developed to help companies to optimize their online marketing performance (e.g., comprehensive online marketing analytics and optimization, essential Web traffic analysis, wireless Website analysis).

defined in Perkowitz and Etzioni (1997, 1998, 1999, 2000a).

Finally, Rossi et al. (2001) introduce an interesting approach based on the *Object-Oriented Hypermedia Design Method (OOHDM)*. They build Web application models as object-oriented views of conceptual models and then refine the views according to users' profiles or preferences to specify personalization. In this context, the linking topology or the contents of individual nodes can be basically personalized.

Moreover, many vendors such as Blue Martini Software Inc., E.piphany, Lumio Software, Net Perceptions, Sane Solutions, WebSideStory Inc, and so forth provide a variety of commercial tools that support mining for Web personalization. Table 1 summarizes a list of the most representative current commercial applications. All these can be integrated directly into a Website server in order to provide users with personalized experiences.

As mentioned before, the techniques applied for Web personalization should be based on standards and languages ensuring interoperability, better utilization of the stored information, as well as personal integrity and privacy (Cingil et al., 2000).

Extensible Markup Language (XML)[b] is a simple, very flexible text format originally designed to meet the challenges of large-scale electronic publishing. XML plays an increasingly important role in the exchange of a wide variety of data on the Web and the *XML Query Language*[c] can be used for extracting data from XML documents.

Resource Description Framework (RDF)[d] is a foundation for processing metadata and constitutes a recommendation of W3C. It provides interoperability between applications that exchange machine-understandable information on the Web and its syntax can use XML. RDF applications include resource discovery, content description/relationships, knowledge sharing and exchange, Web pages' intellectual property rights,

users' privacy preferences, Websites' privacy policies, and so forth.

Platform for Privacy Preferences (P3P)[e] was developed by the W3C in 1999 and comprises a standard that provides a simple and automated way for users to gain more control over their personal information when visiting Websites. Personal profiling is a form of Website visitor surveillance and leads to a number of ethical considerations. Website visitors must be convinced that any collected information will remain confidential and secure. P3P enables Websites to express their privacy practices in a standard format that can be retrieved automatically and interpreted easily by user agents. P3P user agents allow users to be informed of site practices (in both machine and human readable formats) and to automate decision-making based on these practices when appropriate. Thus users need not read the privacy policies at every site they visit. However, while P3P provides a standard mechanism for describing privacy practices, it does not ensure that Websites actually follow them.

Open Profiling Standard (OPS)[f] is a proposed standard by Netscape that enables Web personalization. It allows users to keep profile records on their hard drives, which can be accessed by authorized Web servers. The users have access to these records and can control the presented information. These records can replace cookies and manual online registration. The OPS has been examined by the W3C, and its key ideas have been incorporated into P3P.

Customer Profile Exchange (CPEX)[g] is an open standard for facilitating the privacy-enabled interchange of customer information across disparate enterprise applications and systems. It integrates online/offline customer data in an XML-based data model for use within various enterprise applications both on and off the Web, resulting in a networked, customer-focused environment. The CPEX working group intends to develop open-source reference implementation and developer guidelines to speed adoption of the standard among vendors.

Personalized Information Description Language (PIDL)[h] aims at facilitating personalization of online information by providing enhanced interoperability between applications. PIDL provides a common framework for applications to progressively process original contents and append personalized versions in a compact format. It supports the personalization of different media (e.g., plain text, structured text, graphics, etc.), multiple personalization methods (such as filtering, sorting, replacing, etc.) and different delivery methods (for example SMTP, HTTP, IP-multicasting, etc.). It creates a unified framework for services to both personalize and disseminate information. Using PIDL, services can describe the content and personalization methods used for customizing the information and use a single format for all available access methods.

TRENDS AND CHALLENGES IN PERSONALIZATION RESEARCH

While personalization looks important and appealing for the Web experience, several issues still remain unclear. One such issue is *privacy preserving* and stems from the fact that personalization requires collecting and storing far more personal data than ordinary non-personalized Websites. According to Earp and Baumer (2003), there is little legal protection of consumer information acquired online -- either voluntarily or involuntarily -- while systems try to collect as much data as possible from users, usually without users' initiative and sometimes without their awareness, so as to avoid user distraction. Numerous surveys already available illustrate user preferences concerning online privacy (Kobsa & Schreck, 2003), with the requirement for preservation of anonymity when interacting with an online system prevailing.

A solution to this problem may come from providing *user anonymity,* even thought this may sound controversial, since many believe that anonymity and personalization cannot co-exist. Schafer et al. (2001) claim that "anonymizing techniques are disasters for recommenders, because they make it impossible for the recommender to easily recognize the customer, limiting the ability even to collect data, much less to make accurate recommendations". Kobsa and Schreck, (2003) on the other hand, present a reference model for pseudonymous and secure user modeling that fully preserves personalized interaction. Users' trust in anonymity can be expected to lead to more extensive and frank interaction, and hence to more and better data about the user, and thus better personalization. While this is a comprehensive technical solution for anonymous and personalized user interaction with Web services, a number of obstacles must still be addressed; hardly any readily available distributed anonymisation infrastructures, such as mixes, have been put in place and anonymous interaction is currently difficult to maintain when money, physical goods and non-electronic services are being exchanged.

The deployment of personalized anonymous interaction will thus strongly hinge on social factors (i.e., regulatory provisions that mandate anonymous and pseudonymous access to electronic services). This will give the opportunity to holders of e-shops to apply *intelligent e-marketing* techniques with Web mining and personalization features, as in Perner and Fiss (2002). Intelligent e-marketing is part of the Web intelligence (Yao et al., 2001), where *intelligent Web agents (WA),* acting as computational entities, are making decisions on behalf of their users and self-improving their performance in dynamically changing and unpredictable task environments. WAs provide users with a user-friendly style of presentation (Cheung et al., 2001) that personalizes both interaction and content presentation (referenced in the bibliography as Personalized Multimodal Interface).

A relatively recent development that is foreseen to greatly affect Web personalization (and more specifically the Web mining subtasks) is the creation of the *semantic Web*. Semantic Web mining combines the two fast-developing research areas of semantic Web and Web mining with the purpose of improving Web mining by exploiting the new semantic structures in the Web. Berendt et al. (2002) give an overview of where the two areas meet today, and sketches ways of how a closer integration could be profitable. The Web will reach its full potential when it becomes an environment in which data can be shared and processed by automated tools, as well as by people. The notion of being able to semantically link various resources (documents, images, people, concepts, etc.) is essential for the personalization domain. With this we can begin to move from the current Web of simple hyperlinks to a more expressive, semantically rich web, in which we can incrementally add meaning and express a whole new set of relationships (hasLocation, worksFor, isAuthorOf, hasSubjectOf, dependsOn, etc.) among resources, making explicit the particular contextual relationships that are implicit in the current Web. The semantic Web will allow the application of sophisticated mining techniques (which require more structured input). This will open new doors for effective information integration, management and automated services (Markellos et al., 2003).

Moving away from the promising future potential of the personalization technology, perhaps it is interesting to return to its original motivation. Personalization has one explicit target: people. Users are being offered services or applications that need to be or should be personalized for ease of use, efficiency and satisfaction. Although in the past years different attempts have been proposed for evaluating personalization (Ramakrishnan, 2000; Vassiliou et al., 2002) a more systematic and

integrated approach should be defined for its efficient assessment, justifying on a per application basis the use of such a resource demanding technology. In other words, despite the great potential and how smart a Website can be in changing itself in order to better suit the individual user, or how well it can anticipate and foresee user needs, the fact remains: systems are aware of only a fraction of the total problem-solving process their human partners undergo (Hollan, 1990), and they cannot share an understanding of the situation or state of problem-solving of a human (Suchman, 1987). Personalization, with all the automated adaptations it "triggers" transparently, is a blessing only if the human partner is allowed to control what is adapted automatically and how. This way, locus of control remains at the user side, where it should be. Other than that, numerous issues remain to be addressed: When is personalization required? What data should be used and is there a minimal efficient set? How should data be handled? Is personalization efficient for the user? What about the system's efficiency? Are there any criteria for the efficiency of the methods, in terms of accuracy, speed, privacy and satisfaction?

Technologically, the scene is set for personalization; it is fast developing and constantly improving. What is missing is its wider acceptance that will allow it to prove its full potential. The prerequisite for this final and crucial step is the investigation and resolution of issues connected with the human factor: ethics, trust, privacy, control, satisfaction, respect, and reassurance.

CONCLUSION

As the Web is growing exponentially, the user's capability to find, read, and understand content remains constant. Currently, Web personalization is the most promising approach to alleviate this problem and to provide users with tailored experiences. Web-based applications (e.g., information portals, e-commerce sites, e-learning systems, etc.) improve their performance by addressing the individual needs and preferences of each user, increasing satisfaction, promoting loyalty, and establishing one-to-one relationships. There are many research approaches, initiatives and techniques, as well as commercial tools that provide Web personalization based on business rules, Website contents and structuring, user behavior and navigational history as recorded in Web server logs.

Without disputing the enormous potential of the personalization technology, neither questioning the "noble" motivations behind it, the issue is still unclear: Does personalization really work? The answer is neither trivial nor straightforward. On the one hand the benefits could be significant not only for the Website visitor (being offered more interesting, useful and relevant Web experience) but also for the provider (allowing one-to-one relationships and mass customization, and improving Website performance). On the other hand, personalization requires rich data that are not always easily obtainable and in many cases the output proves unsuccessful in actually understanding and satisfying user needs and goals. Today, the situation is such that providers invest money on personalization technologies without any reassurances concerning actual added value, since users are negative towards the idea of being stereotyped. Finally, the ethical dimension of personalization should also be taken into account: online user activities are recorded for constructing and updating user profiles and this puts privacy in jeopardy.

Summarizing, in this chapter we explored the different faces of personalization. We traced back its roots and ancestors, and followed its progress. We provided detailed descriptions of the modules that typically comprise a personalization process and presented an overview of the interesting research initiatives and representative commercial tools that deploy Web usage mining for producing personalized Web experiences. Finally, we introduced and discussed several open research issues and in some cases, we provided recommendations for solutions.

REFERENCES

Agrawal, R., Imielinski, T., & Swami, A. (1993). Mining association rules between sets of items in large fatabases. *Proceedings of the ACM SIGMOD International Conference on Management of Data* (pp. 207-216).

Agrawal, R., & Srikant, R. (1994). Fast algorithms for mining association rules. *Proceedings of the 20th VLDB Conference,* Santiago, Chile (pp. 487-499).

Ambrosini, L., Cirillo, V., & Micarelli, A. (1997). A hybrid architecture for user-adapted information filtering on the World Wide Web. *Proceedings of the 6th International Conference on User Modelling (UM'97)* (pp. 59-61). Springer-Verlag.

Armstrong, R., Joachims, D., Freitag, D., & Mitchell, T. (1995). WebWatcher: A learning apprentice for the World Wide Web. *Proceedings of the AI Spring Symposium on Information Gathering from Heterogeneous, Distributed Environments,* Stanford, California, USA (pp. 6-13).

Balabanovic, M., & Shoham, Y. (1997). Content-based collaborative recommendation. *Communications of the ACM, 40*(3), 66-72.

Berendt, B., Hotho, A., & Stumme, G. (2002). Towards semantic Web mining. In I. Horrocks & J. Hendler (Eds.), *Proceedings of the ISWC 2002, LNCS 2342* (pp. 264-278). Springer-Verlag Berlin.

Blom, J. (2000). Personalization - A taxonomy. *Proceedings of the CHI 2000 Workshop on Designing Interactive Systems for 1-to-1 Ecommerce.* New York: ACM. Available: http://www.zurich.ibm.com/~mrs/chi2000/

Brusilovsky, P. (1996). Methods and techniques of adaptive hypermedia. *Journal of User Modeling and User-Adaptive Interaction, 6*(2-3), 87-129.

Brusilovsky, P. (2001). Adaptive hypermedia. In A. Kobsa (Ed.), *User modeling and user-adapted interaction, ten year anniversary, 11,* 87-110.

Buchner, M., Baumgarten, M., Anand, S., Mulvenna, M., & Hughes, J. (1999). Navigation pattern discovery from Internet data. *WEBKDD'99.* San Diego, California.

Chen, M., Park, J., & Yu, P. (1996). Data mining for path traversal patterns in a Web environment. *Proceedings of the 16th International Conference on Distributed Computing Systems,* (pp. 385-392).

Chen, M., Park, J., & Yu, P. (1998). Efficient data mining for path traversal patterns. *IEEE Transactions Knowledge and Data Engineering, 10*(2), 209-221.

Cheung, K., Li, C., Lam, E., & Liu, J. (2001). Customized electronic commerce with intelligent software agents. In S.M. Rahman & R.J. Bignall (Eds.), Internet commerce and software agents - Cases, technologies and opportunities (pp. 150-176). Hershey, PA: Idea Group Publishing.

Cingil, I., Dogac, A., & Azgin, A. (2000). A broader approach to personalization. *Communications of the ACM, 43*(8), 136-141.

Cooley, R., Mobasher, B., & Srivastava, J. (1997). Grouping Web page references into transactions for mining World Wide Web browsing patterns. *Knowledge and Data Engineering Workshop,* Newport Beach, CA (pp. 2-9).

Cooley, R., Mobasher, B., & Srivastava, J. (1999a). Data preparation for mining World Wide Web browsing patterns. *Knowledge and Information Systems, 1*(1), 5-32.

Cooley, R., Tan, P., & Srivastava, J. (1999b). *WebSIFT: The Web Site information filter system.*

WEBKDD, San Diego, California. Available: http://www.acm.org/sigkdd/proceedings/web-kdd99/papers/paper11-cooley.ps

Cooley, R., Tan, P., & Srivastava, J. (2000). Discovering of interesting usage patterns from Web data. In M. Spiliopoulou (Ed.), *LNCS/LNAI Series.* Springer-Verlag.

Dennett, D.C. (1991). *Consciousness explained.* Boston, MA: Little, Brown and Co.

Earp, J., & Baumer, D. (2003). Innovative Web use to learn about consumer behavior and online privacy. *Communications of the ACM, 46*(4), 81-83.

Eirinaki, M., & Vazirgiannis, M. (2003, February). Web mining for Web personalization. *ACM Transactions on Internet Technology (TOIT), 3*(1), 1-27. New York: ACM Press.

Hollan, J.D. (1990). User models and user interfaces: A case for domain models, task models, and tailorability. *Proceedings of AAAI-90, Eighth National Conference on Artificial Intelligence,* (p. 1137). Cambridge, MA: AAAI Press/The MIT Press.

Joachims, T., Freitag, D., & Mitchell, T. (1997). WebWatcher: A tour guide for the World Wide Web. *Proceedings of the 15th International Joint Conference on Artificial Intelligence (JCAI97),* (pp. 770-775). Morgan Kaufmann Publishers.

Kobsa, A.J., & Pohl, W. (2001). Personalized hypermedia presentation techniques for improving online customer relationships. *The Knowledge Engineering Review, 16*(2), 111-155.

Kobsa, A., & Schreck, J. (2003). Privacy through pseudonymity in user-adaptive systems. *Transactions on Internet Technology, 3*(2), 149-183.

Kosala, R., & Blockeel, H. (2000). Web mining research: A survey. *SIGKDD Explorations, 2*(1), 1-15.

Kramer, J., Noronha, S., & Vergo, J. (2000). A user-centered design approach to personalization. *Communications of the ACM, 8,* 45-48.

Krishnan, M., Schechter, S., & Smith, M. (1998). Using path profiles to predict http request. *Proceedings of the 7th International World Wide Web Conference,* Brisbane, Qld., Australia, (pp. 457-467).

Lieberman, H. (1995). Letizia: An agent that assists Web browsing. *Proceedings of the 14th International Joint Conference Artificial Intelligence,* Montreal, CA, (pp. 924-929).

Lieberman, H., Van Dyke, N., & Vivacqua, A. (1999). Let's browse: A collaborative Web browsing agent. *Proceedings of the International Conference on Intelligent User Interfaces (IUI'99),* Redondo Beach, USA, (pp. 65-68). ACM Press.

Manber, U., Patel, A., & Robison, J. (2000). Experience with personalization on Yahoo! *Communications of the ACM, 43*(8), 35-39.

Markellos, K., Markellou, P., Rigou, M., & Sirmakessis, S. (2003). Web mining: Past, present and future. In S. Sirmakessis (Ed.), *Proceedings of the 1st International Workshop on Text Mining and its Applications, Studies in Fuzziness.* In press. Springer Verlag Berlin Heidelberg.

Mesquita, C., Barbosa, S.D., & Lucena, C.J. (2002). Towards the identification of concerns in personalization mechanisms via scenarios. *Proceedings of 1st International Conference on Aspect-Oriented Software Development,* Enschede, The Netherlands. Available: http://trese. cs.utwente.nl/AOSD-EarlyAspectsWS/Papers/ Mesquita.pdf

Mladenic, D. (1999). Text learning and related intelligent agents. *IEEE Intelligent Systems and their Applications, 14*(4), 44-54.

Mobasher, B., Cooley, R., & Srivastava, J. (2000b). Automatic personalization based on Web usage mining. *Communications of the ACM, 43*(8), 142-151.

Mobasher, B., & Dai, H. (2003). A road map to more effective Web personalization: Integrating domain knowledge with Web usage mining. *Proceedings of the International Conference on Internet Computing 2003 (IC'03),* Las Vegas, Nevada.

Mobasher, B., Dai, H., Luo, T., Sun, Y., & Zhu, J. (2000a). Integrating Web usage and content mining for more effective personalization. *Proceedings of the 1st International Conference on E-Commerce and Web Technologies (ECWeb2000),* Greenwich, UK, (pp. 165-176).

Mulvenna, M., Anand, S., & Bchner, A. (2000). Personalization on the Net using Web mining. *Communications of the ACM, 43*(8), 122-125.

Ngu, D., & Wu, X. (1997). SiteHelper: A localized agent that helps incremental exploration of the World Wide Web. *Proceedings of the 6th World Wide Web Conference,* Santa Clara, CA.

Nielsen, J. (1994). *Usability engineering.* Morgan Kaufmann.

Nielsen, J. (1998). Personalization is over-rated. Alertbox for October 4, 1998. Available: http:// www.useit.com

Perkowitz, M., & Etzioni, O. (1997). Adaptive Web sites: An AI challenge. *Proceedings of the 15th International Joint Conference on Artificial Intelligence.*

Perkowitz, M., & Etzioni, O. (1998). Adaptive Web sites: Automatically synthesizing Web pages. *Proceedings of the 15th National Conference on Artificial Intelligence.*

Perkowitz, M., & Etzioni, O. (1999). Adaptive Web sites: Conceptual cluster mining. *Proceedings of the 16th International Joint Conference on Artificial Intelligence.*

Mining for Web Personalization

Perkowitz, M., & Etzioni, O. (2000a). Adaptive Web sites. *Communications of the ACM, 43*(8), 152-158.

Perkowitz, M., & Etzioni, O. (2000b). Towards adaptive Web sites: Conceptual framework and case study. *Artificial Intelligence, 118*(1-2), 245-275.

Perner, P., & Fiss, G. (2002). Intelligent E-marketing with Web mining, personalization, and user-adapted interfaces. In P. Perner (Ed.), *Advances in data mining 2002, LNAI 2394* (pp. 37-52). Berlin: Springer-Verlag Berlin Heidelberg.

Pirolli, P., & Card, S. (1999). Information foraging. *Psychological Review, 106*(4), 643-675.

Ramakrishnan, N. (2000). PIPE: Web personalization by partial evaluation. *IEEE Internet Computing, 4*(6), 21-31.

Resnikoff, H. (1989). *The illusion of reality* (p. 97). New York: Springer-Verlag.

Riecken, D. (2000, August). Personalized views of personalization. *Communications of the ACM, 43*(8), 27-28.

Rossi, G., Schwabe, D., & Guimaraes, R. (2001). Designing personalized Web applications. *Proceedings of the WWW10,* Hong Kong, 275-284.

Schafer, J., Konstan, J., & Riedl, J. (2001). E-commerce recommendation applications. *Data Mining and Knowledge Discovery, 5*(1), 115-153.

Smith, E., & Winterhalder, B. (eds.). (1992). Evolutionary ecology and human behavior. New York: de Gruyter.

Spiliopoulou, M. (2000). Web usage mining for Web site evaluation. *Communications of the ACM, 43*(8), 128-134.

Spiliopoulou, M., & Faulstich, L. (1998). *WUM: A Web utilization miner.* EDBT Workshop WebDB98, Valencia, Spain.

Spiliopoulou, M., Faulstich, L., & Wilkler, K. (1999a). A data miner analyzing the navigational behavior of Web users. *Proceedings of the Workshop on Machine Learning in User Modelling of the ACAI99,* Chania, Greece.

Spiliopoulou, M., & Pohle, C. (2000). Data mining for measuring and improving the success of Web sites. *Data Mining and Knowledge Discovery, Special Issue on Electronic Commerce.*

Spiliopoulou, M., Pohle, C., & Faulstich, L. (1999b). Improving the effectiveness of a Web site with Web usage mining. *Proceedings of the WEBKDD99,* San Diego, California (pp. 142-162).

Srivastava, J., Cooley, R., Deshpande, M., & Tan, P. (2000, January). Web usage mining: Discovery and applications of usage patterns from Web data. *ACM SIGKDD, 1*(2), 12-23.

Stephens, D., & Krebs, J. (1986). *Foraging theory.* Princeton, NJ: Princeton University Press.

Suchman, L.A. (1987). Plans and situated actions. Cambridge, UK: Cambridge University Press.

Varian, H. (1995, September). The information economy. *Scientific American,* 200-201.

Vassiliou, C., Stamoulis, D., & Martakos, D. (2002, January). The process of personalizing Web content: Techniques, workflow and evaluation. *Proceedings of the International Conference on Advances in Infrastructure for Electronic Business, Science, and Education on the Internet,* L'Aquila, Italy. Available: http://www.ssgrr.it/en/ssgrr2002s/papers.htm

Wu, K., Yu, P., & Ballman, A. (1998). SpeedTracer: A Web usage mining and analysis tool. *IBM Systems Journal, 37*(1), 89-105.

Yao, Y., Zhong, N., Liu, J., & Ohsuga, S. (2001). Web intelligence (WI) research challenges and trends in the new information age. In N. Zhong et al. (Eds.), *WI 2001, LNAI 2198,* 1-17. Springer Verlag Berlin Heidelberg.

96

ENDNOTES

[a] W3C. World Wide Web Consortium. Available: http://www.w3.org

[b] XML. Extensible Markup Language. Available: http://www.w3.org/XML

[c] XML Query Language. Available: http://www.w3.org/TR/xquery/

[d] RDF. Resource Description Framework. Model and Syntax Specification. Available: http://www.w3.org/TR/REC-rdf-syntax/

[e] P3P. Platform for Privacy Preferences Project. Available: http://www.w3.org/P3P

[f] OPS. Open Profiling Standard. Available: http://developer.netscape.com/ops/ops.html

[g] CPEX. Customer Profile Exchange. Available: http://www.cpexchange.org/

[h] PIDL. Personalized Information Description Language. Available: http://www.w3.org/TR/NOTE-PIDL

This work was previously published in Web Mining: Applications and Techniques, edited by A. Scime, pp. 27-49, copyright 2005 by IGI Publishing, formerly known as Idea Group Publishing (an imprint of IGI Global).

Chapter V
Clustering Web Information Sources

Athena Vakali
Aristotle University of Thessaloniki, Greece

George Pallis
Aristotle University of Thessaloniki, Greece

Lefteris Angelis
Aristotle University of Thessaloniki, Greece

ABSTRACT

The explosive growth of the Web scale has drastically increased information circulation and dissemination rates. As the number of both Web users and Web sources grows significantly everyday, crucial data management issues, such as clustering on the Web, should be addressed and analyzed. Clustering has been proposed towards improving both the information availability and the Web users' personalization. Clusters on the Web are either users' sessions or Web information sources, which are managed in a variation of applications and implementations testbeds. This chapter focuses on the topic of clustering information over the Web, in an effort to overview and survey on the theoretical background and the adopted practices of most popular emerging and challenging clustering research efforts. An up-to-date survey of the existing clustering schemes is given, to be of use for both researchers and practitioners interested in the area of Web data mining.

INTRODUCTION

The explosive growth of the Web has dramatically changed the way in which information is managed and accessed. Thus, several data management solutions such as clustering have been proposed. Specifically, clustering is the process of collecting Web sources into "groups" so that similar objects are in the same group and dissimilar objects are in different groups.

Clustering on the Web has been proposed based on the idea of identifying homogeneous groups of objects from the values of certain attributes (variables) (Jain et al., 1999). In the context of

Web, many clustering approaches have been introduced for identifying Web sources clusters evaluated under a wide range of parameters (such as like their size, content, complexity). A clustering scheme is considered to be efficient if it results in "reliable" Web data grouping within a reasonable time.

Clustering algorithms have their origins in various areas such as statistics, pattern recognition, and machine learning. An "optimal" clustering scheme should mainly satisfy the following criteria:

1. **Compactness:** The data within each cluster should be as close to each other as possible. A common measure of compactness is the "variance", which should be minimized.
2. **Separation:** The clusters should be widely spaced. The notion of "cluster distance" is commonly used for indicating the measure of separation, which should be maximized.

In general, the Web consists of a variety of Web sources. In order to facilitate data availability, accessing, and to meet user preferences, the Web sources are clustered with respect to a certain parameter or characteristic such as: popularity, structure, or content. Clustering on the Web can be one of the following types:

*   **Web users clustering:** the establishment of groups of users exhibiting similar browsing patterns. Such knowledge is especially useful for inferring user statistics in order to perform various actions such as market segmentation in e-commerce applications, personalized Web content to users etc. This type of clustering, helps in better understanding the users' navigation behavior and in improving Web users' requests servicing (by decreasing the lengths in Web navigation pathways),
*   **Web documents clustering:** the grouping of documents with related content. This information is useful in various applications, for example in Web search engines towards improving the information retrieval process (i.e., clustering Web queries). In addition, clustering of Web documents increases Web information accessibility and improves the content delivery on the Web.

Figure 1. Clustering information over the Web

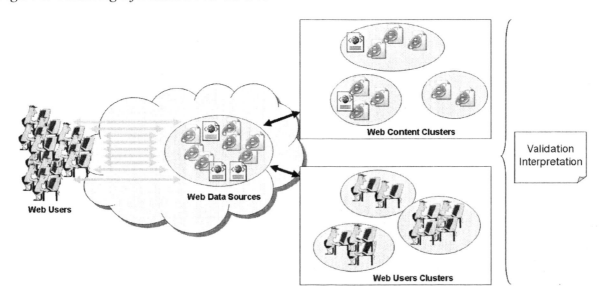

Figure 1 depicts the overall clustering idea as employed on users' accessing to data over the Web. Considering the complexity and the diversity of the information sources on the Web, it is important to understand the relationships between Web data sources and Web users. Due to the fact that the Web data clustering topic is quite challenging and complex, this chapter contributes in understanding the role of clustering mechanisms and methodologies in accessing Web information (such as documents, users' patterns). Thus, it provides a complete view for the existing Web data clustering practices which is essential both for the computing practitioners (e.g., Web sites developers) and for the researchers as well.

Considerable research efforts have focused on clustering information on the Web, and earlier studies have shown that clustering of Web sources is beneficial towards better Web data management (Baldi et al., 2003; Cadez et al, 2003). Some of these benefits are given below:

- *Improvement of the Web searching process*; clustering Web content allows efficient query processing over the large amount of documents stored on the Web servers.
- *Interaction with information retrieval systems*; query clustering helps in discovering frequently asked questions or most popular topics on a search engine.
- *Construction and maintenance of more "intelligent" Web servers* that are able to dynamically adapt their designs to satisfy the future users' needs, providing clues about whether improvements in site design might be useful.
- *Improvement of caching* (temporary storage of objects closer to the end-users) *and prefetching* schemes (predicting future requests for Web objects and fetching those objects into the cache in the background, before an explicit request is made for them) in order to deliver the appropriate content

(products) to the interested users in a timely, scalable, and cost-effective manner.
- *Adaptation of e-commerce sites to* customers' needs; understanding Web users' navigation behavior through e-commerce Web sites can provide valuable insights into customer behavior, recommending new products to Web site visitors, based on their browsing behavior.

In order to identify the Web data clusters, a number of clustering algorithms has been proposed and is available in the literature (Baldi et. al., 2003; Jain et. al., 1999). In general terms, the existing clustering approaches do not provide an indication of the quality of their outcome. For instance, questions, such as "how many clusters are there in the data set?", "does the resulting clustering scheme fits the data set?", "is there a better partitioning for the data set?", show the need for clustering results validation. However, evaluation of the quality of a clustering algorithm is not an easy task since the "correct" clustering is not apriori known and it depends on the different information sources and on the nature of the underlying applications. In this context, a validation scheme is often used for evaluating if the objects have been assigned correctly to the resulted clusters (Stein et. al., 2003; Zaïane et. al. 2002). Another aspect of cluster validation is to justify the number of clusters in a clustering result. Moreover, a further analysis of the resulted clusters is also important since it helps to extract useful information which is often hidden. For example, the experts in an application area have to integrate the clustering results with other experimental evidence and analysis in order to draw the right conclusion. Data mining techniques, statistical analysis and visualization tools are usually used in order to interpret the clusters.

The rest of the chapter is organized as follows: The second Section describes the types of Web sources used for clustering whereas the third

Section presents how these are processed towards clustering. The fourth Section presents the most representative Web data clustering schemes and algorithms. The fifth Section overviews the most indicative validation and interpretation techniques for clustering information over the Web. The sixth Section highlights the most popular Web applications which are favoured from clustering. Finally, the seventh Section summarizes conclusions.

INFORMATION SOURCES USED FOR CLUSTERING

A wide range of information sources are available on the Web. These sources might lie at the server-side, at the client-side, or at proxy servers. Each type of Web information collection differs not only in the location of the Web data source, but also in the formats of data available. In the following paragraphs, we classify the sources which are most commonly available on the Web and describe the way they are processed in order to be used by a clustering scheme.

Web Documents

Web documents are all the objects which are stored in Web servers around the world and can be accessed via a browser. In general, each Web site is considered as a collection of Web documents (a set of related Web resources, such as HTML files, XML files, images, applets, multimedia resources etc.). Typically, documents on the Web have a very large variety of topics; they are differently structured and most of them are not well-structured. Therefore, it is needed to represent Web documents in an effective manner in order for them to be clustered. A typical approach is to pre-process them (either by their content or by their structure) prior clustering.

Web Server Logs

A Web user may visit a Web site from time to time and spend arbitrary amount of time between consecutive visits. All this traffic is logged in a Web server-side log file. In particular, a common log file of any given Web server is a simple text file with one user access record per line. Each user access record consists of the following fields: user's IP address (or host name), access time, request method (e.g. GET, POST etc), URL of the document accessed, protocol, return code, number of bytes transmitted. The format of a common log file line has the following fields separated by a space as shown in Table 1.

The access logs provide most of the data needed for Web servers workload characterization. However, they do not provide all of the information that is of interest, such as identifying the Web users' navigation patterns and certain processing should take place before getting valuable information from Web logs.

Web Proxy Logs

A Web proxy acts as an intermediate level of caching between client browsers and Web servers. Proxy caching can be used to reduce the loading time of a Web document experienced by users as well as the network traffic load at the server and client sides (Pallis et. al., 2003). Proxy traces may reveal the actual HTTP requests from multiple clients to multiple Web servers. This may serve as a data source for characterizing the browsing behavior of a group of anonymous users, sharing a common proxy server.

Proxy servers can be configured to record (in an access log) information about all of the requests and responses processed by the Web servers. Specifically, a proxy log file records all the requests made to Web documents by a certain population of users (e.g., the set of users

Table 1.

[remotehost rfc931 authuser date request status bytes]

- **remotehost:** The remote host name (or IP address number if the DNS [domain name system] host name is not available or was not provided);
- **rfc931:** The remote log-in name of the user (if not available, a minus sign is typically placed in the field);
- **authuser:** The user name with which the user has authenticated himself or herself (if not available, a minus sign is typically placed in the field);
- **date:** Date and time of the request;
- **request:** The request line exactly as it came from the client (i.e., the file name and the method used to retrieve it, typically GET);
- **status:** The HTTP (hypertext transfer protocol) response code returned to the client. It indicates whether or not the file was successfully retrieved, and if not, what error message was returned; and
- **bytes:** The number of bytes transferred.

Table 2.

[time duration remotehost code bytes method URL rfc931 peerstatus/peerhost type]

- **time:** The time when the client socket was closed. The format is Unix time (seconds since January 1, 1970) with millisecond resolution;
- **duration:** The elapsed time of the request, in milliseconds. This is the time between the acceptance and close of the client socket;
- **remotehost:** The client IP address;
- **code:** It encodes the transaction result. The cache result of the request contains information on the kind of request, how it was satisfied, or in what way it failed;
- **bytes:** The amount of data delivered to the client;
- **method:** The HTTP request method;
- **URL:** The requested URL;
- **rfc931:** The remote log-in name of the user (if not available, a minus sign is typically placed in the field);
- **peerstatus/peerhost:** A description of how and where the requested object was fetched; and
- **type:** The content type of the object as seen in the HTTP reply header (if not available, a minus sign is typically placed in the field).

of a certain Internet Service Provider). Each line from the access log contains information on a single request for a document. From each log entry, it is possible to determine the name of the host machine making the request, the time that the request was made, and the name of the requested document. The entry also provides information about the server's response to this request, such as if the server was able to satisfy the request (if not, a reason why the response was unsuccessful is given) and the number of bytes transmitted by the server, if any. The access logs provide most of the data needed for workload characterization studies of Web servers. The format of a proxy log file line consists of the following fields separated by a space as shown in Table 2.

INFORMATION PROCESSING TOWARDS CLUSTERING

Documents Preprocessing

Clustering of documents depends on the quality of representation of the documents content. This representation is characterized by the amount and type of information to be encapsulated and in practice the most important features from each document should be extracted (Moore et. al., 1997). However, since each Web document has a variety of content formats (such as text, graphics, scripts), features' extraction should be facilitated by evicting their useless content. Thus, the so-called cleaning process is an important part of pre-processing and it involves several tasks including parsing, decoding encoded characters, removing tags, detecting word and sentence boundaries. Some learning mechanisms to recognize banner ads, redundant and irrelevant links of Web documents have already been discussed in Jushmerick, 1999 and in Bar-Yossef & Rajagopalan, 2002, where the pre-processing of Web documents is defined as a frequent template detection problem

(a frequency based data mining algorithm detects templates as noise).

After cleaning, each Web document might be represented by a vector or a graph (Hammouda & Kamel, 2004; Yang & Pedersen, 1997; Zamir et. al, 1997). The goal here is to transform each Web document (unstructured format) into a structured format using a vector of feature or attribute's values (which may be binary, nominal, ordinal, interval, or ratio variables). Most of the documents' clustering methods (Baldi et. al., 2003; Chakrabarti, 2003; Jain et. al, 1999; Modha & Sprangler, 2003) that are in use today are based on the Vector Space Model (VSM), which is a very widely used data model for text classification and clustering (Salton et. al., 1975). In particular, the VSM represents documents as feature vectors of the terms (words) that appear in all the document set and each such feature vector is assigned term weights (usually term-frequencies) related to the terms appearing in that document. In its simplest form, each document is represented by the (TF) vector, $v_{tf} = (tf_1, tf_2, ..., tf_V)$, where tf_i is the frequency of the i-th term in the document. Normally very common words are stripped out completely and different forms of a word are reduced to one canonical form. Finally, in order to account for documents of different lengths, each document vector is usually normalized so that it is of unit length. Then, the dissimilarity between two Web documents is measured by applying a metric (such as Euclidean or Manhattan distance) or a cost function to their feature vectors.

Web Server Logs Preprocessing

Web server access logs are undergone a certain pre-processing, such as data cleaning and session identification. Data cleaning removes the records which do not include useful information for the users' navigation behavior, such as graphics, javascripts, small pictures of buttons, advertisements etc. The remaining document requests are usually categorized into different categories.

Users' Session Identification

A user session is defined as a sequence of requests made by a single user over a certain navigation period and a user may have a single (or multiple) session(s) during a period of time. The most popular session identification methods include:

- *Use a timeout threshold*, in which a user poses a sequence of consecutive requests which are separated by an interval less than a predefined threshold. This session identification suffers from the difficulty to set the time threshold, since different users may have different navigation behaviors, and their time intervals between sessions may significantly vary. In order to define the optimal time threshold, earlier research efforts proposed a time threshold of 25.5 minutes based on empirical data (Catledge & Pitkow, 1995), whereas in (Goker & He, 2000) used a wide range of values and concluded that a time range of 10 to 15 minutes was an optimal session interval threshold. In general, the optimal time threshold clearly depends on the specific context and application. Up to now, the most common choice is to use 30 minutes as a default time threshold.
- *Consider the reference length* (Cooley et. al., 1999), i.e. identify sessions by the amount of time a user spends in viewing that document for a specific log entry. The reference length session identification is based on the assumption that the amount of time a user spends on a document correlates to whether the document should be classified as an auxiliary or content document for that user. In addition, in (Chen et. al., 1998) the users' sessions are identified by their maximal forward reference. In this approach, each session is defined as the set of documents from the first

document in a request sequence to the final document before a backward reference is made. Here, a backward reference is defined to be a document that has already occurred in the current session. One advantage of the maximal forward reference method is that it does not have any administrative parameters (e.g., time threshold). However, it has the significant drawback that backward references may not be recorded by the server if caching is enabled at the client site.

- *Identify dynamically the sessions' boundaries* (Huang et. al., 2004), based on an information-theoretic approach by which session boundary detection is based on a statistical n-gram language modeling. In particular, this model predicts the probability of natural requests' sequences. According to this approach, a session boundary is identified by measuring the change of information (is known as entropy) in the sequence of requests. Specifically, when a new object is observed in the sequence, an increase in the entropy of the sequence is observed. Therefore, such an entropy increase serves as a natural signal for session boundary detection and if the change in entropy passes a specific threshold, a session boundary is placed before the new object.

Web Proxy Logs Preprocessing

These data should also be pre-processed in order to extract useful conclusions for the workload and characterize the entire structure of the Web (Pallis et. al., 2003). In general, the Web proxy logs are more difficult to manage than the Web server ones. Thus, a wide range of tools[a] have been implemented in order to manage the Web proxy log file in an efficient way. Furthermore, the Web proxy logs are preprocessed in order to extract users' sessions from Web proxy logs. A lot of approaches have been developed in order to identify users' sessions from Web access logs. However, these approaches may lead to poor performance in the context of proxy Web log mining. In (Lou et. al., 2002) an algorithm is proposed, called Cut-and-Pick, for identifying users' sessions from Web proxy logs. According to this algorithm, the sessions' boundaries are determined by using a Web site clustering algorithm based on site traversal graphs constructed from the proxy logs. In particular, if two consecutive document requests in a proxy log visit two Web sites that fall in two clusters, the two visits are regarded as irrelevant and are therefore classified into two users' sessions.

CLUSTERING ALGORITHMS

Identifying Web Documents Clusters

The main contribution of grouping Web documents is to improve both the Web information retrieval (e.g. search engines) and content delivery on the Web. Clustering of Web documents helps to discover groups of documents having related content. In general, the process of grouping the Web documents into categories is a usual practice (Cadez et. al., 2003; Pallis et. al., 2004), since it improves the data management and in addition eliminates the complexity of the underlying problem (since the number of document categories is smaller than the number of Web documents in a Web site). The approaches that have been proposed in order to group the Web documents into categories can be summarized as follows (Baldi et al., 2003):

- **Content-based:** The individual documents are grouped into semantically similar groups (as determined by the Web site administrator);
- **Functionality-based:** Scanning for specific keywords that occur in the URL string of document request makes the assignment of the document requests to a category;

- **Directory-based:** The documents are categorized according to the directory of Web server where they have been stored.

The schemes which have been developed for clustering Web documents can be categorized on the following two types:

Text-Based Clustering Approach

Text-based clustering approach uses textual document content to estimate the similarity among documents. In text-based clustering, the Web documents are usually represented by Vector Space Models (VSM) in a high dimensional vector space where terms are associated with vector components. Once the Web documents are vectorized, clustering methods of vectors provide Web document clusters (Jain et. al, 2003; Modha, & Spangler, 2003; Wong & Fu, 2000). Similarity between documents is measured using one of several similarity measures that are based on such vectors. Examples include the cosine measure and the Jacard measure (Jain et. al, 1999). However, clustering methods based on this model make use of single-term analysis only. In (Hammouda & Kamel, 2004; Zamir et. al., 1997) the similarity between documents is based on matching phrases (sequence of words) rather than on single words. A drawback of all these approaches is that they are time-consuming since it is required to decompose the texts into terms.

Link-Based Clustering Approach

According to this approach, the Web is treated as a directed graph, where the nodes represent the Web documents with URL addresses and the edges among nodes represent the hyperlinks among Web documents. Link-based techniques use the Website topology in order to cluster the Web documents. In Masada et al. (2004) the Web documents are grouped based only on hyperlink structure. Specifically, each cluster is considered to be a subset of a strongly connected component. In Zhu et al. (2004), the authors presented an hierarchical clustering algorithm, called PageCluster, which clusters documents on each conceptual level of the link hierarchy based on the in-link and out-link similarities between these documents. The link hierarchy of each Web site is constructed by using the Web server log files.

In the same context, other works use link-based clustering techniques in order to identify Web communities (Flake et. al., 2004). A Web community is defined as a set of Web documents that link to more Web documents in the community than to documents outside of the community. A Web community enables Web crawlers to effectively focus on narrow but topically related subsets of the Web. In this framework, a lot of research has been devoted to efficiently identifying them. In (Flake et. al., 2004), communities can be efficiently computed by calculating the s–t minimum cut of the Web site graph (s and t denote the source and sink nodes, respectively). In (Ino et. al., 2005), the authors propose a hierarchical partitioning through repeating partitioning and contraction. Finally, an efficient method for identifying a subclass of communities is given. A different technique for discovering communities from the graph structure of Web documents has been proposed in (Reddy & Kitsuregawa, 2001). The idea is that the set of documents composes a complete bipartite graph such that every hub document contains a link to all authorities. An algorithm for computing Web communities defined as complete bipartite graphs is also proposed. In (Greco et. al., 2004) the authors study the evolution of Web communities and find interesting properties. Then, a new technique for identifying them is proposed on the basis of the above properties.

The notion of Web communities has also been used (implicitly or explicitly) in other contexts as well, but with different meaning and different objectives. For instance, there is a growing interest for compound documents and logical information units (Eiron & McCurley, 2003). A compound document is a logical document authored by (usually) one author presenting an extremely coherent body of material on a single topic, which is split across multiple nodes (URLs). A necessary condition for a set of Web documents to form a compound document is that their link graph should contain a vertex that has a path to every other part of the document. Similarly, a logical information unit is not a single Web document, but it is a connected sub-graph corresponding to one logical document, organized into a set of documents connected via links provided by the document author as "standard navigation routes".

Identifying XML Documents Clusters

With the standardization of XML as an information exchange language over the Web[b], documents formatted in XML have become quite popular. Similarly, clustering XML documents refers to the application of clustering algorithms in order to detect groups that share similar characteristics. Although there have been considerable works on clustering Web documents, new approaches are being proposed in order to exploit the advantages that offers the XML standard. The existing approaches for clustering of XML documents are classified as follows:

- **Text-based approach:** The clustering of XML documents is based on the application of traditional information retrieval techniques (Baeza-Yates & Ribiero-Neto, 1999) in order to define distance metrics that capture the content similarity for pieces of text. Text-based approaches aim at grouping the XML documents of similar topics together. The existing approaches should consider both statistical information for the various parts of the XML documents (e.g., the frequency of a term) and hierarchical indexes for calculating efficiently the distance metrics.

- **Link-based approach:** Based on distances that estimate similarity in terms of the structural relationships of the elements in XML documents. In this approach, each document is represented by a tree model. So, the clustering problem is replaced by a "tree clustering" one. Therefore, most research works focus on finding tree edit distances in order to define metrics that capture structural similarity. Recently, in (Nierman & Jagadish, 2002) a method is proposed to cluster XML documents according to structural similarity between trees using the "edit distance". A quite different approach is presented in (Lian et. al., 2004), where the XML document is represented as a structured graph (s-graph) and a distance metric is used to find similarities.

Identifying Web Users Clusters

In order to cluster the Web users' sessions, each one is usually represented by an n-dimensional vector, where n is the number of Web pages in the session. The values of each vector are the requested Web pages. For simplicity, it is common to group the pages into groups. In addition, a user session may be represented by a graph where the nodes are the visited pages (Baldi et al., 2003; Lou et al., 2002). Up to now, several clustering algorithms have been proposed assigning the Web users sessions with common characteristics into the same cluster (Jain et al, 1999). These may be classified into the following approaches:

- **Similarity-based approach:** In order to decide whether two sessions are clustered together, a distance function (similarity measure) must be defined in advance. Distance functions (e.g. Euclidean, Manhattan, Levenhstein (Scherbina & Kuznetsov, 2004) etc.) can be determined either directly, or indirectly, although the latter is more com-

mon in applications. Hierarchical and partitional are the most indicative approaches that belong to this category. Hierarchical clustering approaches proceed successfully by either merging smaller clusters into larger ones (agglomerative methods), or by splitting larger clusters (divisive methods). In general, differences among the techniques that use hierarchical clustering arise mainly because of the various ways of defining distance (similarity) between two individuals (sessions) or between two groups of individuals[c]. Since the distances have been computed, a hierarchical clustering algorithm is used either to merge or to divide the sessions. The result is represented by a tree of clusters (a two-dimensional diagram which is called dendrogram) and illustrates the relations among them. On the other hand, the partitional algorithms determine a "flat" clustering into a specific number of clusters (e.g. K-means, K-mode etc.). Specifically, a Partition-based clustering scheme decomposes the data set into a pre-defined set of disjoint clusters such that the individuals within each cluster are as homogeneous as possible. Homogeneity is determined by an appropriate score function, such as the distance between each individual and the centroid of the cluster to which it is assigned.

- **Model-based approach:** Model-based clustering is a framework which combines cluster analysis with probabilistic techniques. The objects in such an approach are supposed to follow a finite mixture of probability distributions such that each component distribution expresses a cluster (each cluster has a data-generating model with different parameters for each cluster). The issue in model-based approaches is to learn the parameters for each cluster. Then, the objects are assigned to clusters using a hard assignment policy[d]. In order to learn

Table 3. Web data clustering approaches

Information Source: Web Documents		
Research Work	**Cluster Content**	**Clustering Approach**
k-means (Modha & Spangler, 2003)	*Web documents*	*Text based*
Suffix-Tree Clustering (Zamir et al, 1997)	*Web documents*	*Text based*
Hierarchical Clustering Algorithm (Wong & Fu, 2000)	*Web documents*	*Text based*
Similarity Histogram-Based Clustering (SHC; Hammouda & Kamel, 2004)	*Web documents*	*Text based*
Strongly Connected Components Clustering (Masada et al., 2004)	*Web documents*	*Link based*
The s-t Minimum Cut Algorithm (Flake et al., 2004)	*Web communities*	*Link based*
PageCluster (Zhu et al., 2004)	*Web documents*	*Link based*
Distance-Based Clustering Algorithm (Baeza-Yates & Ribiero-Neto, 1999)	*XML documents*	*Text based*
S-GRACE clustering algorithm (Lian et al., 2004)	*XML documents*	*Link based*
Information Source: Web Server Logs		
Research Work	**Cluster Content**	**Clustering Approach**
Sequence-Alignment Method (SAM; Wang & Zaïane, 2002)	*Web users' sessions*	*Similarity based*
Generalization-Based Clustering (Fu, Sandhu, & Shih, 1999)	*Web users' sessions*	*Similarity based*
Weighted Longest Common Subsequences Clustering (Banerjee & Ghosh, 2001)	*Web users' sessions*	*Similarity based*
Cube-Model Clustering (Huang, Ng, Cheung, Ng, & Ching, 2001)	*Web users' sessions*	*Similarity based*
Path-Mining Clustering (Shahabi, Zarkesh, Adibi, & Shah, 1997)	*Web users' sessions*	*Similarity based*
Hierarchical Clustering Algorithm (Scherbina & Kuznetsov, 2004)	*Web users' sessions*	*Similarity based*
EM (Cadez et al., 2003)	*Web users' sessions*	*Model based*
Self-Organizing Maps (SOMs) Clustering (Smith & Ng, 2003)	*Web users' sessions*	*Model based*

the set of parameters for each cluster, the Expectation-Maximization (EM) algorithm is usually used. The EM algorithm originates from Dempster et al. (1977). In Cadez et al. (2003) a method for employing EM on users' sessions is proposed. The EM algorithm is an iterative procedure that finds the maximum likelihood estimates of the parameter vector by repeating the following steps:

- o **The expectation E-step:** Given a set of parameter estimates the E-step calculates the conditional expectation of the complete-data log likelihood given the observed data and the parameter estimates.
- o **The maximization M-step:** Given a complete-data log likelihood, the M-step finds the parameter estimates to maximize the complete-data log likelihood from the E-step.

The two steps are iterated until the convergence. The complexity of the EM algorithm depends on the complexity of the E and M steps at each iteration (Dempster et. al., 1977). It is important to note that the number of clusters on model-based schemes is estimated by using probabilistic techniques. Specifically, the BIC (Bayesian Information Criterion) and AIC (Akaike Information Criterion) are widely used (Fraley & Raftery, 1998).

Similarity-Based vs. Model-Based

The benefits of similarity-based algorithms are their simplicity and their low complexity as well. However, a drawback of these algorithms is that they do not contain a metric about the structure of the data being clustered. For instance, in hierarchical approaches, the entire hierarchy should be explored at priori and for partitioning approaches, it is essential to predetermine the appropriate number of clusters. On the other hand, the model-based approaches try to solve the above problems by building models that describe the browsing behavior of users on the Web. Modeling can both generate insight into how the users use the Web as well as provide mechanisms for making predictions for a variety of applications (such as Web prefetching, personalization of Web content etc.). Therefore, the model-based schemes are usually favored for clustering Web users' sessions.

In fact, there are a number of reasons why probabilistic modeling is usually selected for describing the dynamic evolution of the Web instead of the other clustering approaches (Baldi et. al., 2003). First of all, model-based schemes enable compact representation of complex data sets (such as Web log files) by being able to exploit regularities present in many real-world systems and the data associated with these systems. Second, model-based schemes can deal with uncertainty and unknown attribute, which is often the typical case in Web data applications. The Web is a high-dimensional system, where measurement of all relevant variables becomes unrealistic, so most of the variables remain hidden and must be revealed using probabilistic methods. Furthermore, the probabilistic models are supported by a sound mathematical background. Another advantage is that model-based schemes can utilize prior knowledge about the domain of interest and combine this knowledge with observed data to build a complete model.

Table 3 presents a summary of the Web data clustering approaches.

VALIDATION AND INTERPRETATION OF CLUSTERS

One of the main challenges with clustering algorithms is that it is difficult to assess the quality of the resulted clusters (Chen & Liu, 2003; Halkidi et. al., 2002a; Halkidi et. al., 2002b; Pallis et. al. 2004). So, an important issue is the evaluation and validation of a clustering scheme.

Another major challenge with clustering algorithms is to efficiently interpret the resulted clusters. No matter how effective a clustering algorithm is, the clustering process might be proven to be inefficient, if it is not accompanied by a sophisticated interpretation of the clusters. Analysis of clusters can provide valuable insights about users' navigation behavior and about the Web site structure. In the following paragraphs, the most representative validating and interpreting approaches are presented.

Clustering Validation

In general, a validation approach is used to decide whether a clustering scheme is valid or not. A cluster validity framework provides insights into the outcomes of the clustering algorithms and assesses the quality of them. Furthermore, a validation technique may be used in order to determine the number of clusters in clustering result (Fraley & Raftery, 1998).

Most of the existing validation approaches for Web data clustering rely on statistical hypothesis testing (Halkidi et. al., 2002a; Halkidi et. al., 2002b). The basic idea is to test whether the points of a data set are randomly structured or not. This analysis involves a Null Hypothesis (H_o) expressed as a statement of random structure of a data set. To test this hypothesis, statistical tests are widely used, which lead to computationally complex procedure. In the literature (Halkidi et. al., 2002a; Halkidi et. al., 2002b), several statistical tests have been proposed for clustering validation, such as Rand Statitistic (R), Cophenetic Correlation Coefficient (CPCC) and χ^2 test (Pallis et. al., 2004). The major drawback of all these approaches is their high computational demands.

A different approach for evaluating cluster validity is to compare the underlying clustering algorithm with other clustering schemes, modifying only the parameter values. The challenge is to choose the best clustering scheme from a set of defined schemes according to a pre-specified criterion, the so-called cluster validation index (a number indicating the quality of a given clustering). Several cluster validation indices have been proposed in the literature. The most indicative are Davies-Bouldin index (DB) (Günter & Bunke, 2003), Frobenius norm (Huang et. al., 2001), and SD (Halkidi et. al., 2002a; Halkidi et. al., 2002b).

Clustering Interpretation

It is quite probable that the information which is obtained by the clusters needs a further analysis, such as in cases of having clusters of Web users' sessions for a commercial Web site, which without any analysis may not provide useful conclusions. An interpretation of the resulted clusters could be important for a number of tasks, such as managing the Web site, identifying malicious visitors, and targeted advertising. It also helps in understanding the Web users' navigation behavior, and therefore, helps in organizing the Web site to better suit the users' needs. Furthermore, interpreting the results of Web data clusters contributes to identify and provide customized services and recommendations to Web users. However, the interpretation of clusters is a difficult and time-consuming process due to large-scale data sets and their complexity.

Several research works in various industrial and academic research communities are focusing on interpreting Web data clusters (e.g., Cadez et al, 2003; Wu et al., 1998)). Statistical methods are usually used in order to interpret the resulted clusters and extract valuable information. For example, a further analysis of the Web users' sessions clusters may reveal interesting relations among clusters and the documents that users visit (Pallis et al., 2004).

A valuable help in cluster interpretation is visualization which can help the Web administrators to visually perceive the clustered results, and sometimes discover hidden patterns in data. In (Vessanto & Alhoniemi, 2000) a visualization method is used in order to interpret Web documents' clusters, based on the Self-Organizing Map (SOM). The SOM is an artificial neural network model that is well suited for mapping high-dimensional data into a 2-dimensional representation space, where clusters can be identified. However, it requires pre-processing and normalization of the data, and the prior specification of the number of clusters. Furthermore, in (Gomory et. al., 1999) a parallel coordinate system has been deployed for interpretation and analysis of users' navigation sessions of online stores. They define "micro-conversion rates" as metrics in e-commerce analysis in order to understand effectiveness of marketing and merchandising efforts. Moreover, a tool (called INSITE) has also been developed for knowledge discovery from users Web site navigation in a real-time fashion (Shahabi et. al, 2000). INSITE visualizes the result of clustering of users' navigation paths in real time. In (Cadez et. al., 2003) a mixture of Markov models is used to predict behavior of user clusters and visualize the classification of users. The authors have developed a tool, called WebCANVAS, which visualizes user navigation paths in each cluster. In this system, user sessions are represented using categories of general topics for Web documents. Another graphical tool, called CLUTO^e, has been implemented for clustering datasets and for analyzing the characteristics of the various clusters. Finally, in Pallis et al. (2005) a visualization method for interpreting the clustering results is presented, revealing interesting features for Web users' navigation behavior and their interaction with the content/structure of Web sites. This method is based on a statistical method, namely the correspondence analysis (CO-AN), which is used for picturing both the inter-cluster and intra-cluster associations.

INTEGRATING CLUSTERING IN APPLICATIONS

A wide range of Web applications can be favored from clustering. Specifically, clustering schemes may be adopted in Web applications in order to manage effectively the large collections of data. Such applications include:

- **Web personalization systems:** In general, Web personalization is defined by (Mobasher et. al., 2000) as any action that adapts the information or services provided by a Web site to the needs of a particular user or a set of users, taking advantage of the knowledge gained from the users' navigational behavior and individual interests, in combination with the content and the structure of the Web site. The challenge of a Web personalization system is to provide users with the information they want, without expecting from them to ask for it explicitly. Personalization effectiveness heavily relies on user profile reliability which, in turn, depends on the accuracy with which user navigation behavior is modeled. In this context, clustering of Web users' sessions improves significantly this process, since an analysis of the resulted clusters helps in modeling and understanding better the human behavior on the Web (Baldi et. al., 2003; Cadez et. al., 2003; Spiliopoulou & Faulstich, 1998).
- **Web prefetching:** Web prefetching is the process of predicting future requests for Web objects and bringing those objects into the cache in the background, before an explicit request is made for them (Nanonopoulos et. al., 2003). Therefore, for a prefetching scheme to be effective there should be an efficient method to predict users' requests. Sophisticated clustering schemes may be adopted in Web prefetching systems, reducing the user perceived Web latency and improving the content management process.

Table 4. Integrating Web data clustering on Web applications

Web Applications	Systems	Improve Information Retrieval	Reduce Traffic	Improve Quality of Service	Improve Content Management	Improve Security
Web personalization	WebPersonalizer (Mobasher et al., 2000), NETMIND[6] (a commercial system from Mindlab that produces multi-user recommendations), WUM (Web usage miner; Spiliopoulou & Faulstich, 1998), SpeedTracer (Wu et al., 1998)	√		√		√
Web prefetching	CacheFlow, NetSonic, Webcelerator		√	√	√	
Search engines	Google, Niagara[7]	√		√	√	
E-mail mining	Popfile,[8] SwiftFile, eMailSift			√		√
CDNs	Akamai,[9] Limelight Network,[10] Mirror Image[11]		√	√	√	

The prefetching process is facilitated by determining clusters of Web documents that are probably requested together. In addition, clustering Web users' sessions helps in predicting the future Web users' requests so as to be prefetched before a request is made for them.

- **Web search engines:** The search engines are the most widely used tools for retrieving Web data. Their goal is to crawl the Web, and retrieve the requested documents with low communication costs, in a reasonable interval of time. Recently, the Web search engines enhance sophisticated clustering schemes in their infrastructure in order to improve the Web search process (Chakrab-

arti, 2003). The objects are clustered either by their popularity statistics or by their structure. Considerable work has also been done on clustering Web queries (Wen et. al, 2001) and Web search results (Zeng et. al., 2004) towards improvement of users' satisfaction.

- **E-mail mining:** The email overload has grown significantly over the past years, becoming a personal headache for users and a financial issue for companies. In order to alleviate this problem, Web mining practices have been developed, which compute the behavior profiles or models of user email accounts (Vel et. al., 2001). Thus, e-mail clustering is useful for report generation and summarization of email archives, as well as for detecting spam mails.

- **CDNs:** Content (different types of information) delivery over the Web has become a mostly crucial practice in improving Web performance. Content Delivery Networks (CDNs) have been proposed, to maximize bandwidth, improve accessibility, and maintain correctness through content replication. Web data clustering techniques seem to offer an effective trend for CDNs, since CDNs manage large collections of data over highly distributed infrastructures (Pallis & Vakali, 2006).

Table 2 highlights some indicative Web applications and systems, which have been favored by clustering in an effort to understand the importance and the challenge in adopting clustering under their framework.

CONCLUSION

The explosive growth of the Web has dramatically changed the way in which information is managed and accessed. Web data mining is an evolving field of high interest to a wide academic and technical community. In this framework, clustering data on the Web has become an emerging research area, raising new difficulties and challenges for the Web community. This chapter addresses the issues involved in the effect of Web data clustering on increasing Web information accessibility, decreasing lengths in navigation patterns, improving users servicing, integrating various data representations standards and extending current Web information organization practices. Furthermore, the most popular methodologies and implementations in terms of Web data clustering are presented.

In summary, clustering is an interesting, useful, and challenging problem. Although, a great deal of research works exists, there is a lot of room for improvement in both theoretical and practical applications. For instance, the emergence of XML standard has as result in developing new clustering schemes. Finally, the rich assortment of dynamic and interactive services on the Web, such as video/audio conferencing, e-commerce, and distance learning, has opened new research issues in terms of Web data clustering.

REFERENCES

Baeza-Yates, R., & Ribiero-Neto, B. (1999). *Modern information retrieval.* Boston: Addison-Wesley.

Baldi, P., Frasconi, P., & Smyth, P. (2003). *Modeling the Internet and the Web.* New York: Wiley.

Banerjee, A., & Ghosh, J. (2001). Clickstream clustering using weighted longest common subsequences. *Proceedings of the Workshop on Web Mining, SIAM Conference on Data Mining,* 33-40.

Bar-Yossef, Z., & Rajagopalan, S. (2002). Template detection via data mining and its applications. *Proceedings of the 11th International World Wide Web Conference (WWW2002)* (pp. 580-591).

Cadez, I. V., Heckerman, D., Meek, C., Smyth, P., & White, S. (2003). Model-based clustering and visualization of navigation patterns on a Web site. *Journal of Data Mining and Knowledge Discovery, 7*(4), 399-424.

Catledge, L., & Pitkow, J. (1995). Characterizing browsing behaviors on the World Wide Web. *Computer Networks and ISDN Systems, 6*(27), 1065-1073.

Chakrabarti, S. (2003). *Mining the Web.* San Francisco: Morgan Kaufmann.

Chen, K., & Liu, L. (2003). Validating and refining clusters via visual rendering. *Proceedings of the 3rd IEEE International Conference on Data Mining (ICDM 2003)* (pp. 501-504).

Chen, M. S., Park, J. S., & Yu, P. S. (1998). Efficient data mining for path traversal patterns. *IEEE Transactions on Knowledge and Data Engineering, 10*(2), 209-221.

Cooley, R., Mobasher, B., & Srivastava, J. (1999). Data preparation for mining World Wide Web browsing patterns. *Knowledge Information Systems, 1*(1), 5-32.

Dempster, A. P., Laird, N. P., & Rubin, D. B. (1977). Maximum likelihood from incomplete data via the EM algorithm. *Journal of the Royal Statistical Society, B, 39,* 1-22.

Eiron, N., & McCurley, K. S. (2003). Untangling compound documents on the Web. *Proceedings of the 14th ACM Conference on Hypertext and Hypermedia* (pp. 85-94).

Flake, G. W., Tarjan, R. E., & Tsioutsiouliklis, K. (2004). Graph clustering and minimum cut trees. *Internet Mathematics, 1*(4), 385-408.

Fraley, C., & Raftery, A. (1998). How many clusters? Which clustering method? Answers via model-based cluster analysis. *Computer Journal, 41,* 578-588.

Fu, Y., Sandhu, K., & Shih, M. Y. (1999). A generalization-based approach to clustering of Web usage sessions. In *Proceedings of the International Workshop on Web Usage Analysis and User Profiling (WEBKDD1999)* (LNCS 1836, pp. 21-38). San Diego: Springer Verlag.

Goker, A., & He, D. (2000). Analysing Web search logs to determine session boundaries for user-oriented learning. In *Proceedings of the International Conference of Adaptive Hypermedia and Adaptive Web-Based Systems (AH2000)* (LNCS 1892, pp. 319-322). Trento, Italy: Springer Verlag.

Gomory, S., Hoch, R., Lee, J., Podlaseck, M., & Schonberg, E. (1999). Analysis and visualization of metrics for online merchandising. In *Proceedings of the International Workshop on Web Usage*

Analysis and User Profiling (WEBKDD1999) (LNCS 1836, pp. 126-141). San Diego, CA: Springer Verlag.

Greco, G., Greco, S., & Zumpano, E. (2004). Web communities: Models and algorithms. *World Wide Web Journal, 7*(1), 58-82.

Günter, S., & Bunke, H. (2003). Validation indices for graph clustering. *Pattern Recognition Letters, 24*(8), 1107-1113.

Halkidi, M., Batistakis, Y., & Vazirgiannis, M. (2002a). Cluster validity methods: Part I. *SIGMOD Record, 31*(2), 40-45.

Halkidi, M., Batistakis, Y., & Vazirgiannis, M. (2002b). Cluster validity methods: Part II. *SIGMOD Record, 31*(3), 19-27.

Hammouda, K. M., & Kamel, M. S. (2004). Efficient phrase-based document indexing for Web document clustering. *IEEE Transactions on Knowledge Data Engineering, 16*(10), 1279-1296.

Huang, X., Peng, F., An, A., & Schuurmans, D. (2004). Dynamic Web log session identification with statistical language models. *Journal of the American Society for Information Science and Technology (JASIST), 55*(14), 1290-1303.

Huang, Z., Ng, J., Cheung, D. W., Ng, M. K., & Ching, W. (2001). A cube model for Web access sessions and cluster analysis. In *Proceedings of the International Workshop on Web Usage Analysis and User Profiling (WEBKDD2001)* (LNCS 2356, pp. 48-67). Hong Kong, China: Springer Verlag.

Huang, Z., Ng, M. K., & Cheung, D. (2001). An empirical study on the visual cluster validation method with fastmap. *Proceedings of the 7th International Conference on Database Systems for Advanced Applications (DASFAA 2001)* (pp. 84-91).

Ino, H., Kudo, M., & Nakamura, A. (2005). Partitioning of Web graphs by community topology. *Proceedings of the 14th International Conference on World Wide Web (WWW 2005)*, 661-669.

Jain, A. K., Murty, M. N., & Flynn, P. J. (1999). Data clustering: A review. *ACM Computing Surveys, 31*(3), 264-323.

Jushmerick, N. (1999). Learning to remove Internet advertisements. *Proceedings of the 3rd Annual Conference on Autonomous Agents* (pp. 175-181).

Lian, W., Cheung, D. W., Mamoulis, N., & Yiu, S. (2004). An efficient and scalable algorithm for clustering XML documents by structure. *IEEE Transactions on Knowledge Data Engineering, 16*(1), 82-96.

Lou, W., Liu, G., Lu, H., & Yang, Q. (2002). Cut-and-pick transactions for proxy log mining. *Proceedings of the 8th International Conference on Extending Database Technology (EDBT 2002)* (pp. 88-105).

Masada, T., Takasu, A., & Adachi, J. (2004). Web page grouping based on parameterized connectivity. *Proceedings of the 9th International Conference on Database Systems for Advanced Applications (DASFAA 2004)* (pp. 374-380).

Mobasher, B., Cooley, R., & Srivastava, J. (2000). Automatic personalization based on Web usage mining. *Communications of the ACM, 43*(8), 142-151.

Modha, D., & Spangler, W. (2003). Feature weighting in *k*-means clustering. *Machine Learning, 52*(3), 217-237.

Moore, J., Han, E., Boley, D., Gini, M., Gross, R., Hastings, K., et al. (1997). Web page categorization and feature selection using association rule and principal component clustering. Proceedings of the 7th *Workshop on Information Technologies and Systems*, Atlanta, GA.

Nanopoulos, A., Katsaros, D., & Manolopoulos, Y. (2003). A data mining algorithm for generalized Web prefetching. *IEEE Transactions on Knowledge Data Engineering, 15*(5), 1155-1169.

Nierman, A., & Jagadish, H. V. (2002). Evaluating structural similarity in XML documents. *Proceedings of the 5th International Workshop on the Web and Databases (WebDB 2002)* (pp. 61-66).

Pallis, G., Angelis, L., & Vakali, A. (2005). Model-based cluster analysis for Web users sessions. In *Proceedings of the 15th International Symposium on Methodologies for Intelligent Systems (IS-MIS 2005)* (LNCS 3488, pp. 219-227). Saratoga Springs, NY: Springer Verlag.

Pallis, G., Angelis, L., Vakali, A., & Pokorny, J. (2004). A probabilistic validation algorithm for Web users' clusters. *Proceedings of the IEEE International Conference on Systems, Man and Cybernetics (SMC 2004)* (pp. 4129-4134).

Pallis, G., & Vakali, A. (2006). Insight and perspectives for content delivery networks. *Communications of the ACM, 49*(1), 101-106.

Pallis, G., Vakali, A., Angelis, L., & Hacid, M. S. (2003). A study on workload characterization for a Web proxy server. *Proceedings of the 21st IASTED International Multi-Conference on Applied Informatics (AI 2003)* (pp. 779-784).

Reddy, P. K., & Kitsuregawa, M. (2001). An approach to relate the Web communities through bipartite graphs. *WISE, 1*, 301-310.

Salton, G., Wong, A., & Yang, C. (1975). A vector space model for automatic indexing. *Communications of the ACM, 18*(11), 613-620.

Scherbina, A., & Kuznetsov, S. (2004). Clustering of Web sessions using Levenshtein metric. In *Proceedings of the 4th Industrial Conference on Data Mining (ICDM 2004)* (LNCS 3275, pp. 127-133). San Jose, CA: Springer Verlag.

Shahabi, C., Faisal, A., Kashani, F. B., & Faruque, J. (2000). INSITE: A tool for interpreting users' interaction with a Web space. *Proceedings of the 26th International Conference on Very Large Data Bases (VLDB 2000)* (pp. 635-638).

Shahabi, C., Zarkesh, A. M., Adibi, J., & Shah, V. (1997). *Knowledge discovery from users Web page navigation.* Proceedings of the 7th International Workshop on Research Issues in Data Engineering (IEEE RIDE), Birmingham, United Kingdom.

Smith, K., & Ng, A. (2003). Web page clustering using a self-organizing map of user navigation patterns. *Decision Support Systems, 35*(2), 245-256.

Spiliopoulou, M., & Faulstich, L. (1998). WUM: A tool for WWW utilization analysis. In *Proceedings of the International Workshop on World Wide Web and Databases (WebDB 1998)* (LNCS 1590, pp. 184-203). Valencia, Spain: Springer Verlag.

Stein, B., Eissen, S. M., & Wibrock, F. (2003). *On cluster validity and the information need of users.* Proceedings of the 3rd IASTED International Conference on Artificial Intelligence and Applications (AIA 2003), Benalmadena, Spain.

Vel, O. D., Anderson, A., Corney, M., & Mohay, G. (2001). Mining e-mail content for author identification forensics. *Special Interest Group on Management of Data Record (SIGMOD Rec.), 30*(4), 55-64.

Vesanto, J., & Alhoniemi, E. (2000). Clustering of self-organizing map. *IEEE Transactions on Neural Networks, 11*(3), 586-600.

Wang, W., & Zaïane, O. R. (2002). Clustering Web sessions by sequence alignment. In *Proceedings of the 13th International Workshop on Database and Expert Systems Applications (DEXA 2002)* (LNCS 2453, pp. 394-398). Aix-en-Provence, France: Springer Verlag.

Wen, J. R., Nie, J. Y., & Zhang, H. (2001). Clustering user queries of a search engine. *Proceedings of the 10th International World Wide Web Conference (WWW2001)* (pp. 162-168).

Wong, W., & Fu, A. (2000). *Incremental document clustering for Web page classification.* Proceedings of the IEEE International Conference on Information Society in the 21st Century: Emerging Technologies and New Challenges (IS2000), Fukushima, Japan.

Wu, K., Yu, P. S., & Ballman, A. (1998). Speedtracer: A Web usage mining and analysis tool. *IBM Systems Journal, 37*(1), 89-105.

Yang, Y., & Pedersen, J. O. (1997). A comparative study on feature selection in text categorization. *Proceedings of the 14th International Conference on Machine Learning (ICML 1997)* (pp. 412-420).

Zaïane, O. R., Foss, A., Lee, C.-H., & Wang, W. (2002). On data clustering analysis: Scalability, constraints, and validation. In *Proceedings of the 6th Pacific-Asia Conference of Advances in Knowledge Discovery and Data Mining (PAKDD 2002)* (LNCS 2336, pp. 28-39). Taipei, Taiwan: Springer Verlag.

Zamir, O., Etzioni, O., Madanim, O., & Karp, R. M. (1997). Fast and intuitive clustering of Web documents. *Proceedings of the 3rd International Conference on Knowledge Discovery and Data Mining (KDD 1997)* (pp. 287-290).

Zeng, H. J., He, Q. C., Chen, Z., Ma, W. Y., & Ma, J. (2004). Learning to cluster Web search results. *Proceedings of the 27th Annual International ACM SIGIR Conference on Research and Development in Information Retrieval* (pp. 210-217).

Zhu, J., Hong, J., & Hughes, J. (2004). PageCluster: Mining conceptual link hierarchies from Web log files for adaptive Web site navigation. *ACM Transactions on Internet Technologies, 4*(2), 185-208.

ENDNOTES

[1]   http://www.mindlab.de

[2]   http://www.cs.wisc.edu/niagara/Introduction.html

[3]   http://popfile.sourceforge.net

[4]   http://www.akamai.org

[5]   http://www.limelightnetworks.com/

[6]   http://www.mirror-image.com

[7]   http://www.squid-cache.org/Scripts

[8]   http://www.w3.org/

[9]   The term proximity is often used as a general term to denote either a measure of similarity or dissimilarity.

[10]   In a hard assignment policy, each object is assigned to only one cluster. On the other hand, a soft assignment policy allows degrees of membership in multiple clusters, which means that one object can be assigned to multiple clusters with certain membership values.

[11]   http://www-users.cs.umn.edu/~karypis/cluto/index.html

Section II
Methods and Practices

Chapter VI
A Conceptual Structure for Designing Personalized Information Seeking and Retrieval Systems in Data-Intensive Domains

Nong Chen
Delft University of Technology, The Netherlands

Ajantha Dahanayake
Georgia College & State University, USA

ABSTRACT

Personalized information seeking and retrieval is regarded as the solution to the problem of information overload in domains such as crisis response and medical networks. Personalization algorithms and techniques are maturing, but their centralized implementation solutions are becoming less efficient for dealing with ever-changing user information needs in data-intensive, dynamic, and distributed environments. In this chapter, we present a conceptual structure for designing personalized, multidisciplinary information seeking and retrieval systems. This conceptual structure is capable of serving as a bridge between information needs coming from an organizational process, and existing implementations of information access services, software, applications, and technical infrastructure; it is also capable of sufficiently describing and inferring users' personalized information needs. We believe that it offers a new way of thinking about the retrieval of personalized information.

INTRODUCTION

The technological developments of the last 50 years have made more information more available to more people than at any other time in human history (Feather, 1998). The increase in widely available Internet communication tools, especially the World Wide Web, has provided a catalyst for a revolution in presenting, gathering, sharing, processing, and using information. Enabled by several distributed infrastructure and technologies based on Microsoft's Component Object Model (COM) and .NET (Microsoft), Object Management Group's (OMG) Common Object Request Broker Architecture (CORBA) (Siegel, 2000), or Java-based tools (Sun Microsystems; Stojanovic, 2003), information is accessible globally today simply via the Internet, middleware, or Web service bus. Furthermore, the availability and popularity of small mobile devices have accelerated the growth of user mobility. Organizations and information seekers now have the privilege of anywhere/anytime information access via wired or wireless networks. Technology availability has significantly encouraged information sharing between business, scientific, or other organizational coordination processes distributed over various independent locations. Attempting to expand the sophistication and scope of data-intensive applications to share and retrieve information over disciplines, organizational, and geographic boundaries stimulates people in domains such as crisis response, medical and healthcare networks, national and international security networks, and so forth to develop complex, Web-enabled, multidisciplinary information seeking and retrieval applications and services. Our world is becoming increasingly interconnected.

This increase in information availability cannot guarantee that organizations and information seekers are able to retrieve and access the information they really need. One of the biggest problems organizations are facing today is the sheer amount of information received and created that has to be catalogued and securely shared. An overwhelming amount of information from many sources must be dealt with as part of their work. The volume of information causes problems with trying to search an immense collection of data for a small and specific set of knowledge, and with dealing with inconsistencies, errors, and useless and conflicting information (Nelson, 2001). Heterogeneous information resources exacerbate the problem of information access. New information types, such as image, animation, video, music, and so forth, and databases or information systems built from a variety of purposes, different technologies, and using different methodologies, make information seeking and retrieval even more complex.

In addition, organizational and information seekers' information needs are changing over time under different situations, scenarios, and even personal preferences; and many of these cannot be predicted or are short lived. The traditional IT approaches that tried to address inter-organizational information access over boundaries are no longer applicable, as the initial assumption of the design paradigm was based on a centralized system. In other words, bringing diverse information into a central store with a predefined data structure to manage and control the solution space cannot efficiently support rapidly changing information needs or the organizational structures to be formed in dynamic and distributed environments. Changes in an organization's or a person's information needs may lead to the need to redesign a complete application.

Obviously, the huge amount of available information, the heterogeneous nature of the information resources, and the dynamically changing information needs of those seeking information make it increasingly difficult to find the "right information" in the "right format" at the "right time." Dealing with the problems of information seeking and retrieval in data-intensive domains shows that it is no longer realistic to design the large information systems of the past. To build such a multiple disciplinary information seeking and retrieval system, the ever-increasing availability of component-based design methods, service-oriented architectures, distributed infrastructures, and other technological achievements provides us with a technical foundation we can use to address the requirement for flexibility and extendibility that we come up against when designing information systems today. Modularization of complex systems into components or services that interoperate primarily via exchanging standardized messages at interfaces is one of the latest products of IT technologies' evolution (Stojanovic, Dahanayake, & Sol, 2004). A new modeling approach is required when applying a service-oriented approach as the design principle of a multidisciplinary, personalized information seeking and retrieval system—that is, personalized information needs are satisfied by dynamically composing required information services, software, or applications that have access to different databases or information management systems of different organizations. This modeling approach should be capable of incorporating information services, software, advanced technologies, and technical infrastructure in a meaningful way to satisfy personalized information needs that are dynamically generated from an organizational process. In other words, a conceptual structure is required to serve as a bridge between personalized information needs coming dynamically from an organizational process, and implementations of required services, software, applications, and technical infrastructure. In this chapter, we present a conceptual structure that is capable of sufficiently describing and inferring users' personalized information needs, and simultaneously is capable of being accepted in a multiple disciplinary environment allowing organizations from the various domains involved to describe which information needs can be satisfied by which information retrieval application, software, or information service.

In the remainder of the chapter, we first present our conceptual structure for supporting the design of personalized information seeking and retrieval systems that address the flexibility and extendibility needed in data-intensive domains. To verify the conceptual structure proposed, we apply it in a problem domain—that is, information seeking and retrieval in crisis response—to test the constituents of this conceptual structure. Finally we present the conclusion.

CONCEPTUAL DESIGN

A way of thinking delineates the view on the problem domain, and it defines the underlying assumptions applied in the process of conceptual structure design. In this section, we present a way of thinking that delineates the view on the problem domain our research faces, and that defines the underlying assumptions applied in the process of designing our conceptual structure. The way of thinking presented in this section consequently influences the way of modeling of our conceptual structure. After that, we present the conceptual structure.

Problem Orientation

Everyday, people are forced to solve many different vital or minor problems connected with their work and normal life. Information needs are stimulated when an information seeker lacks the information required to solve a problem (Wilson, 1998). Sprink and Cole (2004) regard information seeking as a subset of information behavior that includes purposive seeking for information in relation to a goal. Saracevic, Kantor, Chamis, and Trivison (1988) uses the term "problem orientation" and propose that "information provision and information service should focus on solving the problems that trigger information seeking."

Literature shows that problem orientation occupies an important place in the research on information seeking and retrieval (Gaslikova, 1998). Belkin's (1982) "Anomalous States of Knowledge" (ASK) is the first approach that tries to embed the "problem-oriented" way of thinking into the design of information retrieval systems. In this model, an information seeker encounters a problem, but the problem itself and the information needed to solve this problem are not clearly understood. Therefore, the information seeker needs to interact iteratively with the information system to articulate a search request (Marchionini, 1995). ASK has been extended conceptually over the years and applied in numerous studies of problem-oriented information seeking and retrieval (Ingwersen, 1999; Spink, Greisdorf, & Bateman, 1998; Vakkari, 1999), and it serves as a theoretical foundation for the design of interactive information systems (Marchionini, 1995).

Problem orientation in the research of information seeking and retrieval focuses on users' cognitive and internal factors—that is, users' perception of the problem, their individual intended use of the information, their internal knowledge state in respect to the problem, and their estimation of the knowledge available to resolve the problem. Gaslikova (1998) summarizes problem solving in the context of information seeking and retrieval in three stages—problem identification, query formulation, and validation of received information—and he argues that any information seeking and retrieval system must provide suitable software tools for realizing each stage of a problem-solving process. Similar arguments can be found in Wilson (1998), Kuhlthau (1998), and Vakkari (1998), where they consider information seeking and retrieval as a set of processes from

problem authentication to decision making and its quality estimation.

A problem-oriented way of thinking is suitable when we design a conceptual model for building a multidisciplinary information seeking and retrieval system in data-intensive domains. This is because the purpose behind information acquisition—that is, in a process of crisis response—is to deal with and solve the problems arising from a multi-actor, involved disaster relief/ response process. Therefore, information seeking and retrieval in our research is defined as an information acquisition process that is used to satisfy information seekers' information needs stimulated by a problem arising from their work.

A problem-solving model is a scheme for organizing reasoning steps and domain knowledge to construct a solution to a problem. In other words, it provides a conceptual framework for organizing knowledge and a strategy for applying that knowledge. To support the design of information seeking and retrieval systems that are able to realize these three stages of the problem-solving process defined by Gaslikova (1998), the conceptual structure, as the basis of information systems design, should be able to model the

Figure 1. Problem and solution

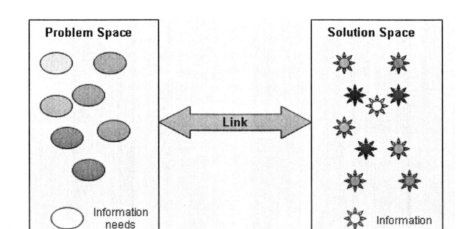

problem space (i.e., to model users' information needs in the context of our research), to model the solution space (i.e., to model the structure of available information), and to model the solution to satisfy the information needs (i.e., to indicate implicitly or explicitly how to use the structured information in the solution space to satisfy the information needs in the problem space). We present this premise in Figure 1.

Service Orientation

To develop complex, Web-enabled, multidisciplinary information seeking and retrieval systems in data-intensive domains, we need to deal with large quantities of information from different organizations. Organizations store and manage their information in distinct independent databases that have been developed at different times, based on different technologies and data management systems. Obviously, the centralized attitude that dominated the IT systems design principles and their solutions are becoming less efficient for today's inter-organizational applications and for the available technology infrastructures. In other words these approaches that try to bring diverse information into a central storage space with predefined data structures to manage and control the solution space are becoming less efficient to support the rapidly changing information needs taking place in dynamic and distributed environments. Changes in organizational or personal information needs may lead to a need to redesign a complete application.

Instead of a centralized system design principle, taking the distributed nature of the organizational process and the distributed nature of information into account is the point of departure for this research. A service-oriented approach provides a design principle for the handling of complex, dynamic, and distributed information systems. Since most software capabilities can be delivered and consumed as services (Sprott & Wilkes, 2004), a service-oriented way of thinking allows building complex applications over geographical boundaries to become a process of selection, reconfiguration, adaptation, assembling, and deployment of services (Papazoglou

Figure 2. Service-oriented way of thinking

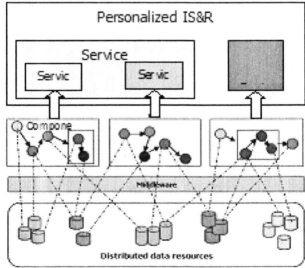

& Georgakopoulos, 2003). Services abstracted from an implementation can represent natural fundamental building blocks that can be used to synchronize the functional requirements and IT implementation perspective: IT is evolving towards modularization of complex systems into components or services that interoperate primarily via exchanging standardized messages at interfaces, and a service-oriented way of thinking runs through our whole research.

Based on a service-oriented way of thinking, we assume that an information seeking and retrieval application, triggered by an information seeker's information needs, can be built using a group of services. Personalization can be provided by composing existing services. Service is a kind of black box that has a specific functionality: information provision in the context of our research. Services are implemented on the basis of well-defined service behaviors and interfaces. The selection of services and the way of grouping services comply with the functional requirements of information seeking and retrieval applications—that is, they form the

functional model of the information seeking and retrieval systems. The concept of service should be consistently used throughout the system development lifecycle, which should be devoted to a real service-oriented design principle.

Services can be built by smaller services. At the level of a simple service, its functionality is realized by grouping a specific collection of software components that determines the behavior requirements of the service (i.e., selection of components) and the way of grouping components form the structural model of a service. In the context of our research, these software components perform the behaviors of accessing the databases or information management systems, and retrieving the information. We present this premise of our conceptual structure in Figure 2.

According to this premise and the problem-oriented way of thinking, the proposed conceptual structure needs to model users' information needs as the elements in the problem space. The information in the solution space shown in Figure 1 therefore needs to be structured as services, and thus the conceptual structure needs to provide a

Figure 3. Problem oriented & service oriented way of thinking

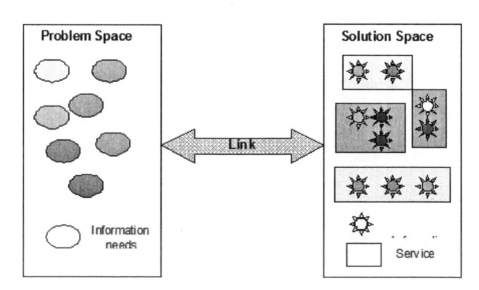

way of describing the services stored in the solution space. Finally, the conceptual structure needs to link the services in the solution space to satisfy the information needs stored in the problem space. We present this premise in Figure 3.

Modeling Users' Personalized Information Needs

Theoretical Foundation

Information seeking and retrieval is a human-IT system interaction activity in the sense of an IT-supported environment. Consideration of users of the information systems and their needs is a natural idea to understand users' information needs better, and eventually better satisfy these needs. Personalized information needs play an essential role in determining the relevance of delivered information. Since information needs are formulated in an information seeker's mental information processing process (Grunig, 1989), unless users explicitly describe their information needs, we can only infer the nature of information needs based on the behavior that an information seeker engenders during information seeking and use (Bruce, 2005).

The research on "information seeking" mainly focuses on how to bring human information seeking behavior into information system design (Johnson, Griffiths, & Hartley, 2003; Järvelin & Wilson, 2003; Bruce, 2005; Wilson, 2006). The literature on information seeking shows that there is a deepening understanding of the concept of information needs and its role in information seeking and retrieval. Currently this research area is concerned with building information behavior models to present a certain section or a full sequence of activities, which lead to obtaining information (Niedźwiedzka, 2003). The major debate exists in the factors that influence and determine an information seeker's information needs. In this section, we look at several dominant approaches in the field. Since the objective of this

section is to determine the influencing factors that determine users' information needs in data-intensive domains, we only look at the research on "problem-oriented" information seeking.

Taylor (1968) and Belkin (1984) argue that users' characteristics determine the information needs of users. Taylor (1968) regards information needs as a personal, psychological, sometimes inexpressible, vague, and unconscious condition, which has laid the foundations for a deeper conceptual understanding of the motivations or triggers for information seeking (Bruce, 2005). Dervin (1999) has been particularly influential in focusing attention on a user's needs through her model based on a human's need to make sense of the world. Her "situation-gap-use" model indicates that people need to go through three phases to make sense of the world—that is, to face and solve their problem. The first phase is to establish the context for information needs, called situation. After that, people find a gap between what they understand and what they need to make sense of the current situation. The answers or hypotheses for these gaps are used to the next situation. According to Dervin's theory of sense-making, information seeking and retrieval is one of the actions people will take to narrow the gap between their understanding of the world and their experience of the world. The "situation-gap-use" has been adopted by researchers in information science as a framework for studying the information seeking process (Marchionini, 1995).

Researchers who apply the social perspective see information users first as members of a particular community, social category, or group. They recognize the social placement or a professional role as the most important determinants of users' information behavior (Niedźwiedzka, 2003). In organizational perspective the most important determinants of information behavior are connected with the type of organization or system in which information seekers work. Wilson's macro-model of information seeking behavior shows that information needs arise from people's environments, social roles, and individual characteristics (Wilson, 1981). Wilson's (1996) extended model presents a complete picture of factors affecting information needs, including psychological, demographic, role-related or interpersonal, environmental, and source characteristic aspects. Wilson (1981, 1996) defines the work task as a central component in information behavior.

The concept of task has gained increasing attention as it provides an important clue to help us to understand why people seek information, what type of information they need, and how they are going to use the information (Byström & Hansen, 2005; Taylor, 1991). As a consequence, the work task has become a central factor for determining a user's information needs (e.g., Byström & Järvelin, 1995; Vakkari, 1999, 2003). Task-oriented information seeking and retrieval has appeared since 1990 (Vakkari, 2003). Järvelin and Ingwersenet (2004) argue that information retrieval research needs to be extended towards including more contexts, and that information seeking research needs to be extended to include tasks. Byström and Järvelin's (1995) work focuses on how work tasks affect the task performers' choice of information sources and information types (Pharo, 2004). Byström and Järvelin's (1995) model of task-based information seeking focuses on how work tasks affect the task performer's choice of information sources and information types. Similar findings are presented in Vakkari (2003). He tries to integrate information retrieval and information seeking by focusing on how work tasks affect information types, search strategies, and relevance assessments. The concept of task provides a framework for analyzing and developing information seeking and retrieval in general, and designing an information retrieval system in particular (Byström & Hansen, 2005).

Combining these approaches, we can distinguish three types of influencing factors used to determine user information needs: (1) user's self characteristics (e.g., user's personality, knowledge, personal interest, and preferences);

(2) user's roles and (work) tasks in society (e.g., user's professional roles connected with occupied positions and their role-related tasks); and (3) the environment or situation.

Modeling Personalized Information Needs

We argue that in a data-intensive domain, an individual's personal interests and preferences may not strongly influence his or her information. Information needs are determined by information seekers' situations, and their roles and tasks in the situations. For example, in the field of crisis response, users' role-based information needs are formed when information seekers become aware of the crisis situation, the professional role they need to adopt, and the work tasks they need to execute. Information needs change as a user's situation changes in response to a crisis situation, and this directly influences a user's judgment regarding information relevance. An individual's personal interests and preferences may not strongly influence his or her information needs, but personality or knowledge may influence his or her search strategies. Although different users may have different knowledge levels about their professional roles, we consider that their knowledge is inherent in the professional roles they perform within their work situations. We assume that the users are well trained, and that they have enough knowledge to detect their information needs based on their professional roles. Therefore, users' role-based information needs are determined by the situation they perceive and the tasks they need to execute when adopting one of their roles in their perceived situation. Consequently, information seekers' personalized information needs are determined by their environment or situation, the professional role they adopt in the environment or situation, and the tasks they need to perform. We show this argument in Figure 4.

Figure 4. Personalized information needs

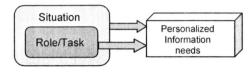

Modeling Situation

The problem that triggers a user's information needs is not directly perceptible. Information seekers need to identify the problem by perceiving where, what happened, when, and who is involved with their perception based on their professional role in a domain. In most research in the field, they used the term *environment,* or the term *context,* or the term *situation* to describe information seekers' perceptions of their surroundings. The term *environment* is regarded as a set of external influencing factors for information needs by many researches in the field. However, the definitions of environment—both in the field of research on information seeking and retrieval, and in dictionaries (Merriam-Webster Dictionary, Cambridge Advanced Learner's Dictionary)—can only be used to describe the stable aspects of the surroundings around an information seeker. The term *context* is defined as "the interrelated conditions in which something exists or occurs" (Merriam-Webster, n.d.). Most work in the field of context-aware computing regards the concept *context* as "knowledge about the user's and IT device's state." Although dynamically obtaining the physical information from sensors and interpreting the physical information as context can be used to describe some dynamic aspects of a situation, the term *context* is not capable of describing where, what happened, when, and who was involved. Instead of the terms *environment* and *context,* we use the term *situation* in our conceptual structure. This is because the term situation implies dynamic changes in an information seeker's surroundings, the influence of changes

on the information seeker, and the information seeker's stable or permanent surroundings.

Information seekers need to be aware of their situation before they realize the roles they need to adopt and the tasks they need to perform, and finally realize their personalized information needs. Situation-awareness in an information seeker is a mental process. Although today's advanced IT technology can replace a huge amount of information processing work, an IT application can only support its users' process of situation-awareness instead of replacing a human's mental information processing process. This also applies to our conceptual design. The information seeking and retrieval systems that are designed based on our conceptual structure need to support the process of situation awareness for information seekers, if the purpose of building these systems is to provide personalized information. In other words, when we model the situation in the conceptual structure, we need to follow a theory of a human's mental processes regarding situation awareness.

The concept of situation awareness (SA) is usually applied to operational situations, especially in the fields of artificial intelligence, agent-based systems, crisis management, the military, and so forth, where people must have SA to perform their operational job (Endsley, Bolte, & Jones, 2003). The objective of SA is to establish a consistent awareness of situations to allow specific users to perform their jobs better. As a result, researches in the field of SA focus mainly on helping users to be aware of their situations so that they can make informed decisions about future actions (Endsley et al., 2003). Endsley and Rodgers' (1998) SA framework, shown in Figure 5, provides a set of well-defined concepts that have been utilized across a wide variety of domains. Endsley and Rodgers (1998) formally define SA as "the perception of elements in the environment along with a comprehension of their meaning and along with a projection of their status in the near future." This definition breaks down into three separate levels,

Figure 5. Endsley's situation awareness model

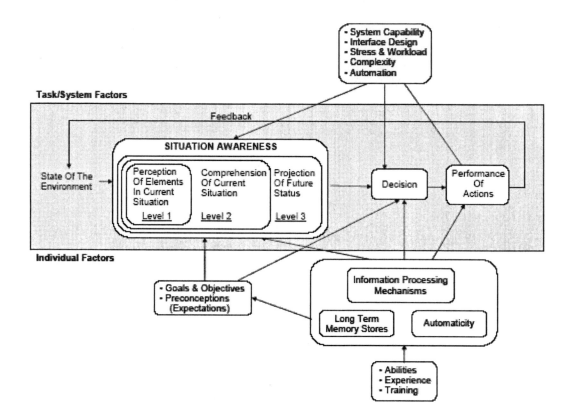

shown below, which reflect the process of how humans are aware of their situations mentally.

- Level 1—Perception of the elements in the environment
- Level 2—Comprehension of the current situation
- Level 3—Projection of future status

We followed Endsley and Rodgers' (1998) SA framework when we modeled the situation in our conceptual structure. It is not feasible to specify all possible situations in the context of information seeking and retrieval for any domain. Detecting situations based on collected historical usage data is required. This is the same as the argument used in Endsley et al.'s (2003) three levels of SA model, which indicates that the situation is derived from known information. The question of what historical data or information is required to be collected at different levels of SA processes for the users to realize their situations becomes important. This leads to the question: What information can be used to describe and model the situation?

Based on Endsley et al.'s (2003) three levels of SA model, to model and describe a situation we need to perceive the elements in the environment (Level 1 in SA) as the information used to comprehend a current situation (Level 2 in SA), to project future status (Level 3 in SA).

The first step in the SA process is to perceive the elements presented in the environment. The information elements that can be directly perceived describe the "things that are known to have happened or to exist" (Merriam-Webster, n.d.). We conceptualize the elements perceived from the environment that describe "things that are known to have happened or to exist" as the concept of fact.

Perceived facts are only direct observations made in the environment. They cannot provide narrative descriptions of the situation. Therefore, facts do not supply sufficient information to understand the situation fully. To support the second level of the user's SA, we use the concept of scenario in our research. We define scenario as a short story reflecting a situation. It describes known outcomes and the casual relationships of a group of detected facts.

Situation is defined in our research as a state of affairs of special or critical significance for information seekers during the course of a cooperation process with respect to their professional role. We claim that the situation can be derived from detecting the information seeker's professional role-relevant scenarios—that is, from those scenarios that directly or indirectly involve the information seeker. Directly involved scenarios are those scenarios in which an information seeker may take actions when adopting his or her professional role. Indirectly involved scenarios are those scenarios that may influence an information seeker's actions. Only when all the information needs have been identified and structured in a meaningful way will the information seekers be able to take any actions to solve the problem. We present the SA process in our research in Figure 6.

Modeling Task

When information seekers are aware of their situations, they are able to determine the professional role they need to adopt and the tasks they need to perform. As mentioned previously, information seekers' roles and tasks determine their information needs in a situation. Tasks have become a central factor for determining a user's information needs. Therefore, we need to model tasks in our conceptual framework.

In the research on task-oriented information retrieval, a task is viewed either as an abstract construction or as a concrete set of actions (Hackman, 1969; Byström & Hansen, 2005). Viewing

Figure 6. Concepts in SA process

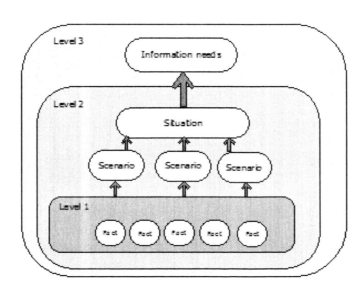

Figure 7. The concept of task

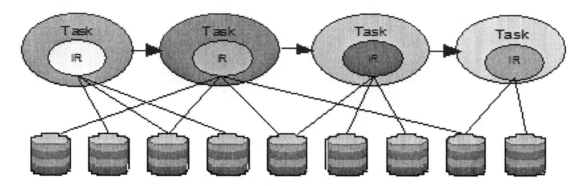

Figure 8. The dimensions of cognitive work analysis (Fidel & Pejtersen, 2004)

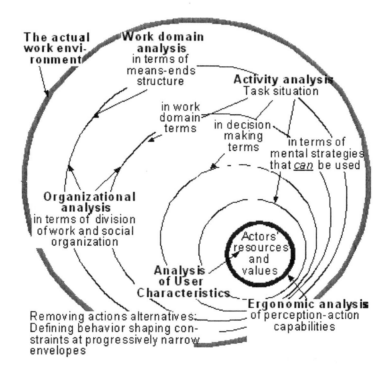

a task as an abstract is used in research, where a task is utilized as a description since individual differences are brought into focus (Hackman, 1969; Byström & Hansen, 2005). We stated in the previous section that we do not take individual interests and preferences into account as influencing factors to determine information needs. Therefore, we take the view that a concrete set of actions can be used to define a task. We regard task as a specific piece of work in which a person or a group of persons undertakes a series of actions. Information retrieval is required when an information seeker lacks the information required to perform a task.

Defining task as a piece of work indicates that it has a performer, a meaningful purpose, and an undertaken situation (Hackman, 1969; Byström & Hansen, 2005). This is also a definition that

Figure 9. Actor, role and task

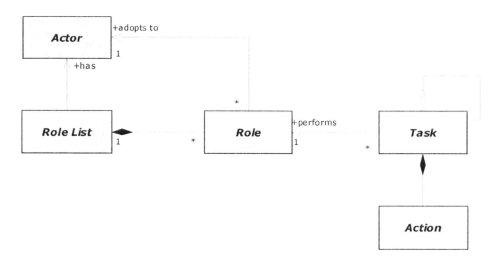

emphasizes the conceptualizing of tasks more from the point of view of the actors and the social context of task performance (Checkland & Holwell, 1998; Suchman, 1995). Literature in the field shows that Cognitive Work Analysis (Fidel & Pejtersen, 2004) is consistent with our definition of task. Cognitive Work Analysis considers people who interact with information as actors involved in their work-related actions, rather than as users of systems. It views human-information interaction in the context of human work activities—that is, it focuses on the tasks actors perform, the environment in which they are carried out, and the perceptual, cognitive, and ergonomic attributes of the people who do the tasks (Fidel & Pejtersen, 2004). A graphic presentation of the framework is given in Figure 8.

Based on Cognitive Work Analysis, we define the organizations or organizational units in a networked environment as actors. Each actor has a list of professional roles. Role is defined by Merriam-Webster (n.d.) as "a function or part performed especially in a particular operation or process." The professional roles of an actor are defined in terms of functions an actor must provide. Therefore, actors are exclusive and are based on the functions they provide (i.e., their professional roles). A task is performed when an

actor adopts one of its professional roles. A task can be composed of smaller tasks. At the level of a simple task, it is constituted of a series of interconnected actions. A meta model of actor, role and task is given in Figure 9.

A task is undertaken in a context (i.e., the situation) where an actor is required to adopt one of its professional roles. According to the definition of task in our research, tasks are required to be identified from an actor's professional roles—that is, from the functions an actor can provide in a situation. However, situation is a dynamic concept, as presented in the SA process defined previously. Since it is not possible to enumerate all possible situations for any domain, it is not feasible to define all tasks corresponding to a specific situation. Instead, the tasks can be defined in facts, which are more concrete and stable. Since a task can be composed of smaller tasks, required tasks in a detected situation can be composed of subtasks identified using the relevant facts. Tasks are undertaken in a process as the solution(s) of an existing fact. We present this meta model in Figure 10.

In this way, information seekers' information needs in a specific situation can be obtained if their roles and tasks are detected from facts.

Figure 10. Task and fact

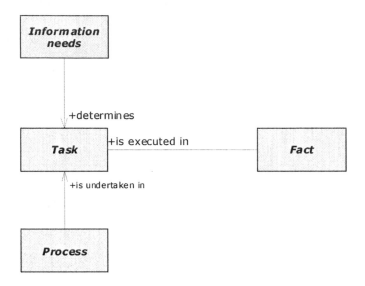

Modeling Service

Methodologies for Information (Software) Systems Developments

Information systems have evolved over the years as a means to integrate legacy assets, third-party software packages, outsourced applications, and newly built functionalities (Stojanovic, 2005). The ability to manage the complexity of information systems and to adapt to rapid changes in both business and IT is widely recognized as a crucial factor in designing software or information systems (Brown & Wallnau, 1998; Gartner Group, 1998). There has been an increasing consensus that to manage complexity and changes effectively, complex IT systems need to be built as a set of discrete building blocks or functionalities that can be integrated to form a meaningful, dedicated whole to provide specific support for specific functions (Heineman & Councill, 2001). The strategy of separation of concerns (i.e., dividing and conquering) and "plug-and-play" used in building IT systems has motivated a number of development paradigms related to building soft-

ware systems from parts, using the concepts of functions, subroutines, modules, units, packages, subsystems, objects, and components (Stojanovic, 2005). Modularization results in a shortened time to market, lower production costs, more evolvable systems, and systems of higher quality (Szyperski, 1998). Object, component, and service are three key concepts in building distributed software systems (Wang & Fung, 2004).

The object-oriented, component-based, and service-oriented paradigms have different features and benefits, and they can be used in a complementary manner (Wang & Fung, 2003). From an implementation perspective, a service's functionality can be implemented by components, and how it is implemented affects its quality properties (Wang & Fung, 2003). According to W3C (the World Wide Web Consortium), a service-oriented architecture consists of a set of components that can be invoked, the interface descriptions of which can be published and discovered (W3C, 2004). A component in relation to a service-oriented design can be viewed as black-box encapsulation of related services (Allen & Frost, 1998). Using components to implement services

Figure 11. Application implementation layers: service, component, objects (Endrei, Ang et al., 2004)

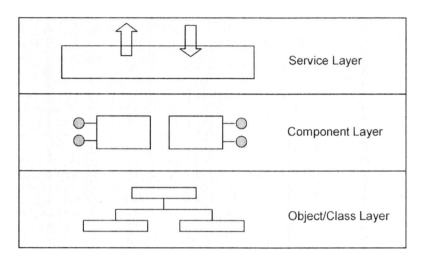

makes a service different from its implementing building blocks—that is, components (Versata, 2004). Similarly, a component's functionality is decomposed into one or more objects as it is implemented in an object-oriented programming language (Wang & Fung, 2003). Object-oriented technology and languages are the best way to implement components (Tewoldeberhan, 2005). Endrei et al. (2004) summarize a three-layer architecture, shown in Figure 11, in which services

Figure 12. Service, component and object

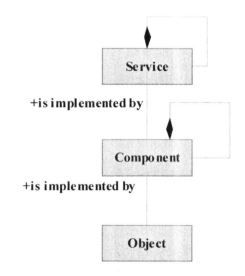

expose an external view of a system, while the internal reuse and composition are done using traditional components and objects (Tewoldeberhan, 2005). Endrei et al.'s (2004) three-layer architecture represents a generic component-based service-oriented architecture.

We stated that our conceptual design is based on a service-oriented way of thinking. Our assumption is that an information seeking and retrieval application, triggered by an information seeker's information needs, is built using a group of services. Service is a kind of black box that has a specific functionality—that is, information provision in the context of our research. The selection of service and the way of grouping services comply with the functional requirements of services that can be built by smaller services. At the level of a simple service, its functionality is realized by grouping a specific collection of software components that determines the behavior requirements of the service. The way of grouping components forms the structural model of a service. This assumption complies with Endrei et al.'s (2004) three-layer architecture. Therefore, the component-based service-oriented architecture forms a logical way to design personalized information seeking and retrieval systems in

Figure 13. SOA

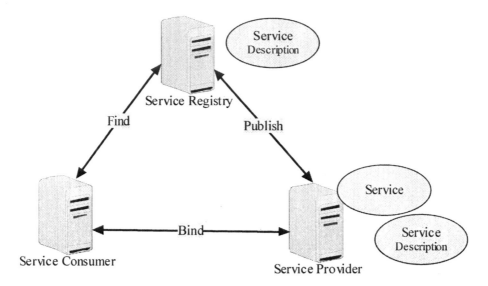

Service-Oriented Architecture and Web Service Standards

A service-oriented architecture comprises three core roles: service consumers, service providers, and service registry. It involves interactions that include publish, find, and bind operations between them. We show the basics of an SOA in Figure 13.

Endrei et al. (2004) define these three roles as follows:

- The service consumer is an application, a software module, or another service that requires a service. It initiates the enquiry of the services registered in a registry, binds to the service over a transport layer, and executes the function of a service according to the interface contract of a service.
- The service provider is a network-addressable entity. This entity publishes its services and interface contract to the service registry.

multidisciplinary, data-intensive domains. Based on Endrei et al. (2004), we present a meta model of service, component, and object in Figure 12.

The service provider accepts and executes the request from the service consumer.
- The service registry contains a repository of available services, and a lookup service that supports the service discovery.

Three operations—publish, find, and bind—are explained by Endrei et al. (2004) as follows:

- **Publish:** A service description must be published so that the service can be discovered and invoked by a service consumer.
- **Find:** A service requestor queries the service registry for a service that meets its search criteria.
- **Bind:** After retrieving the service description, the service consumer invokes the service according to the information in the service description.

Obviously, defining a discoverable service description is the key issue when SOA is applied. Service descriptions need to advertise the functionality of a service, its capability, interface, behavior, and quality (Papazoglou, 2003). The publications of such service descriptions include the necessary means to discover, select, bind, and compose services. The service capability description states the conceptual purpose and expected results of the service, by using terms or concepts defined in an application-specific taxonomy. The service interface description publishes the service signature, such as its input, output, error parameters, and message types. The behavior—that is, the expected behavior during its execution—is described by its service behavior description. The quality of service (QoS) description publishes important functional and non-functional attributes of service quality, such as cost, response time, security attributes, or availability (Casati, Shan, Dayal, & Shan, 2003). Based on SOA, we will define the service description in our conceptual model in the next section.

Information Service

Service Description

As described in the previous section, to apply SOA to design our conceptual structure, we needed to define a discoverable service description that is required for a service provider to subscribe its service for future use. The service description should include the service functionality, capability, interface, behavior, and quality.

- **Functionality:** A service must have a specific functionality. Currently, the functionality of a service defined in SOA, in Web service in particular, is usually defined as a business function (Papazoglou, 2003). We stated that the information stored in the solution space needs to be structured as services. Furthermore, we stated that information is needed when information seekers lack sufficient information to perform their tasks. Therefore, a specific functionality a service must have in the context of our research is that it provides information. To be distinguished

from the definition of service in SOA, or in Web service in particular, we simply define the *services that consume information and provide information as information services.* Information services are stored in a solution space (e.g., a service repository).

- **Capability:** The capability of an information service needs to be explicitly published. The capability description of an information service should state the conceptual purpose and expected results of the information service using terms or concepts defined in an application-specific taxonomy. In the context of our research, we describe the capability of an information service using the concepts of actor, role, task, and description. The actor indicates the category that the service provider belongs to in a domain. The role and task indicate the context where the service is required. The description defines the purpose and expected result of the service. The terminologies utilized in describing the actor, role, task, and description are dependent on the domain taxonomy.

- **Interface:** An information service needs an interface to specify its input and output information, the error message, and the required protocol to invoke it. We assume in this research that it is the service providers' responsibility to define, implement, and maintain their own service interface. We are not able to change the interfaces defined by the service providers. Therefore, the service interface definition falls outside the scope of this research.

- **Behavior:** The behavior description needs to specify the behavior a service provides to or requires from a context, and the conditions or constraints on this behavior. Therefore, besides the purpose and expected result of a service we define in a description, we can also define the conditions or constraints on executing a service, and its behaviors under

Figure 14. Service description

Service name	Provider name	Actor	Role	Task	Description		QoS				location
					Description of functionality and usage context		security	cost	Response time	Status	
					Constraint /Conditions	Behaviors					

specific conditions or constraints in the service description. However, we assume in this research that the service providers are responsible for defining, implementing, and maintaining their own service behavior. We are not able to change constraints/conditions of a service and their corresponding service behaviors. Therefore, the behavior description is out of the scope of this research, although the conditions or constraints of services can be utilized as search criteria for services when necessary.

- **QoS:** We define a set of QoS attributes in the description of a service. This set of QoS attributes includes: (1) security (i.e., access authorization), which specifies which role is authorized to access which service; (2) cost, if a service is not free of charges; (3) response time; and 4) status (i.e., availability of a service). The QoS attributes must be published.

Besides the information on functionality, capability, interface, behavior, and QoS, a service name, a provider name, and the location of the service are required in a service description.

In a summary, to subscribe a service to a repository, a service provider needs to fill in the information defined in Figure 14.

An information service can provide different behaviors according to different conditions. Under this circumstance, the term condition is utilized instead of the term constraint.

Search for a Service

The service providers subscribe their service to a service registry or a repository following the service description. The information that is provided, as shown in Figure 14, should be stored in a service registry or a repository as shown in Figure 13. In SOA, a service registry provides the mechanism for a service search. All the attributes defined in the service description can be used as criteria when searching for suitable services. However, not all attributes are required and suitable during a service search process. We define our service search criteria. The name of a service provider, a service name, and the location of a service are not always known before information seekers start looking for a service to satisfy their information needs. Provider name, service name, and location are not good criteria when defining service search criteria. Furthermore, attributes in description are also inappropriate as service search criteria. A service provider might provide a long description of functionality and usage context of its service. Consequently the description of functionality and usage context might be too long to be a search criterion. Conditions/constraints and their corresponding behaviors are important when searching for a proper service. However, it is the service providers' responsibility to provide, implement, and maintain the conditions/constraints and their corresponding service behavior. Service providers can change the conditions/constraints and service behaviors when necessary. These attributes are not stable enough to be service search criteria. The same arguments can be applied when we argue

Figure 15. Information service and task

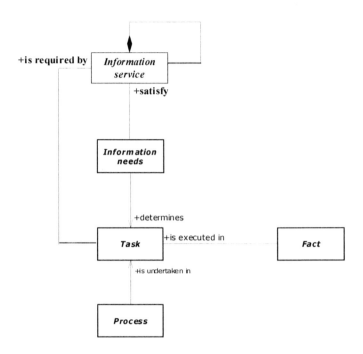

that cost, response time, and status as defined in QoS are not suitable service search criteria.

To search for a proper information service, it is more feasible if we can search using the information provided by an information service and the context within which this information service is required. As mentioned previously, the concept of actor indicates the category that the service provider belongs to in a domain, and the concepts of role and task indicate the context where the information service is required. Tasks implicitly or explicitly indicate the required information; these are satisfied by an information service or a group of information services. We show this in Figure 15.

Therefore, actor, role, and task as defined in the capability description in a service description are proper criteria for search services, and among

them, task is the key attribute in a service search criteria. Each task in a service description can be represented by a set of keywords, which are capable of indicating the information provided by a specific information service. The vocabulary used as a keyword for a task is domain dependent. When information seekers set up a query, they need to specify several keywords to describe their information needs. These keywords set in a query will be compared with the keywords of the tasks in the service description.

Moreover, information on actors and roles will provide more precise information on the suitability and capability of services. Therefore, information seekers are asked to specify the information on actors and roles of information service providers in their search request to narrow down the search scope of services.

Figure 16. Service search process

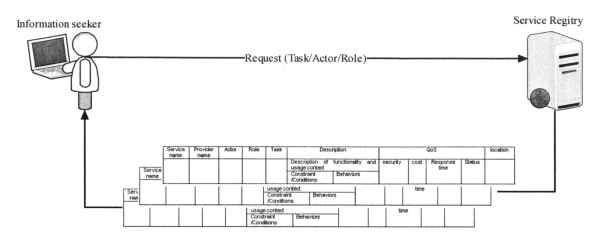

list of services

When a service search request is generated and sent to the service registry, a list of services that satisfy the service search criteria will be returned to the information seekers. Information on returned services includes all the information shown in Figure 14. It is the information seekers' responsibility to determine their required services based on a returned service description that includes "description of functionality and usage context of its service," "conditions/constraints and their corresponding behaviors," and QoS information. We present this process in Figure 16.

As mentioned previously, it is possible to add "description of functionality and usage context of its service," "conditions/constraints and their corresponding behaviors," and QoS information as criteria for a service search. The suitability of adding these criteria into a service search depends on the domains and applications. Adding these attributes may narrow down the service search scope and speed up the service search process. For instance, adding the "attribute access authorization" in "security" as one criterion into a service search will help to return only authorized services to a specific information seeker. However, we need to realize that too many criteria in a service search will filter some relevant information services.

CASE STUDY

In this section, we apply the conceptual structure proposed in the previous section in a typical problem domain, information seeking and retrieval in crisis response, and management in a harbor. The objective of this section is twofold: (1) showing an example of how to apply the conceptual structure to build a Web-enabled multidisciplinary information seeking and retrieval system in a real-life case; and (2) verifying and evaluating the conceptual structure.

Information Seeking and Retrieval in the Processes of Crisis Response

Information acquisition in the event of a crisis in a harbor is a very complex process. Depending on the scale of the disaster, crisis responses in a harbor will range from dealing with a small-scale problem, in which a few organizations might be involved, to a full-scale crisis, in which multiple organizations are required to resolve and to prevent escalation of the crisis. Information relevant for a crisis response may be dispersed across heterogeneous, high-volume, and dis-

Figure 17. Crisis response

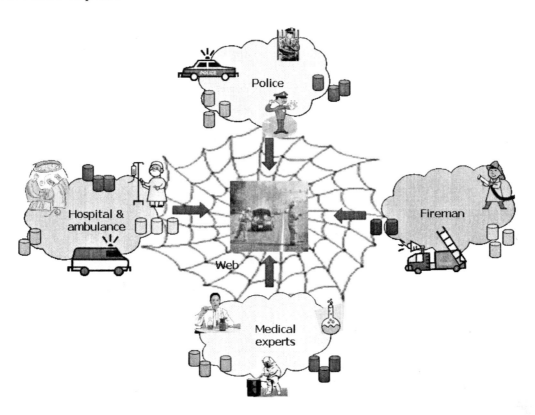

tributed information resources (see Figure 17). Furthermore, such unpredictable crisis situations require the dynamic establishment of a "virtual team" consisting of the various relief/response organizations. In response to an ongoing dynamic crisis situation, membership of the "virtual team" can change accordingly depending on the type of crisis, its magnitude, and how it develops. New relief/response organizations will join the "virtual team" when their services are needed, while others will leave when their response goals have been achieved. Distributed, dynamic, and heterogeneous environments make it difficult for relief organizations to find and retrieve their specific organizational role and crisis-situation-relevant information they can use to inform their crisis relief activities.

To solve this problem, many harbors have built networked crisis response platforms to connect all crisis relief/response organizations, and to allow

them to access, share, and exchange information. One example of such a platform is called the dynamic map, which has been utilized and tested at some harbors. This platform allows relief/response organizations to oversee the disaster area and its surroundings, and to anticipate future developments regarding the crisis (Barosha et al., 2005). The dynamic map provides an efficient way of improving information acquisition in a distributed and dynamic crisis environment. However, these platforms only serve to distribute uniform information to all the relief/response organizations involved in a crisis. It is difficult for an individual organization to select and retrieve information that is specifically relevant for its role and its rescue activities. This can cause delays in information retrieval for its relief/response tasks. Moreover, such networked platforms are built based on the centralized design principle. This traditional approach, which addresses inter-organizational information accesses over boundaries, is no longer the best principle to use when dealing with a dynamic crisis environment. This is because the information needs of the relief/response organization can change dynamically, due to the unpredictable nature of a disaster throughout its course. The tasks and roles of the relief/response organizations will change, and therefore their information needs will change accordingly (van Someren et al., 2005). The centralized design principle satisfies a user's information needs by bundling information from heterogeneous databases. The dynamically changing nature of crises, coupled with the diverse types of crises that can occur, may require a complete redesign of an application to meet the information needs for each possible crisis situation. In summary, there is a need to develop a new crisis response information system based on a more flexible design principle, which is:

1. capable of providing relief/response organizations with a role-related picture of the crises development in a time-critical manner,
2. capable of satisfying changing information needs flexibly,
3. capable of structuring advanced technologies and available technical infrastructures in a meaningful way to realize dynamic changing user information needs during a crisis response flexibly, and
4. extendable when a relief/response organization is required to join relief/response activities.

Concepts and Models

Modeling the Disaster Situation

Fact: The meta model of fact in the context of crisis response can be specified as:

*   **Type of disaster:** At a harbor, disaster types can be fire, explosion, leakage, etc.

*   **Time:** There are two types of time: a time point (e.g., 3:20 p.m.) and a time interval (e.g., 1:00 a.m. to 2:00 a.m., or summer). The choice of time type depends on disaster type.
*   **Place:** The place is the physical location—that is, a region (e.g., an area in the docks, on a ship).
*   **Involved objects:** In the crisis situation, involved objects include personnel, property, or a combination of these two.

A fact can be described as a combination of type of disaster and any or all of the other three concepts. The possible facts observed from a disaster in a harbor might be described as 'a chemical fire, at area (a), at 17:00', 'an explosion in building (n)', 'people have suffered burns', 'a person has fainted in building (n)', 'road (x) is blocked by an overturned truck', and so forth. The type of disaster is the key concept used to describe facts. The description of facts is exclusive. For instance 'a chemical fire, at area (a) at 17:00' and 'a chemical fire, at area (b), at 17:00' would be defined as two different facts, although only the location of the fires differs. Facts cannot be divided into sub-facts.

*   **Scenario:** In the context of crisis response, we define a scenario as a short story reflecting a crisis situation. A scenario describes known outcomes and the casual relationship of a group of determined facts. The scenarios of the disaster example given in the previous paragraph can be described as 'a chemical fire in area (a) blocks road (x)'. 'The chemical fire causes an explosion in building (n)'. 'Personnel suffered burns because of the chemical fire', and 'the gas caused by the chemical fire has poisoned personnel'. Known scenarios in the crisis response are used as historical information that can be analyzed to support level 2 of the users' SA process during a crisis response. Unknown

scenarios can be detected by combining known facts from historical scenarios.

- **Disaster situation:** For example, the problem of information seekers adopting the role of firefighters in the crisis response would be putting out the chemical fire in area (a). Before they take any action to put out the fire, there is a need for information. Information needs are identified using the scenarios that constitute the situation. The information seekers who need to put out the fire will have the following information needs: What type of chemical fire am I dealing with? What sort of equipment/materials should I use to deal with this type of chemical fire? Is it their direct involvement in the scenario of the chemical fire that causes a truck to explode? One of the indirectly involved scenarios of 'a chemical fire in area (a) blocks the road (x)' will give new information needs. These firefighters need to know how to avoid traffic to reach the disaster site.

- **Actor/role:** Crisis response has a social context, where involved organizations or organizational units undertake tasks according to their professional roles in a crisis response process. We define the involved organizations or organizational units as actors. For instance, the actors involved in crisis response might be firefighters, chemical experts, police forces, and hospitals. Each actor has a list of professional roles in the context of crisis response. The professional role of an actor in a crisis response context is defined in terms of functions an actor must provide in a crisis response process. Therefore, actors are exclusive and are detected based on the functions they provide—that is, their professional roles. We believe there are four main actors in any crisis response situation listed below:
  - o **Police:** There are different police forces in a harbor, such as the national police force, the water police, and the harbor police, and they all have different tasks during a crisis response.
  - o **Medical workers:** In an emergency situation, there is a chance that there will be victims who need immediate medical treatment. This will be done by paramedics who are experienced in helping victims at the location of the disaster.
  - o **Firemen:** Firemen should try to control and extinguish any fire as soon as possible. A small fire can quickly become a full-blown crisis if it is not put out promptly.
  - o **Chemical experts:** These experts are, for instance, in charge of measuring the amounts of chemical gas in the air during a crisis situation and giving an indication of the dangers for other emergency workers. They are also required to provide an oversight of hazard developments for all personnel and actors when a crisis is underway.

- **Task:** In the context of crisis response, an example of a task for an information seeker who adopts the role of firefighter might be putting out the fire. The information seeker who executes this task needs to retrieve information about the materials and equipment required to eliminate the fire and a route to the fire.

Information Service

Service Description

We use a simple example in crisis response to specify how a service description can be filled in the domain of crisis response and management. An organization called DCMR provides a service called "dangerous dust measurement." This service is capable of providing information on the development of dangerous dust clouds when the type of dust is known. This service is required

Figure 18. An example of service description

```
Service name: dangerous dust measurement
Provider name: DCMR
Actor: chemical expert
Role: chemical advisor
Task: evacuation of local people because of dangerous dust
Description: This service is capable of providing information on development of
dangerous dusts.
        Constraints: dangerous dust is known
        Behavior: provide information on the development of dangerous dusts
Security: chemical expert & firefighter in the Netherlands
Cost: free
Response time: 5 seconds
Status: available
Location: abc.com/DCMR/dangerous dust/development_cal
```

when a dangerous dust cloud is detected and the evacuation of local people is required during a crisis response. This service can be accessed if an information seeker's ID can be detected in any group of medical experts or firefighters that has been pre-stored in the database of DCMR's database. This service is free of charge. The response time is five seconds, and the current status of this service is available. The location of this service is "abc.com/DCMR/dangerous dust/development_cal." According to the information, DCMR can publish this service as in Figure 18.

An information service can provide different behaviors according to different conditions. Under this circumstance, the term condition is utilized instead of the term constraint. For instance, an information service is capable of providing information on medical solutions for a known epidemic. If this epidemic has been detected in less than five days, this service is able to provide information on medical solution(s) [a], otherwise, information on medical solution(s) [b] is provided. Therefore, two conditions can be "less than 5 days" and "5 days or more"; consequently, service behaviors can be providing information on solution (a) and providing information on solution (b) accordingly.

Search for a Service

An information seeker who needs to perform the task of evacuating people on site where dangerous dust (x) is detected might need information on the development of dangerous dust cloud (x). This information seeker may use keyword "dangerous dust (x) development" when describing this query. Several services that have "dangerous dust," "Dangerous dust (x)," "dust," "chemical dust (x)," "dangerous dust (x) calculation," and so forth as keywords to represent the tasks they serve, might satisfy this query. Therefore, these services will be returned to this information seeker.

If this information seeker is capable of specifying that returned information services need to be provided by "chemical experts" who adopt a role of "chemical advisor," only those information services that are provided by organizations registered as "chemical experts" and act as "chemical advisor" will be returned to this information seeker.

Beside "keyword matching," many well-developed models, methods, and mathematical formulations in indexing techniques can be used to develop the matching mechanism between users' queries and keywords that represented the tasks information services serve.

Figure 19. Ideal implementation architecture

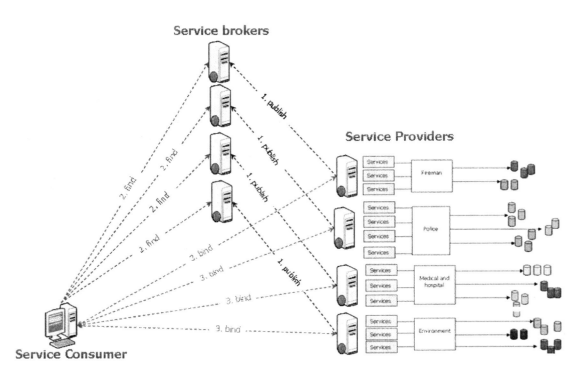

A Proof-of-Concept Demo

Since the development of a complete system is not yet feasible, due to the difficulty of building trust between the various crisis relief/response organizations and getting them to share their information, we built an early demonstration to show that it would be possible to build such a service-oriented architecture to provide role-based, situation-aware information seeking and retrieval services for crisis response.

Ideally, the architecture shown in Figure 19 should be applied. To simplify the process of building the "proof-of-concept" demonstration, we utilized three computers in our demo implementation, representing the service consumers, the service providers, and the service brokers in an SOA shown in Figure 13 respectively. We implemented this prototype based on *jini* technology.

Implementation

Jini Service Provider and Jini Lookup Server

The information provided by the relief/response organizations involved was encapsulated as information services as mentioned in the previous section. We implemented several information services for these four actors shown previously as jini services in our prototype. These jini services must be registered on a jini lookup server. The requested registration information is shown in Figure 16. We have shown a simple example from a chemical expert to display what and how information services are registered in the jini lookup server in Figure 18. Figure 13 presented in the previous section is implemented in a database of the jini lookup server.

Client PC

On the client PC, we used Liferay 4.0[1] as the portal software, and embedded Tomcat 5.0[2] as the Web server to build the "crisis response and management portal." We built two databases, a user administration database and a personalization database, which were used to support role-based information seeking and retrieval applications running on this portal. The user's role-based profiles, stored in a user administration database, were used to control their information access. The personalization database was built, where previous existing crisis situations, their constituting scenarios, scenarios' constituting facts, facts' solutions, and so forth were stored in the tables of situations, scenarios, facts, solutions, and tasks

as historical information. The personalization database was implemented in MySQL.[3]

User Interface Design

User interface design is very important to facilitate users, to help them to generate their role-based information seeking and retrieval service, and to access relevant crisis information. In the crisis response, facts can be directly observed from the environment. It is a very intuitive idea to utilize facts as the starting point of an information acquisition process, and it also matches the previously defined SA process.

However, a myriad of different facts can be detected and defined during a crisis response, and this number increases continuously. It is not

Figure 20. User interface of the proof of concept demo

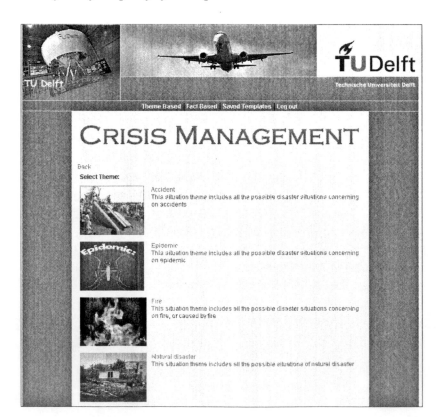

a complex task for a database to record and handle such an amount of information, but it will be a demanding task for a user to extract facts relevant to themselves from those with minor differences within the returned list. Furthermore, a simple crisis can go on to become a very complicated situation, which will further increase the large number of facts that can be observed. Users will need to answer the following questions: what facts can be utilized as a start point, and how can we handle the inter-relationship between the observed facts? These questions may confuse the users; moreover, answers to these questions will bias the information acquisition results. The conceptual design will relieve users from having to deal with this complexity.

It is better to use historical information taken from past crisis situations as the starting point of the information acquisition process—that is, to derive an unknown situation from known situations. We divided historical information on situations into different categories based on theme. This allowed the users to be immediately directed to the category of a similar situation. The user is able to choose a similar situation from a situation description, and the scenarios of the selected situations are retrieved from the personalization database and displayed to the user. Users select relevant scenarios according to the scenario description. The facts of the selected scenarios are then retrieved and displayed to the users. When users select relevant facts from the returned list, they start their SA processes to constitute their picture of the current situation. Once all the facts have been selected and formulated in a correct order, a fact-solution-task linkage as shown in Figure 7 is used to determine the required information services. The service discovery process starts after the required tasks have been identified and linked in a specific order. Tasks are used as keys to search for the required information services provided by the different organizations. When a task is selected, a service search template is generated. The search template is constituted of three

attributes: actor, role, and task. A selected task generates this service search template by filling in the actor name, role name, and task name. The service search template is sent to the jini lookup server to look for the relevant information services based on actor name, role name, and the services descriptions. All the information services of a selected task are returned to the users. Information service name, information service description, service status, and location are returned to the users. It is the users' responsibility to figure out their required information services based on the returned service information. The implementation can be found at *http://kishen.ercotravel. nl/.* Newly detected situations, scenarios, facts, solutions, and tasks can be added to the tables in the personalization database as historical information. Since the portal communicates to the personalization database each time a user sends a request, newly added historical information can be immediately utilized.

When the crisis situation is not complicated, it is more efficient to start the information acquisition process by using facts. For instance, if only a few facts have been observed, a user can search for similar facts based on the keyword "type of disaster." The users can identify the relevant facts and organize the retrieved solutions and their constituting tasks into a logical order based on their observations. In this way, the information seeking and retrieval service can be configured quickly. We show the user interface in Figure 20.

Functional Evaluation

We define the concept situation as the user's situation—that is, crisis situation if applied in the context of crisis response. Based on Endsley's SA three-level model, the concept situation in our design is capable of supporting a relief/response organization as it analyzes and envisions an unpredictable and dynamic crisis situation. Besides the concept situation, we include tasks as an important factor for determining a user's information needs.

Our task model is capable of inferring users' information needs in a crisis response according to their professional role(s) and relief/response tasks during a crisis response. Thus, users' role-based, situation-aware information needs during a crisis response can be sufficiently inferred and well-structured in a meaningful way. We believe that our concepts provide a more specific and a wider ability to deliver users' actual information needs in this type of application.

The development of an early prototype demonstration showed us that our conceptual design is capable of satisfying users' dynamic information needs flexibly during a crisis response. In an unpredictable and dynamically changing crisis situation, users' information needs change when they perceive the need for different relief activities as the crisis evolves. For instance, when a chemical fire leads to an explosion, or to a riot, the information needs of a user adopting a police force role may change from how to control the traffic, to how to disperse personnel, to how to control the riot. Built on our situation model and task model, the prototype is able to infer and construct a user's changing information needs during a crisis. While based on the service-oriented design principle, our prototype is able to support the reconfiguration of information seeking and retrieval services flexibly to access the required information.

Our conceptual models of situation and task can support both service reuse and information reuse. The prototype has shown that the reuse of services in the configuration of information seeking and retrieval applications is possible. The process of selecting and configuring required services is determined through the reuse of historical information. The situation model supports the reuse of information on situations, scenarios, and facts to infer the crisis situation. The exploration of an unknown situation is done through the reuse of facts and scenarios. In this situation, the task model supports information reuse to infer a

user's role-based information needs in order to select services and configure them.

Additionally, the development of an early prototype demonstration showed us that future system extension is feasible. The service-oriented design principle supports the realization of an independent service implementation and service model. Therefore, it provides for the possibility of a future system extension when more relief/response organizations are required to join the crisis response. Our conceptual model is able to provide clear guidance for a newly joined relief/response organization to share its information services and to construct its own role-based, situation-aware information seeking and retrieval services. In addition, due to the possibility to build up the interoperability between jini, Web service, and other service-oriented standards, more commercial and scientific information software and applications can be added to our prototype if they can be implemented in one of the service-oriented standards. This is a very important and necessary improvement to better support information seeking and retrieval during a crisis response. For instance, computational calculations for chemical pollution, which was built as a grid based on a Web service standard, could be used and integrated into the system as information services.

Our conceptual design is independent of the implementation technologies: because of the conceptual underpinning, we were able to implement our prototype using a very low-cost system, free portal software, and free service-oriented middleware. Our prototype is just one of a number of possible implementations for our design. It is also possible to rebuild the whole system using other implementation technologies, for instance, Web service.

CONCLUSION

In this chapter, we presented a new way of thinking of seeking and retrieving personalized information in data-intensive domains based on a service-oriented design principle. Our situation model is capable of reflecting and inferring the unpredictable and dynamic situation users are facing. Our task model is capable of personalizing users' information needs in a dynamic situation according to their professional role(s). The combination of the situation model and task model allows users' role-based personalized, situation-aware information needs to be sufficiently inferred and well structured in a meaningful way. Simultaneously, applying a service-oriented design principle in our conceptual design allows us to realize independent service implementation and service modeling, and quickly to configure information acquisition applications to satisfy users' dynamic information needs by choosing the required services. We believe that our conceptual design provides a possible solution to building a bridge between high-level functional requirements and low-level technology availability.

REFERENCES

Allen, P., & Frost, S. (1998). *Component-based development for enterprise systems applying the SELECT perspective.* Cambridge: Cambridge University Press.

Barosha, N., & Waling, L. (2005). *A service for supporting relief workers in the port, the final assignment in the course of Service Systems Engineering in 2004-2005.* Faculty of Technology, Policy and Management, Delft University of Technology Delft, The Netherlands.

Belkin, N.J. (1984). Cognitive models and information transfer. *Social Science Information Studies, 4,* 111–129.

Brown, A.W., & Wallnau, K.C. (1998). The current status of component-based software engineering. *IEEE Software,* (September/October).

Bruce, H. (2005). Personal, anticipated information need. *Information Research, 10*(3) paper 232. Retrieved from *http://InformationR.net/ir/10-3/paper232.html*

Byström, K., & Hansen, P. (2005). Conceptual framework for tasks in information studies. *Journal of the American Society for Information Science and Technology, 56*(10), 1050–1061. Retrieved from *http://www3.interscience.wiley.com/cgibin/fulltext/110497382/PDFSTART*

Byström, K., & Järvelin, K. (1995). Task complexity affects information seeking and use. *Information Processing & Management, 31*(2), 191–213.

Bui, T., Cho, S., Sankaran, S., & Sovereign, M. (2000). A framework for designing a global information network for multinational humanitarian assistance/disaster relief. *Information Systems Frontiers, 1*(4), 427–442.

Cambridge Advanced Learner's Dictionary. (n.d.). Retrieved from http://dictionary.cambridge.org/results.asp?searchword=environment&x=56&y=7

Casati, F., Shan, E., Dayal, U., & Shan, M. (2003). Business oriented management of Web services. *Communications of the ACM, 46*(10), 55–60.

Checkland, P., & Holwell, S. (1998). *Information, systems and information systems: Making sense of the field.* New York: John Wiley & Sons.

Dervin, B. (1999). On studying information seeking methodologically: The implications of connecting meta theory to method. *Information Processing & Management, 35*(6), 727–750.

Dervin, B., & Nilan, M.S. (1986). Information needs and uses. *Annual Review of Information Science and Technology (ARIST), 21,* 3–33.

Douglas, K.B. (2003). *Web services and service-oriented architectures: The savvy manager's guide.* San Francisco: Morgan Kaufmann.

Endrei, M., Ang, J., Arsanjani, A., Chua, S., Comte, P., & Krogdahl, P. (2004). *Patterns: Service-oriented architecture and Web services.* Retrieved from http://www.redbooks.ibm.com/redbooks/pdfs/sg246303.pdf

Endsley, M.R., Bolte, B., & Jones, D.G. (2003). *Designing for situation awareness: An approach to user-centered design.* London: Taylor & Francis.

Endsley, M.R., & Rodgers, M.D. (1988). Distribution of attention, situation awareness, and workload in a passive air traffic control task: Implications for operational errors and automation. *Air Traffic Control Quarterly, 6*(1), 21–44.

Feather, J. (1998). *In the information society: A study of continuity and change* (p. 11). London: Library Association.

Fidel, R., & Pejtersen, A.M. (2004). From information behavior research to the design of information systems: The Cognitive Work Analysis framework. *Information Research, 10*(1), paper 210. Retrieved from http://InformationR.net/ir/10-1/paper210.html

Gaslikova, I. (1999). Information Seeking in Context and the development of information systems. *Information Research, 5*(1). Retrieved from *http://informationr.net/ir/5-1/paper67.html*

González-Rivera, R. (2006, February). *Information coordination service for situation aware process orchestration: Improving time to action in emergency response.* Draft PhD Proposal, Delft University of Technology, The Netherlands.

Grunig, J. (1989). Publics, audience and market segments: Segmentation principles for campaigns. In C. Salmon (Ed.), *Information campaigns: Balancing social values and social change* (pp. 199–228). Beverly Hills, CA: Sage.

Hackman, J.R. (1969). Towards understanding the role of tasks in behavioral research. *Acta Psychologica, 31,* 97–128.

Heineman, G.T., & Councill, W.T. (2001). *Component based software engineering: Putting the pieces together.* Upper Saddle River, NJ: Addison-Wesley.

Ingwersen, P. (1999). Cognitive information retrieval. *Annual Review of Information Science and Technology, 34,* 3–52.

Järvelin, K., & Ingwersen, P. (2004). Information seeking research needs extension towards tasks and technology. *Information Research, 10*(1), paper 212.

Kim, W. (2002). Personalization: Definition, status, and challenges ahead. *Journal of Object Technology, 1*(1), 29–40.

Kuhlthau, C.C. (1991). Inside the search process: Information seeking from the user's perspective. *Journal of the American Society for Information Science, 42*(5), 361–371.

Magoulas, G.D., & Dimakopoulos, D.N. (2005). Designing personalized information access to structured information spaces. *Proceedings of the Workshop on New Technologies for Personalized Information Access* (pp. 64–73).

Marchionini, G. (1995). *Information seeking in electronic environments.* Cambridge: Pres Syndicate of the University of Cambridge.

Mehrotra, S., Butts, C., Kalashnikov, D., Venkatasubramanian, N., Rao, R., Chockalingam, G., Eguchi, R., Adams, B., & Huyck, C. (2004). Project rescue: Challenges in responding to the unexpected. *SPIE, 5304*(January), 179–192.

Merriam-Webster. (n.d.). Retrieved from http://www.m-w.com

Mork, L. (2002). Technology tools for crisis response. *Risk Management, 49*(10), 44–50.

Nelson, M.R. (2001). *We have the information you want, but getting it will cost you: Being held hostage by information overload.* Retrieved from http://www.acm.org/crossroads/xrds1-1/mnelson.html

Niedźwiedzka, B. (2003). A proposed general model of information behavior. *Information Research, 9*(1) paper 164.

Papazoglou, M.P. (2003, December 10–12). Service-oriented computing: Concepts, characteristics and directions. *Proceedings of the Conference on Web Information Systems Engineering* (WISE 2003) pp. 3–12).

Papazoglou, M.P., & Georgakopoulos, D. (2003). Introduction to service-oriented computing. *Communications of the ACM, 46*(10), 24–28.

Pharo, N. (2004). A new model of information behavior based on the search situation transition schema, library and information science. *Information Research, 10*(1), paper 203.

Saracevic, T., Kantor, P., Chamis, A.Y., & Trivison, D. (1988). A study of information seeking and retrieving, I: Background and methodology. *Journal of the American Society for Information Science, 39,* 161–176.

Siegel, J. (2000). *CORBA 3: Fundamentals and programming.* New York: OMG Press/John Wiley & Sons.

Spink, A., Greisdorf, H., & Bateman, J. (1998). From highly relevant to not relevant: Examining different regions of relevance. *Information Processing & Management, 34*(5), 599–621.

Sprott, D., & Wilkes, L. (2004). Understanding service oriented architecture. *Microsoft Architect Journal,* (January).

Stojanovic, Z. (2003). *An integrated component-oriented framework for effective and flexible enterprise distributed systems development.* Systems Engineering Group, Faculty of Technology, Policy and Management, Delft University of Technology, The Netherlands.

Stojanovic, Z. (2005). *A method for component-based and service-oriented software systems engineering.* Doctoral Dissertation, Delft University of Technology, The Netherlands.

Stojanovic, Z., Dahanayake, A., & Sol, H.G. (2004). *An approach to component based and service-oriented system architecture design.* Faculty of Technology, Policy and Management, Delft University of Technology, The Netherlands.

Szyperski, C. (1998). *Component software: Beyond object orient programming.* Boston: ACM Press/Addison-Wesley.

Taylor, R. (1968). Question negotiation and information seeking in libraries. *College and Research Libraries, 29*(3), 178–194.

Taylor, R. (1991). Information use environments. In B. Dervin & M.J. Voigt (Eds.), *Progress in communication sciences* (pp. 217–255).

Tewoldeberhan, T.W. (2005). *Gaining insight into business networks, a simulation based support environment to improve process orchestration.* PhD Dissertation, Technology University of Delft, The Netherlands.

Turoff, M., Chumer, M., Van de Walle, B., & Yao, X. (2003). The design of emergency response management information systems (ERMIS). *Journal of Information Technology Theory & Application.*

Vakkari, P. (2003). Task-based information searching. *Annual Review of Information Science and Technology (ARIST), 37,* 413–464.

van Someren, M., Netten, N., Evers, V., Cramer, H., de Hoog, R., & Bruinsma, G. (2005, April). A trainable information distribution system to support crisis management. *Proceedings of the Second International ISCRAM Conference,* Brussels, Belgium.

Versata. (2004). *Understanding service-oriented architecture.* Retrieved from http://whitepapers. zdnet.com/whitepaper.aspx?&docid=288390&p romo=100511

Wang, G., & Fung, C.K. (2004, January 5–8). Architecture paradigms and their influences and impacts on component-based software systems. *Proceedings of the 37th Annual Hawaii International Conference on System Sciences.*

Wilson, T.D. (1981). On user studies and information needs. *Journal of Documentation, 37*(1), 3–15.

Wilson, T.D. (1998). Exploring models of information behavior: The 'uncertainty' project. *Information Processing and Management: An International Journal, 35*(6), 839–849.

Yau, S.S., & Huang, D. (2006). Mobile middleware for situation-aware service discovery and coordination. In P. Bellavista & A. Corradi (Eds.), *Handbook of mobile middleware.*

Yau, S.S., Huang, D., Gong, H., & Davulcu, H. (2005, July). Situation-awareness for adaptive coordination in service-based systems. *Proceedings of the 29th Annual International Computer Software and Applications Conference* (COMPSAC 2005) (vol. pp. 107–112).

Yau, S.S., Liu, H., & Yao, D. (2003). Situation-aware personalized information retrieval for mobile Internet. *Proceedings of the 27th Annual International Computer Software and Applications Conference* (p. 638).

ENDNOTES

[1] Information about Liferay can be found at *http://www.liferay.com/web/guest/home.*

[2] Information about Tomcat can be found at *http://tomcat.apache.org/.*

[3] Information about MySQL can be found at *http://www.mysql.com.*

Chapter VII
Privacy Control Requirements for Context-Aware Mobile Services

Amr Ali Eldin
Accenture BV, The Netherlands

Zoran Stojanovic
IBM Nederland BV, The Netherlands

ABSTRACT

With the rapid developments of mobile telecommunications technology over the last two decades, a new computing paradigm known as 'anywhere and anytime' or 'ubiquitous' computing has evolved. Consequently, attention has been given not only to extending current Web services and mobile service models and architectures, but increasingly also to make these services context-aware. Privacy represents one of the hot topics that has questioned the success of these services. In this chapter, we discuss the different requirements of privacy control in context-aware services architectures. Further, we present the different functionalities needed to facilitate this control. The main objective of this control is to help end users make consent decisions regarding their private information collection under conditions of uncertainty. The proposed functionalities have been prototyped and integrated in a UMTS location-based mobile services testbed platform on a university campus. Users have experienced the services in real time. A survey of users' responses on the privacy functionality has been carried out and analyzed as well. Users' collected response on the privacy functionality was positive in most cases. Additionally, results obtained reflected the feasibility and usability of this approach.

INTRODUCTION

Despite the expected benefits behind ambient technology and the need for developing more and more context-aware applications, we enunciate that privacy represents a major challenge for the success and widespread adoption of these services. This is due to the collection of a huge amount of users' contextual information, threatening their privacy concerns. Controlling users' information collection represents a logical way to let users get more acquainted with these context-aware services. Additionally, this control requires users to be able to make what is known as *consent* decisions, which face a high degree of uncertainty due to the nature of this environment and the lack of experience from the user side with information collectors' privacy policies. Therefore, intelligent techniques are required in order to deal with this uncertainty.

Context-aware applications are applications that collect user context and give content that is adapted to it. There have been different scenarios in the literature that describe how a context-aware application would look. Mainly, the idea is that the user's environment is populated with large numbers of sensors that collect information about users in order to provide useful content or services that are adapted to his or her context. Although this personalized functionality would be very helpful for the user, it allows collecting parties to know sensitive information about users that can violate their privacy, unless these applications have taken special measures and practices to support their privacy needs.

Informed consent is one of the requirements of the European Directive (2002). Accordingly, a user should be asked to give his or her informed consent before any context collection. From a usability point of view, it will be difficult to let each user enter his or her response each time context is collected. Increasingly, the type of collected data will highly influence his or her privacy concerns. The problem becomes even more complex when more than one party gets involved in collecting user information, for example third parties. Third parties of a certain information collector represent unknown parties to the user. Despite that the first information collector might list in its privacy policy that user information is being given to those third parties in one way or another, it is not possible yet in the literature (Hauser & Kabatnik, 2001) to provide a means for the user to know which party collects which information. Thus

uncertainty takes over when a user gets pushed information or services from unknown collectors whether to give them consent or not.

PROBLEM DESCRIPTION AND RELATED WORK

In this section, we discuss the motivation behind this work and the type of research problem we are addressing. The problem investigated in this work can be seen as a multidisciplinary problem where legal, social, and technical domains are concerned with providing solutions. In this work, we focus on the technological perspective, taking into consideration requirements set by the other domains.

There is a trade-off between users' privacy needs and their motivation behind giving private information away. Complete privacy is impossible in a society where a user would have to interact with other members of the society such as colleagues, friends, or family members. Each flow of user information would reveal some private information about him or her, at least to the other destination. Since this flow of information is needed and may be initiated by the user, he or she would have to make sure that the other party (the destination) is going to keep his or her privacy requirements. Privacy policies and legal contracts help users and service providers reach an agreement on the type of privacy users would have. However, these contracts do not provide enough flexibility for users on choosing the type of privacy they need. It also does not guarantee that their privacy will not be violated, but it guarantees that the user would have the rights to sew them if these agreed-upon contracts were violated.

Privacy-enhancing technologies (PETs) are assumed to help reduce privacy threats. Privacy threats emerge as a result of the linkage between identities and users' contextual data. Therefore, most literature has focused on the separation between both types of information: whether to control users' identities, by deterring identity capturing through anonymity solutions (Camenisch & Herreweghen, 2002; Chaum, 1985; Lysyanskayal, Rivest, Sahai, & Wolf, 1999); or to control private information perception such as watermarking techniques as in Agrawal and Kiernan (2002), distributing and encrypting of data packets in Clifton, Kantarcioglu, Vaidya, Lin, and Zhu (2002), and physical security through limiting data access within a specified area (Langheinrich, 2001). Most of the previous efforts lack the involvement of users. Stated differently, user control of their privacy has not been taken seriously as a requirement for the design of context-aware services in previous efforts. Instead, a lot of effort has concentrated on developing sophisticated encryption mechanisms that prohibit unauthorized access to private information when stored locally on a database server managed by the information collector or by a trusted third party. We argue that not only user identity information, but also other information with different degrees of confidentiality, can represent a private matter as well, especially when user context is associated with them. Therefore, controlling user contextual information collection could represent a more realistic approach in such context-aware systems. Controlling users' contextual information perception implies making decisions of whether to allow contextual entities to be collected by a certain party or not in what is known as user consent decisions.

The Platform for Privacy Preferences (P3P), submitted by the World Wide Web Consortium (W3C), provides a mechanism to ensure that users can better understand service providers' privacy policies before they submit their personal information, but it does not provide a technical mechanism to enforce privacy protection and to make sure that organizations work according to their stated policies (Cranor, Langheinrich, Marchiori, Presler-Marshall, & Reagle, 2004). However, there have been some efforts to extend P3P to the mobile environment to provide users with control over their location data. Most of these efforts focused more on the technical facilitation of this extension to suit mobile devices and communication protocols, such as Langheinrich (2002) and Nilsson, Lindskog, and Fischer-Hübner (2001). More work is required before the P3P protocol becomes widely applicable for the mobile environment due to its limitations in automating this expression and evaluation of privacy policies, and users preferences by the limited capabilities of the context-aware mobile devices, the dynamic changing context of users, and the large number of context information collectors.

In P3P (Cranor et al., 2004) and APPEL (Cranor, Langheinrich, & Marchiori, 2002), it is assumed that users' consent should be given as one entity per all collected information. In privacy-threatening situations, APPEL evaluation will block only identifying information from being transferred to the collector side. In one effort to design a privacy control architecture, Rodden, Friday, Henk, and Dix (2002) propose a minimal asymmetry approach to control personal location information. A trusted party keeps location information structured in such a way that other parties cannot have full access privileges until they have reached a service agreement. Moreover, user identities are replaced with pseudonyms when other parties collect the location information. Although this approach gives users more control capabilities, it does not provide a means of reducing the intensive involvement of users.

Although a lot of efforts on privacy protection have been exerted in the literature (Ackerman, Darrell, & Weitzner, 2001; Camenisch & Herreweghen, 2002; Casal, 2001), not many have realized the option that privacy can be negotiable. A user might be willing to share his or her information with information collectors in order to get some cheaper service or a better offer. What makes it complex is that users' privacy concerns can be influenced not only by mostly known factors such as culture and age, but also by their context or situation when the information is requested. This influence of context becomes noticeable in environments where the users' context is expected to change.

In the following section, we give a brief overview of the most famous privacy principles.

PRIVACY PRINCIPLES AND REQUIREMENTS

Privacy architectures try to meet the fair information practices (FIP) principles developed since the 1970s. The most well-known principles were set in 1980 by the Organization for Economic Cooperation and Development (OECD) in the form of the Guidelines on the Protection and Transborder Flows of Personal Data. We briefly present these principles (OECD, 2003):

- **Collection limitation principle:** This principle states that there should be limits to personal data collection, and that it should be obtained in a lawful means and with the consent of the user.
- **Data quality principle:** Data collection should be relevant to the purposes for which it was collected.
- **Purpose specification principle:** Purposes should be specified before the collection of the data and not after.
- **Use limitation principle:** Personal data should not be made available or otherwise used for purposes other than those specified, except by the consent of the user or by the authority of law.
- **Security safeguards principle:** Personal data should be protected by reasonable security safeguards against such risks as loss or unauthorized access, destruction, use modification, or disclosure of data.
- **Openness principle:** There should be a general policy of openness about developments, practices, and policies with respect to personal data.

- **Individual participation principle:** An individual should have the right to control his or her data after being collected by erasing, completing, or amending it, and should be able to communicate with the data collector about the type of data being collected.
- **Accountability principle:** The data collector should be accountable for complying with measures that give effect to the principles stated above.

Most of privacy laws and self-regulatory frameworks basically follow the above-mentioned principles. In order to meet the above-mentioned first two principles, users should be notified on what information is being collected, which parties are using the information, for which purpose, and how long it will be used (Ackerman, Darrell, & Weitzner, 2001; Casal, 2001). This notification is mainly done through defining what is called *data practices*. These practices are usually expressed in privacy policies. A privacy policy consists of a number of statements that represent how an information collector is going to deal with the collected information. Most Web sites currently notify users using privacy policies. However, most of these policies are so long that users do not read or understand them completely (Cranor, Guduru, & Arjula, 2006). This leads to the fact that this requirement is not always met, and thus users can lose one of their rights in having control of their private information. Secondly, users should be able to select among different options. The mostly adopted approach, however, "take it or leave it," should not be any longer applied.

Service providers are asked to give the users a number of alternatives to choose from that provide them a flexible way of controlling the way their information is being used. After notifying users and allowing them to select among different choices, it is required that the user explicitly declares his or her acceptance of this type of usage. Most Web sites ask for the user's consent, once and for all, after the user reads the privacy policies (if he or

Figure 1. High-level domain perspective architecture

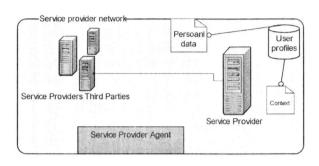

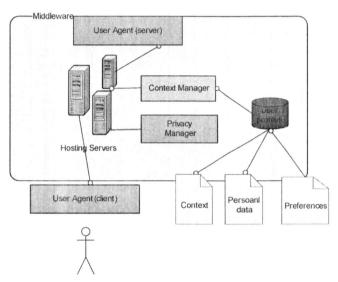

she does): a user will have to accept or object as the previously mentioned option "take it or leave it," and if he or she accepts the policy, then he or she is not allowed to change consent even if his or her preferences change, unless the user stops using the service offered by that Web site.

A PRIVACY CONTROL FUNCTIONAL ARCHITECTURE

With respect to the above-mentioned requirements, we argue that the following functionalities, as shown in Figure 1 in the form of high-level domain architecture, must be taken into consideration to automate privacy management. These

functionalities can be implemented using middleware technology acting as a trusted third party.

System Architecture

When designing a solution for effective privacy management, specifying a proper architecture to provide a basis for implementation is of crucial importance. The standard ANSI/IEEE 1471-2000 that gives recommended practices for describing the architecture of software-intensive systems defines architecture as the fundamental organization of a system—embodied in its components, their relationships, and the environment—and the principles governing its design and evolution (ANSI, 2000). Similarly, in the Rational Unified

Figure 2. Relationships and functionalities model

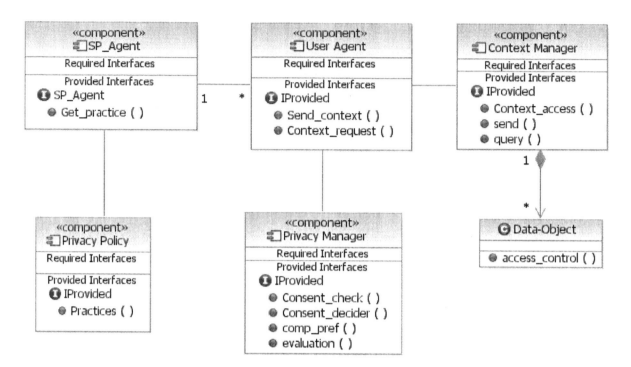

Process (Kruchten, 2003), an architecture is the set of significant decisions about the organization of a software system, the selection of the structural elements, and their interfaces by which the system is composed, together with their behavior as specified in the collaborations among those elements, the composition of these structural and behavioral elements into progressively larger subsystems, and the architectural style that guides this organization, these elements and their interfaces, their collaborations, and their composition (Kruchten, 2003). Therefore, for the purpose of designing an architecture, the main components of the solutions should be identified and specified. The Rational Unified Process defines a component as a non-trivial, nearly independent, and replaceable part of a system solution that fulfils a clear function in the context of a well-defined architecture (Kruchten, 2003). A component interface is an essential element of any component since it is often the only way the consumer of the component knows the function of the component. In UML, an interface is defined as a named collection of operations that are used to specify a service of the component. The interface provides an explicit separation between the outside and the inside of the component, answering the question *what* (What useful services are provided by the particular component to the context of its existence?), but not the question *how* (How are these services actually realized?). A precisely defined component interface allows the component services to be used without knowing how they are actually realized. A component interior is hidden and not important for its environment as long as the component provides services and follows constraints defined by its contractual interface.

Two kinds of interfaces can be distinguished: provided and required interfaces (OMG-UML2, 2004). A component can provide and require interfaces to and from its environment that can include other components. A provided interface represents the services and operations that the component provides to the environment according to its role in it. A required interface specifies the services and operations that the component requires from its environment to perform its role—that is, to provide its services. The main elements of an interface as defined in Heineman and Council (2001) are:

- Names of semantically related operations,
- Their parameters, and
- Valid parameter types.

In the sequel, in defining and creating the different architecture component functionalities, their description and specification, we followed the UML 2.0 standard specification as a modeling method. This version of the UML improves significantly the ability to represent components as not only implementation level artifacts, but also as design-level concepts that, together with classes, represent the main mechanisms used to build a logical system architecture (OMG-UML2, 2004).

Privacy Control Functional Architecture and Components

For the purpose of creating an effective privacy control, a user profile can be defined to consist of user personal information, contextual information, and user preferences. It is expected that every information collector can create local user profiles. In order to ensure the consistency and correctness of the information between the different profiles, an information collector will try to approach the user to update his or her profile on a regular basis, and hence privacy must be rechecked. In order to assign these different functionalities to loosely coupled and highly cohesive functional units (i.e., components), we define five main components of the privacy control solution: user agent, service provider (SP) agent, privacy manager, context manager, and privacy policy, as shown in Figure

2. In what follows, the components will be specified in more detail, and interfaces between them will be defined.

User Agent (Client/Server)

A user agent is needed to handle incoming requests for user information. When it receives a request from an information collector, it should fetch the information collector's privacy policies. The user agent should send these policies to the privacy manager to be processed and to generate a consent decision. After getting a consent decision from the privacy manager, the user agent should contact the context manager (see Figure 2) asking for the required data to be released and then to be propagated back to the service provider agent. Most user agents are implemented locally on the user machine, such as any Internet browser where most of the information requests are made when a user navigates through the Internet. But for a context-aware or mobile environment, most of the requests will be made when the user gets in the range of another registered network using the wireless connectivity in his or her device. Thus, a user agent will be realized as a client/server software program or a service which is partly on the user's device and/or the network, and the user will communicate with his or her user agent through a customized user interface on his or her device.

In this context, the user agent should define the following interfaces with other components in the architecture (see Figure 2):

- **Get_practice:** This is an operation provided on the interface of the SP agent component and is a required interface operation for the user agent component since, by using this operation, the user agent component communicates with the SP agent component to fetch the asked practices of a service provider.

- **Consent_check:** This is an operation provided on the interface of the privacy manager component and is a required interface operation for the user agent component. By using this operation, the user agent component communicates with the privacy manager component to get the required consent type. This operation further uses the Get_practice operation.

- **Context_access:** This is an operation provided on the interface of the context manager component and is a required interface operation for the user agent component. By using this operation, the user agent component communicates with the context manager component to define the type of context allowed to be accessed.

- **Send_context:** This is an operation provided on the interface of the user agent component and is a required interface operation for the SP agent component. Using this operation, the SP agent sends back to the user agent component a response about the type of context to be sent.

Information Collector Agent (SP_Agent)

Each information collector by nature should have a collector agent SP_agent (a representative) that handles all the outgoing requests for information. This functionality can be implemented as a service. It should be responsible for propagating user data to the specified components within the SP_agent organization. This functional component contacts user agent components with all information required, such as a privacy policy that organizes how it deals with users' private information. A single instance of the SP_agent component can be engaged with many instances of the user agent components. The SP_component has the following interfaces with the different components of the architecture:

- **Context_request:** This is an operation provided on the interface of the user agent and is a required interface operation for the SP agent components. By using this operation, the SP agent component communicates with the user agent component with respect to the type of information to be requested.

- **Practices:** This is an operation provided on the interface of the information collector privacy policy components. By using this operation, the SP agent component fetches the asked data practices from the information collector privacy policy component.

Context Manager

The context manager should be responsible for all aspects related to managing users' contextual information such as sensing context and controlling access privileges of users' contextual information and maintaining databases. An example of a context manager can be a distributed database management system where different types of data objects are related to the user and are stored in different databases located at different places, such as network operators or user-sided devices. Usually, this component is implemented at the service provider's side, and users are asked only at the beginning of signing a contract to give their consent—an issue that makes it difficult to enforce any users' preferences.

With the increase awareness of privacy by users, and the more anxiousness expected when using such systems, many third parties—such as Microsoft Passport and Liberty Alliance—are acting as intermediaries in the form of a middleware or a trusted third party between users and service providers in order to guarantee users' privacy. Nevertheless, in addition they have to be trusted by users; these intermediaries do not provide control capabilities to users, but users are forced to accept the providers' ways of dealing with their privacy (the "take it or leave it" option).

The context manager component implements the interfaces context_access and send or send_context with the different components of the user agent. Additionally, it implements the operation query on the interfaces of the data object component.

Privacy Manager

A privacy manager component is needed to make consent decisions on behalf of users. We assume that user consent in context-aware services architectures will be dynamic and therefore should be requested before any collection of any contextual information.

Increasingly, this request for mobile users' consent should be carried out in an autonomous, flexible, and user-friendly way. It is expected that when minimizing user interactions and at the same time taking their requirements into considerations, uncertainty will takeover. In other words, uncertainty represents an obstacle against a good consent decision. Uncertainty is caused by the unknown interaction taking place between (undefined) different factors that influence users' willingness to share their private information, and due to the lack of knowledge about the behavior of the users themselves, when trying to predict their consent decisions. Thus, intelligent techniques are needed to deal with this uncertainty limitation. To deal with this uncertainty in making consent decisions, we can adopt the mechanism developed by Ali Eldin, van den Berg, and Wagenaar (2004) which is based on a fuzzy logic mechanism. The main objective of their work is to provide a consent decision-making mechanism that minimizes users' interactions and meets their privacy concerns at the same time. This consent decision-making mechanism can be implemented in an operation called consent_decider as shown by Figure 2.

Another obstacle that challenges this consent decision making is the effective description of user privacy preferences that matches their privacy requirements and that can be easily evaluated in

a machine-readable way to develop this automatic consent decision. This description should be able to model the dynamic features of context-aware environments. The Platform of Privacy Preferences (Cranor et al., 2004), introduced earlier, has defined a number of data practices that together constitute a P3P privacy policy. A P3P privacy policy is a step towards automating and simplifying users' assessments of an information collector through the use of user agents and APPEL. APPEL, a P3P preference exchange language (Cranor et al., 2002), was also proposed as the language for expressing user preferences. APPEL is a machine-readable specification of user preferences that can be programmatically compared against a privacy policy. This comparison mechanism can be modeled in the form of an operation called comp_pref as shown by Figure 2.

The final step is to combine both outputs of the consent_decider and comp_pref into one Boolean consent output. The evaluator operation *evaluator* takes responsibility of this process. The evaluator rules must be based on the assumption that consent decisions should be as much as possible carefully given because people tend to be rather more conservative when it comes to their privacy (Ali Eldin, 2006). For example, if both outputs are equal, then the final consent output should be the same. But when any of the two outputs is different, we should go for the more strict output.

EXPERIMENTAL WORK

The proposed functional architecture has been prototyped and integrated in developing one of the location-based mobile services on a UMTS testbed offered by MIES (Kar, 2004) and experimented by real users. In the following we present the different features of the implemented service.

The aim was to have a 'privacy-aware finding people service' designed in such a way that it enables users to specify their allowed information practices and privacy attributes in order to evalu-

Figure 3. Finding People menus

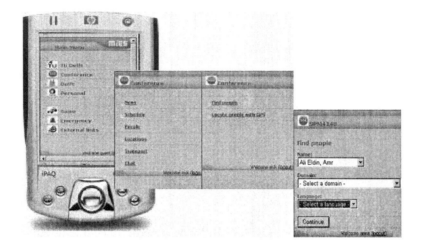

ate consent decisions on any incoming request for users' data. The Finding People service (see Figures 3 and 4) was developed to be one of the services offered by MIES (Kar, 2004). MIES offers GIS location-based services and tourist information to university campus visitors. It also enables users to locate and contact each other. We have implemented the proposed functional architecture for this service to allow users to control their private information collection by other users of MIES.

A service provider agent was implemented in the form of a "search people" script coded in asp. net which is navigated through from the MIES menu on the user iPAQ. In this experiment, information collectors were other users of the service who are looking for others.

The information collector (requesting user) must specify for which purpose he or she is requesting the information, which is known as "purpose of search." Additionally, the requesting user specifies a search criteria based on which user agent is going to find him or her the requested user. The user agent, in the form of an asp script, manages requesting user requests and propagates them to the context manager, which is considered here to be the MS Access database. In user databases, user privacy preferences are stored and taken from Web forms. The privacy manager implemented was the consent decider mechanism presented in Ali Eldin et al. (2004).

EVALUATION TESTS

The participants were asked if they agreed or disagreed with the statements as listed in the questionnaire (see Appendix A). The score could range from "1 highly agree" to "7 highly disagree." From these scores, an average score for each participant for each statement was derived in addition to an overall average of users' responses. Users were asked about the overall performance of the system in terms of their satisfaction of privacy protection, type of preferred control modes, and whether they need to add more preferences to the predefined preferences. Most of the collected response of

Figure 4. Finding People service architecture

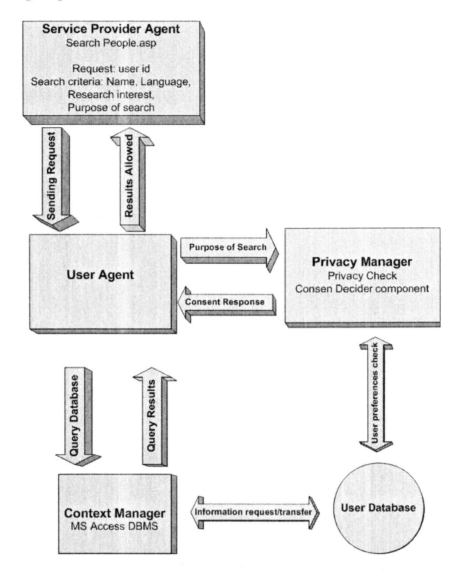

users was positive. However, some users were neutral and very few reacted negatively.

FUTURE TRENDS

Recently, we have noticed that there is a growing research interest in context-aware environments, ad hoc and personal networks, and location-based mobile services. The attention has been given to designing and developing not only theoretically possible, but also operational context-aware applications and services platforms. Among these calls for the next-generation mobile services platforms, research and development on privacy was mainly concentrated on authentication, along with access control mechanisms, biometric solutions, cryptographic mechanisms, and so forth. Most of these privacy solutions were intended for interconnected organizations, where protecting privacy generally means avoiding intrusive access to private information which is stored somewhere,

Figure 5. Basic elements of an SOA

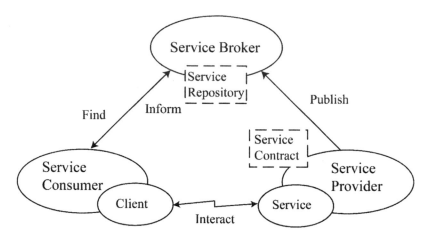

where authorized access is known beforehand and is granted based on different criteria such as roles or activities within these organizations. This chapter, however, sheds light on a new approach of dealing with privacy which is based on user or customer involvement in the consent decision making through the processing of their preferences. Additionally, this chapter gives designers of context-aware services guidelines on how user privacy can be managed and maintained in a way that keeps users aware of their rights and concerns.

A next step will be to prototype the functional architecture in different mobile service scenarios, and check whether this automatic privacy control can be completely accepted by users and in which situations user interactions will be necessary.

During the last few years, we have witnessed the further evolution of the Internet in the form of Web services (Kaye, 2003). Web services have been introduced as a promising way to integrate information systems effectively inside and across the enterprises. They are defined as self-contained and self-describing business-driven functional units that can be plugged in or invoked across the Internet to provide flexible enterprise appli-

cation integration within the Service-Oriented Architecture (SOA) (Kaye, 2003). Using advanced Web service technology such as XML, WSDL, SOAP, and UDDI, the Internet—once solely a repository of various kinds of information—is now evolving into a provider of a variety of business services and applications (Newcomer, 2002). In this manner, Web services technology and SOA are increasingly becoming a business issue based on the new technology's ability to deliver strategic business value (Berry, 2003).

The basic elements of an SOA are a service provider, a service consumer, and a service broker, as shown in Figure 5. The service provider makes the service available and advertises it on the service broker by issuing the service contract. The service consumer finds the service that matches its needs in a service repository of the service broker using the published service contract. The service consumer and the service provider then interact in terms of providing/using the service. It is important to note that the communication between a service provider, a service consumer, and a service broker is performed using the same set of interoperable, technology-independent standards for communication, such as XML, SOAP, and WSDL.

The service in the form of a Web service represents a contractual agreement between provider and consumer. Beside common interface that defines operation signatures, the service also has attributes of its own such as service-level agreement, policies, dependencies, security rules, privacy constraints, and so forth. All these properties of Web services become increasingly important when services are chained in a cascade or organized and orchestrated in a more complex way to provide a higher-level business value. In this case, we potentially have more participants in the collaboration to provide a more valuable business service, for example an Internet-based traveling agency might use the services from a hotel reservation system, a route information system, a rental car system, and a city touristic guide system to provide a complete service to its customers. Such situations put more emphasis on the privacy of the end user being spread over multiple service providers and still need to be effectively maintained.

Therefore, one of the main challenges and further directions of our work is placing our framework of privacy control and maintenance into a fully service-oriented environment.

CONCLUSION

In this chapter, we argued the different requirements of privacy that are triggered by the nature of the context-aware environment. We presented as a proposition a privacy-functional architecture that maintains these requirements. The main objective of these functionalities is to help automate the process of getting users' explicit consent. We enunciate that a consent decision-making mechanism should be able dynamically and automatically to make recommendations to users about their consent decisions. Flexibility means that the recommendation allows users to change their preferences in response to changing circumstances. Users will have different functionalities of

dealing with their privacy. User friendliness here refers to the minimization of the requirements for users to interact and their involvement.

We have prototyped the proposed architecture functionalities in a real-time UMTS personal services platform and experimented with visitors to a university campus. The prototype showed the technical feasibility of the approach in mobile services. Users' reactions showed the satisfaction regarding meeting their privacy needs with the call for a combination of manual and automatic control capabilities according to their context.

At the end, we presented future trends in the field and marked the privacy control in the service-oriented environment as one of our main future research directions.

ACKNOWLEDGMENT

The conceptual development and the experimental work presented here were conducted during the authors' employment for Delft University of Technology, The Netherlands.

REFERENCES

Ackerman, M., Darrell, T., & Weitzner, D.J. (2001). Privacy in context. *HCI, 16*(2), 167–179.

Agrawal, R., & Kiernan, J. (2002). Watermarking relational databases. *Proceedings of the 28th VLDB Conference,* Hong Kong, China.

Ali Eldin, A. (2006). *Private information sharing under uncertainty.* Delft: Amr Ali Eldin.

Ali Eldin, A., van den Berg, J., & Wagenaar, R. (2004). A fuzzy reasoning scheme for context sharing decision making. *Proceedings of the 6th International Conference on Electronic Commerce* (pp. 371–375), Delft, The Netherlands. Retrieved from http://doi.acm.org/10.1145/1052 220.1052267

ANSI. (2000). *ANSI/IEEE 1471-2000 recommended practice for architectural description of software-intensive systems.* Retrieved from http://shop.ieee.org/store/

Camenisch, J., & Herreweghen, E.V. (2002). *Design and implementation of Idemix Anonymous Credential System.* Zurich: IBM Zurich Research Laboratory.

Casal, C.R. (2001). Privacy protection for location based mobile services in Europe. *Proceedings of the 5th World Multi-Conference on Systems, Cybernetics, and Informatics* (SCI2001), Orlando, FL.

Chaum, D. (1985). Security without identification card computers to make big brother obsolete. *Communications of ACM, 28*(10), 1034–1044.

Clifton, C., Kantarcioglu, M., Vaidya, J., Lin, X., & Zhu, M.Y. (2002). Tools for privacy preserving distributed data mining. *ACM SIGKDD Explorations, 4*(2), 28–34.

Cranor, L., Langheinrich, M., & Marchiori, M. (2002). *A P3P Preference Exchange Language 1.0 (APPEL1.0).* Working Draft, W3C.

Cranor, L., Langheinrich, M., Marchiori, M., Presler-Marshall, M., & Reagle, J. (2004). *The Platform for Privacy Preferences 1.1 (P3P1.1) specification.* Working Draft, W3C.

Cranor, L.F., Guduru, P., & Arjula, M. (2006). User interfaces for privacy agents. *ACM Transactions on Human Computer Interactions.*

European Directive. (2002). Directive 2002/58/EC of the European Parliament and of the Council of 12 July 2002, electronic communications sector (directive on privacy and electronic communications). *Official Journal of European Communities, L,* 201–237.

Hauser, C., & Kabatnik, M. (2001). Towards privacy support in a global location service. *Proceedings of the IFIP Workshop on IP and ATM Traffic Management* (WATM/EUNICE 2001), Paris.

Heineman, G.T., & Council, W.T. (2001). *Component-based software engineering: Putting the pieces together.* Boston: Addison-Wesley Longman.

Kar, E.A.M. (2004). *Designing mobile information services: An approach for organisations in a value network.* Unpublished Doctoral Dissertation, Delft University of Technology, The Netherlands.

Kaye, D. (2003). *Loosely coupled: The missing pieces of Web services* (1st ed.). RDS Associates.

Kruchten, P. (2003). *The Rational Unified Process: An introduction* (3rd ed.). Boston: Addison-Wesley.

Langheinrich, M. (2001). Privacy by design—principles of privacy-aware ubiquitous systems. *Proceedings of the 3rd International Conference on Ubiquitous Computing* (Ubicomp2001).

Langheinrich, M. (2002). A privacy awareness system for ubiquitous computing environments. *Proceedings of the 4th International Conference on Ubiquitous Computing* (UbiComp2002).

Lysyanskayal, A., Rivest, R.L., Sahai, A., & Wolf, S. (1999). Pseudonym systems. *Proceedings of the 6th Annual Workshop on Selected Areas in Cryptography* (SAC'99).

Nilsson, M., Lindskog, H., & Fischer-Hübner, S. (2001). Privacy enhancements in the mobile Internet. *Proceedings of the IFIP WG 9.6/11.7 Working Conference on Security and Control of IT in Society,* Bratislava.

OECD. (2003). Privacy online. In OECD (Ed.), *OECD guidance on policy and practice* (p. 40). Paris: OECD.

OMG-UML2. (2004). *Unified Modeling Language version 2.0.* Retrieved from http://www.uml.org

Rodden, T., Friday, A., Henk, M., & Dix, A. (2002). *A lightweight approach to managing privacy in location-based services* (No. Equator-02-058), University of Nottingham and Lancaster, UK.

Stojanovic, Z. (2005). *A method for component based and service oriented software systems engineering.* Unpublished PhD Thesis, Delft University of Technology, The Netherlands.

APPENDIX A: QUESTIONNAIRE

Statements	Highly agree	Agree	Almost agree	Neutral	Almost disagree	Disagree	Highly disagree
	1	2	3	4	5	6	7
I could easily define my privacy settings.							
People could contact me, though I did not ask for that.							
My privacy should always automatically handle requests for my WHAinfo.							
I should always be asked before letting others contact me.							
I need to add new privacy preferences.							
I was able to self-control my privacy.							
My privacy was guaranteed.							

Chapter VIII
User and Context–Aware Quality Filters Based on Web Metadata Retrieval

Ricardo Barros
Federal University of Rio de Janeiro, Brazil

Geraldo Xexéo
Federal University of Rio de Janeiro, Brazil

Wallace A. Pinheiro
Federal University of Rio de Janeiro, Brazil

Jano de Souza
Federal University of Rio de Janeiro, Brazil

ABSTRACT

Due to the amount of information on the Web being so large and being of varying levels of quality, it is becoming increasingly difficult to find precisely what is required on the Web, particularly if the information consumer does not have precise knowledge of his or her information needs. On the Web, while searching for information, users can find data that is old, imprecise, invalid, intentionally wrong, or biased, due to this large amount of available data and comparative ease of access. In this environment users·constantly receive useless, outdated, or false data, which they have no means to assess. This chapter addresses the issues regarding the large amount and low quality of Web information by proposing a methodology that adopts user and context-aware quality filters based on Web metadata retrieval. This starts with an initial evaluation and adjusts it to consider context characteristics and user perspectives to obtain aggregated evaluation values.

INTRODUCTION

Years ago, data storage was scarce and had to be cleaned periodically. In those times, a database project would include rules for longevity of data, for migration from secondary memory (disks) to archival memory (tapes), and for deletion of unused data. Current practice, however, is to leave data lingering around, or at most, transfer them to data warehouses to be used opportunely.

Specifically, data available on the Internet is overwhelming. Lyman and Hal (2003) estimate that there are 167 terabytes of data in fixed Web pages, and also that Web pages created on demand use more than 91.850 terabytes of data stored in databases. To that we can add 440.606 terabytes of new e-mails per year, approximately one-third of which is spam.

Due to the amount of information[1] being so large and being of varying levels of quality, it is becoming increasingly difficult to find precisely what is required on the Web, particularly if the information consumer does not have precise

knowledge of his or her information needs (Burgess, Gray, & Fiddian, 2004). On the Web, while searching for information, users can find data that is old, imprecise, invalid, intentionally wrong, or biased, due to this large amount of available data and comparative ease of access. Web search engines are a good example of this situation: in a reply from these mechanisms, one can usually find links to replicated or conflicting information. In this environment, users constantly receive useless, outdated, or false data, which they have no means to assess.

Moreover, the range of suppliers also results in a diverse variety of formats in which information is stored and presented. It is possible to search for information on an unlimited number of contexts and categories across a wide range of information environments, such as databases, application systems, electronic library systems, corporate intranets, as well as the Internet. This information presents different levels of quality, with original sources ranging from multi-national corporations to individuals with limited knowledge. With so

Figure 1. Producer-consumer schema and selection filters

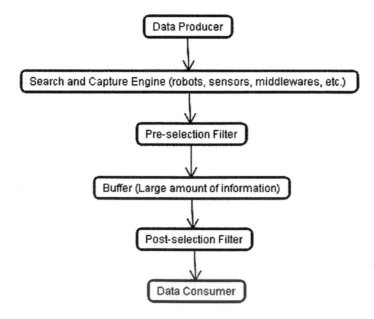

much information available, quality has become an important discriminator when deciding which information to use and which to discard (Burgess et al., 2004).

In this sense, the difficulties to identify, separate, and assess quality of information have caused financial losses and compromised decision-making processes (Eckerson, 2002; English, 1999; Redman, 1998).

In order to illustrate this scenario, Figure 1 introduces a producer-consumer schema and selection filters. Obviously, the schema is quite simple and only incorporates the most important components normally found in these cases. These main components include:

- **Data producer:** All kinds of data sources are represented by this single component. It provides data on many subjects in heterogeneous formats, such as satellites, security cameras, or any other system that produces data. For example, meteorological satellites take photos of a specific region and send a sequence of images. Moreover, there are metadata, such as publishing date, sources, authors, subject of an article, size, and so forth. These metadata should be retrieved, since they are useful to organize and refine the stored data according to some users' requirements.
- **Data consumer:** This is external to the systems and represents all kinds of users that access data. It can be a person, a browser, a specific system of a company, a database, and so forth. It is important to trace and store the preferences of the consumer, such as usually visited sites and specific domains, in order to help the data quality assessment.
- **Buffer:** This component represents the data repository to provide data availability to the data consumer. It stores all kinds of data, data structures, and metadata for an unlimited time, depending on the users' requirements. To reduce the ambiguity, the

adoption of ontologies is an approach that becomes very interesting to organize data in a semantic meaning. For example, if the data consumer works within the computer science domain, a search with the word "net" will return concepts like "network." Concepts such as "fishnet" or "net" (to hair) will be avoided (Pinheiro & Moura, 2004). As the amount of available information has dramatically increased, the managing of information becomes more difficult, which can lead to the related problems mentioned before.

- **Search and capture engine:** This component represents the mechanism to search and capture data provided by the data producer. It can be a sensor, a robot, or a kind of middleware that presumes a proactive behavior. For instance, a search engine should access Web pages just after the new generations or the update of the living ones, in order to minimize the "impedance matching" between data update and data search times.
- **Pre-selection filter:** This component represents the mechanism to filter data resulting from the searcher and capturer engine. There is a content analysis after the search part, according to a set of user specifications—for instance, a search engine that analyzes the page contents to filter and capture those pages really relevant to a consumer, in terms of a search argument.
- **Post-selection filter:** This component represents the mechanism to data filtering from the buffer. There is a content analysis, according to the metadata, the context, and the defined user' characteristics—for instance, a post-selection to filter those pages really relevant to a data consumer, in terms of the quality dimensions *completeness, timeliness,* and *reputation* for a context *economy.*

Then, the selection filters intend to eliminate low-quality information to reduce the amount of data to be stored, consequently minimizing the related effects as a whole.

In spite of the extensive discussion in literature, there is no consensus on an appropriate approach to improve the quality of information, as for the effectiveness of proposals and the expected benefits. However, there is a consensus that the effort to reach a good information quality standard must have high priority (Eckerson, 2002; Redman, 1998).

This chapter addresses the issues regarding the large amount and low quality of Web documents by proposing a methodology that adopts user and context-aware quality filters based on Web metadata retrieval. This starts with an initial evaluation and adjusts it to consider context characteristics and user perspectives to obtain aggregated evaluation values.

This methodology provides the theory to implement a post-query or browse support mechanisms. Furthermore, this can be embodied as a final step of a Web information retrieval engine or as a recommender system running in collaboration with a browser.

We apply the fuzzy theory approach to obtain the values of quality dimensions from metadata values and to evaluate the quality of the retrieved Web documents set, taking advantage of fuzzy logic's ability to capture humans' imprecise knowledge and deal with different concepts.

We also apply the fuzzy theory approach to identify user expectations about information quality through the weights attributed to quality dimensions according to the specific contexts and user requirements (Zadeh, 1988; Yager, 1991; Xexéo, Belchior, & da Rocha, 1996).

We adopted an ontology represented by a UML (*www.uml.org*) model to formalize, keep, and share the concepts and its instances used in all steps of the information quality evaluation process (*www.w3.org/2004/OWL*).

There is an example to illustrate how it has been used, taking the metadata *update date, query time, update time, forward links, backwards links, hubs,* and *authorities,* and applying them as a basis to evaluate the quality dimensions *timeliness, reputation,* and *completeness* in an *economy* context.

The remainder of this chapter is organized as follows. In the next section, we present a background. Afterwards we demonstrate our proposal, and show the architecture of the system and some technical details. Finally, before the conclusion, we delineate the expected results by an example and discuss future and emerging trends.

BACKGROUND

Brief Introduction to Fuzzy Theory

Fuzzy logic is also another extension realized in Boolean logic that may be considered a generalization of multi-valued logic. By modeling the uncertainties of natural language through concepts of partial truth—truth-values falling somewhere between completely true and completely false (Kantrowitz, Horstkotte, & Joslyn, 1997)—fuzzy logic deals with such values through fuzzy sets in the interval [0,1]. These characteristics allow fuzzy logic to manipulate real-world objects that possess imprecise limits. Utilizing fuzzy predicates (old, new, high, etc.), fuzzy quantifiers (many, few, almost all, etc.), fuzzy truth-values (completely true, more or less true) (Dubois & Prade, 1991), and generalizing the meaning of connectors and logical operators, fuzzy logic is seen as a means of approximate reasoning (Grauel, 1999).

It was introduced by Lotfi Zadeh of UC/Berkeley in the 1960s as a way to model the uncertainty of natural language. Zadeh (1965) says that rather than regarding fuzzy theory as a single theory, we should regard the process of "fuzzification" as a methodology to generalize any specific theory from a crisp (discrete) to a continuous (fuzzy) form.

Thus, recently researchers have also introduced "fuzzy calculus," "fuzzy differential equations," "fuzzy systems," "fuzzy logic with engineering applications," and so on (Cox, 1994; Klir & Yuan, 1995; Kantrowitz et al., 1997).

Just as there is a strong relationship between Boolean logic and the concept of a subset, there is a similar strong relationship between fuzzy logic and fuzzy set theory.

In classical set theory, a subset A of a set X can be defined as a mapping from the elements of A to the elements of the set $\{0,1\}$, $A:X \to \{0,1\}$.

This mapping may be represented as a set of ordered pairs, with exactly one ordered pair present for each element of X. The first element of the ordered pair is an element of the set X, and the second element is an element of the set $\{0,1\}$. The value "zero" is used to represent non-membership, and the value "one" is used to represent membership. The truth or falsity of the statement *x is in A* is determined by finding the ordered pair whose first element is x. The statement is true if the second element of the ordered pair is 1, and the statement is false if it is 0.

Similarly, a fuzzy subset A of a set X can be defined as a set of ordered pairs, each with the first element from X and the second element from the interval [0,1], with exactly one ordered pair present for each element of X. This defines a mapping between elements of the set X and values in the interval [0,1]. In extreme cases, the degree of membership is 0, in which case the element is not a member of the set, or the degree of membership is 1, if the element is a 100% member of the set. The set X is referred to as the universe of discourse for the fuzzy subset A.

The membership of an element within a certain set becomes a question of degree, substituting the actual dichotomist process imposed by *crisp* sets when this treatment is not suitable (Turksen, 1991; Zimmermann, 1991).

Frequently, the mapping is described as a function, the membership function of A. The degree to which the statement *x is in A* is true is determined

by finding the ordered pair whose first element is x. The degree of truth of the statement is the second element of the ordered pair. In practice, the terms "membership function" and "fuzzy set" get used interchangeably.

Summarizing, a fuzzy set is characterized by a membership function, which maps the elements of a domain, space, or discourse universe X for a real number in [0, 1]. Formally, $\tilde{A}:X \to [0,1]$. Thus, a fuzzy set is presented as a set of ordered pairs in which the first element is $x \in X$, and the second $\mu_{\tilde{A}}(x)$ is the degree of membership or the membership function of x into $\tilde{A}$, which maps x in the interval [0,1] or $\tilde{A} = \{x, \mu_{\tilde{A}}(x) \mid x \in X\}$ (Zadeh, 1965; Klir & Yuan, 1995).

Therefore, here is an example. Let us talk about people and "age." In this case, the set $X = \{5, 10, 20, 30, 40, 50, 60, 70, 80\}$ (the universe of discourse) is the set of "ages."

Let us define fuzzy subsets "child," "young," "adult," and "old," which will answer the question "to what membership degree is person x "child," "young," "adult," and "old"? Zadeh (1965) describes "age" as a linguistic variable, which represents our cognitive category "age group." To each person in the universe of discourse, we have to assign a degree of membership in the fuzzy subsets. The easiest way to do this is with a membership function based on the person's age. The fuzzy set $\tilde{A}$, young, could be described as:

$$\tilde{A} = \{(5,1)(10,1)(20,0.8)(30,0.5)(40,0.2)(50,0.1)(60,0)(70,0)(80,0)\}$$

Then, a fuzzy set emerges from the "enlargement" of a *crisp* set that begins to incorporate aspects of uncertainty. This process is called *fuzzification*.

Nevertheless, the literature already contains families of parameterized membership functions such as triangular, exponential, and Gauss functions. Each one of these functions is characterized by a fuzzy number that is a convex and normalized fuzzy set defined in the set of the real numbers R, such that its membership function has the form

Table 1. Examples of quality evaluation approaches

Initiatives	Approaches
(Strong, 1994)	Presents a framework that captures the aspects of data quality that are important to Data Consumers.
(Wand, 1996)	Suggests rigorous definition of data quality dimensions by anchoring them in ontological foundations, and show how such dimensions can provide guidance to systems designers on data quality issues.
(Redman, 1998)	Categorizes every questions related to low data quality impact on the three levels of the organizations: operational , tactical and strategic.
(English, 1999)	Proposes a method for reducing costs and increasing profits improving the Data Warehouse and business information quality.
(Twidale, 1999)	Outlines a new collaborative approach to data quality management.
(Lee, 2004)	Finds that experienced practitioners solve data quality problems by reflecting on and explicating knowledge about contexts embedded in, or missing from, data.
(Loshin, 2001)	Analyzes data quality under knowledge management point of view. It defines data quality as "adequacy for the use" and stands out that quality evaluation is dependent of the user' context.
(Pipino, 2002)	Describes the subjective and objective assessments of data quality, and present three functional forms for developing objective data quality metrics.
(Burgess, 2004)	Proposes a hierarchical generic model of quality that can be used by the information consumer to assist in information searching, by focusing the returned result set based on personal quality preferences.
(Peralta, 2004)	Addresses the problem, in the context of data integration systems, using cost graphic models, which enable the definition of evaluation methods and demonstration of propositions in terms of graph properties.
(Kim, 2005)	Applies the concepts of data quality in the context of e-business systems.

$[250, 750]$: $\mu_{\tilde{A}} : R \rightarrow [0,1]$ (Klir & Yuan, 1995; Zimmermann, 1991).

Defuzzification is the inverse process, that is, it is the conversion of a fuzzy set into a *crisp* value (or a vector of values) (Zimmermann, 1991). Theoretically, any function in the form of $\tilde{A} : X \rightarrow [0,1]$ can be associated with a fuzzy set depending on the concepts and properties that need to be represented along with the context in which the set is inserted.

There are many defuzzification methods (at least 30), such as centroid (centroid of area), bisector (bisector of area), MOM (mean value of maximum), SOM (smallest absolute value of maximum), and LOM (largest absolute value of maximum), among others. The more common techniques are the centroid and maximum methods. In the centroid method, the crisp value of the output variable is computed by finding the variable value of the center of gravity of the membership function for the fuzzy value. In the maximum method, one of the variable values at which the fuzzy subset has its maximum truth value is chosen as the crisp value for the output variable (Kantrowitz et al., 1997; Klir & Yuan, 1995; Cox, 1994).

The main concepts of our proposal and how these concepts have been extended by fuzzy set and fuzzy logic theory will be shown later.

Quality and Information Quality

In spite of the existence of different efforts to create a definition of quality, "no single definition or standard of quality exists" (Smart, 2002, p. 130). Pipino, Lee, and Wang (2002) state that quality is a multidimensional concept, since users must deal with both subjective perceptions of the individuals involved with the data and objective measurements based on the dataset under evaluation.

Previous initiatives, exemplified in Table 1, tried to define, organize, and prioritize the required information, improving its quality to the end user.

Quality and information quality has attracted the interest of many researchers in a great number of disciplines, including computer science, library science, information science, and management of information systems. Certainly, a strong commercial interest in this last area exists, with emphasis on the costs and the impact for the organizations in consequence of low data quality. These impacts can influence directly some competitive differential paradigms in most of enterprises (Redman, 1998).

Metadata

The most common definition of *metadata* is the literal translation: "Metadata is data about data," and *Web metadata* "is machine-understandable description of things on (and about) the Web" (*www.w3.org/Metadata*).

In some approaches presented in Table 1, different metadata can be associated with data, including metadata to improve or restrict quality, according to some set of dimensions. Rothenberg (1996) outlines a range of metadata fields that can be used in this way. We only focus on a subpart of his wider analysis, which references the data-value level metadata, such as source information (source, derivation, time of generation/entry, etc.).

These initiatives, however, did not explore the benefits of using Web metadata. In this case, there are several alternatives to be considered to capture metadata. For instance, search engine APIs (*www.google.com/apis*), third-party services, using protocols like W3C PICS (Platform for Internet Content Selection),[2] and also metadata provided by the original data source, such as the proposed Dublin Core (*www.dublincore.org*). Table 2 illustrates each one of these sources to capture metadata.

In our approach, we developed a crawler to retrieve Web documents and adopt the JUNG - Java Universal Network/Graph Framework (*jung. sourceforge.net*) to obtain derived metadata, such as *hubs* and *authorities* (Kleinberg, 1998).

Kleinberg (1998) says that the Internet is annotated with precisely the type of human judgment we need to identify authority (p. 670). Based on this, he developed a set of algorithms, called *HITS (Hyperlink Induced Topic Search),* for extracting information from the hyperlink structures of those environments. He states that the annotation on the Internet almost says something about the way the Web has evolved. He thinks it's about the way people link information in general, not just on the Web (pp. 670-671).

The goal of HITS is to rank pages on the Web through the discovery of related authoritative information sources. HITS introduced two concepts: *authorities* and *hubs.* Authorities are sites other Web pages link to frequently on a particular topic. Hubs are sites that cite many of these authorities. He observed that there is a certain natural type of equilibrium between hubs and authorities in

Table 2. Sources to capture metadata

Google	PICS	Meta-Tags of Dublin Core
Query parameters	**Attributes of Service**	
key, **q**: query terms, start, maxresults, filter, restricts, safesearch, **lr**: language restrict, **ie**: input encoding, **oe**: output encoding.	category, default, description, extension, icon, name, PICS-version, rating-service, and rating-system.	
Query special Operators	**Attributes of Categories**	Title, Creator, Subject, Description, Publisher, Contributor, Date, Type, Format, Identifier, Source, Language, Relation, Coverage, Rights, etc.
Special Query Capability, Include Query Term, Exclude Query Term, Phrase Search, Boolean OR Search, Site Restricted Search, Date Restricted Search Title Search (term), Title Search (all), URL Search (term), URL Search (all) Text Only Search (all), Links Only, Search (all), File Type Filtering, File Type Exclusion, Web Document Info, Back Links, Related Links, Cached Results Page.	description, extension, icon, integer, label, label-only, max, min, multivalue, name, transmit-as, and unordered.	
Returned Results		
<summary>, <URL>, <snippet>, <title>, <cachedSize>, <directoryTitle>, <hostName>, <relatedInformationPresent>, <directoryCategory>.		
Categories of Directories		
<fullViewableName>, <specialEncoding>		

the graph defined by the network structure of a hyperlinked environment, and he exploited this to develop a set of algorithms that identifies both types of pages simultaneously. Kleinberg's method says that the best *authorities* will be those that point to the best hubs, and the best hubs will be the ones that point to the best authorities. This calculation is repeated several times. Each time the program increases the authority weight to sites that link to sites with more hub weight, and it increases hub weight to sites that link to sites with more authority weight. He says that 10 repetitions are enough to return surprisingly focused lists of authorities and hubs. In practice convergence is achieved after only 10-20 iterations. HITS operates on *focused subgraphs* of the Web that are constructed from the output of a text-based Web search engine, like Google or Alta Vista. From there on, text is ignored, and the application only looks at the way pages in the expanded set are linked to one another.

Quality Dimensions

Despite the frequent use of some terms to indicate data quality, there is not a rigorously defined or

Table 3. Data quality dimensions (Pipino, 2002)

Dimensions	Definitions (The extent to which...)
Accessibility	data is available, or easily and quickly retrievable.
Appropriate Amount of Data	the volume of data is appropriate for the task at hand.
Believability	data is regarded as true and credible.
Completeness	data is not missing and is of sufficient breadth and depth for the task at hand.
Concise Representation	data is compactly represented.
Consistent Representation	data is presented in the same format.
Easy of Manipulation	data is easy to manipulate and apply to different tasks.
Free-of-Error	data is correct and reliable.
Interpretability	data is in appropriate languages, symbols, and units and the definitions are clear
Objectivity	data is unbiased, unprejudiced, and impartial.
Relevancy	data is applicable and helpful for the task at hand.
Reputation	data is highly regarded in terms of its source or content.
Security	access to data is restricted appropriately to maintain its security.
Timeliness	data is sufficiently up to date for the task at hand.
Understandability	data is easily comprehended.
Value-Added	data is beneficial and provides advantages from its use.

standardized set of data quality dimensions. Table 3 shows the set of data quality dimensions able to represent users' quality expectations (Pipino et al., 2002).

To carry out information quality evaluation, we need first to identify the set of quality dimensions. The most appropriate set depends on the user application, the selection of metrics, and the implementation of the evaluation algorithms that measure or estimate such quality dimension (Peralta et al., 2004). Wand and Wang (1996) state that the choice of these dimensions is primarily based on intuitive understanding, industrial experience, or literature review. Tillman (2003) emphasizes that we need to have in mind the current state of the Internet, to adopt generic criteria for information quality evaluation. This understanding is very important to determine the best set of quality dimensions, due to the constant changes in the Web.

There is an example provided later to illustrate our approach, where we work with *completeness, reputation,* and *timeliness.*

Context

Dey (2001) states:

Context is any information that can be used to characterize the situation of an entity. An entity is a person, place, or object that is considered relevant to the interaction between a user and an application, including the user and applications themselves ... This definition makes it easier for an application developer to enumerate the context for a given application scenario. If a piece of information can be used to characterize the situation of a participant in an interaction, then that information is context. (pp. 3–4)

The context specifies a scope or a boundary for a knowledge domain. In practice, contexts have been implicit in information quality management, yet they have been a critical part of resolving information quality problems (Lee, 2004; Dey, 2001; Pinheiro & Moura, 2004). Google (*www.google.com/dirhp*) and similar Web sites have organized hierarchical structures by topics into categories, such as *Maths, Economics, Social Sciences,* and *Technology.*

Pipino et al. (2002) classifies the objective assessments into task-independent or task-dependent metrics. Task-independent metrics reflect states of the data without the contextual knowledge of the application and can be applied to any data set, regardless of the tasks at hand.

In contrast, task-dependent metrics are developed in specific application contexts, which include the organization's business rules, company and government regulations, and constraints provided by the database administrator.

We focus on the task-dependent metrics classification, considering that our approach proposal involves semantic contextualization and user perspectives.

A USER AND CONTEXT-AWARE QUALITY FILTER BASED ON WEB METADATA RETRIEVAL

Figure 2 shows a UML diagram that would be seen as a taxonomy to define terms and relationships among these terms, and additionally a set of

transformation and membership functions responsible for keeping some real semantic constraints. Hence, according to this ontology, searched Web documents are evaluated and filtered, taking into account their metadata, the semantic contextualization, and the user perspectives.

Web Document Class

This class defines the set of retrieved Web documents to be evaluated.

Definition 1. The Web document is a set:

$$WebDoc = \{webdoc_1, webdoc_2, ... webdoc_n\}$$

where each $webdoc_i, 1 \leq i \leq n$, is an instance of Web document.

Metadata Class

This class defines the set of Web metadata used as a base for the information quality evaluation. Original metadata is retrieved "as-is" with the information, while derived metadata is obtained by transformation functions.

Definition 2. Metadata of a document (*Document_Metadata Association Class*) is some information about the document and the document data—that is, its contents. The metadata class represents a set:

$$M = \{m_1, m_2, ... m_n\}$$

where each $m_i, 1 \leq i \leq n$, is an instance of metadata.

Definition 3. Original metadata is metadata that can be directly retrieved from a document or from a third-party engine using a document as a key. The Original Metadata Class represents a set:

Figure 2. User and context aware quality ontology based on Web metadata

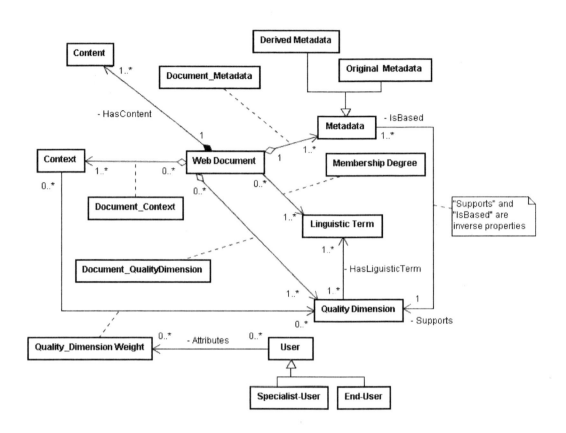

$$OM = \left\{ om_1, om_2,...om_n \right\}$$

where each $om_i, 1 \le i \le n$, is an instance of original metadata. A simple example of original metadata is its *query date*.

Definition 4. Derived metadata is metadata that cannot be directly retrieved from a document or a third-party engine, but rather must be derived from metadata through some computable function. We use *m* to represent metadata, *om* to represent original metadata, and *dm* to represent derived metadata, indexed when necessary. To represent a function that calculates the value of a specific derived metadata dm_i, we use the notation fd_i. The Derived Metadata Class represents a set:

$$DM = \left\{ dm_1, dm_2,...dm_n \right\}$$

where each $dm_i, 1 \le i \le n$, is an instance of derived metadata. A simple example of derived metadata is its *update time*.

We also define $M = OM \cup DM$ and $OM \cap DM = \phi$.

Table 4 gives four examples of original metadata and three examples of derived metadata. The first example, *Update Time*, derives from the original metadata: *Update Date* and *Query Date*. The second and third ones adopt the concepts of *authorities* and *hubs* (Kleinberg, 1998).

Quality Dimension and Linguistic Term Classes

The Quality Dimensions Class defines the set of quality dimensions. It represents the adopted information quality evaluation criteria and factors. The operation of fuzzification to transform derived metadata to quality dimensions instances is a membership function of fuzzy sets. The Linguistic Term Class defines a set of adjectives or adverbs related to the linguistic variables.

Definition 5. A quality dimension is defined as some user perspective about document quality. The Quality Dimension Class represents a set:

$$QD = \{qd_1, qd_2, ... qd_n\}$$

where each $qd_i, 1 \leq i \leq n$, is an instance of a quality dimension. A simple example of quality dimension is *completeness*.

At this point we should clarify one important point of the model. While metadata describes documents and is created with the possible information that one can, directly or indirectly, obtain about a document or its contents, the quality dimensions describe the user perspective about the expected quality of a document (*Document_QualityDimensions*

Association Class), regardless of the possibility to calculate it. In this model we presume that it is possible to make a direct relationship between one quality dimension and another, specific metadata. Therefore, the relationships "*Supports*" and "*IsBased*" indicate that a quality dimension can be represented, with some degree of uncertainty, from a metadata value. This relationship represents this association as an inverse property.

Definition 6. A quality dimension qd_i is represented as a linguistic variable (*HasLinguisticTerm relationship*) that can assume, possibly simultaneously, the values of its applicable fuzzy linguistic term (*Linguistic Term Class*) lt_{ij}, where j is a specific linguistic term and i is a specific variable linguistic. When evaluating a document according to a quality dimension, the model provides a linguistic interpretation of the respective metadata value for that document (*Membership Degree Association Class*). This is illustrated by three following examples.

Let R be the referential set for all possible values for the quality dimension *reputation*.

Table 4. Original and the derived metadata

Original Metadata	Functions to obtain Derived Metadata *(fd)*
ud_i – update date of a Web document i	**(1)** *(UT) Update Time =* $ut_i = qt_i - ud_i$
qt_i – query date of a Web document i	**(2)** *Authority* $= a_i = \sum h_j$, *where*: $j \in BL_i$
	(3) *Hub* $= h_i = \sum a_j$, *where*: $j \in FL_i$
BL_i – number of links which points to the Web document i on a context	The calculation of *Authorities* and *hubs* considers a set S of documents on a context. It is an iterative process where all of weights initialize on 1. Afterwards, *hub* and *authority* weights are calculated and the results are normalized. This process is repeated until the convergence of values a and h of all documents. We adopt JUNG to obtain the values of *hubs* and *authorities*.
FL_i – number of links going out of the Web document i on a context	

Reputation assumes the corresponding metadata *authority* as the base data for the linguistic variable. For a given document, based on the *authority* to the document *i* on a context (its *reputation*), the model should provide its membership value for all sets defined by the linguistic variables.

Let *C* be the referential set for all possible values for the quality dimension *completeness*. *Completeness* assumes the corresponding metadata *hub* as the base data for the linguistic variable. For a given document, based on the *hub* for document *i* on a context (its *completeness*), the model should provide its membership value for all defined sets defined by the linguistic variables.

Let *T* be the referential set for all possible values for the quality dimension *timeliness*. *Timeliness* assumes the corresponding metadata *update time* as the base data for the linguistic variable. For a given document, based on how many hours ago the document was updated (its *update time*), the model should provide its membership value for all sets defined by the linguistic variables.

The number of linguistic terms for subjective evaluation can be established in accordance with the project convenience, possible application domain peculiarities, or determination of the managing team of quality. Based on previous work (Ross, 2004; Kantrowitz et al., 1997; Klir & Yuan, 1995; Cox, 1994), we know that at least five or seven linguistic terms are more indicated to obtain a better classification. For the sake of simplification, here we only define three linguistic terms to describe *timeliness, reputation,* and *completeness* as linguistic variables. The linguistic terms are classified as *bad, regular,* and *good,* involving, for instance, every possibility of fuzzy subsets of *T, C,* and *R* denoted by $\tilde{N}(T)$, $\tilde{N}(C)$, and $\tilde{N}(R)$, respectively.

To exemplify the definitions above, Figure 3 illustrates the linguistic variable *timeliness*

and its possible values, the linguistic terms *Bad, Regular,* and *Good* denoted as $\tilde{B}$, $\tilde{R}$, and $\tilde{G}$:

$$\tilde{B} = \left\{ \left(ut_i, \mu_{\tilde{B}}(ut_i)\right) \middle| ut_i \in UT \right\}$$

$$\tilde{R} = \left\{ \left(ut_i, \mu_{\tilde{R}}(ut_i)\right) \middle| ut_i \in UT \right\}$$

$$\tilde{G} = \left\{ \left(ut_i, \mu_{\tilde{G}}(ut_i)\right) \middle| ut_i \in UT \right\}$$

where $\mu_{\tilde{B}}(ut_i): UT \to [0,1]$, $\mu_{\tilde{R}}(ut_i): UT \to [0,1]$, $\mu_{\tilde{G}}(ut_i): UT \to [0,1]$ represent fuzzy membership functions that map the element ut_i (*update time* of a Web document) into $\tilde{B}$, $\tilde{R}$, and $\tilde{G}$, respectively.

Content Class

This class defines the set of values representing data, metadata, and context of a Web document (*HasContent relationship*). This is defined as the intrinsic aspects of data representation—for example, all stored data, metadata attributes, context, user categories, and their values for which the results are interesting to some user.

Definition 7. The Content Class represents a set:

$$T = \left\{ Content_1, Content_2, ... Content_n \right\}$$

where each $Content_i, 1 \le i \le n$, is a content instance.

User Class

This class defines the set of specialist users and end users. We use *su* to represent specialist users and *eu* to represent end users, indexed when necessary.

Definition 8. User is a set:

$$U = \{u_1, u_2, \ldots u_n\}$$

where each $u_i, 1 \le i \le n$, is an instance of an user.

Definition 9. Specialist-User Class represents a set:

$$SU = \{su_1, su_2, \ldots su_n\}$$

where each $su_i, 1 \le i \le n$, is the instance of a specialist user. Simple examples of specialist users are *economists and mathematicians.*

Definition 10. The End-User Class represents a set:

$$EU = \{eu_1, eu_2, \ldots eu_n\}$$

where each $eu_i, 1 \le i \le n$, is an instance of an end user.

We also define: $U = SU \cup EU$ and $SU \cap EU = \phi$.

Context Class

This class defines the set of contexts. They are retrieved together with the information, as with metadata.

Definition 11. The Context is a set:

$$C = \{c_1, c_2, \ldots c_n\}$$

where each $c_i, 1 \le i \le n$, is a name associated to a context. Simple examples of contexts are *economy* and *mathematics.*

Considering that quality dimensions present different relevance depending on

Figure 3. Linguistic variable "Timeliness" (Adapted from Klir, 1995)

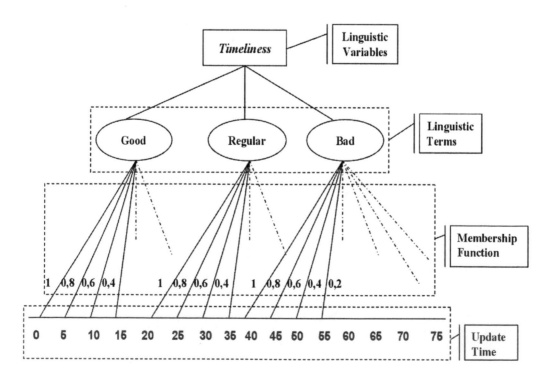

Table 5. Scale of importance degrees (Adapted from Xexéo, 1996)

Importance Degrees	Explanation
0	Indicates that the evaluated quality dimension has no importance.
1	Indicates that the evaluated quality dimension has a small importance.
2	Indicates that the evaluated quality dimension is important in some circumstances, but not always.
3	Indicates that the evaluated quality dimension is very important.
4	Indicates that the evaluated quality dimension is essential.

the context, the specialist users attribute an importance degree to each quality dimension considering a specific context. Thus, based on the selection of quality dimensions and importance weightings of them, it is defined as a context weight vector to be used later during the defuzzification stage. Table 5 shows the scale of importance degrees to be used by the specialist users.

Definition 12. The context weight vector is represented by:

$$CQD = \langle w(c,qd_1) \quad w(c,qd_2) \quad ... \quad w(c,qd_n) \rangle$$

where c = is a specific context. qd_n is a quality dimension.

$w(c, qd_n)$ is the importance degree attributed by specialist-users to one qd_n in a specific c. A simple example is to attribute "3" to *timeliness* in *math*. To simplify, in this representation we consider the arithmetic average of all degrees attributed by the specialist users to one qd_n.

CQD represents the vector of weights to each qd_n in a specific c, attributed by specialist users.

Besides the semantic contextualization, this is also considered the end user perspec-

tive. They attribute the importance degree of each quality dimension, similarly to preceding procedure, now considering their specific requirements. Then, it is defined as an end user weight vector also to be used later during the defuzzification stage.

Definition 13. The end user weight vector is represented by:

$$UQD = \langle w(c,qd_1) \quad w(c,qd_2) \quad ... \quad w(c,qd_n) \rangle$$

where UQD represents the vector of weights to each qd_n attributed by end users.

There are a *Quality_Dimension Weight Association Class* and the relationship "*Attributes*" to represent these attributions.

We understand that it could be difficult to find specialist users to define CQD for every context, so there is the alternative of using multiple UQD to compose CQD.

So far, we have dealt with the evaluation results, separately, by content and by each considered linguistic term defined by each linguist variable (quality dimension). In this work, we name these results *Single Quality Evaluation Results—SQER*.

For example, there are three *SQER* $(\mu_{\tilde{B}}(ut_i),$ $\mu_{\tilde{R}}(ut_i),$ and $\mu_{\tilde{G}}(ut_i))$ for each Web document that take into account the linguistic terms *Bad, Regular,* and *Good* and the linguistic variable *Timeliness.*

These *SQER* are the fuzzy input sets. From these *SQER*, we calculate the *CQER—Composed Quality Evaluation Results* for each Web document. The operation to obtain *CQER* from *SQER* is a fuzzy logic aggregated function, and *CQER* represents the fuzzy output sets.

Here it is important to emphasize that the fuzzy logic approach allows handling linguistic variable compositions from different concepts.

In a composition, all of the fuzzy subsets assigned to each output variable are combined together to form composed fuzzy subsets for each output variable. Usually, MAX or SUM inferences are used. In MAX composition, the combined output fuzzy subset is constructed by taking the point-wise maximum over all of the fuzzy subsets assigned to a variable by the inference rule (fuzzy logic OR). In SUM composition, the combined output fuzzy subset is constructed by taking the point-wise sum over all of the fuzzy subsets assigned to the output variable by the inference rule (Kantrowitz et al., 1997).

In our proposal, we adopt the weighted arithmetic average to obtain the output fuzzy subsets. Definition 14 depicts these concepts.

Definition 14. The composition values formed from the fuzzy subsets is represented by:

$$CQER_j = \left(\sum_{i=1}^{n} cqd_i.uqd_i\, SQER_{ij}\right) \Big/ \left(\sum_{i=1}^{n} cqd_i.uqd_i\right)$$

where

- j is a specific linguistic term, in our example *bad, regular,* and *good*;
- i is a specific variable linguistic, in our example *timeliness, reputation,* and *completeness*;
- cqd represents the weight to each qd_n in a specific c, estimated by specialist users;
- udq represents the weight to each qd_n estimated by end users; and
- $CQER_j$ represents the output fuzzy subsets of a specific linguistic term j.

Finally, there is the defuzzification, which is used when it is useful to convert the fuzzy output set to a crisp number. This is executed after the fuzzy inference aggregation. The defuzzification is very important in our approach, in order to rank the Web documents set by their quality evaluation. These result-set ranking orders are then used by data consumers to filter and personalize the information searches according to their quality level preference values.

As we have read, there are many defuzzification methods. In this work, we adopt the centroid as defuzzification method.

SYSTEM ARCHITECTURE AND TECHNICAL DETAILS

Figure 4 shows the system architecture. Its components are described as follows:

- **Web information quality awareness layer:** This layer is responsible for controlling and mediating the processing and flow of information among the other components.
- **Crawler:** This component was developed in Java to retrieve Web documents and the original metadata in a breadth-first strategy (Baeza-Yates, Castillo, Marin, & Rodriguez, 2005). It also generates the graphs (vertices and arcs) from Web documents to *JUNG*

component in the *Pajek* format (*vlado.fmf. uni-lj.si/pub/networks/pajek/*).

- **JUNG:** This is a software library that provides a common and extendable language for modeling, analysis, and visualization of data that can be represented as a graph or network. We adopt *JUNG* to calculate the *hubs* and *authorities* of Web documents using *Pajek* format. It is written in Java, which allows JUNG-based applications to make use of the extensive built-in capabilities of the Java API, as well as those of other existing third-party Java libraries (*jung. sourceforge.net*).

- **Matlab Fuzzy Logic Toolbox:** This is a collection of functions built on the *MATLAB* numeric computing environment (*www. mathworks.com*). It provides tools to create

and edit fuzzy inference systems within the framework of *MATLAB*.

- **User and Context-Aware Quality Ontology Based on Web Metadata:** This ontology was described above.

EXPECTED RESULTS

To illustrate our approach, we prepared an example using *timeliness, reputation,* and *completeness* as specific quality dimensions. We consider one specific scenario for the *economy* context. There are five steps in this process. Table 6 presents the five first obtained results by our crawler.

The first step defines the metadata sets *OM* e *DM* according to Table 4:

Figure 4. System architecture and technical details

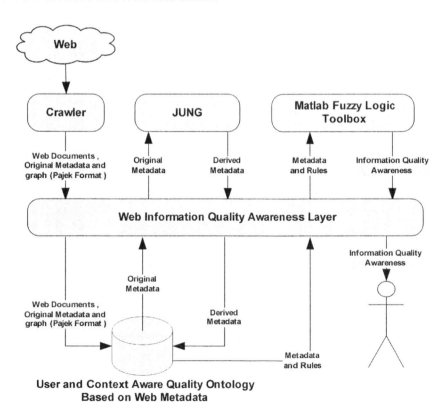

Table 6. Original and derived metadata values

Query Context: *economy*	Original Metadata		Derived Metadata		
Web Sites	**UD**	**QT**	**UT**	**Authority**	**Hub**
Economist. com Surveys[1]	Nov 25th	Nov 28th	72	0.019793	0.026939
Economist Conferences[2]	Nov 23rd	Nov 28th	120	0.018074	0.022909
The World In 2007[3]	Nov 21st	Nov 28th	168	0.017019	0.017008
Economist.com Opinion[4]	Nov 28th	Nov 28th	12	0.012019	0.053238
Scottrade[5]	Nov 22nd	Nov 28th	144	0.007503	0.007331

(Endnotes)
1   http://www.economist.com/surveys/
2   http://www.economistconferences.com/
3   http://www.theworldin.com/
4   http://www.economist.com/opinion
5   http://www.scottrade.com/index.asp?supbid=68597

$$OM_i = \{ud_i, qt_i\}$$
$$DM_i = fd(OM_i) = \{ut_i, a_i, h_i,\}$$

The second step defines the fuzzy membership sets for *timeliness, reputation,* and *completeness* that represent the fuzzy input sets and *CQER* that represent the fuzzy output set, respectively. Figures 5a and 5b show the mapping of membership functions for the fuzzy set *bad, regular,* and *good.* The triangular numbers, which compose each set, have the same base width. The triangular number related to the regular set is in the middle of the metadata numeric interval.

Based on Figures 5a and 5b, it is possible to accomplish the fuzzification mapping from metadata values presented in Table 6, and to obtain the membership degrees of the linguistic variables (quality dimensions) to each fuzzy set (*bad, regular,* and *good*). The results of this operation are shown in Table 7. Notice that Table 7 provides *Dmin* and *Dmax* by the smallest and largest value of each derived metadata. This table

does not provide the *CQER* values to *Dmin* and *Dmax,* and in this case we assume *Dmin=0* and *Dmax=1.*

The third step defines the context weight vector *CQD*. The specialist users attribute weights to the quality dimensions *timeliness (tim), reputation (rep),* and *completeness (com),* considering the context *economy (eco).*

$$CQD = \langle w(eco,tim) \quad w(eco,com) \quad w(eco,rep) \rangle$$

This example considers the arithmetic average of all degrees attributed by the specialist users to one qd_n. This way we assume the following weights:

$$CQD = \langle 2 \quad 3 \quad 4 \rangle$$

- *timeliness* = 2 (*timeliness* is important in some circumstances, but not always);
- *reputation* = 3 (*reputation* is very important);
- *completeness* = 4 (*completeness* is essential).

Figure 5a. Graph of fuzzy membership functions to Timelines

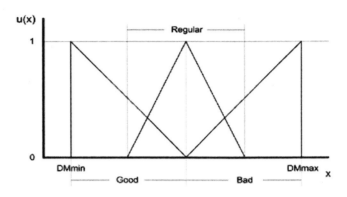

Figure 5b. Graph of fuzzy membership functions to Reputation, Completeness

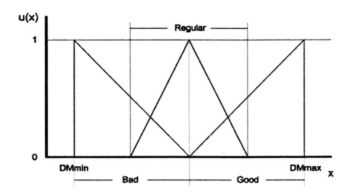

The fourth step defines the end user weight vector *UQD*. The end users attribute weights to the quality dimensions *timeliness (tim), completeness (com),* and *reputation (rep),* considering the context *economy (eco)* and their specific requirements.

$$UQD = \langle w(eco,tim) \quad w(eco,com) \quad w(eco,rep) \rangle$$

This example considers the arithmetic average of all degrees attributed by the end users to one qd_n. This way we assume the following weights:

$$UQD = \langle 3 \quad 2 \quad 4 \rangle$$

- *timeliness* = 3 (*timeliness* is very important);
- *reputation* = 2 (*reputation* is important in some circumstances, but not always);
- *completeness* = 4 (*completeness* is essential).

The fifth step defines the **co**mposition values $CQER_j$ from the fuzzy input subsets. It defines also the subsequent defuzzification. Each $CQER_j$ represents the maximum value of the set given by *j*. Figures 6a, 6b, 6c, 6d, and 6e present the fuzzy output set $CQER_j$ and the defuzzification results for each Web document. It is appropriate to remember that the centroid method was adopted.

Table 7. Fuzzification results

Query Context: *economy*	*Fuzzification* **Results**		
Web Sites	*Timeliness*	*Reputation*	*Completeness*
Economist.com Surveys	$\mu_{\tilde{B}}(ut_i)=0.25$ $\mu_{\tilde{R}}(ut_i)=0.55$ $\mu_{\tilde{G}}(ut_i)=0$	$\mu_{\tilde{B}}(a_i)=0$ $\mu_{\tilde{R}}(a_i)=0$ $\mu_{\tilde{G}}(a_i)=1$	$\mu_{\tilde{B}}(h_i)=0,167110$ $\mu_{\tilde{R}}(h_i)=0,7157852$ $\mu_{\tilde{G}}(h_i)=0$
Economist Conferences	$\mu_{\tilde{B}}(ut_i)=0$ $\mu_{\tilde{R}}(ut_i)=0.25$ $\mu_{\tilde{G}}(ut_i)=0.4$	$\mu_{\tilde{B}}(a_i)=0$ $\mu_{\tilde{R}}(a_i)=0$ $\mu_{\tilde{G}}(a_i)=0,727254$	$\mu_{\tilde{B}}(h_i)=0,33829$ $\mu_{\tilde{R}}(h_i)=0,3734191$ $\mu_{\tilde{G}}(h_i)=0$
The World In 2007	$\mu_{\tilde{B}}(ut_i)=0$ $\mu_{\tilde{R}}(ut_i)=0$ $\mu_{\tilde{G}}(ut_i)=1$	$\mu_{\tilde{B}}(a_i)=0$ $\mu_{\tilde{R}}(a_i)=0$ $\mu_{\tilde{G}}(a_i)=0,559862$	$\mu_{\tilde{B}}(h_i)=0,58895$ $\mu_{\tilde{R}}(h_i)=0$ $\mu_{\tilde{G}}(h_i)=0$
Economist.com Opinion	$\mu_{\tilde{B}}(ut_i)=1$ $\mu_{\tilde{R}}(ut_i)=0$ $\mu_{\tilde{G}}(ut_i)=0$	$\mu_{\tilde{B}}(a_i)=0,283470$ $\mu_{\tilde{R}}(a_i)=0,4830675$ $\mu_{\tilde{G}}(a_i)=0$	$\mu_{\tilde{B}}(h_i)=0$ $\mu_{\tilde{R}}(h_i)=0$ $\mu_{\tilde{G}}(h_i)=1$
Scottrade	$\mu_{\tilde{B}}(ut_i)=0$ $\mu_{\tilde{R}}(ut_i)=0$ $\mu_{\tilde{G}}(ut_i)=0.7$	$\mu_{\tilde{B}}(a_i)=1$ $\mu_{\tilde{R}}(a_i)=0$ $\mu_{\tilde{G}}(a_i)=0$	$\mu_{\tilde{B}}(h_i)=1$ $\mu_{\tilde{R}}(h_i)=0$ $\mu_{\tilde{G}}(h_i)=0$

Table 8 shows the rank of the pages obtained from the defuzzification results. Notice that in these examples, Web documents with the largest values for good sets were in the first positions. However, the attributed weights could affect and compensate or not the final results by increasing or decreasing these positions.

FUTURE TRENDS

The current version of the prototype already implements the fuzzy theory approach to obtain the graphs and the fuzzy membership sets, in order to identify users' quality level expectations on their retrieved Web documents. This would carry forward into extra research tasks, including:

- Detailing of fuzzy membership sets, aggregation mappings, and the defuzzification process, to work with five or seven linguistic terms, in order to obtain a better-refined classification of the Web documents; and
- Development or adoption of a policy to assess the competencies of the specialist users.

These assessment results will be weighted in the context weight vector definition.

Figure 6a. The defuzzification results to http://www.economist.com/surveys/

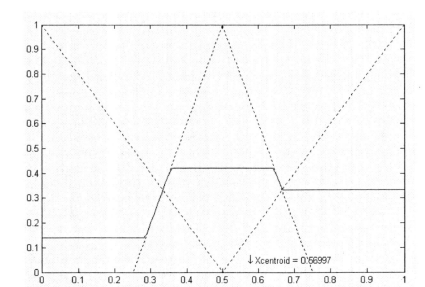

Figure 6b. The defuzzification results to http://www.economistconferences.com/

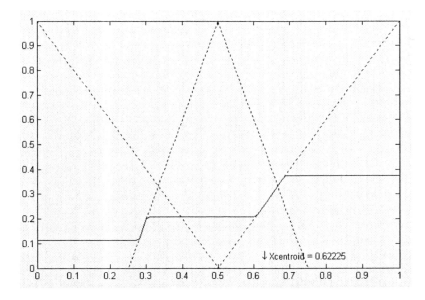

Future research should expand the model and the prototype, including in the evaluation process others quality dimensions and metadata in order to improve the quality evaluation results as a whole.

Besides there are some applications and technologies possible to be implemented based on knowledge of User and Context Aware Quality Ontology.

As we have seen previously with the continuous growth of the available information volume on the Web, users can have difficulty finding relevant information, although the information retrieval area has carried out a fundamental role in this direction, providing techniques that make

Figure 6c. The defuzzification results to http://www.theworldin.com/

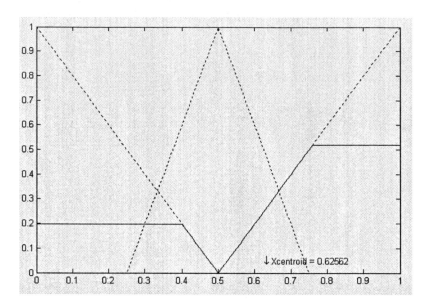

Figure 6d. The defuzzification results to http://www.economist.com/opinion

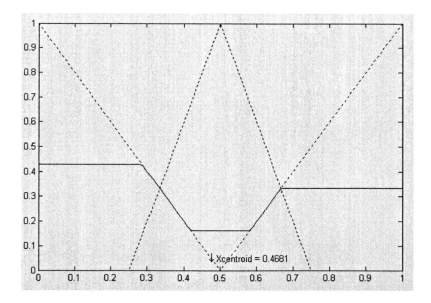

possible more efficient searches (Baeza-Yates & Ribeiro-Neto, 1999).

This fact occurs due to the volume of data to be processed, the heterogeneity and distribution of the information sources, the lack of a metadata standard to describe the data semantics on Web pages, and the difficulty of the users to express theirs information needs through a search that adopts keywords (Lawrence, 2000; Mizzaro, 1997; Moura, 2003).

Another aspect to be considered is that the search systems do not store information on the user, nor on the context in which the search is requested (Lawrence, 2000). In this sense, the

Figure 6e. The defuzzification results to http://www.scottrade.com/index.asp? supbid=68597

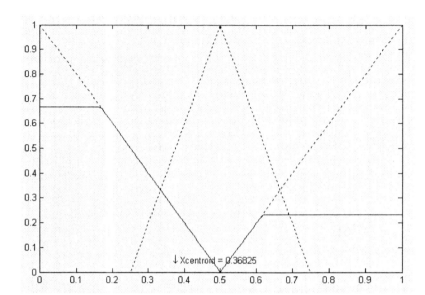

Table 8. The defuzzification results and the ranking of the Web documents

Query Context: *Economy*	Defuzzification	Ranking
Economist.com Surveys	0.56997	3°
Economist Conferences	0.62225	2°
The World In 2007	0.62562	1°
Economist.com Opinion	0.46810	4°
Scottrade	0.36825	5°

information filtering area deals with the information overload problem, considering the use of filters to eliminate irrelevant information (Belkin & Croft, 1992). Filtering generally uses user profiles to represent the user information needs and uses intelligent agents to eliminate items from the information flow (Maes, 1994).

Another proposal to deal with this problem uses recommender systems. These systems are personalized services developed to help people with the diversity and the information overload, since they make possible that they share opinions and experiences. The main approach of this solution is to find interesting items to users, instead of eliminating irrelevant items.

People generally appeal from recommendations of friends, specialists, or specialized publications when they need to make a decision, even to choose a product to buy or to decide which film to see. Thus as we appeal from these trivial resources, to know the opinion of other people would help to select relevant information in situations where there is a great volume of information.

Recommender systems automatize this process, since they allow sharing opinions and exchange of experience between people (Terveen & Hill, 2001). These systems have been used for entertainment sites, games, and forums; in e-commerce (Schafer, Konstan, & Riedl, 2001); as well as in digital libraries (Paepcke, 1996; Borgman,

1999). Amazon (*www.amazon.com*), for example, uses one technique of recommendation as part of its CRM (Customer Relationship Management) policies.

As another venue for future trends, we also intend to develop a recommender system based on acquired results, integrating this activity as a final step of the proposed evaluation process. We believe this is a fertile area for research, and one that has not been totally explored yet.

Data cleaning is one of the other possible applications that can help the improvement of data quality. This treatment includes the aggregation, the organization, and the cleanness of data. Most cleanness operations involve correcting the defects of the data elements and records by the modification of incorrect values or replacement of lost values, returning them to the initial standards. These corrections can be made by insertions of the pre-defined values (e.g., "unknown value"), by the use of a correct value captured from another database or asking who knows and can inform the correct values.

The prevention of errors involves the education of people responsible for data entry, the modification or application of new validations for systems, the update of codes, the update of the systems and the models, and the changes in the processes and the business rules.

In some cases, the correction of errors cannot be desirable because of the involved costs or some other impossibility. In these situations, the errors need to be recorded and users need to be notified through reports of error detention (Eckerson, 2002; Maletic & Marcus, 2000).

According to Eckerson (2002), if the problems related to data quality cannot be prevented, there exist some places where they can be corrected: in the source of information, in a storage area, or in the date warehouses ETL process. He considers that the best place for data cleaning is in the source of information, where the dissemination of errors can be blocked before its flow for other systems or databases. In this in case, the main objective

is to guarantee that data reach the user with the highest possible degree of quality.

CONCLUSION

This work is related to some study areas such as data quality and metadata, processes of quality evaluation, fuzzy logic and fuzzy sets for quality evaluation, contexts, and ontologies. It aims the investigation and aggregated application of the advantages inherent to each one of these areas to acquire solutions to identified problems. In this sense, we hope to contribute to the generation of new alternative answers that lead to innovative results.

The problems regarding information quality involve many different users' profiles. Beyond the Internet users, they occur similarly in complex corporative environments that keep their proper Web as one or more intranets. The awareness of problems inherent to low information quality is the first obstacle to succeeding when looking for alternative solutions. The more tangible impacts—such as the dissatisfactions of the users and the organizations, the increase of costs, the inefficient decision-making processes, and the reduction of the ability to execute the strategy—are sufficiently bad already. Other minor impacts can make these problems worse. But this does not have to be this way: the mechanisms to improve data quality are available and have been effectively applied in some projects.

The possibility to evaluate and rank the Web documents based on their quality criteria leads to new opportunities and more efficient strategies when data consumers decide to filter and personalize the information searches according to their quality-level perspectives, in view of so much information available (Lyman & Hal, 2003; Burgess et al., 2004). Therefore, taking into account that information quality is dependent on its own context, metadata contexts are adopted as a base to quality evaluation indicators.

As stated in our chapter, the aim of this project is to produce a user and context-aware quality filters strategy based on Web metadata retrieval that can be adopted by end users. Our proposed solution aims to provide better and novel mechanisms to improve the quality evaluation results and increase the trustworthiness in information retrieval processes as a whole. The final results can be compared with the results of other studies developed in the area.

Finally, this methodology formalizes the different components involved in a quality evaluation process, and surely other research is necessary to explore its computational and social consequences, as well as the effective costs of this quality improvement. The main and immediate costs regard the adaptation of environments and systems to adopt the methodology.

REFERENCES

Baeza-Yates, R., Castillo, C., Marin, M., & Rodriguez, A. (2005). Crawling a country: Better strategies than breadth-first for Web page ordering. *Proceedings of the Industrial and Practical Experience Track of the 14th Conference on the World Wide Web* (pp. 864–872), Chiba, Japan.

Baeza-Yates, R., & Ribeiro-Neto, B. (1999). *Modern information retrieval.* Boston: Addison-Wesley-Longman.

Belkin, N.J., & Croft, W.B. (1992). Information filtering and information retrieval: Two sides of the same coin? *Communications of the ACM, 35,* 29–38.

Borgman, C. (1999). What are digital libraries? Competing visions. *Information Processing and Management: An International Journal, 35*(5), 227–243.

Burgess, M.S.E., Gray, W.A., & Fiddian, N.J. (2004). Quality measures and the information consumer. *Proceedings of the 9th International Conference on Information Quality* (ICIQ-04) (pp. 373–388). Retrieved June 25, 2006, from *http://www.iqconference.org/ICIQ/iqpapers. aspx?iciqyear=2004*

Cox, E. (1994). *The fuzzy systems handbook: A practitioner's guide to building, using, and maintaining fuzzy systems.* London: Academic Press.

Dey, A.K. (2001). Understanding and using context. *Personal and Ubiquitous Computing Journal, 5,* 4–7.

Dubois, D., & Prade, H. (1991). Fuzzy sets in approximate reasoning. Part 1: Inference with possibility distributions. In IFSA (Ed.), *Fuzzy sets and systems. Special memorial volume: 25 years of fuzzy sets.* Amsterdam: North-Holland.

Eckerson, W. (2002). *Data quality and the bottom line: Achieving business success through a commitment to high quality data.* Report Series (vol. 1, pp. 1–32), Data Warehousing Institute.

English, L.P. (1999). *Improving data warehouse and business information quality—methods for reducing costs and increasing profits.* New York: John Wiley & Sons.

Grauel, A. (1999). Analytical and structural considerations in fuzzy modeling. *Fuzzy Sets and Systems, 101,* 205–206.

Kantrowitz, M., Horstkotte, E., & Joslyn, C. (1997). *Answers to questions about fuzzy logic and fuzzy expert systems.* Retrieved June 25, 2006, from *http://www-cgi.cs.cmu.edu/afs/cs/project/ai-repository/ai/areas/fuzzy/faq/fuzzy.faq*

Kim, Y.J., Kishore, R., & Sanders, R.L. (2005). DQ to EQ: Understanding data quality in the context of e-business systems. *Communications of the ACM, 48,* 75–81.

Kleinberg, J.M. (1998). Authoritative sources in a hyperlinked environment. *Proceedings of the 9th*

ACM-SIAM Symposium on Discrete Algorithms (pp. 668–677). Retrieved June 25, 2006, from *http://www.cs.cornell.edu/home/kleinber/auth.pdf*

Klir, G.J., & Yuan, B. (1995). *Fuzzy sets and fuzzy logic: Theory and applications.* Englewood Cliffs, NJ: Prentice Hall.

Lawrence, S. (2000). Context in Web search. *IEEE Data Engineering Bulletin, 23,* 25–32.

Lee, Y.W. (2004). Crafting rules: Context-reflective data quality problem solving. *Journal of Management Information Systems, 20*(Winter), 93–119.

Loshin, D. (2001). *Enterprise knowledge management—the data quality approach.* San Francisco: Morgan Kaufman.

Lyman, P., & Hal, R.V. (2003). *How much information?* Retrieved June 25, 2006, from http://www.sims.berkeley.edu/how-much-info-2003

Maes, P. (1994). Social interface agents: Acquiring competence by learning from users and other agents. *Proceedings of the AAAI Spring Symposium on Software Agents* (pp. 71–78), Stanford, CA.

Maletic, J.I., & Marcus, A. (2000). Data cleansing: Beyond integrity checking. *Proceedings of the Conference on Information Quality* (IQ2000) (pp. 200–209).

Mizzaro, S. (1997). Relevance: The whole history. *Journal of the American Society for Information Science, 48*(9), 810–832.

Moura, A.M. (2003). The semantic Web: Fundamentals, technologies, trends. *Proceedings of the 17th Brazilian Symposium of Databases,* Gramado, Brazil.

Paepcke, A. (1996). *Digital libraries: Searching is not enough.* Retrieved June 25, 2006, from *http://dlib.org/dlib/may96/stanford/05paepcke.html*

Peralta, V., Ruggia, R., Kedad, Z., & Mokrane, B. (2004). A framework for data quality evaluation in a data integration system. *Proceedings of the Brazilian Symposium of Databases* (pp. 134–147).

Pinheiro, W.A., & Moura, A.M.C. (2004). An ontology based-approach for semantic search in portals. *Database and Expert Systems Applications, 15,* 127–131.

Pipino, L.L., Lee, Y.W., & Wang, R.Y. (2002). Data quality assessment. *Communications of the ACM, 45,* 211–218.

Redman, T.C. (1998). The impact of poor data quality on the typical enterprise. *Communications of the ACM, 41,* 79–81.

Ross, T.J. (2004). Fuzzy Logic with Engineering Applications (2nd ed.). West Sussex, England: John Wiley & Sons.

Rothenberg, J. (1996). Metadata to support data quality and longevity. *Proceedings of the 1st IEEE Metadata Conference* (pp. 16–18).

Schafer, J.B., Konstan, J.A., & Riedl, J. (2001). E-commerce recommendation applications. *Proceedings of the Conference on Data Mining and Knowledge Discovery* (pp. 115–153).

Smart, K.L. (2002). Assessing quality documents. *ACM Journal of Computer Documentation, 26*(3), 130–140.

Strong, D., Wang, R.Y., & Guarascio, M.L. (1994). Beyond accuracy: What data quality means to data consumers. TDQM Research Program. *Journal of Management Information Systems, 12*(4), 5–33.

Terveen, L., & Hill, W. (2001). Beyond recommender system: Helping people to find each other. *Proceedings of HCI in the New Millennium.*

Tillman, H.N. (2003). *Evaluating quality on the Net.* Retrieved June 25, 2006, from *http://www.hopetillman.com/findqual.html*

Turksen, I.B. (1991). Measurement of membership functions and their acquisition. In ITSA (Ed.), *Fuzzy sets and systems. Special memorial volume: 25 years of fuzzy sets.* Amsterdam: North-Holland.

Twidale, M.B., & Marty, P.F. (1999). *An investigation of data quality and collaboration.* Technical Report UIUCLIS—1999/9+CSCW, University of Illinois at Urbana-Champaign, USA.

Wand, Y., & Wang, R. (1996). Anchoring data quality dimensions in ontological foundations. *Communications of the ACM, 39,* 86–95.

Xexéo, G., Belchior, A., & da Rocha, A.R.C. (1996). Aplicação da teoria fuzzy em requisitos de qualidade de software. *Memorias-I, XXII CLEI,* Santafé de Bogotá, Colombia, Junio (pp. 3–7).

Yager, R.R. (1991). Connectives and quantifiers in fuzzy sets. In IFSA (Ed.), *Fuzzy sets and systems. Special memorial volume: 25 years of fuzzy sets.* Amsterdam: North-Holland.

Zadeh, L.A. (1965). Fuzzy sets. *Information and Control, 8,* 338–353.

Zadeh, L.A. (1988). Fuzzy logic. *IEEE Transactions in Computing,* 83-92.

Zimmermann, H.J. (1991). *Fuzzy set theory and its applications* (2nd revised ed.). Boston: Kluwer.

ENDNOTES

[1] The reader must be aware of the subtle difference between data and information. In this chapter, we consider that data is the representation (notation) and information is the meaning (denotation), and we use these terms indistinctly.

[2] The PICS™ specification enables labels (metadata) to be associated with Internet content. It was originally designed to help parents and teachers control what children access on the Internet, but it also facilitates other uses for labels, including code signing and privacy. The PICS platform is one on which other rating services and filtering software have been built (*http://www.w3.org/PICS/#RDF*).

[3] *http://www.economist.com/surveys/*

[4] *http://www.economistconferences.com/*

[5] *http://www.theworldin.com/*

[6] *http://www.economist.com/opinion*

[7] *http://www.scottrade.com/index.asp?supbid=68597*

Chapter IX
Personalized Content–Based Image Retrieval

Iker Gondra
St. Francis Xavier University, Canada

ABSTRACT

In content-based image retrieval (CBIR), a set of low-level features are extracted from an image to represent its visual content. Retrieval is performed by image example where a query image is given as input by the user and an appropriate similarity measure is used to find the best matches in the corresponding feature space. This approach suffers from the fact that there is a large discrepancy between the low-level visual features that one can extract from an image and the semantic interpretation of the image's content that a particular user may have in a given situation. That is, users seek semantic similarity, but we can only provide similarity based on low-level visual features extracted from the raw pixel data, a situation known as the semantic gap. The selection of an appropriate similarity measure is thus an important problem. Since visual content can be represented by different attributes, the combination and importance of each set of features varies according to the user's semantic intent. Thus, the retrieval strategy should be adaptive so that it can accommodate the preferences of different users. Relevance feedback (RF) learning has been proposed as a technique aimed at reducing the semantic gap. It works by gathering semantic information from user interaction. Based on the user's feedback on the retrieval results, the retrieval scheme is adjusted. By providing an image similarity measure under human perception, RF learning can be seen as a form of supervised learning that finds relations between high-level semantic interpretations and low-level visual properties. That is, the feedback obtained within a single query session is used to personalize the retrieval strategy and thus enhance retrieval performance. In this chapter we present an overview of CBIR and related work on RF learning. We also present our own previous work on a RF learning-based probabilistic region relevance learning algorithm for automatically estimating the importance of each region in an image based on the user's semantic intent.

INTRODUCTION

In recent years, the rapid development of information technologies and the advent of the Web have accelerated the growth of digital media and, in particular, image collections. As a result and in order to realize the full potential of these technologies, the need for effective mechanisms to search large image collections becomes evident. The management of text information has been studied thoroughly, and there have been many successful approaches for handling text databases (see Salton, 1986). However, the progress in research and development of multimedia database systems has been slow due to the difficulties and challenges of the problem.

The development of concise representations of images that can capture the essence of their visual content is an important task. However, as the saying "a picture is worth a thousand words" suggests, representing visual content is a very difficult task. The human ability to extract semantics from an image by using knowledge of the world is remarkable, though probably difficult to emulate.

At present, the most common way to represent the visual content of an image is to assign a set of descriptive keywords to it. Then, image retrieval is performed by matching the query text with the stored keywords (Rui & Huang, 1998). However, there are many problems associated with this simple keyword matching approach. First, it is usually the case that all the information contained in an image cannot be captured by a few keywords. Furthermore, a large amount of effort is needed to do keyword assignments in a large image database. Also, because different people may have different interpretations of an image's content, there will be inconsistencies (Rui & Huang, 1998). Consider the image in Figure 1. One might describe it as "mountains," "trees," and/or "lake." However, that particular description would not be able to respond to user queries for "water," "landscape," "peaceful," or "water reflection."

In order to alleviate some of the problems associated with text-based approaches, content-based image retrieval (CBIR) was proposed (see Faloutsos et al., 1993, for examples of early approaches). The idea is to search on the images

Figure 1. Sample image

Figure 2. General CBIR computational framework

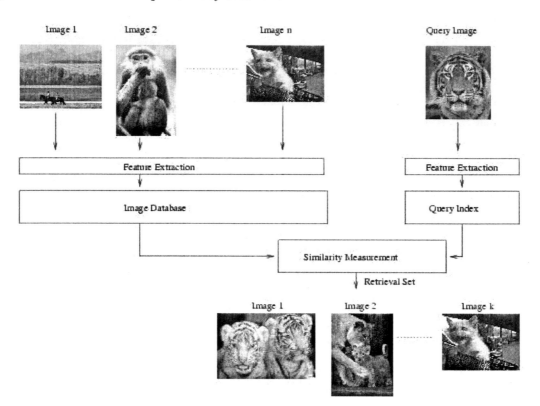

directly. A set of low-level features (such as color, texture, and shape) are extracted from the image to characterize its visual content. In traditional approaches (Faloutsos et al., 1993; Gupta & Jain, 1997; Hara, Hirata, Takano, & Kawasaki, 1997; Kelly, Cannon, & Hush, 1995; Mehrotra, Rui, Ortega, & Huang, 1997; Pentland, Picard, & Sclaroff, 1994; Samadani, Han, & Katragadda, 1993; Sclaroff, Taycher, & Cascia, 1997; Smith & Chang, 1996, 1997; Stone & Li, 1996; Wang, Wiederhold, Firschein, & Sha, 1998), each image is represented by a set of global features that are calculated by means of uniform processing over the entire image and describe its visual content (e.g., color, texture). The features are then the components of a feature vector which makes the image correspond to a point in a feature space.

Users usually look for particular objects when describing the semantic interpretation of an image. Thus, due to global image properties affecting

the recognition of certain objects depicted in an image, low retrieval performance is often attained when using global features. In region-based image representations (Carson, 2002; Chen & Wang, 2002; Li, Wang, & Wiederhold, 2000; Li, Chen, & Zhang, 2002; Ma & Majunath 1997; Smith & Li, 1999; Wang, Li, & Wiederhold, 2001), the use of local features that describe each of a set of segmented regions in an image provides a more meaningful characterization that is closer to a user's perception of an image's content. That is, instead of looking at the image as a whole, we look at its objects and their relationships. Many image segmentation algorithms have been proposed. However, robust and accurate segmentation remains a difficult problem.

Retrieval in CBIR is performed by image example where a query image is given as input by the user and an appropriate similarity measure is used to find the best matches in the corresponding feature space. Thus, the system views the query and database images as a collection of features. The relevance of a database image to the query image is then proportional to their feature-based similarity. The general computational framework of a CBIR system is depicted in Figure 2. In order to create the image database, images are processed by a feature extraction algorithm and their feature representations are stored in the database. The same feature extraction algorithm is used to obtain the features that represent the query image. The similarity measure compares the representation of the query image with the representation of each database image. Those feature representations deemed the most "similar" are returned to the user as the retrieval set.

This approach suffers from the fact that there is a large discrepancy between the low-level visual features that one can extract from an image and the semantic interpretation of the image's content that a particular user may have in a given situation. That is, users seek semantic similarity but we can only provide similarity based on low-level visual features extracted from the raw pixel data. The human notion of similarity is usually based on high-level abstractions such as activities, events, or emotions displayed in an image. Therefore, a database image with a high feature similarity to the query image may be completely different from the query in terms of user-defined semantics. This discrepancy between low-level features and high-level concepts is known as the *semantic gap* (Smeulders, Worring, Santini, Gupta, & Jain, 2000). This situation is exacerbated when the retrieval task is to be performed in broad image domains (e.g., the Web) where images with similar semantic interpretations may have unpredictable and large variability in their low-level visual content. In contrast, when the retrieval task is performed in narrow domains (e.g., medical images, frontal views of faces), usually there are specific assumptions particular to the application that, for a given semantic interpretation, limit the variability of its corresponding

low-level visual content. As a result, it is easier to find links between low-level visual content and semantic interpretations (i.e., the semantic gap is smaller). The selection of an appropriate similarity measure is thus an important problem. Since visual content can be represented by different attributes, the combination and importance of each set of features varies according to the user's semantic intent. Thus, the retrieval strategy should be adaptive so that it can accommodate the preferences of different users.

Relevance feedback (RF) learning, originally developed for information retrieval (Rocchio & Salton, 1971), has been proposed as a learning technique aimed at reducing the semantic gap. It works by gathering semantic information from user interaction. Based on the user's feedback on the retrieval results, the retrieval scheme is adjusted. By providing an image similarity measure under human perception, RF learning can be seen as a form of supervised learning that finds relations between high-level semantic interpretations and low-level visual properties. That is, the feedback obtained within a single query session is used to personalize the retrieval strategy and thus enhance retrieval performance.

CONTENT-BASED IMAGE RETRIEVAL

As described in the previous section, early approaches to image retrieval were mainly text-based techniques consisting of the manual annotation of images with descriptive keywords. This manual annotation is very time consuming and cumbersome for large image databases. Furthermore, it is very subjective and error-prone. Recently, some approaches for automatic image labeling (Ono, Amano, Hakaridani, Satoh, & Sakauchi, 1996; Shen, Ooi, & Tan, 2000; Srihari, Zhang, & Rao, 2000) have been proposed as an attempt to improve this manual annotation process. Ono et al. (1996) use image recognition techniques to automatically assign descriptive keywords to images. Their approach uses only a limited number of keywords. Furthermore, because image recognition techniques are not completely reliable, automatically assigned keywords still must be verified by a human. Shen et al. (2000) use the textual context of images in a Web page to automatically extract descriptive keywords. The collateral text that usually accompanies an image (e.g., captions) is exploited in Srihari et al. (2000). The performance of those approaches is not as high as that obtained with manual annotation, and their applicability is limited in situations where there is no textual context (e.g., a photo album). Wenyin et al. (2001) propose a semi-automatic annotation that assigns images to keywords based on users' RF. Their approach uses both keyword- and content-based retrieval strategies. A weighted sum of the keyword-based and visual feature-based similarity measures is used to calculate the overall similarity of an image. Based on the user's RF, the annotation of each image in the retrieval set is updated. The experiments conducted in Wenyin et al. (2001) indicate that this strategy of semi-automatic annotation outperforms manual annotation in terms of efficiency and automatic annotation in terms of accuracy. However, the performance of this approach depends heavily on the performance of the particular CBIR and RF algorithms used, especially when there is no initial annotation in the database at all (Wenyin et al., 2001).

In order to overcome the above-mentioned drawbacks associated with text-based approaches, it would be more suitable to search on the images directly based on their visual content. In the early 1990s, CBIR was proposed as a way of allowing a user to search target images in terms of the content represented by visual features. Since then, many CBIR systems have been developed including Blobworld (Carson, 2002), QBIC (Faloutsos et al., 1993), IRM (Li et al., 2000), NeTra (Ma & Majunath, 1997), MARS (Mehrotra et al., 1997), Photobook (Pentland et al., 1994), WebSEEK

(Smith & Change, 1997), and SIMPLIcity (Wang et al., 2001), just to name a few.

Retrieval is performed by image example, where a query image is given as input by the user and an appropriate similarity measure is used to find the best matches in the corresponding feature space. Thus, the system views the query and database images as a collection of features. The relevance of a database image to the query image is then proportional to their feature-based similarity. The general computational framework of a CBIR system is depicted in Figure 2. In order to create the image database, images are processed by a feature extraction algorithm and their feature representations are stored in the database. The same feature extraction algorithm is used to obtain the features that represent the query image. The similarity measure compares the representation of the query image with the representation of each database image. Those feature representations deemed the most "similar" are returned to the user as the retrieval set. For example, when retrieving similar images based on color, most existing techniques use a color histogram generated from the entire image (Jain & Vailaya, 1996). In Swain & Ballard (1991), image similarity was based solely on color. The distribution of color was represented by color histograms. The similarity between two images was then based on a similarity measure between their corresponding histograms called the "normalized histogram intersection."

Conversely, we can measure distance between images. In this case, small distances between feature representations correspond to large similarities, and large distances correspond to small similarities. Thus, distance is a measure of dissimilarity. One way to transform between a distance measure and a similarity measure is to take the reciprocal. Some commonly used distance measures are the Euclidean (also known as the L2-distance) and city-block distances (also known as the Manhattan distance or L1-distance) (Bimbo, 1999). For example, Netra (Ma & Majunath, 1997) uses Euclidean distance on color and shape features; MARS (Mehrotra et al., 1997) uses Euclidean distance on texture features; Blobworld (Carson, 2002) uses Euclidean distance on texture and shape features. IBM's QBIC (Faloutsos et al., 1993) was the first commercial system that implemented CBIR. It addressed the problems of non-Euclidean distance measuring and high dimensionality of feature vectors. MIT's Photobook (Pentland et al., 1994) implements a set of interactive tools for browsing and searching images. It consists of three subsystems: one that allows the user to search based on appearance, one that uses 2D shape, and one that allows search based on textural properties. While searching, these image features can be combined with each other and with keywords to improve retrieval performance.

Similarity Measure

The selection of an appropriate similarity (or distance) measure is an important problem. Since visual content can be represented by different attributes, the combination and importance of each set of features varies according to the user's semantic intent. Thus, the retrieval strategy should be adaptive so that it can accommodate the preferences of different users. Note that with (uniformly weighted) Euclidean distance, every feature is treated equally. However, some features may be more important than others. Similarly, in region-based approaches (where similarity between regions of two images must be computed), some regions may be more important than others in determining overall image-to-image similarity. Thus, the weight of each feature (or region) should be based on its discriminative power between the relevant and non-relevant images for the current query (see Figure 4). Then, the similarity measure of images can be based on a weighted distance in the feature space. The querying system developed in Smith and Li (1999) decomposes and image into regions with characterizations pre-defined

in a finite pattern library. In Blobworld (Carson, 2002), images are partitioned into regions that have similar color and texture. Each pixel is then associated with a set of color, texture, and spatial features. The distribution of pixels for each region is calculated and the distance between two images is equal to the distance between their regions in terms of color and texture. In NeTra (Ma & Majunath, 1997), regions are segmented based on color. Then, texture, shape, color, and spatial properties are used to determine similarity. Both Blobworld (Carson, 2002) and NeTra (Ma & Majunath, 1997) require the user to select the region(s) of interest from the segmented query image. This information is then used for determining similarity with database images. Ravela, Manmatha, and Riseman (1996) use a system that uses a measure of correlation to indicate similarity. This system works for a variety of images, but it requires the user to select the region(s) of interest from the images.

Image Segmentation

A major problem with systems that use region-based image representations is that the segmented regions they produce usually do not correspond to actual objects in the image. For instance, an object may be partitioned into several regions, with none of them being representative of the object. Object (or strong) segmentation is defined as a grouping of the image pixels into regions such that each region contains all the pixels of a single physical object and nothing else. It is an extremely difficult image processing task mainly due to the fact that most segmentation algorithms use low-level data-driven properties to generate regions that are homogeneous according to some criterion. Unfortunately, it is very often the case that such regions do not correspond to meaningful units (i.e., physical objects). Thus, due to the great difficulty of accurately segmenting an image into regions that correspond to a human's perception of an object, several approaches have been proposed

(Chen & Wang, 2002; Li et al., 2002; Smith & Li, 1999; Wang et al., 2001) that consider all regions in an image for determining similarity. As a result, the problems of inaccurate segmentation are reduced. Integrated region matching (IRM) (Li et al., 2002) is proposed as a measure that allows a many-to-many region mapping relationship between two images by matching a region of one image to several regions of another image. Thus, by having a similarity measure that is a weighted sum of distances between all regions from different images, IRM is more robust to inaccurate segmentation. Recently, a fuzzy logic approach, unified feature matching (UFM) (Chen & Wang, 2002), was proposed as an improved alternative to IRM. UFM uses the same segmentation algorithm as IRM. In UFM, an image is characterized by a fuzzy feature denoting color, texture, and shape characteristics. Because fuzzy features can characterize the gradual transition between regions in an image, segmentation-related inaccuracies are implicitly considered by viewing them as blurring boundaries between segmented regions. As a result, a feature vector can belong to multiple regions with different degrees of membership, as opposed to classical region representations in which a feature vector belongs to only one region. The similarity between two images is then defined as the overall similarity between two sets of fuzzy features.

A key factor in these types of systems that consider all the regions to perform an overall image-to-image similarity is the weighting of regions. The weight that is assigned to each region for determining similarity is usually based on prior assumptions such as that larger regions, or regions that are close to the center of the image, should have larger weights. For example, in IRM, an *area percentage scheme,* which is based on the assumption that important objects in an image tend to occupy larger areas, is used to assign weights to regions. The location of a region is also taken into consideration. For example, higher weights are assigned to regions in the center of an image

than to those around boundaries. These region weighting heuristics are often inconsistent with human perception. For instance, a facial region may be the most important when the user is looking for images of people, while other larger regions such as the background may be much less relevant. Some RF approaches are motivated by the need to have a similarity measure that is flexible to user preferences. Later in this chapter, we present our previous work on a learning algorithm that can be used in region-based CBIR systems for estimating region weights in an image.

RELEVANCE FEEDBACK LEARNING

CBIR suffers from what is known as the semantic gap, or the large discrepancy between the low-level visual features that one can extract from an image and the semantic interpretation of the image's content that a particular user may have in a given situation. This situation is exacerbated when the retrieval task is to be performed in broad image domains (e.g., the Web) where images with similar semantic interpretations may have unpredictable and large variability in their low-level visual content. Thus with the exception of some constrained applications such as face and fingerprint recognition, low-level features do not capture the high-level semantics of images (Rui, Huang, & Chang, 1999). The selection of an appropriate similarity measure is thus an important problem. Since visual content can be represented by different attributes, the combination and importance of each set of features varies according to the user's semantic intent. Thus, the retrieval strategy should be adaptive so that it can accommodate the preferences of different users.

Relevance feedback learning, originally developed for information retrieval (Rocchio & Salton, 1971), has been proposed as a learning technique aimed at reducing the semantic gap. It works by gathering semantic information from user interaction. Based on the user's feedback on the retrieval results, the retrieval scheme is adjusted. By providing an image similarity measure under human perception, RF learning can be seen as a form of supervised learning that finds relations between high-level semantic interpretations and low-level visual properties. That is, the feedback obtained within a single query session is used to personalize the retrieval strategy and thus enhance retrieval performance. In order to learn a user's query concept, the user labels each image returned in the previous query round as relevant or non-relevant. Based on the feedback, the retrieval scheme is adjusted and the next set of images is presented to the user for labeling. This process iterates until the user is satisfied with the retrieved images or stops searching.

Relevance Feedback Learning Strategies

The key issue in RF is how to use the positive and negative examples to adjust the retrieval scheme so that the number of relevant images in the next retrieval set will increase. Two main RF strategies have been proposed in CBIR: query modification

(Rui, Huang, & Mehrotra, 1997) and distance reweighing (Buckley & Salton, 1995; Ishikawa, Subramanys, & Faloutsos, 1998; Peng, Bhanu, & Qing, 1999; Rui & Huang, 1998; Shaw, 1995). Query modification changes the representation of the user's query in a form that is closer (hopefully) to the semantic intent of the user. In particular, query shifting involves moving the query towards the region of the feature space containing relevant images and away from the region containing non-relevant images (see Figure 3). This is based on the assumption that relevant images have similar feature vectors and cluster together in feature space. Based on RF, the next query location can be determined with the standard Rocchio formula (Salton & McGill, 1998):

$$q' \leftarrow \alpha q + \beta \left(\frac{1}{|R^+|} \sum_{x \in R^+} x \right) - \gamma \left(\frac{1}{|R^-|} \sum_{x \in R^-} x \right)$$

where q is the initial query, q' is the new query location, R^+ is the set of relevant retrievals, and R^- is the set of non-relevant retrievals. Thus, the new query location q' is a linear combination of the mean feature vectors of the relevant and non-relevant retrieved images so that q' is close to

Figure 3. Query shifting. The query is moved towards the region of the feature space containing user-labeled relevant images (squares) and away from the region containing user labeled non-relevant images (circles).

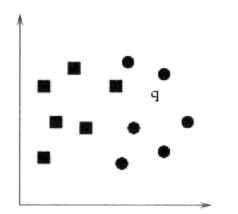
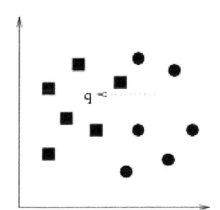

Figure 4. Features are unequal in their differential relevance for computing similarity. The neighborhoods of queries b and c should be elongated along the less relevant Y and X axis respectively. For query a, features X and Y have equal discriminating strength.

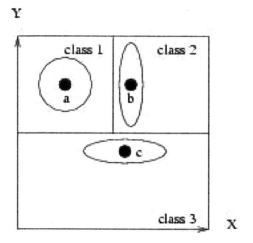

the relevant mean and far from the non-relevant mean. The values for the parameters α, β, and γ are usually chosen by experimental runs. Note that the refined query vector represents an ideal query point and not longer corresponds to any actual image.

Distance reweighing changes the calculation of image to image similarity to strengthen the contribution of relevant image components in regard to the current query. Thus, the task is to determine the features that help the most in retrieving relevant images and increase their importance in determining similarity. In Rui and Huang (1998), the weight and representation of each feature is updated according to their ability to discriminate between the set of relevant and non-relevant images in the current query. Peng et al. (1999) present a probabilistic feature relevance learning (PFRL) method that automatically captures feature relevance based on RF. It computes flexible retrieval metrics for producing neighborhoods that are elongated along less relevant feature dimensions and constricted along most influential ones (see Figure 4). PFRL is an

application of the approach described in Friedman (1994) for learning local feature relevance. Friedman (1994) observes that input variables of low relevance can degrade the performance of nearest-neighbor classifiers if they are allowed to be equally influential with those of high relevance in defining the distance from the point to be classified. Thus, if the relative local relevance of each input variable was known, this information would be used to construct a distance metric that provides an optimal differential weighting for the input variables (Friedman, 1994).

Some methods for incorporating both query shifting and feature relevance weighting have also been proposed (Heisterkamp, Peng, & Dai 2000; Ishikawa et al., 1998). Heisterkamp et al. (2000) propose a retrieval method that combines feature relevance learning and query shifting to achieve the best of both worlds. This method uses a linear discriminant analysis to compute the new query and exploit the local neighborhood structure centered at the new query by using PFRL.

Heisterkamp et al. (2001) further use distance in the feature space associated with a kernel to rank relevant images. An adaptive quasiconformal mapping based on RF is used to generate successive new kernels. The kernel is constructed in such a way that the spatial resolution is contracted around relevant images and dilated around non-relevant images. Then, the distance from the query to new images is measured in this new space. Instead of updating individual feature weights, we could also select from a pre-defined set of similarity measures. For example, Sclaroff et al. (1997) describe an approach that minimizes mean distance between user-labeled relevant images by selecting from a set of pre-defined distance metrics.

In PicHunter (Ingemar & Cox, 2000), a Bayesian framework is used to associate each image with a probability that it corresponds to the user's query concept. The probability is updated based on the user's feedback at each iteration. Tieu and Viola (2000) propose a "boosting" algorithm to improve RF learning. Recently, Support Vector Machine (SVM) learning has been applied to CBIR systems with RF to significantly improve retrieval performance (Chen, Zhou, & Huang, 2001; Hong, Tian, & Huang, 2000; Tong & Chang, 2001; Zhang, Goldman, Yu, & Fritts, 2002). Basically, the probability density of relevant images can be estimated by using SVMs. For instance, Chen et al. (2001) use a one-class SVM to include as many relevant images as possible into a hypersphere of minimum size. That is, relevant images are used to estimate the distribution of target images by fitting a tight hypersphere in the non-linearly transformed feature space. Zhang et al. (2002) regard the problem as a two-class classification problem, and a maximum margin hyperplane in the non-linearly transformed feature space is used to separate relevant images from non-relevant images. Many other approaches, such as Heisterkamp et al. (2002), Peng, Banerjee, and Heisterkamp (2002) and Zhou and Huang (2001), have provided improved alternatives for utilizing kernel methods in CBIR.

Other classical machine learning approaches, such as decision trees (MacArthur, Bradley, & Shyu, 2000), nearest-neighbor classifiers (Wu & Manjunath, 2001), and artificial neural networks (Laaksonen, Koskela, & Oja, 1999) have also been applied for RF learning in CBIR. MacArthur et al. (2000) use a decision tree to sequentially split the feature space until all points within a partition are of the same class. Then, images that are classified as relevant are returned as the nearest neighbors of the query image.

Although RF learning has been successfully applied to CBIR systems that use global image representations, not much research has been conducted on RF learning methods for region-based CBIR. By referring to an image as a bag and a region in the image as an instance, multiple instance learning (MIL) has been applied to image classification and retrieval (Andrews, Tsochantaridis, & Hofmann, 2003; Maron & Lakshmi Ratan, 1998; Yang & Lozano Perez, 2000; Zhang et al.,

2002). The Diverse Density technique (Maron & Lozano Perez, 1997) is applied in Maron and Lakshmi Ratan (1998), Yang and Lozano Perez (2000), and Zhang et al. (2002). Basically, an objective function is used that looks for a feature vector that is close to many instances from different positive bags and far from all instances from negative bags. Such a vector is likely to represent the concept (i.e., object in the image) that matches the concept the user has in mind.

Maron and Lakshmi Ratan (1998) applied MIL to the task of learning to recognize a person from a set of images that are labeled positive if they contain the person and negative otherwise. They also used this model to learn descriptions of natural images (such as sunsets or mountains) and then used the learned concept to retrieve similar images from an image database. Their system uses the set of cumulative user-labeled relevant and non-relevant images to learn a scene concept which is used to retrieve similar images. This is done by using the Diverse Density algorithm to find out what regions are in common between the relevant images, and the differences between those and the non-relevant images. The confidence that an image is relevant to the user's query concept can be measured by the distance from the ideal point (as computed by the Diverse Density algorithm) to the closest region in the image. However, not all region features are equally important. Thus, in this approach, the distance measure is not restricted to a normal Euclidean distance, but may be defined as a weighted Euclidean distance where important features have larger weights. The Diverse Density algorithm is also capable of determining these weights. However, by introducing weights, the number of dimensions over which Diverse Density has to be maximized is doubled. This method is improved in Yang and Lozano Perez (2000) by allowing a broader range of images. Yang and Lozano Perez (2000) define the image similarity measure as the correlation coefficient of corresponding regions. This similarity measure is further refined by allowing different weights for different locations. Zhang et al. (2002) present a comparison of performance obtained with the Diverse Density and EM-DD (Zhang & Goldman, 2001) algorithms when using a wide variety of image processing techniques and a broader range of images.

Based on the assumption that important regions should appear more often in relevant images than unimportant regions, an *RF*IIF*

Figure 5. Regions are unequal in their differential relevance for computing similarity. Given that the user is looking for images of people, region R_1 may be the most important, perhaps followed by R_2 and R_3. Thus, the neighborhood of the similarity metric should be elongated along the direction of R_1 and constricted along the direction of R_3.

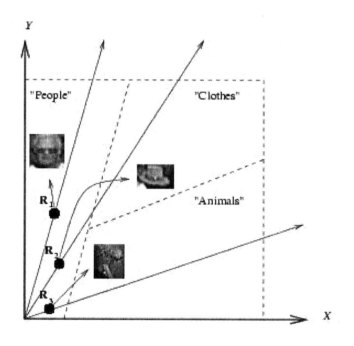

Query Image

(Region Frequency * Inverse Image Frequency) weighting scheme is proposed in Jing, Li, Zhang, Zhang, and Zhang (2003). Let $D = \{x_i\}_1^m$ be the set of all images in the database, x be the query image, $\{R_i\}_1^n$ be the set of all regions in x, and R^+ be the set of cumulative relevant retrieved images for x. The region frequency (RF) of a region R_i is defined as:

$$RF(R_i) = \sum_{x_j \in R^+} s(R_i, x_j)$$

where $s(R_i, x_j) = 1$ if at least one region of x_j is similar to R_i, and 0 otherwise. Two regions are deemed similar if their L1-distance (also known as the Manhattan distance or city-block distance) is smaller than a predefined threshold. The inverse image frequency (IIF) of R_i is defined as:

$$IIF(R_i) = \log\left(\frac{m}{\sum_{x_j \in D} s(R_i, x_j)}\right)$$

The region importance RI (i.e., weight) of R_i is then:

$$RI(R_i) = \frac{RF(R_i) * IIF(R_i)}{\sum_{j=1}^{n}(RF(R_j) * IIF(R_j))}$$

PROBABILISTIC REGION RELEVANCE LEARNING

A key factor in region-based CBIR approaches that consider all the regions to perform an overall image-to-image similarity is the weighting of regions. The weight that is assigned to each region for determining similarity is usually based on prior assumptions such as that larger regions, or regions that are close to the center of the image, should have larger weights. For example, in integrated region matching (IRM) (Li et al., 2002), an *area percentage scheme,* which is based on the

assumption that important objects in an image tend to occupy larger areas, is used to assign weights to regions. The location of a region is also taken into consideration. For example, higher weights are assigned to regions in the center of an image than to those around boundaries. These region weighting heuristics are often inconsistent with human perception. For instance, a facial region may be the most important when the user is looking for images of people, while other larger regions such as the background may be much less relevant.

Based on the observation that regions in an image have unequal importance for computing image similarity (see Figure 5), we proposed a probabilistic method inspired by probabilistic feature relevance learning (PFRL) (Peng et al., 1999) and probabilistic region relevance learning (PRRL) (Gondra & Heisterkamp, 2004) for automatically capturing region relevance based on user's feedback. PRRL can be used to set region weights in region-based image retrieval frameworks that use an overall image-to-image similarity measure.

Region Relevance Measure

Given a query image $x = \{R_i\}_1^n$, where R_i represents the features extracted from a region in the image, let the class label (i.e., relevant or not relevant) $y \in \{1, 0\}$ at x be treated as a random variable from a distribution with the probabilities $\{\Pr(1|x)\ \Pr(0|x)\}$. Consider the function f of n arguments:

$$f(x) \doteq \Pr(1|x) = \Pr(y=1|x) = E(y|x)$$

In the absence of any argument assignments, the least-squared estimate for $f(x)$ is simply its expected (average) value:

$$E[f] = \int f(x)p(x)dx$$

where $p(x)$ is the joint probability density. Now, suppose that we know the value of x at a particular region R_i. The least-squares estimate becomes:

$$E[f \mid R_i] = \int f(x)p(x \mid R_i)dx$$

where $p(x \mid R_i)$ is the conditional density of the other regions. Because $f(x) = 1$ (i.e., the query image is always relevant), $(f(x) - 0)$ is the maximum error that can be made when assigning 0 to the probability that x is relevant when the probability is in fact 1. On the other hand, $(f(x) - E[f \mid R_i])$ is the error that is made by predicting $E[f \mid R_i]$ to be the probability that x is relevant. Therefore:

$$[(f(x) - 0) - (f(x) - E[f \mid R_i])] = E[f \mid R_i]$$

represents a reduction in error between the two predictions. Therefore, a measure of the relevance of region R_i for x can be defined as:

$$r_i(x) = E[f \mid R_i] \qquad (1)$$

The relative relevance can then be used as the weight of region R_i in a weighted similarity measure:

$$w_i = \frac{e^{Tr_i(x)}}{\sum_{j=1}^{n} e^{Tr_j(x)}} \qquad (2)$$

where T is a parameter that can be chosen to maximize (minimize) the influence of r_i on w_i.

Estimation of Region Relevance

Retrieved images with RF are used to estimate region relevance. Let $A = \{(x_j, y_j)\}_1^m$ be the set of cumulative retrievals for x. Let $x_j = \{R'_i\}_1^z$. Let $0 \leq s(R_i, R'_j) \leq 1$ denote the similarity between region R_i in x and region R'_j in x_j in a region-based CBIR system. Also, let $\hat{s}(R_i, x_j) = \max_{j \in \{1,2,\ldots,z\}} (s(R_i, R'_j))$. We can use A to estimate $r_i(x)$ and hence w_i. Note that $E[f \mid R_i] = E[y \mid R_i]$. However, since there may be no $x_j \in A$ for which $R'_j = R_i$ (i.e., no R'_j such that $s(R_i, R'_j) = 1$), a strategy suggested in Friedman (1994) is followed, and we look for data in the vicinity of R_i (i.e., we allow $s(R_i, R'_j)$ to be smaller than 1). Thus, w_i is estimated by:

$$\hat{E}[y \mid R_i] = \frac{\sum_{j=1}^{m} y_j \mathbf{1}(\hat{s}(R_i, x_j) > \varepsilon)}{\sum_{j=1}^{m} \mathbf{1}(\hat{s}(R_i, x_j) > \varepsilon)} \qquad (3)$$

Figure 6. The probabilistic region relevance learning (PRRL) algorithm

1. Use a segmentation method to extract regions and represent current query by $x = \{R_i\}_1^n$; initialize region weight vector w to $\left\{\frac{1}{n}\right\}_1^n$; $A = \phi$.
2. Compute the K most similar images to x with an overall image-to-image similarity measure using w for the weighting of regions in x.
3. User marks the K images as relevant or not relevant.

4. While more RF iterations Do
   4.1. $A \leftarrow A \cup \{marked\ K\ images\}$.
   4.2. Update w from Eqs. (3) and (2) using A.
   4.3. Compute the K most similar images to x with an overall image-to-image similarity measure using w for the weighting of regions in x.
   4.4. User marks the K images as relevant or not relevant.

Figure 7. A typical RF process

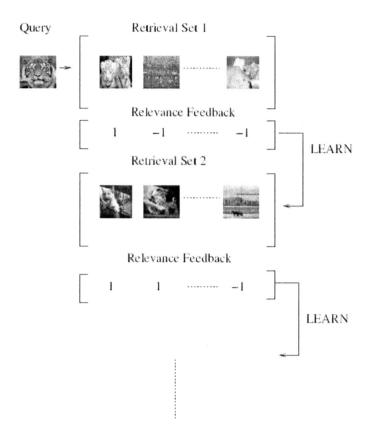

where $1(\cdot)$ returns 1 if its argument is true, and 0 otherwise. Thus, $0 \leq \varepsilon \leq 1$ is an adaptive similarity threshold that changes so that there is sufficient data for the estimation of $r_i(x)$. The value of ε is chosen so that:

$$\sum_{j=1}^{m} 1(\hat{s}(R_i, x_j) > \varepsilon) = G,$$

where $G \leq m$. The probabilistic region relevance algorithm is summarized in Figure 6.

Usage Scenario

We present in this subsection a typical usage scenario in an RF-based CBIR system and show how the PRRL algorithm presented improves the retrieval performance of such system. As previously discussed, the goal of RF learning is to reduce the semantic gap by gathering semantic information from user interaction. Based on the user's feedback on the retrieval results, the retrieval scheme is adjusted. By providing an image similarity measure under human perception, RF learning can be seen as a form of supervised learning that finds relations between high-level semantic interpretations and low-level visual properties. That is, the feedback obtained within a single query session is used to personalize the retrieval strategy and thus enhance retrieval performance. As illustrated in Figure 7, in order to learn a user's query concept, the user labels each image returned in the previous query round as relevant (denoted by a 1 in Figure 7) or non-relevant (denoted by a -1 in Figure 7). Based on the feedback, the retrieval scheme is adjusted and

Figure 8. Retrieval results on random query image (top leftmost) from subset of COREL image database. The images are sorted based on their similarity to the query image. The ranks descend from left to right and from top to bottom.

Initial Retrieval Set with UFM, precision = 0.3

Retrieval Set with UFM+PRRL after 2 RF iterations, precision = 0.75

the next set of images is presented to the user for labeling. After each such RF iteration, the number of relevant images (e.g., images of cats in Figure 7) in the retrieval set increases and thus retrieval performance is improved. This process iterates until the user is satisfied with the retrieved images or stops searching.

After each RF iteration, the PRRL algorithm automatically captures the relevance/importance of the different regions in an image. Suppose that a particular user of the CBIR system would like

to obtain other images that are similar to a query image (e.g., the top leftmost image in Figure 8). The top box in Figure 8 shows the top 20 images that the CBIR system would return to the user if using UFM (without RF learning) as the similarity measure. The retrieval precision is only 0.3 (i.e., only 30% of the images in the retrieval set are relevant to the user's query concept). On the other hand, if the CBIR system uses the PRRL algorithm, after only two RF iterations the retrieval performance is much higher (i.e., a precision of

0.75 is obtained), as illustrated by the retrieval set in the bottom box of Figure 8.

Experimental Results

Next we present experimental results obtained with PRRL. *Precision* and *recall* are common measures that are used to evaluate the performance of an image retrieval system. Consider an image database consisting of a set of images D. Let x be a query image and $A \subset D$ be the subset of images in D that are relevant to x. Assume that a given image retrieval strategy processes x and generates $R \subset D$ as the retrieval set. Then, $R^+ = R \cap A$ is the set of relevant images to x that appear in R. Similarly, $R^- = R - A$ is the set of non-relevant images to x that appear in R. Figure 9 illustrates these sets. Precision measures the ability to retrieve only relevant images and is defined as $precision = |R^+|/|R|$. Recall measures the ability

Figure 9. Image retrieval performance measures: D is the set of all database images; A is the set of all images relevant to a query; R is the retrieval set in response to the query; precision is $|R^+|/|R|$; recall is $|R^+|/|A|$.

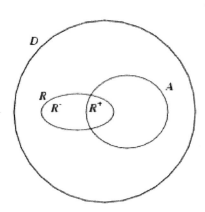

Figure 10. Sample images from COREL data set

to retrieval all relevant images and is defined as $recall = |R^+|/|A|$.

Both high recall and high precision are desirable, though not often obtainable. That is, in many cases, improvement of one leads to the deterioration of the other. Note that perfect recall could be achieved simply by letting $R = D$ (i.e., by retrieving all images in the database in response to x). However, obviously users would probably not be happy with this approach. Thus, recall by itself is not a good measure of the performance of an image retrieval system. Instead, users want the database images to be ranked according to their relevance to x and then be presented with only the K most relevant images so that $|R| = K < |D|$. Therefore, in order to account for the quality of image rankings, precision at a cut-off point (e.g., K) is commonly used. For example, if $K = 20$ and the top 20 ranked images are all relevant to x, then R contains only relevant images and thus precision is 1. On the other hand, if $K = 40$ and

only the first top 20 images are all relevant to x, then half of the images in R are non-relevant to x and thus precision is only 0.5. A common way to depict the degradation of precision as K increases is to plot a precision-recall graph.

Ideally, in order to evaluate the practical usability of an RF-based CBIR system, large-scale experiments with real users should be conducted. However, such experiments are costly and difficult to set up. As a result, the evaluation and comparison of RF algorithms rely on the use of image ground-truth databases and on the emulation of the behaviour of real users. In an image ground-truth database, all images are labeled according to their category (i.e., all images that belong to the same category such as "cat" have the same label). Thus, it is known whether an image in a retrieval set would be labeled as relevant (in case it has the same label as that of the query image) or non-relevant (in case its label is different from that of the query image). Therefore, the user's feedback on a retrieval set can be emulated by automatically

Figure 11. Retrieval performance at different number of RF iterations with PRRL and other methods on COREL data

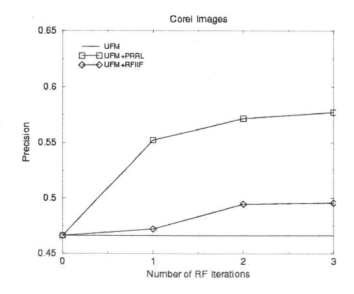

labeling all returned images as either relevant or non-relevant without any mistake.

A subset of 2000 labeled images from the general purpose COREL image database was used as the ground-truth for evaluation. There are 20 image categories, each containing 100 pictures. The region-based feature vectors of those images are obtained with the IRM/UFM segmentation algorithm. Sample images are shown in Figure 10.

We tested the performance of unified feature matching (UFM) (Chen & Wang, 2002), UFM with PRRL (UFM+PRRL), and UFM with the RF*IIF method (Jing et al., 2003) (UFM+RFIIF). Every image is used as a query image. A uniform weighting scheme is used to set the region weights of each query and target images. For UFM+PRRL and UFM+RFIIF, user feedback was simulated by carrying out three RF iterations for each query. Because the images in the data set are labeled according to their category, it is known whether an image in a retrieval set would be labeled as relevant or non-relevant by a user.

The average precision of the 2000 queries with respect to different number of RF iterations is shown in Figure 11. The size of the retrieval set is 20. Figures 12 through 15 show the precision-recall curves after each RF iteration. We can observe that UFM+PRRL has the best performance. It can be seen that, even after only one RF iteration, the region weights learned by PRRL result in a very significant performance improvement.

CONCLUSION

Content-based image retrieval (CBIR) suffers from the fact that there is a large discrepancy between the low-level visual features that one can extract from an image and the semantic interpretation of the image's content that a particular user may have in a given situation. That is, users seek semantic similarity, but we can only provide similarity based on low-level visual features extracted from the raw pixel data. The selection of an appropriate similarity measure is thus an

Figure 12. Retrieval performance in initial retrieval set with PRRL and other methods on COREL data

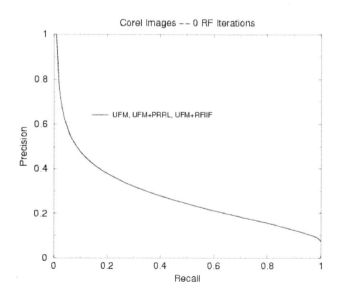

Figure 13. Retrieval performance after one RF iteration with PRRL and other methods on COREL data

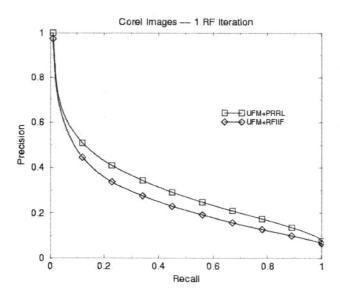

Figure 14. Retrieval performance after two RF iterations with PRRL and other methods on COREL data

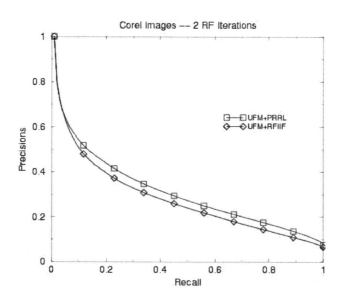

Figure 15. Retrieval performance after three RF iterations with PRRL and other methods on COREL data

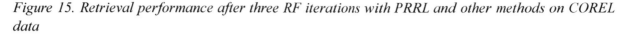
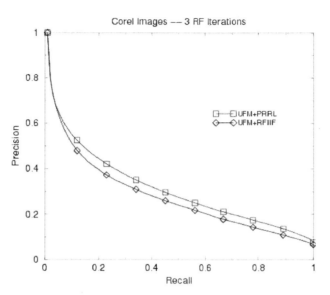

important problem. Since visual content can be represented by different attributes, the combination and importance of each set of features varies according to the user's semantic intent. Thus, the retrieval strategy should be adaptive so that it can accommodate the preferences of different users. Relevance feedback (RF) learning has been proposed as a technique aimed at reducing the semantic gap. By providing an image similarity measure under human perception, RF learning can be seen as a form of supervised learning that finds relations between high-level semantic interpretations and low-level visual properties. That is, the feedback obtained within a single query session is used to personalize the retrieval strategy and thus enhance retrieval performance. In this chapter we presented an overview of CBIR and related work on RF learning. We also presented our own previous work on an RF learning-based probabilistic region relevance learning algorithm for automatically estimating the importance of each region in an image based on the user's semantic intent.

A fundamental observation when designing a personalized CBIR system is that, ultimately, the semantic interpretation of an image is defined by humans and thus people are an indispensable part of such system. This is reinforced by the fact that, in contrast to early literature which emphasizes the search for a "single best feature," more recent research is focused on "human in the loop" approaches. Therefore, when attempting to reduce the semantic gap and thus meet the performance challenges encountered in practical CBIR applications, RF learning remains a very promising research direction.

FUTURE RESEARCH DIRECTIONS

We can distinguish two different types of information provided by RF: the short-term learning obtained within a single query session is intra-query learning; the long-term learning accumulated over the course of many query sessions is inter-query learning. By accumulating knowledge from users, long-term learning can be used to enhance future retrieval performance. The fact that two images were regarded as similar by a previous user is a cue for similarities in their semantic content. This is because, although different people may associate the same image into different concepts, there is some common semantic agreement. While short-term learning has been widely used in the literature, less research has been focused on exploiting long-term learning (several references to previous work on long-term learning are given in the Additional Reading section). Currently, PRRL only performs intra-query learning. That is, for each given query, the user's feedback is used to learn the relevance of the regions in the query, and the learning process starts from ground up for each new query. However, it is also possible to exploit inter-query learning to enhance the retrieval performance of future queries. Thus, for a new query, instead of starting the learning process from the ground up, we could exploit the previously learned region importance of similar queries. This would be very beneficial especially in the initial retrieval set since, instead of using uniform weighting or some other weighting heuristic, we could make a more informed initial estimate of the relevance of regions in the new query. We plan to investigate the possibility of incorporating inter-query learning into the PRRL framework as part of our future work

REFERENCES

Andrews, S., Tsochantaridis, I., & Hofmann, T. (2003). Support vector machines for multiple-instance learning. In S. Becker, S. Thrun, & K. Obermayer (Eds.), *Advances in neural information processing systems* (vol. 15, pp. 561–568). Cambridge, MA: MIT Press.

Bimbo, A. (1999). *Visual information retrieval.* San Francisco: Morgan Kaufmann.

Buckley, C., & Salton, G. (1995). Optimization of relevance feedback weights. In E.A. Fox, P.

Ingwersen, & R. Fidel (Eds.), *Proceedings of the Annual International ACM SIGIR Conference on Research and Development in Information Retrieval* (pp. 351–357).

Carson, C. (2002). Blobworld: Image segmentation using expectation-maximization and its applications to image querying. *IEEE Transactions on Pattern Analysis and Machine Intelligence, 24*(8), 1026–1038.

Chen, Y., Zhou, X., & Huang, T. (2001). One-class SVM for learning in image retrieval. *Proceedings of the IEEE International Conference on Image Processing* (vol. 1, pp. 34–37).

Chen, Y., & Wang, J. (2002). A region-based fuzzy feature matching approach to content-based image retrieval. *IEEE Transactions on Pattern Analysis and Machine Intelligence, 24*(9), 1252–1267.

Faloutsos, C., Flicker, M., Niblack, W., Petkovic, D., Equitz, W., & Barber, R. (1993). *Efficient and effective querying by image content.* Technical Report, IBM, USA.

Friedman, J. (1994). *Flexible metric nearest neighbor classification.* Technical Report, Department of Statistics, Stanford University, USA.

Gondra, I., & Heisterkamp, D.R. (2004). Probabilistic region relevance learning for content-based image retrieval. *Proceedings of the International Conference on Imaging Science, Systems, and Technology* (pp. 434–440).

Gupta, A., & Jain, R. (1997). Visual information retrieval. *Communications of the ACM, 40*(5), 70–79.

Hara, Y., Hirata, K., Takano, H., & Kawasaki, S. (1997). Hypermedia navigation and content-based retrieval for distributed multimedia databases. *Proceedings of the NEC Research Symposium on Multimedia Computing* (pp. 133–148).

Heisterkamp, D.R. (2002). Building a latent semantic index of an image database from patterns of relevance feedback. *Proceedings of the International Conference on Pattern Recognition* (vol. 4, pp. 134–137).

Heisterkamp, D.R., Peng, J., & Dai, H.K. (2000). Feature relevance learning with query shifting for content-based image retrieval. *Proceedings of the International Conference on Pattern Recognition* (vol. 4, pp. 4250–4253).

Heisterkamp, D.R., Peng, J., & Dai, H. (2001). Adaptive quasiconformal kernel metric for image retrieval. *Proceedings of the IEEE International Conference on Computer Vision and Pattern Recognition* (vol. 2, pp. 388–393).

Hong, P., Tian, Q., & Huang, T. (2000). Incorporate support vector machines to content-based image retrieval with relevance feedback. *Proceedings of the IEEE International Conference on Image Processing* (pp. 750–753).

Ingemar, J., & Cox, J. (2000). The Bayesian image retrieval system, PicHunter: Theory, implementation, and psychological experiments. *IEEE Transactions on Image Processing, 9*(1), 20–37.

Ishikawa, Y., Subramanys, R., & Faloutsos, C. (1998). MindReader: Querying databases through multiple examples. *Proceedings of the International Conference on Very Large Databases* (pp. 218–227).

Jain, A.K., & Vailaya, A. (1996). Image retrieval using color and shape. *Pattern Recognition, 29*(8), 1233–1244.

Jing, F., Li, M., Zhang, L., Zhang, H., & Zhang, B. (2003). Learning in region-based image retrieval. *Proceedings of the International Conference on Image and Video Retrieval* (vol. 2728, pp. 206–215).

Kelly, P.M., Cannon, T.M., & Hush, D.R. (1995). Query by image example: The CANDID approach. In W. Niblack & R. Jain (Eds.), *Proceedings of the SPIE Storage and Retrieval for Image and Video Databases* (vol. 2420, pp. 238–248).

Laaksonen, J., Koskela, M., & Oja, E. (1999). Picsom: Self-organizing maps for content-based image retrieval. *Proceedings of the International Joint Conference on Neural Networks* (vol. 4, pp. 2470–2473).

Li, J., Wang, J., & Wiederhold, G. (2000). IRM: Integrated region matching for image retrieval. *Proceedings of the ACM International Conference on Multimedia* (pp. 147–156).

Li, M., Chen, Z., & Zhang, H. (2002). Statistical correlation analysis in image retrieval. *Pattern Recognition, 35*(12), 2687–2693.

Ma, W., & Majunath, B. (1997). NeTra: A toolbox for navigating large image databases. *Proceedings of the IEEE International Conference on Image Processing* (vol. 1, pp. 568–571).

MacArthur, S.D., Bradley, C.E., & Shyu, C.R. (2000). Relevance feedback decision trees in content-based image retrieval. *Proceedings of the IEEE Workshop on Content-Based Access of Image and Video Libraries* (pp. 68–72).

Maron, O., & Lakshmi Ratan, A. (1998). Multiple-instance learning for natural scene classification. In J.W. Shavlik (Ed.), *Proceedings of the International Conference on Machine Learning* (vol. 15, pp. 341–349).

Maron, O., & Lozano Perez, T. (1997). A framework for multiple-instance learning. In M.I. Jordan, M.J. Kearns, & S.A. Solla (Eds.), *Advances in neural information processing systems* (vol. 10, pp. 570–576). Cambridge, MA: MIT Press.

Mehrotra, S., Rui, Y., Ortega, M., & Huang, T. (1997). Supporting content-based queries over images in MARS. *Proceedings of the IEEE International Conference on Multimedia Computing and Systems* (pp. 632–633).

Ono, A., Amano, M., Hakaridani, M., Satoh, T., & Sakauchi, M. (1996). A flexible content-based image retrieval system with combined scene description keywords. *Proceedings of the IEEE*

International Conference on Multimedia Computing and Systems (pp. 201–208).

Peng, J., Banerjee, B., & Heisterkamp, D.R. (2002). Kernel index for relevance feedback retrieval in large image databases. *Proceedings of the International Conference on Neural Information Processing* (pp. 187–191).

Peng, J., Bhanu, B., & Qing, S. (1999). Probabilistic feature relevance learning for content-based image retrieval. *Computer Vision and Image Understanding, 75*(1/2), 150–164.

Pentland, A., Picard, R., & Sclaroff, S. (1994). PhotoBOOK: Tools for content-based manipulation of image databases. In W. Niblack & R. Jain (Eds.), *Proceedings of the SPIE Storage and Retrieval for Image Databases* (vol. 2, pp. 34–47).

Ravela, S., Manmatha, R., & Riseman, E.M. (1996). Scale-space matching and image retrieval. *Proceedings of the Image Understanding Workshop* (vol. 2, pp. 1199–1207).

Rocchio, J., & Salton, G. (1971). The SMART retrieval system: Experiments in automatic document processing. In *Relevance feedback in information retrieval* (pp. 313–323). Englewood Cliffs, NJ: Prentice Hall.

Rui, Y., & Huang, T. (1998). Relevance feedback: A power tool for interactive content-based image retrieval. *IEEE Transactions on Circuits and Systems for Video Technology, 8*(5), 644–655.

Rui, Y., Huang, T., & Chang, S. (1999). Image retrieval: Past, present, and future. *Journal of Visual Communication and Image Representation, 10*, 1-23.

Rui, Y., Huang, T., & Mehrotra, S. (1997). Content-based image retrieval with relevance feedback in MARS. *Proceedings of the IEEE International Conference on Image Processing* (vol. 2, pp. 815–818).

Salton, G. (1986). Another look at automatic text-retrieval systems. *Communications of the ACM, 29*(7), 648–656.

Salton, G., & McGill, M. (1998). *Introduction to modern information retrieval*. New York: McGraw-Hill.

Samadani, R., Han, C., & Katragadda, L.K. (1993). Content-based event selection from satellite image of the aurora. In W. Niblack (Ed.), *Proceedings of the SPIE Storage and Retrieval for Image and Video Databases* (vol. 1908, pp. 50–59).

Sclaroff, S., Taycher, L., & Cascia, M.L. (1997). *ImageRover: A content-based image browser for the World Wide Web*. Technical Report No. 97-005, Computer Science Department, Boston University, USA.

Shaw, W.M. (1995). Term-relevance computations and perfect retrieval performance. *Information Processing and Management: An International Journal, 31*(4), 491–498.

Shen, H.T., Ooi, B.C., & Tan, K.L. (2000). Giving meanings to WWW images. *Proceedings of the ACM Multimedia* (pp. 39–47).

Smeulders, A.W.M., Worring, M., Santini, S., Gupta, A., & Jain, R. (2000). Content-based image retrieval at the end of the early years. *IEEE Transactions on Pattern Analysis and Machine Intelligence, 22*(12), 1349–1380.

Smith, J., & Chang, S. (1996). VisualSEEk: A fully automated content-based image query system. *Proceedings of the ACM Conference on Multimedia* (pp. 87–98).

Smith, J., & Chang, S. (1997). An image and video search engine for the World Wide Web. *Proceedings of the SPIE Storage and Retrieval for Image and Video Databases* (vol. 5, pp. 84–95).

Smith, J.R., & Li, C.S. (1999). Image classification and querying using composite region templates.

Computer Vision and Image Understanding, *75*(1/2), 165–174.

Srihari, R.K., Zhang, Z., & Rao, A. (2000). Intelligent indexing and semantic retricval of multimedia documents. *Information Retrieval, 2,* 245–275.

Stone, H.S., & Li, C.S. (1996). Image matching by means of intensity and texture matching in the Fourier domain. In I.K. Sethi & R. Jain (Eds.), *Proceedings of the SPIE Conference on Image and Video Databases* (vol. 2670, pp. 337–349).

Swain, M., & Ballard, D. (1991). Color indexing. *International Journal of Computer Vision, 7*(1), 11–32.

Tieu, K., & Viola, P. (2000). Boosting image retrieval. *Proceedings of the IEEE Conference in Computer Vision and Pattern Recognition* (pp. 1228–1235).

Tong, S., & Chang, E. (2001). Support vector machine active learning for image retrieval. *Proceedings of the ACM International Conference on Multimedia* (pp. 107–118).

Wang, J., Li, G., & Wiederhold, G. (2001). Simplicity: Semantic-sensitive integrated matching for picture libraries. *IEEE Transactions on Pattern Analysis and Machine Intelligence, 23,* 947–963.

Wang, J., Wiederhold, G., Firschein, O., & Sha, X. (1998). Content-based image indexing and searching using Daubechies' wavelets. *International Journal of Digital Libraries, 1*(4), 311–328.

Wenyin, L., Dumais, S., Sun, Y., Zhang, H., Czerwinski, M., & Field, B. (2001). Semiautomatic image annotation. *Proceedings of the International Conference on Human-Computer Interaction* (vol. 1, pp. 326–334).

Wu, P., & Manjunath, B.S. (2001). Adaptive nearest neighbor search for relevance feedback in large image databases. *Proceedings of the ACM Conference on Multimedia* (pp. 89–97).

Yang, C., & Lozano Perez, T. (2000). Image database retrieval with multiple instance learning techniques. *Proceedings of the IEEE International Conference on Data Engineering* (pp. 233–243).

Zhang, Q., & Goldman, S.A. (2001). EM-DD: An improved multiple-instance learning technique. In T.G. Dietterich, S. Becker, & Z. Ghahramani (Eds.), *Advances in neural information processing systems* (vol. 14, pp. 1073–1080). Cambridge, MA: MIT Press.

Zhang, Q., Goldman, S.A., Yu, W., & Fritts, J. (2002). Content-based image retrieval using multiple-instance learning. In C. Sammut & A.G. Hoffmann (Eds.), *Proceedings of the International Conference on Machine Learning* (pp. 682–689).

Zhou, X., & Huang, T. (2001). Small sample learning during multimedia retrieval using BiasMap. *Proceedings of the IEEE International Conference on Computer Vision and Pattern Recognition* (vol. 1, pp. 11–17).

ADDITIONAL READING

Benitez, A.B. (1998). Using relevance feedback in content-based image metasearch. *IEEE Internet Computing, 2*(4), 59–69.

Campadelli, P., Medici, D., & Schettini, R. (1997). Color image segmentation using Hopfield networks. *Image and Vision Computing, 15*(3), 161–166.

Ciaccia, P., Patella, M., & Zezula, P. (1997). M-tree: An efficient access method for similarity search in metric spaces. *Proceedings of the International Conference on Very Large Databases* (pp. 426–435).

Cox, J., Miller, M.L., Minka, T.P., & Yianilos, P.N. (1998). An optimized interaction strategy for Bayesian relevance feedback. *Proceedings of the IEEE Conference on Computer Vision and Pattern Recognition* (pp. 553–558).

Gondra, I., & Heisterkamp, D.R. (2004). Adaptive and efficient image retrieval with one-class support vector machines for inter-query learning. *WSEAS Transactions on Circuits and Systems, 3*(2), 324–329.

Gondra, I., & Heisterkamp, D.R. (2004). Improving image retrieval performance by inter-query learning with one-class support vector machines. *Neural Computing and Applications, 13*(2), 130–139.

Gondra, I., & Heisterkamp, D.R. (2004). Learning in region-based image retrieval with generalized support vector machines. *Proceedings of the IEEE Conference on Computer Vision and Pattern Recognition Workshops.*

Gondra, I., & Heisterkamp, D.R. (2004). Semantic similarity for adaptive exploitation of inter-query learning. *Proceedings of the International Conference on Computing, Communications, and Control Technologies* (pp. 142–147).

Gondra. I., & Heisterkamp, D.R. (2004). Summarizing inter-query knowledge in content-based image retrieval via incremental semantic clustering. *Proceedings of the IEEE International Conference on Information Technology* (pp. 18–22).

Gondra, I., & Heisterkamp, D.R. (2005). A Kolmogorov complexity-based normalized information distance for image retrieval. *Proceedings of the International Conference on Imaging Science, Systems, and Technology: Computer Graphics* (pp. 3–7).

Gondra, I., Heisterkamp, D.R., & Peng, J. (2003). Improving the initial image retrieval set by inter-query learning with one-class support vector machines. *Proceedings of the International*

Conference on Intelligent Systems Design and Applications (pp. 393–402).

Guttman, A. (1984). R-trees: A dynamic index structure for spatial searching. *Proceedings of the ACM SIGMOD International Conference on Management of Data* (pp. 47–57).

Guy, G., & Medioni, G. (1996). Inferring global perceptual contours from local features. *International Journal of Computer Vision, 20*(12), 113–133.

Haralick, R.M., Shanmugam, K., & Dinstein, I. (1973). Texture features for image classification. *IEEE Transactions on Systems, Man, and Cybernetics, 3*(6), 610–621.

He, X., King, O., Ma, W., Li, M., & Zhang, H. (2003). Learning a semantic space from user's relevance feedback for image retrieval. *IEEE Transactions on Circuits and Systems for Video Technology, 13*(1), 39–48.

Heisterkamp, D.R. (2002). Building a latent semantic index of an image database from patterns of relevance feedback. *Proceedings of the International Conference on Pattern Recognition* (pp. 132–135).

Koskela, M., & Laaksonen, J. (2003). Using long-term learning to improve efficiency of content-based image retrieval. *Proceedings of the International Workshop on Pattern Recognition in Information Systems* (pp. 72–79).

Lee, C., Ma, W.Y., & Zhang, H.J. (1999). Information embedding based on user's relevance feedback for image retrieval. *Proceedings of the SPIE International Conference on Multimedia Storage and Archiving Systems* (pp. 19–22).

Minka, T., & Picard, R. (1997). Interactive learning using a society of models. *Pattern Recognition, 30*(4), 565–581.

Sull, S., Oh, J., Oh, S., Song, S., & Lee, S. (2000). Relevance graph-based image retrieval. *Proceed-*

ings of the IEEE International Conference on Multimedia and Expo (pp. 713–716).

Vasconcelos, N., & Lippman, A. (2000). Learning over multiple temporal scales in image databases. *Proceedings of the European Conference on Computer Vision* (pp. 33–47).

Yin, P., Bhanu, B., & Chang, K. (2002). Improving retrieval performance by long-term relevance information. *Proceedings of the International Conference on Pattern Recognition* (pp. 533–536).

Zhang, C., & Chen, T. (2002). An active learning framework for content-based information retrieval. *IEEE Transactions on Multimedia, 4*(2), 260–268.

Zhang, Y.J. (1996). A survey on evaluation methods for image segmentation. *Pattern Recognition, 29*(8), 1335–1346.

Zhang, Y.J. (2001). A review of recent evaluation methods for image segmentation. *Proceedings of the International Symposium on Signal Processing and its Applications* (pp. 13–16).

Chapter X
Service–Oriented Architectures for Context–Aware Information Retrieval and Access

Lu Yan
University College London, UK

ABSTRACT

Humans are quite successful at conveying ideas to each other and retrieving information from interactions appropriately. This is due to many factors: the richness of the language they share, the common understanding of how the world works, and an implicit understanding of everyday situations (Dey & Abowd, 1999). When humans talk with humans, they are able to use implicit situational information (i.e., context) to enhance the information exchange process. Context (Cool & Spink, 2002) plays a vital part in adaptive and personalized information retrieval and access. Unfortunately, computer communications lacks this ability to provide auxiliary context in addition to the substantial content of information. As computers are becoming more and more ubiquitous and mobile, there is a need and possibility to provide information "personalized, any time, and anywhere" (ITU, 2006). In these scenarios, large amounts of information circulate in order to create smart and proactive environments that will significantly enhance both the work and leisure experiences of people. Context-awareness plays an important role to enable personalized information retrieval and access according to the current situation with minimal human intervention. Although context-aware information retrieval systems have been researched for a decade (Korkea-aho, 2000), the rise of mobile and ubiquitous computing put new challenges to issue, and therefore we are motivated to come up with new solutions to achieve non-intrusive, personalized information access on the mobile service platforms and heterogeneous wireless environments.

LITERATURE REVIEW

Current research on context-aware information retrieval systems is focused on Web information systems, search techniques, and digital memory systems (Jones, 2005). The "Stuff I've Seen" (SIS) system (Dumais et al, 2003) is a search engineering approach to context-aware information retrieval. SIS stores most information, which people have interacted previously with, along with a context index. It also provides recommendations with heuristic algorithms. Though the approach is straightforward, as search techniques are mature nowadays, the requirement of search-driven will limit the scope of exploration of the system; yet it is not suitable for mobile users as well, since many user inputs are required. Moreover, it is built on the data level, and no service provisioning issues are considered.

CAR is a pioneer attempt to address the challenges of context-aware information in the ubiquitous computing environment (Jones & Brown, 2003). CAR is part of the infrastructure needed by a range of applications that detect and exploit context in mobile devices such as PDAs and mobile phones. CAR uses context-of-interests to personalize the information seeking process and manage that information accordingly. However, no implementation detail was given and the system does not consider any service selection issues in mobile platforms either.

MyLifeBits is a Microsoft Research project to create a "lifetime store of everything" (Bell et al., 2006). It is the fulfillment of the Memex vision (Bush, 1945) including full-text search, text and audio annotations, and hyperlinks. This project has raised many interesting questions relating to the reuse of captured data and context, but research into useful applications exploiting these resources is currently at a very early stage. Like the above previous approaches, this project uses context to personalize data representations and does not touch the service selections which we believe are of importance to mobile users.

OUR APPROACH AND PROPOSAL

Service-oriented architecture (SOA) is an evolution of distributed computing based on the request/reply design paradigm for synchronous and asynchronous applications. An application's business logic or individual functions are modularized and presented as services for consumer/client applications. What is key to these services is their loosely coupled nature—that is, the service interface is independent of the implementation. Application developers or system integrators can build applications by composing one or more services without knowing the services' underlying implementations.

Due to the heterogeneity of mobile computing devices and the variety of widespread network communication technologies, nowadays users have more possibilities to access various services. However, having alternative networks and services does not bring ease to users immediately, but often results in increased burdens in terms of repetitive configuration and reconfiguration, though users are only interested in the actual use of the appropriate services.

We propose tackling this problem with SOA in a context-aware manner, aiming to facilitate users' ability to make use of different services in a smart way, based on adaptive services which exploit their awareness of users' context. In this chapter, we present the SOA architecture, along with the context-aware action systems that provide a systematic method for managing and processing context information (Back & Sere, 1996). Action systems are intended to be developed in a stepwise manner within an associated refinement calculus (Back & Wright, 1998). Hence, the development and reasoning about the proposed systems can be carried out within this calculus, ensuring the correctness of derived mobile applications (Sere & Walden, 1997).

Using the proposed architecture, we can now model ubiquitous computing in an extremely dynamic context: location changes all the time while moving around with our portable devices, and so do the services and devices in reach; local resource availability varies quickly as well, such as memory availability, bandwidth, and battery power. In order to maintain reasonable QoS to the users, applications must be context-aware.

CONFERENCE ASSISTANT EXAMPLE

Initial work in context-aware computing resulted in the development of applications that can use context definitions to support everyday behaviors, such as Active Badge (Harter & Hopper, 1994) and PARCTab (Want, 1995). Another kind of typical context-aware application relates to the development of guides, for example Cyberguide (Abowd et al., 1997) and GUIDE (Cheverst, Davies, Mitchell, Friday, & Efstratiou, 2000). Therefore, we present a context-aware scenario similar to

Day, Salber, Abowd, and Futakawa (1999) and Asthana, Cravatts, and Kryzyzanowski (1994) as an example to show how this context-aware action system's framework can be effectively used to model context-aware services for mobile applications.

Imagine that Kaisa is attending a conference with her own smart phone. When arriving at the conference location, she is provided with a mobile application to be installed on her own portable device that, based on a wireless network infrastructure, allows attendees to access the proceedings online, browse through the technical program, select the presentation they wish to attend, and exchange messages with other attendees. These services may have to be delivered in different ways when requested in different contexts, in order to meet the users' needs.

MODELING THE ENVIRONMENT

The ideas behind this scenario are rooted in the notion that mobile application development could be simplified if the retrieval and maintenance of context information were to be delegated to the software support infrastructure without loss of flexibility and generality as shown in Figure 1.

To ease the prototyping of a context-aware application, we proposed a middleware for network-centric ubiquitous systems (Yan, 2004) from which an application developer can derive specific services. This layer takes care of most low-level context-aware functions—collecting sensor data, combining data from multiple sensors, and translating sensor data into alternate formats—and contains the infrastructure required for distributed peer-to-peer storage, communication via XML over HTTP, and software event monitoring.

Here we introduce a simplified model of the environment which retrieves and maintains necessary environment variables:

Figure 1. Overall infrastructure

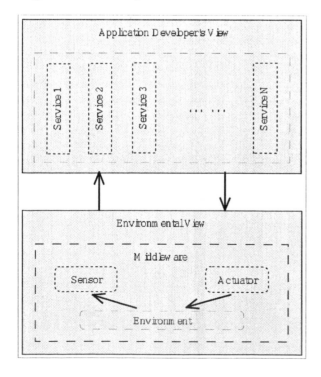

Table 1. Sensor and actuator

$$
\begin{aligned}
S_{ensor} \quad = \quad &|[\text{ import } read \\
&\text{export } value; \\
&\text{var } \quad env \\
&\text{do} \\
&\qquad read = true \rightarrow value = env \\
&\qquad\qquad\qquad read = false \\
&\text{od} \\
&]| \\
\\
A_{ctuator} \quad = \quad &|[\text{ import } write, value; \\
&\text{var } \quad v\,ar; \\
&\text{do} \\
&\qquad write = true \rightarrow env = value \\
&\qquad\qquad\qquad write = false \\
&\text{od} \\
&]|
\end{aligned}
$$

$$M_{iddleware} = S_{ensor} \parallel A_{ctuator}$$

where *sensor* and *actuator,* modeled via classical action systems in Table 1, make the context information accessible and updated from the application developer's view; more sophisticated models can be found in Yan, Sere, Zhou, and Pang (2004). The benefit of this approach is obvious: since context information actually belongs to the environmental view, given proper middleware, application developers will usually focus on service construct and not necessarily care too much about the low-level context-aware operations; thus it will ease application development by taking advantage of this abstraction.

REMINDING SERVICE

Let us consider a reminding service that alerts an attendee of the coming presentation to attend five minutes before it starts. Based on the functionality of Kaisa's smart phone, the following profiles can be used to remind her of coming events: sound alert, particularly useful to capture user attention in noisy and open air places; and vibra alert, to capture user attention without disturbing anyone else (e.g., when attending a talk).

We model the reminding service in context-aware action systems as follows. The reminding service $R_{eminder}$ is a parallel composition of sound alter service A_{sound} and vibra alert service A_{vibra} in Table 2:

$$R_{eminder} = A_{sound} \parallel A_{vibra}$$

We model the current time and the coming presentation as imported variables *now* and *talk,* and current status of our service as an export variable *alert.* Then, we store our preference in the variable *schedule* for reference. The context-aware action system formalism has context information *c* to constrain at what situation a service is delivered.

Table 2. Alert service

$$
\begin{aligned}
A_{sound} \ = \ &|[\ \text{imp}\ now, talk; \\
&\quad \text{exp}\ alert \\
&\quad \text{var}\ schedule \\
&\quad \text{do} \\
&\qquad schedule.time - now > 5 \vee now > schedule.time \rightarrow alert := off \\
&\qquad [] \ 0 < schedule.time < 5 \rightarrow \ \text{if}\ schedule.title = talk \\
&\qquad\qquad\qquad\qquad\qquad\qquad\qquad\qquad alert = sound\ \text{fi} \\
&\quad \text{od} \\
&]|@outdoor \\[8pt]
A_{vibra} \ = \ &|[\ \text{imp}\ now, talk; \\
&\quad \text{exp}\ alert \\
&\quad \text{var}\ schedule \\
&\quad \text{do} \\
&\qquad schedule.time - now > 5 \vee now > schedule.time \rightarrow alert := off \\
&\qquad [] \ 0 < schedule.time < 5 \rightarrow \ \text{if}\ schedule.title = talk \\
&\qquad\qquad\qquad\qquad\qquad\qquad\qquad\qquad alert = vibra\ \text{fi} \\
&\quad \text{od} \\
&]|@conference
\end{aligned}
$$

For the reminding service we define, there are two sorts of context: *outdoor* profile and *conference* profile, where:

ourdoor = {location = outside}
conference = {location = conferenceRoom}

Using the properties presented in the previous section and the techniques discussed in Sere and Walden (1997) and Petre, Sere, and Walden (1999), we can transform these context-aware action systems into one action system and further refine it within its associated refinement calculus (Back & Wright, 1998). A possible result is shown in Table 3.

With the above refined specification, we can derive a design pattern (Buschmann, Meunier, Rohnert, Sommerlad, & Stal, 1996) as shown in

Figure 2 to ease the software development for *reminding service*: as an attendee moves around the conference places, his or her context variable, *location,* defined to contain the current location information, changes in response to the available context. If the new context matches some particular locations, the attendee's reminding policy is updated to adapt the application to the new environment.

MESSAGING SERVICE

The messaging service enables an attendee to exchange messages with other attendees. Attendees can exchange messages using the following profiles: *SMS,* to exchange messages in plain text; *MMS,* to send messages comprising a combina-

Table 3. Reminding service

$$
\begin{aligned}
R_{e\min der} \; = \; |[\; &\text{context} \quad outdoor, conference; \\
&\text{imp} \qquad now \; talk, location; \\
&\text{exp} \qquad alert \\
&\text{var} \qquad schedule \\
&\text{do} \\
&\qquad schedule.time - now > 5 \vee now > schedule.time \rightarrow alert := off \\
&\qquad [] \; 0 < schedule.time < 5 \rightarrow \; \text{if} \; schedule.title = talk \\
&\qquad\qquad\qquad\qquad\qquad i \rightarrow \text{f} \; location = outside \\
&\qquad\qquad\qquad\qquad\qquad :\rightarrow alert = sound \\
&\qquad\qquad\qquad\qquad\qquad [] \; location = conferenceRoom \\
&\qquad\qquad\qquad\qquad\qquad :\rightarrow alert = vibra \; \text{fi} \\
&\qquad\qquad\qquad\qquad \text{fi} \\
&\text{od} \\
]|&
\end{aligned}
$$

Figure 2. Reminding service

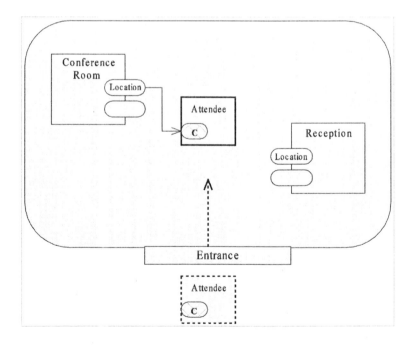

tion of text, sounds, images, and video; *EMS,* to send encrypted messages. The messaging service is an example of peer-to-peer service, where any number of peers may participate in the delivery of the service.

Let us assume, for example, another attendee Lu is willing to exchange messages with Kaisa, but he is using a PDA, which has a different profiling policy than the smart phone. We model this with two context-aware action systems:

$$K_{aisa} = SMS_{phone} \parallel MMS_{phone} \parallel EMS_{phone}$$
$$L_{u} = SMS_{PDA} \parallel MMS_{PDA} \parallel EMS_{PDA}$$

where the contexts are defined in Table 4. Note that no context information is associated to the SMS_{phone} context of Kaisa's profile: this means that this action is always available, regardless of current context. At any time, attendees may change their preferences through the user interface that the conference application provides; the application, in turn, dynamically updates the context

information encoded in their profiles, in order to take the new preference into account.

The interesting part of the messaging service is the specification of context itself. Let us consider, for example, the messaging service is requested when Kaisa's bandwidth is greater than 70% and battery availability is greater than 50%: all three profiles SMS_{phone}, MMS_{phone}, and EMS_{phone} can be applied. In this sample, the messaging service will be delivered via *SMS, MMS,* and *EMS* simultaneously, which is unnecessary and should be avoided in the real world.

In case we need to ensure that a service is delivered via *only* one context-aware action system, even if several different context-aware action systems can be used, a *conflict* may arise due to the different contexts themselves or due to changes in context. There has been some research on conflict resolution, and several schemes are proposed. A critical literature review in this area can be found in Lamsweerde, Darimont, and Letier (1998). In the context-aware action system framework, we implement a priority

Table 4. Context for smart phone and PDA

Profile	Context
SMS_{phone}	
MMS_{phone}	$bandwidth > 70\%$
	$battery > 50\%$
EMS_{phone}	$battery > 20\%$
SMS_{PDA}	$bandwidth > 5\%$
MMS_{PDA}	$bandwidth > 40\%$
	$battery > 25\%$
EMS_{PDA}	$bandwidth > 75\%$

assignment scheme (Sivasankaran, Stankovic, Towsley, Purimetla, & Ramamritham, 1996) for conflict resolution, where the order of prioritizing composition reflects the user's preferences (Sekerinski & Sere, 1996).

$$K_{aisa} = MMS_{phone} \parallel EMS_{phone} \parallel SMS_{phone}$$
$$L_u = EMS_{PDA} \parallel MMS_{PDA} \parallel SMS_{PDA}$$

THE WHOLE SYSTEM

Let us imagine that, at the moment, the attendee Lu opens his tablet PC to enable better communication with Kaisa. Obviously, this kind of mobile device has a different profiling policy than the previous two. We model the situation with a new context-aware action system L_u':

$$L_u' = L_{u1} \parallel L_{u2}$$
$$L_{u1} = EMS_{PDA} \parallel MMS_{PDA} \parallel SMS_{PDA}$$
$$L_{u2} = MMS_{tab} \parallel EMS_{tab} \parallel SMS_{tab}$$

where the contexts are defined in Table 5. As the result, the messaging service is now modeled as follows:

$$K_{aisa} \parallel L_u' = K_{aisa} \parallel (L_{u1} \parallel L_{u2})$$

The final application is a parallel composition of all involved service providers:

$$S_{ervices} = R_{eminder} \parallel (K_{aisa} \parallel L_u')$$
$$(= A_{sound} \parallel A_{vibra}) \parallel (K_{aisa} \parallel (L_{u1} \parallel L_{u2}))$$
$$\models A_{sound} \mid A_{vibra} \parallel (MMS_{phone} \mathbin{/\!/} EMS_{phone} \mathbin{/\!/} SMS_{phone}) \parallel$$
$$(EMS_{PDA} \mathbin{/\!/} MMS_{PDA} \mathbin{/\!/} SMS_{PDA}) \parallel (MMS_{tab} \mathbin{/\!/} EMS_{tab} \mathbin{/\!/} SMS_{tab})$$

and the whole system is modeled as the interaction between the application view and the environment view:

$$S_{ystem} = S_{ervices} \parallel M_{iddleware}$$

where services lead to the final program to be deployed into attendees' mobile devices, and middleware is the supporting software existed in attendees' mobile devices and preinstalled at the conference venue.

CONCLUSION

The increasing popularity of portable devices and recent advances in wireless network technologies are facilitating the engineering of new classes of distributed systems, which present challenging problems to designers. To harness the flexibility and power of these rapidly evolving network and

Table 5. Context for tablet PC

Profile	Context
SMS_{tab}	
MMS_{tab}	*bandwidth > 25%*
	battery > 10%
EMS_{tab}	*bandwidth > 5%*

ubiquitous computing systems, and in particular to meet the need for context-awareness and adaptation, we need to come up with new foundational ideas and effective principles for building and analyzing such systems.

In this chapter, we have described a formal approach to context-aware mobile computing: we present SOA along with context-aware action systems framework, which provides a systematic method for managing and processing context information. Besides the essential notions and properties of this framework, we demonstrate how this approach can effectively be used to derive context-aware services for mobile applications with examples.

FUTURE RESEARCH DIRECTIONS

Context-aware delivery of information to mobile users from SOAs and other sources combines all the issues explored in this chapter. Currently we are implementing a prototype of this system based on the proposed formalism and principles. While putting together a system that can deliver information to a user is only part of the goal; the information delivered must be useful and enrich the user's experience of his or her environment. Information delivery must be reliable and timely, and in a form suitable for the user's current activities (Jones, 2005).

This raises issues of detecting the user's likely current activity, and deciding if or when to deliver information, and how much information and in what media it should be delivered. This would require a further study of context-awareness on the principle ground, combining many different but overlapping aspects such as software technology, ubiquitous computing, HCI, and social sciences.

REFERENCES

Abowd, G., Atkeson, C., Hong, J., Long, S., Kooper, R., & Pinkerton, M. (1997). Cyberguide: A mobile context-aware tour guide. *ACM Wireless Networks.*

Asthana, A., Cravatts, M., & Kryzyzanowski, P. (1994). An indoor wireless system for personalized shopping assistance. *Proceedings of the IEEE Workshop on Mobile Computing Systems and Applications,* Santa Cruz, CA.

Back, R.J.R., & Sere, K. (1996). From action systems to modular systems. *Software—Concepts and Tools.*

Back, R.J.R., & Wright, J. (1998). *Refinement calculus: A systematic introduction.* Berlin: Springer-Verlag (Graduate Texts in Computer Science).

Buschmann, F., Meunier, R., Rohnert, H., Sommerlad, P., & Stal, M. (1996). *Pattern-oriented software architecture, a system of patterns.* New York: John Wiley & Sons.

Bush, V. (1945). As we may think. *Atlantic Monthly,176*(1), 101–108.

Cheverst, K., Davies, N., Mitchell, K., Friday, A., & Efstratiou, C. (2000). Experiences of developing and deploying a context-aware tourist guide: The GUIDE project. *Proceedings of the 6ᵗʰ Annual International Conference on Mobile Computing and Networking.*

Cool, C., & Spink, A. (2002). Issues of context in information retrieval (IR): An introduction to the special issue. *Information Processing and Management: An International Journal, 38*(5), 605–611.

Day, A.K., Salber, D., Abowd, G.D., & Futakawa, M. (1999). The conference assistant: Combining context-awareness with wearable computing.

Proceedings of the 3rd International Symposium on Wearable Computers, San Francisco.

Dey, A.K., & Abowd, G.D. (1999). *Towards a better understanding of context and context-awareness.* Technical Report, Georgia Institute of Technology, USA.

Dumais, S., Cutrell, E., Cadiz, J., Jancke, G., Sarin, R., & Robbins, D.C. (2003). Stuff I've Seen: A system for personal information retrieval and re-use. *Proceedings of the 26th Annual International ACM SIGIR Conference on Research and Development in Information Retrieval.*

Gemmell, J., Bell, G., & Lueder, R. (2006). My-LifeBits: A personal database for everything. *Communications of the ACM, 49*(1).

Harter, A., & Hopper, A. (1994). A distributed location system for the active office. *IEEE Networks.*

ITU (International Telecommunication Union). (2006). *ITU Internet reports 2006.* Author.

Jones, G.J.F. (2005). Challenges and opportunities of context-aware information access. *Proceedings of the International Workshop on Ubiquitous Data Management.*

Jones, G.J.F., & Brown, P.J. (2003). Context-aware retrieval for ubiquitous computing environments. *Proceedings of the Workshop on Mobile and Ubiquitous Information Access of the 5th International Symposium on Human Computer Interaction with Mobile Devices and Services* (Mobile HCI 2003).

Korkea-aho, M. (2000, Spring). Context-aware applications survey. *Proceedings of the Internetworking Seminar,* Helsinki, Finland.

Lamsweerde, A.V., Darimont, R., & Letier, E. (1998). Managing conflicts in goal-driven requirements engineering. *IEEE Transactions on Software Engineering.*

Petre, L., Sere, K., & Walden, M. (1999). A topological approach to distributed computing. *Proceedings of the Workshop on Distributed Systems* (WDS'99).

Sekerinski, E., & Sere, K. (1996). A theory of prioritizing composition. *The Computer Journal.*

Sere, K., & Walden, M. (1997). Data refinement of remote procedures. *Proceedings of the International Symposium on Theoretical Aspects of Computer Software,* Sendai, Japan. Berlin: Springer-Verlag (LNCS 1281).

Sivasankaran, R.M., Stankovic, J.A., Towsley, D., Purimetla, B., & Ramamritham, K. (1996). Priority assignment in real-time active databases. *International Journal on Very Large Data Bases.*

Want, R. (1995). An overview of the PARCTab ubiquitous computing environment. *IEEE Personal Communications.*

Yan, L. (2004). MIN: Middleware for network-centric ubiquitous systems. *IEEE Pervasive Computing.*

Yan, L., Sere, K., Zhou, X., & Pang, J. (2004). Towards an integrated architecture for peer-to-peer and ad hoc overlay network applications. *Proceedings of the 10th IEEE International Workshop on Future Trends of Distributed Computing Systems* (FTDCS 2004).

ADDITIONAL READING

Aizawa, K., Tancharoen, D., Kawasaki S., & Yamasaki, T. (2004). Efficient retrieval of life log based on context and content. *Proceedings of the 1st ACM Workshop on Continuous Archival and Retrieval of Personal Experiences.*

Barry, B., & Davenport, G. (2003). Documenting life: Videography and common sense. *Proceedings of the IEEE International Conference on Multimedia.*

Bradley, N.A., & Dunlop, M.D. (2004). Towards a user-centric and multidisciplinary framework for designing context-aware applications. *Proceedings of the Workshop on Advanced Context Modeling, Reasoning and Management at Ubicomp 2004.*

Bradley, N.A., & Dunlop, M.D. (2007). Navigation AT: Context-aware computing. *Assistive Technology for Vision-Impaired and Blind People.*

Brown, P.J., & Jones, G.J.F. (2002). Exploiting contextual change in context-aware retrieval. *Proceedings of the 2002 ACM Symposium on Applied Computing.*

Budzik, J., & Hammond, K.J. (2000). User interactions with everyday applications as context for just-in-time information access. *Proceedings of the ACM Intelligent User Interfaces Conference.*

Budzik, J.L., & Hammond, K.J. (2003). *Information access in context: Experiences with the Watson system.*

Cheverst, K., Davies, N., Mitchel, K., & Smith, P. (2000). Providing tailored (context-aware) information to city visitors. *Proceedings of the International Conference on Adaptive Hypermedia and Adaptive Web-Based Systems.*

Dourish, P. (2001). Seeking a foundation for context-aware computing. *Human-Computer Interaction, 16*(2–3).

Dourish, P. (2004). What we talk about when we talk about context. *Personal and Ubiquitous Computing, 8*(1).

Dunlop, M.D., Glen, A., Motaparti, S., & Patel, S. (2006). AdapTex: Contextually adaptive text entry for mobiles. *Proceedings of the 8th Conference on Human-Computer Interaction with Mobile Devices and Services.*

Fischer, G., & Ye, Y. (2001). Exploiting context to make delivered information relevant to tasks and users. *Proceedings of the Workshop on User Modeling for Context-Aware Applications.*

Göker, A., Watt, S., Myrhaug, H.I., Whitehead, N., Yakici, M., Bierig, R., Nuti, S.K., & Cumming, H. (2004). An ambient, personalised, and context-sensitive information system for mobile users. *Proceedings of the 2nd European Union Symposium on Ambient Intelligence.*

Grand, B.L., Aufaure, M.A., & Soto, M. (2006). Semantic and conceptual context-aware. *Proceedings of the ACM IEEE International Conference on Signal-Image Technology & Internet-Based Systems.*

He, D., Göker, A., & Harper, D.J. (2002). Combining evidence for automatic Web session identification. *Information Processing and Management: An International Journal, 38*(5), 727–742.

Hirsch, H., Basu, C., & Davison, B.D. (2000). Learning to personalize. *CACM, 43*(8).

Hong, J.I., & Landay, J.A. (2004). An architecture for privacy-sensitive ubiquitous computing. *Proceedings of the 2nd International Conference on Mobile Systems, Applications, and Services.*

Järvelin, K., & Kekäläinen, J. (2002). IR evaluation methods for retrieving highly relevant documents. *Proceedings of the 23rd Annual International ACM SIGIR Conference on Research and Development in Information Retrieval.*

Jones, G.J.F., & Brown, P.J. (2000). Information access for context-aware appliances. *Proceedings of the 23rd Annual International ACM SIGIR Conference on Research and Development in Information Retrieval.*

Jones, G.J.F., & Brown, P.J. (2001). Context-aware retrieval: Exploring a new environment for information retrieval and information filtering. *Personal and Ubiquitous Computing, 5*(4).

Kammanahalli, H., Gopalan, S., Sridhar, V., & Ramamritham, K. (2004). Context aware retrieval in Web-based collaborations. *Proceedings of the 2nd IEEE Annual Conference on Pervasive Computing and Communications Workshops.*

Kammanahalli, H., Gopalan, S., Sridhar, V., & Ramamritham, K. (2003). CART: An information system for context-aware information access during synchronous Web-based collaboration. *Proceedings of (408) Communications, Internet, and Information Technology.*

Kraft, R., Maghoul, F., & Chang, C.C. (2005). Y!Q: Contextual search at the point of inspiration. *Proceedings of the 14th ACM International Conference on Information and Knowledge Management.*

Lawrence, S. (2000). Context in Web search. *IEEE Data Engineering Bulletin, 23*(3), 25–32.

Lieberman, H., & Liu, H. (2002). Adaptive linking between text and photos using common sense reasoning. *Proceedings of the Conference on Adaptive Hypermedia and Adaptive Web Systems.*

Liu, H., Lieberman, H., & Selker, T. (2002). GOOSE: A goal-oriented search engine. *Proceedings of the Conference on Adaptive Hypermedia and Adaptive Web Systems.*

Mikalsen, M., & Kofod-Petersen, A. (2004). Representing and reasoning about context in a mobile environment. *Modeling and Retrieval of Context.*

Ng, K.B. (2002). Toward a theoretical framework for understanding the relationship between situated action and planned action models of behavior in information retrieval contexts: Contributions from phenomenology. *Information Processing and Management: An International Journal, 38*(5), 613–626.

Oulasvirta, A., Tamminen, S., & Höök, K. (2005). Comparing two approaches to context: Realism and constructivism. *Proceedings of the 4th Decennial Conference on Critical Computing: Between Sense and Sensibility.*

Page, L., Brin, S., Motwani, R., & Winograd, T. (1998). *The Pagerank citation ranking: Bringing order to the Web.* Technical Report.

Rhodes, B.J., & Maes, P. (2000). Just-in-time information retrieval agents. *IBM Systems Journal, 39*(3&4):685–704.

Rodríguez, M., & Preciado, A. (2004). An agent based system for the contextual retrieval of medical information. *Advances in Web Intelligence.*

Shen, X., Tan, B., & Zhai, C. (2005). Context-sensitive information retrieval using implicit feedback. *Proceedings of the 28th Annual International ACM SIGIR Conference on Research and Development in Information Retrieval.*

Silva, J.M., & Favela, J. (2006). Context aware retrieval of health information on the Web. *Proceedings of the 4th Latin American Web Congress.*

Singhal. A. (2001). Modern information retrieval: A brief overview. *IEEE Data Engineering Bulletin, 24*(4), 35–43.

Suchman, L.A. (1987). *Plans and situated actions: The problem of human-machine communications.* Cambridge: Cambridge Press.

Teevan, J., Dumais, S.T., & Horvitz, E. (2005). Personalizing search via automated analysis of interests and activities. *Proceedings of the 28th Annual International ACM SIGIR Conference on Research and Development in Information Retrieval.*

Wen, Z., Zhou, M.X., & Aggarwal, V. (2007). Context-aware, adaptive information retrieval for investigative tasks. *Proceedings of the 12th International Conference on Intelligent User Interfaces.*

Chapter XI
On Personalizing
Web Services Using Context

Zakaria Maamar
Zayed University, UAE

Soraya Kouadri Mostéfaoui
Fribourg University, Switzerland

Qusay H. Mahmoud
Guelph University, Canada

ABSTRACT

This chapter presents a context-based approach for Web services personalization so that user preferences are accommodated. Preferences are of different types, varying from when the execution of a Web service should start to where the outcome of this execution should be delivered according to user location. Besides user preferences, it will be discussed in this chapter that the computing resources on which the Web services operate have an impact on their personalization. Indeed, resources schedule the execution requests that originate from multiple Web services. To track the personalization of a Web service from a temporal perspective (i.e., what did happen, what is happening, and what will happen), three types of contexts are devised and referred to as user context, Web service context, and resource context.

INTRODUCTION AND MOTIVATIONS

With the latest development of information and communication technologies, academia and industries are proposing several concepts that can hide the complexity of developing a new generation of user applications. Among these concepts are Web services (Papazoglou & Georgakopoulos, 2003), which are suitable candidates for achieving the integration of distributed and heterogeneous applications.

A Web service is an accessible application that other applications and humans can discover and trigger to satisfy various needs. It is known that Web services (also called *services* in the rest of this paper) have the capacity to be composed into high-level business processes known as *composite services*. Composing services rather than accessing a single service is essential and offers better benefits to users (Casati et al., 2003; Maamar et al., 2004b). Composition addresses the situation of a user's request that cannot be satisfied by any available service, whereas a composite service obtained by combining a set of available services might be used (Berardi et al., 2003). For example, applying online for a loan requires identifying the Web site of the appropriate financial institution, filling in an application, submitting the application for assessment, and collecting the analysts' comments for decision-making and applicant notification. In this paper, composition is a kind of collaborative interaction that emerges when each participant has some, but not all, of the information and abilities required to perform an operation.

Because users' expectations and requirements constantly change, it is important to include their preferences in the composition and provisioning of Web services. Indeed, some users, while on the move, would like to receive answers according to their current locations (Maamar et al., 2004c). This simple example sheds light on personalization and its impact on making applications adjustable. Personalization is of an explicit or implicit type (Muldoon et al., 2003). Explicit personalization calls for a direct participation of users in the adjustment of applications. Users clearly indicate the information that needs to be treated or discarded. Implicit personalization does not call for any user involvement and can be built upon learning strategies that automatically track users' behaviors. Personalization is motivated by the recognition that a user has needs and that meeting them successfully is likely to lead to a successful relationship with the user (Riecken, 2000).

Personalization depends on the features of the environment in which it is expected to happen. These features can be about users (e.g., stationary user, mobile user), computing resources (e.g., fixed device, handheld device), time of day (e.g., in the afternoon, in the evening), and physical locations (e.g., meeting room, shopping center). Sensing,

collecting, assessing, and refining the features of a situation permit the definition of its context. Context is the information that characterizes the interaction between humans, applications, and the surrounding environment (Brézillon, 2003). Prior to integrating context into Web services, various issues need to be addressed (adapted from Satyanarayanan, 2001): how is context structured, how does a Web service bind to context, where is context stored, how frequently does a Web service consult context, how are changes detected and assessed for context update purposes, and what is the overload on a Web service of taking context into account?

Web services composition and provisioning are a very active area of R&D (Papazoglou & Georgakopoulos, 2003). However, very little has been accomplished to date regarding their context-based personalization. Several obstacles still hinder personalization such as (1) current Web services are not active components that can be embedded with context-awareness mechanisms, (2) existing Web services composition languages (e.g., WSFL and BPEL) typically facilitate choreography only, while neglecting context of users, Web services, and computing resources, and (3) there is a lack of support techniques for modeling and specifying the integration of personalization into Web services. In this paper, we present our approach for personalizing Web services using context. The major features of this approach are as follows and will be detailed throughout this paper:

- Three types of contexts are devised and correspond to U-context to denote user context, W-context to denote Web service context, and R-context to denote Resource context.
- Three types of policies are developed for regulating personalization of Web services. These policies guarantee that the Web services still do what they are supposed to do, despite being subject to personalization.

- Web services initiate conversations with appropriate components during their personalization. The flow of exchange and progress of conversations also are context-dependent.

The rest of this paper is organized as follows. The next section provides a scenario that explains our view on Web services personalization. Next, we overview some basic concepts such as Web service, context, and personalization. The approach for personalizing Web services is presented later on. This is followed by a discussion on the value-added of policies and conversations to Web services personalization, respectively. The implementation of the suggested personalization approach is discussed next. Prior to concluding the paper, some related works are presented.

BASIC SCENARIO

Our motivating scenario concerns Melissa, a tourist who just landed in Dubai. She is equipped with a PDA and plans to use it as a platform for running Tourist MobileBook (TMB) application, rather than carrying brochures and booklets (these are outdated most of the time). Upon arrival at the airport, she downloads this application into her PDA, as tourism authorities offer it free-of-charge. TMB application is the front-end of two Web services that concern tourism in Dubai; namely, sightseeing and shopping. It should be noted that both Web services can be combined according to a certain composition pattern1.

Melissa's plans are to visit places in the morning and go shopping in the afternoon. TMB application, among other things, prompts Melissa to select some places based on her interests, indicate the pickup/drop-off places and times of the various activities, and express her need for a guide during the visits. In fact, Melissa is asked to adjust the execution of sightseeing and shopping Web services according to various parameters,

among them time and location. Melissa wishes to receive news about the daily events happening in Dubai every morning so that she can plan the rest of her day. In addition, she wishes to receive an historical background about places (e.g., museums) only when she is nearby and before going in. The scheduling of Melissa's activities has to guarantee that places are open to the public on the days that Melissa has opted for, and that transportation and guides are arranged.

SOME DEFINITIONS

Benatallah et al. (2003) associate the following properties with a Web service: independent as much as possible from specific platforms and computing paradigms; primarily developed for interorganizational situations; and easily composable so that developing complex adapters for the needs of composition are not required. Several standards back the development of Web services, such as UDDI, WSDL, and SOAP, which define service discovery, description, and messaging protocols, respectively (Milanovic & Malek, 2004). For composition requirements, a composite service is always associated with a specification that describes, among other things, the list of component Web services that participate in the composite service, the execution order of these component Web services, and the corrective strategies in case of exception handling.

Dey (2001) defines context as any information that is relevant to the interactions between a user and an environment. This information is about the circumstances, objects, or conditions by which the user is surrounded. Many other researchers have attempted to define context (Brézillon, 2003; Doulkeridis et al., 2003), among them Schilit et al. (1994), who decompose context into three categories: computing context, such as network connectivity and nearby resources; user context, such as profile and location; and physical context, such as lighting and temperature. In an environment populated with mobile devices, context awareness has been categorized along three components (Spriestersbach et al., 2001): activity, environment, and self. The activity component describes a user's habits while he or she performs a certain task. The environment component describes the physical and social surroundings of the user in terms of current location, ongoing activities, and others. Finally, the self component contains the current status of the mobile device itself.

Personalization has attracted the attention of several researchers (Schiaffino & Amandi, 2004). It aims at integrating users' preferences into the process of delivering any information-related content or outcome of service computing. Preferences are of multiple types and vary from content and format to time and location. It is shown, for instance, that the needs of mobile users regarding information access are quite different from the needs of stationary users. Needs of mobile users are not about browsing the Web, but about receiving personalized content that is highly sensitive to their immediate environment and respective requirements.

A conversation is a sequence of messages that involves two or more participants who intend to achieve a particular purpose (Smith et al., 1998). A conversation either succeeds or fails. A conversation succeeds because the outcome that is expected out of the conversation has been achieved (e.g., action implemented). However, a conversation fails because the conversation faced some technical difficulties (e.g., communication medium disconnected) or didn't achieve what was expected out of the conversation (e.g., information exchanged is misunderstood).

WEB SERVICES PERSONALIZATION: FOUNDATIONS AND OPERATION

Foundations

Figure 1 illustrates the proposed approach for the personalization of Web services. The core concept in this approach is context from which three subcontexts are derived: U-Context, W-Context, and R-Context.

Muldoon et al. (2003) define the user context of a user as an aggregation of the user's location, previous activities, and preferences. Sun adopts the same definition of the user context and adds physiological information to this Context (Sun, 2003). In this paper, we comply with Muldoon et al.'s definition. We define the Web service context of a Web service as an aggregation of its simultaneous participations in composite services, locations, and times of execution that users set, and constraints during execution. Finally we define the resource context of a resource as an aggregation of its current status, periods of unavailability, and capacities of meeting the execution requirements of Web services. According to Bellavista et al. (2003), provisioning a service in a specific context identifies the logical set of resources that are accessible to a user during a service session. This accessibility depends on various factors such as user location, access device capabilities, subscribed services, user preferences, and level of trust.

In Figure 1, U-context, W-context, and R-context are interconnected. From R-context to W-context, execution adjustment relationship identifies the execution constraints on a Web service (e.g., execution time, execution location, flow dependency) vs. the execution capabilities of a resource (e.g., next period of availability, scheduling policy) on which the Web service will operate. A resource checks its status before it agrees to support the execution of an additional Web service. From U-context to W-context, provi-

Figure 1. Representation of the context-based personalization approach

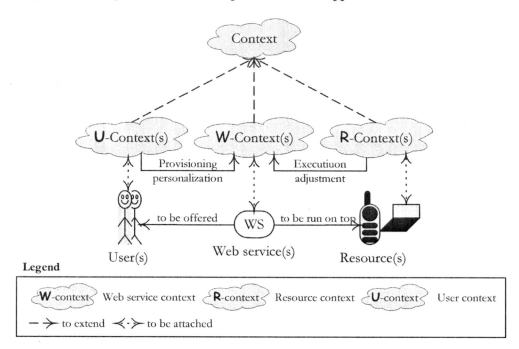

sioning personalization relationship identifies the preferences of a user (e.g., when and where a Web service needs to be executed, and when and where the execution's outcome needs to be returned) vs. the capabilities of a Web service to accommodate these preferences (e.g., can a service be executed at a certain time or in a certain location?). A Web service checks its status before it agrees to satisfy an extra user's need. W-context is the common element between U-context and R-context. A Web service has to conciliate between what a user wishes and what a resource permits.

A Web service is context-aware if it can transparently adapt its behavior or the content it processes to the requirements of the entities for which it works (Hegering et al., 2003). Users or peers in case of composition are samples of these entities. The execution of a Web service is adjusted (i.e., postponed) once details on resources are known. These details concern the status of a

resource (e.g., idle, operational, busy) and exist in its R-context. R-context acts now as a context source for the Web service. Once a Web service is adjusted to the availability of a resource, its W-context is updated. The same description applies to supplying Web services to users. Before a Web service gets invoked, the user's preferences are handled. Preferences are about the user's current location and activities, and the current time. User preferences are contained in the U-context which acts as a context source for the Web service. Once a Web service is adjusted to the preferences of a user, its W-context is updated again.

A Web service is personalized because of user preferences and adjusted because of resource availabilities. Users and resources are the triggers that make Web services change so that they can accommodate preferences and consider availabilities. Besides both triggers, a third one exists, which is a personalized Web service. The personalization of a Web service can trigger the personalization of other peers, which is in relationship with this personalized Web service. We call this type of relationship *causal*. For example, if a service is personalized in order to accommodate a certain time preference, it is important to ensure that the preceding services all are successfully executed before the time that features the execution of this service. This means that the respective execution times of these services have to be checked and adjusted, if needed.

Types and Roles of Context

In Figure 1, each context type is attached to a specific component whether user, Web service, or resource. User is the most dynamic component. The user's needs, requirements, and preferences always change. Resource is nearly the most stable component. The computing features of and constraints on a resource can be known, to a certain

extent, in-advance. Therefore, the capabilities of a resource can be tuned in order to meet certain requirements, such as communication access reliability and efficiency of security mechanisms. The Web service component is between user and resource. It is responsible for finding a compromise between what users prefer and what resources permit.

The role of U-context is to track the current status of a user and reflect the user's personal preferences in terms of execution location or execution time of services. The following parameters populate U-context (Table 1): label, previous locations/services, current location/services, next locations/services, previous periods of time/services, current period of time/services, next periods of time/services, and date. "Previous locations" and "previous periods of time" parameters illustrate the Web services that were executed in the past. "Next locations" and "next periods of times" illustrate the Web services that will be executed

Table 1. Description of U-context's parameters

Label: corresponds to the identifier of the user.
Previous locations/services: keeps track of all the locations, as indicated by the user, that have featured in the past the execution of services (null if there are no predecessor locations).
Current location/services: indicates the current location (as indicated by the user) that should feature now the execution of services.
Next locations/services: indicates all the locations (as indicated by the user) that will feature the execution of services (null if there are no next locations).
Previous periods of time/services: keeps track of all the periods of time, as indicated by the user, that have featured the execution of services (null if there are no predecessor periods of time).
Current period of time/services: indicates the current time (as indicated by the user) that should feature now the execution of services.
Next periods of time/services: keeps track of all the periods of time (as indicated by the user) that will feature the execution of services (null if there are no next periods of time).
Date: identifies the time of updating the parameters above.
Application to Melissa scenario
(previous locations/services: City Center Mall/Shopping) - Shopping Web service was executed when Melissa was in City Center Mall, as per Melissa's request.
(next periods of time/services: 12pm/Transportation) - Transportation Web service will be executed at noon, as per Melissa's request.

Table 2. Description of W-context's parameters

Label: corresponds to the identifier of the Web service.
Status per participation: informs about the current status of the service with regard to each composite service in which the service takes part. Status can be of type in-progress, suspended, aborted, or terminated.
Previous services per participation: indicates whether there are services before the service with regard to each composite service (null if there are no predecessors).
Next services per participation: indicates whether there are services after the service with regard to each composite service (null if there are no successors).
Regular actions: illustrates the actions that the service normally performs.
Starting time per participation (requested and effective): informs when the execution of the service should start as requested by the user (i.e., user-related), and has effectively started with regard to each composite service (i.e., execution-related).
Location per participation (requested and effective): informs where the execution of the service should happen as requested by the user (i.e., user-related) and has effectively happened (i.e., execution-related) with regard to each composite service.
Reasons of failure: informs about the reasons that are behind the failure of the execution of the service with regard to each composite service.
Corrective actions: illustrates the actions that the service has to perform in case its execution fails. The actions depend on the reasons of failure.
Date: identifies the time of updating the parameters above.
Application to Melissa scenario (Sightseeing Web service)   (previous services per participation: Weather Forecasts) - Weather Forecasts Web service is executed before Sightseeing Web service, according to a specific composition pattern.   (location per participation (requested and effective): City Center Mall/City Center Mall) - Sightseeing Web service was requested to be executed when Melissa is at City Center Mall, and the execution has effectively happened when Melissa was at City Center Mall.

in the future. Appendix 1 illustrates the XML code associated with U-context.

The role of W-context is to oversee the current status of a Web service and its respective execution constraints. These constraints are tightly dependent on the preferences of users of type "execution-time requested" and "execution-location requested". A Web service is triggered each time it receives an invitation of participation in a composite service (details are given in Maamar et al. [2004a] on what an invitation of participation stands for). Before a service accepts an invitation, it carries out some verifications, among them the number of current participations vs. number of allowed participations, expected completion time of current participations, and features of the newly-received invitation with regard to execu-

tion time and execution location. It happens that a Web service refuses an invitation of participation in a composite service because of multiple reasons (e.g., period of unavailability for some maintenance work, resource unavailability, or overloaded status).

The following parameters populate W-context (Table 2): label, status per participation, previous services per participation, next services per participation, regular actions, starting time per participation (requested and effective), location per participation (requested and effective), reasons of failure, corrective actions, and date. "Previous services per participation" parameter illustrates the predecessor Web services to the current Web service that were executed in the past. "Next services per participation" parameter illustrates

Table 3. Description of R-context's parameters

Label: corresponds to the identifier of the resource.

Previous periods of time/services: keeps track of the periods of time, as indicated by the user, that have featured the execution of services with regard to each composite service (null if there are no predecessor periods of time). The effective periods of time of the execution of services are also reported in this parameter.

Current period of time/services: indicates the current time (as indicated by the user) that should feature now the execution of services with regard to each composite service.

Next periods of time/services: keeps track of all the periods of time (as indicated by the user) that will feature the execution of services with regard to each composite service (null if there are no next periods of time).

Previous locations/services: keeps track of the locations (as indicated by the user) that have featured the execution of services with regard to each composite service (null if there are no predecessor periods of time). The effective locations of the execution of services are also reported in this parameter.

Current location/services: indicates the current location (as indicated by the user) that should feature now the execution of services with regard to each composite service.

Next locations/services: keeps track of all the locations (as indicated by the user) that will feature the execution of services with regard to each composite service (null if there are no next periods of time).

Date: identifies the time of updating the parameters above.

Application to Melissa scenario
(Current period of time/services: 2pm/Transportation) - The current time, which is 2pm, is featured by the execution of Transportation Web service.

the successor Web services to the current Web service that are expected to be executed in the future. It should be noted that "per participation" in the aforementioned list of parameters stands for each composite service in which a Web service takes part. Mechanisms that allow a Web service to participate in several composite services are detailed in Maamar et al. (2005).

In "time-requested" and "location-requested" parameters are user dependently; user assigns values to both parameters. "Time-effective" and "location-effective" parameters are execution-dependent, (i.e., when and where the execution has really happened). Values to assign to "time effective" parameter are obtained from the resource on which a service was executed, whereas values to assign to the "location effective" parameter are obtained from users (we argue later why a manual detection of the user's location is adopted).

To verify that time and location preferences of a user have been properly considered during the deployment of a Web service, the values of "time-requested" or "location-requested" parameters should respectively be equal to the values of "time-effective" or "location-effective" parameters (a negligible difference is also acceptable). Any discrepancy between a parameter of type requested and a parameter of type effective indicates that the user adjustment in term of execution location or execution time of a Web service has not been handled correctly. The user needs to be informed about this discrepancy so that he or she can update (or through a third component acting on the user's behalf) the relevant parameters of U-context: "previous locations/services" or "previous periods of time/services." In addition, the Web service needs to determine the reasons for this discrepancy with regard to what was requested and what has effectively happened. With regard

Table 4. Parameter overlapping between U-context

U-context	W-context	R-context
Current location/services	Location per participation effective	Current location/services
Next locations/services	Location per participation requested	Next locations/services
Current period of time/services	Starting time per participation effective	Current period of time/services
Next periods of time/services	Starting time per participation requested	Next periods of time/services

to the preference of type location, we recall that users have to explicitly announce their location. A user who forgets to announce his or her location constitutes a valid reason for delaying the execution of a Web service.

The role of R-context is to monitor the current status of a resource. Before a resource accepts supporting the execution of a service, it performs some verifications, including number of Web services currently executed vs. maximum number of Web services under execution, approximate completion time of ongoing executions, and execution time of the newly-received request. It happens that a resource turns down a request of executing a Web service because of multiple reasons: period of unavailability due to some maintenance work or potential overloaded status.

The following parameters define R-context (Table 3): label, previous periods of time/services, current period of time/services, next periods of time/services, previous locations/services, current location/services, next locations/services, and date. "Previous periods of time" parameter illustrates the periods of time with regard to a particular period of time that has featured the execution of Web services on a resource in the past. "Next periods of time" parameter illustrates the periods of time with regard to a particular

period of time that will feature the execution of Web services on a resource in the future.

In Figure 1, "provisioning personalization" and "execution adjustment" relationships are identified with the common semantics that some of the parameters of U-context, W-context, and R-context share, as well (Table 1, Table 2, and Table 3). For instance, "starting-time requested per participation" and "location requested per participation" parameters of W-context have as counterpart the "multiple time and location" parameters of U-context. A similar comment is made on "starting-time requested per participation" parameter of W-context, which has as counterpart the "various time" parameters of R-context. illustrates the correspondence between the parameters of these three contexts.

Operation

Figure 2 represents the interaction diagram of context-based personalization of Web services. When a user selects a Web service, he or she proceeds next with its personalization according to time and location preferences. On the one hand, time preference is organized along two parts: (1) when the execution of the service should start, and (2) when the outcome of this execution should be returned to the user. Melissa could request to start the execution of "sightseeing" Web service at 2:00 P.M. and to return the outcome of this execution at 5:00 P.M., as she will be having a nap. It happens that execution time and delivery time are equal, if the time that the execution lasts is excluded or negligible. On the other hand, location preference is organized along two parts: (1) where the execution of the service should occur, and (2) where the outcome of this execution should be returned to the user. Melissa could ask to start the execution of "location mall" Web service once she leaves her hotel and to return the outcome of this execution when she is in the vicinity of the

mall. It also happens that execution location and delivery location are the same.

Once the user's preferences are submitted to the Web service, this one ensures that the dates and locations are valid and that no conflicts could emerge during deployment. For instance, the delivery time cannot occur before the execution time of a service. Moreover, the user has to be reminded continuously that he or she has to explicitly identify his or her current location so that execution location and delivery location are both properly handled[2]. Prior to identifying the resources on which it will be executed, the Web

Figure 2. Interactions between participants of personalized Web services

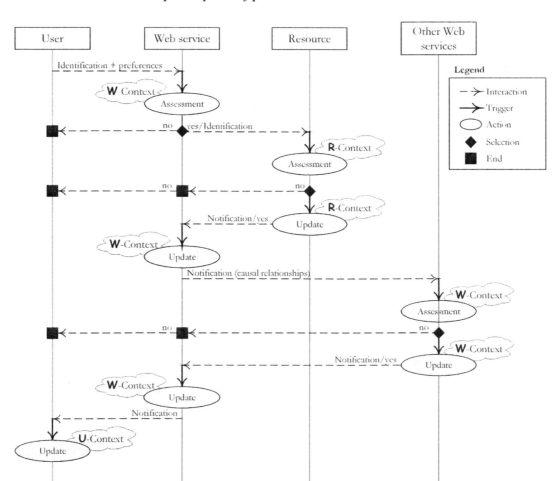

service checks its W-context with regard to the number of Web services currently under execution vs. the maximum number of Web services under execution, and the next period of unavailability. After a positive check of the W-context, the identification of a resource now can be launched. A resource mainly needs to accommodate two things: the starting time of the execution of a service, and the time that the execution of a service lasts, since the outcome of this execution needs to consider the delivery time as per user indication. To this purpose, a resource checks its R-context with regard to the next periods of time that will feature the execution of Web services and the next period of maintenance. After a positive check, the resource notifies the service, which notifies the user. User notification means updating the following parameters:

- "Next locations/services" and "next periods of time/services" of U-context (Table 1).
- "Next services per participation," "starting-time requested per participation," and "location requested per participation" of W-context (Table 2).
- "Next periods of time/services" and "next locations/services" of R-context (Table 3).

The update of these parameters and particularly those that feature the next actions to take is a good indication of the assessment that occurs in terms of (1) which Web services are involved and in which composite services, (2) which resources are considered, and (3) which locations or periods of time will feature the execution of Web services. This type of assessment enables first predicting the situations that will happen and second, preparing the relevant corrective plans in case of exceptions.

Before the personalized Web service notifies the user, as shown in Figure 2, an additional personalization process is triggered. This process consists of adjusting the Web services that are linked, through the causal relationship to the re-

cently personalized Web service. The description given in the previous paragraphs also applies to the extra Web services, which assess their current status through their respective W-contexts and search for the resources on which they will operate. To keep Figure 2 clean, the interactions that the extra personalized Web services undertake to search for the resources are not represented. Once all the Web services are personalized, a final notification is sent out to the user about the deployment of the Web service that he or she initially requested.

MANAGING PERSONALIZATION THROUGH POLICIES

In the introduction of this paper, the use of policies for managing the integration of personalization into Web services was suggested. In fact, policy-based approaches provide many benefits including reusability, efficiency, extensibility, and context-sensitivity (Uszok et al., 2004). Because of user preferences and resource availabilities, a Web service has to be adjusted so that it accommodates these preferences and takes into account these availabilities. To ensure that the adjustment of a Web service is efficient, we developed three types of policies (owners of Web services are normally responsible for developing the policies). The first type, called consistency, checks the status of a Web service after being personalized. The second type, called feasibility, ensures that a personalized Web service can find a resource on that it executes according to the constraints of time and location. Finally, the third type, called inspection, ensures that the deployment of a personalized Web service complies with the adjusted specification.

Before we detail each policy type, the arguments that constitute a Web service are defined. According to Medjahed et al. (2003), a Web service has a name, a description of its features, and a set of operations it performs. Interactions with the Web service are conducted using a specific binding (e.g., SOAP over HTTP), which defines message format and protocol details. Medjahed et al. (2003) also suggest purpose and category arguments to define a Web service. However, at this stage of our research, they are excluded. Therefore, a Web service WS_i is defined with the triple (Description$_i$, OP$_i$, Bindings$_i$).

When Web service WS_i is personalized, the outcome is $P.WS_i$ (P for personalized) that is defined with the triple (Description$_i$, P.OP$_i$, P.Bindings$_i$). The description of a service does not change after personalization. However, a new set of operations (OP$_i$ included in P.OP$_i$) and a new set of binding protocols (Bindings$_i$ included in P.Bindings$_i$) might be attached to the personalized Web service. The extra operations and bindings should not affect the initial outcome of the Web service. It should be noted that the personalization does not always call for new operations (OP$_i$ = P.OP$_i$) or for new bindings (Bindings$_i$ = P.Bindings$_i$).

A consistency policy guarantees that a Web service still does exactly what it is supposed to do after personalization. Personalization could alter the initial specification of a Web service, when, for instance, it comes to the list of regular events that trigger the Web service. Indeed, time- and location-related parameters are now new events to add to the list of regular events. Moreover, because of QoS-related parameters (e.g., response time and throughput) of a Web service (Menascé, 2002), it is important to verify that these QoS parameters did not change and are still satisfied, despite the personalization. For illustration, because a user would like to initiate the execution of a service at 2:00 P.M., which corresponds to the peak-time period of receiving requests, the response time QoS of the service might be disrupted.

A feasibility policy guarantees that a personalized Web service always succeeds in the identification of a resource on which it will operate. Because services have different requirements (e.g., periods of request, periods of delivery), and resources have different constraints (e.g., period of availabilities, maximum capacity), an agreement has to be reached between what services need in terms of resources and what resources offer in terms of capabilities. Furthermore, the feasibility policy checks that the new operations (P.OP$_i$ - OP$_i$) and new binding protocols (P.Bindings$_i$ - Bindings$_i$) of the personalized Web service (P.WS$_i$) can be handled by the existing resources. For example, if a new operation, which is the result of a personalization, requires a wireless connection, this connection should be made available.

An inspection policy is a means by which various aspects are considered, such as what to track (time, location, etc.), who asked to track (user, service itself, or both), when to track (continuously, intermittently), when and how to update the arguments of the different contexts, and how to react if a discrepancy is noticed between what was requested and what has effectively happened. The inspection policy is mainly tightened to the parameters of type requested and effective of the W-context of a Web service (Table 2). If there is a discrepancy between these parameters, the reasons have to be determined, assessed, and reported. One of the reasons could be the lack of appropriate resources on which the personalized service needs to be executed. It should be noted that this reason is in contradiction with the aim of the feasibility policy.

SUPPORTING PERSONALIZATION THROUGH CONVERSATIONS

Figure 2 illustrates multiple interactions that involve users, Web services to be personalized, and resources. In the following section, we outline how some of these interactions are leveraged to conversations. Two things are highlighted at this stage of the paper:

- In addition to contexts of user, Web service, and resource, an additional context type is deemed appropriate at the conversation level. In Maamar et al. (2004a), we argued the importance of having context for conversations. C-context denotes this context, and its arguments are explained later on.

- In addition to the consistency, feasibility, and inspection policies that manage personalization, a fourth type of policy is deemed appropriate at the conversation level, too.

A conversation is an exchange of messages that takes place between participants. It is accepted that a conversation is more complex than a simple interaction, as several rounds of exchange are required (e.g., propose/counter-propose/accept or reject or counter-propose, etc.) before the outcome expected from the conversation is reached. This is not the case with interactions where a single round of exchange is judged sufficient (i.e., question/answer). In addition, during conversations, participants have to adjust their behavior based on the messages they receive and submit and the environment in which they run. This is not the case with participants who, for example, adopt a question/answer interaction pattern. Backing our claim on the importance of conversations, Ardissono et al. (2003) observe that current Web services standards (e.g., WSDL) are integrated into systems featured by simple interactions, and, thus, expressing complex interactions by using conversations is required. The same comment is made by Benatallah et al. (2004), who noticed that, despite the growing interest in Web services,

several issues remain to be addressed so that Web services can benefit from the technologies of traditional integration middleware. Benatallah et al.'s (2004) suggestion for enhancing Web services is to develop a conversational metamodel. The integration of conversations into Web services requires addressing the following issues: (1) how to format the messages that are to be sent; (2) how to parse the messages that are to be received; and (3) how to constraint the sequencing of multiple messages.

We decompose a conversation into two parts: static and dynamic. The static part is about the format of a conversation in terms of parameters (e.g., from, to, content, context) and their valid values. Context parameter is a reference to the progress of a conversation that is assessed based on the active state that the conversation takes. A series of states that work toward achieving the same objective are aggregated into a common session. Conversation sessions are of multiple types, including the conversations between users and Web services and the conversations between Web services and resources.

The dynamic part of a conversation is about the evolution happening in a conversation session and is specified with conversation policies. A conversation shifts from one state/session to another state/session because some events have occurred, some messages are received, or some actions are performed. Conversation policies

Figure 3. Extended state chart diagram for conversation-session specification

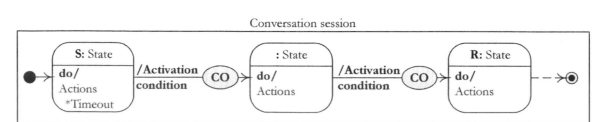

specify various aspects such as admissible turns, state/session changes, conflict resolutions, and corrective actions in case of unsuccessful conversations or exceptions. In this paper, we specify conversation policies with state chart diagrams (Harel & Naamad, 1996) after we enrich them with extra details. First, we discuss the rationale of using state chart diagrams and then continue with presenting the details that enrich these diagrams. A state chart diagram possesses a formal semantics, which is essential for reasoning on the content of conversations. Next, a state chart diagram is becoming a standard process-modeling language as it is being integrated into UML. This process modeling helps manage admissible turns, decision-makings, and timeouts during conversations. Finally, a state chart diagram offers various control-flow constructs that can turn out to be useful in modeling real conversations such as branching and looping. Figure 3 represents what we refer to as an extended state chart diagram

for the specification of conversation sessions. In addition to the traditional components of state and transition that a state chart diagram encompasses, the following elements are added:

- Name of a state is annotated either with label S (sender) or label R (receiver). In case of no annotation, the state identifies the communication middleware.
- Name of a transition is annotated with activation condition and content of conversation. The content is referred to as conversation object (CO).
- Actions of a state implement the information that a CO conveys. In case some acknowledgements from receivers to senders are required, a timeout action for monitoring purposes is added to the list of actions of the receiver's state.
- A complete extended state chart diagram represents a conversation session.

Figure 4. Representation of (personalized service, resource) conversation session

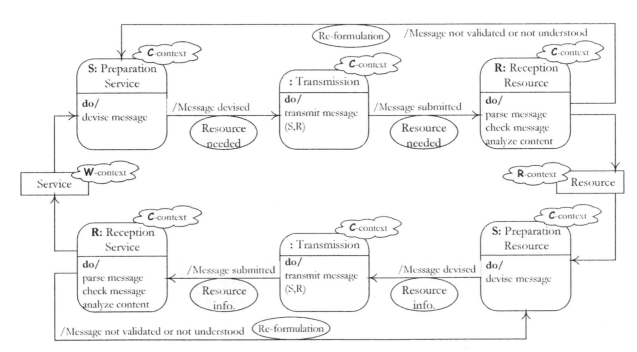

Table 5. Description of C-context's parameters

> Label: corresponds to the identifier of the conversation.
> Conversation session: corresponds to the identifier of the session in which the conversation is being conducted.
> Conversation policy: corresponds to the identifier of the conversation policy that is being used.
> Participants: lists the names of participant in the conversation (users, Web services, resources).
> Previous states: is used for tracing purposes and succinctly lists all the previous states that the conversation has taken.
> Current active state: illustrates the state the conversation currently takes.
> Potential next state: illustrates the next state that the conversation could take according to the current active state.
> Time: illustrates the time elapsed since the conversation has taken the first state.
> Date: identifies the time of updating the parameters above.

Currently, we have identified three types of conversation sessions each featuring different participants: (user, service), (personalized service, resource), and (personalized service, service). For illustration purposes, (personalized service, resource) conversation session is described. In this session, the objective is to identify the resource on which a personalized Web service will operate (Figure 4). Depending on the current commitments of a resource toward other personalized services, the personalized service may need to be adjusted because of these commitments.

Once a Web service is personalized, the appropriate parameters of its W-context are updated ("starting-time requested per participation" and "location requested per participation"). Next, the personalized Web service initiates a conversation with one of the available resources (it is assumed that these resources are known). This is illustrated with the state (S:preparation - service) in Figure 4. Once the message is devised, it is sent to the resource as the state (R:reception - resource) shows. Prior to that, the conversation takes the state (: transmission), which consists of transferring the message from the service to the resource through a communication middleware. Once the message is received, the resource parses it and analyzes its content. The message is sent back to the sender in case of no-validity, otherwise, it makes the resource take appropriate actions. The resource checks its status using its respective R-context and particularly "current period of time/services" and "next periods of time/services" parameters of Table 3. Finally, the resource gets back to the service with its availabilities. This feedback also is conducted through conversation as the states (S:preparation - resource), (:transmission), and (R:reception - service) show.

In the beginning of this section, we emphasized the importance of associating context with conversation. The following parameters define the C-context of a conversation (Table 5): label, conversation session, conversation policy, participants, previous states, current active state, potential next state, time, and date.

IMPLEMENTATION STATUS

We overview the progress of implementing the context-based approach for Web services personalization. After assessing our objectives and constraints, we decided to focus on a rapid prototyping of this approach rather than low-

Figure 5. Architecture of the prototype for Web services personalization

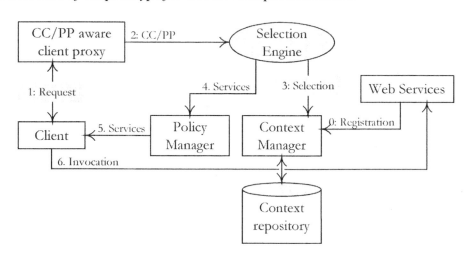

level details implementation. Therefore, we have adopted Sun Microsystems' J2EE 1.4 for the creation of Web services and their reference implementation of JSR 188 (Composite Capability/ Preference Profile Processing Specification)[3] for context information representation and processing. The Composite Capability/Preferences Profile (CC/PP)[4] is an industry standard of the W3C that provides a way for client devices to transmit their capabilities and user preferences. CC/PP is based on the Resource Description Framework (RDF), which is an approach for representing statements, each of which contain a subject, predicate, and an object. CC/PP uses the XML serialization of RDF. A concrete implementation and extension of the CC/PP is the UAProf[5], which was developed by the Open Mobile Alliance (OMA) for WAP-enabled devices.

In order to ensure that any Web browser can be used with our prototype, Figure 5 illustrates the multi-tier architecture that we have devised. Instead of using a custom CC/PP aware Web browser, we have developed a CC/PP aware client proxy that receives the client request and inserts

CC/PP headers that correspond to the client profile. Reference profiles and client preferences are sent as part of the proxy request to the CC/PP aware server that acts as a "Selection Engine". This one interacts with the "Context Manager" in collaboration with the "Context Repository" to first select the most appropriate Web services and, second, to send their addresses to the client so that he or she can interact with them. The "Context Repository" keeps track of U-, W-, and R-contexts. Before sending the selected Web services' addresses to the client, the "Policy Manager" ensures that these Web services comply with the policies reported earlier. Currently, we are experiencing several policy description languages, among them Ponder[6].

We emphasized the value-added of integrating conversations into Web services personalization. These conversations are specified using extended state chart diagrams, as illustrated in Figure 4. Details of conversation sessions are structured as XML files. We are in the process of developing a dedicated XML editor in order to create, validate, test, and monitor the different XML files (Figure

Figure 6. Graphical editor for conversation sessions specification

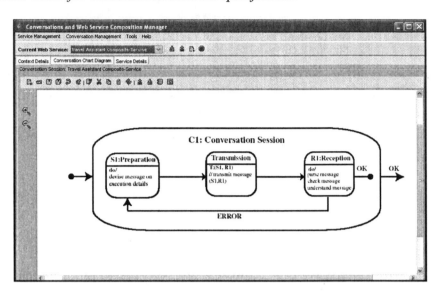

7). The validation of these files is based on their compliance with conversations.xsd XML schema. The graphical editor is a means for directly manipulating conversations graphically using drag and drop operations.

RELATED WORK

Web services are a very active area of R&D. However, few projects have aimed at personalizing Web services using context. We present in the following some of the works that have inspired shaping the context-based personalization approach of this paper.

Hegering et al. (2003) present a strategy that homogenizes the notion of context through the use of three categories: device, environment, and user. The three categories greatly overlap with the types of context of Figure 1. Independently of the user context, the device context category corresponds to the resource context, and the environment context corresponds to the Web service context.

Zuidweg et al. (2003) use the W3C's Platform for Privacy Preferences (P3P) standard (W3C, 2003) in a Web service-based context-aware application. The intention of P3P is to automatically negotiate on a Web site's privacy practice. A user defines his or her privacy preferences and stores them in a machine-readable format such as APPEL (W3C, 2003). When a user wants to browse a Web site, a user agent that resides in the user's browser retrieves first the Web site's P3P policy. Next, the user agent compares the policy with the user's preferences. If the policy complies with these preferences, then the Web site will be made available. Otherwise, the user may be prompted to further evaluate the Web site; otherwise, the user's request will be cancelled. While we have discussed in this paper that preferences are related to execution time and execution location of Web services, preferences also can be associated with privacy, when it comes, for instance, to disclosing some sensitive information on users.

Barkhuus and Dey (2003) have identified three levels of interactivity for context-aware applications: personalization, active context-awareness, and passive context-awareness. According to the authors, personalization, also referred to as customization and tailoring, is motivated by the diversity and dynamics featuring today's applications. In an active context-awareness mode, it concerns applications that, on the basis of sensor data, change their content autonomously. In a passive context-awareness mode, applications merely present the updated context to the user and let the user specify how the application should change. In this paper, we adopted a passive context-awareness style with the manual feeding of the user's current location. While we mentioned that this type of feeding presents some limitations vs. an automatic feeding, this has, however, enabled an efficient handling of the privacy concern of users.

In Table 2, parameters of type requested vs. parameters of type effective has a major overlapping with the QoS of type advertised (or "promised") vs. QoS of type delivered. Ouzzani and Bouguettaya (2004) report that a key feature in distinguishing between competing Web services is their QoS, which encompasses several qualitative and quantitative parameters that measure how well the Web service delivers its functionalities. A Web service may not always fulfill its advertised QoS parameters due to various fluctuations related, for example, to the network status or resource availability. Therefore, some differences between QoS advertised and QoS delivered values occur. However, large differences indicate that the Web service is suffering performance degradation in delivering its functionalities. The same comment is made on parameters of type requested vs. parameters of type effective, when it comes to service personalization. A major difference between the values of these respective parameters indicates the non-consideration of a user's personal preferences in terms of execution time or execution location.

In this paper, context is used for overseeing Web services personalization. Other projects such as Breener and Schiffers (2003) use Web services

for managing context provisioning. Breener and Schiffers (2003) envision that context information typically will be provided by autonomous organizations (or context providers), which means heterogeneity and distribution challenges to deal with. Additional challenges are cited in Breener and Schiffers (2003), including (1) what is the optimal sequence for gathering and combining the required context information? (2) how to secure the whole context provisioning process; and (3) how is the cooperation between the providers of context achieved, and even enforced?

The separation of concerns among user, Web service, and resource is backed by Poladian et al. (2004). In their dynamic configuration of resource-aware services project, they have considered three spaces: user utility, application capability, and computing resources; and two mappings. A mapping from capability space to utility space expresses the user's needs and preferences (similar to "provisioning personalization" in Figure 1). A mapping from capability space to resource space expresses the fidelity profiles of available application (similar to "execution adjustment" in Figure 1). In Poladian et al. (2004), by configuring the system, it is meant finding a point in the capability space that first maximizes user utility and, second, satisfies the resource constraints. In our Web services personalization approach, a Web service could represent this point, since it aims at conciliating between what a user needs and what resources offer.

CONCLUSION

In this paper, we presented our context-based approach for Web services personalization. Three types of contexts (i.e., U-context, W-context, and R-context) are the cornerstone of the approach by storing details related to personalization such as preferred execution-time and preferred execution-location of Web services. The effect of changes of a Web service because of user preferences and resource availabilities has required the development of three types of policies referred to as consistency, feasibility, and inspection. Our use of policies has guaranteed that the Web services still do what they are supposed to do, despite personalization. As future work, an extension is planned for the context structure so that security concerns can be handled. Some of the elements that could be identified through the use of a security context are multiple, such as the identification of the security violations that have happened and the corrective actions that have been taken in case of any attempt to misuse a resource.

Despite the widespread use of Web services, we have shown that they still lack the capabilities that propel them to the acceptance level of traditional integration middleware. Services are still unaware of the environment in which they operate. However, there are several situations that call for Web services self-assessment and self-management so that the requirements of scalability, adaptability, and autonomy are satisfied. By scalability, we mean the capacity of a Web service to interact with a small or large community of Web services without having its expected performance either disrupted or reduced. By adaptability, we mean the capacity of a service to adjust its behavior by selecting the appropriate operations that accommodate the situation in which it operates. Finally, by autonomy, we mean the capacity of a service to accept demands of participation in composite services, reject such demands in case of unappealing rewards, or even propose other alternatives for its participation by recommending other peers. To satisfy these requirements, Web services first have to assess their current capabilities and ongoing commitments and, second, their surrounding environment prior to binding to any composition. Web services need to be context-aware.

REFERENCES

Ardissono, L., Goy, A., & Petrone, G. (2003). Enabling conversations with Web services. *Proceedings of the 2nd International Joint Conference on Autonomous Agents & Multi-Agent Systems (AAMAS'2003)*, Melbourne, Australia.

Barkhuus, L., & Dey, A. (2003). Is context-aware computing taking control away from the user? Three levels of interactivity examined. *Proceedings of the 5th International Conference on Ubiquitous Computing (UbiComp'2003)*, Seattle, Washington.

Bellavista, P., Corradi, A., Montanari, R., & Stefanelli, C. (2003). Context-aware middleware for resource management in the wireless Internet. *IEEE Transactions on Software Engineering, Special Issue on Software Engineering for the Wireless Internet, 29*(12).

Benatallah, B., Casati, F., & Toumani, F. (2004). Web service conversation modeling: A cornerstone for e-business automation. *IEEE Internet Computing, 8*(1).

Benatallah, B., Sheng, Q. Z., & Dumas, M. (2003). The self-serv environment for Web services composition. *IEEE Internet Computing, 7*(1).

Berardi, D., Calvanese, D., De Giacomo, G., Lenzerini, M., & Mecella, M. (2003). A foundational vision for e-services. *Proceedings of the Workshop on Web Services, e-Business, and the Semantic Web (WES'2003) held in conjunction with the 15th Conference On Advanced Information Systems Engineering (CAiSE'2003)*, Klagenfurt/Velden, Austria.

Breener, M., & Schiffers, M. (2003). Applying Web services technologies to the management of context provisioning. *Proceedings of the 10th Workshop of the OpenView University Association (OVUA'2003)*, Geneva, Switzerland.

Brézillon, P. (2003). Focusing on context in human-centered computing. *IEEE Intelligent Systems, 18*(3).

Casati, F., Shan, E., Dayal, U., & Shan, M.C. (2003). Business-oriented management of Web services. *Communications of the ACM, 46*(10).

Dey, A.K., Abowd, G.D., & Salber, D. (2001). A conceptual framework and a toolkit for supporting the rapid prototyping of context-aware applications. *Human-Computer Interaction Journal, Special Issue on Context-Aware Computing, 16*(1).

Doulkeridis, C., Valavanis, E., & Vazirgiannis, M. (2003). Towards a context-aware service directory. *Proceedings of the 4th Workshop on Technologies for E-Services (TES'03) held in conjunction with the 29th International Conference on Very Large Data Bases (VLDB'2003)*, Berlin, Germany.

Harel, D., & Naamad, A. (1996). The STATE-MATE semantics of statecharts. *ACM Transactions on Software Engineering and Methodology, 5*(4).

Hegering, H.G., Kupper, A., Linnhoff-Popien, C., & Reiser, H. (2003). Management challenges of context-aware services in ubiquitous environments. *Proceedings of the 14th IFIP/IEEE International Workshop on Distributed Systems: Operations and Management (DSOM'2003)*, Heidelberg, Germany.

Maamar, Z., Kouadri Mostéfaoui, S., & Bataineh, E. (2004a). A conceptual analysis of the role of conversations in Web services composition. *Proceedings of the 2004 IEEE International Conference on e-Technology, e-Commerce and e-Service (EEE-04)*, Taipei, Taiwan.

Maamar, Z., Kouadri Mostéfaoui, S., & Yahyaoui, H. (2005). Towards an agent-based and context-oriented approach for Web services composition. *IEEE Transactions on Knowledge and Data Engineering, 17*(5).

Maamar, Z., Sheng, Q.Z., & Benatallah, B. (2004b). On composite Web services provisioning in an environment of fixed and mobile computing resources. *Information Technology and Management Journal, Special Issue on Workflow and e-Business, Kluwer Academic Publishers, 5*(3).

Maamar, Z., Yahyaoui, H., & Mansoor, W. (2004c). Design and development of an m-commerce environment: The E-CWE project. *Journal of Organizational Computing and Electronic Commerce, Lawrence Erlbaum Associates Publishers, 14*(4).

Medjahed, B., Bouguettaya, A., & Elmagarmid, A. (2003). Composing Web services on the semantic Web. *The VLDB Journal, Special Issue on the Semantic Web, Springer Verlag, 12*(4).

Menascé, D.A. (2002). QoS issues in Web services. *IEEE Internet Computing, 6*(6).

Milanovic, N. and Malek, M. (2004). Current Solutions for Web Service Composition. *IEEE Internet Computing, 8*(6).

Muldoon, C., O'Hare, G., Phelan, D., Strahan, R., & Collier, R. (2003). ACCESS: An agent architecture for ubiquitous service delivery. *Proceedings of the 7th International Workshop on Cooperative Information Agents (CIA'2003)*, Helsinki, Finland.

Ouzzani, M., & Bouguettaya, A. (2004). Efficient access to Web services. *IEEE Internet Computing, 8*(2).

Papazoglou, M., & Georgakopoulos, D. (2003). Introduction to the special issue on service-oriented computing. *Communications of the ACM, 46*(10).

Poladian, V., Pedro Sousa, J., Garlan, D., & Shaw, M. (2004). Dynamic configuration of resource-aware services. *Proceedings of the 26th International Conference on Software Engineering (ICSE'2004)*, Edinburgh, Scotland.

Ratsimor, O., Korolev, V., Joshi, A., & Finin, T. (2001). Agents2Go: An infrastructure for location-dependent service discovery in the mobile electronic commerce environment. *Proceedings of the 1st ACM International Workshop on Mobile Commerce (WMC'2001) held in conjunction with the Seventh Annual International Conference on Mobile Computing and Networking (Mobi-Com'2001)*, Rome, Italy.

Riecken, D. (2000). Personalized views of personalization. *Communications of the ACM, 43*(18).

Satyanarayanan, M. (2001). Pervasive computing: Vision and challenges. *IEEE Personal Communications, 8*(4).

Schiaffino, S., & Amandi, A. (2004). User-interface agent interaction: Personalization issues. *International Journal of Human Computer Studies, Elsevier Sciences Publisher, 60*(1).

Schilit, B., Adams, N., & Want, R. (1994). Context-aware computing applications. *Proceedings of the IEEE Workshop on Mobile Computing Systems and Applications*, Santa Cruz, California.

Smith, I.A., Cohen, P.R., Bradshaw, J.M., Greaves, M., & Holmback, H. (1998). Designing conversation policies using joint intention theory. *Proceedings of the 3rd International Conference on Multi-Agent Systems (ICMAS'1998)*, Paris, France.

Spriestersbach, A., Volger, H., Lehmann, F., & Ziegert, T. (2001). Integrating context information into enterprise applications for the mobile workforce—A case study. *Proceedings of the 1st ACM International Workshop on Mobile Commerce (WMC'2001) held in conjunction with the Seventh Annual International Conference on Mobile Computing and Networking (Mobi-Com'2001)*, Rome, Italy.

Sun, J. (2003). Information requirement elicitation in mobile commerce. *Communications of the ACM, 46(*12).

Uszok, A., et al. Policy and contract management for semantic Web services. *Proceedings of the 2004 AAAI Spring Symposium on Semantic Web Services Series*, Stanford, California.

W3C (2003). Platform for privacy preferences (P3P) project. Retrieved June 2004, from *http://www.w3.org/P3P/*

Zuidweg, M., Pereira Filho, J.G., & van Sinderen, M. (2003). Using P3P in a Web services-based context-aware application platform. *Proceedings of the 9th Open European Summer School and IFIP Workshop on Next Generation Networks (EUNICE'2003)*, Balatonfured, Hungary.

ENDNOTES

[1] In our previous research, we leveraged the interactions between Web services during composition to the level of conversations (Maamar et al., 2004a).

[2] While a manual feeding of the current location of users has some limitations, this type of feeding allows a better handling of the privacy issue, since users only reveal the locations that they wish to be known to others. The manual feeding is in line with the privacy control that is considered in the design of context-aware computing platforms (Zuidweg et al., 2003). An automatic feeding of the location of users also is doable in the proposed personalization approach and can be based on satellite-based techniques (Ratsimor et al., 2001).

[3] www.jcp.org/en/jsr/detail?id=188.

[4] www.w3.org/TR/2004/REC-CCPP-struct-vocab-20040115.

[5] www.wapforum.org/what/technical/SPEC-UAProf-19991110.pdf.

[6] http://www.doc.ic.ac.uk/old-doc/deptechrep/DTR00-1.pdf

APPENDIX 1. XML CODE OF U-CONTEXT

```
<?xml version="1.0" encoding="ISO-8859-1"?>
<!DOCTYPE c:ucontext SYSTEM "C:\context.dtd">
<c:ucontext number="1" xmlns:s="http://www.../Usercontexttest">
<c:header>
        <c:title>User context</c:title>
</c:header>
<c:uelement>
        <label>user1</label>
        <previouslocations/services>mallshopping</previouslocations/services>
        <currentlocation/services>cafeteriamovietheater</currentlocation/services>
        <nextlocations/services>null</nextlocations/services>
        <previousperiodsoftime/services>null</previousperiodsoftime/services>
        <currentperiodoftime/services>12pmtransportation</currentperiodoftime/services>
<nextperiodsoftime/services>null</nextperiodsoftime/services>
        <date>12/12/2003</date>
</c:uelement>
</c:ucontext>
```

This work was previously published in International Journal of E-Business Research, Vol. 1, No. 3, pp. 41-62, copyright 2005 by IGI Publishing, formerly known as Idea Group Publishing (an imprint of IGI Global).

Chapter XII
Role–Based
Multi–Agent Systems

Haibin Zhu
Nipissing University, Canada

MengChu Zhou
New Jersey Institute of Technology, USA

ABSTRACT

Agent system design is a complex task challenging designers to simulate intelligent collaborative behavior. Roles can reduce the complexity of agent system design by categorizing the roles played by agents. The role concepts can also be used in agent systems to describe the collaboration among cooperative agents. In this chapter, we introduce roles as a means to support interaction and collaboration among agents in multi-agent systems. We review the application of roles in current agent systems at first, then describe the fundamental principles of role-based collaboration and propose the basic methodologies of how to apply roles into agent systems (i.e., the revised E-CARGO model). After that, we demonstrate a case study: a soccer robot team designed with role specifications. Finally, we present the potentiality to apply roles into information personalization.

INTRODUCTION

Artificial intelligence is the discipline aimed at understanding intelligent beings by constructing intelligent systems (Castelfranchi, 1998). From a behaviorist's perspective, intelligent systems are those that can simulate human beings' work that requires intelligence, including logic reasoning, problem solving, deduction, and induction. A distributed system is composed of many comput- ers interconnected via communication networks, which cooperate and coordinate to accomplish a common task or goal (Coulouris, Dollimore, & Kindberg, 2005). Multi-agent systems are intelligent systems built on a distributed computer system. They are based on the use of cooperative agents and organized with hardware/software components. In such systems, each agent independently handles a small set of specialized tasks and cooperates to achieve the system-level goals and a high degree of flexibility (Ahn, Lee, & Park, 2003; Gruver, 2004).

Multi-agent systems are becoming more relevant to artificial intelligence (AI) (Bowling & Veloso, 2002) and can be used to implement distributed AI (DAI). The agent concept evolves from objects. It is a combination of object-orientation and AI. The AI community claims intelligence as a natural quality of agents and uses the traditional symbolic representation to describe agents.

Maes (1994) defines agents as computational systems that inhabit a complex dynamic environment, sense and act autonomously in this environment, and by doing so realize a set of goals or tasks for which they are designed. Wooldridge and Jennings (1995; Jennings & Wooldridge, 1996) define agents as hardware-based or software-based computer systems that possess the following properties:

- **Autonomy:** Agents operate without the direct intervention of humans or others, and have some kind of control over their actions and internal state.
- **Social ability:** Agents interact with other agents (and possibly humans) via a kind of agent-communication language.
- **Reactivity:** Agents perceive their environment, which may be the physical world, a user via a graphical user interface, a collection of other agents, or perhaps all of these combined, and respond in a timely fashion to changes that occur in it.
- **Pro-activeness:** Agents do not simply act in response to their environment. They are able to exhibit goal-directed behavior by taking an initiative.

Normal objects can be thought of as passive because they wait for a message before performing an operation. Once invoked, they execute their method and go back to "sleep" until the next message arrives. A current trend is to design objects that not only react to events in their environment, but also behave proactively. Therefore, in addition to traditional object properties, an agent should also have the following characteristics:

- **Active:** An agent may act according to its internal states and goals. Note that an object in its conventional meaning can only respond to the messages sent to it even though many acclaim that everything is an object.
- **Autonomous:** An agent is not controlled directly by people.
- **Collaborative:** Agents need to collaborate with others to accomplish a complex task.

Every agent is responsible for accomplishing a certain task. It can be considered as a self-contained object of some class and involves itself with a specific environment. The environment exists before agents are created. Agents should be designed such that they can adapt to a constantly changing environment.

Agent design is a complex task challenging designers to simulate intelligent human behavior. Searching and retrieving are considered expressions of intelligence. Roles can reduce the complexity of agent design by categorizing agent responsibilities. Based on the theory of search and retrieval, such separation greatly shrinks the search space and tends to significantly increase agent efficiency in response to messages or events relevant to a specific role.

In fact, multi-agent systems are simulations of human societies or virtual societies. To simulate real societies, we need to understand their nature. A well-organized society should encourage member contributions (Mills & Simmons, 1999). Similarly, distributed intelligent systems should establish a healthy platform or environment for virtual participants who contribute and work effectively. One can consider agents as virtual citizens in intelligent systems. A capable political system promotes a harmonious and flourishing society. Good architecture leads to a beautiful and long-lasting building. Clearly, a distributed intelligent system requires good system architecture. A role-based design can provide such architecture.

Organizational and social psychological theory suggests that an organization is composed of three key elements: participants, goals, and roles (Cyert & MacCrimmon, 1968). A goal is a mental representation of a process that expresses an agent's internal anticipation and regulations (Castelfranchi, 1998). Therefore, it is meaningful to use roles to express a participant's goal in an organization (Zhu, 2005). Furthermore, it can be said that roles, role relationships, role players (agents), and role playing constitute all the aspects for distributed intelligent systems.

Roles are commonly applied concepts in many fields, such as sociology, psychology, social psychology, behavioral science, management, and drama. Roles can be applied into people's natural organizations, task distributions, and system analysis, system design, and system construction (Alon, 2003). Therefore, the introduction of roles has many potential benefits such as encouraging people's contributions to collaboration (Zhu, 2005), even task distribution, evolutionary expression, and reuse and the reduction of agent complexity.

An important goal of multi-agent systems is to obtain collective intelligence (Heylighen, 1999) through the organization of numerous agents. This chapter discusses the fundamentals of Role-based Multi-Agent Systems (RMASs) by applying roles into the design and implementation of multi-agent systems. This work is based on our previous one—the Environments, Classes, Agents, Roles, Groups, and Objects (E-CARGO) model (Zhu & Zhou, 2006a).

This chapter is arranged as follows. The next section reviews the applications of role concepts in agent systems. We then describe the revised E-CARGO model for RMAS and demonstrate a role-based architecture for multi-agent systems. We discuss the agent evolution expressed by roles, as well as the benefits and challenges of RMAS, and conclude the chapter and propose topics for future research.

REVIEW OF ROLE CONCEPTS IN AGENT SYSTEMS

Betcht et al. (1999) propose an agent system, ROPE, which includes roles. They point out that roles provide a well-defined interface between agents and cooperative processes. This allows an agent to read and follow normative rules established by the cooperation process even if not previously known by the agent. Their major motivation to introduce such roles is to increase the agent system's adaptability to structural changes. They formally define a role as an entity consisting of a set of required permissions, a set of granted permissions, a directed graph of service invocations, and a state visible to the runtime environment but not to other agents. Roles in ROPE are used to describe the separate behavior of an agent. Their paper describes the architecture of ROPE, but lacks a prototype system to demonstrate the practicability and usability of this architecture.

Stone and Veloso (1999) point out that a role consists of a specification of an agent's internal and external behavior. They state that roles may be rigid (completely specifying an agent's behavior) or flexible (leaving a certain degree of autonomy to the agent filling the role). They introduce role concepts from their research on AI and model them via a robot soccer team.

Depke, Heckel, and Kuster (2001) study role concepts in agent systems. In their approach, roles are modeled as traditional classes. Thus roles are the latter's instances. Roles encapsulate certain tasks, responsibilities, and goals of an agent. They conclude that roles can be applied into agent systems for the following purposes: (1) to express the organizational structure of a multi-agent system, (2) to specify interactions in a generic way; and (3) to serve as agent-building blocks in class diagrams. A shortcoming of this approach is that a role is deleted when the adopting agent is destroyed. This can be an inaccurate depiction of reality. For example, should the president of a country die while in office, people must elect another but not eliminate that societal role.

In agent-oriented software engineering, Gaia methodology (Wooldridge, Jennings, & Kinny, 2000; Zambonelli, Jennings, & Wooldridge, 2003) is proposed to support system analysis and design by taking a multi-agent system as an organization. Analysis and design are well-separated phases—that is, analysis aims to develop an understanding of the system structures through role and interaction models, while the design phase aims to define agent details within the system. An important contribution of Gaia is in modeling roles that accommodate agent rights or permissions. In Gaia, roles are described with responsibilities, permissions, interaction protocols, and activities. The ideas on role application in agent-oriented software engineering are similar to those expressed in our previous work (Zhu, 2006d; Zhu & Zhou, 2006b).

In an Organization-Centered Multi-Agent System (OCMAS) (Ferber, Gutknechtl, & Michell, 2004), roles are emphasized as an important element of organizations. A role is the abstract representation of a functional agent position in a group. It helps overcome the drawbacks of agent-centered multi-agent systems—that is, an agent is open for the entire system, there are no constraints on inter-agent accessibility, and agent interaction occurs directly. The roles in OCMAS are similar to those in Wooddridge et al. (2003). Group roles, as mentioned in Ferber et al. (2004), refer to roles in a group—that is, an agent must play a role in a group. This definitely incurs an argument that should be based on the other: roles or groups (Zhu & Zhou, 2006a).

Cabri, Ferrari, and Leonardi (2005a, 2005b) discuss how to introduce roles into agent systems. The role ideas in both Role-Based Access Control (RBAC) and modeling methodologies are reviewed. Supporting roles at the implementation level are emphasized. Roles can be exploited by agents at runtime in order to enhance their capabilities. A role can be thought of as a set of behaviors and capabilities that agents can exploit to perform their tasks in a given context. A role is temporary in that an agent must perform it within a specified period of time or context. It is generic, in the sense that it is not tightly bound to a specific application, but expresses general properties that can be used in different applications by different agents. Roles are related to contexts so that each environment can impose its own rules and can grant some local capabilities, forcing agents to assume specific roles. A role is described by four elements in the XRole language (Cabri et al., 2002, 2005a, 2005b)—name, description, keyword, and action. A unique name precisely identifies a role. The description allows designers to understand role objectives in human-readable sentences. Keywords can also be used in role identification. Actions allow for interactions among agents or execution environments. Roles in agent systems are significant on two important fronts. From an environmental point of view, a role imposes a defined behavior on the entities assuming it. From the application perspective, it expresses a set of capabilities, which can be exploited by agents in carrying out their tasks; and it can be used to support the separation of concerns of agents (Botha & Eloff, 2001).

It is arguable that roles are temporary. We can say that a person may play a role temporarily. However, the lifetime of a role is often longer than an object or agent. For example, Bill Clinton played a role as U.S. President for eight years, while there is always the role called 'U.S. President'. A role serves as an abstract description of functions which must be fulfilled in reaching an assigned goal. In the agent-oriented approaches, roles are a proper means of refining agent-oriented modeling. However, they still lack a clear definition (e.g., how a role is defined for a special agent). They still consider a role as a property of an agent that is similar to the ideas in object modeling. There are some important aspects of roles left unconsidered.

Odell, Van Dyke Parunak, and Fleischer (2003) and Odell, Nodine, and Levy (2005) consider the aspects of roles from the viewpoint of theaters and behavioral science. They refer to Biddle and Thomas's (1966) and other psychologists' work, and cite Shakespeare's role concepts in theaters. They state that roles specify normative behavioral repertoires for agents, and provide both the building blocks for social agents and the requirements by which agents interact. They emphasize the diversity and limited capability of the roles agents can play.

Partsakoulakis and Vouros (2004) survey role concepts and mechanisms in multi-agent systems. Roles are viewed as tools to manage the complexity of tasks and environments. Roles are intuitively used to analyze agent systems, model social activities, and construct coherent and robust teams of agents. A high degree of interactions, environment changes, and distributivity of roles are emphasized.

Roles are a useful concept in assisting designers and developers with the need for interactions. They can help system designers focus on those conditions where social determinants are more influential (Odell et al., 2003). Roles help the agent-application developers/designers to model the execution environment. They also allow agents to actively recognize the environment themselves (Cabri, 2004).

Agent systems are currently among the most active fields in role application. Most approaches to agent-oriented modeling use only a few of the possible aspects of roles. Role concepts are generally used in agent systems to describe the collaboration among cooperative processes or agents. We call these roles agent-roles.

In agent systems, the following principles related to a role are widely accepted:

1. A role instance is deleted when an agent is destroyed, that is, its lifetime depends on its agents.

2. Roles are used to form different interfaces for agents in order to restrict the visibility of features and to handle permissions for the access to the internal state and role services of agents.
3. Roles have three functions: comprise special behavior, form the behavior of an agent, and take a position in a group of agents.
4. A role specifies a position and a set of responsibilities that are made up of services and tasks.
5. Roles are modeled as stereotyped classes.
6. Roles can be used for expressing the organizational structure of a multi-agent system.
7. Roles can be used for specifying interactions in a generic way.
8. Roles can be used as agent-building blocks in class diagrams.

From Table 1, one can obtain a good picture of the literature on roles as modeling mechanisms in agent systems.

FUNDAMENTAL PRINCIPLES OF RMAS

Roles are appropriate tools for designing multi-agent systems since they can provide platforms for agents to execute their tasks. A role describes both the service requirement and the ability to provide services. With provided services, an agent does not need to bring with it many things that are required by traditional mobile agents. In a traditional method, an agent should be able to have its own facility to provide required services. Role-based methods reduce further the traffic requirement for mobile agents.

Although role concepts and agent systems have been investigated for decades, their combination attracted attention only a few years ago. Only recently, in an agent community, have roles been considered as an important concept and mecha-

Table 1. Role as modeling mechanisms in agent systems

Year	Authors	Motivations	Contributions	Conclusions
1999	Becht	To increase the agent system's adaptability to structural change	Propose an architecure ROPE to support roles in agent systems	Roles can be used to support the coooperative processes among agents.
1999	Stone Veloso	To provide a well-defined team strucutre	Propose a teamwork structure with roles	Agents can respond to changing envrionments by dynamically changing their roles.
2001	Depke Heckel Kuster	To analyse the application of roles in agent systems	Analyze the role requirement and propose a method to transform UML diagrams into code	Roles can be used in many ways in modeling agent systems, such as expressing an organizational structure, specifying interactions, and being agent–building blocks.
2003	Odell, *et al.*	To simplify the design of sophisticated agent systems	Enforce that the roles for agent systems should be consistent with those in behavioral science	Roles are good implications of how agents behave in a group.
2004	Partsako-ulakis Vouros	To support the collaboration among agents	Emphasize the improtance of roles for agent systems by analyzing the properties of roles in agent systems.	The extensive use of roles in implemented systems shows the need for role-oriented thinking and modeling in agent system development.
2004	Cabri Ferrari Leonardi	To investigate how the concept of role can be exploited in agent systems and how to simplify the related tasks	Propose the framework BRAIN that exploits the concept of role in different phases of the development based on a simple yet general role-based model for interactions	The use of roles can bring different advantages, in terms of separation of concerns between algorithmic issues and interaction issues, generality of approaches, locality, and reuse of solutions and experiences.
2004	Ferber	To overcome the drawbacks of agent-centered multi-agent systems	Propose organization-centered multi-agent systems by introducing roles	The OCMAS with roles overcomes the drawbacks of agent-centered multi-agent systems.
2005	Cabri Ferrari Leonardi	To support agent interactions and increase agents' adaptabilities	Implement a role interaction infrastructure that enables Java agents to dynamically assume and use roles at runtime	Roles can be more useful to design, develop, and even maintain complex applications, where there are many interactions among interacting agents.
2005	Odell Nodine Levy	To design a metamodel for agents and groups	Continue their work of 2003 and propose a metamodel for agents, roles and groups	The metamodel enhances the predictabilitiy, reliability and stability of agent systems.

nism in assisting agents' interaction, coordination, and collaboration.

Although there is a common belief that roles are important concepts, until now no consensus has been reached as to how roles should be represented and integrated into agent systems. Even though role theory has been investigated in social psychology for several decades, there is neither a unified theory nor commonly accepted specification tool for roles. Roles can be taken as a highly abstract concept that is very flexible for players to enact. For example, a *manager* role is highly abstract, different people taking the role *manager* differently. On the other hand, roles can be a very concrete process description for players to follow. For example, a labor worker role in a manufacturing production line is to perform rigid operations and processes. Its players must conduct these operations and processes. There is little or no flexibility in playing such a role.

From the literature relevant to roles, the aspects of roles are discussed in Figure 1. Considering role expression, we have:

Figure 1. The different views of roles

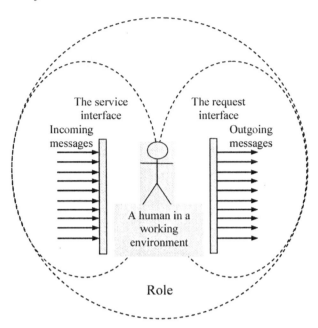

- **Rights:** Roles are entities that facilitate users (agents) in accessing system resources (files, objects, and devices). Roles are tags or tickets attached to users to access objects.
- **Responsibilities:** Roles are entities that express different aspects of an object at a different context and time. They provide different services to the outside world. The rights of an object are taken for granted by all the objects in its context or scope.
- **Both rights and responsibilities:** In social psychology, people who live in a society should take responsibilities and hold rights when playing a role.

On the subject of concrete role specification, we have:

- **Interfaces:** Roles are abstract entities to express the interfaces between objects, agents, or people in collaboration. In this sense, roles only specify what the services are and what the requests are. How the services and requests are processed depends on their players. We can call them interface-roles.

- **Processes:** Roles are concrete behavior describers in specifying the functions of an object, agent, or human. They specify not only what services and requests are, but also how services and requests are processed. We can call them process-roles.

To support role-based agent collaboration, it is necessary to construct a role-based agent system that allows for agent cooperation and successful collaborative results. We must understand the fundamental principles with which we need to comply. They can be established based on many principles learned from modeling methodologies, software engineering, and intelligent system development.

With object-oriented principles, we can conceptually construct the underlying components of a role-based system including classes, objects, messages, interfaces, agents, roles, and groups. We can use agents to simulate human behaviors. The following four sets of principles related to object, agent, role, and group (Zhu, 2006a; Zhu & Zhou, 2006a) must be addressed when one builds RMAS.

Object Principles

Object-oriented methodologies are widely used in system modeling and software engineering. A multi-agent system can also be considered as an object system at first. Its development should obey the following object principles (Meyer, 1988; Kay, 1993; Zhu & Zhou, 2003):

O1: Everything in the world is an object. An object can be used to express everything in a collaborative system.

O2: Every system is composed of objects and a system is also an object.

O3: The evolution and development of a system is caused by the interactions among the objects inside or outside the system.

O4: Objects can be created, modified, and deleted.

O5: A message is a way to activate services of an object.

O6: An interface is a list of message patterns.

O6: The interactions among objects are expressed by sending messages that are requests to invoke objects' actions.

O7: Each object is an instance of a class. A class shows the commonality of a group of objects.

O8: A class X may inherit another class Y. Y is called a superclass, while X is called a subclass.

O9: Classes can be taken as templates of objects.

Agent Principles

To make real multi-agent systems and overpass object systems, agents should be distinguished from objects. The agent principles are as follows:

A1: Agents are special objects that simulate the behavior of people.

A2: Agents can be created, modified, and deleted.

A3: Agents are autonomous. They should be able to reply to incoming messages and send outgoing messages based on their situations (Etzioni & Weld, 1995; Jennings, Sycara, & Wooldridge, 1998; Russell & Norvig, 2003).

A4: Agents are adaptive. They should be able to understand their environment, and take actions to change the environment and make it better for them to live in (Etzioni & Weld, 1995; Russell & Norvig, 2003).

A5: Agents are social. They should be able to interact with other agents (Jennings et al., 1998; Russell & Norvig, 2003).

A6: Agents are collaborative. They may join a group to work for a common goal or quit a group if they do not want to cooperate more.

A7: Agents are flexible. Not all actions of agents are predicted. They can dynamically choose which actions to invoke, and in what sequence, in response to the state of its environment (Jennings et al., 1998; Russell & Norvig, 2003).

A8: Agents are mobile. They are able to transport them from one site to another in a system (Etzioni & Weld, 1995).

Role Principles

Based on the discussion above, we derive the following role principles:

R1: A role is independent of agents. A role should be defined separately. It is commonly understood that a role depends on objects in object systems. In collaboration, however, collaborators do not necessarily care about who services them as long as the service is performed to their expectation. For example, professor X in a university may ask for services from the technology service department. X does not care who provides the service so long as he or she is performing the role of technician.

R2: A role can be created, changed, and deleted. A role includes both responsibilities (the service interface) when an agent is taken as a server and rights (the request interface) when the agent is taken as a client. To specify a role means to specify both responsibilities and rights. A role does not accomplish the tasks specified by the responsibilities. Only agents playing the role accomplish the tasks.

R3: Roles can be interface-roles. As for the service interface, a role is actually a filter of messages sent to an agent. This filter only allows passage of the messages relating to the role played by the agent. As for the request interface, a role expresses or restricts the accessibility of an agent to the system.

R4: Roles can be process-roles. In such roles, what to do, how to do it, and what to access are all rigidly specified.

R5: Roles are taken as media for interactions. Interactions among agents are based on their roles—that is, a message to request collaboration with other agents is sent to the relevant roles they are playing. Roles emphasize that the message receivers are firstly roles but not agents. Any available agent playing a role can respond to the messages received by the role.

R6: Playing a role means that the agent is attached to a role. A role can be played by one or more agents at the same time.

R7: An agent may adopt one or more roles but can perform only one at a time.

R8: Roles can be used to support indirect and direct interactions. For direct interactions, each role has exactly one agent to play. For indirect interactions, each role has multiple agents to play. In the former case, identifying a role means identifying an agent. In the latter, identifying a role does not mean identifying an agent.

R9: Roles can have hierarchy relationships. Higher-level roles can be taken as goals for agents playing roles at lower levels. In long-term collaboration, autonomous agents such as human beings may hope to play higher-level roles as their careers advance.

Group Principles

In reality, people work in a group and may hold multiple roles. Every work setting involves groups of individuals. To accomplish a common task, the group members (i.e., agents) interact with each other. We should follow the principles as follows:

G1: A group is necessary to build a multi-agent system.

G2: A group can be created, changed, and deleted (Chockler, Keidar, & Vitenberg, 2001).

G3: Before specifying a group, we must specify all the roles in it.

G4: Group formation allows agents to join the group and play roles. They are named as the members of this group.

G5: A group can be embedded, that is, one group may be an object in another (Tanenbaum & van Steen, 2002).

G6: A group can be overlapped with other groups, that is, the members may belong to two or more groups (Tanenbaum & van Steen, 2002).

G7: A group can be public or private (WebBoard, 2006). Public means that all the agents in the system can join the group. Private means that joining a group is controlled by a special agent who plays a special role called moderator.

G8: A group can be open or closed (Coulouris et al., 2005). Open groups mean that new agents are permitted to join the groups, while closed ones allow no further membership.

The above four sets of principles are reflected in the revised E-CARGO model to be discussed next.

THE REVISED E-CARGO MODEL FOR RMAS

To collaborate, people generally join a group or organization. All individuals should have clear positions within a group, and their roles should be related without causing interference (Zhu & Zhou, 2006a). Unclear role specification may create dysfunctional ambiguity and conflict in an organization (Bostrom, 1980), while clear role definition and specification can help people collaborate effectively in a group (Becht, Gurzki, Klarmann, & Muscholl, 1999). Role conflict and ambiguity are causes of stress in organizations. Role conflict means situations in which individuals do not know how they should behave due to differing expectations. Role ambiguity means a situation in which individuals do not know exactly how they are expected to behave based on of vague, abstract expectations (Ashforth, 2001; Miner, 1992). A collaborative learning environment may have to establish and assign well-defined roles to participants to foster interaction (Singley, Singh, Fairweather, Farrell, & Swerling, 2000). Dynamic role assignment requires a stable basis to improve productivity and performance. By "dynamic" we mean that role assignment and reassignment occur during collaboration. People may be expected to dynamically change their roles according to the needs of the group and organization (Dafoulas & Macaulay, 2001; Ould, 1995). Therefore, roles are required to be taken as underlying mechanisms in collaboration, yielding a concept of role-based collaboration (Zhu, 2006a; Zhu & Zhou, 2006a, 2006b).

The E-CARGO (Zhu & Zhou, 2006a) model is proposed to support collaboration among people by using computer systems. It formulates role-based collaboration by providing underlying components such as classes, objects, agents, roles, environments, and groups. With the support of the E-CARGO model, people can practice role-based collaboration easily and naturally.

Based on the principles discussed above, the E-CARGO model needs to be revised to support RMAS. In this revised model, human users *H* in the original E-CARGO model are removed to emphasize the autonomy of agents.

Object and Class

From the viewpoint that everything in the world is an *object* and every object has a *class*, an object must be (Kay, 1993; Meyer, 1988; Zhu & Zhou, 2003):

- Uniquely identified, that is, any object should carry a unique identification;
- Created or destroyed; and
- Communicative, that is, an object can exchange messages with other objects.

It may be:

- Nested, that is, a complex object has other objects as its components (which in turn may have object components);
- Active and autonomous, that is, an object may respond to messages without people's intervention; and
- Collaborative, that is, collaborative relationships among objects arise when they exchange messages.

We use agents to express the objects that possess all the properties discussed above. Considering the general meaning and properties of objects, we can express a *class* by a quadruple.

Definition 1: class. c ::= <n, D, F, X> where:

- n is the identification of the class.
- D is a data structure description for storing the state of an object.
- F is a set of the function definitions or implementations.

- X is a unified interface of all the objects of this class. It is a set of all the message patterns relevant to the functions of this class. A message pattern tells how to send a message to invoke a function.

We use c to express a specific class and C the set of all classes. Next, we define an *object* based on a class.

Definition 2: object. $o ::= < n, c, s >$ where:

- n is the identification of the object.
- c is the object's class identified by the class identification or name.
- s is a data structure whose values are called attributes, properties, or states.

We use o to express a specific object and O the set of all the objects. The above two definitions comply with object principles O1–9.

Agent

An agent is defined as an entity consisting of a set of provided services (Castelfranchi, 1998). An *agent* a is a special object that can simulate the intelligent behavior of a human being. It is different from objects in that it responds to messages based on its current state, but conventional objects respond to messages directly.

Definition 3: agent. $a ::= <n, c_a, s, r_c, R_p, N_g, e_t, e_s, \psi, u >$, where:

- n and s have the same meanings as those in Definition 2.
- c_a is a special class that describes the common properties of agents.
- r_c means a role that the agent is currently playing. If it is empty, then this agent is free.
- R_p means a set of roles that the agent is potential to play ($r_c \notin a.R_p$).

- N_g means a set of identifications of groups that the agent belongs to.
- $<e_t, e_s>$ expresses the processing capacity for an agent, where e_t expresses how many units of free time it has, and e_s expresses how much memory space it has. $<e_t, e_s>$ can be reset based on the performance of an agent's services. Even though the time in one day is 24 hours, a person may have different e_t and e_s based on their processing capacities including the working efficiency, attitudes, and goals.
- ψ expresses the past performance or credits of serving others.
- u expresses the workload of the agent.

This definition complies with agent principles A1–8. c_a and s are used to reflect A1–2. N_r, N_g, e_t, e_s, ψ, and u are used to reflect A3–8. To support its functionality, an agent should have the knowledge about groups, classes, objects, and other agents in the system. A denotes the set of all agents.

Message

Interaction is a necessary entity for collaboration. To facilitate interactions among roles while following the principles O3–5, messages are used.

Definition 4: message. $m ::= < n, v, l, P, t, \psi >$ where:

- n is the identification of the message.
- v is null or the receiver of the message expressed by an identification of a role.
- l is the pattern of a message, specifying the types, sequence, and number of parameters.
- P is a set of objects taken as parameters with the message pattern l, where $P \subset O$.
- t is a tag that expresses any, some, or all-message.
- ψ is the weight for an agent to collect its credit for promotion. If an agent responds to

this message, the agent receives the weight and adds it to its credit.

In a traditional object model, we concentrate mainly on objects and their classes because executable programs run automatically with little interaction with users at the system level. A traditional object-oriented paradigm emphasizes the messages accepted by a class of objects. However, it does not give much consideration to the messages an object may send out. In this model, we emphasize that a role is a message receiver and a user sends messages through roles. In this definition, if v is null, this message is an incoming one to be dispatched by the role to an agent, and P and t are meaningless. If v is an identification of a role, it is an outgoing message that should be dispatched by the role specified by the message. Outgoing messages should be filled with P (it can be empty) and t. We divide the outgoing messages into three categories by t: *any-message, some-message,* and *all-message.* By any-message we mean that the message may be sent to any agent who plays the role. Some-message means the messages should be sent to some agents playing the role, and all-message means that the messages should be sent to all the agents who play the role.

We use m to express a message and M the set of all messages. We call m a message template if its P is not specified completely.

Role

A *role* can show the specialties of some users. It provides them with not only message patterns to serve others, but also message patterns to access objects, classes, groups, and other roles.

Definition 5: role. $r ::= <n, I, N_a, N_o, e_t, e_s, R_m, R_b, \psi>$ where:

- n is the identification of the role.
- $I ::= < M_{in}, M_{out} >$ denotes a set of messages, wherein, M_{in} expresses the incoming

messages to the relevant agents, and M_{out} expresses a set of outgoing messages or message templates to roles (i.e., M_{in}, M_{out} $\subset M$).

- N_a is a set of identifications of agents that are playing this role.
- N_o is a set of identifications of objects including classes, environments, roles, and groups that can be accessed by the agents playing this role.
- e_t and e_s are used to express the processing capacity requirement, where e_t expresses how many units of free time it requires and e_s expresses how many units of space it requires. $<e_t, e_s>$ expresses that an agent must possess at least $<e_t, e_s>$ to play this role.
- R_m is the super roles.
- R_b is the subordinate roles.
- ψ is the required credits for an agent to play this role.

This definition follows role principles R1–10. I is used to reflect R3–7. N_a and N_o are used to reflect R8–10.

In a run-time system, M_{in} is a subset of X (interface) of C_a (set of special classes describing common properties of users) of an agent a that plays this role. The elements of M_{out} are constructed with the subsets of M_{in} of other roles. Suppose that we have at least one agent playing a role, for roles r_i and r_j $(i \neq j)$:

$$\forall m_{in}(m_{in} \in r_i.M_{in} \rightarrow \exists a(m_{in} \in a.C_a.X \wedge a.n \in r_i.N_a))$$
$$\forall m_{out}(m_{out} \in r_i.M_{out} \rightarrow \exists r_j(i \neq j, \exists m_{in}(m_{in} \in r_j.M_{in} \wedge m_{in}.t = m_{out}.t)))$$

where m_{in} expresses an incoming message $m_{in} \in M_{in}$ and m_{out} an outgoing message $(m_{out} \in M_{out})$.

In Definition 5, accessing means obtaining all the services the objects provide. Note that we separate agents from objects to emphasize that a role is the media to access agents. The only way to interact with other agents is by sending messages to roles. Denote by R the set of all roles.

N_a in Definition 5 and N_r in Definition 3 are just sets of identifications of agents and roles. They might be empty at the beginning. They are used to express the dynamic properties of roles and agents. If $|N_r|=0$, the user represented by the agent is playing no role. If $|N_a|=0$, the role has not been played by any agent. When we issue a message r.addAgent(a), we mean that we add the identification of agent a to role r and the identification of r to a.

To facilitate role playing, roles should constitute a hierarchy. A role hierarchy is actually a partial order on roles R and a relation >, that is, (R , >). $r_1 > r_2$ means that r_1 is a super role of r_2. To express this hierarchy, we need an item in the role entity to accommodate the identifications of subordinate roles and super roles. Note that this relationship expresses the promotion direction for roles.

Environment

In reality, people collaborate in an environment. People normally build groups in an environment. We can mimic a play on a stage. The stage is the environment. The play or collaboration is performed by a group of actors. Therefore, we introduce a new concept to facilitate the definition of a group.

Definition 6: environment. e ::= <n, B> where:

- n is the identification of the environment.
- B is a set of tuples of role, number range, and an object set, B ={< n_r, q, N_o>}. The number range q tells how many users may play this role in this environment, and q is expressed by (lower, upper). For example, q might be (1, 1), (2, 2), (1, 10), and (3, 50). It states how many agents may play the same role r in the group. The object set N_o consists of the objects accessed by the agents who play the relevant role. By "complex" we mean they are composed of other objects.

The complex objects in N_o are mutually exclusive, that is, one complex object in this set can only be accessed by one agent (user). For each tuple, we have the inequality: $q.lower \leq |N_o| \leq q.upper$. In fact, $|N_o|$ expresses the number of resources for agents to access.

For example, a computer science department can be expressed as an environment:

- n = Department of Computer Science.
- B has five tuples as its members: B = {<chairperson, [1, 1], {a chairperson office}>, <associate chairperson, [1,3], { one to three offices for associate chairpersons}>, <secretary, [1,5], { one to five offices for secretaries }>, <computer administrator, [1,4), { one to four offices for administrators }>, <faculty, [3, 15], {three to fifteen faculty offices}>}. It implies one chairperson, one chairperson office; one to three associate chairpersons and one to three offices for associate chairpersons; one to five secretaries and one to five offices for secretaries; one to four computer system administrators and one to four offices for administrators; three to fifteen faculties and three to fifteen faculty offices.

Denote by E the set of all the environments in a system. All the roles in an environment have access to it. With this definition, we know that prior to environment creation, roles must be specified. At the same time, before we specify a role, we need to create objects for the roles to access.

Group

Agents work in a group and hold roles. Every work setting involves groups of individuals. In a group, to accomplish a task, the group members (agents) interact with each other. We can define a group as a set of agents playing roles in an environment.

Definition 7: g = <n, e, J> where:

- n is the identification of the group.
- e is an environment for the group to work.
- J is a set of tuples of identifications of an agent and role, that is, $J = \{<n_a, n_r, n_o>|$ $\exists q, n_o (n_o \in N_o) \wedge (<n_r, q, N_o> \in e.B)\}$.

Definitions 6–7 comply with group principles G1–8. n and e are used to reflect G1–3; e and J are used to reflect principles G4 and G5.

Suppose U ($|\{n_a| \exists n_r, n_o (<n_a, n_r, n_o> \in J)\}|$) agents in the group, V ($|\{n_r| \exists n_a, n_o (<n_a, n_r, n_o> \in J)\}|$) roles in the environment e of a group, and one agent plays exactly one role in the group. q_i means the role number range for the *i*th role, $q_i.upper$ means the upper limit of the number of the agents playing the ith role, and $q_i.lower$ means the lower limit, then we have the following inequality for a group:

$$\sum_{i=1}^{V} q_i.lower \leq U \leq \sum_{i=1}^{V} q_i.upper.$$

This means that every agent must play a role in a group, an agent may join the group only when vacancies are available for a role, and there must be a number of agents to play relevant roles. It also follows principle G8 (i.e., an open group). The group is closed if:

$$U = \sum_{i=1}^{V} q_i.upper.$$

If we want the resources in an environment to be fully used without waste, we should keep the equality:

$$\sum_{i=1}^{V} b_i . | N_o | = | J |$$

for each $b_i \in B$ in group g.

Clearly, $\sum_{i=1}^{V} b_i . | N_o | > | J |$ means that there are more resources than required, while $\sum_{i=1}^{V} b_i . | N_o | < | J |$ means that there are not enough resources.

For principle G6, we can state that g_1 is embedded in g_2 if:

$$\{n_r | \exists q, N_o (<n_r, q, N_o> \in g_1.e.B)\} \subset \{n_r | \exists q, N_o (<n_r, q, N_o> \in g_2.e.B)\}$$
$$\{n_o | \exists n_r, n_o (<n_a, n_r, n_o> \in g_1.J)\} \subset \{n_o | \exists n_r, n_o (<n_a, n_r, n_o> \in g_2.J)\}.$$

For G7, we can state that g_1 is overlapped with g_2 if:

$$\{n_r | \exists q, N_o (<n_r, q, N_o> \in g_1.e.B)\} \cap \{n_r | \exists q, N_o (<n_r, q, N_o> \in g_2.e.B)\} \neq \phi$$
$$\{n_o | \exists n_r, n_o (<n_a, n_r, n_o> \in g_1.J)\} \cap \{n_o | \exists n_r, n_o (<n_a, n_r, n_o> \in g_2.J)\} \neq \phi$$

For G8, we can state that g is public if g is in all the roles' object sets ($\forall r(r \in R \rightarrow g.n \in r.N_o)$) and g is private if g is in only some roles' object sets ($\exists r(r \in R, g.n \notin r.N_o)$).

The computer science department of Nipissing University is a group, where:

- n = CS department of Nipissing University.
- e = the computer science department environment.
- J includes all the <agent, role, object> tuples expressing its members, their roles, and their accessible offices.

The above definition of a group states this fact that without the users' participation, no collaboration would be performed.

We use g to express a specific group and G the set of all groups. The relationship between an agent and a group is similar to that between an agent and a role.

After a group is built, users can log into the system, join it by playing a role, access a relevant object, and interact with each other. To support a group to work is basically the routine function of a collaborative system. In this definition, for group g, role r, agent a, and an object o, we have such a relationship:

Figure 2. Role net: Architecture design

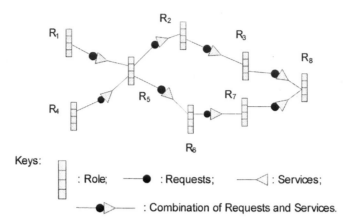

Figure 3. Agents: Implementation of role players

$$a.n \in \{b \,|< b,r,o \geq g.J\} \rightarrow a.n \in r.N_a.$$

That is, joining a group means playing a role, but not vise versa. Therefore, a role is independent of groups.

Now, a role-based multi-agent system Σ can be described as an 8-tuple $\Sigma ::= <C, O, A, M, R, E, G, s_0>$, where:

- C is a set of classes.
- O is a set of objects.
- A is a set of agents.
- M is a set of messages.
- R is a set of roles.
- E is a set of environments.
- G is a set of groups.

- s_0 is the initial state of the system.

With the above revised E-CARGO model, we can restate what Shakespeare ("As You Like It," Act II, Scene 7) said with the above notation: "All the world (C, O) is a stage (E), and all the men and women merely players (A); they all have their exits and entrances (Σ, G, s_0); and one man in his time plays many parts (R)."

ARCHITECTURE OF RMAS

We can specify an agent's role using two components: the service interface, including incoming messages, and the request interface, including outgoing messages (Zhu & Zhou, 2006a). The human icon in Figure 1 can be an agent, object, group, or system. Hence, the roles applied in an agent system should be concerned with two aspects of roles—responsibilities and rights—because a player (an agent, or an object) should perform the service upon request and send out messages to seek other players' services. With the revised E-CARGO model, we know that every group has an environment in which agents play roles.

With roles, to form a group of agents who collaborate to complete a defined task, we suggest the following steps:

- define roles required by the task (r);
- connect the roles with structures (e, c, o);
- design agents based on roles (a); and
- release agents to play roles in the group (g).

To accomplish the above tasks, we need to provide tools as follows:

- role specification;
- role registration;
- role match;
- agent release; and
- agent migration.

To develop an RMAS, the main tasks are specifying roles and the relationships among them, specifying role players, and assigning roles to them. In the system design, roles are created, specified, and connected into a net, called role net (Figure 2). A system architecture, in fact, is an environment e of the E-CARGO model.

To provide a concrete system, we need to obtain the architecture with roles and role relationships, create agents that can play roles, assign agents with roles, and then allow agents to play roles. Hence, to develop an RMAS, we have the following steps: architecture design, agent implementation, and system integration (Zhu, 2006b).

Architecture Design

In this step, the major task is to build role nets (Figure 2). A role net is a blueprint of agent collaboration and is composed of roles, requests, and services. The basic procedure is as follows:

- **Identify roles:** Analysts extract roles from the problem descriptions.
- **Specify roles:** Designers describe the incoming and outgoing messages for the roles.
- **Specify the role relationships:** Designers describe the relationships among the roles, such as classification, promotion, request/ service, and conflict.

Agent Implementation

The major tasks in this step are to design and implement qualified role players, that is, agents (Figure 3).

RMAS implementers are mainly concerned with implementing agents. An agent might be a machine, a computer, a robot, a hardware component such as a sensor, or a software component such as a process.

There are two possible explanations as to why an agent does not work: one is that the designers have not specified enough requests (or rights) for the roles, or the agent developers have not completely applied the specified requests (or rights). Designers should concentrate on specifying roles and the relevant requests and services. They need only care about high-level role specifications and role request/service relationships—that is, which roles should be in a system, which rights roles should possess, and which services roles should provide. Agent developers will work primarily on how to implement the services with the provided requests.

Figure 4. System integration: Assigning roles to agents

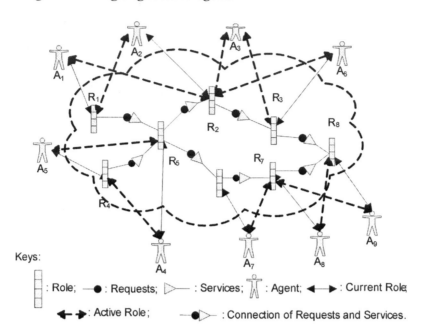

Keys:

⊟ : Role; ──●─ : Requests; ▷── : Services; 🯅 : Agent; ◀──▶ : Current Role;

◀─ ─▶ : Active Role; ──●▷─ : Connection of Requests and Services.

System Integration

The major task of system integration is to have agents play roles (Figure 4), where "active roles" means that the relevant agents are qualified to play the relevant roles and "current roles" means the agents are currently playing the roles. They are discussed in detail below. Agents and roles are combined together to make a whole intelligent system executable.

A multi-agent system can be built by integration, that is, assigning agents with roles or having agents play roles. This step builds a deliverable and workable intelligent system (Figure 4). At this step, agents are put onto the role nets, and match a role or roles to play. If each role has a relevant agent to play it and the agent can provide enough space and speed required by that role, the system is completed and workable.

Evidently, the above three steps can be done by specialists such as designers, agent providers, and system integrators who possess differing levels of experience and training. The integration step shows significant scaling capabilities based on assignment of sufficient agents to perform a single role. The efficiencies of agents as supplied by different agent providers may vary. Based on these differences, the managers of a development team must have concrete evaluation criteria for these providers.

From Figures 2–4, we find that a system is designed when roles are designed and specified. System construction involves the design of agents that are qualified to play roles then arrange for agents to play those roles.

From Figures 2 and 3, we know that software design establishes roles and their relationships while system implementation calls agents and has them play roles.

Based on the above discussion, we find that the specialization of designers and that of agent providers are totally different. Designers are experts in role specification, role relationship analysis, and role structure design. Agent providers are experts from different professions with special skills in the creation and provision of agents qualified to play roles as specified by designers. They require different consideration, expertise, and knowledge.

This specialization really separates designers and agent providers. This will lead to the real separation between system design and system implementation.

We also need other experienced specialists to match agents and roles. They understand agents and roles. They are matchmakers for roles and agents. They are the bridges between design and implementation. Matchmaking is their major task. These specialists are a totally new type of system developer.

AGENT EVOLUTION IN RMAS

To build RMAS, we need to take roles as nodes in a distributed structure or architecture. Agents will be placed on it to do jobs. An agent can be an organization, group, person, system, machine (computer), or component of a machine.

Agents in a system work actively and collaboratively toward the common goal of the system. Introduction of a new agent to the system is done for a specific reason. Role performance is the reason why agents are created, modified, and transferred. An agent should be able to adopt appropriate roles as demonstration of its ability, and transfer roles to demonstrate mobility.

The evolution of agents is based on their adaptabilities (Hayes-Roth, 1999). Agents are required to adapt five aspects of an intelligent system: perception strategy, control mode, reasoning tasks, reasoning methods, and meta-control strategy. Roles are a great tool to describe the evolution of agents in an intelligent system and improve their adaptability in the system. Past, active, current, and future roles can well express the evolution of agents.

Future Roles

In our society, people strive to be a great person within a great group. This situation was described early in 1970s by Maslow's (1970) hierarchy of needs. Every person has a goal in a society. A goal is a controlling or guiding state that determines the action of search and selection, and qualifies a person's success or failure.

In a society, roles are organized in a ladder mode to encourage people to pursue higher positions and obtain increased respect. These ladder modes can be seen almost everywhere. In a university, there is a ladder from assistant professor to full professor. In a software company, there is a ladder from programmer to senior programmer. In an army, there is a ladder from the lowest rank, recruit, to the highest rank, general. All of these ladders aim at encouraging people to work in order to obtain progressive promotion. Figure 5 indicates examples of role hierarchy (or a ladder). A role hierarchy is actually a partial relation of roles, say $<R,,<>$, where R is as defined earlier and $r_1 < r_2$ means r_1 is a sub-role of r_2 and r_2 is a super-role of r_1—for example, in Figure 5, *Assistant Professor <Associate Professor, Full Professor < Distinguished Professor,* and *Research Member < Research Fellow.*

When an agent lives in a role net, it tries to achieve its *future roles* through hard work. By "future," we mean the roles an agent hopes to play in the future. To be qualified to play the future role, the agent must collect credits by serving other agents in the system. Therefore, roles can be taken as goals for agents in a role-based agent system. Gradually, agents approach their goals.

The Current Roles and Active Roles

From daily lives, we know that a person may play many roles during a period. For example, a person might be a professor, technical consultant, and project manager in the same year. To express this situation while obeying the principle "a player

Figure 5. Examples of role ladders for (a) a researcher and (b) a software developer

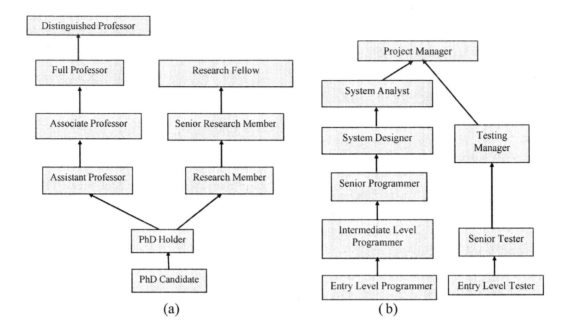

(a) (b)

Figure 6. The role play graph showing the roles an agent plays

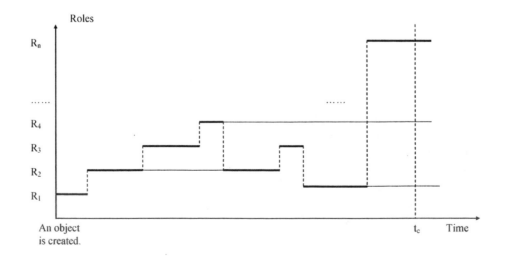

plays only one role at a time" (Zhu & Zhou, 2006a), we need to differentiate the concepts of *active roles* (R_p in E-CARGO) and *the current role* (r_c in E-CARGO). By "active roles," we mean the player still responds to the messages relevant to these roles, but with delayed or scheduled responses. Sometimes, an active role should be transferred to the current role to respond to the messages. By "current," we mean the agent is currently playing this role, that is, it directly responds to the messages relevant to this role. These concepts are used to express the current state of an agent.

Active roles are the roles a player is holding and they are ready to respond to messages. The current role is the role that can immediately respond to messages coming to it. That is to say, a role player can hold many active roles at the same time, but it holds only one current role at a time. By holding only one current role, we can avoid role-role conflicts (Nyanchama & Osborn, 1999). Active roles can also be used to express the meaningfulness of role transition, (i.e., changing the current role from one active role to another).

Past Roles

To express an agent's dynamic and evolving situation, we must consider the passage of time. To completely express a live agent, we need to track past, current, active, and future roles.

This requires tracking of a historical record. We are then able to answer a question such as: What roles did an agent play in the past? To accomplish this task, we need to introduce the concept of *past roles*. By "past roles," we mean those already performed by an agent then discarded. Figure 6 shows the roles and the time segment used by an agent in their performance.

Suppose a person plays a student role again after playing a project manager role. Should we create a new role instance or replay the original role instance? This will depend on actual requirements and the situation. If it is really a different one, say, a graduate student, we need to create

a new role instance. If he or she really plays the same student role instance as before, he or she should replay the original role instance.

The horizontal axis stands for time and the vertical one for roles. To view an agent's evolution, we can concentrate on its role transition along the time axis. In Figure 6, the current roles are expressed by the bold line segments and the active roles by thin lines. A bold line segment expresses a past role. Suppose that the current time is t_c. The past roles of the agent in Figure 6 were R_1–R_3, the active ones are R_1, R_4, and R_n, and the current one is R_n.

Role-Playing Rules

To accommodate agent evolution, there should be a role engine that provides a method to attach an agent to a role and a method to find an agent to execute the message. These methods affect the promotion of the agents, that is, to play more high-level roles. They should check if the agent can be attached to the role and return true or false as a result and dispatch the messages evenly and without bias.

To determine if an agent is qualified to play a role, there are several criteria:

- The agent must provide methods to cover all the incoming messages for the role.
- The agent must collect enough credits.
- The agent must have the needed processing capacities.
- At least one role the agent is playing belongs to the sub-roles of this role if the role has sub-roles.
- When a role is approved for an agent, the processing capacity $<e_t, e_s>$ of the agent should be decreased When an agent releases a role, $<e_t, e_s>$ should be increased.

To manage credits, we assign a weight for each incoming message of a role. When we specify a role, we can assign incoming messages to a role and set the specific weight for the role. That is to say, the same incoming messages can have different weights for different roles. When an agent successfully executes a method relevant to an incoming message, it collects the weight of the message to increase its credits.

CASE STUDY

With the revised E-CARGO model as discussed above, we can define a soccer team with the 4-4-2 formulation as an environment as e_1 = {<goalie, [1], f>, <defender, [4], f>, <midfield, [4], f>, <forward, [2], f>, <goalie, [1], f>}, where, f = {the gate, the field, the ball}. A 3-6-1 formulation can be described as e_2 = {<defender, [3], f>, <midfield, [6], f>, <forward, [1], f>, <goalie, [1], f>} (Zhu, 2006c).

If we specify the team in a more clear way, the environments are: e_1 = {<goalie, [1], f>, <left-defender, [1], f>, <right-defender, [1] , f>, <mid-defender, [2], f>, <left-midfield, [1], f>, <right-midfield, [1], f >, <mid-midfield, [2], f>, <left-forward, [1], f>, <right-forward, [1], f>, <goalie, [1], f>}. e_2 = {<left-defender, [1], f>, <right-defender, [1], f>, <mid-defender, [1], f>, <left-midfield, [2], f>, <right-midfield, [2], f>, <mid-midfield, [2], f>, <left-forward, [1], f>, <goalie, [1], f>}.

The environment e_1 can be shown as in Figure 7, where R_1–R_4 are defender role instances, R_5–R_8 are midfielder role instances, R_9–R_{10} are forward role instances, and R_0 is the goalie role instance. Figure 7 also shows some relationships among roles. For example, R_0 can request R_1, R_2, R_3, and R_4; R_2 can request R_5 and R_6; and R_3 can request R_7 and R_8.

Robots are designed and built to possess similar hardware abilities. They can sense, move, control a ball, and kick a ball.

For roles in a robot soccer team, a role can be specified as how to behave with Java (Zhu, 2007). For example, a forward role segment can be specified as shown in Box 1.

Figure 7. An environment for a soccer team with the 4-4-2 formation

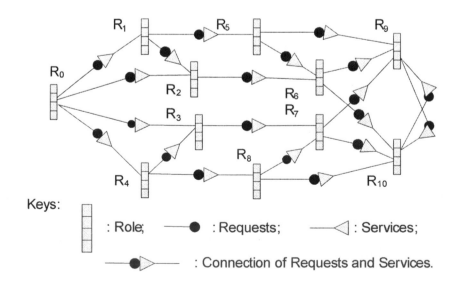

Box 1.

```
public class forward extends Role {
public forward(Robot nearest)    //Constructor of the Forward class
{//initialize the states of a forward at the beginning of a game
distanceToNearestForward=140;          //half of the field width
distanceToGate=230;                    //less than the half of the field length
distanceToGoal=30;                     //It depends on the power of the robot
newrestForward=nearest;
ballHoldState=false;
blockedToGoal=true;
}
public void start(){
while (true)
        {        if (!ballHoldState) moveToBall();
                 if ((ballHoldState)
&& (distanceToGate >= distanceToNearestForward)
&& (distanceToGoal >= distanceToGate)
&& (!blockedToGoal) )
                        goal();
                 if ((ballHoldState) && (!blockedToGoal))
                        pass(newrestForward);
}
}
private void moveToBall()
{//move to the ball;
}
private void goal()
{//kick the ball to the gate;
}
private void pass(Robot r)
{//pass the ball to the robot r;
}
private double distanceToNearestForward;
//in centimeters. The field size is 440 cm x 280 cm (Weiss & Reusch, 2005).
private double distanceToGate;  //in centimeters
private double distanceToGoal;          //in centimeters
private Robot newrestForward;
//an robot playing a Forward role. Robot is a class to describe all robots.
private Boolean ballHoldState;          //true means holding the ball and false not.
private Boolean blockedToGoal;          //true means blocked and false not.
}
```

Figure 8. A robot soccer team

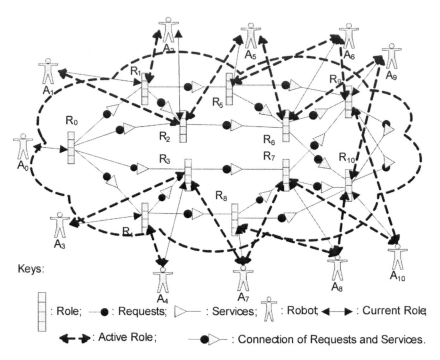

Keys:

☐ : Role; ━●━ : Requests; ▷── : Services; ⛷ : Robot; ◄──► : Current Role;

◄─►: Active Role; ━●▷ : Connection of Requests and Services.

To organize a robot soccer team specified by Figure 7, we can have 11 robots and assign them role instances (Figure 8). Robots with limited power (electric and computing) and memories are often assigned to play similar roles as shown in Figure 8. In such a situation, the role transfer for each robot is limited. When robots are developed with enough power and memories, many or all roles can be assigned to every robot. Role transfers are triggered with events activated by the sensors and conditions predefined. Figure 8 expresses that this formation is dynamic. It is initially 4-4-2. When attacking, it might evolve into 2-4-4. When blocking, it might be 4-6-0. This totally supports the dynamic role allocations for agent that are required in a robot agent team (Chaimowicz, Campos, & Kumar, 2002; Stone & Veloso, 1999).

INFORMATION PERSONALIZATION WITH ROLES

Because of the vast quantity of information on the Internet, it is difficult for users to find information appropriate to their interests. It is necessary to filter irrelevant information from that presented to Internet users (Abidi & Zeng, 2006). Information personalization refers to the automatic adjustment of information content, structure, and presentation tailored to an individual user. It is obtained by reducing information overload and customizing information access. Information personalization is important in the development of a user-friendly interface to the Internet. It constitutes the mechanisms and technologies required to customize information access to end users.

However, it is difficult to capture requirement specifications independent of particular personalization algorithms or techniques (Haase,

Ehrig, Hotho, & Schnizler, 2004; Perugini & Ramakrishnan, 2003; Ramakrishnan, Rosson, & Carroll, 2007). It is not practical for users to set their personal filtering preferences, because many lack sufficient computer literacy and they wish to limit their experience to clicking buttons or selecting menu items. Role-based approaches are a good trade-off between an easy end user experience and the filtering out of irrelevant information. Roles enable users to easily set interface preferences relevant to their jobs. Through roles, common interfaces for specialized information can be designed thus filtering much irrelevant information.

Information personalization needs to address the following requirements (Abidi & Zeng, 2006):

1. The personalized information should be relevant to the interests of the user. The user may choose the degree of relevance to include either all or a partial list of topics of interest.
2. The personalized information should be factually consistent, that is, the set of documents being presented to users should mutually satisfy the consistency constraint.
3. The information personalization process should attempt to find the largest set of consistent documents in terms of the coverage of topics defined by users.

Using roles, we can support: by indicating specific concerns, by setting server agents to provide role-related information, and by matching requests with agents performing the same role.

Based on the E-CARGO model, the scenario of role-based information personalization on the Internet is as follows:

1. Users use client computers to retrieve *information* stored in Internet server computers (client/server architecture).

2. All the information is stored and expressed in the format of *objects* and *classes*.
3. All the information is distributed across Internet *server* computers that form an *environment*.
4. In each *server* computer, there is one or many prescribed *roles*.
5. *Agents* are put into the computers to form a *group*.
6. Each *agent* plays one or many *roles* in the *group* to manage the information relevant to the *roles*.
7. In each *client* computer (personal computer), there is one *agent* that serves its user.
8. When a user logs in a *client* computer, an *agent* will present him or her with *roles*.
9. Each time the user retrieves information, he or she plays a *role*.
10. It is much easier for users to set the criteria to search for information because each *role* helps him or her concentrate on a specific concern.
11. All the requests from users will be issued through their current *roles*.
12. The information request with its *role* identification is issued to an *agent* playing a specific *role broker* (Siegel, 1998).
13. This *agent* matches the *request* with the *service* of some *agents*.
14. The users obtain the *information* from the server *agent*.

In the above scenario, *agents* at the server computers can be specially designed to play roles for certain information efficiently and effectively; *roles* at the server computers can be used to shrink the information space to be searched and retrieved by a special request; *roles* at the client are used to concentrate on the information preferred by the user; and the *agents* at the client are used to collect the users' personal preferences and retrieval history. With this personal information, *roles* can be used to represent the user's preferences. The above process significantly increases the precision of the requested information.

FUTURE RESEARCH DIRECTIONS AND CONCLUSION

The human world can be characterized by three major statements:

- A society has people and roles.
- Roles are organized in structures.
- People play roles.

To develop a role-based agent system, the main tasks are to specify roles and the relationships among roles, specify role players, and assign roles to their players. In the system design, roles are created, specified, and connected into a net, called role net. System architecture, in fact, is an environment of the E-CARGO model. To provide a concrete system, we need to obtain the architecture with roles and role relationships, create agents that can play roles, assign agents with roles, and then let agents play roles.

That is to say, to develop a role-based agent system, we have the following steps: architecture design, agent implementation, and system integration.

Roles are fundamental for multi-agent systems and information personalization. Using a role-based architecture, a multi-agent system can be designed by role and role relationship specification. We can consider a computer or a computer group as an agent in the networked systems. Every computer or computer group added to the network is to play a role or a group of roles in order to make the distributed system perform better.

A role-based architecture is a great guideline for distributed MAS builders and designers to plan and architect a distributed intelligent system. It is also an engine to help agents evolve to automatically join the architecture and cooperate with other agents to make MAS perform better. It

is an exciting future job to design agent factories on networked multi-computer systems. They are built to meet the requirement of roles to solve a special practical problem.

Role-based information personalization is an exciting topic to investigate. It inherently incorporates the requirement of information personalization.

The revised E-CARGO model has demonstrated the abstract mechanisms for role specification. We still need to provide concrete tools to specify, store, manage, transfer, and apply roles in intelligent system development. Future work can be investigated in the following aspects:

- Design and implement role-based grid environment for agents.
- Design and implement role-based information personalization systems.
- Develop role-based robot collaboration, such as robot soccer teams, with better role assignment and role transfer strategies.
- Design role-based agent development tools.
- Build simulation systems with roles and agents to help analyze human world community.

REFERENCES

Abidi, S.S.R., & Zeng, Y. (2006). Intelligent information personalization leveraging constraint satisfaction and association rule methods. In L. Lamontagne & M. Marchand (Eds.), *Proceedings of Canadian AI 2006* (pp. 134–145). Berlin: Springer-Verlag (LNAI 4013).

Ahn, H.J., Lee, H., & Park, S.J. (2003). A flexible agent system for change adaptation in supply chains. *Expert Systems with Applications, 25*(4), 603–618.

Alon, I. (2003). *Chinese culture, organizational behavior, and international business management.* Westport, CT: Greenwood.

Ashforth, B.E. (2001). *Role transitions in organizational life: An identity-based perspective.* Mahwah, NJ: Lawrence Erlbaum.

Becht, M., Gurzki, T., Klarmann, J., & Muscholl, M. (1999). ROPE: Role oriented programming environment for multiagent systems. *Proceedings of the 4th IECIS International Conference of Cooperative Information Systems* (pp. 325–333).

Bellavista, P., Corradi, A., & Stefanelli, C. (2001). Mobile agent middleware for mobile computing. *IEEE Computer, 34*(3), 73–81.

Bostrom, R.P. (1980). Role conflict and ambiguity: Critical variables in the MIS user-designer relationship. *Proceedings of the 17th Annual Computer Personnel Research Conference* (pp. 88–115), Miami, FL.

Botha, R.A., & Eloff, J.H.P. (2001). Designing role hierarchies for access control in workflow systems. *Proceedings of the 25th Annual International Computer Software and Applications Conference* (COMPSAC'01) (pp. 117–122), Chicago, IL.

Bowling, M., & Veloso, M. (2002). Multiagent learning using a variable learning rate. *Artificial Intelligence, 136*(2), 215–250.

Cabri, G., Ferrari, L., & Leonardi, L. (2005a). Injecting roles in Java agents through runtime bytecode manipulation. *IBM Systems Journal, 44*(1), 185–208.

Cabri, G., Ferrari, L., & Leonardi, L. (2005b, July). Supporting the development of multi-agent interactions via roles. *Proceedings of the 6th International Workshop on Agent-Oriented Software Engineering at AAMAS 2005* (pp. 54–166), Utrecht, The Netherlands. Berlin: Springer-Verlag (LNCS 3950).

Cao, L.B., Zhang, C.Q., & Dai. R.W. (2005a). The OSOAD methodology for open complex agent systems. *International Journal of Intelligent Control and Systems, 10*(4), 277–285.

Cao, L.B., Zhang, C.Q., & Dai. R.W. (2005b). Organization-oriented analysis of open complex agent systems. *International Journal of Intelligent Control and Systems, 10*(2), 114–122.

Castelfranchi, C. (1998). Modeling social action for AI agents. *Artificial Intelligence, 103,* 157–182.

Chaimowicz, L., Campos, M.F.M., & Kumar, R.V. (2002). Dynamic role assignment for cooperative robots. *Proceedings of the IEEE International Conference on Robotics and Automation* (ICRA'02) (pp. 293–298), Washington, DC.

Chockler, G.V., Keidar, I., & Vitenberg, I. (2001). Group communication specifications: A comprehensive study. *ACM Computing Surveys, 33*(4), 427–469.

Coulouris, G., Dollimore, J., & Kindberg, T. (2005), *Distributed systems: Concepts and design* (4th ed.). Reading, MA: Addison-Wesley.

Cristiano, C. (1998). Modeling social action for AI agents. *Artificial Intelligence, 103*(1–2), 157–182.

Cyert, R.M., & MacCrimmon, K.R. (1968). Organizations. In G. Lindzey & E. Aronson (Eds.), *The handbook of social psychology* (pp. 568–611). Reading, MA: Addison-Wesley.

Dafoulas, G.A., & Macaulay, L.A. (2001, June 25-29). Facilitating group formation and role allocation in software engineering groups. *Proceedings of the ACS/IEEE International Conference of Computer Systems and Applications* (pp. 352–359), Beirut, Lebanon.

Esteva, M., Rodríguez-Aguilar, J.A., Sierra C., Garcia, P., & Arcos, J.L. (2001). *On the formal specifications of electronic institutions* (pp. 126–147). Berlin: Springer-Verlag (LNCS 1991).

Etzioni, O., & Weld, D.S. (1995). Intelligent agents on the Internet: Fact, fiction, and forecast. *IEEE Expert: Intelligent Systems and Their Applications, 10*(4), 44–49.

Ferber, J., Gutknechtl, O., & Michell, F. (2004). From agents to organizations: An organizational view of multi-agent systems. In P. Giorgini, J. Müller, & J. Odell (Eds.), *Agent-Oriented Software Engineering (AOSE) IV* (pp. 214–230). Berlin: Springer-Verlag (LNCS 2935).

Genesereth, M.R., & Ketchpel, S.P. (1994). Software agents. *Communications of the ACM, 37*(7), 48–55.

Green, S., Hurst, L., Nangle, B., Cunningham, P., Somers, F., & Evans, R. (1997). *Software agents: A review.* Technical Report TCD-CS-1997-06, Trinity College, Ireland.

Gruver, W. (2004). Technologies and applications of distributed intelligent systems. *Proceedings of the IEEE MTT-Chapter Presentation,* Waterloo, Canada.

Hayes-Roth, B. (1995). An architecture for adaptive intelligent systems. *Artificial Intelligence, 72*(1–2), 329–365.

Haase, P., Ehrig, M., Hotho, A., & Schnizler, B. (2004). Personalized information access in a bibliographic peer-to-peer system. *Proceedings of the AAAI Workshop on Semantic Web Personalization.* Retrieved March 22, 2007, from http://citeseer.ist.psu.edu/haase04personalized.html

Heylighen, F. (1999). Collective intelligence and its implementation on the Web. *Computational & Mathematical Organization Theory, 5*(3), 253–280.

Jennings, N., Sycara, K., & Wooldridge, M. (1998). A roadmap of agent research and development. *Autonomous Agents and Multi-Agent Systems, 42*(1), 7–38.

Jennings, N., & Wooldridge, M. (1996). Software agents. *IEE Review, 42*(1), 17–20.

Kay, A. (1993). The early history of Smalltalk. *Proceedings of the 2nd ACM SIGPLAN Conference on History of Programming Languages* (pp. 69–95), Cambridge, MA.

Kephart, J.O., Hanson, J.E., & Greenwald, A.R. (2000). Dynamic pricing by software agents. *Computer Networks.*

Lavender, R.G., & Schmidt, D.C. (1996). Active object: An object behavioral pattern for concurrent programming. In J.O. Coplien, J. Vlissides, & N. Kerth (Eds.), *Pattern languages of program design.* Boston: Addison-Wesley.

Louden, K.C. (2003). *Programming languages: Principles and practice* (2nd ed.). Brooks/Cole.

Maes, P. (1994). Modeling adaptive autonomous agents. *Artificial Life, 1*(1), 135–162.

Maslow, A. (1970). *Motivation and personality* (2nd ed.). New York: Harper & Row.

Meyer, B. (1988). *Object-oriented software construction.* Englewood Cliffs, NJ: Prentice Hall.

Mills, A.J., & Simmons, A.M. (1999). *Reading organization theory.* Toronto: Garamond.

Miner, J.B. (1992). *Industrial-organizational psychology.* New York: McGraw-Hill.

Nwana H.S. (1996). Software agents: An overview. *Knowledge Engineering Review, 11*(3), 205–244.

Nwana, H.S., Lee, L., & Jennings, N.R. (1996). Coordination in software agent systems. *BT Technology Journal, 14*(4), 79–89.

Nyanchama, M., & Osborn, S. (1999). The role graph model and conflict of interest. *ACM Transactions on Information and System Security, 2*(1), 3–33.

Odell, J., Nodine, M., & Levy, R.(2005). A metamodel for agents, roles, and groups. In J. Odell, P. Giorgini, & J. Müller (Eds.), *Agent-oriented software engineering* (pp. 78–92). Berlin: Springer-Verlag (LNCS 3382).

Odell, J., Van Dyke Parunak, H., & Fleischer, M. (2003). The role of roles in designing effective agent organizations. In A. Garcia, C. Lucena, F. Zambonelli, A. Omicini, & J. Castro (Eds.), *Software engineering for large-scale multi-agent systems* (pp. 27–38). Berlin: Springer-Verlag (LNCS 2603).

Ould, M.A. (1995). *Business processes: Modeling and analysis for re-engineering and improvement.* New York: John Wiley & Sons.

Papazoglou, M.P. (2001). Agent-oriented technology in support of e-business. *Communications of the ACM, 44*(4), 71–77.

Perugini, S., & Ramakrishnan, N. (2003). Personalizing interactions with information systems. In M. Zelkowitz (Ed.), *Advances in computers* (vol. 57, pp. 323–382). Academic Press.

Pham, V.A., & Karmouch, A. (1998). Mobile software agents: An overview. *IEEE Communications Magazine,* (July), 26–37.

Ramakrishnan, N., Rosson, M.B., & Carroll, J.M. (2007). *Explaining scenarios for information personalization.* Retrieved April 10, 2007, from http://arxiv.org/pdf/cs/0111007v1

Russell, D., & Norvig, P. (2003). *Artificial intelligence: A modern approach* (2nd ed.). Upper Saddle River, NJ: Pearson Education.

Scherer, A.G. (2003). Modes of explanation in organization theory. In H. Tsoukas & C. Knudsen (Eds.), *The Oxford handbook of organizational theory* (pp. 310–344). Oxford: Oxford University Press.

Siegel, J. (1998). OMG overview: CORBA and the OMA in enterprise computing. *Communications of the ACM, 41*(10), 37–43.

Singley, M.K., Singh, M., Fairweather, P., Farrell, R., & Swerling, S. (2000). Algebra jam: Supporting teamwork and managing roles in a collaborative learning environment. *Proceedings of CSCW'00* (pp. 145–154), Philadelphia.

Stone, P., & Veloso, M. (1999). Task decomposition, dynamic role assignment, and low-bandwidth communication for real-time strategic teamwork. *Artificial Intelligence, 110,* 241–273.

Tanenbaum, A.S., & van Steen, M. (2002), *Distributed systems: Principles and paradigms.* Englewood Cliffs, NJ: Prentice Hall.

WebBoard™. (2006). *WebBoard discussion forum and collaboration software.* Retrieved March 10, 2007, from http://www.webboard.com/

Webber, A.B. (2003). *Modern programming languages.* Franklin, Beedle & Associates.

Weiss, N., & Reusch, B. (2005). Current and future trends and challenges in robot soccer. In R. Moreno Díaz et al. (Eds.), *EUROCAST 2005* (pp. 559–564). Berlin: Springer-Verlag (LNCS 3643).

Wooldridge, M., & Jennings, N. (1995). Intelligent agents: Theory and practice. *The Knowledge Engineering Review, 10*(2), 115–152.

Wooldridge, M., Jennings, N.R., & Kinny, D. (2000). The Gaia methodology for agent-oriented analysis and design. *Journal of Autonomous Agents and Multi-Agent Systems, 3*(3), 285–312.

Zambonelli, F., Jennings, N.R., & Wooldridge, M. (2003). Developing multiagent systems: The Gaia methodology. *ACM Transactions on Software Engineering Methodology, 12*(3). 317–370.

Zhu, H. (2005, October). Encourage contributions by roles. *Proceedings of the IEEE International Conference on Systems, Man and Cybernetics* (pp. 1574–1579).

Zhu, H. (2006a). Role mechanisms in collaborative systems. *International Journal of Production Research, 41*(1), 181–193.

Zhu, H. (2006b). A role-based architecture for intelligent agent systems. *Proceedings of the International Workshop on Distributed Intel-*

ligent Systems (pp. 354–359), Prague, Czech Republic.

Zhu, H. (2006c, October). A role-based approach to robot agent team design. *Proceedings of the IEEE International Conference on Systems, Man and Cybernetics* (pp. 4861–4866), Taipei, China.

Zhu, H. (2006d). Separating design from implementations: Role-based software development. *Proceedings of the 5th IEEE International Conference on Cognitive Informatics* (pp. 141–148), Beijing, China.

Zhu, H. (2007). *Role playing Java documents.* Retrieved April 10, 2007, from http://www.nipissingu.ca/faculty/haibinz/RolePlaying/

Zhu, H., & Zhou, M.C. (2003, October). Methodology first and language second: A way to teach object-oriented programming. *Companion of the ACM International Conference of Object-Oriented Programming, Systems, Languages and Applications* (OOPSLA'03) (pp. 140–147).

Zhu, H., & Zhou, M.C. (2006a). Role-based collaboration and its kernel mechanisms. *IEEE Transactions on Systems, Man and Cybernetics, Part C, 36*(4), 578–589.

Zhu, H., & Zhou, M.C. (2006b). Supporting software development with roles. *IEEE Transactions on Systems, Man and Cybernetics, Part A, 36*(6), 1110–1123.

ADDITIONAL READING

Readers who are interested in agent systems could refer to the publications below. The following two papers provide a good overview of research and development activities in the field of autonomous agents and multi-agent systems. They discuss the key concepts and applications, and highlight a range of open issues and future challenges.

Jennings, N., & Wooldridge, M. (1996). Software agents. *IEE Review, 42*(1), 17–20.

Jennings, N., Sycara, K., & Wooldridge, M. (1998). A roadmap of agent research and development. *Autonomous Agents and Multi-Agent Systems, 42*(1), 7–38.

This paper discusses autonomous agents from the point of view of animal behaviors. From this point of view, it extracts its main ideas, evaluates what contributions have been made so far, and identifies its current limitations and open problems.

Maes, P. (1994). Modeling adaptive autonomous agents. *Artificial Life,* 1(1), 135–162.

This paper reviews software agents and contains some strong opinions that are not necessarily widely accepted by the agent community.

Nwana H.S. (1996). Software agents: An overview. *Knowledge Engineering Review, 11*(3), 205–244.

This paper examines coordination in multi-agent systems and highlights the necessity for coordination in agent systems, overviews briefly various coordination techniques, and presents some conclusions and challenges drawn from this literature.

Nwana, H.S., Lee, L., & Jennings, N.R. (1996). Coordination in software agent systems. *BT Technology Journal, 14*(4), 79–89.

This book is the current standard college text book on artificial intelligence (AI). The authors present the subject of AI in a unified manner using the concept of an intelligent agent to develop a common framework for problem solving. The theory and practice of intelligent agent design are given equal weight in the text.

Russell, D., & Norvig, P. (2003). *Artificial intelligence: A modern approach* (2nd ed.). Upper Saddle River, NJ: Pearson Education.

This paper identifies and elaborates on the most important issues of intelligent agents. It provides a short review of applications of agent technology at that time.

Wooldridge, M., & Jennings, N. (1995). Intelligent agents: Theory and practice. *The Knowledge Engineering Review, 10*(2), 115–152.

Artificial intelligence has a long history of research. There would be a much longer list for a full list of recommended readings. The list here only helps readers understand the initiatives of applying roles in multi-agent systems. The above readings give good overviews of agents and agent (mobile or multi-agent) systems. Readers could understand the general principles and important challenges related with agents, agent systems, and collaboration among agents.

Readers who are interested in roles in agent systems could refer to the publications reviewed in this chapter as follows:

Becht, M., Gurzki, T., Klarmann, J., & Muscholl M. (1999, September). ROPE: Role oriented programming environment for multiagent systems. *Proceedings of the 4th IECIS International Conference on Cooperative Information Systems* (pp. 325–333).

Cabri, G., Ferrari, L., & Leonardi, L. (2005a). Injecting roles in Java agents through runtime bytecode manipulation. *IBM Systems Journal, 44*(1), 185–208.

Cabri, G., Ferrari, L., & Leonardi, L. (2005b, July). Supporting the development of multi-agent interactions via roles. *Proceedings of the 6th International Workshop on Agent-Oriented Software Engineering at AAMAS 2005* (pp. 54–166), Utrecht, The Netherlands. Berlin: Springer-Verlag (LNCS 3950).

Cao, L.B., Zhang, C.Q., & Dai. R.W. (2005a). The OSOAD methodology for open complex agent systems. *International Journal of Intelligent Control and Systems, 10*(4), 277–285.

Cao, L.B., Zhang, C.Q., & Dai. R.W. (2005b). Organization-oriented analysis of open complex agent systems. *International Journal of Intelligent Control and Systems, 10*(2), 114–122.

Depke, R., Heckel, R., & Kuster, J.M. (2001). Roles in agent-oriented modeling. *International Journal of Software Engineering and Knowledge Engineering, 11*(3), 281–302.

Ferber, J., Gutknechtl, O., & Michell, F. (2004). From agents to organizations: An organizational view of multi-agent systems. In P. Giorgini, J. Müller, & J. Odell (Eds.), *Agent-oriented software engineering IV* (pp. 214–230). Berlin: Springer-Verlag (LNCS 2935).

Odell, J., Nodine, M., & Levy, R. (2005). A metamodel for agents, roles, and groups. In J. Odell, P. Giorgini, & J. Müller (Eds.), *Agent-oriented software engineering* (pp. 78–92). Berlin: Springer-Verlag (LNCS 3382).

Odell, J., Van Dyke Parunak, H., & Fleischer, M. (2003). The role of roles in designing effective agent organizations. In A. Garcia, C. Lucena, F. Zambonelli, A. Omicini, & J. Castro (Eds.), *Software engineering for large-scale multi-agent systems* (pp. 27–38). Berlin: Springer-Verlag (LNCS 2603).

Partsakoulakis, I., & Vouros G. (2004). Roles in MAS: Managing the complexity of tasks and environments. In T. Wagner (Ed.), *An application science for multi-agent systems* (pp. 133–154). Berlin: Springer-Verlag.

Stone, P., & Veloso, M. (1999). Task decomposition, dynamic role assignment, and low-bandwidth communication for real-time strategic teamwork. *Artificial Intelligence, 110,* 241–273.

Wooldridge, M., Jennings, N.R., & Kinny, D. (2000). The Gaia methodology for agent-oriented analysis and design. *Journal of Autonomous Agents and Multi-Agent Systems, 3*(3), 285–312.

Zambonelli, F., Jennings, N.R., & Wooldridge, M. (2003). Developing multiagent systems: The Gaia methodology. *ACM Transactions on Software Engineering Methodology, 12*(3), 317–370.

Agent systems are currently the most active research field that applies role concepts and mechanisms. The above readings can activate readers to think and understand the importance of roles in agent systems. They also give readers a good overview of how roles have been applied in agent systems and what aspects of roles are currently emphasized. From these readings, readers will find that roles can be abstract like interfaces and concrete like processes. Roles have many aspects to consider in different usages.

Readers who are interested in the general ideas of information personalization could further refer the publications as follows:

Abidi, S.S.R., & Zeng, Y. (2006). Intelligent information personalization leveraging constraint satisfaction and association rule methods. In L. Lamontagne & M. Marchand (Eds.), *Proceedings of Canadian AI 2006* (pp. 134–145). Berlin: Springer-Verlag (LNAI 4013).

Haase, P., Ehrig, M., Hotho, A., & Schnizler, B. (2004). Personalized information access in a bibliographic peer-to-peer system. *Proceedings of the AAAI Workshop on Semantic Web Personalization.* Retrieved March 22, 2007, from http://citeseer.ist.psu.edu/haase04personalized.html

Perugini, S., & Ramakrishnan, N. (2003). Personalizing interactions with information systems. In M. Zelkowitz (Ed.), *Advances in computers* (vol. 57, pp. 323–382). Academic Press.

Ramakrishnan, N., Rosson, M.B., & Carroll, J.M. (2007). *Explaining scenarios for information personalization.* Retrieved April 10, 2007, from http://arxiv.org/pdf/cs/0111007v1

Information personalization is a new frontier of information technology. The above readings can activate readers to think and understand the importance of roles in information personalization. They also give readers a good overview of the challenges of information personalization. From these readings, readers will find that roles discussed in this chapter are good potential ways to solve the issues from the basic requirement of information personalization.

Readers who are interested in role-based collaboration could further refer to the following publications:

Zhu, H. (2005, October). Encourage contributions by roles. *Proceedings of the IEEE International Conference on Systems, Man and Cybernetics* (pp. 1574–1579).

Zhu, H. (2006a). Role mechanisms in collaborative systems. *International Journal of Production Research, 41*(1), 181–193.

Zhu, H. (2006b). A role-based architecture for intelligent agent systems. *Proceedings of the International Workshop on Distributed Intelligent Systems* (pp. 354–359), Prague, Czech Republic.

Zhu, H. (2006c, October). A role-based approach to robot agent team design. *Proceedings of the IEEE International Conference on Systems, Man and Cybernetics* (pp. 4861–4866), Taipei, China.

Zhu, H. (2006d). Separating design from implementations: Role-based software development. *Proceedings of the 5th IEEE International Conference on Cognitive Informatics* (pp. 141–148), Beijing, China.

Zhu, H., & Zhou, M.C. (2006a). Role-based collaboration and its kernel mechanisms. *IEEE*

Transactions on Systems, Man and Cybernetics, Part C, 36(4), 578–589.

Zhu, H., & Zhou, M.C. (2006b). Supporting software development with roles. *IEEE Transactions on Systems, Man and Cybernetics, Part A, 36*(6), 1110–1123.

Role-based collaboration is an emerging technology that can be applied to many fields. The above papers discuss systematically the principles of role-based collaboration (Zhu & Zhou, 2006a) and present some possible application of role-based methodology (Zhu, 2005, 2006a, 2006b, 2006c, 2006d; Zhu & Zhou, 2006b). They are helpful for people to understand role-based collaboration and apply role-based methodology to their particular applications.

Chapter XIII
Towards a Context Definition for Multi–Agent Systems

Tarek Ben Mena
RIADI-ENSI, Tunisia GRIC-IRIT, France

Narjès Bellamine-Ben Saoud
RIADI-ENSI, Tunisia

Mohamed Ben Ahmed
RIADI-ENSI, Tunisia

Bernard Pavard
GRIC-IRIT, France

ABSTRACT

This chapter aims to define context notion for multi-agent systems (MAS). Starting from the state of the art on context in different disciplines, we present context as a generic and abstract notion. We argue that context depends on three characteristics: domain, entity, and problem. By specifying this definition with MAS, we initially consider context from an extensional point of view as three components—actant, role, and situation—and then from an intensional one, which represents the context model for agents in MAS which consist of information on environment, other objects, agents, and relations between them. Therefore, we underline a new way of representing agent knowledge, building context on this knowledge, and using it. Furthermore, we prove the applicability of contextual agent solution for other research fields, particularly in personalized information retrieval by taking into account as agents: crawlers and as objects: documents.

INTRODUCTION

The notion of context is a well-known concept in cognitive psychology, philosophy of language, and in linguistics as well. Nevertheless, it has emerged in the Artificial Intelligence field only since 1980 (Weyhrauch, 1980).

Indeed, it was during the 13th International Joint Conference on Artificial Intelligence that context came to be considered more significant when Giunchiglia (1993) and McCarthy (1993) introduced contexts as formal objects.

The term "context" itself has always been ostensible in the English language, and the scrutiny of the concept which it represents has been the object of study in various fields and according to various points of view. However, the focus of the present study is on the field of Artificial Intelligence (AI), particularly on those studies that have been carried out to apply the results obtained in the field of the representation of knowledge.

There is no single definition of the notion of context. Each field has its own terminology to define a context according to various aims. On one dimension, Hirst (1997) shows that there is no theory of context, and that context in a natural language is not the same as context in the representation of knowledge. On another dimension, Hoffman (2004) states that the AI does not seek to define what the term context really stands, for but AI often describes context as being a local model representing a point of view on a field.

In this chapter, we aim to provide a definition of context with regard to multi-agent systems and then underline a new way of building on it as well as using it. Therefore, we progressively define context as an abstract and general notion, then we consider an extensional point of view, to end up with a specific definition for multi-agent system (MAS) from an intensional viewpoint presented as a context model. We apply this model in a case study for representing knowledge and reasoning at a context-aware agent.

BACKGROUND: CONTEXT AND AI

Theoretically, in artificial intelligence, contexts have been introduced as means of partitioning knowledge into manageable sets (Hendrix, 1997). A precursory idea of context can be traced back to Peirce's *existential graphs* (Roberts, 1973). Existential graphs use a logical form of context called

a *cut* which shows in a topological manner the scope of a negative context on a sheet of paper (the *sheet of assertion*). Context as a concept was first introduced in AI with Weyhrauch (1980) works on the mechanization of the logical theories in an interactive system of theorems demonstration. Sowa (1985) introduced *conceptual graphs* as an extension of the existential graphs and defined *contexts* as concepts whose referent contains one or more conceptual graphs (Sowa's *situations*).

Context and Logic

In logic, the context mechanism was introduced into the CYC project (www.cyc.com) in 1990 to simplify the construction of the commonsense-knowledge base (Lenat, Sierra, & Guha, 1990). In 1991, CYC contained more than 1.5 million sentences and covered a wide range of phenomena (Guha, 1991). Contexts are considered as rich objects in a first-order framework, extending the logic as required (Lenat, 1993). Contexts have also been considered as logical constructs that facilitate reasoning activities. In 1993, McCarthy (1993) defines context as the generalization of a collection of assumptions. According to this definition, contexts are treated as *formal objects* and have been made first-class objects in first-order logic. The basic relation *ist(c, p)* proposed by McCarthy asserts that the proposition p is true in the context c, where c is meant to capture all that is not explicit in p that is required to make p a meaningful statement representing what it is intended to state. Such a basic relation is always given in a context. Buvač (1996; Buvač & Mason, 1993) treats *ist* as a modality. Brézillion (1999) proposed the consequences of the formula *ist(c, p)* presented by McCarthy:

1. A context is always related to another context.
2. Contexts have an infinite dimension.
3. Contexts cannot be completely described.

4. When several contexts occur in a discussion, there is a common context above all the others in which all the terms and the predicates can be raised.

Later, Theodorakis and Spyratos (2002) presented consequences of the relation *specialize(c_1, c_2)* defined by McCarthy (1993) which states that c_2 does not imply more assumptions than c_1 and each significant proposal in c_1 is translatable in a proposal significant in c_2:

1. Contexts can be hidden in any depth.
2. Contexts are connected to others with various relations.

Based on McCarthy's work on context logic, Farquhar, Dappert, and Fikes (1995) present an approach to integrating disparate heterogeneous information sources. They show that the use of context logic reduces the up-front cost of integration path, and allows semantic conflicts within a single information source or between information sources to be expressed and resolved.

Context and Knowledge Representation and Reasoning (KRR)

Giunchiglia and Bouquet (1996) argue that the majority of the notions suggested with regard to context can be looked at with a prospect for unification. They give a very general notion of context as a collection of "things" (parameters, assumptions, presuppositions, etc.) a representation depends upon. The fact that a representation depends upon these "things" is called *context dependence*. Context can metaphorically be thought of as a sort of "box" (Giunchiglia & Bouquet, 1996). Each box has its own laws and draws a kind of limit between what is inside and what is outside. In Demonstrative Logic, Kaplan (1978) defines a context c as quadrupled $<c_A, c_T, c_P, c_W>$

where c_A is called the agent of c, c_T is time, c_P is the position, and c_W is the world of c.

The goal of KRR is to provide and study formal languages that can be used to represent what an agent of a certain kind knows about the world, and to show how this knowledge can be used in a reasoning process to infer new knowledge from that already available.

Interestingly enough, KRR seems to share this intuition with other related areas. Two examples will illustrate this "family resemblance." Sperber and Wilson (1986), in their book on relevance, express a similar intuition from a psycholinguistic perspective:

The set of premises used in interpreting an utterance…constitutes what is generally known as the context. A context is a psychological construct, a subset of the hearer's assumptions about the world. (p. 15)

And Kokinov (1995), in his paper on a dynamic approach to context modeling, says:

Context is the set of all entities that influence human (or system's) cognitive behavior on a particular occasion. (p. 200)

Despite the evidence of a shared intuition, we argue that there are at least two different types of theories of context that have been proposed in KRR (Bouquet, Ghidini, & Giunchiglia, 2003):

- A context seen as a way of partitioning (and giving a more articulated internal structure to) a global theory of the world; and
- A context seen as a local theory, namely a (partial, approximate) representation of the world, in a network of relations with other local theories.

The context also plays a significant role in:

a. the formalization of reasoning about beliefs (Giunchiglia, 1993; Giunchiglia & Giunchiglia, 1996; Benerecetti, Bouquet, & Ghidini, 1998a):

b. the meta-reasoning and propositional attitudes (Giunchiglia & Serafini, 1994);

c. the reasoning with viewpoints (Attardi & Simi, 1995);

d. the reasoning about action (Bouquet & Giunchiglia, 1995); and

e. in the integration of heterogeneous and autonomous knowledge databases (Farquhar et al., 1995; Mylopoulos & Motschnig-Pitrik, 1995; Ghidini & Giunchiglia, 2001).

Context and Agent

According to Agentlink Roadmap (2005), the current challenges of research on multi-agent systems are to build autonomous agents able to adapt to and reason on the modifications of the environment, of the users, and of the context in general. Edmonds (2002) argues that context has not been much utilized in agents. Hence, in this section, we present the attempts of using context in agents.

Kokinov (1994) proposes DUAL as a hybrid cognitive architecture: symbolic system and connectionist. It is a multi-agent system composed of a great number of non-cognitive and relatively simple agents, and system behavior emerges from the behavior of these simple agents and the interactions between them. The agents in this architecture do not have any internal knowledge base nor any goal. Kokinov did not define the context concept explicitly. Therefore, the connectionist aspect of architecture "restructures" continuously the system knowledge base represented by the symbolic aspect, ordering consequently the set of possible inferences. This makes the knowledge base dynamic and sensitive to the context.

Contexts have been used for the specification of architectures for argumentative agents (Parsons, Sierra, & Jennings, 1998). In a nutshell, the idea is to use the notion of context to represent the different components of agent architecture, and to specify the interaction between the different components as appropriate rules between contexts. Especially, in BDI (Believes, Desires, Intentions) agent architecture, Parsons defined four contexts related to B, D, I, and communication (Parsons, Jennings, & Sabater, 2002).

Ballim and Wilks (1991) proposed ViewGen as a framework to model agents which have beliefs, intentions, and goals representation of the other agents implied in a dialogue. ViewGen supposes that each agent taking part in a dialogue has an environment of beliefs which includes attitudes about what the other agents believe, want, and allow for. Such attitudes are represented as overlapping structures. Each structure contains the propositions which can be grouped by a particular subject or a stereotype; each structure is considered as a context as well as the overlapping structures.

The context notion was applied to formalize various aspects of intentional context, and particularly the beliefs context (Giunchiglia & Serafini, 1994; Cimatti & Serafini, 1995). Benerecetti et al. (1998a) use the beliefs context to solve opaque and transparent belief report reading problem. This approach of representation of belief is called *hierarchical belief,* which presents the notion of belief context also called *view* (Benerecetti, Giunchiglia, & Serafini, 1998b). Edmonds (2002) proposed an algorithm to learn the appropriate context along with the knowledge relevant to that context. Such an algorithm gets around these difficulties and opened the way for the exploitation of context in agent design.

Lately, several context-aware systems based on agents interested in data exploitation resulting from the surrounding environment were implemented: GAIA (Ranganathan & Campbell, 2003), CoBrA (context broker structures) (Chen & Finin,

2003), SOCAM (service-oriented context-aware middleware) (Gu, Wang, & Pung, 2004), and MySAM (Bucur, Beaune, & Boissier, 2005), an architecture where agents manage the diary of their users. Bucur (2004) defines the context as a pair made up of *finality* and a set of contextual information called *contextual attributes*. The finality is any information able to recognize the relevant attributes. The relevant contextual attributes gather all the attributes which can help to reach finality.

Context and Personalized Information Retrieval

The fundamental objective of an information retrieval system is to turn over, starting from a documentation collection, those that are relevant, with a requirement in information expressed by the user, through a request generally made up of keywords. The problem is not only with the availability of information, but it is mainly related to its relevance in a particular context of use. This is why work (Allan, Jay Aslam, & Belkin, 2002; Cool & Spink, 2002) is directed towards the revision of the information access chain with a view to integrate the user as a component of the total model of research; the aim is to deliver relevant information, adapted to the user's definite needs, context, and preferences.

More precisely, the global approaches of personalized information access (Tamine, Boughanem, & Chrisment, 2006) are focused particularly on two aspects. The first aspect relates to the representation of the user's interest. The second aspect relates to the integration of these contexts in a decisional model of information access. Indeed two fundamental reasons plead for personalization (Su & Lee, 2003): (a) the users have different objectives, different contexts, and perceptions which are different from the concept of relevance; and (b) the same user can have various needs at various moments.

Work is currently directed towards a broader definition of the user and his or her context, which gave rise to a research trend known as *the retrieval contextual information*, which defines as the whole the context and/or user profile as the set of cognitive and social dimensions (social, professional, and cultural environment) which characterizes it like its goals and intentions during a research session. Research on contextual information retrieval then approaches more or less one or the other of these questions: How do you represent the user? How do you integrate the user in the cycle of life of the request?

The profile construction represents a process which allows the instantiation of his or her representation. This process, generally implicit, is based on a process of inference of the context and preferences of the user according to his or her behavior during the use of an information access system (Kelly, 2004) or various other applications (McGowan, 2003; Dumais, Cadiz Cuttrel, & Jancke, 2003). Personalization can also relate to the definition of the relevance calculation function. In this direction, we find in Fan, Gordon, and Pathak (2004) a proposal for the adaptation of the parameters of the function of relevance to the user context, by using the techniques of genetic programming. Jeh and Widom (2003) proposed a personalized alternative of the PageRank algorithm PPV (Personalized PageRank Vector).

In Challam (2004), Speretta and Gauch (2004), and Teevan, Dumais, and Horvitz (2005), another oriented context approach of personalization of relevance measurement function is proposed. It consists of reordering the results provided by the process of selection by combining the order produced with the process of selection and that given by the user context, represented by a list of keywords resulting from the selected documents, via a calculation of similarity. Shen, Tan, and Zhai (2005) propose a probabilistic model of using access to the information of the sources of belief related to the contexts.

Discussion

We conclude that even though context has been more or less considered in many AI-related fields, and in different ways, defining context univocally is a hard issue. Although Giunchiglia and Bouquet (1996) attempted to give a unified definition, it proved to be too general, especially by defining context as an infinite set of "things." The importance of the notion of context in modeling human activities (reasoning, perception, language comprehension, etc.), as well as in social sciences and in computing, is an established fact. The traditional approaches of AI highlighted the theoretical difficulties associated with the formalization of this concept. Indeed, within the framework of representational AI theories, context can be identified with difficulty by a finished list of factors (Guha, 1991; McCarthy, 1993). These difficulties will be reflected on the proposition of a generic context definition.

We also notice that context is used for various goals with various granularities from knowledge represented as facts and rules to agent architecture through beliefs representation and reasoning.

We additionally observe that, in the proposals for using context, there is an absence of differentiation between the conceptual and the operational levels. These two levels are not taken into account and are often confused. We think that the conceptual and the operational levels should be differentiated while using context.

Many researchers consider context in its static form only—that is, context is considered as a fixed set of attributes to which they affect values thereafter. If the context is a set of beliefs, knowledge, or rules, these definitions consider context as the whole knowledge in an exhaustive way with relevant and not relevant knowledge. We also notice the absence of a context "building" approach.

Concerning context-aware systems, we notice that they present the same centralized architecture made up of three levels: a context recognition level, a context management level, and a use of context level. The first level collects information known as contextual from the surrounding physical environment via sensors and provides the context to the intermediate level. The intermediate level is composed of the context manager having a context base and an inference engine of reasoning on context. This level is called "context synthesizer" (Ranganathan & Campbell, 2003) in GAIA, "context broker" (Chen & Finin, 2003) in CoBrA, "context interpreter" (Gu et al., 2004) in SOCAM, and "context manager" (Bucur et al., 2005) in MySAM. The third and last level uses contexts managed by the second level by questioning the context manager for any necessary contextual knowledge. We think that such a centralized architecture presents disadvantages from a final use point of view.

We notice that the few approaches using agents in personalization and retrieval information do not present multi-agent architectures. In the project Cairsweb (Context-Aware Retrieval Information in the Semantic Web) (Woerndl & Groh, 2005), an attempt of an agent-based use for context-aware personalization in the Semantic Web is presented, but this published work misses the user and context model development. Moreover, all the approaches define context independently from environment architecture. They consider only the context user. However, the systems of information retrieval are deployed in a dynamic environment (the Web for example) using several components (number of connected machine, databases, devices, etc.) and other individuals. Thus, when taking context into account, the focus should not only be on the user context, but also on these components. Context could represent the processing power of peers and the network throughput, or it could be seen as the knowledge domain of the user or even the set of external interaction conditions. In a multi-agent architecture, it is necessary to try to model context from the point of view of the agent, taking into account simultaneously: the user, the environment, and physical or software components in the process of research.

DEFINING CONTEXT FOR MULTI-AGENT SYSTEM

Generic Context Definition

We suggest, hereafter, to define context as an abstract notion. Firstly, as shown in the previous section, defining and studying context depends highly on the field or *domain* and objectives of each study.

Secondly, we can say that context is an abstract concept because it has meaning only related to its object which we call the *entity of the context*. In fact, context is always related to an entity—for example the context of a sentence, the context of an agent, or the context of the user. Moreover, a given context exists only by existence of the entity to which it is related. The entity can be for example a proposition, a sentence, an object, a user, or a system.

Thirdly, it is noticeable that in all the aforementioned definitions, context is introduced mainly to facilitate comprehension, remove ambiguities, clear up a situation, help make a choice, enable and/or improve a decision-making process, select a choice, clarify a situation, contribute to interpretation, and optimize a treatment. To summarize, context is necessary to solve a *problem* within a particular field or *domain.*

Consequently, we state that any context depends on these three characterizing abstract components: *domain, entity,* and *problem.* In fact, given a specific *domain,* an *entity* which has (or is topic of) *a problem* requires a *context* to solve it. For example, in linguistics (domain) as soon as a sentence (entity) causes ambiguities (problem), we require a context for its comprehension. Also, in personalized information retrieval and access (domain), an information retrieval system or a search engine or a crawler agent requires identify-

ing user (entity) context to answer relevantly the user request (problem). In addition, in multi-agent systems (domain), an agent (entity) that needs to make a decision (problem) requires a context to reason and decide.

These three concepts are closely interdependent for the definition of each. In fact, an entity belongs to a domain and the problem can be explicitly defined only in one domain. A domain is characterized by a set of elements and a set of relations, functions, operations, and rules on the elements. For example, the linguistic domain is a set of words, sentences, languages, semantic rules, grammatical rules, spelling rules, and so forth. As we mentioned above, an entity is an element of a specific domain; it can be a datum, information, knowledge, object, set of objects, concept, agent, relation, user, system, and so forth. A problem is always related to an entity in a domain.

By defining context in this way, we provide a generic concept which may be adopted and specialized for each field. In what follows, we briefly study the mapping of our definition of context with those identified in the various fields. We take again the definition of context found in the literature by identifying the three concepts. For the notation, the **domain** is in bold, the *entity* is the part in italic, and the problem is the underlined part of definition:

- In **cognitive sciences**, Sperber and Wilson (1986) present the context like a manner of structuring *knowledge* and its use in problem resolution tasks.
- In **logic**, McCarthy (1987) states that all times that we fix an *axiom,* a criticism can say that the axiom is not true only in a certain context.
- In **logic** (McCarthy, 1993), *ist*(*c, p*) asserts that a *proposition p* is true in a context c, where c supposes capture all what is not explicit in p.
- In **AI**, Kokinov (1994) states: "Context is the whole of all the entities which influ-

ence the *human* cognitive behavior (or *the system*) on a particular occasion." We think that the problem is to make the situation particular.

- In **logic,** Motschnig-Pitrik (1995) states: "It seems often useful to represent the *situations* themselves *inside the model...*the denotation of a situation in a model is regarded as context...."

- In **logic,** Sharma (1995) states that the context of a set of logical sentences (a theory) is defined as: the assumptions of the environment which are not axiomatisables (*the problem is that we cannot axiomatize every thing*) and consequently are formalized as an abstracted object, relative so that the *language* (entity) and the sentences in this language are stated for the theory.

- In **knowledge representation and reasoning,** Giunchiglia and Bouquet (1996) define the context like a collection of (parameters, intentions, presuppositions, etc.). A possible *representation* will depend on this collection, since the principal interest is the design of formal systems for modeling the reasoning.

- Brown, Bovey, and Chen (1997), Pascoe (1998), and Dey, Salber, and Futakawa (1999) work on the **interactive systems**; their idea is that the context covers all information being able to be used for characterizing the situation of an *entity*.

- In **human machine interaction:**
  - For Schilit and Theimer (1994), studying the context is to answer the questions: Where are you? With whom are you? Which resources do you have in the proximity? In this case the *user* is the entity on which the context is dependent.
  - For Gaëtan (2001), the context at the moment t is the addition of the situations

between t_0 and t for the realization of the task T by the *user*.

- In **multi-agent systems,** Bucur (2004) defined the context like a pair made up of the finality and a set of contextual information called contextual attributes. In this definition, the entity is that which seeks to reach the finality.

Therefore, we can conclude that our abstract definition of context is general enough and embodies all previous definitions in a unified frame.

Specializing Context Definition for MAS

We notice that the proposed context definition is at the same time generic and abstract. It is defined at a conceptual level, and thus it can be used and applied only by the means of an approach, making it possible to get from the conceptual abstract level on a concrete operational one. We already mentioned the absence of approaches, allowing identification and building of adequate contexts to follow during the development of a system. On the basis of this context definition, we present below a process allowing definition and identification of the context for multi-agent systems. This process is made up of two interrelated phases:

1. We start by analyzing the domain of MAS to identify the set of entities and factors related to the problem to solve. We identify also possible relations between entities. We call this fist phase: *conceptualization.*

2. We then identify the possible contexts related to each entity. A context of an entity *e* is the set of entities and relations related to *e* and intervening directly or indirectly in the problem associated with *e*. We call this phase: *contextualization.*

Conceptualization

Let us first summarize the principal concepts related to a multi-agent system: a multi-agent system is composed of elements such as environment, objects, relations between objects, agents with their characteristics: knowledge, beliefs, intentions, desires, roles, goals, capacities, perception, reasoning, and so forth. By considering MAS definitions according to Demazeau (1995) and Ferber (1995), we can generalize the modeling of such a system according to three concepts: *agent, object,* and *relation*. From one point of view, we can define multi-agent system by the triplet *<Agent, Object, Relation>*.

We notice that objects encapsulate a broad part of knowledge on the world (environment) in which they evolve. The environment is largely described by the objects which constitute it. We can sometimes say that the environment exists only by the existence of objects which it contains.

From a conceptual view, the agent has knowledge relating to various objects which constitute the environment. The characteristics of these objects can be implicitly propagated in the environment and then considered as environment characteristics. We can then simplify the problem by assigning to the agent environment-related knowledge.

In suggested agent definitions (Shoham, 1993; Wooldridge & Jennings, 1995; Ferber, 1995; Demazeau, 1995; Russell, 1997), the agent must be able to perceive and act on environment, to communicate and interact with the other agents, to obey to a standard of organization. Thus, we can consider multi-agent systems as relations between agents themselves and objects constituting the environment. Indeed, we distinguish:

- Simple relations between two objects or a set of objects O^* *(1 or many),* for example an object is above another: *Relation = R (O*, O*).*

- Action of an agent on another one or an object is a relation between *actant* and the entity which undergoes action *{A, O}*. This relation has the capacity to change the entity state: *Action = R (A, {A, O}).*

- Perception of the environment (objects and other agents that surround the observer) is a relation between the agent and percept object which surrounds it (objects O^*, agents A^* perceived, and relations between them $R (A^*, O^*)$ and $R (O^*, O^*)$): *Perception = R (A, O*, A*, R (A*, O*), R (O*, O*)).*

- Interaction is a relation of exchange (communication and collaboration) between the agent and one or more agents A^*: *Interaction = R (A, A*).*

- Organization is a relation of structuring dependency between several cooperative agents A^* to carry out their common objective: *Organization = R (A*, A*).*

After this multi-agent domain analysis, it is obvious that the central entity of this domain is the agent which represents the principal *actant* in this case. Indeed, the tasks of resolution of identified problems will be assigned to various agents. The global problem resolution will be the common objective of the agent society, and the sub-problems resolution will be individual objectives and goals of agents. The resolution of a problem by an agent represents the *role* affected to it which will be used in an instantaneous *situation*. The agent must be able to reason dynamically in front of an evolutionary environment, and thus must be aware and sensitive to context.

Synthesis of the first phase: Context definition for MAS: An extensional point of view—We can thus from an extensional point of view define an agent context as a triplet *<Actant, Role, Situation>*. Indeed, we notice that *context* emerges as soon as *actant* needs to choose "the best" alternative to achieve its *role* in the frame of a *situation*. The agent (actant) is characterized by its knowledge and its capacities. An agent role is mainly a set of tasks, actions, and strategy. The situation represents the instantaneous environment in which agents perform their tasks and act according to strategies. One should not confuse context and situation, because the latter is included in the context and it is often regarded as instantaneous.

Contextualization: Context definition for MAS: An intentional point of view—In the preceding part we defined the conceptual model which is composed of agents, objects, and five kinds of relations: simple relation, perception, action, interaction, and organization. Let us now structure context contents according to entities and relations defined during the first phase. We point out that the entity is the agent and that agent-related context must then describe the system from entity point of view. An agent is characterized by its autonomy. However, an agent will have a subjective vision of context: its goal is to collect information (which requires a certain capacity of recognition of context) relating to his problem, in order to fix a resolution space; he or she will define the context like a set of conditions and surrounding influences, which make the situation single and make it possible to be understood (Brézillion, 1999).

Considering an agent *A*, we propose that the context must contain:

- Information on the agent *A* itself (its knowledge, its state, its goal, its beliefs and desires and intentions);
- Information on the environment perceived by *A*;
- Information on the perceived objects by *A* including the other agents;
- Information on the nature of known relations between objects from the agent point of view;
- Information on the nature of agents' operations; and
- Information on the other agents in relation to the considered agent.

In what follows, we introduce a set of attributes characterizing agent in context. The fundamental components of MAS are: *objects* and in particular *agents, relations* between the objects and in particular *action* or *operations* of the agents on

Figure 1. Context model for MAS (UML notation)

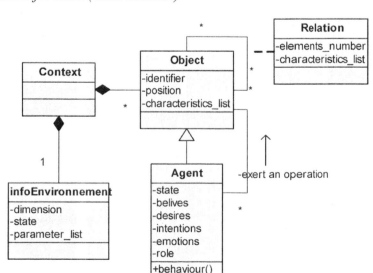

the objects, and information on *environment.* However, with each one of these components will be associated a set of information forming context. We underline that the context relates to the agent, and we describe therefore the components from the agent's point of view. Figure 1 presents a UML (Unified Modeling Language) diagram of this notion of context.

- The **object** is characterized by:
  o   an identifier;
  o   a position in the environment;
  o   a list of physical characteristics; and
  o   a set of relations with the other objects and especially other agents. A relation is characterized by the number of elements participating in the relation and by its type (Simple Relation, Interaction, Action, Organization).
- The **environment information** is characterized mainly by:
  o   dimensions;
  o   an environment state; and
  o   a parameter list related to the physical or/and concrete aspect of environment.
- The **agent from the point of view of the agent (actant)** is characterized by the same attributes as the object since it is a particular object. It is also mainly characterized by:
  o   a state;
  o   a set of beliefs, desires, intentions, knowledge, emotions; and
  o   its behavior (what it is doing and what it can do).

Knowledge Representation

Context must be closely related to an agent. Agent knowledge in mental agent representation must be represented according to this model. Each agent belonging to SMA builds progressively its mental and social representations according to its perception with these three concepts in the

form of a network, for example. In its simplest representation, a network consists of units, called *nodes* or *summits,* and relations with particular types which link them, called *links* or *arcs.* In the case of this representation, the nodes are of three types: *agent, object,* and *relation.* To simplify such a representation, we assume that the relations of perception are not taken into account in this representation because an agent cannot know what the other agents perceived. So we keep four kinds of relations: Simple Relation (R), Interaction (I), Action (A), and Organization (O).

Building and Using Context by an Agent

We describe in the following section the stages of the observation process of a context by an agent facing a problem in a situation:

1.   **Information collection:** Perception of the environment and other objects and especially other agents. The agent represents perceived knowledge and builds progressively its knowledge according to context model.
2.   **Context identification:** Reasoning to define context from acquired knowledge and of new collected knowledge and problem to solve. The defined context is an instance of the context model.
3.   **Context categorization:** Comparison between recognized context and existing contexts in a context base to benefit from the experiment.
4.   **Learning:** Addition of the new context in the base of contexts.

During process iteration, the agent builds its representation of the external world (environment) and acts in consequence on the environment to achieve its role. Consequently, the environment may evolve after the agents' actions; therefore, during the next iteration, an agent will perceive the new state of the environment and, consequently, will adapt its behavior accordingly.

Case Study: Agent-Based Virtual Environment of Accident Emergency Rescue

Description of the Case Study

In this case study, we intend to develop an agent-based simulator in order to support organizing emergency rescue plans of a large-scale accident. A catastrophic situation can be defined as a situation where there is brutal inadequacy between needs for help and available means. The purpose of rescue plans is to manage the rescue process in catastrophic situations and large-scale accidents. All rescuers collaborate to minimize losses by evacuating the highest number of victims and reducing delays.

In this study, decision making is far from being an easy task, especially in the case of social complex systems operating under many constraints and utilizing several human agents, several technical features which collaborate and cooperate according to evolutionary social networks, and via various communication networks.

In fact, these social agents must reason dynamically according to the system evolution and adapt their behavior to the current situation. In this case, the decision to be made depends on the experience of the decision maker and his or her capacity to recognize the situation where he or she is. These social agents must thus take into account context while reasoning. The analysis of real rescue activities has been conducted in collaboration with medical experts and based on French rescue plans—ORSEC (ORganisation de SECours: Rescue Organization), Red Plan (CDSP91 & SAMU91, 2000), White Plan (Ecollan, 1998)—in order to understand the collaborative process and the involved actors and features. Based on the emergency analysis, a first agent-based model and simulator was constructed (Bellamine-Ben Saoud, Ben Mena, & Dugdale, 2006).

Agentification

In Ben Mena, Bellamine-Ben Saoud, and Ben Ahmed (2006), we proposed an iterative approach of unification which allows defining a multi-agent model for complex social systems on the basis of field studies. This approach is based on two stages: a first stage of identification and a second one of iterative unification.

The principal of this approach is as follows:

Stage 1

Step 1: Identify the Real Actors: From the analysis of field data, we must build the set of all existing actors and all related roles in the organization.

Step 2: Identify the Relevant Criteria of Unification: According to the aim of the study, we define a set of criteria and sort them by priority. To identify such criterion, we consider at least five distinct dimensions related to the bricks of the Vowels approach (Demazeau, 1995) *{A, E, I, O, U}* as follows:

- A-criterion related to Agent (e.g., roles, goals, beliefs).
- E-criterion related to Environment (e.g., position, metric, objects).
- I-criterion related to Interactions (e.g., communication, operations).
- O-criterion related to Organization (e.g., cooperation, collaboration).
- U-criterion related to User (e.g., user profile, interactivity).

Stage 2

Step 3: Unify the Actors: by criterion of decreasing priority (apply from the criterion having the greatest priority to that having the weakest one).

Step 4: Repeat (3): until the unification becomes impossible.

Figure 2. Simulator architecture

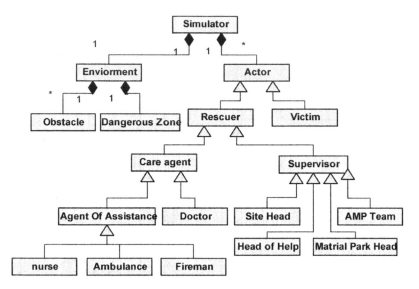

By applying this approach to our case study, we obtained a consistent agent model. A first iteration enabled us to move from 20 actors (18 human actors and 2 centers) to 11 actors to end up at the end of the second iteration with only 7 key agents. Consequently, we reduced the number of inter-communications from 34 to only **8**. Thus we reduced the complexity of the model while keeping the coherence of the original one (Ben Mena et al., 2006).

The resulting agent model is composed of an environment which represents the site of the accident, and actors who interact with the environment and with each other (Figure 2). An actor in the simulator can be a victim or a rescuer. The rescuers are divided into two types: (1) the decision makers, chiefs evolving in the site; and (2) the care agents. The latter are the doctors treating the victims, the nurses and the firemen who assist the doctors. We consider also the ambulance teams who transport victims to hospitals. The chiefs are of four types: the *head of rescue* who supervises the site, the *site head* who coordinates the rescue activities on the critical zone (disaster area of the site), the *AMP (advanced medical post)*

team represents the team assigned to the AMP, and finally the *material park head* is in charge of logistics.

Agent Knowledge Representation and Reasoning Based on Context Model

Figure 3 presents a network representing with semiformal notation knowledge of an *agent,* for example a fireman, which knows that:

- *Head of help* directs, organizes, and supervises the rescues and rescuers, especially the site head, park material head, and AMP team.
- *Site head* directs a team of three doctors—Doctor 1, Doctor 2, and Doctor 3—who collaborate together
- *Doctor 1* directs a team of three nurses and two firemen.
- *Doctor 2* is moving.
- *Doctor 3* treats a *victim* in position x = 10 and y=6.
- The *AMP team* asks the *material park head* for an *ambulance* for transporting *victim 2.*

Figure 3. An example of an agent (fireman) mental representation

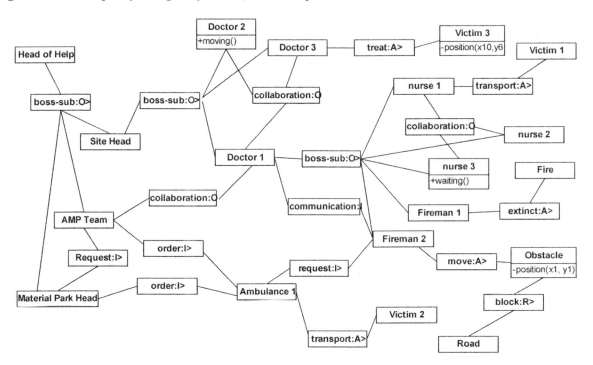

- *Doctor 1* asks *fireman 2* to move an *obstacle* blocking the *road 1*.
- *Fireman 1* extinguishes a *fire*.

Each sub-network can be considered as an instance of a context. In fact each sub-network is composed from instances of agents, objects, and relations. The agent must determine, according to the problem, the set of knowledge related to entities and relations which intervene and help in problem solving. We call this set *resolution context*.

Let us now take a sample of the observation context process for contextual reasoning: Suppose that a *trunk* blocks *road 1* near the *obstacle*, *doctor 1* orders the *fireman* "*to move the trunk*" (the problem for him). Figure 3 represents the knowledge of the fireman. We notice that the fireman is not aware of what a trunk is. The fireman is in front of two overlapping problems, the first is "*to move the trunk*," and the second is not being aware of what a trunk is. The context base of the fireman

is empty for the moment. To achieve his goal, the fireman needs the recognition of a context. He then carries out the process of observation of context from his point of view:

Stage 1: Information collection: After perception, the fireman updates his mental representation (Figure 4). The fireman adds that an unknown object blocks *road 1*.

Stage 2: Context identification *Context 1*: The fireman's problem is that *doctor 1* orders him to move the trunk. He is not aware what a trunk is. So he needs a context to solve his problem. He identifies the set of entities related to his problem (doctor 1, fireman 2, obstacle, road 1, unknown) and relations between them. Figure 4 shows the instance of context *context 1*:

- *Doctor 1* is the speaker.
- *Doctor 1* ordered *fireman 2* to move *obstacle*.
- *Doctor 1* is the boss of *fireman 1*.

Figure 4. A new instance of context after perception (update of Figure 3)

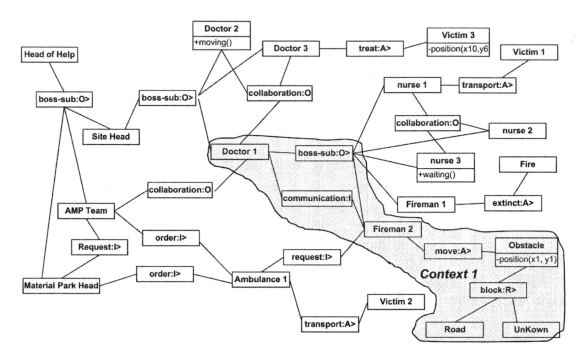

- *Fireman 2* is moving *obstacle*.
- *Obstacle* blocks *road 1*.
- *Unknown* blocks *road 1*.

Stage 3: Context categorization: The context base *CB* of the fireman is empty.

Stage 4: Learning: Add in *CB* the context *context 1* associated with the reasoning adopted. We try to present his reasoning:

1. I have the order to move an unknown object.
2. I can move.
3. The order is from *doctor 1*, and *doctor 1* is a boss ⇒ impossibility to reject the order.
4. What is a trunk?
5. I saw the object *unknown* blocking *road 1*.
6. *Doctor 1* ordered *fireman 2* to move *obstacle*.
7. *Doctor 1* is the boss of *fireman 2*.
8. The *obstacle* blocks *road 1*.
9. *Fireman 2* is moving the *obstacle*.
    ⇒ The unknown object can be the trunk.

In spite of the use of the *context 1,* the fireman could not define exactly what a trunk is. It can then:

1. Ask for an explanation from *doctor 1,* who can answer: *"Trunk = what blocking road 1."* Thus it can deduce from (5) that *unknown* = trunk and then update its knowledge and its *context 1.*
2. Or *fireman* takes the initiative to move *unknown.* In this case, firstly he is mistaken and *doctor 1* corrects him, which brings us to the higher behavior, or he is succeeded and at the end of a certain time it deduces that it was right and updates its knowledge.

FUTURE TRENDS

We can see the trends of research as the meeting point of several diverse fields: the personalized information retrieval, multi-agent systems, and the notion of context. A conceptual model of context for multi-agent systems is applicable to various fields, particularly personalized information retrieval. What would also be interesting, in addition to user context modeling, is the modeling of other contexts. Indeed, a user searches for Web documents produced by other users in different contexts, a possible matching between these various contexts would allow a more relevant research. What would also be noteworthy is the dynamic reasoning on this contextual information. Indeed, in an environment as dynamic as the Web, while crawling, agents must adapt their reasoning according to the global environment's evolution—the addition, suppression, displacement, or update of the documents—by giving more importance to the time dimension in the information retrieval.

We have shown throughout this chapter that the difficulties to define the context are due to the absence of a context construction approach. We have proposed a definition of context for multi-agent systems. On the basis of the domain of the SMA, this definition was closely related to the components of MAS. We think that it is possible to define a generic approach facilitating and allowing the definition of the context in a dynamic way for different other domains by identifying the set of entities and relations of the fixed field. This approach must allow the level crossing from the abstracted conceptual level to the concrete operational level. We did not limit ourselves only to future research, but these will enable us to specify other future trends. We distinguish in this research project two short-term perspectives stemming out from two axes. In the first axis of software engineering, we specify and improve the process of context identification in a methodology of taking into account context in the development of the context-sensitive applications. In this work, by fixing the field at the multi-agent systems, we could define the context model to be taken into account in these systems' development. We can thus think of applying this methodology to other fields such as personalized information retrieval and access with contextual search engines.

In the second axis of the multi-agent systems, we will be interested in the behavior models of context-sensitive agents. Knowledge representation and contextual reasoning allow agents to adapt their behaviors to situations. In a cooperative system, where several cognitive agents cooperate together with an aim of achieving a common goal (with the example of crawlers), these agents will adopt their behaviors according to the contexts: knowledge and competences of the other distributed agents. At the same time, cognitive entities are distributed; consequently knowledge is distributed and entities reasoning and decision making are situated—that is, the entity makes a decision in a particular situation and takes into account distributed and exchanged knowledge with the other entities. We are in the presence of cognitive, cooperative, distributed, and situated systems. It is the case of a new generation of search meta-engines which:

- Are *cognitive* by knowledge on users and their profiles (who change according to the context), and reasoning of decision making in the personalization information retrieval and access;

- *Cooperate* with other search engines specific to other fields—this cooperation requires the contextual pairing of ontology (another research field);

- Are *distributed* on the network through the mobile cognitive agents which take into account in their mobility and choice of their destination the starting context (profile of the user) and the instantaneous context (result of the cooperation); and

- Are *situated* because each component of these systems takes its local decisions according to its situation, and this action will have an impact on the system's global decisions.

CONCLUSION

Currently, there is no single definition of the concept of context. Researchers in various fields employ their own terminologies to define context and use such definitions for various aims. We have presented a general definition of context based on three characteristics: domain, entity, and problem. In fact, in a given domain, an entity requires a context to solve a problem. We also have presented two definitions of context multi-agent systems from extensional and intensional points of view. The extensional point of view presents context as a triplet *<Actant, Role, Situation>*. The intensional point of view defines context as a model based on agent, object, and relation. We also presented a case study showing an example where we made use of the suggested model of context. Then, based on this model, we proposed a knowledge representation of an agent, and context identification and reasoning process of a context-sensitive agent.

The proposed context model for multi-agent systems is generic. Thus, by choosing an application field and by opting for a multi-agent solution, we can instantiate the context model to be taken into account in this field. Indeed, we can extend the proposed context model to agent-based systems in the field of information retrieval and access. The agents would be user and/or profile agents, crawler agents, indexing agents, semantic agents, and so forth. The objects will be principally documents, databases having as attributes: physical, logical, and semantic descriptions, as well as social and cultural dimensions. As for relations, we will find the simple relations between documents as hypertext, and semantic link the organization and interaction relations between various agents.

FUTURE RESEARCH DIRECTIONS

In personalizing the behavior of any other system, there are three major stages one must go through, with each stage raising its own diverse set of problems: *user modeling,* where particular user characteristics, interests, preferences, abilities, and so forth, are identified as critical for the applications of concern and placed within an appropriate framework or model; *user profiling,* where, through observations of a user's behavior or through direct input, a particular profile for the user is created following the structure of the user model of choice; and *personalization,* where the particular profile is used to modify some aspects of the system behavior. These three stages may be similarly identified for contextualization, giving rise to analogous sets of research problems. Furthermore, exploring the possible relations between contextualization and personalization is of particular interest. First, contextualization can be used as a personalization mechanism by viewing a user's profile as a particular case of context. Alternatively, users may have different profiles depending on the context in which they operate each time.

The multi-agent systems field also relates to the design engineering of systems composed of a set of autonomous entities (agents) in interaction with each other and with their environment, and having to carry out a given task collectively. It proposes models, methodologies, techniques, and tools to answer various problems such as the development of the decentralized information processing systems where the MAS approach allows flexible integration and the cooperation of software and autonomous services. Several problems considered as fundamental to the MAS, such as the artificial intelligence, target the topic of the models of behaviors, which is a current subject of research for the implementation of evolved behavior and reasoning; of balance between individual decision and group decision, like cooperative information retrieval; and finally for which it is necessary to add a contextual dimension.

REFERENCES

Agentlink Roadmap. (2005). Retrieved from *http://www.agentlink.org/roadmap/*

Allan, J., Jay Aslam, J., & Belkin, N. (2002). Challenges in information retrieval and language modeling. *Proceedings of the Workshop held at the Center for Intelligent Information Retrieval.*

Attardi, G., & Simi, M. (1995). A formalisation of viewpoints. *Fundamenta Informatica, 23*(2–4), 149–174.

Ballim, A., & Wilks, Y. (1991). *Artificial believers: The ascription of belief.* Hillsdale, NJ: Lawrence Erlbaum.

Bellamine-Ben Saoud, N., Ben Mena, T., & Dugdale, J. (2006) Assessing large scale emergency rescue plans: An agent based approach. *International Journal of Intelligent Control and Systems, 11*(4), 260–271.

Benerecetti, M., Bouquet, P., & Ghidini, C. (1998a). Formalizing belief reports—the approach and a case study. In F. Giunchiglia (Ed.), *Proceedings of the 8th International Conference on Artificial Intelligence, Methodology, Systems, and Applications* (pp. 62–75). Berlin: Springer-Verlag.

Benerecetti, M., Giunchiglia, F., & Serafini, L. (1998b). Model checking multiagent systems. *Journal of Logic and Computation, Special Issue on Computational and Logical Aspects of Multiagent Systems, 8*(3), 401–423.

Ben Mena, T., Bellamine-Ben Saoud, N., & Ben Ahmed, M. (2006). Towards a unification approach for agent based modeling of complex social systems. *Proceedings of the 17th IASTED International Conference on Modeling and Simulation.*

Bouquet, P., Ghidini, C., & Giunchiglia, F. (2003). Theories and uses of context in knowledge representation and reasoning. *Journal of Pragmatics, 35*(3), 455–484.

Bouquet, P., & Giunchiglia, F. (1995). Reasoning about theory adequacy. A new solution to the qualification problems. *Fundamenta Informaticae, 23*(2–4), 247–262.

Brézillon, P. (1999). Context in artificial intelligence: I. A survey of the literature. *Knowledge Engineering Review, 14*(1), 1–34.

Brown, P.J., Bovey, J.D., & Chen, X. (1997). Context-aware applications: From the laboratory to the marketplace. *IEEE Personal Communications,* 58–64.

Bucur, O. (2004). *Modélisation du contexte pour un apprentissage multi-agent des préférences utilisateurs.* Unpublished Doctoral Dissertation, High National School of Saint Étienne, France.

Bucur, O., Beaune, P., & Boissier, O. (2005). Representing context in an agent architecture for context-based decision making. In L. Serafini & P. Bouquet (Eds.), Proceedings of the CRR'05 Workshop on Context Representation and Reasoning.

Buvač, S. (1996). Quantificational logic of context. *Proceedings of the 30th American National Conference on Artificial Intelligence.*

Buvač, S., & Mason, I.A. (1993). Propositional logic of context. *Proceedings of the 11th American National Conference on Artificial Intelligence* (pp. 412–419).

CDSP91 & SAMU91. (2000). *Plan rouge: Plan destiné porter secours de nombreuses victimes.* France.

Challam, V.K.R. (2004). *Contextual information retrieval using ontology based user profiles.* Hyderabad, India: Jawaharlal Nehru Technological University.

Chen, H., & Finin, T. (2003). An ontology for context-aware pervasive computing environments. *The Knowledge Engineering Review, 18*(3), 197–207.

Cimatti, A., & Serafini, L. (1995). Multi-agent reasoning with belief contexts: The approach and a case study. In M. Wooldridge & N.R. Jennings (Eds.), *Intelligent Agents, Proceedings of the Workshop on Agent Theories, Architectures, and Languages* (pp. 71–85).

Cool, C. & Spink, A. (2002). Issues of context in information retrieval: An introduction to the special issue. *Journal of Information Processing and Management, 38*(55), 605–611.

Demazeau, Y. (1995). From interactions to collective behaviour in agent-based systems. *Proceedings of the 1st European Conference on Cognitive Science* (pp. 117-132), Saint Malo, France.

Dey, A.K., Salber, D., & Futakawa, M. (1999). *An architecture to support context-aware applications.* Technical Report GIT-GVU-99-23, Georgia Institute of Technology, USA.

Dumais, S., Cadiz Cuttrel, E., & Jancke, J.J. (2003). Stuff I've seen: A system for a personal information retrieval and reuse. *Proceedings of the 26th ACM SIGIR International Conference on Research and Development* (pp. 72–79).

Ecollan, P. (1989). *Le plan blanc.* Unpublished Doctoral Dissertation, Faculty of Medicine, PITIESALPETRIERE, France.

Edmonds, B. (2002). Learning and exploiting context in agents. *Proceedings of the 1st International Joint Conference on Autonomous Agents and Multiagent Systems* (AAMAS'02) (pp. 1231–1238).

Fan, W., Gordon, M.D., & Pathak, P. (2004). *Discovery of context specific ranking functions for effective information retrieval using genetic programming* (vol. 16, pp. 523–527).

Farquhar, A., Dappert, J., & Fikes, R. (1995). *Integrating information sources using context logic.* Technical Report KSL-95-12, Knowledge Systems Laboratory, USA.

Ferber, J. (1995). *Les systèmes multi-agents, vers une intelligence collective.* InterEditions.

Gaëtan, R. (2001). *Systèmes interactifs sensibles au contexte.* Unpublished Doctoral Dissertation, Polytechnic National Institute of Grenoble, France.

Ghidini, C., & Giunchiglia, F. (2001). Local models semantics, or contextual reasoning = locality + compatibility. *Artificial Intelligence, 127*(4), 221–259.

Giunchiglia, E., & Giunchiglia, F. (1996). Ideal and real belief about belief. *Proceedings of the International Conference on Formal and Applied Practical Reasoning* (pp. 261–275).

Giunchiglia, F. (1993). Contextual reasoning. *Proceedings of the IJCAI'93 Workshop on Using Knowledge in its Context* (pp. 39–48).

Giunchiglia, F., & Bouquet, P. (1996). Introduction to contextual reasoning: An artificial intelligence perspective. In B. Kokinov (Ed.), *Perspectives on cognitive science* (vol. 3, pp. 138–159). Sofia: NBU Press.

Giunchiglia, F., & Serafini, L. (1994). Multi-language hierarchical logics (or: how we can do without modal logics). *Artificial Intelligence, 65,* 29–70.

Gu, T., Wang, X.H., & Pung, H.K. (2004). An ontology-based context model in intelligent environments. *Proceedings of the Communication Networks and Distributed Systems Modeling and Simulation Conference,* San Diego, CA.

Guha, R.V. (1991). *Contexts: A formalization and some applications.* Unpublished Doctoral Dissertation, Stanford University, USA.

Hendrix, G. (1979). Encoding knowledge in partitioned networks. In N. Findler (Ed.), *Associative networks.* New York: Academic Press.

Hirst, G. (1997). Context as a spurious concept. *Unpublished Invited Talk at the AAAI Fall Sym-*

posium on Context in Knowledge Representation and Natural Language, Cambridge, MA.

Hoffmann, P. (2004). *Appariement contextuel d'ontologies.* Unpublished Doctoral Dissertation, University of Claude Bernard, France.

Jeh, G., & Widom, J. (2003). Scaling personalized Web search. *Proceedings of the 12th International World Wide Web Conference* (pp. 271–279).

Kaplan, D. (1978). On the logic of demonstratives. *Journal of Philosophical Logic, 8,* 81–98.

Kelly, N.J. (2004). *Understanding implicit feedback and document preference: A naturalistic study.* Unpublished Doctoral Dissertation, Rutgers University, USA.

Kokinov, B. (1994). The context-sensitive cognitive architecture DUAL. *Proceedings of 16th Annual Conference of the Cognitive Science Society.*

Kokinov, B. (1995). A dynamic approach to context modelling. In P. Brezillon & S. Abu-Hakima (Eds.), *Working Notes of the IJCAI-95 Workshop on Modelling Context in Knowledge Representation and Reasoning,* Montreal, Canada.

Lenat, D.B. (1993). Context dependence of representations in CYC. *Proceedings of Colloque ICO'93,* Montréal, Canada.

Lenat, D.B., Sierra, C., & Guha, R.V. (1990). Cyc: Toward programs with common sense. *Communications of the ACM, 33*(8), 30–49.

McCarthy, J. (1993). Notes on formalizing context. *Proceedings of the 13th International Joint Conference on Artificial Intelligence* (pp. 555–560), Chambery, France.

McGowan, J.P. (2003). *A multiple model approach to personalised information access.* Unpublished Doctoral Dissertation, Faculty of Science, University College Dublin, Ireland.

Motschnig-Pitrik, R. (1995). An integrated view on the viewing abstraction: Contexts and perspectives in software development, AI, and databases. *Journal of Systems Integration 5*(1), 23–60.

Mylopoulos, J., & Motschnig-Pitrik, R. (1995). Partitioning information bases with contexts. *Proceedings of CoopIS'95* (pp. 44–55), Vienna, Austria.

Parsons, S., Jennings, N.R., & Sabater, J. (2002). *Agent specification using multi-context systems.*

Parsons, S., Sierra, C., & Jennings, N.R. (1998). Multi-context argumentative agents. *Proceedings of the 4th International Symposium on Logical Formalizations of Commonsense Reasoning.*

Pascoe, J. (1998). Adding generic contextual capabilities to wearable computers. *Proceedings of the 2nd International Symposium on Wearable Computers* (pp. 92–99).

Ranganathan, A., & Campbell, R.H. (2003). *An infrastructure for context-awareness based on first order logic.* London: Springer-Verlag.

Roberts, D.D. (1973). *The existential graphs of Charles S. Peirce.* The Hague: Mouton.

Russell, S.J. (1997). Rationality and intelligence. *Artificial Intelligence, 94,* 57–77.

Schilit, B.N., & Theimer, M. (1994). Disseminating active map information to mobile hosts. *IEEE Network,* 22–32.

Sharma, N. (1995). *On formalizing and reasoning with contexts.* Technical Report, Department of Computer Science, University of Queensland, Australia.

Shen, X., Tan, B., & Zhai, J.C. (2005). Context-sensitive information retrieval using implicit feedback. *Proceedings of the 29th Annual International ACM SIGIR Conference on Research and Development in Information Retrieval* (pp. 43–50).

Shoham, Y. (1993). Agent-oriented programming. *Artificial Intelligence, 60,* 51–92.

Sowa, J.F. (1995). Syntax, semantics, and pragmatics of context. *Proceedings of the 3rd International Conference on Conceptual Structures* (ICCS'95) (pp. 1–15), Santa Cruz, CA. Berlin: Springer-Verlag (LNAI 954).

Sperber, D., & Wilson, D. (1986). *Relevance: Communication and cognition.* Basil Blackwell.

Speretta, M., & Gauch, S. (2004). Personalizing search based user search histories. *Proceedings of the 13th International Conference on Information Knowledge and Management* (CIKM) (pp. 238–239).

Su, J., & Lee, M. (2003). An exploration in personalized and context-sensitive search. *Proceedings of the 7th Annual UK Special Interest Group for Computational Linguists Research Colloquium.*

Tamine, L., Boughanem, M., & Chrisment, C. (2006). Accès personnalisé à l'information: Vers un modèle basé sur les diagrammes d'influence. *Information—Interaction—Intelligence, 6*(1), 69–90).

Teevan, J., Dumais, S., & Horvitz, E. (2005). Personalizing search via automated analysis of interests and activities. *Proceedings of the 28th Annual ACM Conference on Research and Development in Information Retrieval* (pp.449–456).

Theodorakis, M., & Spyratos, N. (2002). Context in artificial intelligent and information modeling. *Proceedings of the 2nd Hellenic Conference on AI* (SETN-2002) (companion vol., pp. 27–38).

Weyhrauch, R.W. (1980). Prolegomena to a theory of mechanized formal reasoning. *Artificial Intelligence, 13*(1), 133–176.

Woerndl, W., & Groh, G. (2005). A proposal for an agent-based architecture for context-aware personalization in the Semantic Web. *Proceedings of the 9th International Joint Conference on Artificial Intelligence, Multi-Agent Information Retrieval and Recommender Systems* (pp. 75–79).

Wooldridge, M., & Jennings, N.R. (1995). Agent theories, architectures, and languages. In *Intelligent agents* (pp.1–22). Berlin: Springer-Verlag.

ADDITIONAL READING

Boughanem, M., Chrisment, C., & Tamine, L. (2002). On using genetic algorithms for multimodal relevance optimization in information retrieval. *Journal of American Society in Information Systems, 53*(11), 934–942.

Bouquet, P., & Serafini, L. (2001). Two formalizations of context: A comparison. *Proceedings of the 3rd International and Interdisciplinary Conference on Modelling and Using Context* (CONTEXT'01). Berlin: Springer-Verlag (LNAI 2116).

Bouquet, P., & Serafini, L., (2003). On the difference between bridge rules and lifting axioms. *Proceedings of the 4th International and Interdisciplinary Conference on Modeling and Using Context* (pp. 80–93). Berlin: Springer-Verlag (LNAI 2680).

Bouzeghoub, M., & Kostadinov, D. (2005). Personnalisation de l'information: Aperçu de l'état de l'art et définition d'un modèle flexible de définition de profils. *Actes de la 2nde Conférence en Recherche d'Information et Applications* (pp. 201–218).

Brézillion, P. (2003). Context dynamic and explanation in contextual graphs. In P. Blackburn, C. Ghidini, R.M. Turner, & F. Giunchiglia (Eds.), *Proceedings of CONTEXT'03* (pp. 94–106). Berlin: Springer-Verlag (LNAI 2680).

Brini, A., Boughanem, M., & Dubois., D. (2005). A model for information retrieval based on possibilistic networks. *Proceedings of the Symposium on String Processing and Information Retrieval* (SPIRE) (pp. 271–282).

Carver, L., & Turoff, M. (2007). Human-computer interaction: The human and computer as a team in emergency management information systems. *Communications of the ACM, 50*(3), 33–38.

Coutaz, J., Crowley, J.L., & Dobson, S. (2005). Context is key. *Communications of the ACM, 48*(3), 49–53.

Deloach, S.A. (2005). Multiagent systems engineering of organization-based multiagent systems. *Proceedings of SELMAS'05 at ICSE'05,* St. Louis, MO.

DeSaeger, S., & Shimojima, A. (2005). Contextual reasoning in concept spaces. *Proceedings of CONTEXT'05.*

Ferber, J., Michel, F., & Baez, J. (2005). AGRE: Integrating environments with organizations. In Weyns et al. (Eds.) (2005a). Berlin: Springer-Verlag.

Fiedrich, F., & Burghardt, P. (2007). Agent-based systems for disaster management. *Communications of the ACM, 50*(3), 41–42.

Helleboogh, A., Vizzari, G., & Uhrmacher, A. (2007). Modeling dynamic environments in multi-agent simulation. *Journal of Autonomous Agent Multi-Agent Systems 14,* 87–116.

Hernandez, N., Mothe, J., & Chrisment, C. (2007). Modeling context through domain ontologies. *Journal of Information Retrieval,* (Special Issue on Contextual Information Retrieval).

Lin, C., Xue, G.R., & Zeng, H.J. (2005). Using probabilistic latent semantic analysis for personalised Web search. *Proceedings of the APWeb Conference* (pp. 707–711).

Marc, F. (2005). *Planification multi-agent sous contraintes dans un contexte dynamique.* Unpublished Doctoral Dissertation, Doctoral School of Computer Science and Telecommunication, University Pierre and Marie Curie, France.

Nair, R., & Tambe, M. (2005). Hybrid BDI-POMDP framework for multiagent teaming. *Journal of AI Research, 23,* 367–420.

Nakayama, L., Nóbile de Almeida, V., & Vicari, R. (2004). A personalized information retrieval service for an educational environment, In J.C. Lester et al. (Eds.), *Proceedings of ITS 2004* (pp. 842–844). Berlin: Springer-Verlag (LNCS 3220).

Pasquier, L., Brezillon, P., & Pomerol, J.C. (2003). Learning and explanation in a context-sensitive adaptive support system. In C. Faucher, L. Jain, & N. Ichalkaranje (Eds.), *Innovative knowledge engineering.* Berlin: Springer-Verlag.

Schelfthout, K., Holvoet, T., & Berbers, Y. (2005). Views: Customizable abstractions for context-aware applications in MANETs. *Proceedings of the 4th International Workshop on Software Engineering for Large-Scale Multiagent Systems* (SELMAS 2005), St. Louis, MO.

Tamine, L., & Bahsoun, W. (2006). Définition d'un profil multi-dimensionnel de l'utilisateur: Vers une technique basée sur l'interaction entre dimensions. *Actes de la 3ème Conférence en Recherche d'Information et Application.*

Weyns, D., Omicini, A., & Odell, J. (2007). Environment as a first class abstraction in multiagent systems. *Journal of Autonomous Agent Multi-Agent Systems, 14,* 5–30.

Zacarias, M., Sofia Pinto, H., & Tribolet, J. (2005). *Notion, theories and models of context: Engineering, cognitive and social perspectives.* Technical Report.

Compilation of References

Abidi, S., & Chong, Y. (2004). Constraint satisfaction methods for information personalization. *Lecture Notes in Artificial Intelligence, 3060,* 261–276.

Abidi, S.S.R., & Zeng, Y. (2006). Intelligent information personalization leveraging constraint satisfaction and association rule methods. In L. Lamontagne & M. Marchand (Eds.), *Proceedings of Canadian AI 2006* (pp. 134–145). Berlin: Springer-Verlag (LNAI 4013).

Abowd, G., Atkeson, C., Hong, J., Long, S., Kooper, R., & Pinkerton, M. (1997). Cyberguide: A mobile context-aware tour guide. *ACM Wireless Networks.*

Ackerman, M., Darrell, T., & Weitzner, D.J. (2001). Privacy in context. *HCI, 16*(2), 167–179.

Adomavicius, G., & Tuzhilin, A. (2005). Towards the next generation of recommender systems: A survey of the state-of-the-art and possible extensions. *IEEE Transactions on Knowledge and Data Engineering, 17*(6), 734–749.

Agentlink Roadmap. (2005). Retrieved from *http://www.agentlink.org/roadmap/*

Aggarwal, C.C., Wolf, J.L., Wu, K.-L., & Yu, P.S. (1999). Horting hatches an egg: A new graph-theoretic approach to collaborative filtering. *Proceedings of the ACM SIGKDD International Conference on Knowledge Discovery and Data Mining.*

Agrawal, R., & Kiernan, J. (2002). Watermarking relational databases. *Proceedings of the 28th VLDB Conference,* Hong Kong, China.

Agrawal, R., & Srikant, R. (1994). Fast algorithms for mining association rules. *Proceedings of the 20th VLDB Conference,* Santiago, Chile (pp. 487-499).

Agrawal, R., Imielinski, T., & Swami, A. (1993). Mining association rules between sets of items in large fatabases. *Proceedings of the ACM SIGMOD International Conference on Management of Data* (pp. 207-216).

Agrawala, A.K., Larsen, R.L., & Szajda, D. (2000). Information dynamics: An information-centric approach to system design. *Proceedings of the International Conference on Virtual Worlds and Simulation,* San Diego, CA.

Aha, D.W., Kibler, D., & Albert, M.K. (1991). Instance-based learning algorithms. *Machine Learning, 6,* 37–66.

Ahn, H.J., Lee, H., & Park, S.J. (2003). A flexible agent system for change adaptation in supply chains. *Expert Systems with Applications, 25*(4), 603–618.

Alahakoon, D., Halgamuge, S.K., & Srinivasan, B. (2000). Dynamic self-organizing-maps with controlled growth for knowledge discovery. *IEEE Transactions on Neural Networks, 11*(3), 601–614.

Alchourron, C.E., Gärdenfors, P., & Makinson, D. (1985). On the logic of theory change: Partial meet contraction and revision functions. *Journal of Symbolic Logic, 50*(2), 510–530.

Ali Eldin, A. (2006). *Private information sharing under uncertainty.* Delft: Amr Ali Eldin.

Ali Eldin, A., van den Berg, J., & Wagenaar, R. (2004). A fuzzy reasoning scheme for context sharing decision making. *Proceedings of the 6th International Conference on Electronic Commerce* (pp. 371–375), Delft, The Netherlands. Retrieved from http://doi.acm.org/10.1145/1052220.1052267

Allan, J., Jay Aslam, J., & Belkin, N. (2002). Challenges in information retrieval and language modeling. *Proceedings of the Workshop held at the Center for Intelligent Information Retrieval.*

Allen, P., & Frost, S. (1998). *Component-based development for enterprise systems applying the SELECT perspective.* Cambridge: Cambridge University Press.

Alon, I. (2003). *Chinese culture, organizational behavior, and international business management.* Westport, CT: Greenwood.

Ambrosini, L., Cirillo, V., & Micarelli, A. (1997). A hybrid architecture for user-adapted information filtering on the World Wide Web. *Proceedings of the 6th International Conference on User Modelling (UM'97)* (pp. 59-61). Springer-Verlag.

Andrews, S., Tsochantaridis, I., & Hofmann, T. (2003). Support vector machines for multiple-instance learning. In S. Becker, S. Thrun, & K. Obermayer (Eds.), *Advances in neural information processing systems* (vol. 15, pp. 561–568). Cambridge, MA: MIT Press.

Ankolekar, A., Seo, Y.-W., & Sycara, K. (2003). Investigating semantic knowledge for text learning. *Proceedings of the ACM SIGIR Workshop on the Semantic Web.* Retrieved from http://www-cgi.cs.cmu.edu/~softagents/papers/ywseo_sigir_03.pdf

ANSI. (2000). *ANSI/IEEE 1471-2000 recommended practice for architectural description of software-intensive systems.* Retrieved from http://shop.ieee.org/store/

Ardissono, L., Goy, A., & Petrone, G. (2003). Enabling conversations with Web services. *Proceedings of the 2nd International Joint Conference on Autonomous Agents & Multi-Agent Systems (AAMAS'2003),* Melbourne, Australia.

Armstrong, R., Joachims, D., Freitag, D., & Mitchell, T. (1995). WebWatcher: A learning apprentice for the World Wide Web. *Proceedings of the AI Spring Symposium on Information Gathering from Heterogeneous, Distributed Environments,* Stanford, California, USA (pp. 6-13).

Ashforth, B.E. (2001). *Role transitions in organizational life: An identity-based perspective.* Mahwah, NJ: Lawrence Erlbaum.

Asthana, A., Cravatts, M., & Kryzyzanowski, P. (1994). An indoor wireless system for personalized shopping assistance. *Proceedings of the IEEE Workshop on Mobile Computing Systems and Applications,* Santa Cruz, CA.

Atoji, Y., Koiso, T., & Nishida, S. (2000). Information filtering for emergency management. *Proceedings of the 2000 IEEE International Workshop on Robot and Human Interactive Communication.*

Attardi, G., & Simi, M. (1995). A formalisation of viewpoints. *Fundamenta Informatica, 23*(2–4), 149–174.

Bachimont, B., Isaac, A., & Troncy, R. (2002). Semantic commitment for designing ontologies: A proposal. *Proceedings of the 13th International Conference on Knowledge Engineering and Knowledge Management. Ontologies and the Semantic Web* (EKAW'02) (pp. 114–121). London: Springer-Verlag.

Back, R.J.R., & Sere, K. (1996). From action systems to modular systems. *Software—Concepts and Tools.*

Back, R.J.R., & Wright, J. (1998). *Refinement calculus: A systematic introduction.* Berlin: Springer-Verlag (Graduate Texts in Computer Science).

Baeza-Yates, R., & Ribeiro-Neto, B. (1999). *Modern information retrieval.* Boston: Addison-Wesley-Longman.

Baeza-Yates, R., Castillo, C., Marin, M., & Rodriguez, A. (2005). Crawling a country: Better strategies than breadth-first for Web page ordering. *Proceedings of the Industrial and Practical Experience Track of the 14th Conference on the World Wide Web* (pp. 864–872), Chiba, Japan.

Balabanovic, M., & Shoham, Y. (1997). Content-based collaborative recommendation. *Communications of the ACM, 40*(3), 66-72.

Baldi, P., Frasconi, P., & Smyth, P. (2003). *Modeling the Internet and the Web.* New York: Wiley.

Ballim, A., & Wilks, Y. (1991). *Artificial believers: The ascription of belief.* Hillsdale, NJ: Lawrence Erlbaum.

Banerjee, A., & Ghosh, J. (2001). Clickstream clustering using weighted longest common subsequences. *Proceedings of the Workshop on Web Mining, SIAM Conference on Data Mining*, 33-40.

Barkhuus, L., & Dey, A. (2003). Is context-aware computing taking control away from the user? Three levels of interactivity examined. *Proceedings of the 5th International Conference on Ubiquitous Computing (UbiComp'2003)*, Seattle, Washington.

Barnes, P., & Oloruntoba, R. (2005). Assurance of security in maritime supply chains: Conceptual issues of vulnerability and crisis management. *Journal of Information Management, 11*, 519–540.

Barosha, N., & Waling, L. (2005). *A service for supporting relief workers in the port, the final assignment in the course of Service Systems Engineering in 2004-2005.* Faculty of Technology, Policy and Management, Delft University of Technology Delft, The Netherlands.

Bar-Yossef, Z., & Rajagopalan, S. (2002). Template detection via data mining and its applications. *Proceedings of the 11th International World Wide Web Conference (WWW2002)* (pp. 580-591).

Barzilay, R., McKeown, K., & Elhadad, M. (1999). Information fusion in the context of multi-document summarization. *Proceedings of the 37th Annual Meeting of the Association for Computational Linguistics on Computational Linguistics* (pp. 550–557).

Baudisch, P. (2001). *Dynamic information filtering.* PhD Thesis, Darmstad Technical University (GMD Research Series, 16), Germany.

Becht, M., Gurzki, T., Klarmann, J., & Muscholl, M. (1999). ROPE: Role oriented programming environment

for multiagent systems. *Proceedings of the 4th IECIS International Conference of Cooperative Information Systems* (pp. 325–333).

Belkin, N.J. (1984). Cognitive models and information transfer. *Social Science Information Studies, 4*, 111–129.

Belkin, N.J., & Croft, W.B. (1992). Information filtering and information retrieval: Two sides of the same coin? *Communications of the ACM, 35*(12), 29–38.

Bellamine-Ben Saoud, N., Ben Mena, T., & Dugdale, J. (2006) Assessing large scale emergency rescue plans: An agent based approach. *International Journal of Intelligent Control and Systems, 11*(4), 260–271.

Bellavista, P., Corradi, A., & Stefanelli, C. (2001). Mobile agent middleware for mobile computing. *IEEE Computer, 34*(3), 73–81.

Bellavista, P., Corradi, A., Montanari, R., & Stefanelli, C. (2003). Context-aware middleware for resource management in the wireless Internet. *IEEE Transactions on Software Engineering, Special Issue on Software Engineering for the Wireless Internet, 29*(12).

Ben Mena, T., Bellamine-Ben Saoud, N., & Ben Ahmed, M. (2006). Towards a unification approach for agent based modeling of complex social systems. *Proceedings of the 17th IASTED International Conference on Modeling and Simulation.*

Benatallah, B., Casati, F., & Toumani, F. (2004). Web service conversation modeling: A cornerstone for e-business automation. *IEEE Internet Computing, 8*(1).

Benatallah, B., Sheng, Q. Z., & Dumas, M. (2003). The self-serv environment for Web services composition. *IEEE Internet Computing, 7*(1).

Benerecetti, M., Bouquet, P., & Ghidini, C. (1998a). Formalizing belief reports—the approach and a case study. In F. Giunchiglia (Ed.), *Proceedings of the 8th International Conference on Artificial Intelligence, Methodology, Systems, and Applications* (pp. 62–75). Berlin: Springer-Verlag.

Benerecetti, M., Giunchiglia, F., & Serafini, L. (1998b). Model checking multiagent systems. *Journal of Logic and Computation, Special Issue on Computational and Logical Aspects of Multiagent Systems, 8*(3), 401–423.

Benferhat, S., Kaci, S., Berre, D.L., & Williams, M.-A. (2004). Weakening conflicting information for iterated revision and knowledge integration. *Artificial Intelligence, 153*(1–2), 339-371.

Berardi, D., Calvanese, D., De Giacomo, G., Lenzerini, M., & Mecella, M. (2003). A foundational vision for e-services. *Proceedings of the Workshop on Web Services, e-Business, and the Semantic Web (WES'2003) held in conjunction with the 15th Conference On Advanced Information Systems Engineering (CAiSE'2003)*, Klagenfurt/Velden, Austria.

Berendt, B., Hotho, A., & Stumme, G. (2002). Towards semantic Web mining. In I. Horrocks & J. Hendler (Eds.), *Proceedings of the ISWC 2002, LNCS 2342* (pp. 264-278). Springer-Verlag Berlin.

Berkhin, P. (2002). *Survey of clustering data mining techniques.* Technical Report, Accrue Software, USA. Retrieved from http://www.accrue.com/products/rp_cluster_review.pdf

Bimbo, A. (1999). *Visual information retrieval.* San Francisco: Morgan Kaufmann.

Bloehdorn, S., Cimiano, P., & Hotho, A. (2006, March 9–11). Learning ontologies to improve text clustering and classification. In M. Spiliopoulou, R. Kruse, A. Nurnberger, C. Borgelt, & W. Gaul (Eds.), *From Data and Information Analysis to Knowledge Engineering: Proceedings of the 29th Annual Conference of the German Classification Society* (GFKL 2005) (vol. 30, pp. 334–341), Magdeburg, Germany. Berlin: Springer-Verlag.

Blom, J. (2000). Personalization - A taxonomy. *Proceedings of the CHI 2000 Workshop on Designing Interactive Systems for 1-to-1 Ecommerce.* New York: ACM. Available: http://www.zurich.ibm.com/~mrs/chi2000/

Bloodsworth, P., & Greenwood, S. (2005). COSMOA: An ontology-centric multi-agent system for coordinating

medical responses to large-scale disasters. *AI Communications, 18,* 229–240.

Borgatti, S.P., & Cross, R. (2003). A relational view of information seeking and learning in social networks. *Management Science, 49*(4), 432–445.

Borges, J.L. (1979). *Borges oral, emcee.* Buenos Aires: Alianza.

Borgman, C. (1999). What are digital libraries? Competing visions. *Information Processing and Management: An International Journal, 35*(5), 227–243.

Borst, P. (1997). *Construction of engineering ontologies for knowledge sharing and reuse.* Unpublished Doctoral Dissertation, Universiteit Twente, the Netherlands.

Bostrom, R.P. (1980). Role conflict and ambiguity: Critical variables in the MIS user-designer relationship. *Proceedings of the 17th Annual Computer Personnel Research Conference* (pp. 88–115), Miami, FL.

Botha, R.A., & Eloff, J.H.P. (2001). Designing role hierarchies for access control in workflow systems. *Proceedings of the 25th Annual International Computer Software and Applications Conference* (COMPSAC'01) (pp. 117–122), Chicago, IL.

Bouquet, P., & Giunchiglia, F. (1995). Reasoning about theory adequacy. A new solution to the qualification problems. *Fundamenta Informaticae, 23*(2–4), 247–262.

Bouquet, P., Ghidini, C., & Giunchiglia, F. (2003). Theories and uses of context in knowledge representation and reasoning. *Journal of Pragmatics, 35*(3), 455–484.

Bowling, M., & Veloso, M. (2002). Multiagent learning using a variable learning rate. *Artificial Intelligence, 136*(2), 215–250.

Breener, M., & Schiffers, M. (2003). Applying Web services technologies to the management of context provisioning. *Proceedings of the 10th Workshop of the OpenView University Association (OVUA'2003)*, Geneva, Switzerland.

Breese, J.S., Heckerman, D., & Kadie, C. (1998). Empirical analysis of predictive algorithms for collaborative filtering. *Proceedings of the 14th Conference on Uncertainty in Artificial Intelligence.*

Brézillon, P. (1999). Context in artificial intelligence: I. A survey of the literature. *Knowledge Engineering Review, 14*(1), 1–34.

Brézillon, P. (2003). Focusing on context in human-centered computing. *IEEE Intelligent Systems, 18*(3).

Brown, A.W., & Wallnau, K.C. (1998). The current status of component-based software engineering. *IEEE Software,* (September/October).

Brown, J., & Duguid, O. (1994). Borderline issues: Social and material aspects of design. *Human-Computer Interaction, 9,* 3–36.

Brown, P.J., Bovey, J.D., & Chen, X. (1997). Context-aware applications: From the laboratory to the marketplace. *IEEE Personal Communications,* 58–64.

Bruce, H. (2005). Personal, anticipated information need. *Information Research, 10*(3) paper 232. Retrieved from *http://InformationR.net/ir/10-3/paper232.html*

Brusilovsky, P. (1996). Methods and techniques of adaptive hypermedia. *Journal of User Modeling and User-Adaptive Interaction, 6*(2-3), 87-129.

Brusilovsky, P. (2001). Adaptive hypermedia. In A. Kobsa (Ed.), *User modeling and user-adapted interaction, ten year anniversary, 11,* 87-110.

Buchner, M., Baumgarten, M., Anand, S., Mulvenna, M., & Hughes, J. (1999). Navigation pattern discovery from Internet data. *WEBKDD'99.* San Diego, California.

Buckley, C., & Salton, G. (1995). Optimization of relevance feedback weights. In E.A. Fox, P. Ingwersen, & R. Fidel (Eds.), *Proceedings of the Annual International ACM SIGIR Conference on Research and Development in Information Retrieval* (pp. 351–357).

Bucur, O. (2004). *Modélisation du contexte pour un apprentissage multi-agent des préférences utilisateurs.* Unpublished Doctoral Dissertation, High National School of Saint Étienne, France.

Bucur, O., Beaune, P., & Boissier, O. (2005). Representing context in an agent architecture for context-based decision making. In L. Serafini & P. Bouquet (Eds.), Proceedings of the CRR'05 Workshop on Context Representation and Reasoning.

Bui, T., Cho, S., Sankaran, S., & Sovereign, M. (2000). A framework for designing a global information network for multinational humanitarian assistance/disaster relief. *Information Systems Frontiers, 1*(4), 427–442.

Bui, T., Cho, S., Sankaran, S., & Sovereign, M. (2000). A framework for designing a global information network for multinational humanitarian assistance/disaster relief. *Information Systems Frontiers, 1*(4), 427–442.

Buitelaar, P., Cimiano, P., & Magnini, B. (Eds.). (2005). *Ontology learning from text: Methods, evaluation and applications.* Amsterdam: IOS Press.

Burgess, M.S.E., Gray, W.A., & Fiddian, N.J. (2004). Quality measures and the information consumer. *Proceedings of the 9th International Conference on Information Quality* (ICIQ-04) (pp. 373–388). Retrieved June 25, 2006, from *http://www.iqconference.org/ICIQ/iqpapers. aspx?iciqyear=2004*

Burgin, M. (2003). Information theory: A mutlifaceted model of information. *Entropy, 5*(2), 146–160.

Burke, R. (2002). Hybrid recommender systems: Survey and experiments. *User Modeling and User-Adapted Interaction, 12,* 331–370.

Buschmann, F., Meunier, R., Rohnert, H., Sommerlad, P., & Stal, M. (1996). *Pattern-oriented software architecture, a system of patterns.* New York: John Wiley & Sons.

Bush, V. (1945). As we may think. *Atlantic Monthly,176*(1), 101–108.

Buvač, S. (1996). Quantificational logic of context. *Proceedings of the 30th American National Conference on Artificial Intelligence.*

Buvač, S., & Mason, I.A. (1993). Propositional logic of context. *Proceedings of the 11th American National Conference on Artificial Intelligence* (pp. 412–419).

Byström, K., & Hansen, P. (2005). Conceptual framework for tasks in information studies. *Journal of the American Society for Information Science and Technology, 56*(10), 1050–1061. Retrieved from *http://www3.interscience. wiley.com/cgibin/fulltext/110497382/PDFSTART*

Byström, K., & Järvelin, K. (1995). Task complexity affects information seeking and use. *Information Processing & Management, 31*(2), 191–213.

Cabri, G., Ferrari, L., & Leonardi, L. (2005a). Injecting roles in Java agents through runtime bytecode manipulation. *IBM Systems Journal, 44*(1), 185–208.

Cabri, G., Ferrari, L., & Leonardi, L. (2005b, July). Supporting the development of multi-agent interactions via roles. *Proceedings of the 6th International Workshop on Agent-Oriented Software Engineering at AAMAS 2005* (pp. 54–166), Utrecht, The Netherlands. Berlin: Springer-Verlag (LNCS 3950).

Cadez, I. V., Heckerman, D., Meek, C., Smyth, P., & White, S. (2003). Model-based clustering and visualization of navigation patterns on a Web site. *Journal of Data Mining and Knowledge Discovery, 7*(4), 399-424.

Cambridge Advanced Learner's Dictionary. (n.d.). Retrieved from http://dictionary.cambridge.org/results. asp?searchword=environment&x=56&y=7

Camenisch, J., & Herreweghen, E.V. (2002). *Design and implementation of Idemix Anonymous Credential System.* Zurich: IBM Zurich Research Laboratory.

Cao, L.B., Zhang, C.Q., & Dai. R.W. (2005a). The OSOAD methodology for open complex agent systems. *International Journal of Intelligent Control and Systems, 10*(4), 277–285.

Cao, L.B., Zhang, C.Q., & Dai. R.W. (2005b). Organization-oriented analysis of open complex agent systems. *International Journal of Intelligent Control and Systems, 10*(2), 114–122.

Carson, C. (2002). Blobworld: Image segmentation using expectation-maximization and its applications to image querying. *IEEE Transactions on Pattern Analysis and Machine Intelligence, 24*(8), 1026–1038.

Casal, C.R. (2001). Privacy protection for location based mobile services in Europe. *Proceedings of the 5th World Multi-Conference on Systems, Cybernetics, and Informatics* (SCI2001), Orlando, FL.

Casati, F., Shan, E., Dayal, U., & Shan, M. (2003). Business oriented management of Web services. *Communications of the ACM, 46*(10), 55–60.

Casati, F., Shan, E., Dayal, U., & Shan, M.C. (2003). Business-oriented management of Web services. *Communications of the ACM, 46*(10).

Castelfranchi, C. (1998). Modeling social action for AI agents. *Artificial Intelligence, 103,* 157–182.

Catledge, L., & Pitkow, J. (1995). Characterizing browsing behaviors on the World Wide Web. *Computer Networks and ISDN Systems, 6*(27), 1065-1073.

CDSP91 & SAMU91. (2000). *Plan rouge: Plan destiné porter secours de nombreuses victimes.* France.

Celjuska, D. (2004). *Semi-automatic construction of ontologies from text.* Unpublished Master's Thesis, Technical University Koice, Slovak Republic.

Chaimowicz, L., Campos, M.F.M., & Kumar, R.V. (2002). Dynamic role assignment for cooperative robots. *Proceedings of the IEEE International Conference on Robotics and Automation* (ICRA'02) (pp. 293–298), Washington, DC.

Chakrabarti, S. (2003). *Mining the Web.* San Francisco: Morgan Kaufmann.

Challam, V.K.R. (2004). *Contextual information retrieval using ontology based user profiles.* Hyderabad, India: Jawaharlal Nehru Technological University.

Chaum, D. (1985). Security without identification card computers to make big brother obsolete. *Communications of ACM, 28*(10), 1034–1044.

Checkland, P., & Holwell, S. (1998). *Information, systems and information systems: Making sense of the field.* New York: John Wiley & Sons.

Chen, H., & Finin, T. (2003). An ontology for context-aware pervasive computing environments. *The Knowledge Engineering Review, 18*(3), 197–207.

Chen, K., & Liu, L. (2003). Validating and refining clusters via visual rendering. *Proceedings of the 3rd IEEE International Conference on Data Mining (ICDM 2003)* (pp. 501-504).

Chen, M. S., Park, J. S., & Yu, P. S. (1998). Efficient data mining for path traversal patterns. *IEEE Transactions on Knowledge and Data Engineering, 10*(2), 209-221.

Chen, M., Park, J., & Yu, P. (1996). Data mining for path traversal patterns in a Web environment. *Proceedings of the 16th International Conference on Distributed Computing Systems,* (pp. 385-392).

Chen, M., Park, J., & Yu, P. (1998). Efficient data mining for path traversal patterns. *IEEE Transactions Knowledge and Data Engineering, 10*(2), 209-221.

Chen, R., Sharman, R., Rao, H.R., & Upadhyaya, S. (2005). Design principles of coordinated multi-incident emergency response systems. In P. Kantor et al. (Eds.), *Proceedings of the IEEE International Conference on Intelligence and Security Informatics* (ISI 2005) (pp. 19–20). Berlin: Springer-Verlag.

Chen, S. (2006). *Ontology discovery from text: A hybrid framework.* Unpublished Master's Thesis, Monash University, Australia.

Chen, S., Alahakoon, D., & Indrawan, M. (2004). An unsupervised neural network approach for ontology discovery from text. *Proceedings of the Workshop on Semantic Web Mining and Reasoning* (SWMR 2004) (pp. 1–8), Beijing.

Chen, S., Alahakoon, D., & Indrawan, M. (2005). Background knowledge driven ontology discovery. *Proceedings of the 2005 IEEE International Conference on E-Technology, E-Commerce and E-Service* (EEE'05) (pp. 202–207).

Chen, S., Alahakoon, D., & Indrawan, M. (2006). Building an adaptive hierarchy of clusters for text data. *Proceedings of the International Conference on Intel-ligent Agents, Web Technology and Internet Commerce* (IAWTIC'2005) (pp. 7–12).

Chen, Y., & Wang, J. (2002). A region-based fuzzy feature matching approach to content-based image retrieval. *IEEE Transactions on Pattern Analysis and Machine Intelligence, 24*(9), 1252–1267.

Chen, Y., Zhou, X., & Huang, T. (2001). One-class SVM for learning in image retrieval. *Proceedings of the IEEE International Conference on Image Processing* (vol. 1, pp. 34–37).

Cheung, K., Li, C., Lam, E., & Liu, J. (2001). Customized electronic commerce with intelligent software agents. In S.M. Rahman & R.J. Bignall (Eds.), Internet commerce and software agents - Cases, technologies and opportunities (pp. 150-176). Hershey, PA: Idea Group Publishing.

Cheverst, K., Davies, N., Mitchell, K., Friday, A., & Efstratiou, C. (2000). Experiences of developing and deploying a context-aware tourist guide: The GUIDE project. *Proceedings of the 6th Annual International Conference on Mobile Computing and Networking.*

Cho, Y.B., Cho, Y.H., & Kim, S.H. (2005). Mining changes in customer buying behavior for collaborative recommendations. *Expert Systems with Applications, 28,* 359–369.

Cho, Y.H., Kim, J.K., & Kim, S.H. (2002). A personalized recommender system based on Web usage mining and decision tree induction. *Expert System with Applications, 23,* 329–342.

Chockler, G.V., Keidar, I., & Vitenberg, I. (2001). Group communication specifications: A comprehensive study. *ACM Computing Surveys, 33*(4), 427–469.

Chuang, S.-L., & Chien, L.-F. (2005). Taxonomy generation for text segments: A practical Web-based approach. *ACM Transactions on Information Systems, 23*(4), 363–396.

Cimatti, A., & Serafini, L. (1995). Multi-agent reasoning with belief contexts: The approach and a case study. In M. Wooldridge & N.R. Jennings (Eds.), *Intelligent*

Agents, Proceedings of the Workshop on Agent Theories, Architectures, and Languages (pp. 71–85).

Cimiano, P., Hotho, A., & Staab, S. (2005). Learning concept hierarchies from text corpora using formal concept analysis. *Journal of Artificial Intelligence Research, 24,* 305–339.

Cingil, I., Dogac, A., & Azgin, A. (2000). A broader approach to personalization. *Communications of the ACM, 43*(8), 136-141.

Clifton, C., Kantarcioglu, M., Vaidya, J., Lin, X., & Zhu, M.Y. (2002). Tools for privacy preserving distributed data mining. *ACM SIGKDD Explorations, 4*(2), 28–34.

Comfort, L., Ko, K., & Zagorecki, A. (2004). Coordination in rapidly evolving disaster response systems: The role of information. *American Behavioral Scientist, 48*(3), 295–313.

Cool, C. & Spink, A. (2002). Issues of context in information retrieval: An introduction to the special issue. *Journal of Information Processing and Management, 38*(55), 605–611.

Cooley, R., Mobasher, B., & Srivastava, J. (1997). Grouping Web page references into transactions for mining World Wide Web browsing patterns. *Knowledge and Data Engineering Workshop,* Newport Beach, CA (pp. 2-9).

Cooley, R., Mobasher, B., & Srivastava, J. (1999). Data preparation for mining World Wide Web browsing patterns. *Knowledge Information Systems, 1*(1), 5-32.

Cooley, R., Mobasher, B., & Srivastava, J. (1999a). Data preparation for mining World Wide Web browsing patterns. *Knowledge and Information Systems, 1*(1), 5-32.

Cooley, R., Tan, P., & Srivastava, J. (1999b). *WebSIFT: The Web Site information filter system.* WEBKDD, San Diego, California. Available: http://www.acm.org/sigkdd/proceedings/webkdd99/papers/paper11-cooley.ps

Cooley, R., Tan, P., & Srivastava, J. (2000). Discovering of interesting usage patterns from Web data. In M. Spiliopoulou (Ed.), *LNCS/LNAI Series.* Springer-Verlag.

Corcho, O., Fernández-López, M., & Gómez-Pérez, A. (2003). Methodologies, tools and languages for building ontologies: Where is their meeting point? *Data Knowledge Engineering, 46*(1), 41–64.

Coulouris, G., Dollimore, J., & Kindberg, T. (2005), *Distributed systems: Concepts and design* (4th ed.). Reading, MA: Addison-Wesley.

Cover, T.M., & Hart, P.E. (1967). Nearest neighbor pattern classification. *IEEE Transactions on Information Theory, 13*(1), 21–27.

Cover, T.M., & Thomas, J.A. (1991). *Elements of information theory.* New York: John Wiley & Sons.

Cox, E. (1994). *The fuzzy systems handbook: A practitioner's guide to building, using, and maintaining fuzzy systems.* London: Academic Press.

Cranor, L., Langheinrich, M., & Marchiori, M. (2002). *A P3P Preference Exchange Language 1.0 (APPEL1.0).* Working Draft, W3C.

Cranor, L., Langheinrich, M., Marchiori, M., Presler-Marshall, M., & Reagle, J. (2004). *The Platform for Privacy Preferences 1.1 (P3P1.1) specification.* Working Draft, W3C.

Cranor, L.F., Guduru, P., & Arjula, M. (2006). User interfaces for privacy agents. *ACM Transactions on Human Computer Interactions.*

Cristiano, C. (1998). Modeling social action for AI agents. *Artificial Intelligence, 103*(1–2), 157–182.

Cyert, R.M., & MacCrimmon, K.R. (1968). Organizations. In G. Lindzey & E. Aronson (Eds.), *The handbook of social psychology* (pp. 568–611). Reading, MA: Addison-Wesley.

Dafoulas, G.A., & Macaulay, L.A. (2001, June 25-29). Facilitating group formation and role allocation in software engineering groups. *Proceedings of the ACS/IEEE International Conference of Computer Systems and Applications* (pp. 352–359), Beirut, Lebanon.

Dagan, I., Glickman, O., & Magnini, B. (2005, April 11–13). The PASCAL recognising textual entailment challenge. *Revised Selected Papers of the Machine Learning Challenges, Evaluating Predictive Uncertainty, Visual Object Classification and Recognizing Textual Entailment, 1st PASCAL Machine Learning Challenges Workshop* (MLCW 2005) (vol. 3944, pp. 177–190), Southampton, UK. Berlin: Springer-Verlag.

Day, A.K., Salber, D., Abowd, G.D., & Futakawa, M. (1999). The conference assistant: Combining context-awareness with wearable computing. *Proceedings of the 3rd International Symposium on Wearable Computers,* San Francisco.

de la Rosa, J.L., Montaner, M., & Lopez, J.M. (2006). Opinion based filtering. *Proceedings of the International Workshop on Recommender Systems, 17th European Conference on Artificial Intelligence* (ECAI 2006), Riva del Garda, Italy.

Delgado, J., & Ishii, N. (1999). Memory-based weighted-majority prediction for recommender systems. *Proceedings of the ACM-SIGIR'99 Recommender Systems Workshop,* Berkeley, CA.

Demazeau, Y. (1995). From interactions to collective behaviour in agent-based systems. *Proceedings of the 1st European Conference on Cognitive Science* (pp. 117-132), Saint Malo, France.

Dempster, A. P., Laird, N. P., & Rubin, D. B. (1977). Maximum likelihood from incomplete data via the EM algorithm. *Journal of the Royal Statistical Society, B, 39,* 1-22.

Dennett, D.C. (1991). *Consciousness explained.* Boston, MA: Little, Brown and Co.

Dervin, B. (1999). On studying information seeking methodologically: The implications of connecting meta theory to method. *Information Processing & Management, 35*(6), 727–750.

Dervin, B., & Nilan, M.S. (1986). Information needs and uses. *Annual Review of Information Science and Technology (ARIST), 21,* 3–33.

Deshpande, M., & Karypis, G. (2004). Item-based Top-N recommendation algorithms. *ACM Transactions on Information Systems, 22*(1), 143–177.

Dey, A.K. (2001). Understanding and using context. *Personal and Ubiquitous Computing Journal, 5,* 4–7.

Dey, A.K., & Abowd, G.D. (1999). *Towards a better understanding of context and context-awareness.* Technical Report, Georgia Institute of Technology, USA.

Dey, A.K., Abowd, G.D., & Salber, D. (2001). A conceptual framework and a toolkit for supporting the rapid prototyping of context-aware applications. *Human-Computer Interaction Journal, Special Issue on Context-Aware Computing, 16*(1).

Dey, A.K., Salber, D., & Futakawa, M. (1999). *An architecture to support context-aware applications.* Technical Report GIT-GVU-99-23, Georgia Institute of Technology, USA.

Dittenbach, M., Berger, H., & Merll, D. (2004). Improving domain ontologies by mining semantics from text. *Proceedings of the 1st Asian-Pacific Conference on Conceptual Modeling* (APCCM'04) (pp. 91–100). Darlinghurst, Australia: Australian Computer Society.

Dittenbach, M., Merkl, D., & Rauber, A. (2002). Organizing and exploring high-dimensional data with the growing hierarchical self-organizing map. In L. Wang, S. Halgamuge, & X. Yao (Eds.), *Proceedings of the 1st International Conference on Fuzzy Systems and Knowledge Discovery* (FSKD 2002) (vol. 2, pp. 626–630), Singapore.

Dopazo, J., & Carazo, J.M. (1997). Phylogenetic reconstruction using an unsupervised growing neural network that adopts the topology of a phylogenetic tree. *Journal of Molecular Evolution, 44,* 226–233.

Douglas, K.B. (2003). *Web services and service-oriented architectures: The savvy manager's guide.* San Francisco: Morgan Kaufmann.

Doulkeridis, C., Valavanis, E., & Vazirgiannis, M. (2003). Towards a context-aware service directory. *Proceedings of the 4th Workshop on Technologies for E-Services*

(TES'03) held in conjunction with the 29th International Conference on Very Large Data Bases (VLDB'2003), Berlin, Germany.

Dubois, D., & Prade, H. (1991). Fuzzy sets in approximate reasoning. Part 1: Inference with possibility distributions. In IFSA (Ed.), *Fuzzy sets and systems. Special memorial volume: 25 years of fuzzy sets.* Amsterdam: North-Holland.

Dubois, D., & Prade, H. (2004). On the use of aggregation operations in information fusion processes. *Fuzzy Sets and Systems, 142*(1), 143–161.

Dumais, S., Cadiz Cuttrel, E., & Jancke, J.J. (2003). Stuff I've seen: A system for a personal information retrieval and reuse. *Proceedings of the 26th ACM SIGIR International Conference on Research and Development* (pp. 72–79).

Dumais, S., Cutrell, E., Cadiz, J., Jancke, G., Sarin, R., & Robbins, D.C. (2003). Stuff I've Seen: A system for personal information retrieval and re-use. *Proceedings of the 26th Annual International ACM SIGIR Conference on Research and Development in Information Retrieval.*

Earp, J., & Baumer, D. (2003). Innovative Web use to learn about consumer behavior and online privacy. *Communications of the ACM, 46*(4), 81-83.

Eckerson, W. (2002). *Data quality and the bottom line: Achieving business success through a commitment to high quality data.* Report Series (vol. 1, pp. 1–32), Data Warehousing Institute.

Ecollan, P. (1989). *Le plan blanc.* Unpublished Doctoral Dissertation, Faculty of Medicine, PITIESALPETRIERE, France.

Edmonds, B. (2002). Learning and exploiting context in agents. *Proceedings of the 1st International Joint Conference on Autonomous Agents and Multiagent Systems* (AAMAS'02) (pp. 1231–1238).

Eirinaki, M., & Vazirgiannis, M. (2003). Web mining for Web personalization. *ACM Transactions on Internet Technology, 3*(1), 1–27.

Eirinaki, M., & Vazirgiannis, M. (2003, February). Web mining for Web personalization. *ACM Transactions on Internet Technology (TOIT), 3*(1), 1-27. New York: ACM Press.

Eiron, N., & McCurley, K. S. (2003). Untangling compound documents on the Web. *Proceedings of the 14th ACM Conference on Hypertext and Hypermedia* (pp. 85-94).

Endrei, M., Ang, J., Arsanjani, A., Chua, S., Comte, P., & Krogdahl, P. (2004). *Patterns: Service-oriented architecture and Web services.* Retrieved from http://www.redbooks.ibm.com/redbooks/pdfs/sg246303.pdf

Endsley, M.R., & Rodgers, M.D. (1988). Distribution of attention, situation awareness, and workload in a passive air traffic control task: Implications for operational errors and automation. *Air Traffic Control Quarterly, 6*(1), 21–44.

Endsley, M.R., Bolte, B., & Jones, D.G. (2003). *Designing for situation awareness: An approach to user-centered design.* London: Taylor & Francis.

English, L.P. (1999). *Improving data warehouse and business information quality methods for reducing costs and increasing profits.* New York: John Wiley & Sons.

Eppler, M., & Mengis, J. (2004). The concept of information overload: A review of literature from organization science, accounting, marketing, MIS, and related disciplines. *The Information Society, 20*(5), 325–344.

Esteva, M., Rodríguez-Aguilar, J.A., Sierra C., Garcia, P., & Arcos, J.L. (2001). *On the formal specifications of electronic institutions* (pp. 126–147). Berlin: Springer-Verlag (LNCS 1991).

Etzioni, O., & Weld, D.S. (1995). Intelligent agents on the Internet: Fact, fiction, and forecast. *IEEE Expert: Intelligent Systems and Their Applications, 10*(4), 44–49.

Etzioni, O., Cafarella, M., Downey, D., Kok, S., Popescu, A.-M., Shaked, T. et al. (2004). Web-scale information extraction in Knowitall: (preliminary results). *Proceedings of the 13th International Conference on the World Wide Web* (WWW'04) (pp. 100–110). New York: ACM Press.

European Directive. (2002). Directive 2002/58/EC of the European Parliament and of the Council of 12 July 2002, electronic communications sector (directive on privacy and electronic communications). *Official Journal of European Communities, L,* 201–237.

Faloutsos, C., Flicker, M., Niblack, W., Petkovic, D., Equitz, W., & Barber, R. (1993). *Efficient and effective querying by image content.* Technical Report, IBM, USA.

Fan, W., Gordon, M.D., & Pathak, P. (2004). *Discovery of context specific ranking functions for effective information retrieval using genetic programming* (vol. 16, pp. 523–527).

Farquhar, A., Dappert, J., & Fikes, R. (1995). *Integrating information sources using context logic.* Technical Report KSL-95-12, Knowledge Systems Laboratory, USA.

Faure, D., & Nédellec, C. (1998). ASIUM: Learning subcategorization frames and restrictions of selection. In Y. Kodratoff (Ed.), *Proceedings of the 10th Conference on Machine Learning, Workshop on Text Mining* (ECML'98), Chemnitz, Germany.

Feather, J. (1998). *In the information society: A study of continuity and change* (p. 11). London: Library Association.

Fellbaum, C. (Ed.). (1998). *WordNet: An electronic lexical database.* Cambridge, MA: MIT Press.

Ferber, J. (1995). *Les systèmes multi-agents, vers une intelligence collective.* InterEditions.

Ferber, J., Gutknechtl, O., & Michell, F. (2004). From agents to organizations: An organizational view of multi-agent systems. In P. Giorgini, J. Müller, & J. Odell (Eds.), *Agent-Oriented Software Engineering (AOSE) IV* (pp. 214–230). Berlin: Springer-Verlag (LNCS 2935).

Fernández-López, M., & Gómez-Pérez, A. (2002). *OntoWeb—a survey on methodologies for developing, maintaining, evaluating and reengineering ontologies.* OntoWeb Deliverable 1.4, IST Programme of the Commission of the European Communities, IST-2000-29243.

Fernández-López, M., Gómez-Pérez, A., & Juristo, N. (1997). METHONTOLOGY: From ontological art towards ontological engineering. *Proceedings of the Symposium on Ontological Engineering of AAAI* (pp. 33–40), Stanford, CA.

Fernández-López, M., Gómez-Pérez, A., Sierra, J.P., & Sierra, A.P. (1999). Building a chemical ontology using methontology and the ontology design environment. *IEEE Intelligent Systems, 14*(1), 37–46.

Fidel, R., & Pejtersen, A.M. (2004). From information behavior research to the design of information systems: The Cognitive Work Analysis framework. *Information Research, 10*(1), paper 210. Retrieved from http://InformationR.net/ir/10-1/paper210.html

Flake, G. W., Tarjan, R. E., & Tsioutsiouliklis, K. (2004). Graph clustering and minimum cut trees. *Internet Mathematics, 1*(4), 385-408.

Foo, N.Y. (1995, August 14–18). Ontology revision. In G. Ellis, R. Levinson, W. Rich, & J.F. Sowa (Eds.), *Proceedings of Conceptual Structures: Applications, Implementation and Theory, the 3rd International Conference on Conceptual Structures* (ICCS'95) (pp. 16–31), Santa Cruz, CA.

Fraley, C., & Raftery, A. (1998). How many clusters? Which clustering method? Answers via model-based cluster analysis. *Computer Journal, 41,* 578-588.

Friedman, J. (1994). *Flexible metric nearest neighbor classification.* Technical Report, Department of Statistics, Stanford University, USA.

Fu, Y., Sandhu, K., & Shih, M. Y. (1999). A generalization-based approach to clustering of Web usage sessions. In *Proceedings of the International Workshop on Web Usage Analysis and User Profiling (WEBKDD1999)* (LNCS 1836, pp. 21-38). San Diego: Springer Verlag.

Gaëtan, R. (2001). *Systèmes interactifs sensibles au contexte.* Unpublished Doctoral Dissertation, Polytechnic National Institute of Grenoble, France.

Galbraith, J. (1974). Organization design: An information processing view. *Interfaces, 4*(3), 28–36.

Galbraith, J., Downey, D., & Kates, A. (2002). How networks undergird the lateral capability of an organization—where the work gets done. *Journal of Organizational Excellence, 21*(2), 67–78.

Gandon, F. (2002). *Ontology engineering: A survey and a return on experience.* Rapport de Recherche No. 4396, INRIA.

Ganter, B. (1999). *The Dresden formal concept analysis page.* Retrieved February 21, 2005, from http://www.math.tu-dresden.de/~ganter/fba.html

Gärdenfors, P., & Williams, M.-A. (2003). Building rich and grounded robot world models from sensors and knowledge resources: A conceptual spaces approach. *Proceedings of the 2nd International Symposium on Autonomous Mini-Robots for Research and Edutainment* (pp. 34–45).

Gaslikova, I. (1999). Information Seeking in Context and the development of information systems. *Information Research, 5*(1). Retrieved from *http://informationr.net/ir/5-1/paper67.html*

Gemmell, J., Bell, G., & Lueder, R. (2006). MyLifeBits: A personal database for everything. *Communications of the ACM, 49*(1).

Genesereth, M.R., & Ketchpel, S.P. (1994). Software agents. *Communications of the ACM, 37*(7), 48–55.

Genesereth, M.R., & Nilsson, N.J. (1987). *Logical foundations of artificial intelligence.* San Francisco: Morgan Kaufmann.

Ghidini, C., & Giunchiglia, F. (2001). Local models semantics, or contextual reasoning = locality + compatibility. *Artificial Intelligence, 127*(4), 221–259.

Giunchiglia, E., & Giunchiglia, F. (1996). Ideal and real belief about belief. *Proceedings of the International Conference on Formal and Applied Practical Reasoning* (pp. 261–275).

Giunchiglia, F. (1993). Contextual reasoning. *Proceedings of the IJCAI'93 Workshop on Using Knowledge in its Context* (pp. 39–48).

Giunchiglia, F., & Bouquet, P. (1996). Introduction to contextual reasoning: An artificial intelligence perspective. In B. Kokinov (Ed.), *Perspectives on cognitive science* (vol. 3, pp. 138–159). Sofia: NBU Press.

Giunchiglia, F., & Serafini, L. (1994). Multilanguage hierarchical logics (or: how we can do without modal logics). *Artificial Intelligence, 65,* 29–70.

Goh, O., & Fung, C. (2005). Automated knowledge extraction from Internet for a crisis communication portal. *Lecture Notes in Artificial Intelligence, 3614,* 1226–1235.

Goker, A., & He, D. (2000). Analysing Web search logs to determine session boundaries for user-oriented learning. In *Proceedings of the International Conference of Adaptive Hypermedia and Adaptive Web-Based Systems (AH2000)* (LNCS 1892, pp. 319-322). Trento, Italy: Springer Verlag.

Goldberg, K., Roeder, T., Gupta, D., & Perkins, C. (2001). Eigentaste: A constant time collaborative filtering algorithm. *Information Retrieval Journal, 4*(2), 133–151.

Gómez-Pérez, A., Fernández-López, M., & Corcho, O. (2004). *Ontological engineering: With examples from the areas of knowledge management, e-commerce and the Semantic Web (advanced information and knowledge processing).* London/New York: Springer-Verlag.

Gomory, S., Hoch, R., Lee, J., Podlaseck, M., & Schonberg, E. (1999). Analysis and visualization of metrics for online merchandising. In *Proceedings of the International Workshop on Web Usage Analysis and User Profiling (WEBKDD1999)* (LNCS 1836, pp. 126-141). San Diego, CA: Springer Verlag.

Gondra, I., & Heisterkamp, D.R. (2004). Probabilistic region relevance learning for content-based image retrieval. *Proceedings of the International Conference on Imaging Science, Systems, and Technology* (pp. 434–440).

González-Rivera, R. (2006, February). *Information coordination service for situation aware process orchestration: Improving time to action in emergency response.* Draft PhD Proposal, Delft University of Technology, The Netherlands.

Grauel, A. (1999). Analytical and structural considerations in fuzzy modeling. *Fuzzy Sets and Systems, 101,* 205–206.

Greco, G., Greco, S., & Zumpano, E. (2004). Web communities: Models and algorithms. *World Wide Web Journal, 7*(1), 58-82.

Green, S., Hurst, L., Nangle, B., Cunningham, P., Somers, F., & Evans, R. (1997). *Software agents: A review.* Technical Report TCD-CS-1997-06, Trinity College, Ireland.

Greening, D. (1997). *Building consumer trust with accurate product recommendations.* LikeMinds White Paper, LMWSWP-210-6966.

Gruber, T.R. (1993). A translation approach to portable ontology specifications. *Knowledge Acquisition, 5*(2), 199–220.

Grunig, J. (1989). Publics, audience and market segments: Segmentation principles for campaigns. In C. Salmon (Ed.), *Information campaigns: Balancing social values and social change* (pp. 199–228). Beverly Hills, CA: Sage.

Grüninger, M., & Fox, M. (1995). Methodology for the design and evaluation of ontologies. *Proceedings of IJCAI'95, Workshop on Basic Ontological Issues in Knowledge Sharing.*

Gruver, W. (2004). Technologies and applications of distributed intelligent systems. *Proceedings of the IEEE MTT-Chapter Presentation,* Waterloo, Canada.

Gu, T., Wang, X.H., & Pung, H.K. (2004). An ontology-based context model in intelligent environments. *Proceedings of the Communication Networks and Distributed Systems Modeling and Simulation Conference,* San Diego, CA.

Guarino, N. (1998). Formal ontology and information systems. *Proceedings of the 1st International Conference on Formal Ontologies in Information Systems* (FOIS'98) (pp. 3–5), Trento, Italy. Amsterdam: IOS Press.

Guarino, N., & Giaretta, P. (1995). Ontologies and knowledge bases: Towards a terminological clarification. In N.J.I. Mars (Ed.), *Towards very large knowledge bases* (pp. 25–32). Amsterdam: IOS Press.

Guha, R.V. (1991). *Contexts: A formalization and some applications.* Unpublished Doctoral Dissertation, Stanford University, USA.

Günter, S., & Bunke, H. (2003). Validation indices for graph clustering. *Pattern Recognition Letters, 24*(8), 1107-1113.

Gupta, A., & Jain, R. (1997). Visual information retrieval. *Communications of the ACM, 40*(5), 70–79.

Haase, P., Ehrig, M., Hotho, A., & Schnizler, B. (2004). Personalized information access in a bibliographic peer-to-peer system. *Proceedings of the AAAI Workshop on Semantic Web Personalization.* Retrieved March 22, 2007, from http://citeseer.ist.psu.edu/haase04personalized.html

Hackman, J.R. (1969). Towards understanding the role of tasks in behavioral research. *Acta Psychologica, 31,* 97–128.

Halkidi, M., Batistakis, Y., & Vazirgiannis, M. (2002a). Cluster validity methods: Part I. *SIGMOD Record, 31*(2), 40-45.

Halkidi, M., Batistakis, Y., & Vazirgiannis, M. (2002b). Cluster validity methods: Part II. *SIGMOD Record, 31*(3), 19-27.

Hammouda, K. M., & Kamel, M. S. (2004). Efficient phrase-based document indexing for Web document clustering. *IEEE Transactions on Knowledge Data Engineering, 16*(10), 1279-1296.

Hanani, U., Shapira, B., & Shoval, P. (2001). Information filtering: Overview of issues, research and systems. *User Modeling and User-Adapted Interaction, 11,* 203–259.

Hanani, U., Shapira, B., & Shoval, P. (2001). Information filtering: Overview of issues, research and systems. *User Modeling and User-Adapted Interaction, 11*(3), 203–259.

Hara, Y., Hirata, K., Takano, H., & Kawasaki, S. (1997). Hypermedia navigation and content-based retrieval for distributed multimedia databases. *Proceedings of the NEC Research Symposium on Multimedia Computing* (pp. 133–148).

Harel, D., & Naamad, A. (1996). The STATEMATE semantics of statecharts. *ACM Transactions on Software Engineering and Methodology, 5*(4).

Harter, A., & Hopper, A. (1994). A distributed location system for the active office. *IEEE Networks.*

Hauser, C., & Kabatnik, M. (2001). Towards privacy support in a global location service. *Proceedings of the IFIP Workshop on IP and ATM Traffic Management* (WATM/EUNICE 2001), Paris.

Hayes, R.M. (1993). Measurement of information. *Information Processing & Management, 29*(1), 1–11.

Hayes-Roth, B. (1995). An architecture for adaptive intelligent systems. *Artificial Intelligence, 72*(1–2), 329–365.

Heflin, J., & Hendler, J.A. (2000). Dynamic ontologies on the Web. *Proceedings of the 17th National Conference on Artificial Intelligence and 12th Conference on Innovative Applications of Artificial Intelligence* (pp. 443–449). Cambridge, MA: AAAI Press/MIT Press.

Hegering, H.G., Kupper, A., Linnhoff-Popien, C., & Reiser, H. (2003). Management challenges of context-aware services in ubiquitous environments. *Proceedings of the 14th IFIP/IEEE International Workshop on Distributed Systems: Operations and Management (DSOM'2003),* Heidelberg, Germany.

Heineman, G.T., & Council, W.T. (2001). *Component-based software engineering: Putting the pieces together.* Boston: Addison-Wesley Longman.

Heineman, G.T., & Councill, W.T. (2001). *Component based software engineering: Putting the pieces together.* Upper Saddle River, NJ: Addison-Wesley.

Heisterkamp, D.R. (2002). Building a latent semantic index of an image database from patterns of relevance feedback. *Proceedings of the International Conference on Pattern Recognition* (vol. 4, pp. 134–137).

Heisterkamp, D.R., Peng, J., & Dai, H. (2001). Adaptive quasiconformal kernel metric for image retrieval. *Proceedings of the IEEE International Conference on Computer Vision and Pattern Recognition* (vol. 2, pp. 388–393).

Heisterkamp, D.R., Peng, J., & Dai, H.K. (2000). Feature relevance learning with query shifting for content-based image retrieval. *Proceedings of the International Conference on Pattern Recognition* (vol. 4, pp. 4250–4253).

Hendrix, G. (1979). Encoding knowledge in partitioned networks. In N. Findler (Ed.), *Associative networks.* New York: Academic Press.

Herlocker, J., Konstan, J.A., & Riedl, J. (2002). An empirical analysis of design choices in neighborhood-based collaborative filtering algorithms. *Information Retrieval, 5,* 287–310.

Herlocker, J.L., Konstan, J.A., Terveen, L.G., & Riedl, J.T. (2004). Evaluating collaborative filtering recommender systems. *ACM Transactions in Information Systems, 22*(1), 5–53.

Heylighen, F. (1999). Collective intelligence and its implementation on the Web. *Computational & Mathematical Organization Theory, 5*(3), 253–280.

Hirst, G. (1997). Context as a spurious concept. *Unpublished Invited Talk at the AAAI Fall Symposium on Context in Knowledge Representation and Natural Language,* Cambridge, MA.

Hoffman, T. (2003). Collaborative filtering via Gaussian probabilistic latent semantic analysis. *Proceedings of the International ACM SIGIR Conference on Research and Development in Information Retrieval* (SIGIR'03), Toronto, Canada.

Hoffmann, P. (2004). *Appariement contextuel d'ontologies.* Unpublished Doctoral Dissertation, University of Claude Bernard, France.

Hollan, J.D. (1990). User models and user interfaces: A case for domain models, task models, and tailorability. *Proceedings of AAAI-90, Eighth National Conference on Artificial Intelligence,* (p. 1137). Cambridge, MA: AAAI Press/The MIT Press.

Hong, P., Tian, Q., & Huang, T. (2000). Incorporate support vector machines to content-based image retrieval with relevance feedback. *Proceedings of the IEEE International Conference on Image Processing* (pp. 750–753).

Hotho, A., Staab, S., & Stumme, G. (2003). WordNet improves text document clustering. *Proceedings of the SIGIR 2003 Semantic Web Workshop, 26th Annual International ACM SIGIR Conference.*

Huang, X., Peng, F., An, A., & Schuurmans, D. (2004). Dynamic Web log session identification with statistical language models. *Journal of the American Society for Information Science and Technology (JASIST), 55*(14), 1290-1303.

Huang, Z., Ng, J., Cheung, D. W., Ng, M. K., & Ching, W. (2001). A cube model for Web access sessions and cluster analysis. In *Proceedings of the International Workshop on Web Usage Analysis and User Profiling (WEBKDD2001)* (LNCS 2356, pp. 48-67). Hong Kong, China: Springer Verlag.

Huang, Z., Ng, M. K., & Cheung, D. (2001). An empirical study on the visual cluster validation method with fastmap. *Proceedings of the 7th International Conference on Database Systems for Advanced Applications (DASFAA 2001)* (pp. 84-91).

Huberman, B., & Adamic, L. (2004). Information dynamics in the networked world. *Lecture Notes in Physics, 650,* 371–398.

Hunter, A., & Liu, W. (2006). Fusion rules for merging uncertain information. *Information Fusion, 7*(1), 97–134.

Huokka, D., & Harada, L. (1998). Matchmaking for information agents. In M. Huhns & M. Singh (Eds.), *Readings in agents.* San Francisco: Morgan Kaufmann.

IEEE. (1996). *IEEE standard for developing software life cycle processes.* Standard 1074-1995, IEEE Computer Society, USA.

Ingemar, J., & Cox, J. (2000). The Bayesian image retrieval system, PicHunter: Theory, implementation, and psychological experiments. *IEEE Transactions on Image Processing, 9*(1), 20–37.

Ingwersen, P. (1999). Cognitive information retrieval. *Annual Review of Information Science and Technology, 34,* 3–52.

Ino, H., Kudo, M., & Nakamura, A. (2005). Partitioning of Web graphs by community topology. *Proceedings of the 14th International Conference on World Wide Web (WWW 2005),* 661-669.

Ishikawa, Y., Subramanys, R., & Faloutsos, C. (1998). MindReader: Querying databases through multiple examples. *Proceedings of the International Conference on Very Large Databases* (pp. 218–227).

ITU (International Telecommunication Union). (2006). *ITU Internet reports 2006.* Author.

Jain, A. K., Murty, M. N., & Flynn, P. J. (1999). Data clustering: A review. *ACM Computing Surveys, 31*(3), 264-323.

Jain, A.K., & Vailaya, A. (1996). Image retrieval using color and shape. *Pattern Recognition, 29*(8), 1233–1244.

Jain, A.K., Murty, M.N., & Flynn, P.J. (1999). Data clustering: A review. *ACM Computing Surveys, 31*(3), 264–323.

Järvelin, K., & Ingwersen, P. (2004). Information seeking research needs extension towards tasks and technology. *Information Research, 10*(1), paper 212.

Jeh, G., & Widom, J. (2003). Scaling personalized Web search. *Proceedings of the 12th International World Wide Web Conference* (pp. 271–279).

Jennings, N., & Wooldridge, M. (1996). Software agents. *IEE Review, 42*(1), 17–20.

Jennings, N., Sycara, K., & Wooldridge, M. (1998). A roadmap of agent research and development. *Autonomous Agents and Multi-Agent Systems, 42*(1), 7–38.

Jenvald, J., Morin, M., & Kincaid, J.P. (2001). A framework for Web-based dissemination of models and lessons learned from emergency-response exercises and operations. *International Journal of Emergency Management, 1*(1), 82–94.

Jhingran, A.D., Mattos, N., & Pirahesh, H. (2002). Information integration: A research agenda. *IBM Systems Journal, 41*(4), 555–562.

Jin, R., & Si, L. (2004). A study of methods for normalizing user ratings in collaborative filtering. *Proceedings of the International ACM SIGIR Conference on Research and Development in Information Retrieval* (SIGIR'04), Sheffield, UK.

Jin, R., Zhai, C., & Callan, J. (2003). Collaborative filtering with decoupled models for preferences and ratings. *Proceedings of CIKM'03,* New Orleans, LA.

Jing, F., Li, M., Zhang, L., Zhang, H., & Zhang, B. (2003). Learning in region-based image retrieval. *Proceedings of the International Conference on Image and Video Retrieval* (vol. 2728, pp. 206–215).

Joachims, T., Freitag, D., & Mitchell, T. (1997). WebWatcher: A tour guide for the World Wide Web. *Proceedings of the 15th International Joint Conference on Artificial Intelligence (JCAI97),* (pp. 770-775). Morgan Kaufmann Publishers.

Jones, G.J.F. (2005). Challenges and opportunities of context-aware information access. *Proceedings of the International Workshop on Ubiquitous Data Management.*

Jones, G.J.F., & Brown, P.J. (2003). Context-aware retrieval for ubiquitous computing environments. *Proceedings of the Workshop on Mobile and Ubiquitous Information Access of the 5th International Symposium on Human Computer Interaction with Mobile Devices and Services* (Mobile HCI 2003).

Jushmerick, N. (1999). Learning to remove Internet advertisements. *Proceedings of the 3rd Annual Conference on Autonomous Agents* (pp. 175-181).

Kang, S.H., & Lau, S.K. (2004, September 20–25). Ontology revision using the concept of belief revision. *Proceedings of the 8th International Conference on Knowledge-Based Intelligent Information and Engineer-*ing Systems (KES 2004) (pt. 3, pp. 8–15), Wellington, New Zealand.

Kantrowitz, M., Horstkotte, E., & Joslyn, C. (1997). *Answers to questions about fuzzy logic and fuzzy expert systems.* Retrieved June 25, 2006, from *http://www-cgi. cs.cmu.edu/afs/cs/project/ai-repository/ai/areas/fuzzy/ faq/fuzzy.faq*

Kaplan, D. (1978). On the logic of demonstratives. *Journal of Philosophical Logic, 8,* 81–98.

Kar, E.A.M. (2004). *Designing mobile information services: An approach for organisations in a value network.* Unpublished Doctoral Dissertation, Delft University of Technology, The Netherlands.

Kaufman, L., & Rousseeuw, P.J. (1990). *Finding groups in data: An introduction to cluster analysis.* New York: John Wiley & Sons.

Kay, A. (1993). The early history of Smalltalk. *Proceedings of the 2nd ACM SIGPLAN Conference on History of Programming Languages* (pp. 69–95), Cambridge, MA.

Kaye, D. (2003). *Loosely coupled: The missing pieces of Web services* (1st ed.). RDS Associates.

Kelly, N.J. (2004). *Understanding implicit feedback and document preference: A naturalistic study.* Unpublished Doctoral Dissertation, Rutgers University, USA.

Kelly, P.M., Cannon, T.M., & Hush, D.R. (1995). Query by image example: The CANDID approach. In W. Niblack & R. Jain (Eds.), *Proceedings of the SPIE Storage and Retrieval for Image and Video Databases* (vol. 2420, pp. 238–248).

Kephart, J.O., Hanson, J.E., & Greenwald, A.R. (2000). Dynamic pricing by software agents. *Computer Networks.*

Khan, L., & Luo, F. (2002). Ontology construction for information selection. *Proceedings of the 14th IEEE International Conference on Tools with Artificial Intelligence* (ICTAI'02) (pp. 122–127), Washington, DC.

Kim, H., Kim, J., & Herlocker, J. (2004). Feature-based prediction of unknown preferences for nearest-neighbor collaborative filtering. *Proceedings of the IEEE International Conference on Data Mining* (ICDM'04).

Kim, T.-H., & Yang, S.-B. (2004). Using attributes to improve prediction quality in collaborative filtering. *Proceedings of the 5th International Conference on E-Commerce and Web Technologies* (EC-Web 2004), Zaragoza, Spain.

Kim, W. (2002). Personalization: Definition, status, and challenges ahead. *Journal of Object Technology, 1*(1), 29–40.

Kim, Y.J., Kishore, R., & Sanders, R.L. (2005). DQ to EQ: Understanding data quality in the context of e-business systems. *Communications of the ACM, 48,* 75–81.

Kim, Y.S., Yum, B.-J., & Kim, S.M. (2005). Development of a recommender system based on navigational and behavioral patterns of customers in e-commerce sites. *Expert Systems with Applications, 28,* 381–393.

Kleinberg, J.M. (1998). Authoritative sources in a hyperlinked environment. *Proceedings of the 9th ACM-SIAM Symposium on Discrete Algorithms* (pp. 668–677). Retrieved June 25, 2006, from *http://www.cs.cornell.edu/home/kleinber/auth.pdf*

Klir, G.J., & Yuan, B. (1995). *Fuzzy sets and fuzzy logic: Theory and applications.* Englewood Cliffs, NJ: Prentice Hall.

Kobsa, A., & Schreck, J. (2003). Privacy through pseudonymity in user-adaptive systems. *Transactions on Internet Technology, 3*(2), 149-183.

Kobsa, A.J., & Pohl, W. (2001). Personalized hypermedia presentation techniques for improving online customer relationships. *The Knowledge Engineering Review, 16*(2), 111-155.

Kohonen, T. (1989). *Self-organization and associative memory* (3rd ed.). New York: Springer-Verlag.

Kokar, M., Tomasik, J., & Weyman, J. (2004). Formalizing classes of information fusion systems. *Information Fusion, 5*(3), 189–202.

Kokinov, B. (1994). The context-sensitive cognitive architecture DUAL. *Proceedings of 16th Annual Conference of the Cognitive Science Society.*

Kokinov, B. (1995). A dynamic approach to context modelling. In P. Brezillon & S. Abu-Hakima (Eds.), *Working Notes of the IJCAI-95 Workshop on Modelling Context in Knowledge Representation and Reasoning,* Montreal, Canada.

Konstan, J.A. (2004). Introduction to recommender systems: Algorithms and evaluation. *ACM Transactions on Information Systems, 22*(1), 1–4.

Konstan, J.A., Miller, B.N., Maltz, D., Herlocker, J.L., Gordon, L.R., & Riedl, J. (1997). Grouplens: Applying collaborative filtering to Usenet news. *Communications of the ACM, 40*(3), 77–87.

Korkea-aho, M. (2000, Spring). Context-aware applications survey. *Proceedings of the Internetworking Seminar,* Helsinki, Finland.

Kosala, R., & Blockeel, H. (2000). Web mining research: A survey. *SIGKDD Explor. Newsletter, 2*(1), 1–15.

Kosala, R., & Blockeel, H. (2000). Web mining research: A survey. *SIGKDD Explorations, 2*(1), 1-15.

Kramer, J., Noronha, S., & Vergo, J. (2000). A user-centered design approach to personalization. *Communications of the ACM, 8,* 45-48.

Krishnan, M., Schechter, S., & Smith, M. (1998). Using path profiles to predict http request. *Proceedings of the 7th International World Wide Web Conference,* Brisbane, Qld., Australia, (pp. 457-467).

Kruchten, P. (2003). *The Rational Unified Process: An introduction* (3rd ed.). Boston: Addison-Wesley.

Kuhlthau, C.C. (1991). Inside the search process: Information seeking from the user's perspective. *Journal of the American Society for Information Science, 42*(5), 361–371.

Laaksonen, J., Koskela, M., & Oja, E. (1999). Picsom: Self-organizing maps for content-based image retrieval. *Proceedings of the International Joint Conference on Neural Networks* (vol. 4, pp. 2470–2473).

Lamsweerde, A.V., Darimont, R., & Letier, E. (1998). Managing conflicts in goal-driven requirements engineering. *IEEE Transactions on Software Engineering.*

Langheinrich, M. (2001). Privacy by design—principles of privacy-aware ubiquitous systems. *Proceedings of the 3rd International Conference on Ubiquitous Computing* (Ubicomp2001).

Langheinrich, M. (2002). A privacy awareness system for ubiquitous computing environments. *Proceedings of the 4th International Conference on Ubiquitous Computing* (UbiComp2002).

Lassila, O., & McGuinness, D. (2001). *The role of frame-based representation on the Semantic Web.* Technical Report No. KSL-01-02, Stanford University, USA.

Lau, R.Y.K., Hao, J.X., Tang, M., & Zhou, X. (2007, January 3–6). Towards context-sensitive domain ontology extraction. *Abstract Proceedings of the 40th Hawaii International Conference on Systems Science* (HICSS-40 2007) (p. 60), Waikoloa, Big Island, HI.

Lavender, R.G., & Schmidt, D.C. (1996). Active object: An object behavioral pattern for concurrent programming. In J.O. Coplien, J. Vlissides, & N. Kerth (Eds.), *Pattern languages of program design.* Boston: Addison-Wesley.

Lawrence, S. (2000). Context in Web search. *IEEE Data Engineering Bulletin, 23,* 25–32.

Lee, J.-S., Jun, C.-H., Lee, J., & Kim, S. (2005). Classification-based collaborative filtering using market basket data. *Expert Systems with Applications, 29,* 700–704.

Lee, Y.W. (2004). Crafting rules: Context-reflective data quality problem solving. *Journal of Management Information Systems, 20*(Winter), 93–119.

Lenat, D.B. (1993). Context dependence of representations in CYC. *Proceedings of Colloque ICO'93,* Montréal, Canada.

Lenat, D.B. (1995). CYC: A large-scale investment in knowledge infrastructure. *Communications of the ACM, 38*(11), 33–38.

Lenat, D.B., & Guha, R.V. (1989). *Building large knowledge-based systems: Representation and inference in the Cyc Project.* Boston: Addison-Wesley Longman.

Lenat, D.B., Sierra, C., & Guha, R.V. (1990). Cyc: Toward programs with common sense. *Communications of the ACM, 33*(8), 30–49.

Lenz, H. (1998). Multi-data sources and data fusion. *Proceedings of the International Seminar on New Techniques & Technologies for Statistics* (NTTS '98) (pp. 139–146), Sorrento.

Li, J., Wang, J., & Wiederhold, G. (2000). IRM: Integrated region matching for image retrieval. *Proceedings of the ACM International Conference on Multimedia* (pp. 147–156).

Li, M., Chen, Z., & Zhang, H. (2002). Statistical correlation analysis in image retrieval. *Pattern Recognition, 35*(12), 2687–2693.

Lian, W., Cheung, D. W., Mamoulis, N., & Yiu, S. (2004). An efficient and scalable algorithm for clustering XML documents by structure. *IEEE Transactions on Knowledge Data Engineering, 16*(1), 82-96.

Lieberman, H. (1995). Letizia: An agent that assists Web browsing. *Proceedings of the 14th International Joint Conference Artificial Intelligence,* Montreal, CA, (pp. 924-929).

Lieberman, H., Van Dyke, N., & Vivacqua, A. (1999). Let's browse: A collaborative Web browsing agent. *Proceedings of the International Conference on Intelligent User Interfaces (IUI'99),* Redondo Beach, USA, (pp. 65-68). ACM Press.

Liu, K. (2004). Agent-based resource discovery architecture for environmental emergency management. *Expert Systems with Applications, 27,* 77–95.

Liu, T., Liu, S., Chen, Z., & Ma, W.-Y. (2003). An evaluation on feature selection for text clustering. *Proceedings of the 20th International Conference on Machine Learning* (ICML 2003) (pp. 488–495).

Losee, R.M. (1997). A discipline independent definition of information. *Journal of the American Society for Information Science, 48*(3), 254–269.

Loshin, D. (2001). *Enterprise knowledge management—the data quality approach.* San Francisco: Morgan Kaufman.

Lou, W., Liu, G., Lu, H., & Yang, Q. (2002). Cut-and-pick transactions for proxy log mining. *Proceedings of the 8th International Conference on Extending Database Technology (EDBT 2002)* (pp. 88-105).

Louden, K.C. (2003). *Programming languages: Principles and practice* (2nd ed.). Brooks/Cole.

Lyman, P., & Hal, R.V. (2003). *How much information?* Retrieved June 25, 2006, from http://www.sims.berkeley.edu/how-much-info-2003

Lysyanskayal, A., Rivest, R.L., Sahai, A., & Wolf, S. (1999). Pseudonym systems. *Proceedings of the 6th Annual Workshop on Selected Areas in Cryptography (SAC'99).*

Ma, W., & Majunath, B. (1997). NeTra: A toolbox for navigating large image databases. *Proceedings of the IEEE International Conference on Image Processing* (vol. 1, pp. 568–571).

Maamar, Z., Kouadri Mostéfaoui, S., & Bataineh, E. (2004a). A conceptual analysis of the role of conversations in Web services composition. *Proceedings of the 2004 IEEE International Conference on e-Technology, e-Commerce and e-Service (EEE-04)*, Taipei, Taiwan.

Maamar, Z., Kouadri Mostéfaoui, S., & Yahyaoui, H. (2005). Towards an agent-based and context-oriented approach for Web services composition. *IEEE Transactions on Knowledge and Data Engineering, 17*(5).

Maamar, Z., Sheng, Q.Z., & Benatallah, B. (2004b). On composite Web services provisioning in an environment of fixed and mobile computing resources. *Information Technology and Management Journal, Special Issue on Workflow and e-Business, Kluwer Academic Publishers, 5*(3).

Maamar, Z., Yahyaoui, H., & Mansoor, W. (2004c). Design and development of an m-commerce environment: The E-CWE project. *Journal of Organizational Computing and Electronic Commerce, Lawrence Erlbaum Associates Publishers, 14*(4).

MacArthur, S.D., Bradley, C.E., & Shyu, C.R. (2000). Relevance feedback decision trees in content-based image retrieval. *Proceedings of the IEEE Workshop on Content-Based Access of Image and Video Libraries* (pp. 68–72).

Maedche, A. (2003). *Ontology learning for the Semantic Web.* Boston: Kluwer Academic.

Maedche, A., & Staab, S. (2000). Discovering conceptual relations from text. *Proceedings of ECAI* (pp. 321–325).

Maedche, A., & Staab, S. (2001). Ontology learning for the Semantic Web. *IEEE Intelligent Systems, 16*(2), 72–79.

Maes, P. (1994). Agents that reduce work and information overload. *Communications of the ACM, 37*(7), 30–40.

Maes, P. (1994). Modeling adaptive autonomous agents. *Artificial Life, 1*(1), 135–162.

Maes, P. (1994). Social interface agents: Acquiring competence by learning from users and other agents. *Proceedings of the AAAI Spring Symposium on Software Agents* (pp. 71–78), Stanford, CA.

Magoulas, G.D., & Dimakopoulos, D.N. (2005). Designing personalized information access to structured information spaces. *Proceedings of the Workshop on New Technologies for Personalized Information Access* (pp. 64–73).

Maletic, J.I., & Marcus, A. (2000). Data cleansing: Beyond integrity checking. *Proceedings of the Conference on Information Quality* (IQ2000) (pp. 200–209).

Malone, T., Grant, K., Turbak, F., Brobst, S., & Cohen, M. (1987). Intelligent information sharing systems. *Communications of the ACM, 30*(5), 390–402.

Malone, T.W., Grant, K.R., Turbak, F.A., Brobost, S.A., & Cohen, M.D. (1987). Intelligent information-sharing systems. *Communications of the ACM, 30*(5), 390–402.

Manber, U., Patel, A., & Robison, J. (2000). Experience with personalization on Yahoo! *Communications of the ACM, 43*(8), 35-39.

Manouselis, N., & Costopoulou, C. (2006a). *Designing multi-attribute utility algorithms for collaborative filtering.* Technical Report No. 181, Informatics Laboratory, Agricultural University of Athens, Greece.

Manouselis, N., & Costopoulou, C. (2006b). A Web-based testing tool for multi-criteria recommender systems. *Engineering Letters, Special Issue on Web Engineering, 13*(3).

Manouselis, N., & Costopoulou, C. (2007a). Analysis and classification of multi-criteria recommender systems. *World Wide Web: Internet and Web Information Systems, Special Issue on Multi-Channel Adaptive Information Systems on the World Wide Web.*

Manouselis, N., & Costopoulou, C. (2007b). Experimental analysis of design choices in multi-attribute utility collaborative filtering. *International Journal of Pattern Recognition and Artificial Intelligence, Special Issue on Personalization Techniques for Recommender Systems and Intelligent User Interfaces, 21*(2), 311-331.

Marchionini, G. (1995). *Information seeking in electronic environments.* Cambridge: Pres Syndicate of the University of Cambridge.

Marinescu, D. (2002). *Internet-based workflow management: Toward a semantic we.* New York: John Wiley & Sons.

Maritza, L., Gonzalez-Caro, C.N., Perez-Alcazar, J.J., Garcia-Diaz, J.C., & Delgado, J. (2004). A comparison of several predictive algorithms for collaborative filtering on multi-valued ratings. *Proceedings of the 2004 ACM Symposium on Applied Computing* (SAC'04), Nicosia, Cyprus.

Markellos, K., Markellou, P., Rigou, M., & Sirmakessis, S. (2003). Web mining: Past, present and future. In S. Sirmakessis (Ed.), *Proceedings of the 1st International Workshop on Text Mining and its Applications, Studies in Fuzziness.* In press. Springer Verlag Berlin Heidelberg.

Maron, O., & Lakshmi Ratan, A. (1998). Multiple-instance learning for natural scene classification. In J.W. Shavlik (Ed.), *Proceedings of the International Conference on Machine Learning* (vol. 15, pp. 341-349).

Maron, O., & Lozano Perez, T. (1997). A framework for multiple-instance learning. In M.I. Jordan, M.J. Kearns, & S.A. Solla (Eds.), *Advances in neural information processing systems* (vol. 10, pp. 570-576). Cambridge, MA: MIT Press.

Martin-Guerrero, J.D., Palomares, A., Balaguer-Ballester, E., Soria-Olivas, E., Gomez-Sanchis, J., & Soriano-Asensi, A. (2006). Studying the feasibility of a recommender in a citizen Web portal based on user modeling and clustering algorithms. *Expert Systems with Applications, 30*(2), 299-312.

Masada, T., Takasu, A., & Adachi, J. (2004). Web page grouping based on parameterized connectivity. *Proceedings of the 9th International Conference on Database Systems for Advanced Applications (DASFAA 2004)* (pp. 374-380).

Maslow, A. (1970). *Motivation and personality* (2nd ed.). New York: Harper & Row.

McCarthy, J. (1993). Notes on formalizing context. *Proceedings of the 13th International Joint Conference on Artificial Intelligence* (pp. 555-560), Chambery, France.

McCarthy, J. (2003). *Elaboration tolerance.* Retrieved May 17, 2007, from *http://www-formal.stanford.edu/jmc/elaboration/elaboration.html*

McGowan, J.P. (2003). *A multiple model approach to personalised information access.* Unpublished Doctoral Dissertation, Faculty of Science, University College Dublin, Ireland.

McLaughlin, M.R., & Herlocker, J.L. (2004). A collaborative filtering algorithm and evaluation metric that accurately model the user experience. *Proceedings of the International ACM SIGIR Conference on Research and Development in Information Retrieval* (SIGIR'04), Sheffield, UK.

McLuhan, M., & Fiore, Q. (1967). *The medium is the massage.* London: Penguin.

Medjahed, B., Bouguettaya, A., & Elmagarmid, A. (2003). Composing Web services on the semantic Web. *The VLDB Journal, Special Issue on the Semantic Web, Springer Verlag, 12*(4).

Mehrotra, S., Butts, C., Kalashnikov, D., Venkatasubramanian, N., Rao, R., Chockalingam, G., Eguchi, R., Adams, B., & Huyck, C. (2004). Project rescue: Challenges in responding to the unexpected. *SPIE, 5304*(January), 179–192.

Mehrotra, S., Rui, Y., Ortega, M., & Huang, T. (1997). Supporting content-based queries over images in MARS. *Proceedings of the IEEE International Conference on Multimedia Computing and Systems* (pp. 632–633).

Menascé, D.A. (2002). QoS issues in Web services. *IEEE Internet Computing, 6*(6).

Merriam-Webster. (n.d.). Retrieved from http://www.m-w.com

Mesquita, C., Barbosa, S.D., & Lucena, C.J. (2002). Towards the identification of concerns in personalization mechanisms via scenarios. *Proceedings of 1st International Conference on Aspect-Oriented Software Development,* Enschede, The Netherlands. Available: http://trese.cs.utwente.nl/AOSD-EarlyAspectsWS/Papers/Mesquita.pdf

Meyer, B. (1988). *Object-oriented software construction.* Englewood Cliffs, NJ: Prentice Hall.

Michigan State University School of Criminal Justice. (2000). *Critical incident protocol—a public and private partnership.* Retrieved December 18, 2006, from *http://www.cj.msu.edu/%7Eoutreach/CIP/CIP.pdf*

Milanovic, N. and Malek, M. (2004). Current Solutions for Web Service Composition. *IEEE Internet Computing, 8*(6).

Miller, B.N., Konstan, J.A., & Riedl, J. (2004). PocketLens: Toward a personal recommender system. *ACM Transactions on Information Systems, 22*(3), 437–476.

Mills, A.J., & Simmons, A.M. (1999). *Reading organization theory.* Toronto: Garamond.

Min, S.-H., & Han, I. (2005). Detection of the customer time-invariant pattern for improving recommender systems. *Expert Systems with Applications, 28,* 189–199.

Miner, J.B. (1992). *Industrial-organizational psychology.* New York: McGraw-Hill.

Missikof, M., Navigli, R., & Velardi, P. (2002). Integrated approach to Web ontology learning and engineering. *Computer, 35*(11), 60–63.

Mizoguchi, R., Ikeda, M., & Sinitsa, K. (1997). Roles of shared ontology in AI-ED research. *Proceedings of the Conference on Intelligence, Conceptualization, Standardization, and Reusability* (AI-ED97) (pp. 537–544).

Mizzaro, S. (1997). Relevance: The whole history. *Journal of the American Society for Information Science, 48*(9), 810–832.

Mladenic, D. (1999). Text learning and related intelligent agents. *IEEE Intelligent Systems and their Applications, 14*(4), 44-54.

Mobasher, B., & Dai, H. (2003). A road map to more effective Web personalization: Integrating domain knowledge with Web usage mining. *Proceedings of the International Conference on Internet Computing 2003 (IC'03),* Las Vegas, Nevada.

Mobasher, B., Cooley, R., & Srivastava, J. (2000). Automatic personalization based on Web usage mining. *Communications of the ACM, 43*(8), 142–151.

Mobasher, B., Cooley, R., & Srivastava, J. (2000). Automatic personalization based on Web usage mining. *Communications of the ACM, 43*(8), 142-151.

Mobasher, B., Cooley, R., & Srivastava, J. (2000b). Automatic personalization based on Web usage mining. *Communications of the ACM, 43*(8), 142-151.

Mobasher, B., Dai, H., Luo, T., Sun, Y., & Zhu, J. (2000a). Integrating Web usage and content mining for more effective personalization. *Proceedings of the 1st International*

Conference on E-Commerce and Web Technologies (ECWeb2000), Greenwich, UK, (pp. 165-176).

Modha, D., & Spangler, W. (2003). Feature weighting in k-means clustering. *Machine Learning, 52*(3), 217-237.

Moore, J., Han, E., Boley, D., Gini, M., Gross, R., Hastings, K., et al. (1997). Web page categorization and feature selection using association rule and principal component clustering. Proceedings of the *7th Workshop on Information Technologies and Systems*, Atlanta, GA.

Mork, L. (2002). Technology tools for crisis response. *Risk Management, 49*(10), 44–50.

Motschnig-Pitrik, R. (1995). An integrated view on the viewing abstraction: Contexts and perspectives in software development, AI, and databases. *Journal of Systems Integration 5*(1), 23–60.

Moukas, A. (1997). Amalthea: Information discovery and filtering using a multiagent evolving ecosystem. *Applied Artificial Intelligence, 11,* 437–457.

Moura, A.M. (2003). The semantic Web: Fundamentals, technologies, trends. *Proceedings of the 17th Brazilian Symposium of Databases,* Gramado, Brazil.

Muldoon, C., O'Hare, G., Phelan, D., Strahan, R., & Collier, R. (2003). ACCESS: An agent architecture for ubiquitous service delivery. *Proceedings of the 7th International Workshop on Cooperative Information Agents (CIA'2003)*, Helsinki, Finland.

Mulvenna, M., Anand, S., & Bchner, A. (2000). Personalization on the Net using Web mining. *Communications of the ACM, 43*(8), 122-125.

Mylopoulos, J., & Motschnig-Pitrik, R. (1995). Partitioning information bases with contexts. *Proceedings of CoopIS'95* (pp. 44–55), Vienna, Austria.

Nakamura, A., & Abe, N. (1998). Collaborative filtering using weighted majority prediction algorithms. *Proceedings of the 15th International Conference on Machine Learning* (ICML'98). San Francisco: Morgan Kaufman.

Nanopoulos, A., Katsaros, D., & Manolopoulos, Y. (2003). A data mining algorithm for generalized Web prefetching. *IEEE Transactions on Knowledge Data Engineering, 15*(5), 1155-1169.

Navigli, R., Velardi, P., & Gangemi, A. (2003). Ontology learning and its application to automated terminology translation. *IEEE Intelligent Systems, 18*(1), 22–31.

Nelson, M.R. (2001). *We have the information you want, but getting it will cost you: Being held hostage by information overload.* Retrieved from *http://www.acm.org/crossroads/xrds1-1/mnelson.html*

Ngu, D., & Wu, X. (1997). SiteHelper: A localized agent that helps incremental exploration of the World Wide Web. *Proceedings of the 6th World Wide Web Conference,* Santa Clara, CA.

Niedźwiedzka, B. (2003). A proposed general model of information behavior. *Information Research, 9*(1) paper 164.

Nielsen, J. (1994). *Usability engineering.* Morgan Kaufmann.

Nielsen, J. (1998). Personalization is over-rated. Alertbox for October 4, 1998. Available: http://www.useit.com

Nierman, A., & Jagadish, H. V. (2002). Evaluating structural similarity in XML documents. *Proceedings of the 5th International Workshop on the Web and Databases (WebDB 2002)* (pp. 61-66).

Nilsson, M., Lindskog, H., & Fischer-Hübner, S. (2001). Privacy enhancements in the mobile Internet. *Proceedings of the IFIP WG 9.6/11.7 Working Conference on Security and Control of IT in Society,* Bratislava.

Nurnberger, A. (2001). Clustering of document collections using a growing self-organizing map. *Proceedings of the BISC International Workshop on Fuzzy Logic and the Internet* (FLINT 2001) (pp. 136–141).

Nwana H.S. (1996). Software agents: An overview. *Knowledge Engineering Review, 11*(3), 205–244.

Nwana, H.S., Lee, L., & Jennings, N.R. (1996). Coordination in software agent systems. *BT Technology Journal, 14*(4), 79–89.

Nyanchama, M., & Osborn, S. (1999). The role graph model and conflict of interest. *ACM Transactions on Information and System Security, 2*(1), 3–33.

Odell, J., Nodine, M., & Levy, R.(2005). A metamodel for agents, roles, and groups. In J. Odell, P. Giorgini, & J. Müller (Eds.), *Agent-oriented software engineering* (pp. 78–92). Berlin: Springer-Verlag (LNCS 3382).

Odell, J., Van Dyke Parunak, H., & Fleischer, M. (2003). The role of roles in designing effective agent organizations. In A. Garcia, C. Lucena, F. Zambonelli, A. Omicini, & J. Castro (Eds.), *Software engineering for large-scale multi-agent systems* (pp. 27–38). Berlin: Springer-Verlag (LNCS 2603).

OECD. (2003). Privacy online. In OECD (Ed.), *OECD guidance on policy and practice* (p. 40). Paris: OECD.

OMG-UML2. (2004). *Unified Modeling Language version 2.0.* Retrieved from http://www.uml.org

Ono, A., Amano, M., Hakaridani, M., Satoh, T., & Sakauchi, M. (1996). A flexible content-based image retrieval system with combined scene description keywords. *Proceedings of the IEEE International Conference on Multimedia Computing and Systems* (pp. 201–208).

Osiski, S. (2004). *Dimensionality reduction techniques for search results clustering.* Unpublished Master's Thesis, Department of Computer Science, University of Sheffield, UK.

Ould, M.A. (1995). *Business processes: Modeling and analysis for re-engineering and improvement.* New York: John Wiley & Sons.

Ouzzani, M., & Bouguettaya, A. (2004). Efficient access to Web services. *IEEE Internet Computing, 8*(2).

Paepcke, A. (1996). *Digital libraries: Searching is not enough.* Retrieved June 25, 2006, from *http://dlib.org/dlib/may96/stanford/05paepcke.html*

Pallis, G., & Vakali, A. (2006). Insight and perspectives for content delivery networks. *Communications of the ACM, 49*(1), 101-106.

Pallis, G., Angelis, L., & Vakali, A. (2005). Model-based cluster analysis for Web users sessions. In *Proceedings of the 15th International Symposium on Methodologies for Intelligent Systems (ISMIS 2005)* (LNCS 3488, pp. 219-227). Saratoga Springs, NY: Springer Verlag.

Pallis, G., Angelis, L., Vakali, A., & Pokorny, J. (2004). A probabilistic validation algorithm for Web users' clusters. *Proceedings of the IEEE International Conference on Systems, Man and Cybernetics (SMC 2004)* (pp. 4129-4134).

Pallis, G., Vakali, A., Angelis, L., & Hacid, M. S. (2003). A study on workload characterization for a Web proxy server. *Proceedings of the 21st IASTED International Multi-Conference on Applied Informatics (AI 2003)* (pp. 779-784).

Papagelis, M., & Plexousakis, D. (2005). Qualitative analysis of user-based and item-based prediction algorithms for recommendation agents. *Engineering Applications of Artificial Intelligence, 18,* 781–789.

Papagelis, M., Rousidis, I., Plexousakis, D., & Theoharopoulos, E. (2005). Incremental collaborative filtering for highly-scalable recommendation algorithms. *Proceedings of ISMIS 2005* (pp. 553–561). Berlin: Springer-Verlag (LNAI 3488).

Papazoglou, M., & Georgakopoulos, D. (2003). Introduction to the special issue on service-oriented computing. *Communications of the ACM, 46*(10).

Papazoglou, M.P. (2001). Agent-oriented technology in support of e-business. *Communications of the ACM, 44*(4), 71–77.

Papazoglou, M.P. (2003, December 10–12). Service-oriented computing: Concepts, characteristics and directions. *Proceedings of the Conference on Web Information Systems Engineering* (WISE 2003) pp. 3–12).

Papazoglou, M.P., & Georgakopoulos, D. (2003). Introduction to service-oriented computing. *Communications of the ACM, 46*(10), 24–28.

Parsons, S., Jennings, N.R., & Sabater, J. (2002). *Agent specification using multi-context systems.*

Parsons, S., Sierra, C., & Jennings, N.R. (1998). Multi-context argumentative agents. *Proceedings of the 4ᵗʰ International Symposium on Logical Formalizations of Commonsense Reasoning.*

Pascoe, J. (1998). Adding generic contextual capabilities to wearable computers. *Proceedings of the 2ⁿᵈ International Symposium on Wearable Computers* (pp. 92–99).

Pavlin, G., de Oude, P., & Nunnink, J. (2005). A MAS approach to fusion of heterogeneous information. *Proceedings of the 2005 IEEE/WIC/ACM International Conference on Web Intelligence* (WI'05) (pp. 802–804).

Peng, J., Banerjee, B., & Heisterkamp, D.R. (2002). Kernel index for relevance feedback retrieval in large image databases. *Proceedings of the International Conference on Neural Information Processing* (pp. 187–191).

Peng, J., Bhanu, B., & Qing, S. (1999). Probabilistic feature relevance learning for content-based image retrieval. *Computer Vision and Image Understanding, 75*(1/2), 150–164.

Pentland, A., Picard, R., & Sclaroff, S. (1994). PhotoBOOK: Tools for content-based manipulation of image databases. In W. Niblack & R. Jain (Eds.), *Proceedings of the SPIE Storage and Retrieval for Image Databases* (vol. 2, pp. 34–47).

Peralta, V., Ruggia, R., Kedad, Z., & Mokrane, B. (2004). A framework for data quality evaluation in a data integration system. *Proceedings of the Brazilian Symposium of Databases* (pp. 134–147).

Perkowitz, M., & Etzioni, O. (1997). Adaptive Web sites: An AI challenge. *Proceedings of the 15th International Joint Conference on Artificial Intelligence.*

Perkowitz, M., & Etzioni, O. (1998). Adaptive Web sites: Automatically synthesizing Web pages. *Proceedings of the 15th National Conference on Artificial Intelligence.*

Perkowitz, M., & Etzioni, O. (1999). Adaptive Web sites: Conceptual cluster mining. *Proceedings of the 16th International Joint Conference on Artificial Intelligence.*

Perkowitz, M., & Etzioni, O. (2000a). Adaptive Web sites. *Communications of the ACM, 43*(8), 152-158.

Perkowitz, M., & Etzioni, O. (2000b). Towards adaptive Web sites: Conceptual framework and case study. *Artificial Intelligence, 118*(1-2), 245-275.

Perner, P., & Fiss, G. (2002). Intelligent E-marketing with Web mining, personalization, and user-adapted interfaces. In P. Perner (Ed.), *Advances in data mining 2002, LNAI 2394* (pp. 37-52). Berlin: Springer-Verlag Berlin Heidelberg.

Perugini, S., & Ramakrishnan, N. (2003). Personalizing interactions with information systems. In M. Zelkowitz (Ed.), *Advances in computers* (vol. 57, pp. 323–382). Academic Press.

Petit-Rozé, C., & Grislin-Le Strugeon, E. (2006). MAPIS, a multi-agent system for information personalization. *Information and Software Technology, 48,* 107–120.

Petre, L., Sere, K., & Walden, M. (1999). A topological approach to distributed computing. *Proceedings of the Workshop on Distributed Systems* (WDS'99).

Pham, V.A., & Karmouch, A. (1998). Mobile software agents: An overview. *IEEE Communications Magazine,* (July), 26–37.

Pharo, N. (2004). A new model of information behavior based on the search situation transition schema, library and information science. *Information Research, 10*(1), paper 203.

Pierrakos, D., Paliouras, G., Papatheodorou, C., & Spyropoulos, C.D. (2003). Web usage mining as a tool for personalization: A survey. *User Modeling and User-Adapted Interaction, 13*(4), 311–372.

Pinheiro, W.A., & Moura, A.M.C. (2004). An ontology based-approach for semantic search in portals. *Database and Expert Systems Applications, 15,* 127–131.

Pinto, H.S., & Martins, J.P. (2004). Ontologies: How can they be built? *Knowledge and Information Systems, 6*(4), 441–464.

Pipino, L.L., Lee, Y.W., & Wang, R.Y. (2002). Data quality assessment. *Communications of the ACM, 45,* 211–218.

Pirolli, P., & Card, S. (1999). Information foraging. *Psychological Review, 106*(4), 643-675.

Poladian, V., Pedro Sousa, J., Garlan, D., & Shaw, M. (2004). Dynamic configuration of resource-aware services. *Proceedings of the 26th International Conference on Software Engineering (ICSE'2004)*, Edinburgh, Scotland.

Proper, H.A., & Bruza, P.D. (1999). What is information discovery about? *Journal of the American Society for Information Science, 50*(9), 737–750.

Ramakrishnan, N. (2000). PIPE: Web personalization by partial evaluation. *IEEE Internet Computing, 4*(6), 21-31.

Ramakrishnan, N., Rosson, M.B., & Carroll, J.M. (2007). *Explaining scenarios for information personalization.* Retrieved April 10, 2007, from http://arxiv.org/pdf/cs/0111007v1

Ranganathan, A., & Campbell, R.H. (2003). *An infrastructure for context-awareness based on first order logic.* London: Springer-Verlag.

Ratsimor, O., Korolev, V., Joshi, A., & Finin, T. (2001). Agents2Go: An infrastructure for location-dependent service discovery in the mobile electronic commerce environment. *Proceedings of the 1st ACM International Workshop on Mobile Commerce (WMC'2001) held in conjunction with the Seventh Annual International Conference on Mobile Computing and Networking (MobiCom'2001)*, Rome, Italy.

Rauber, A., & Merkl, D. (1999). Using self-organizing maps to organize document archives and to characterize subject matter: How to make a map tell the news of the world. *Proceedings of the 10th International Conference on Database and Expert Systems Applications (DEXA'99)* (pp. 302–311). London: Springer-Verlag.

Ravela, S., Manmatha, R., & Riseman, E.M. (1996). Scale-space matching and image retrieval. *Proceed-ings of the Image Understanding Workshop* (vol. 2, pp. 1199–1207).

Reddy, P. K., & Kitsuregawa, M. (2001). An approach to relate the Web communities through bipartite graphs. *WISE, 1,* 301-310.

Redman, T.C. (1998). The impact of poor data quality on the typical enterprise. *Communications of the ACM, 41,* 79–81.

Resnick, P., Iacovou, N., Suchak, M., Bergstrom, P., & Riedl, J. (1994). GroupLens: An open architecture for collaborative filtering. *Proceedings of ACM CSCW'94* (pp. 175–186).

Resnikoff, H. (1989). *The illusion of reality* (p. 97). New York: Springer-Verlag.

Rhodes, B.J., & Maes, P. (2000). Just-in-time information retrieval agents. *IBM Systems Journal, 39*(3–4), 685–704.

Riecken, D. (2000). Personalized views of personalization. *Communications of the ACM, 43*(18).

Roberts, D.D. (1973). *The existential graphs of Charles S. Peirce.* The Hague: Mouton.

Rocchio, J., & Salton, G. (1971). The SMART retrieval system: Experiments in automatic document processing. In *Relevance feedback in information retrieval* (pp. 313–323). Englewood Cliffs, NJ: Prentice Hall.

Rodden, T., Friday, A., Henk, M., & Dix, A. (2002). *A lightweight approach to managing privacy in location-based services* (No. Equator-02-058), University of Nottingham and Lancaster, UK.

Roh, T.H., Oh, K.J., & Han, I. (2003). The collaborative filtering recommendation based on SOM cluster-indexing CBR. *Expert Systems with Applications, 25,* 413–423.

Ross, T.J. (2004). Fuzzy Logic with Engineering Applications (2nd ed.). West Sussex, England: John Wiley & Sons.

Rossi, G., Schwabe, D., & Guimaraes, R. (2001). Designing personalized Web applications. *Proceedings of the WWW10,* Hong Kong, 275-284.

Roth, G., & Dicke, U. (2005). Evolution of the brain and intelligence. *Trends in Cognitive Sciences, 9*(5), 250–257.

Rothenberg, J. (1996). Metadata to support data quality and longevity. *Proceedings of the 1st IEEE Metadata Conference* (pp. 16–18).

Rui, Y., & Huang, T. (1998). Relevance feedback: A power tool for interactive content-based image retrieval. *IEEE Transactions on Circuits and Systems for Video Technology, 8*(5), 644–655.

Rui, Y., Huang, T., & Chang, S. (1999). Image retrieval: Past, present, and future. *Journal of Visual Communication and Image Representation, 10,* 1-23.

Rui, Y., Huang, T., & Mehrotra, S. (1997). Content-based image retrieval with relevance feedback in MARS. *Proceedings of the IEEE International Conference on Image Processing* (vol. 2, pp. 815–818).

Russell, D., & Norvig, P. (2003). *Artificial intelligence: A modern approach* (2nd ed.). Upper Saddle River, NJ: Pearson Education.

Russell, S.J. (1997). Rationality and intelligence. *Artificial Intelligence, 94,* 57–77.

Salton, G. (1986). Another look at automatic text-retrieval systems. *Communications of the ACM, 29*(7), 648–656.

Salton, G. (1989). *Automatic text processing: The transformation, analysis and retrieval of information by computer.* Reading, MA: Addison-Wesley.

Salton, G., & McGill, M. (1983). *Introduction to modern information retrieval.* New York: McGraw-Hill.

Salton, G., & McGill, M. (1998). *Introduction to modern information retrieval.* New York: McGraw-Hill.

Salton, G., Wong, A., & Yang, C. (1975). A vector space model for automatic indexing. *Communications of the ACM, 18*(11), 613-620.

Samadani, R., Han, C., & Katragadda, L.K. (1993). Content-based event selection from satellite image of the aurora. In W. Niblack (Ed.), *Proceedings of the SPIE Storage and Retrieval for Image and Video Databases* (vol. 1908, pp. 50–59).

Saracevic, T., Kantor, P., Chamis, A.Y., & Trivison, D. (1988). A study of information seeking and retrieving, I: Background and methodology. *Journal of the American Society for Information Science, 39,* 161–176.

Sarwar, B., Karypis, G., Konstan, J., & Riedl, J. (2000). Analysis of recommendation algorithms for e-commerce. *Proceedings of ACM EC'00,* Minneapolis, MN.

Sarwar, B.M. (2001). *Sparsity, scalability, and distribution in recommender systems.* PhD Thesis, University of Minnesota, USA.

Satyanarayanan, M. (2001). Pervasive computing: Vision and challenges. *IEEE Personal Communications, 8*(4).

Schafer, J., Konstan, J., & Riedl, J. (2001). E-commerce recommendation applications. *Data Mining and Knowledge Discovery, 5*(1), 115-153.

Schafer, J.B., Konstan, J.A., & Riedl, J. (2001). E-commerce recommendation applications. *Proceedings of the Conference on Data Mining and Knowledge Discovery* (pp. 115–153).

Scherbina, A., & Kuznetsov, S. (2004). Clustering of Web sessions using Levenshtein metric. In *Proceedings of the 4th Industrial Conference on Data Mining (ICDM 2004)* (LNCS 3275, pp. 127-133). San Jose, CA: Springer Verlag.

Scherer, A.G. (2003). Modes of explanation in organization theory. In H. Tsoukas & C. Knudsen (Eds.), *The Oxford handbook of organizational theory* (pp. 310–344). Oxford: Oxford University Press.

Schiaffino, S., & Amandi, A. (2004). User-interface agent interaction: Personalization issues. *International Journal of Human Computer Studies, Elsevier Sciences Publisher, 60*(1).

Schilit, B., Adams, N., & Want, R. (1994). Context-aware computing applications. *Proceedings of the IEEE Workshop on Mobile Computing Systems and Applications,* Santa Cruz, California.

Schilit, B.N., & Theimer, M. (1994). Disseminating active map information to mobile hosts. *IEEE Network,* 22–32.

Schreiber, A.T., Wielinga, B.J., & Jansweijer, W.H.J. (1995). The KACTUS view on the 'O' word. *Proceedings of the IJCAI Workshop on Basic Ontological Issues in Knowledge Sharing.*

Sclaroff, S., Taycher, L., & Cascia, M.L. (1997). *ImageRover: A content-based image browser for the World Wide Web.* Technical Report No. 97-005, Computer Science Department, Boston University, USA.

Sekerinski, E., & Sere, K. (1996). A theory of prioritizing composition. *The Computer Journal.*

Sere, K., & Walden, M. (1997). Data refinement of remote procedures. *Proceedings of the International Symposium on Theoretical Aspects of Computer Software,* Sendai, Japan. Berlin: Springer-Verlag (LNCS 1281).

Shadbolt, N., Berners-Lee, T., & Hall, W. (2006). The Semantic Web revisited. *IEEE Intelligent Systems, 21*(3), 96–101.

Shahabi, C., & Chen, Y. (2003). Web information personalization: Challenges and approaches. *Lecture Notes in Computer Science, 2822,* 5–15.

Shahabi, C., Faisal, A., Kashani, F. B., & Faruque, J. (2000). INSITE: A tool for interpreting users' interaction with a Web space. *Proceedings of the 26th International Conference on Very Large Data Bases (VLDB 2000)* (pp. 635-638).

Shahabi, C., Zarkesh, A. M., Adibi, J., & Shah, V. (1997). *Knowledge discovery from users Web page navigation.* Proceedings of the 7th International Workshop on Research Issues in Data Engineering (IEEE RIDE), Birmingham, United Kingdom.

Shakshuki, E., Ghenniwa, H., & Kamel, M. (2003). An architecture for cooperative information systems. *Knowledge-Based Systems, 16,* 17–27.

Shardanand, U., & Maes, P. (1995). Social information filtering: Algorithms for automatic 'word of mouth'.

Proceedings of the Conference on Human Factors in Computing Systems (CHI'95), Denver CO.

Sharma, N. (1995). *On formalizing and reasoning with contexts.* Technical Report, Department of Computer Science, University of Queensland, Australia.

Shaw, W.M. (1995). Term-relevance computations and perfect retrieval performance. *Information Processing and Management: An International Journal, 31*(4), 491–498.

Shen, H.T., Ooi, B.C., & Tan, K.L. (2000). Giving meanings to WWW images. *Proceedings of the ACM Multimedia* (pp. 39–47).

Shen, X., Tan, B., & Zhai, J.C. (2005). Context-sensitive information retrieval using implicit feedback. *Proceedings of the 29th Annual International ACM SIGIR Conference on Research and Development in Information Retrieval* (pp. 43–50).

Shoham, Y. (1993). Agent-oriented programming. *Artificial Intelligence, 60,* 51–92.

Siegel, J. (1998). OMG overview: CORBA and the OMA in enterprise computing. *Communications of the ACM, 41*(10), 37–43.

Siegel, J. (2000). *CORBA 3: Fundamentals and programming.* New York: OMG Press/John Wiley & Sons.

Singley, M.K., Singh, M., Fairweather, P., Farrell, R., & Swerling, S. (2000). Algebra jam: Supporting teamwork and managing roles in a collaborative learning environment. *Proceedings of CSCW'00* (pp. 145–154), Philadelphia.

Sivasankaran, R.M., Stankovic, J.A., Towsley, D., Purimetla, B., & Ramamritham, K. (1996). Priority assignment in real-time active databases. *International Journal on Very Large Data Bases.*

Smart, K.L. (2002). Assessing quality documents. *ACM Journal of Computer Documentation, 26*(3), 130–140.

Smeulders, A.W.M., Worring, M., Santini, S., Gupta, A., & Jain, R. (2000). Content-based image retrieval at the end of the early years. *IEEE Transactions on Pattern Analysis and Machine Intelligence, 22*(12), 1349–1380.

Smith, E., & Winterhalder, B. (eds.). (1992). Evolutionary ecology and human behavior. New York: de Gruyter.

Smith, I.A., Cohen, P.R., Bradshaw, J.M., Greaves, M., & Holmback, H. (1998). Designing conversation policies using joint intention theory. *Proceedings of the 3rd International Conference on Multi-Agent Systems (ICMAS'1998)*, Paris, France.

Smith, J., & Chang, S. (1996). VisualSEEk: A fully automated content-based image query system. *Proceedings of the ACM Conference on Multimedia* (pp. 87–98).

Smith, J., & Chang, S. (1997). An image and video search engine for the World Wide Web. *Proceedings of the SPIE Storage and Retrieval for Image and Video Databases* (vol. 5, pp. 84–95).

Smith, J.R., & Li, C.S. (1999). Image classification and querying using composite region templates. *Computer Vision and Image Understanding, 75*(1/2), 165–174.

Smith, K., & Ng, A. (2003). Web page clustering using a self-organizing map of user navigation patterns. *Decision Support Systems, 35*(2), 245-256.

Sowa, J.F. (1995). Syntax, semantics, and pragmatics of context. *Proceedings of the 3rd International Conference on Conceptual Structures* (ICCS'95) (pp. 1–15), Santa Cruz, CA. Berlin: Springer-Verlag (LNAI 954).

Sperber, D., & Wilson, D. (1986). *Relevance: Communication and cognition.* Basil Blackwell.

Speretta, M., & Gauch, S. (2004). Personalizing search based user search histories. *Proceedings of the 13th International Conference on Information Knowledge and Management* (CIKM) (pp. 238–239).

Spertus, E., Sahami, M., & Buyukkokten, O. (2005, August 21–24). Evaluating similarity measures: A large-scale study in the Orkut Social Network. *Proceedings of KDD'05.*

Spiliopoulou, M. (2000). Web usage mining for Web site evaluation. *Communications of the ACM, 43*(8), 128-134.

Spiliopoulou, M., & Faulstich, L. (1998). WUM: A tool for WWW utilization analysis. In *Proceedings of the International Workshop on World Wide Web and Databases (WebDB 1998)* (LNCS 1590, pp. 184-203). Valencia, Spain: Springer Verlag.

Spiliopoulou, M., & Faulstich, L. (1998). *WUM: A Web utilization miner.* EDBT Workshop WebDB98, Valencia, Spain.

Spiliopoulou, M., & Pohle, C. (2000). Data mining for measuring and improving the success of Web sites. *Data Mining and Knowledge Discovery, Special Issue on Electronic Commerce.*

Spiliopoulou, M., Faulstich, L., & Wilkler, K. (1999a). A data miner analyzing the navigational behavior of Web users. *Proceedings of the Workshop on Machine Learning in User Modelling of the ACAI99*, Chania, Greece.

Spiliopoulou, M., Pohle, C., & Faulstich, L. (1999b). Improving the effectiveness of a Web site with Web usage mining. *Proceedings of the WEBKDD99*, San Diego, California (pp. 142-162).

Spink, A., & Saracevic, T. (1997). Interaction in information retrieval: Selection and effectiveness of search terms. *Journal of the American Society for Information Science, 48*(8), 741–761.

Spink, A., Greisdorf, H., & Bateman, J. (1998). From highly relevant to not relevant: Examining different regions of relevance. *Information Processing & Management, 34*(5), 599–621.

Spriestersbach, A., Volger, H., Lehmann, F., & Ziegert, T. (2001). Integrating context information into enterprise applications for the mobile workforce—A case study. *Proceedings of the 1st ACM International Workshop on Mobile Commerce (WMC'2001) held in conjunction with the Seventh Annual International Conference on Mobile Computing and Networking (MobiCom'2001)*, Rome, Italy.

Sprott, D., & Wilkes, L. (2004). Understanding service oriented architecture. *Microsoft Architect Journal,* (January).

Srihari, R.K., Zhang, Z., & Rao, A. (2000). Intelligent indexing and semantic retrieval of multimedia documents. *Information Retrieval, 2,* 245–275.

Srivastava, J., Cooley, R., Deshpande, M., & Tan, P. (2000, January). Web usage mining: Discovery and applications of usage patterns from Web data. *ACM SIGKDD, 1*(2), 12-23.

Stein, B., Eissen, S. M., & Wibrock, F. (2003). *On cluster validity and the information need of users.* Proceedings of the 3rd IASTED International Conference on Artificial Intelligence and Applications (AIA 2003), Benalmadena, Spain.

Steinberg, L., & Cruz, A. (2004). When natural and technological disasters collide: Lessons from the Turkey earthquake of August 17, 1999. *Natural Hazards Review, 5*(3).

Stephens, D., & Krebs, J. (1986). *Foraging theory.* Princeton, NJ: Princeton University Press.

Stojanovic, Z. (2003). *An integrated component-oriented framework for effective and flexible enterprise distributed systems development.* Systems Engineering Group, Faculty of Technology, Policy and Management, Delft University of Technology, The Netherlands.

Stojanovic, Z. (2005). *A method for component based and service oriented software systems engineering.* Unpublished PhD Thesis, Delft University of Technology, The Netherlands.

Stojanovic, Z. (2005). *A method for component-based and service-oriented software systems engineering.* Doctoral Dissertation, Delft University of Technology, The Netherlands.

Stojanovic, Z., Dahanayake, A., & Sol, H.G. (2004). *An approach to component based and service-oriented system architecture design.* Faculty of Technology, Policy and Management, Delft University of Technology, The Netherlands.

Stone, H.S., & Li, C.S. (1996). Image matching by means of intensity and texture matching in the Fourier domain. In I.K. Sethi & R. Jain (Eds.), *Proceedings of the SPIE Conference on Image and Video Databases* (vol. 2670, pp. 337–349).

Stone, P., & Veloso, M. (1999). Task decomposition, dynamic role assignment, and low-bandwidth communication for real-time strategic teamwork. *Artificial Intelligence, 110,* 241–273.

Strong, D., Wang, R.Y., & Guarascio, M.L. (1994). Beyond accuracy: What data quality means to data consumers. TDQM Research Program. *Journal of Management Information Systems, 12*(4), 5–33.

Studer, R., Benjamins, V.R., & Fensel, D. (1998). Knowledge engineering: Principles and methods. *Data Knowledge Engineering, 25*(1–2), 161–197.

Su, J., & Lee, M. (2003). An exploration in personalized and context-sensitive search. *Proceedings of the 7th Annual UK Special Interest Group for Computational Linguists Research Colloquium.*

Suchman, L.A. (1987). Plans and situated actions. Cambridge, UK: Cambridge University Press.

Sun, J. (2003). Information requirement elicitation in mobile commerce. *Communications of the ACM, 46*(12).

Sure, Y., & Studer, R. (2002a). *On-To-Knowledge methodology□expanded version.* Technical Report No. OTK/2001/D17/v1.0, Institute AIFB, University of Karlsruhe, Germany.

Sure, Y., & Studer, R. (2002b). *On-To-Knowledge methodology□final version.* Technical Report No. OTK/2002/D18/v1.0, Institute AIFB, University of Karlsruhe, Germany.

Swain, M., & Ballard, D. (1991). Color indexing. *International Journal of Computer Vision, 7*(1), 11–32.

Swartout, B., Patil, R., Knight, K., & Russ, T. (1997). Toward distributed use of large-scale ontologies. *Proceedings of the Symposium on Ontological Engineering of AAAI* (pp. 138–148), Stanford University, USA.

Szathmáry, E., & Maynard Smith, J. (1995). The major evolutionary transitions. *Nature, 374*(16), 227–232.

Szyperski, C. (1998). *Component software: Beyond object orient programming.* Boston: ACM Press/Addison-Wesley.

Tamine, L., Boughanem, M., & Chrisment, C. (2006). Accès personnalisé à l'information: Vers un modèle basé sur les diagrammes d'influence. *Information—Interaction—Intelligence, 6*(1), 69–90).

Tanenbaum, A.S., & van Steen, M. (2002), *Distributed systems: Principles and paradigms.* Englewood Cliffs, NJ: Prentice Hall.

Taylor, R. (1968). Question negotiation and information seeking in libraries. *College and Research Libraries, 29*(3), 178–194.

Taylor, R. (1991). Information use environments. In B. Dervin & M.J. Voigt (Eds.), *Progress in communication sciences* (pp. 217–255).

Teevan, J., Dumais, S., & Horvitz, E. (2005). Personalizing search via automated analysis of interests and activities. *Proceedings of the 28th Annual ACM Conference on Research and Development in Information Retrieval* (pp.449–456).

Terveen, L.,& Hill, W. (2001). Beyond recommender system: Helping people to find each other. *Proceedings of HCI in the New Millennium.*

Tewoldeberhan, T.W. (2005). *Gaining insight into business networks, a simulation based support environment to improve process orchestration.* PhD Dissertation, Technology University of Delft, The Netherlands.

Theodorakis, M., & Spyratos, N. (2002). Context in artificial intelligent and information modeling. *Proceedings of the 2nd Hellenic Conference on AI* (SETN-2002) (companion vol., pp. 27–38).

Tieu, K., & Viola, P. (2000). Boosting image retrieval. *Proceedings of the IEEE Conference in Computer Vision and Pattern Recognition* (pp. 1228–1235).

Tillman, H.N. (2003). *Evaluating quality on the Net.* Retrieved June 25, 2006, from *http://www.hopetillman.com/findqual.html*

Tong, S., & Chang, E. (2001). Support vector machine active learning for image retrieval. *Proceedings of the ACM International Conference on Multimedia* (pp. 107–118).

Tsai, K.H., Chiu, T.K., Lee, M.C., & Wang, T.I. (2006). A learning objects recommendation model based on the preference and ontological approaches. *Proceedings of the 6th IEEE International Conference on Advanced Learning Technologies* (ICALT'06).

Tu, H., & Hsiang, J. (2000). An architecture and category knowledge for intelligent information retrieval agents. *Decision Support Systems, 28*(3), 255–268.

Turksen, I.B. (1991). Measurement of membership functions and their acquisition. In ITSA (Ed.), *Fuzzy sets and systems. Special memorial volume: 25 years of fuzzy sets.* Amsterdam: North-Holland.

Turoff, M., Chumer, M., Van de Walle, B., & Yao, X. (2003). The design of emergency response management information systems (ERMIS). *Journal of Information Technology Theory & Application.*

Twidale, M.B., & Marty, P.F. (1999). *An investigation of data quality and collaboration.* Technical Report UIUCLIS—1999/9+CSCW, University of Illinois at Urbana-Champaign, USA.

Uschold, M., & Grüninger, M. (1996). Ontologies: Principles, methods, and applications. *Knowledge Engineering Review, 11*(2), 93–155.

Uszok, A., et al. Policy and contract management for semantic Web services. *Proceedings of the 2004 AAAI Spring Symposium on Semantic Web Services Series,* Stanford, California.

Vakkari, P. (2003). Task-based information searching. *Annual Review of Information Science and Technology (ARIST), 37,* 413–464.

Valet, L., Mauris, G., & Bolon, P. (2001). A statistical overview of recent literature in information fusion. *IEEE AESS Systems Magazine, 16*(3), 7–14.

van Rijsbergen, C.J., & Lalmas, M. (1996). Information calculus for information retrieval. *Journal of the American*

Society for Information Science, 47(5), 385–398.

van Someren, M., Netten, N., Evers, V., Cramer, H., de Hoog, R., & Bruinsma, G. (2005, April). A trainable information distribution system to support crisis management. *Proceedings of the Second International ISCRAM Conference,* Brussels, Belgium.

Varian, H. (1995, September). The information economy. *Scientific American,* 200-201.

Vassiliou, C., Stamoulis, D., & Martakos, D. (2002, January). The process of personalizing Web content: Techniques, workflow and evaluation. *Proceedings of the International Conference on Advances in Infrastructure for Electronic Business, Science, and Education on the Internet,* L'Aquila, Italy. Available: http://www.ssgrr. it/en/ssgrr2002s/papers.htm

Vel, O. D., Anderson, A., Corney, M., & Mohay, G. (2001). Mining e-mail content for author identification forensics. *Special Interest Group on Management of Data Record (SIGMOD Rec.), 30*(4), 55-64.

Versata. (2004). *Understanding service-oriented architecture.* Retrieved from http://whitepapers.zdnet.com/ whitepaper.aspx?&docid=288390&promo=100511

Vesanto, J., & Alhoniemi, E. (2000). Clustering of self-organizing map. *IEEE Transactions on Neural Networks, 11*(3), 586-600.

Vozalis, E., & Margaritis, K.G. (2003). Analysis of recommender systems' algorithms. *Proceedings of the 6th Hellenic-European Conference on Computer Mathematics and its Applications* (HERCMA), Athens, Greece.

W3C (2003). Platform for privacy preferences (P3P) project. Retrieved June 2004, from *http://www.w3.org/ P3P/*

Wand, Y., & Wang, R. (1996). Anchoring data quality dimensions in ontological foundations. *Communications of the ACM, 39,* 86–95.

Wang, G., & Fung, C.K. (2004, January 5–8). Architecture paradigms and their influences and impacts on component-based software systems. *Proceedings of*

the 37th Annual Hawaii International Conference on System Sciences.

Wang, J., Li, G., & Wiederhold, G. (2001). Simplicity: Semantic-sensitive integrated matching for picture libraries. *IEEE Transactions on Pattern Analysis and Machine Intelligence, 23,* 947–963.

Wang, J., Wiederhold, G., Firschein, O., & Sha, X. (1998). Content-based image indexing and searching using Daubechies' wavelets. *International Journal of Digital Libraries, 1*(4), 311–328.

Wang, W., & Zaïane, O. R. (2002). Clustering Web sessions by sequence alignment. In *Proceedings of the 13th International Workshop on Database and Expert Systems Applications (DEXA 2002)* (LNCS 2453, pp. 394-398). Aix-en-Provence, France: Springer Verlag.

Want, R. (1995). An overview of the PARCTab ubiquitous computing environment. *IEEE Personal Communications.*

Webber, A.B. (2003). *Modern programming languages.* Franklin, Beedle & Associates.

WebBoard™. (2006). *WebBoard discussion forum and collaboration software.* Retrieved March 10, 2007, from http://www.webboard.com/

Weiss, N., & Reusch, B. (2005). Current and future trends and challenges in robot soccer. In R. Moreno Díaz et al. (Eds.), *EUROCAST 2005* (pp. 559–564). Berlin: Springer-Verlag (LNCS 3643).

Wen, J. R., Nie, J. Y., & Zhang, H. (2001). Clustering user queries of a search engine. *Proceedings of the 10th International World Wide Web Conference (WWW2001)* (pp. 162-168).

Wenyin, L., Dumais, S., Sun, Y., Zhang, H., Czerwinski, M., & Field, B. (2001). Semiautomatic image annotation. *Proceedings of the International Conference on Human-Computer Interaction* (vol. 1, pp. 326–334).

Weyhrauch, R.W. (1980). Prolegomena to a theory of mechanized formal reasoning. *Artificial Intelligence, 13*(1), 133–176.

Williams, M.-A. (1997). Anytime belief revision. *Proceedings of the International Joint Conference on Artificial Intelligence* (pp. 74–80).

Williams, M.-A. (1998). Applications of belief revision. *Proceedings of the International Seminar on Logic Databases and the Meaning of Change, Transactions and Change in Logic Databases* (ILPS'97) (pp. 287–316). London: Springer-Verlag.

Williams, M.-A., Gärdenfors, P., McCarthy, J., Karol, A., & Stanton, C. (2005). A framework for grounding representations. *Proceedings of the IJCAI Workshop on Agents in Real-Time and Dynamic Environments.*

Wilson, T.D. (1981). On user studies and information needs. *Journal of Documentation, 37*(1), 3–15.

Wilson, T.D. (1998). Exploring models of information behavior: The 'uncertainty' project. *Information Processing and Management: An International Journal, 35*(6), 839–849.

Woerndl, W., & Groh, G. (2005). A proposal for an agent-based architecture for context-aware personalization in the Semantic Web. *Proceedings of the 9ᵗʰ International Joint Conference on Artificial Intelligence, Multi-Agent Information Retrieval and Recommender Systems* (pp. 75–79).

Wong, W., & Fu, A. (2000). *Incremental document clustering for Web page classification.* Proceedings of the IEEE International Conference on Information Society in the 21ˢᵗ Century: Emerging Technologies and New Challenges (IS2000), Fukushima, Japan.

Wooldridge, M., & Jennings, N. (1995). Intelligent agents: Theory and practice. *The Knowledge Engineering Review, 10*(2), 115–152.

Wooldridge, M., & Jennings, N.R. (1995). Agent theories, architectures, and languages. In *Intelligent agents* (pp.1–22). Berlin: Springer-Verlag

Wooldridge, M., Jennings, N.R., & Kinny, D. (2000). The Gaia methodology for agent-oriented analysis and design. *Journal of Autonomous Agents and Multi-Agent Systems, 3*(3), 285–312.

WordNet. (n.d.). Retrieved July 5, 2004, from http://www.cogsci.princeton.edu /wn/

Wu, K., Yu, P. S., & Ballman, A. (1998). Speedtracer: A Web usage mining and analysis tool. *IBM Systems Journal, 37*(1), 89-105.

Wu, K., Yu, P., & Ballman, A. (1998). SpeedTracer: A Web usage mining and analysis tool. *IBM Systems Journal, 37*(1), 89-105.

Wu, P., & Manjunath, B.S. (2001). Adaptive nearest neighbor search for relevance feedback in large image databases. *Proceedings of the ACM Conference on Multimedia* (pp. 89–97).

Xexéo, G., Belchior, A., & da Rocha, A.R.C. (1996). Aplicação da teoria fuzzy em requisitos de qualidade de software. *Memorias-I, XXII CLEI*, Santafé de Bogotá, Colombia, Junio (pp. 3–7).

Xue, G.-R., Lin, C., Yang, Q., Xi, W., Zeng, H.-J., Yu, Y., & Chen, Z. (2005). Scalable collaborative filtering using cluster-based smoothing. *Proceedings of the 2005 Conference on Research and Development in Information Retrieval* (SIGIR 2005), Salvador, Brazil.

Yager, R.R. (1991). Connectives and quantifiers in fuzzy sets. In IFSA (Ed.), *Fuzzy sets and systems. Special memorial volume: 25 years of fuzzy sets.* Amsterdam: North-Holland.

Yan, L. (2004). MIN: Middleware for network-centric ubiquitous systems. *IEEE Pervasive Computing.*

Yan, L., Sere, K., Zhou, X., & Pang, J. (2004). Towards an integrated architecture for peer-to-peer and ad hoc overlay network applications. *Proceedings of the 10th IEEE International Workshop on Future Trends of Distributed Computing Systems* (FTDCS 2004).

Yang, C., & Lozano Perez, T. (2000). Image database retrieval with multiple instance learning techniques. *Proceedings of the IEEE International Conference on Data Engineering* (pp. 233–243).

Yang, Y. (1995). Noise reduction in a statistical approach to text categorization. In E.A. Fox, P. Ingwersen, & R. Fidel (Eds.), *Proceedings of the 18ᵗʰ ACM International*

Conference on Research and Development in Information Retrieval (SIGIR-95) (pp. 256–263), Seattle, WA. New York: ACM Press.

Yang, Y., & Pedersen, J. O. (1997). A comparative study on feature selection in text categorization. *Proceedings of the 14th International Conference on Machine Learning (ICML 1997)* (pp. 412-420).

Yang, Y., & Pedersen, J.O. (1997). A comparative study on feature selection in text categorization. *Proceedings of the 14th International Conference on Machine Learning* (ICML'97) (pp. 412– 420). San Francisco: Morgan Kaufmann.

Yao, Y., Zhong, N., Liu, J., & Ohsuga, S. (2001). Web intelligence (WI) research challenges and trends in the new information age. In N. Zhong et al. (Eds.), *WI 2001, LNAI 2198*, 1-17. Springer Verlag Berlin Heidelberg.

Yau, S.S., & Huang, D. (2006). Mobile middleware for situation-aware service discovery and coordination. In P. Bellavista & A. Corradi (Eds.), *Handbook of mobile middleware*.

Yau, S.S., Huang, D., Gong, H., & Davulcu, H. (2005, July). Situation-awareness for adaptive coordination in service-based systems. *Proceedings of the 29th Annual International Computer Software and Applications Conference* (COMPSAC 2005) (vol. pp. 107–112).

Yau, S.S., Liu, H., & Yao, D. (2003). Situation-aware personalized information retrieval for mobile Internet. *Proceedings of the 27th Annual International Computer Software and Applications Conference* (p. 638).

Yu, K., Schwaighofer, A., Tresp, V., Xu, X., & Kriegel, H.-P. (2004). Probabilistic memory-based collaborative filtering. *IEEE Transactions on Knowledge and Data Engineering, 16*(1), 56–68.

Yu, K., Wen, Z., Xu, X., & Ester, M. (2001). Feature weighting and instance selection for collaborative filtering. *Proceedings of the 2nd International Workshop on Management of Information on the Web—Web Data and Text Mining* (MIW'01).

Yu, K., Xu, X., Ester, M., & Kriegel, H.-P. (2003). Feature weighting and instance selection for collaborative filtering: An information-theoretic approach. *Knowledge and Information Systems, 5*(2), 201–224.

Zadeh, L.A. (1965). Fuzzy sets. *Information and Control, 8,* 338–353.

Zadeh, L.A. (1988). Fuzzy logic. *IEEE Transactions in Computing,* 83-92.

Zadrozny, W. (1995). *Context and ontology in understanding of dialogs.* CoRR, cmp-lg/9505032.

Zaïane, O. R., Foss, A., Lee, C.-H., & Wang, W. (2002). On data clustering analysis: Scalability, constraints, and validation. In *Proceedings of the 6th Pacific-Asia Conference of Advances in Knowledge Discovery and Data Mining (PAKDD 2002)* (LNCS 2336, pp. 28-39). Taipei, Taiwan: Springer Verlag.

Zambonelli, F., Jennings, N.R., & Wooldridge, M. (2003). Developing multiagent systems: The Gaia methodology. *ACM Transactions on Software Engineering Methodology, 12*(3). 317–370.

Zamir, O., Etzioni, O., Madanim, O., & Karp, R. M. (1997). Fast and intuitive clustering of Web documents. *Proceedings of the 3rd International Conference on Knowledge Discovery and Data Mining (KDD 1997)* (pp. 287-290).

Zeng, C., Xing, C.-X., Zhou, L.-Z., & Zheng, X.-H. (2004). Similarity measure and instance selection for collaborative filtering. *International Journal of Electronic Commerce, 8*(4), 115–129.

Zeng, H. J., He, Q. C., Chen, Z., Ma, W. Y., & Ma, J. (2004). Learning to cluster Web search results. *Proceedings of the 27th Annual International ACM SIGIR Conference on Research and Development in Information Retrieval* (pp. 210-217).

Zhang, Q., & Goldman, S.A. (2001). EM-DD: An improved multiple-instance learning technique. In T.G. Dietterich, S. Becker, & Z. Ghahramani (Eds.), *Advances in neural information processing systems* (vol. 14, pp. 1073–1080). Cambridge, MA: MIT Press.

Zhang, Q., Goldman, S.A., Yu, W., & Fritts, J. (2002). Content-based image retrieval using multiple-instance learning. In C. Sammut & A.G. Hoffmann (Eds.), *Proceedings of the International Conference on Machine Learning* (pp. 682–689).

Zhou, X., & Huang, T. (2001). Small sample learning during multimedia retrieval using BiasMap. *Proceedings of the IEEE International Conference on Computer Vision and Pattern Recognition* (vol. 1, pp. 11–17).

Zhu, H. (2005, October). Encourage contributions by roles. *Proceedings of the IEEE International Conference on Systems, Man and Cybernetics* (pp. 1574–1579).

Zhu, H. (2006a). Role mechanisms in collaborative systems. *International Journal of Production Research, 41*(1), 181–193.

Zhu, H. (2006b). A role-based architecture for intelligent agent systems. *Proceedings of the International Workshop on Distributed Intelligent Systems* (pp. 354–359), Prague, Czech Republic.

Zhu, H. (2006c, October). A role-based approach to robot agent team design. *Proceedings of the IEEE International Conference on Systems, Man and Cybernetics* (pp. 4861–4866), Taipei, China.

Zhu, H. (2006d). Separating design from implementations: Role-based software development. *Proceedings of the 5th IEEE International Conference on Cognitive Informatics* (pp. 141–148), Beijing, China.

Zhu, H. (2007). *Role playing Java documents.* Retrieved April 10, 2007, from http://www.nipissingu.ca/faculty/haibinz/RolePlaying/

Zhu, H., & Zhou, M.C. (2003, October). Methodology first and language second: A way to teach object-oriented programming. *Companion of the ACM International Conference of Object-Oriented Programming, Systems, Languages and Applications* (OOPSLA'03) (pp. 140–147).

Zhu, H., & Zhou, M.C. (2006a). Role-based collaboration and its kernel mechanisms. *IEEE Transactions on Systems, Man and Cybernetics, Part C, 36*(4), 578–589.

Zhu, H., & Zhou, M.C. (2006b). Supporting software development with roles. *IEEE Transactions on Systems, Man and Cybernetics, Part A, 36*(6), 1110–1123.

Zhu, J., Hong, J., & Hughes, J. (2004). PageCluster: Mining conceptual link hierarchies from Web log files for adaptive Web site navigation. *ACM Transactions on Internet Technologies, 4*(2), 185-208.

Zimmermann, H.J. (1991). *Fuzzy set theory and its applications* (2nd revised ed.). Boston: Kluwe

Zuidweg, M., Pereira Filho, J.G., & van Sinderen, M. (2003). Using P3P in a Web services-based context-aware application platform. *Proceedings of the 9th Open European Summer School and IFIP Workshop on Next Generation Networks (EUNICE'2003)*, Balatonfured, Hungary.

About the Contributors

Rafael Andrés Gonzalez has been assistant professor in the areas of information systems and software engineering at Javeriana University, Bogotá, Colombia, in addition to acting as an IT consultant. He is currently a PhD student in the Technology, Policy and Management Faculty, Delft University of Technology, The Netherlands. His present research focuses on information systems for supporting coordination in the domain of crisis management. He holds a Systems Engineering degree from Javeriana University and an MSc in computer science from Delft University of Technology.

Nong Chen is a researcher at the Faculty of Technology, Police and Management, Delft University of Technology, The Netherlands. She received a BSc in industrial engineering from the School of Economy and Management, Beijing University of Technology, China. She received an MSc in technical informatics from the Faculty of Electrical Engineering, Mathematics and Computer Science, Delft University of Technology. Her research interests are personalized information seeking and retrieval, system modeling and architecture, crisis response and management, geographic information systems, and location-based services.

Ajantha Dahanayake is a professor of information systems at the J. Whitney Bunting School of Business, Georgia College & State University, USA. She is also an associate professor of the Faculty of Technology, Police and Management, Delft University of Technology, The Netherlands. She previously served as an associate professor in the Department of Information Systems and Algorithms of the Faculty of Information Technology and Systems. She received a BSc and MSc in computer science from the University of Leiden and a PhD in information systems from Delft University of Technology. She has served in a number of Dutch research and academic institutions. Her research interests are distributed Web-enabled systems, CASE, methodology engineering, component-based development, and m-business. She was the research director of the research program, Building Blocks for Telematics Applications Development and Evaluation (BETADE).

* * *

Ricardo Barros is a doctorate candidate in the Computer Science Department of the Federal University of Rio de Janeiro. He received an MS in computer systems engineering from the Military Institute of Engineering in 1996, and a bachelor's degree in accounting from Oswaldo Aranha Foundation in 1982. His current research focuses on information quality, cooperative work and ontologies, information retrieval, and fuzzy logic. He worked in many consultant projects at home and abroad for public and private organizations.

Narjès Bellamine-Ben Saoud is an associate professor of computer science at the University of Tunis, Tunisia, and a researcher at the RIADI-GDL Laboratory of the National School of Computer Science of Tunis. She received an engineering diploma and master's degree from ENSEEIHT Toulouse, and a PhD on computer-supported collaborative work and groupware design from the University of Toulouse, France. Her main research interests concern complexity paradigm, agent-based modeling, and simulation of cooperative socio-technical systems, computer-supported collaborative learning, groupware development, and software engineering. Her current research projects include modeling and simulation of emergency rescue activities for large-scale accidents.

Mohamed Ben Ahmed is emeritus professor at the National School of Computer Science, University of La Manouba, Tunisia. Among his main research interests are complexity, knowledge, linguistics and Arabic, and epistemology.

Tarek Ben Mena is preparing his PhD on multiagent systems and contexts at the RIADI-GDL Laboratory, National School of Computer Science of Tunis, Tunisia, in collaboration with the Cognitive Engineering Research Laboratory of the Computer Science Research Institute of Toulouse, France. He received his computer science engineering diploma and master's degree from the National School of Computer Science, Tunisia.

Shan Chen is pursuing a PhD at the University of Technology, Sydney, Australia. She holds a master's research degree in information technology and a bachelor's degree in computer science. She has wide experience working in the IT industry and Australian university IT departments, including commercial software product development, research, and teaching. Her current research interests lie in the area of ontologies, in particular the ontology evolution and its neighborhood.

Constantina Costopoulou is an assistant professor at the Informatics Laboratory of the AUA. She holds a BSc in mathematics from the National and Kapodistrian University of Athens, Greece, an MSc in software engineering from Cranfield Institute of Technology, UK, and a PhD from the National Technical University of Athens, Greece. Her research interests include rural area networks, Web services, intelligent agents, and e-services for the agricultural sector. She has published more than 90 papers in edited volumes, scientific journals, and refereed conferences. She has also served as the scientific responsible or member of the working group of several funded projects in the above research areas.

Amr Ali Eldin graduated in 1997 with Bachelor of Science in electronics engineering from Mansoura University. He was ranked first in his class with the general grade of Excellent. He has received the following scientific honor degree awards: Bahrain Kingdom (1990), El-Dakahleya state (1992, 1998), and Mansoura University (1997). He was awarded the Master of Science in automatic control engineering in April 2001. He was awarded the Doctoral of Philosophy in information systems engineering from Delft University of Technology, The Netherlands. He supervised master's and bachelor's students, and participated in teaching and research projects at Delft University of Technology. Dr. Ali Eldin has more than 15 publications in international conferences, workshops, and book chapters. Recently, he joined the Technology Architecture team at Accenture, The Netherlands, where he applies his knowledge and experience in providing solutions for high-potential IT architecture integration and design projects.

Iker Gondra received BS, MS, and PhD degrees in computer science from Oklahoma State University, USA (1998, 2002, and 2005, respectively). Since 2005, he has been an assistant professor of mathematics, statistics and computer science at St. Francis Xavier University, Canada. His research interests include machine learning, content-based image retrieval, and evolutionary algorithms.

Nikos Manouselis is a researcher at the Informatics Laboratory of the Agricultural University of Athens. He has a diploma in electronics & computer engineering, a master's degree in operational research, as well as a master's degree in electronics & computer engineering from the Technical University of Crete, Greece. Manouselis was previously affiliated with the Informatics & Telematics Institute of the Center for Research & Technology, Greece, as well as the Decision Support Systems Laboratory and the Multimedia Systems & Applications Laboratory of the Technical University of Crete, Greece. His research interests involve the design, development, and evaluation of electronic services, and their applications for the agricultural sector.

Bernard Pavard is manager of the Cognitive Engineering Research Laboratory in Toulouse, France. His research team works on the simulation and conception of complex socio-technical systems. Using complex system theory, the team has designed simulation platforms that have been extensively used to design regulation centers such as emergency control rooms, air traffic control centers, disaster management PCs, and so forth. His research is now extended to cooperation in virtual worlds. The challenge is to allow practitioners to collaborate in virtual worlds, taking into account emotional interaction.

Wallace A. Pinheiro is a doctorate student of computer science at the Federal University of Rio de Janeiro. He has an electronic engineering degree from the Federal University of Rio de Janeiro, from where graduated in 1998. He received his master's degree in science from the Military Institute of Engineering in 2004. His recent works involve information quality, autonomic computing, cooperative work, and ontologies. His current research focuses on ontologies, fuzzy logic, and information quality.

Jano de Souza is a professor of computer science at the Graduate School of Engineering (COPPE) and Mathematics Institute of the Federal University of Rio de Janeiro (UFRJ). His area of specialization is databases, and he is involved in research in fields such as CSCW, DB, DSS, KM, and GIS. He received his bachelor's degree in mechanical engineering (1974) and his master's degree (1978) in system engineering from UFRJ, and his PhD in information systems (1986) from the University of East Anglia, UK. He has published more than 200 papers in journals and conference proceedings, and supervised about 50 theses and dissertations.

Zoran Stojanovic is an IT architect at IBM Global Services Netherlands. He has been active since 1993 in various areas of IT, software engineering, and GIS—in both industry and academia—as an enterprise IT architect, consultant, researcher, and lecturer. His research interests are in the areas of service-oriented architecture, enterprise architecture, Web services, business process management, and model-driven development. He received his PhD from Delft University of Technology. He has authored a number of publications in international journals and conferences.

Mary-Anne Williams is a leading scientist in areas of belief revision, agent technologies, knowledge representation, and reasoning. She is past president of KR Inc., an international scientific foundation and peak body for knowledge representation and reasoning, and director of the Innovation and Technology Research Laboratory at UTS. She has developed several belief revision systems that have been used in a range of applications, and she published more than 100 papers, books, and book chapters, many of them in leading journals and conferences, and highly cited. She has chaired several prestigious international conferences and served on the senior program committee of key conferences in the field of AI, including IJCAI and AAAI. She is also a guest professor at the University of Science and Technology China, where she teaches classes on knowledge representation.

Geraldo Xexéo is a professor of computer science at the Graduate School of Engineering (COPPE) and Mathematics Institute of the Federal University of Rio de Janeiro (UFRJ). He has an electronic engineering degree from the Military Institute of Engineering (1988) and received his DSc in computer sciences from UFRJ in 1994. His area of specialization is computer science, with emphasis in databases and software engineering, and he is involved in research in fields such as peer-to-peer, information retrieval, information quality, and fuzzy logic. He has worked in many consultant projects for public and private organizations.

Lu Yan is a research fellow at University College London and a visiting fellow at the University of Cambridge. Previously, he was with the Department of Information Technologies at Åbo Akademi University, the Distributed Systems Design Laboratory at the Turku Center for Computer Science, and the Institute of Microelectronics at Peking University. He holds visiting professor positions in both École Supérieure d'Ingénieurs Generalists and École Supérieure de Commerce de Rouen.

MengChu Zhou received a BS from Nanjing University of Science and Technology, an MS from Beijing Institute of Technology, and a PhD from Rensselaer Polytechnic Institute. He joined the New Jersey Institute of Technology in 1990 where he is currently a professor of electrical and computer engineering. His interests are in computer-integrated systems and Petri nets. He has 250+ publications including six books and 100+ journal papers. He is managing editor of *IEEE Transactions on Systems, Man and Cybernetics*, associate editor of *IEEE Transactions on Industrial Informatics*, and editor-in-chief of the *International Journal of Intelligent Control and Systems*. He has served as general and program chair of many international conferences, is a life member and former president of the Chinese Association for Science and Technology – USA, and is a fellow of IEEE.

Haibin Zhu is an associate professor of computer science and math at Nipissing University. He has published 60+ papers and five books on object-oriented programming, distributed systems, collaborative systems, and computer architecture. He is a senior member of IEEE and a member of ACM. He is serving and served as co-chair of the technical committee of distributed intelligent systems of the IEEE SMC Society, guest editor for three special issues of prestigious journals, PC vice-chair for SIWN CODS'07, publicity chair for IEEE CTS'07, organizer of the workshop on "Role-Based Collaboration (RBC)" for CSCW'06, organizer for seven special sessions for the IEEE International Conference on SMC and WDIS'06, and a PC member for 10+ international conferences. He is the recipient of the Best Paper Award from ISPE/CE'04, two IBM EIG awards, and the Educator's Fellowship of OOPSLA'03. He also received many research awards from the government of China.

Index

A

agent system, role concepts in 256
agent system design 254
agglomerative clustering 19
application ontology 5
artificial intelligence 254
autonomy 255

C

clustering 19, 83, 98
clustering, agglomerative 19
clustering, divisive 19
clustering, hierarchical 19
clustering, link-based 105
clustering, text-based 105
clustering, Web documents 99
clustering, Web users 99
clustering algorithms 105
cluster labeling 13
cognitive filtering 31
collaborative filtering 30–54
conceptualization 3–5
conceptualization, shared 3–5
content-based image retrieval (CBIR) 194–219

D

default voting 35
divisive clustering 19
domain ontology 5

E

E-CARGO model 262
Euclidian distance formula 38
existential graph 287

F

filtering 64
filtering, cognitive 31
filtering, collaborative 79
filtering, sociological 31
formal concept analysis (FCA) 18
fuzzy theory, introduction to 170

H

hierarchical clustering 19
human machine interaction 293

I

image keywords 198
image segmentation 199
information discovery 62
information dynamics 60, 70
information filtering 63
information fusion 65
information heterogeneity 58–76, 69
information overload 59, 69
information personalization 67
information problem 55–76
information quality 173
information retrieval 62, 220
in integrated region matching (IRM) 205
integrated region matching (IRM) 200

J

jini technology 143
JUNG 183

K

knowledge representation 293

knowledge representation and reasoning (KRR) 288

L

learning, machine 2
learning, multiple instance 203
learning, ontology 1, 8
learning, probabilistic feature relevance 205
learning, relevance feedback 194–219

M

machine learning 2
MESSAGING SERVICE 224–231
multi-agent system (MAS) 286
multiple instance learning (MIL) 203

O

OntoDiscFM 13
OntoLearn 20
ontologies, classification of 4
ontologies, definitions and overviews 2–4
ontology, application 5
ontology, domain 5
ontology, task 5
ontology, top-level 5
ontology engineering 5–6
ontology learning 1, 8
ontology learning, from text 8
orientation, problem 121
orientation, service 123

P

pattern analysis 84
personalization 15, 67, 79–97
personalization, check-box 79
personalization, observational 79
personalization process 80
personalization research 91
personalized information retrieval 290
personalized information seeking 119–150
personalizing, Web services 232–253
Platform for Privacy Preferences (P3P) 153
privacy 151–166
probabilistic feature relevance learning (PFRL) 205

problem orientation 121

Q

quality 173
quality filters 167–193

R

relevance feedback (RF) learning 194
reminding service 223–231

S

semantic feature extraction 13
service-oriented architecture (SOA) 221–231
service orientation 123
shared conceptualization 3–5
similarity measure 199
sociological filtering 31

T

task ontology 5
top-level ontology 5
Tourist MobileBook 234

U

user agent 157
user profile data 15

W

Web data 15
Web personalization 1, 77–97
Web service personalization 232–253
word sense disambiguation (WSD) 10, 23